# THE LAST GREAT VICTORY

Also by Stanley Weintraub

*Disraeli: A Biography*
*Long Day's Journey into War*
*Victoria: An Intimate Biography*
*A Stillness Heard Round the World*

· STANLEY WEINTRAUB ·

# THE LAST
# GREAT
# VICTORY

## THE END OF WORLD WAR II
### July/August 1945

KONECKY&KONECKY

Konecky & Konecky
72 Ayers Point Rd.
Old Saybrook, CT. 06475

This edition published by special arrangement
with Dutton, a division of Penguin books USA, Inc.

ISBN:1-56852-346-7

Printed and bound in the USA

*for my cousins—and uncle—who won the war*
*before I got old enough for a uniform:*
*Arnold, Ben, Gene, Harold, Hy, Irv,*
*Leonard, Morris, Myer*

*summer grasses*
*where soldiers dreamed*
—MATSUO BASHŌ (1644–1694)

# · CONTENTS ·

NORTH SEA

DENMARK

BALTIC SEA

Königsberg

RUSSIAN ADMINISTERED

EAST PRUSSIA

POLISH ADMINISTERED AREA

Bremerhaven

Lübeck

Rostock

Swinemünde

Stettin

Danzig

HOLLAND

Arnhem

Bremen

Hamburg

RUSSIAN

Wittenberg

INTERNATIONAL OCCUPATION

BERLIN

Brunswick

Magdeburg

ZONE

R. Vistula

Warsaw

POLAND

BELGIUM

BRITISH ZONE

Cologne

Kassel

Leipzig

TERRITORY

Erfurt

YIELDED TO U.S.S.R.

Dresden

Breslau

RUSSIAN ADMINISTERED AREA

Frankfurt

FRENCH ZONE

Mainz

Würzburg

Karlsbad

Pilsen

Prague

Cracow

Karlsruhe

Nuremberg

Regensburg

CZECHOSLOVAKIA

Stuttgart

R. Danube

Budejovice

AMERICAN ZONE

Münich

Linz

RUSSIAN OCCUPATION ZONE

Vienna

INTERNATIONAL OCCUPATION

Salzburg

R. Danube

Budapest

L. Constance

Innsbruck

FRENCH ZONE

AUSTRIA

BRITISH ZONE

HUNGARY

SWITZERLAND

Klagenfurt

ITALY

YUGOSLAVIA

### THE WITHDRAWAL OF THE WESTERN ALLIES, July 1945

Boundaries of Zones ———
National Frontiers, 1937 —·—·—

0    50    100    150    200    250 MILES

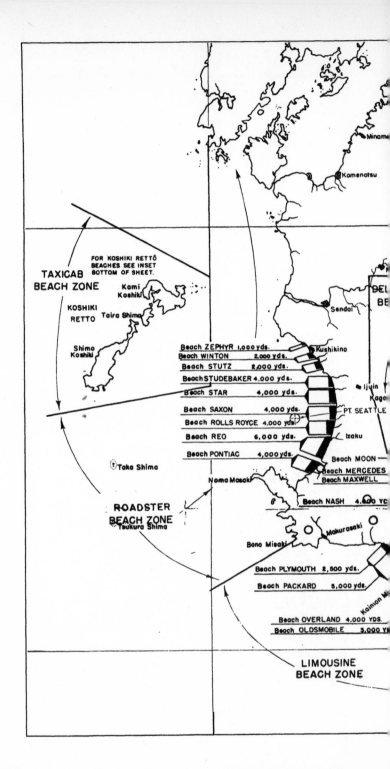

TAXICAB
BEACH ZONE

FOR KOSHIKI RETTŌ
BEACHES SEE INSET
BOTTOM OF SHEET.

KOSHIKI
RETTO

Kami
Koshiki

Taira Shima

Shimo
Koshiki

Taka Shima

ROADSTER
BEACH ZONE

Tsukura Shima

Noma Masaki

Bono Misaki

LIMOUSINE
BEACH ZONE

Minama

Komenotsu

Sendai

BEL
BE

Kushikino

Ijuin

Kago

PT. SEATTLE

Izaku

Beach ZEPHYR 1,000 yds.
Beach WINTON       2,000 yds.
Beach STUTZ        2,000 yds.
Beach STUDEBAKER 4,000 yds.
Beach STAR         4,000 yds.
Beach SAXON        4,000 yds.
Beach ROLLS ROYCE 4,000 yds.
Beach REO          6,000 yds.
Beach PONTIAC      4,000yds.

Beach MOON
Beach MERCEDES
Beach MAXWELL
Beach NASH      4,000 YC

Makurasaki

Kaimon Mi

Beach PLYMOUTH  2,500 yds.
Beach PACKARD   5,000 yds.
Beach OVERLAND  4,000 YDS.
Beach OLDSMOBILE  3,000 Y

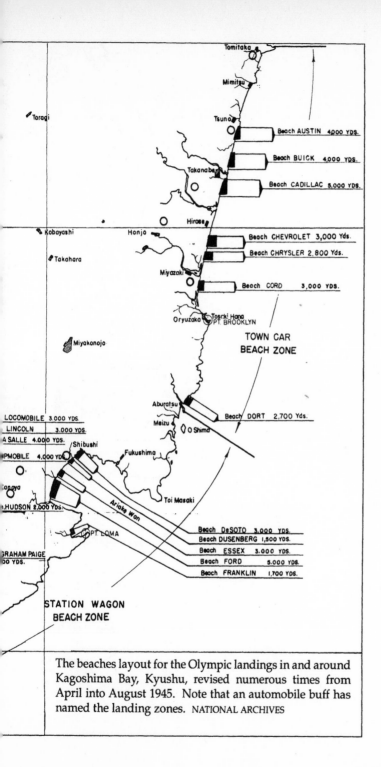

The beaches layout for the Olympic landings in and around Kagoshima Bay, Kyushu, revised numerous times from April into August 1945. Note that an automobile buff has named the landing zones. NATIONAL ARCHIVES

# · PROLOGUE ·

The war winding down in East Asia and the Pacific began long before the war in Europe—in Manchuria ten years earlier than Pearl Harbor, four years earlier in China itself—and it went on longer and over a larger expanse of the earth's surface. As the conflict came to a close in the waning summer, the greatest amphibious invasion ever planned was in preparation and the most awesome technology ever devised for war was being relentlessly employed over Japan. The overwhelming victories of mid-1945 seemed a hopeless dream in 1941. Poland in 1939 had been indefensible. France in 1940 proved a facade. Communist slogans in June 1941 were worthless against the *Wehrmacht*. Pearl Harbor that December was the ultimate embarrassment. After the first Japanese strikes from Hong Kong to Hawaii, from Mandalay to Manila, the Rising Sun seemed destined to fly over a colonial empire rivaling Hitler's continental dominion in Europe.

That the United States would be enmeshed, East and West, was inevitable, but before war came many Americans were akin to patients in denial of the gravity of their illnesses. With German submarines strangling a Britain already reeling from the Blitz, Franklin Roosevelt had stretched his presidential powers to the limit, and beyond, to save what he saw as the free world's stationary aircraft carrier off *Festung Europa*. If America were drawn in, Roosevelt felt, so much the better. If Britain fell before then, the United States would be alone against Hitler. Neither the White House nor the military expected the blow to fall, first, in the Pacific. A two-ocean war in any case would compound the unpreparedness that was the legacy of isolationist complacency in Congress. While Japan would continue to collect colonies deprived by Hitler of absentee masters, the United States took itself as too formidable to challenge. Conventional wisdom was that America could defeat Japan, if necessary, in six weeks. Or was it six months?

In Washington the service chiefs knew better. The army trained reluctant peacetime draftees with broomstick rifles while armored units maneuvered in trucks imaginatively labeled TANK. The signs were that Japan might take advantage of American unreadiness, and ten days before *Kido Butai*—"strike force"—unleashed its torpedo planes and dive bombers against Pearl Harbor, George C. Marshall radioed "war warnings" to key headquarters at home and abroad. No zone proved ready on December 7, 1941. Three hundred planes from five undetected carriers sank eight battleships at anchor. Ten other ships were beached or sunk; over 350 aircraft were destroyed; 2,403 Americans were killed and 1,178 were wounded. Nine hours later, half of General Douglas MacArthur's air force in the Philippines was wiped out at Clark Field.

The deepest wound was to the American psyche, yet the Japanese commander responsible for the victory, Admiral Isoroku Yamamoto, realized that the dangerous operation might become a self-inflicted wound. He knew America's industrial potential and Japan's potential for depletion. While his fleet units rehearsed the attack, he wrote to the Navy Minister, Vice Admiral Shigetaro Shimada, that "following four years of exhausting operations in China" it seemed to him "risky and illogical" to go to war against America and Britain as well, "with the possibility of fighting Russia also having to be kept in mind." The Japanese might have to "sustain ourselves unassisted for ten years or more in a protracted war over an area several times more vast than the European war theater." No "ordinary strategy" would succeed, he explained. Japan would have to "deal a blow, material and moral," from which the enemy would not be able to recover until it was too late to matter.

The American public would not know how heavy the blows were, materially, until the war was over, which perhaps prevented the moral blow—defeatism. Instead, outrage arose, exemplified in Roosevelt's war message about a date that would "live in infamy." The battle cry spawned from the Sunday morning nightmare, "Remember Pearl Harbor," exuded confidence and vowed victory.

Hitler's rush to exploit military weaknesses unknown to most Americans was an unexpected turn. The Nazi declaration of war four days later made a debate in Congress about the inadvisability of a two-front war unnecessary, but the first enemy seemed to be Japan, and the events of the first hours of the war for the United States belied the quick optimism. As the proudest ships of the Pacific Fleet lay shattered on the muddy bottom of Pearl Harbor, the West Coast was in a panic. Invasion jitters sowed hysteria from the Panama Canal to Seattle. At the Presidio, somnolent until that Sunday, the commanding general of the Fourth Army claimed certainty that Japanese bombers had overflown San Francisco. Rumors flew that enemy aircraft carriers lay offshore. Japanese farmers and fishermen were arrested wholesale. Untrained troops were rushed to deserted California beaches. Guards were posted at aircraft plants still gearing up for production. In Washington, soldiers set up antiaircraft guns on government buildings although they had no shells to fit them.

Forty-one months later, the Japanese threat to the American mainland had become real, but only in a haphazard way that demonstrated how the war had gone into reverse. Across the Pacific from their endangered home islands, now under siege by military technology that had not existed in December 1941, a deflated Japanese paper balloon made from mulberry tree pulp had lain in the quiet Oregon woods near Lakeview for two months when a picnicking party of a minister, his wife, and five children discovered the curious object. There was a rush toward it, and the Reverend Archie Mitchell shouted, too late, "Don't touch it!"

The forty-foot balloon, glued together from six hundred tatami-sized sheets by conscripted schoolgirls at a makeshift factory in Kokura, had carried a bomb package across the Pacific jet stream. A Japanese officer had urged the girls as they gathered in predawn darkness, "You will be defeating America with these arms. Work to your utmost! Achieve your goals!" Contributing nothing to the defeat of America, the balloon bomb exploded.

The Japanese girls wore headbands displaying the characters for SPECIAL ATTACK FORCE. Prior to twelve-hour shifts without breaks they had recited daily the Imperial Precepts for Soldiers and Sailors. But in March 1945 there was neither paper nor paste. As submarine and air blockades cut the home islands off from raw materials formerly supplied by the vast empire seized in the first months of the war, Japan was running out of everything. Even the powdered *konnyaku* paste sealant was being covertly consumed as food. Yet the remaining 9,300 balloons continued to be launched into the west wind, even into the summer of 1945, touching down as far east as Ontario and Michigan. The woman and children killed in Oregon on May 5, 1945, on the eve of the German surrender in Europe, were the only wartime deaths due to enemy action in any of the forty-eight states.

Kokura* was among the seventeen targets then under study by a secret American committee to advise the new president, Harry S. Truman, where to drop the first atomic bombs—if a test device actually worked. Areas already destroyed by conventional explosives would be deleted from the list. Émigre mathematician John von Neumann was delegated to oversee computations of atomic shock waves and damage potential. (A year later he would establish the practicality of a digital computer.) The committee was to meet again in mid-May in J. Robert Oppenheimer's office in Los Alamos, New Mexico.

The atomic bomb worked on paper. The West had feared throughout the war that somehow the Nazis would make the technological breakthrough. In Germany, scientific experts were in the vanguard of each Allied division. One team, "Operation Lusty," found an extravagant aeronautical research institute at Volkenrode, and at the I.G. Farben scientific complex searchers discovered a lethal nerve gas, Tabun, and its even more effective derivative, Sarin, which, if loaded on a V-2 missile, might have decimated London. Close to the end, underground enemy factories, their technicians assisted by slave laborers replaced as they died of malnutrition and overwork, continued turning out rockets and jet engines although the fuel to power them was all but gone. On May 5, a British scientific mission followed

---

*Kokura and the steel-manufacturing city of Yamata were absorbed after the American occupation into a single conurbation renamed Kitakyushu (literally, "North Kyushu").

troops of the Fifth King's Regiment into the Walterwerke in Lübeck, where revolutionary high-speed submarines driven by peroxide were being constructed. Production had ceased only two days earlier, and the new U-1410s lay disabled by the workmen and seamen unable to send them to sea.

In the last days and hours of the war in Europe, the American "Alsos" mission,* anxious about enemy equivalents to the Manhattan Engineering District atomic establishment, rounded up scientists considered by the Nazis as *kriegswichtig* ("war-valuable") and confined them in a detention center in Versailles, the Chateau du Chesnay, code-named "Dustbin." Led by refugee physicist Samuel A. Goudsmit, "Alsos" had followed the troops after D-Day. By November 1944 Goudsmit had become convinced there was no likely German Bomb. At the end "Alsos" raced through a gap in the Black Forest and plucked leading nuclear scientists from the relocated Kaiser Wilhelm Institut für Physik. One was missing, but traced. On May 5, as Germany's premier physicist, Werner Heisenberg, seized at his hilltop retreat at Urfeld, was being hurried toward Heidelberg in the back of Lieutenant Colonel Boris Pash's jeep, "Alsos" still had a lot to learn about German war technology.

In the Allied capitals, everything occurring after a cerebral hemorrhage on April 12 had caused the sudden death of President Franklin Roosevelt seemed anticlimactic. Mussolini had been executed by Italian partisans, and Hitler had shot himself in his bunker in Berlin, leaving orders to be cremated with some of the little gasoline remaining rather than permit his corpse to be a trophy for Stalin.†
    The capture of Berlin, the creation of the United Nations (a conference was taking place in San Francisco), and the celebrations of Victory-in-Europe Day were headline events, yet the euphoria over V-E Day seemed premature to many. Obscure Nine-Section in the Burmese jungle had it right. While demobilization and peacetime re-

---

*Alsos* was Greek for "grove," an ego-tripping pun on the name of General Leslie A. Groves, who ran the Bomb project for the Army.
†Stalin obtained what was left of the corpse nonetheless. The charred remains were first buried in a shell crater by the Russians, after which troops of the Soviet Third Army carried them as far as Magdeburg, near the line that would divide East and West Germany. When Stalin ordered a sample of the evidence for the archives, he was secretly brought a jaw and part of a skull. The Magdeburg site was destroyed in 1970. The jaw and skull fragment disappeared during the chaos of the dissolution of the Soviet state. (*The New York Times*, September 18, 1992, p. A10)

tooling were already beginning, the war in Asia was still to be won. As the British embassy put it in a May 13 report from Washington to Whitehall, the Pacific burden was largely America's: "We must naturally be prepared for criticism from some quarters no matter what we do. If we prosecute [the] Eastern [Asia] War with might and main, we shall be told by some people that we are really fighting for our colonial possessions the better to exploit them and that American blood is being shed to better purpose than to help ourselves and [the] Dutch and French to perpetuate our unregenerate colonial Empires; while if we are judged not to have gone all out, that is because we are letting America fight her own war with little aid after having her pull our chestnuts out of [the] European fire."

The embassy was certain, the report went on, that the U.S. Navy wanted it that way, "torn as they are by desires to make [the] Pacific victory as purely an American victory as possible and yet not to let us off too great a share of the heat and burden of the day." It was some consolation that "Despite flood of bigger news, acknowledgement of British achievement in Burma appeared very widely."

In the back of beyond, near the silty Sittang River on the outskirts of Pegu in Burma, Nine-Section of the 17th "Black Cat" Division, a young Scot, George MacDonald Fraser, was about to go out "to lay ambushes." A village on the Sittang was reputed to be in enemy hands, and the sweaty men in their green jungle uniforms and broad-brimmed Australian bush hats with him were checking assignments. Although realizing that if the Japanese had not withdrawn toward Rangoon the company could be wiped out, a veteran offered a Salvation Army parody: "Sister Anna will carry the banner," he joked to gloss over their anxiety; "Sister Kate will carry the plate. . . ." A solitary Spitfire rumbled over—they usually arrived too late to matter—and as its roar died away an officer (new, Fraser realized) ran out and shouted, "Men! The war in Europe is over!"

The soldiers gazed silently into the heat haze; then someone laughed, and derision swelled through the company. "Ev ye told Tojo, like?" scoffed one. "Hey, son," shouted another, unconcerned about the young officer's rank, "is it awreet if we a' gan yam [go home]?"

Indifference was the widespread reaction in Asia and the Pacific to victory in Europe. It meant nothing unless forces there were redeployed to finish off Japan. "Uh-huh," said GIs on Okinawa, Air Force Sergeant Edward Fry remembered: "The hell it's over! When will the troops from Europe come here and help us really end this thing?" In the Philippines, however, it meant a great deal to the refugee communities in cities like Iloilo, on the island of Panay, which survived the war because the Japanese were indifferent about expired German passports. In Manila, the Viennese conductor Herbert Zipper, an escapee from Dachau, had promised himself that he would mark the fall of Hitler's regime with a thanksgiving performance of Beethoven's *Eroica.* Accordingly, on May 10, 1945, the Manila Symphony made good his vow. Their instruments and library, hidden since 1941, had been retrieved, and the surviving players were augmented by American army volunteers. (The concertmaster was dead; also the entire horn section.) Since few venues in which to perform had survived the violent Japanese retreat from Manila earlier in the year, the musicians gathered in the roofless nave of the old Church of Santa Cruz, between the shattered, echoing stone walls. The music soared nevertheless. "The *Eroica* has been performed by many greater orchestras," Bill Dunn of CBS reported—he had been in Burma at the time of Pearl Harbor—"but never with greater feeling."

The war did not conclude conveniently in a single place at a predetermined time. The signing of surrenders, the laying down of arms, the announcements from commanders and heads of state, all spread over global time zones, suggest a variety of dates for the ending of World War II. "V-E Day" and "V-J Day" depended upon the capitals from which they were proclaimed, the political intent of the declarations, and even upon the legal ramifications of declaring an official end. Yet in a practical sense the war with the "Thousand-Year Reich" that endured only twelve years and three months effectively ended with the Potsdam Conference of July 16 through August 2, eighty-seven days after the shooting stopped. There was an ironic resonance to Potsdam, a suburb of Berlin that had once been the seat of Frederick the Great. Hitler had so identified himself with the eighteenth-century Prussian hero that he considered home to be wherever he carried the king's ornate oval portrait.

Americans had been traditionally reluctant to enter distant wars, and only General George C. Marshall's personal appeal to Congress in July 1941 to extend the grudgingly approved first peacetime draft had pushed it into passage by a single vote. In November, Major General George S. Patton's 2nd Armored Division, on maneuvers in Louisiana, had to be fueled from roadside gas stations and paid for out of Patton's wallet, as were replacement bolts for his tanks ordered from Sears Roebuck. When the surprise attack came at Pearl Harbor, Captain Ellis M. Zacharias of the *Salt Lake City*, returning to the stricken, smoke-filled base from maneuvers the next day, told his shocked crew on the cruiser's intercom that the sneak attack had destroyed only the obsolete old navy. In the summer of 1945 he would be broadcasting, in Japanese, to Tokyo that further resistance was useless. In the summer of 1945 Patton's new tanks would be in Bavaria, and the new navy, including ships lifted from the mud of Pearl Harbor and modernized for a war of a nature no one imagined in 1941, was battering the home islands of Japan.

The new fleet was already under construction as Zacharias brought the *Salt Lake City* in, but little of it was afloat when the Japanese were halted in the Coral Sea off Australia early in May. Although the first carrier-to-carrier battle in history came out a draw, it thwarted Japanese expansion toward defenseless Australia, which possessed one Hurricane fighter plane—for training. Much of the Aussie army not fighting in North Africa had been forced to surrender in February at Singapore, a humiliation owed to miscalculations in London. The final American humiliation came at Corregidor while the Battle of the Coral Sea raged. Landing on Corregidor, the Japanese forced the surrender of the pathetic remnants of MacArthur's Philippines garrison, left to Major General Jonathan Wainwright when MacArthur was ordered to Australia to plan his way back.

The new American B-29 Superfortresses, which would set Japan afire in 1945, were still on the drawing board early in 1942, and the Air Force's B-17 (Flying Fortress) predecessor would prove useless a month later against the Japanese armada heading for Midway Island and the domination of the Pacific. Level bombers were ineffective against moving ships. But the Japanese had found no aircraft carriers at Pearl Harbor, which Admiral Yamamoto, even from the distance of his flagship in Hiroshima Bay, had realized was ominously crucial. The battleship war had been the *last* one. On June 4, American carrier planes made the difference, sinking four Japanese carriers with many of their aircraft aboard and reversing the momentum of December 1941. Once American marines began retaking Guadalcanal in the Solomons in August, the tide had effectively turned, and the Japanese were mired in the protracted war they could not win. American industrial capacity would overtake the early enemy successes.

•     •     •

Across the world the Axis tide was also turning: by November 1942 the Russians were reducing Stalingrad; the breakout of British and Commonwealth forces from El Alamein that would carry them across Libya had begun; and, in French North Africa, General Dwight D. Eisenhower's "Operation Torch" was putting American and British forces ashore in the first step toward the liberation of Europe.

Early in 1943 Roosevelt and Churchill met in Casablanca to plan the next Western moves and issue the first call for "Unconditional Surrender," a demand that seemed arrogant, given Japanese control of nearly seven thousand miles of the Pacific and Indian oceans and German occupation of nearly all of Europe. Stalin remained so suspicious of Anglo-American intentions—a separate peace with Hitler would leave Germany free to crush Russia—that the United States and Britain had to declare that their aims in both Europe and Asia were unwavering. Eisenhower's deal with Vichy's Admiral Darlan in Algeria had suggested that further compromises with Fascism could follow. Shabby bargains were not unknown to the Soviets, whose pact with the Nazis in August 1939 permitted the Russian aggrandizement from Finland to Romania.

Although the unconditional surrender formula would lock the West into positions from which negotiation was impossible, the slogan seemed opportunely timed. On February 2 General Paulus surrendered what was left of his huge Nazi army at Stalingrad; on the eighth the American Eighth Army entered Tunisia, while on the nineteenth the Japanese Seventeenth Army evacuated the last of its troops from Guadalcanal. Some temporary German successes in March gave the Red Army pause, but in July at Kursk the largest tank battle in history ended German hopes to hold on to anything of Russia.

An epic of heroism, the Warsaw Ghetto uprising of April 19, 1943, had become, by May 16, a lonely failure as no one came to the doomed inhabitants' aid. The Russians had no interest in the matter, and it would take the West until mid-July to get as close as Sicily, still offshore from the European continent. But the imminence of the invasion of Italy itself led to the fall of the first of the Axis dictators, Mussolini. Forced to resign on July 25, he was arrested. By September, Italy had surrendered and changed sides, but the Germans poured in, rescuing the hapless *Duce* and keeping the Allies from moving north into what Churchill had touted as the "soft underbelly" of Europe. A second front across the Channel was still essential, and Stalin grew impatient waiting for it to take some of the pressure off the Eastern Front.

That the Germans were able to fight multifront campaigns against demographically and materially overwhelming adversaries was a continuing triumph of generalship, technology, and the ruthless employment of slave labor and the occupation economy. Resources, however, had their limits. The Nazi war machine now depended upon synthetic oil and rubber and the diversion of crucial materials from one priority to another. Raids by American and British heavy bombers forced plants underground, although not out of action, yet the German war effort had become entirely defensive. *Festung Europa* had considerable fight left, but the Nazis could no longer carry the war to the enemy except through submarine warfare, which for many months had sunk more Allied tonnage than could be replaced. With new sonar and better convoy protection, even that strategy was no longer effective in the final months of 1943.

For the Japanese, dependent for resources on the captured colonies, the American submarine offensive, erratic and inefficient through 1942 (Navy torpedoes often failed to explode), had become grimly effective, cutting off resupply of the Japanese home islands. Meanwhile, American forces island-hopped, often at great human cost, across Pacific atolls toward Japan. Tarawa was taken in November, Kwajalein in January (1944), Eniwetok in February, Saipan in June. The Air Force was now able to reach Japan itself from the Pacific.

From England, American and British bombers—the newly manufactured B-29s were being reserved for Japan—were firebombing German cities such as Hamburg and Bremen daily and nightly, often at heavy cost in airmen, attempting to interdict supplies for the Second Front and diminishing by attrition Göring's dwindling squadrons of fighter planes. In the south of England the buildup for the D-Day seaborne invasion first planned for May 1944 was masked by a fake mobilization near Dover—closer, the Germans thought, to the Rhine-Ruhr industrial heart of the Nazi empire. With the Red Army sweeping into Poland in the spring of 1944, the Soviets appeared so irresistible that "Overlord" across the Channel seemed necessary if only to check the Russians at the Rhine. That nearly all of Europe seemed inevitably lost to communism in mid-1944 also explains Western concessions to Stalin at Tehran, ratified later at Yalta. To guarantee freedom to some of Europe meant conceding what already appeared lost. The Red Army was already in prewar Poland when Rome fell on June 5. D-Day—delayed by Channel storms—succeeded on June 6. Vastly outnumbered and almost without any presence in the air, the Germans held Eisenhower's forces to small beachheads through effective artillery fire. Yet Allied footholds were held and expanded, and by the time the belated von Stauffenberg plot to kill Hitler at his East Prussian headquarters failed on July 20, Eisenhower's forces were about to break through at Saint-Lô.

As Tinian and Guam were taken in early August—creating, with Saipan, a huge airfield in the Marianas within Superfortress distance to Japan—desperate German strategy, with defeat looming, began to turn to superweapons and to political guile. The West might be put into disarray if its own island operations center, England, were attacked by the new German technological marvels, the V-1 "buzz bomb," a pilotless explosive with wings, and the far more frightening V-2 rocket bomb, a first-generation space missile that lifted off from North Sea pens and struck without warning. (The first V-2s hit London on September 8.) Only in December 1944 did the Americans capture a V-weapon factory, at Wittring, but stockpiled missiles still landed. That the Rhine now proved accessible, despite fierce resistance—the unexpected Battle of the Bulge, in the snowy Ardennes the week before Christmas, was the last Allied defeat—resulted from Hitler's decision to slow the Russians at the expense of accelerating the Allied advance. There was still hope that superweapons and the fear that Communism would overrun Europe might induce the West to strike a deal preserving some of Germany in order to contain Stalinism. Anglo-American insistence on unconditional surrender kept the wary alliance intact, but Stalin remained suspicious about what seemed easy successes by the Americans and British, and capitulations to them of large German forces while the Red Army was encountering stubborn resistance in eastern Hungary and central Poland.

In the Pacific, Japanese resistance as the home islands became threatened increased from fierce to fanatical to suicidal, and all the while the changing governments in Tokyo (on July 18, 1944, Tojo had been sacked) looked cautiously west to Russia as a possible predator as the now-dead Yamamoto had feared, or, more hopefully, as peacemaker. Soviet mediation might permit Japan to keep some of its gains, and the military government replacing the regime that had begun the war now saw victory as hopeless—especially after the Philippines were invaded late in October and much of the remaining Japanese fleet was destroyed off Leyte in a carrier-plane encounter eclipsing even Midway in losses. By the close of 1944 the Japanese had no offensive capability in the air or on the sea and could not prevent a landing on Luzon. When Manila fell on February 24, 1945, it was a ravaged hulk—the Japanese had fired the city as they retreated into the hills— but both the Philippines and the Marianas now became vast staging areas for the planned invasion of Japan.

It took American forces until January 16 to eliminate the Ardennes salient that had upset the timetable to the Rhine, but two weeks later General Omar Bradley's divisions reached the Siegfried Line of pre-war Germany, and major cities, many of them long blasted from the air, began to fall. To support the Russian advance from the east and to impede German retreat, the Western Allies, who had little reason for further saturation bombing of indefensible cities closer at hand, hit Dresden, which had extensive railway marshaling yards, on the night of February 13, raising a firestorm exceeded only when the massive B-29 raids on Japan began in March of the same year. In Dresden a hundred thousand civilians died, leaving little of the city for the Red Army to plunder.

With only twenty-six understrength divisions against Eisen-hower's eighty-five augmented divisions, *Wehrmacht* resistance broke down. The Germans tried to hold on to their North Sea missile sites to the end, but on March 27, 1945, the last V-2 landed in Britain. It was the day before Eisenhower, recognizing the occupation con-straints agreed upon at Tehran and Yalta, when it appeared likely that the Red juggernaut would roll into Berlin before the Western Al-lies could reach the Rhine, shifted his advancing armies away from the capital. Politically motivated cries of sellout came later from crit-ics blind to how the strategy looked at the time the decisions had to be made. Allied forces moved southward instead into Bavaria and Austria, and northwest into Holland, North Germany, and Denmark, liberating Belsen and Buchenwald on April 12 and taking the Nazi holy city of Nuremberg on April 20. Some Allied regiments would rove beyond the agreed occupation zones, even into Czechoslovakia, but these would pull back. Armies from East and West met at the Elbe on April 25. The *Wehrmacht* was no longer fighting to defend territory, but to avoid the clutches of the Soviets, burdening the West with millions of prisoners of war and refugees it could neither shelter nor feed.

By then the Russians had Berlin under siege, and Hitler was directing a fantasy war from his bunker beneath the Chancellery. On April 22 he permitted his Supreme Command—the OKW—to flee north to Schleswig-Holstein in the few planes left. The Berlin command had been reduced to a ten-mile strip little more than three miles wide. But like the Japanese leadership, Hitler had no intention of surrendering. His was not the case of the captain going down with his ship but of the captain taking the ship down with him—to the Japanese, a *kamikaze* conclusion.

"We are vomiting up our victories," a disillusioned German officer would concede. Unpleasant as the metaphor was, it reflected the realities for both Germany and Japan. Both were faced with demands for unconditional surrender. For Germany the vast European empire was gone and there was little left, at the end of April 1945, to surrender, even of the *Heimat*. For Japan the sprawling colonies were as good as lost, but the home islands might be rescued—or ravaged. What kind of summer it would be for Japan would be determined in Tokyo, in the tunneled corridors of the War Ministry on Ichigaya Hill.

# CHAPTER I

## · THE ROAD TO POTSDAM ·

For the Germans early in May 1945 *die Stunde Null* had come—the Hour Zero when the Nazi nation, touted by its founder to last a thousand years, ceased to exist. Allied troops streaming across what was once the frontier found warnings posted by their predecessors: "Here ends the civilized world. Fraternizing prohibited." Exhausted Germans raised their own ironic signs amid the ruins—*"Das verdanken wir Hitler"* ("For this we thank Hitler")—recalling the Party invocation during the years of pride. Puzzling at first to the Americans and the British, a scattering of messages read, defiantly, "88"—shorthand for the eighth letter of the alphabet and proclaiming, as the Third Reich disappeared, "Heil Hitler!" More mordantly clever was the "USA" lettering seemingly a welcome to the occupiers. To unregenerate Nazis it was code for *unser seliger Adolf*—"our blessed Adolf." Yet in that context *seliger* also meant "deceased."

The end of the *Hitlerzeit* had been signaled by Hitler's own. The news that he had committed suicide in his bunker in Berlin on April 30 made it clear to Dwight Eisenhower that the *Führer*'s successor, Admiral Karl Dönitz, trapped at his base in Flensburg, just south of the Danish border, would soon negotiate the end. The rump regime hoped to surrender as many of its forces as possible to the West rather than to the dreaded Red Army. The surrender of Admiral Hans von Friedeburg to Field Marshal Bernard Montgomery at Lüneburg occurred on the fourth, enabling him to go to Reims on a British plane to sign, for Dönitz, a general surrender.

At Supreme Headquarters, a red-brick "schoolhouse"—actually a technical college—in Reims, Eisenhower had already determined that he would not meet personally with Friedeburg. The American general was effectively a head of state, master of a grand coalition. The German represented a commander with doubtful credentials only his for a few days. Besides, Eisenhower knew little German and preferred to leave Friedeburg to chief of staff Walter Bedell Smith and intelligence chief Sir Kenneth S. D. Strong. Playing for time, so that further hundreds of thousands of the *Wehrmacht* might evade Russian encirclement and capitulate to the West, Dönitz's emissaries dragged on what were supposed to be unconditional surrender negotiations into the next morning, claiming that they were not authorized to sign a surrender that included Russia. In a nearby room, however anxious about developments, Eisenhower tried lulling himself with his favorite bedtime reading. He had a Western by William Colt MacDonald in the oblong two-columned paperback Armed Forces Edition—*Cartridge Carnival*. It was the thirty-third and newest novel by the author of *Six-Shooter Showdown*, in which gunslinger Stormy Knight relentlessly pursues cattle rancher Rufe Harper's mean-eyed, fast-shooting henchmen. With some of the book's 215 pages still to go, Eisenhower summed it up to Mamie as "terrible. I could write better ones, left-handed."

While Eisenhower waited, Dönitz instructed Colonel General Alfred Jodl, chief of operations for the High Command, to surrender to Montgomery, who was close to Flensburg. Winston Churchill was already preparing his victory broadcast when Jodl threw Downing Street off schedule. The general, Montgomery telegraphed London, was seeking forty-eight additional hours in which to get surrender orders to his troops.

Abandoning *Cartridge Carnival*, Eisenhower insisted impatiently through his deputies, as Jodl flashed to Dönitz that "we sign today otherwise Allied lines will be closed even to persons attempting to surrender individually and negotiations broken off. See no alternative but chaos or signature." The forty-eight hours would be timed from that midnight.

In Reims at 0241 on May 7, in the presence of British, American, French, and Russian witnesses, Jodl signed. The effective date was to be midnight the next day, after which Churchill and Truman would make simultaneous broadcasts. Yet the German High Command rushed to announce the surrender, eager to hasten its troops into Allied rather than Soviet hands. After the breach of pledged silence, news services followed with their own bulletins, the Associated Press first to the wire.

When Jodl and Friedeburg* were returned to Flensburg with a copy of the surrender documents, with them also was a copy of the American service newspaper *Stars and Stripes,* which had published photographs of Buchenwald. Dönitz would later claim that for most of the *Wehrmacht* brass it was the first revelation of the death camps, which were largely under SS control.

That night, at Bancroft Hall at the Naval Academy in Annapolis, midshipmen wondered whether the Japanese would hold out long enough for some of them to get a taste of war. Probably, said James Earl Carter, but not long enough for him, as he was a member of the class of '46. He was due only for a summer tour aboard a battleship unlikely to leave the peaceful Atlantic.

While Truman and Churchill rushed to microphones—jubilation had already reached the streets—Stalin refused to recognize the tripartite surrender his representative in Reims had been given no instructions to sign. "Churchill was trying to make me break faith with the Russians," Truman wrote in his diary. He was new to high politics but understood that Churchill wanted to renege on agreements made at Yalta because the Russians were already failing to keep their part of the trade-offs. A victory announcement from the West would take some of the gloss off Soviet achievements and help Churchill politically. As a maneuvering tactic, Churchill also wanted to delay withdrawal of British and American troops from their farthermost penetrations into Austria, Czechoslovakia, and northern Germany. These were in future Soviet zones of occupation agreed upon at Yalta, seized while the Russians were preoccupied with the prize of

---

*Friedeburg committed suicide by poison on May 23 as the British were taking the officer corps at Flensburg into custody.

Berlin. American evidences of good faith included Eisenhower's refusal on May 4 to advance upon Berlin and Prague, and his denying
prisoner of war refuge to a million or more Germans conducting a
fighting retreat in the East while attempting to surrender to the West.

The Yalta concessions by Franklin Roosevelt recognized military
and geopolitical facts. The Big Three had convened on February 4,
only a month after the Americans had been pushed back in what became known as the Battle of the Bulge; Allied troops would not reach
the Rhine until Yalta had adjourned. In the East, hundreds of Russian
divisions had penetrated the heartland of Germany. Once the Americans withdrew troops to the Pacific, the Red Army could overwhelm
all of eastern and central Europe. Tough Communist parties, practiced
at subverting the electoral process, were already active in Italy,
Greece, and France. On the plus side, a Russian invasion of Manchuria
and Korea, endangering the home islands, might push Japan out of
the war before a costly American invasion was mounted. As a show of
unity the three powers had agreed at Yalta on a public German surrender, in Berlin. The capitulation at Reims had bypassed that.

The eighth of May would acquire a grim resonance in Germany.
Heinrich Boll's first novel, written in 1950 but opening in a gutted
city like Cologne on May 8, 1945, has its hero, a soldier on the run,
survive via a stolen rubber stamp to officialize documents that keep
altering his identity and to authorize ration coupons for food. Now
the occupation places him in new jeopardy. "Peace?" he inquires as
he rummages through his dirty, reddish coupons to secure precious
bread. "Since when?"

"Since this morning," a woman with a "gray face and dead
eyes" explains.

"I know," he says. "It's been over for a long time, but peace?"

"We've capitulated; don't you believe it?" To confirm the surrender she calls over an amputee who sits on the remnants of a wall.

The scene in *The Silent Angel* encapsulated urban Germany as the
war ended—the weedy rubble, the amputee, the beggary, the fearful
soldier under death sentence by one side for desertion, evading the
uncertainties of a POW camp on the other. The ruins almost obliterate
memory. "So this is Grosse Strasse?" he asks a man with a threadbare
sack of potatoes, one of the "ghosts whose path and goal could not be
ascertained: figures with packages and sacks, cartons and crates. . . ."
Yet it was worse in the east, where the Russians had come.

A hurried second signing in Berlin, the show Stalin wanted,

would be an anticlimax, but it made possible a Russian celebration of victory on the ninth.

Three million people thronged Red Square, Gorki Street, and the Moscow River embankments. They danced and sang and shouted "Hurray for Roosevelt!" The dead President had become synonymous with America. The fireworks were spectacular, and even from cell 53 of Lubyanka Prison shaven-headed former sergeant Aleksandr Solzhenitsyn, charged at the front with counterrevolutionary statements, could see the tracery through the bars and hear the forty-gun salute. Having fought across the Ukraine, Belorussia, Poland, and East Prussia before political indiscretions in his letters were discovered, Solzhenitsyn was as filled with emotion as if he had not fought for nothing. He had known a few hours earlier that something unusual was happening when for supper he received two bowls of gruel and a ladle of soup.

Dönitz ordered all U-boats to surface and surrender. Many others were scuttled in port. Of the Type XXIII superboats, new to the service, only one, the *U-2511*, was at sea, in the Atlantic. The giant 22,000-ton *U-234*, on its way from Kiel to Kure with war material for which Germans no longer had any need, was unable to pick up signals from home after May 2, until one of the repetitions of Dönitz's order was overheard. On May 10, Lieutenant Commander Adelbert Schnee, out of a Norwegian base and nearing the Faroe Islands, had just found a British cruiser in his sights. Still, the order, "Cease all military activity," held. Captain Johann Heinrich Fehler surfaced and headed for the American mainland. Two Japanese officers aboard warned that they would kill themselves rather than surrender. Given submarine conditions, Fehler ruled out ritual disembowelment. They settled for cyanide. Five hundred miles out, on May 14, the *U-234* was boarded by a U.S. Navy crew that took it into Portsmouth, New Hampshire. An inventory of its cargo included 560 kilos of uranium oxide. The Nazis had failed to make wartime use of it. Now the Japanese would lose the opportunity.

Although advance American forces were kept under tight surveillance by suspicious Russians, on May 8, the day the *Wehrmacht* on the Eastern Front finally surrendered to the Soviet Army, Anglo-American intelligence in Berlin learned that conditions at the end had prevented Japanese embassy officials from totally destroying their

Type B cipher machine. Buried in the floor, it was discovered later, were four key pieces, with cogwheels and wiring largely intact. (The "PURPLE" device would help keep tabs on the Japanese.) Also found intact, at the Hotel Mozart in Bad Gastein, was General Hiroshi Oshima, the Japanese ambassador to Berlin throughout the war. General Maxwell Taylor would remove Oshima and the embassy staff and take over the hotel.

The most significant broadcast on V-E Day was not heard in Europe or the Americas. At the microphone in a studio in the Department of the Interior at 11:00 A.M. on May 8, as a heavy rain was drenching Washington, was the former captain of the *Salt Lake City*, who remembered Pearl Harbor. Ellis Zacharias's excellent Japanese was the product of prewar service as an attaché. He translated his own words into English, his voice penetrating the home islands via transmitters in Honolulu and Saipan. American listening posts quickly traced the reception of the blunt message in Japan:

> Nazi Germany has been defeated.
> The Japanese people have felt the weight of our land, air, and naval attacks. So long as their leaders and the armed forces continue the war the striking power and intensity of our blows will steadily increase and will bring utter destruction to Japan's industrial production, to its shipping, and to everything that supports its military activity.
> The longer the war lasts, the greater will be the suffering and hardships which the people of Japan will undergo— all in vain. Our blows will not cease until the Japanese military and naval forces lay down their arms in *unconditional surrender.*
> Just what does the unconditional surrender of the armed forces mean to the Japanese people?
> It means the end of the war.
> It means the termination of the influence of the military leaders who have brought Japan to the present brink of disaster.
> It means provision for the return of soldiers and sailors to their families, their farms, their jobs.
> It means not prolonging the present agony and suffering of the Japanese in the vain hope of victory.

> *Unconditional surrender does not mean the extermination or
> enslavement of the Japanese people.*

Following the adage that a nation has interests rather than
friends or enemies, American listening posts intercepted messages
originating overseas from allies, neutrals, and enemies. The neutral
nations that maintained diplomatic missions in Japan (as had been
true in Germany) became inadvertent American sources when they
reported home, while allies were watched as well as enemies. Was it
in the American interest, for example, for De Gaulle's France to regain Syria and Indochina, or for Britain and Holland to return to
Southeast Asian possessions eager for independence? The Japanese
had promised freedom to almost every territory seized except for
Singapore, which was to be the Imperial colony of Syonan. That
Russian signals had to be monitored was hardly a decision made by
anti-Red ideologues. Stalin had connived with Hitler to carve up
Poland, to seize the Baltic states, and now intended to carry Communism as far west in Europe as he could. The goal was a public one,
dating back to Lenin. Responding to the Russian record, American
officials as junior as Assistant Secretary of State Nelson A. Rockefeller
and Assistant Secretary of War John J. McCloy were privately referring to the Soviets in terms formerly reserved for the Nazis. On the
very day the Soviets officially proclaimed victory, fifteen Polish leaders recommended by Britain to Russia as possible members of a multiparty future government were arrested and taken to prison in
Moscow. "I do not see what we can do now in this interlude of joy-
making," Churchill minuted to his Foreign Office. Seized German
generals predicted openly that the West would need the *Wehrmacht*
to fight the inevitable next war against expansionist Russia.

Admiral Dönitz's formal surrender as the *Führer's* heir included
every remnant of German-occupied territory, leaving such quislings
as Vidkun Quisling himself, the Minister President of Norway, isolated. News of the signing at Reims reached the man who had given
his notorious name to the English language in 1940 at mid-afternoon
on May 7, but he knew it was coming because his Belgian counterpart, *Reichskommissar* Leon Degrelle, who had escaped to Denmark,
had flown to Oslo the day before. In Norway all of Quisling's trap-
pings of power had vanished. Home Forces materialized to take over
police stations and prisons, but faithful to Scandinavian niceties, no

Norwegian administrators assumed office until the surrender took formal effect one minute after midnight on the ninth. By then the *Reichskommissar* for Norway, a onetime Rhineland politician named Josef Terboven, had retired to his mansion, Skaugum, accompanied by the head of the *Sichersheitpolizei*, Friedrich Rediess, responsible for the occupation's tortures and murders. Steeling shaky resolve with drink, each waited for the other to follow his *Führer*. Finally Rediess put a pistol to his head and pulled the trigger. Terboven dragged the body to his concrete bunker in the garden, where he lit an explosive charge, reenacting in his own way the end in the Berlin Chancellery.

Quisling was eager to surrender his evaporated authority to Crown Prince Olav, who had not followed his father, King Haakon, into exile. When Olav refused the Nazi credentials, Quisling left in his *"forer*-car," a bulletproof gift from Hitler, and in the early hours of the morning gave himself up to the new acting chief of police in Oslo, Henrik Meyer. There the puppet traitor was booked; his suitcases of liquor, chocolate, and cigars for comfortable internment were confiscated, and a cell prepared at Mollergaten.*

With both Denmark and Norway untenable, Leon Degrelle fled once more, this time to Spain and the protection of Francisco Franco, whose services to escaping Nazis were rivaled in Europe only by the Vatican. More than a thousand war criminals would emigrate, with papal passports, to Paraguay and Argentina. (Degrelle, of whom Hitler said, "If I had a son, I would have liked him to be like you," died in 1994 at eighty-seven, a Spanish citizen with a villa near Málaga.) Kastrup Airport in Copenhagen still held hundreds of warplanes the Germans had abandoned, along with small arms neatly stored inside the terminal building. A small British mission had arrived by air the day before V-E Day to find that the Danes and Germans had already arranged matters. A thousand paratroopers followed to supervise the surrender of the 400,000 *Wehrmacht* troops in Denmark, and according to an American officer in the military mission, Robert Strauss, "there was no difficulty whatsoever. Field Marshal Montgomery issued orders to the German Commanding General that his soldiers were to stack their arms and march out of Denmark on foot to Germany, and these orders were carried out exactly as issued."

Compliance signified much more than Teutonic discipline. Anything was preferable to capitulation to the Russians, which could

*Sentenced on September 10, Quisling was executed for treason on October 24.

mean, and often did, years of slave labor in Siberia, followed by death, rather than repatriation along the lines of the Geneva Convention. Inevitably there were millions who had no choice.

Field Marshal Albert Kesselring, the Nazi commander in the south who had executed a brilliant delaying operation in Italy, was seized at his Alpine headquarters, Heinrich Himmler's former special train, on a siding in Saalfelden. With his weapons, medals, and marshal's baton, Kesselring was flown to the Grand Hotel in Mondorf-les-Bains, Luxembourg, which would be temporary home for politicians and generals too exalted for ordinary POW stockades. Removal there of his symbols of rank began what he called "a bitter progress" through interrogations and confinement—yet less painful for him than for political generals certain of war crimes charges.

Near Plön, just south of Kiel, English sergeant Norman Turgel arrested Field Marshal Erich von Manstein. "I ordered him to take off his shoelaces and braces, which is normal procedure. He said to me, 'Do you realize that I am a field marshal? I expect to be [formally] arrested by someone of the same rank.' I turned to him and said, 'Well, Field Marshal Montgomery is too busy and he asked me to do it.' " Turgel had already been involved in the liberation of Belsen, where he discovered an inmate named Gena, who for all her emaciation still looked beautiful to him. A few months later he married her, in the first Jewish wedding in Lübeck since the Nazis had banned them.

Already in Allied custody was *Reichsmarschall* Hermann Göring, picked up by the 36th Infantry Division near Augsburg. Bloated and bemedalled—he weighed 264 pounds at capture—Göring was first treated by the Americans—to his delight—as an exotic curiosity, but Germans scoffed that the only medal he deserved was the *Kriegsverlustkreuz* ("the war-losing cross"). To be transferred to Mondorf in a small six-seater plane on May 20, he had to be stuffed aboard through the cargo hatch.

Flown to Mondorf the next day with Dönitz and Jodl was Hitler's architect and industrial planner, Albert Speer. He was amazed at the company he would keep: "The whole hierarchy was there: ministers, Field Marshals, *Reichsleiters*, state secretaries, and generals. It was a ghastly experience." Soon quarrels over precedence began among the Nazi hierarchy. Göring claimed primacy as acknowledged successor to Hitler of many years' standing. Dönitz had been designated leader at the end. "Soon the two principals avoided meeting ... while each took the presiding seat at two different tables in the dining room."

The same day, Heinrich Himmler was picked up by the British in Bremervörde. At first he was unrecognized, as he had shaved his mustache and clamped a patch over one eye, but walking along with two of his adjutants he did not appear to be an ordinary disabled veteran. At Lüneburg, where he was taken for examination, he bit into a concealed cyanide capsule and escaped the dining room at Mondorf and the dock at Nuremberg.

Dead or alive, the Nazis who had craved the succession could not have faulted Dönitz's unrepentant proclamation from the "sovereign territory" of his castle just below the Danish frontier to what was left of the German armed forces. "As of midnight," he had declared as the eighth of May became the ninth, "the guns have fallen silent on all fronts." On his orders, broadcasts to the field announced,

> The *Wehrmacht* has ceased the struggle, which has become hopeless. With that, almost six years of heroic struggle are at an end. It has brought us great victories and grave defeats. In the end, the German *Wehrmacht* honorably succumbed to forces vastly superior in number.
>
> True to his oath, the German soldier has given his utmost for his people, achieving unforgettable deeds. To the very end, our homeland supported him with all its might, sustaining heavy sacrifices. The unparalleled achievement of both the military and the civilian population will receive its definitive recognition when the just verdict of history is handed down at some later date.
>
> Even the enemy cannot fail to respect the achievements and sacrifices of the German soldier on land, on sea, and in the air. Every soldier can therefore lay down his arms with pride and dignity and, in these gravest hours of our history, bravely and confidently go to work to assure that our people may live forever.
>
> In this grave hour, the *Wehrmacht* remembers its fallen comrades. The dead enjoin us to manifest unconditional loyalty, obedience, and discipline toward our Fatherland, bleeding now from countless wounds.

It seemed no coincidence that the word *struggle—Kampf—*evoked the fallen *Führer*, whom few Germans knew had committed suicide, and that it evaded the fact of unconditional surrender, or guilt for the war. Dönitz's deputy, Graf Schwerin von Krosigk, in a passionate broadcast to the few Germans who might be listening, was realistically contrite, hoping that the nation might have a future in which it could return to "the innermost and best forces of German nature which have given to the world imperishable works and values." In the aftermath of "the heroic struggle" of his people, he vowed to "combine with our pride the will to contribute, as a member of Western culture, honest, peaceful labor . . . [in] the best traditions of our nation. May God not forsake us in our distress and bless us in our heavy task." While Krosigk, Dönitz's finance minister, had been a loyal Nazi, it was the most un-Hitlerian public statement in Germany in thirteen years. Yet it also followed the Goebbels line that the real enemy of the West remained Communist Russia. "In the East," Krosigk had also said, "the iron curtain behind which, unseen by the eyes of the world, the work of destruction [of civilization] goes on, is moving steadily forward."

For the defeated—the victors had an enemy farther east to subdue—the war at least was over. At Grand Ligne Camp in Quebec, Afrika Korps General Johann van Ravenstein, captured in 1941, told POWs after the commandant had read the proclamation of surrender: "My young comrades, I know it is a sad thing for a soldier to have said to him, 'You have lost.' But let me tell you this: it is better for Germany, better for us, that we have lost, because if we had won we would have lost ourselves."

"As we walked thoughtfully away," a *Leutnant* Boettger, captured at Alamein a year after the general, recalled, "there were those who said he was a traitor. But I and many others will never forget his words as long as we live. With them he gave us a new beginning." A somber mood descended on the camp, muting the old defiance.

On the same day, Private Erich Leverkus was one of a shipful of prisoners about to dock at Newport News. He felt a different kind of relief. "Unconditional Surrender of Germany = end of the war," he wrote in his diary. "First bowel movement since being captured five weeks ago." The next day he added, "Arrival Newport. Amazed at American talent for organization, unimaginably large material resources and mechanical equipment. Bath, delousing, then while still naked[,] interview by young woman reporter."

•   •   •

On the day that Jodl had arrived in Reims, the American 11th Armored Division entered the unguarded gates of the death camp at Mauthausen in Austria, just east of Hitler's birthplace in Linz, where the *Führer* had envisioned a huge Nazi museum. Seven hundred unburied bodies littered the ground. Of the eighteen thousand bewildered survivors, mostly Jews, two hundred were dying of starvation and disease daily. Shocked troops struggled to keep from retching as they tried to bring in food and medicine and remove the corpses. Similar scenes had occurred at Dachau, Belsen, Buchenwald, and elsewhere, townspeople nearby claiming surprise and disbelief at the enormities.

On the same day, Russian tanks arrived at Theresienstadt, which for a week had flown only the flag of the Swiss Red Cross. The Nazis had hauled down the Swastika and fled. Rabbi Leo Baeck and a council of elders had issued a proclamation to fellow survivors the day before asking them to remain in the camp. "In Theresienstadt you are safe," it declared in what must have seemed a rueful irony to the half-dead. "The war is not yet ended. Those of you who might leave . . . expose yourself to many dangers." The Russians distributed bread, sugar, and even tobacco, and wild celebrations went on through the night. But when the Soviet authorities reported the liberation, the overwhelming Jewishness of the inmate remnant was suppressed. Until his death in 1953 Stalin forbade mention of the millions of Jewish victims of the war, many of them Russian, and of the Jewish identity of many heroes of the Red Army itself. Of the saintly Baeck one of the survivors wrote that the hell of the camp "did not seem to exist near him; none of the filth could touch him. Peace emanated from him." But few victims of the horrors could handle their experience serenely, as one American GI discovered.

In Linz itself, Private Michael M. Dembo of the 1126th Combat Engineers remembered, May 8 found him with several other enlisted men and their captain watching the crowds go by the two-story house they had just commandeered as quarters. Conspicuous in the bright sunlight among the well-dressed Austrians were freed concentration camp inmates, their gauntness emphasized by striped prison garb. "Then two boys, perhaps my age, twenty or twenty-one, came up to us pulling a middle-aged man along. . . . The boys claimed that the man had mistreated them in the camp, and they wanted to kill him. The officer took his sidearm, a .45-caliber pistol, from his holster and removed the magazine. He took a round from the magazine and slammed it into the chamber. I can recall the sharp sound. The officer then handed the pistol to the young men, indicating they could do what they wanted. They took him around the corner of the building and we heard the shot. Then they returned, gave the captain his pistol, and left. The man's body lay in the street with a bullet in his head. We all went on our way."

The survivors were almost as much of a problem as the dead stacked in bony emaciation like cordwood. Corpses could hardly be buried now, Nazi style, in a pit, or incinerated. And the living kept dying. Food was too much for the far gone, and the stubbornly alive, in their rags, seemed hardly able to act human—or, at least, civilized. They pushed each other aside in desperate attempts to get to the soup kettles and the abundant loaves of bread. Dazed by privation and brutality, they sometimes seemed uninterested in personal cleanliness and stubbornly refused showers, which many still took to be jets emitting deadly Zyklon-B. Disparate groups, even when of the same religious faiths, despised each other. Poles, Germans, Czechs, Hungarians, Gypsies, Balts, Romanians, and Slavs complained about unequal treatment and lived by a selfish, rather than selfless, survivalist ethic. And in the chaos, reporters, photographers, social workers, soldiers, and politicians gawked at the pathetic circuses the camps had become. The stench of excrement, corruption, and death was everywhere, and the occupants resented being kept in the filthy camps behind the familiar barbed wire while their former oppressors, now fawningly friendly to the occupiers, came and went as they liked in their tidy villages and towns. Often too suspicious, or too listless, to help themselves, survivors in the camps refused to sign anything, or to obey what seemed to be orders. Occupation troops preferred the clean, disciplined, respectful, uncomplaining Germans and Austrians, and detested the victims with their babel of strange languages.

"Displaced Persons"—a new category—wandered everywhere, between and into the lines. Survivors all, some were fleeing the collapsed security zones of concentration camps or slave labor barracks; others were enemy troops who had shed their uniforms. An SS badge could earn the wearer a severe beating, or worse, and storm troopers who looked too well fed in ill-fitting civilian clothes often underwent a simple screening. A blood-type tattoo gave them away. (But a shrewd SS official, the infamous Josef Mengele, saw to it that he had none, and escaped detection as a farmhand.) Thousands of apparent displaced persons were actually Russian prisoners escaping German

POW compounds into the West, or former Russian prisoners who had fought for the Germans and faced certain execution. Liberation led to new abuses and new anxieties. Polish captives at Mauthausen threatened to riot if Jewish services were held, and the few Polish Jews who found their way back to expropriated homes and farms were often murdered en route, or by the new occupants. (At Kielce the next year a full-scale pogrom eliminated hundreds of Jewish survivors who tried to resettle in Poland.)

In Austrian Carinthia and Italian Istria, astride the Yugoslav border, tens of thousands of the "Vlasov Army"—troops of turncoat General Andrei Vlasov, who had recruited POWs like himself to fight the Communists—faced repatriation to Russia. Some, a few with their families, jumped off eastbound trains to their deaths, or slit their throats. Vlasovites in one POW barracks set fire to the building and stood in the flames with linked arms. Another plunged his head through a window and twisted it until his throat was cut. British and American troops who forcibly escorted previous groups of repatriates saw them shot on the docks of Odessa, or heard from witnesses of their extermination and mass burial elsewhere. Turncoat generals would be hanged together in Moscow, but in line with complete Stalinist silence about the movement, on August 2, 1946, *Pravda* listed them only by surname and made no mention of their ranks or anything else but the crime of treachery to the Motherland.

Allied governments had wanted Russia in the war with Japan, and even more, they wanted their own POWs and internees back. With little choice, Roosevelt and Churchill had agreed at Yalta that Soviet citizens as of the 1939 frontiers would be returned to Russia, although the Geneva Convention stated that "prisoners of war are entitled to be treated on the basis of the uniform worn at the time of capture and the detaining power shall not without their consent look behind the uniforms to determine questions of citizenship or nationality." In implicit hostage the Soviets held an estimated one hundred thousand Americans and British liberated from Nazi camps. (Also, they held Americans, mostly airmen, interned after crashing or chuting into Russian space after missions over Japan. It was correct behavior for a neutral.) In the same chaotic border areas as were Vlasov's troops, Marshal Josip Broz Tito's Yugoslav Communists were busy settling scores with rivals and trying to seize portions of adjacent Austria and Italy as spoils of war. As the Allied commander, Field Marshal Alexander, telegraphed to Whitehall, he was faced with a possible war with an ally if he were to forestall illegal seizures of territory. Also, Tito had Soviet-style ideas about renegade prisoners: he wanted them back alive, but he did not want them kept alive very long after that.

While DPs and concentration camp inmates had nearly nothing, the populations of Germany and Austria not made homeless by bombings had lived relatively well until 1945, enjoying if only indirectly the plunder of Europe. Now, East and West, soldiers pilfered from them whatever could be carried away—watches and pistols from prisoners, pictures and anything else portable from churches and museums, silver and liquor from private homes, chickens and pigs from farms, even iron crosses or battle flags from an abandoned headquarters. In Berlin and elsewhere in the East, Russians preferred watches and women. The Red Army seemed to wear watches from wrist to shoulder, seized—it could cost an arm to resist—from soldier and civilian alike, and raped women from schoolgirls to grandmothers.

To many survivors the Russians were a new Mongol horde, evidencing a savagery that did not bother Stalin as he believed the enemy had earned it after its own brutalities. To Yugoslav partisan leader Milovan Djilas, Stalin observed lightly, "Imagine a man who has fought from Stalingrad to Belgrade—over thousands of kilometers of his own devastated land, across the dead bodies of his comrades and dearest ones. How can such a man react normally? And what is so awful in his having fun with a woman after such horrors? You have imagined the Red Army to be ideal. And it is not ideal, nor can it be. . . . The important thing is that it fights Germans—and it is fighting them very well. The rest does not matter." In Berlin, Lalli Horstmann, the wife of a diplomat, evaded assault by escaping through a window. "Masses of soldiers," she recalled, "swarmed ceaselessly in and out of the house like pigeons in a pigeon loft."

Footsore from walking homeward, pilot-candidate James Krüss, having discarded his blue uniform for nondescript fatigues, made his own way among the many. It was not the disciplined march of postarmistice 1918. "I could hear the German of the Banat, the German of the Baltic provinces—I could hear German from Alsace and German from Tyrol; I heard Silesian, German from the Rhineland, Bavaria and Hesse, Hamburg, Thuringia, Swabia, and Baden, and Steyr. This was the last scene of the *danse macabre.* . . ." From a farmhouse a young woman ran screaming and pulled at his sleeve. "My mother! My mother!" she cried. "Help her!" Krüss found a body in the attic, hanging and beyond help. With a pair of hedge clippers he cut her down. The body fell grotesquely to the floor. He was sick in the stomach. "The old woman had been raped by seven Russian soldiers. Then she had climbed up to the attic and competently hanged herself. The soldier who had been the instigator of the crime . . . was shot on the open road by a commissar after a short trial. . . . He lay face down in the gutter."

Death was omnipresent on the roads home. For Krüss the violence had begun when, in Lower Saxony, his major defied the T-34 tanks in the distance. He would piss on them, he shouted, and thrust out his "Zeppelin" to consummate the act. A shot obliterated him, and Krüss crawled away. At each village and town he repeated his story. "He is from an island in the North Sea. Its name is Helgoland. . . . He was supposed to be a pilot, but they had no fuel left. He came on foot. He wants to go home to his island."

To escape the Russian zone Krüss would have to cross the Elbe, where checkpoints blocked the flow to the West, but the British and the Americans were still moving back to positions agreed upon at Yalta. In one town a resourceful typist in the *Bürgermeister*'s office put into English ostensible travel orders for him to Helgoland, stamping it as if by order of the mayor. He still had a long way to go. The next town was Greiz, north of the westernmost tip of what had been Czechoslovakia.

In Berlin, collection points were set up by the Soviets for all radios, telephones, and typewriters. To be found with contraband after the deadline risked a firing squad. Where the Soviets occupied swaths of Germany, the victors made a point about who had won the war by changing to Moscow time on May 20. (The Nazis had done the same to Paris in 1940.) "A beautiful morning tonight," was the rueful joke. Defeat had literally meant *die Stunde Null,* and the lack of watches and clocks, and the artificial new time, was disconcerting. "Everybody who still owns a watch sets the time two hours ahead," Ruth Andreas-Friedrich noted in her diary. "There are not many watches left in Berlin. At least among Germans. Time stands still on the public clocks. As if frozen with horror when the bombs tore up the power supply. Ultimately one gets used to timelessness. In any case, the lack of electric light . . . still rules our daily routines."

In some cases the lack of electric power made no difference because there was nothing for it to run. Rumors quickly arose that Berlin would be occupied by the four Allied powers—it had been agreed upon at Yalta—and Berliners, one of them recalled, began guessing what sectors would be assigned to which flags. "And we had certain aids in our guesses. When we heard that the Russians . . . were taking the electric motors from the *S-Bahn* trains which ran through this district, and also machinery from the Zehlendorf Station, then other Germans would say to us who lived in this area: 'Aha! This means that your district will be in the British or American zone! Congratulations!' "

Few services were restored in the first weeks, but on the grounds of the ruined Titania Palace in the waning daylight of May 26, there had been a symbolic beginning. Without conductor Wilhelm Furtwangler, a Nazi favorite who had fled to Switzerland, the remnants of the Berlin Philharmonic had performed a concert of Mozart, Mendelssohn, and Tchaikovsky, the latter two long banned. Goebbels had prohibited the music of Felix Mendelssohn as a "Jewish concoction," although he had been baptized as a boy. A thousand Berliners came, on foot and on precious bicycles, soon also to be Russian prizes. Later—an index to the chaos—the conductor of the concert, Leo Borchard, inadvertently drove through a roadblock and was shot to death.

Outside the smashed cities conditions were better. The German countryside in some places bloomed; crops were planted up to roadsides and hedgerows. In the south, largely spared the ground fighting, villages and towns were intact, and, independent of the shattered food distribution system, relatively prosperous. Destroyed trackage and bridges and buildings elsewhere, in an economy ruthlessly built upon slave labor, had little impact in picture postcard settings that now became recreation areas for the occupiers. The price of defeat showed only in that it was a country of old men and boys, and run by women. Many men would never return.

One expert flown to Germany shortly after the surrender—the idea would have been abhorrent to the late President—was between-the-wars hero Charles Lindbergh, who had preferred Hitler's Germany as ally rather than enemy, and had opposed the war. United Aircraft flew him to Munich on May 17 as part of a technical mission to see what could be learned from advanced German aircraft to help finish off Japan, a mockery of logic given the industrial lead time to get a weapon into production. The "mass of rubble" that had been Munich and the plight of city dwellers in the ruins left him complaining about American GIs who lived in luxury while the Müncheners appeared near starvation. "What right have we to stuff ourselves?" he asked himself in his diary. "What right have we to damn the Nazis and Japs while we carry on with such callousness and hatred in our hearts?"

Two weeks later he inspected the V-2 rocket factory at Nordhausen, for which adjacent Camp Dora had furnished mostly Jewish slave labor that was worked to death, then cremated by the tens of thousands. Suddenly revolted, he wrote of the scene as "the lowest form of degradation," then backtracked by charging that in the South Pacific some Americans had been equally barbaric to the Japanese, shooting prisoners and keeping their skulls as souvenirs. He had seen such incidents, he claimed, but Lindbergh failed to keep the savagery in scale. "We," he deplored, equating millions with dozens, "who claimed that the German was defiling humanity in his treatment of the Jew, were doing the same thing in our treatment of the Jap."

In the first anarchic weeks in Europe after the war, the rules were that there were no rules if the capacity for enforcement failed to exist. In the Austrian and Bavarian Alps, impromptu hunting parties of the victors blew deer and mountain goats away with weapons meant for combat in order to make a meal of venison or secure a souvenir antler, or merely for what was described as sport. Cigarettes in the West, and food in the East, bought sex, and looted liquor bought hours of a different sort of bliss, later paid for by lax company punishment. Officers, Russian and Allied, quickly settled into confiscated Nazi functionary villas complete with Mercedes-Benz, wine and cigars, and often a resident blonde. Lower ranks had little difficulty, whatever the lightly monitored ban on fraternization, in securing *Ruinenmaüschen*—("mice from the ruins"), as less well fed Germans scornfully called them.

The behavior of troops without a war to fight was often worse elsewhere. The Russians were boorish when on their best behavior, bestial when it was obvious that their commanders would look the other way—and Poland, Hungary, Romania, and Czechoslovakia were treated little better than Germany. In the West, the French, given occupation areas carved from the British and American sectors, dragooned German prisoners into hard labor back home, but, having collaborated—whether actively or passively—with the Nazi occupation, became occupiers themselves on similar principles. With their history of running colonies efficiently, the British were interested in getting essential services going again in the north—and in going home. They had been at war since 1939.

Americans in postwar France were bored with inactivity and anxious about the possibility of reshipment to fight the Japanese. Many were reserve troops who had seen no action. Less than a year after D-Day, freed France seemed remote from war, unlike drab, battered Britain, which had withstood years of attack and privation after its ally had hurriedly surrendered and become a Nazi satellite. In some places the liberation of 1944 had done more damage than the invasion of 1940, but farmers in Normandy plowed around the smashed tanks, and cattle grazed in open spaces around wrecked villages being rebuilt with POW labor. A visiting American Congressman observed from his Army transport plane that the destruction was minimal as they approached Paris, which had spared itself by welcoming the invader. "The Tricolor of France increased in display from window after window.... Everybody seems to be a patriot now. Where are the collaborationists? . . . There is something unreal, something definitely phony about this whole business," he wrote after watching what seemed to be an army of Americans enjoying themselves in the bistros and cabarets with ladies of the evening who had plied their trade with only minimal interruption. "The Montmartre never closed during the reign and rule of the Germans. Life was normal and except for the color and nationality of the uniform, soldiers ruled the roost as they rule the roost now. . . ."

Whether in liberated lands or occupied ones, troops were sometimes bereft of good examples higher up, and the breakdowns in discipline led to behavior that would have been headlined as scandalous, or worse, had it been reported in the press. Yet, one-time private Herschel Liebowitz remembered, although the army furnished holidays at the Riviera or in Switzerland, even classes for interested GIs at the Sorbonne, there was also casual fishing in Rhenish trout streams by the rodless method of tossing in a grenade, or firing into an angler's paradise with an assault weapon. Many in the 75th Division proudly referred to the "7 lootin' 5 shootin' Infantry." But censorship still prevailed, and most photos that made American papers were of the variety that showed GIs giving chocolate bars to children.

Murder, rape, and robbery reached such proportions that there was a bottleneck in carrying out hangings when the British official hangman—the Americans had none—was unavailable. The provost marshal's office at Eisenhower's headquarters, with at least 252 executions for capital crimes on hold, according to a legal officer and future judge, was offered, as a courtesy by the French, the use of a guillotine, but the gesture was declined. In France and Germany, American troops were proving so undependable at policing areas to remove unexploded ammunition and abandoned weapons that German officers were sent out with German troops to do the job. Americans persevered only long enough to collect souvenirs, or booty to black-market, often merely to purchase sex, and afterwards refused hazardous duty. "Us do such dangerous work? We won the war, didn't we?"

Unexploded shells detonated in German fields and forests rattled windows miles away and were a feature of daily life for months. For boys they were dangerously thrilling toys that would cost, if they went off, a limb or an eye. Even more exciting was the pastime that made the job of occupier early in the *Zusammenbruch*—the "collapse"—menacing beyond the occasional overlooked mine or overdue time bomb. The omnipresent open jeep often sported an angle iron welded perpendicularly to the front bumper, rising well above the hood. It was to break wires which resentful Germans stretched across the roads nightly—at just the height to decapitate GIs. The showcase Nazi city of Nuremberg, nearly destroyed in February by Eighth Air Force B-17s, was especially hazardous.

Most GIs, for whom a good time meant something more boring, but doing it in their own hometowns, added up their "points" or other measuring units of service time and awards, and yearned for home. If short on points a GI was likely to face a sprawling camp in France named for his favorite smoke—a Camp Lucky Strike, Philip Morris, or Old Gold—and shipment, possibly after a Stateside furlough, to the Pacific.

In the Pacific itself, soldiers and sailors hoping for home before the biggest push of all joked in mimeographed mock circulars in blackly humorous bureaucratese about eligibility to apply. One category was men over fifty-five who had completed forty-four years of faithful service overseas. Also eligible were "men who have become deceased, providing the fatality was incurred in line of duty and his name has been properly submitted to the Graves Registration Office." Other eligibles for release were "men in lower ranks who formerly held the rank of Major General or above, providing the reduction in grade was not due to misconduct." Exceptions were men dying "while waiting to be rotated home," as that would be interpreted as not wishing to return, automatically cancelling the application. "Furthermore, if it is established that he has accepted mortality without authorization, his corpse is subject to disciplinary action under AW 96, Deliberate Circumvention of Authorized Dying Procedure."

To drastically augment forces in the Pacific and to replace the seasoned servicemen actually rotated to the States, American officers in Europe from platoon leader up were asked informally for the names and service numbers of problem soldiers whom they wanted to get rid of. "These," Major Ed Buss of the 101st Airborne remembered, "were cut orders for redeployment to units tapped for the invasion of Japan."

"I believe that war lowers mankind," said Konrad Adenauer, newly installed as civilian mayor of Cologne, when interviewed by the OSS on June 22; "that every war encourages the worst instincts of both victor and the vanquished."

In the Rhenish city of Krefeld a twenty-two-year-old sergeant in the 84th Division, no expert on local government but fluent in German and clearly smart, was delegated to oversee restoration of municipal services. Seven years earlier as a teenager he had exited Germany as an *Untermensch*. In a few days "Mr. Henry" had organized civil employees who hadn't fled—he had the power of arrest— and the community of two hundred thousand was working again, while Sergeant Kissinger found himself a cottage and confiscated from a Nazi a white 1938 Mercedes-Benz. Moved soon to run a larger district in Hesse, he took his Mercedes to the hillside suburb of Bensheim and occupied a villa previously named "Adolf Hitler."

On May 25, 1945, Eisenhower moved his headquarters to the sprawling I.G. Farben headquarters in Frankfurt. His WAC private secretary Kay Summersby spoke happily of "no more schoolhouses." A visiting congressional committee chaired by Representative Lyndon Baines Johnson* saw the vacated offices in Reims in different terms. It was not, Louisiana Representative F. Edward Hebert reported, "the kind of schoolhouse we have been misled into believing it is as a result of certain newspaper articles describing the German surrender.... Now as a matter of fact this so-called 'Little Red School House' has probably more floor space than the House Office Building in Washington. It covers about 10 or more acres.... In peacetime it was the leading school of technology in France."

The I.G. Farben complex was less institutional, "a small city in it-

---

*After Pearl Harbor, Johnson picked up a quick Navy commission as lieutenant commander, went on a combat patrol in the South Pacific as an observer, and arranged to be awarded a Distinguished Flying Cross before returning to Washington.

self," Sergeant Summersby noted. "It was very elegant—lots of marble and fountains and indoor flower gardens, great curving staircases and very luxurious offices. Several tennis courts could have been fitted into Ike's office." Stories arose that Eisenhower had ordered the buildings spared from bombing because he intended to occupy them. More sinister suspicions arose from the long and reciprocal relationships between the German chemical colossus and powerful American corporations. While Eisenhower was now elevated above innuendo, he could not evade the outcries at home about the coddling of Nazi war criminals gathered together for security in a resort hotel in Luxembourg, and the propensity of outspoken anti-Communists among the high brass—George Patton of the Third Army in particular—to openly co-opt Nazi officers and bureaucrats for the occupation rather than the formerly cowed or imprisoned opposition, many from the political left.

Complaints from Britain and the United States about the apparent failure to pursue a vindictive, punishing peace were not shared by the Germans, who interpreted the quickly detested *Fragenbogen* as revenge. The long questionnaire to screen German job holders and job applicants required detailing past positions, memberships, honors, and a plethora of personal and professional data that might expose a Nazi past.

For Libussa von Oldershausen in eastern Pomerania (soon to be Poland), waiting for a husband who would never return from the war, the indignation of her inconvenienced neighbors was exasperating. "Property owners were complaining about the propertyless, the locals about the refugees, who were allegedly taking everything. And for their part, the refugees were complaining about the lack of sympathy, the coldness, greed, and arrogance of the locals. . . . And then I heard people saying, 'Oh, look at the occupying powers . . . handing out questionnaires on everyone's past political posture and affiliations! I ask you, my dear, what did we know, what could we do about it? Actually, I was always opposed; whenever it was safe. I would always say 'Good Morning' instead of 'Heil Hitler.' But what choice did you have but to go along with it?"

Another *Bürger* would explain that although he had worn the swastika, he was never a member of the Party. "I was only a candidate for admission. I never became a member, although it would have simplified many things for me. If only you knew what I did to stay out of the Party! God knows, it wasn't easy not to be drawn in."

Failure to complete a *Fragenbogen* that was *Persilschein*—the reference was to a popular laundry soap that guaranteed cleanliness—could bar a person from a job or the practice of a profession. Humiliation over defeat and occupation focused on the questionnaire, but public resentment was only possible afterward, when it made Ernst von Salomon's novel *Der Fragenbogen* a best-seller in 1951. Perhaps it helped that Salomon was remembered as a diehard Rightist and anti-Semite who had been implicated in the murder of the Weimar Republic's foreign minister, Walther Rathenau, a Jew, in 1922.

Patton flagrantly violated rules about employing Nazis, and Eisenhower had to step in and admonish him. Ike, so Patton maintained, was naive. Germans had joined the Party to get jobs, he contended, just as an American might have to be registered in the party in power to become a postmaster. Yet he was employing Nazis rather than others with clean bills of political health because non-Nazis were possibly Communist, and he saw the next enemy as the Russians across the occupation frontier. Japan came first, he understood, and he was eager to be relieved of his command in Bavaria if that meant he could lead troops in the Pacific. But there was no shortage of generals eager for another star, and the Army was already beginning to downsize.

Patton was far from alone in seeing Russia as eager for all of Europe, and in the Pentagon there was concern not only about overwhelming Soviet manpower for which Stalin might seek further employment, but about the potential of Russian weaponry. Their tanks and artillery were the best in use, and no one scientifically knowledgeable in the West underestimated Russian potential to produce, in time, an atomic weapon equivalent to the Los Alamos devices. An army management type, General Leslie Groves, who oversaw Manhattan District, looked at the cost and the complexity and foresaw a long uphill struggle for the Soviets. Allegedly they were technologically clumsy. James Bryant Conant guessed that once the Russians examined what the West had done, they could catch up in two or three years, and American intelligence was well aware of Russian competition to capture Nazi weapons experts as they penetrated into Germany. (Even the Americans, British, and French vied fiercely with each other to spirit Nazi scientists into their own enterprises. In American code it was "Operation Paperclip.") Some émigré physicists recalled that Russian nuclear expert Igor Tamm had asked his prewar students, once German physicist Werner Heisenberg had described how the uranium isotope, if separated and combined with others in sufficient mass, might be made to explode, "Do you know what this discovery means? It means a bomb can be built that will destroy a city out to a radius of maybe ten kilometers."*

While the United States guessed that German physicists were Russia's likely route to the Bomb, at four in the afternoon of Saturday, June 2, when it was too hot for most tourists to be out in the streets, two Soviet spies met at the Castillo Bridge in Santa Fe, New Mexico. Harry Gold, an obscure New York chemist with Moscow contacts, had taken a transcontinental train to Albuquerque, and a bus from the station to Santa Fe. Klaus Fuchs, an émigré physicist (and Communist) who had been a British subject since August 1942 and one of its contributions to Manhattan District, drove to the bridge in his old Buick with a packet of details about plutonium bomb manufacture. Passing it to Gold, he noted casually that he didn't think the weapon would be ready for use before the end of the war.

Drawings of the bomb's implosion lens stolen by a young soldier at Los Alamos with Communist connections in New York were offered to Gold the next morning. From the Hotel Hilton he telephoned Sergeant David Greenglass, allegedly identifying himself with the words "Julius sent me." (Julius Rosenberg was married to the sergeant's sister, Ethel.) At 209 North High Street, Gold confidently knocked on the door, received the plans of the triggering mechanism, and left Greenglass five hundred dollars for his expenses. "Fat Man" would be no secret to the Soviets.

Like Hitler before him, Stalin saw little reason to invest substantial resources in a weapon unlikely to be ready by the end of the war. Yet the Bomb was behind American reluctance to rush into a "Big Three" meeting with Stalin and Churchill on postwar Europe and the war against Japan. General Groves had promised Truman a deliverable device sometime in July. Also, Churchill had announced national elections when the war ended. Recalling Lloyd George's "Khaki Election" in December 1918, which gave him a huge majority, the Prime Minister wanted to turn V-E Day to similar political advantage.

The opportunity arose when at a Labour Party conference at Blackpool on May 18 Herbert Morrison and Clement Attlee refused to support an extension of the wartime coalition beyond October,

*Tamm, a future Nobel laureate, would design, with his postwar student Andrei Sakharov, the first Russian thermonuclear device—the "H-Bomb."

whether or not Japan had been defeated by then. Since it would take time after Churchill's formal resignation of his government on May 23—his answer to Labour—to issue ballots to military personnel worldwide, and return them for counting, the campaign would have a long fuse. At home the polling date was set for July 5, with results to be announced three weeks later, on July 26. Labour politician Ernest Bevin would even make a partisan issue out of victory, complaining in the House of Commons that the vacuum of power in Europe created by unconditional surrender and the sweeping out of government at every level left the occupying forces "a Germany without laws, without a constitution, without a single person with whom we could negotiate, without a single institution with which we could master the situation. We had to rebuild with absolutely nothing as a basis."

After twelve years of Nazi infiltration down to the level of postman and policeman, beginning again from absolutely nothing might have been desirable, but the old bureaucracy would be back, as it had been in 1919. Nevertheless, Labour's views would be represented at Potsdam by Attlee, who would furnish continuity if the elections went against Churchill, who expected nothing of the sort. A meeting with Stalin in mid-July with victory in prospect, he figured, might strengthen his negotiating position.

Sensitive to any suggestions that Britain would have to relinquish restive colonies and be reduced to a second-class power like France, Churchill intended to campaign as leader of the party that had won the war, and was outraged when the press picked up a comment by Field Marshal Montgomery that without American involvement Britain could not have defeated Germany. The P.M. wired his displeasure by inquiring whether the field marshal had been correctly reported. The Minister for War warned Monty to expect "fuliginous minutes" from Churchill, as insensitive remarks would be exploited by the "awful lot of near-Communists among the newspaper correspondents."

A onetime torpedo boat lieutenant invalided out of the Navy because of injuries suffered when his vessel was sunk off the Solomons by the Japanese, John Fitzgerald Kennedy, twenty-eight, predicted from London, where he was a correspondent for the Hearst syndicate, that despite Tory confidence, "there is a definite possibility that Prime Minister Winston Churchill and his Conservative Party may be defeated. This may come as a surprise to most Americans, who feel Churchill is as indomitable at the polls as he was in war. However Churchill is fighting a tide that is surging through Europe, washing away monarchies and conservative governments everywhere, and that tide flows powerfully in England."

Hearst had employed young Kennedy because his father was a millionaire conservative Democrat and inimical to Roosevelt. It never occurred to him that young Jack Kennedy was also a shrewd and articulate reporter, and he may not have liked what Kennedy dispatched on June 23—that England was "moving towards some form of socialism."

At a White House meeting with Foreign Secretary Anthony Eden on May 14, Truman had suggested a Big Three conference in "early July." He wanted Russia in the Pacific war. A week later, disheartened by Russian duplicity in Europe, he was not so sure, and cabled Churchill that a date and place for a tripartite meeting would be set somewhat later "if Stalin agrees to participate." To diplomatically arrange a delay in the conference that would accommodate Churchill's political needs as well as the schedule of the Manhattan District, Truman sent Harry Hopkins, long Roosevelt's confidential emissary but now a very sick, even dying, man, to Moscow. While Stalin was eager to talk about redrawing the map of Europe, he was already putting his plans into place, and expected to have his rewards in East Asia in exchange for cooperation against Japan. If not, he would move without Western approval, and had made his independence obvious by boldly putting Communist puppets in charge in Berlin and installing his own regime in Poland. Even before he knew of Hitler's suicide, Stalin packed off from Moscow Airport in an American DC-3 a group of German expatriates led by Walter Ulbricht to become the postwar government of Soviet-occupied areas.

The Ulbricht mission belies the founding myth of the German Democratic Republic, which was that Buchenwald inmates, led by members of Communist cells in the camp, liberated themselves in an armed rebellion and became the core of the new republic. Buchenwald was the "Red Olympus," in which Ernst Thälmann, head of the prewar German Communist Party, had been imprisoned and murdered, and the leading GDR shrine until the satrapy disappeared. Yet the camp had been liberated by Patton's troops on April 11, the SS guards fleeing or surrendering at the approach of American tanks. But perception is history, and a "Buchenwald Oath" of freed Communists on the day of liberation was celebrated annually and Patton's tanks forgotten in Prime Minister Otto Grotewohl's utopia.

With the fighting in Berlin still in progress, Ulbricht (who would be Grotewohl's successor) and his party landed at a temporary airstrip near Kustrin, on the Oder, arriving in Berlin on May 2, the day the Germans surrendered what was left of the city. Making contact with old party members who had survived the Nazis, the Communists had the nucleus of a government. From Stalin's standpoint the fate of Germany was settled, however much he denied to Hopkins that he wanted to dismember the country. To the east, Polish occupation of German territories east of the Oder and the Neisse was a fait accompli, with the army of the Lublin government driving Pomeranians and Silesians from homes and farms they had occupied for centuries. It was Stalin's reimbursement for the half of Poland he had seized in 1939 in concert with Hitler—and bought cheaply with land neither Russian nor Polish but now being rendered *deutschrein* with a brutality for which the Nazis had furnished the example.

At Yalta, Stalin had agreed to broaden his Polish government to include all parties, and to establish democratic freedoms. The concessions were already a charade. Conceding the political facts, Truman and Churchill, once Hopkins returned, withdrew recognition from the London émigré government and on July 5 recognized the Red regime now moved from Lublin to Warsaw.

Churchill understood the powerlessness of the West where Red Army occupation existed, and recognized that Sovietization was likely to harden into the new reality of Europe. On May 12 he had already sent a long, pessimistic cable to Truman, "profoundly concerned" about the future: "I learn that half the American Air Force in Europe has already begun to move to the Pacific theatre." Even the newspapers were describing "the great movements of the American armies out of Europe." Churchill saw new political configurations arising from Soviet power and intransigence: "An iron curtain* is drawn down upon their front. . . . There seems little doubt that the whole of the regions east of the line Lübeck–Trieste–Corfu will soon be completely in their hands." And they would also possess the territory Eisenhower's armies had taken but would relinquish under the

---

*Churchill had not coined the term but his public usage would give it currency. On February 25, 1945, referring to Russia, Goebbels had spoken of *"ein eisener Vorhang."* Vasily Rozanov, in his postrevolution *Apocalypse of Our Time* (1918), wrote, "With a rumble and a roar, an iron curtain is descending on Russian history." Two years later, in her book *Through Bolshevik Russia* (1920), Ethel Snowden wrote that she had returned from behind an "iron curtain." And Churchill may well have seen the text of Schwerin von Krosigk's broadcast in *The Times* of May 3.

occupation zones agreed upon at Yalta. There would be an "enormous Muscovite advance into the centre of Europe," and the West would have to make the best of it, for "it would be open to the Russians in a very short time to advance if they chose to the waters of the North Sea and the Atlantic."

What would later be labeled a Cold War had been developing during the hot one. The allies of convenience—and both sides had understood that from the first day of Hitler's invasion of Russia in 1941—were rivals for dominance in an unsettled world. Realizing that, a weary Churchill and an anxious Truman faced up to their mid-July appointment with Stalin. "Wish I didn't have to go," Truman wrote to his mother in Missouri on his way to Potsdam. "It is a chore." Camaraderie with Russia had never been made easy by Stalin, whose suspicions of the West were paranoid. His ambitions for Europe were as open as his support of Communist parties in each country. In France and Italy, these were major political forces.

In Moscow late in May, Hopkins and Harriman recognized the bleak outlook for accommodation with Stalin but negotiated on the premise that mutual self-interest required it. For the Potsdam meetings to take place there had to be some likelihood of acceptable results. During his grueling ten days of talks, Hopkins was informed, as if it were of little importance beyond evidence of Soviet good faith, of "peace feelers" from Tokyo. They were of little interest to Stalin. He had agreed at Yalta to enter the war as an opportunity to Sovietize East Asia. Washington knew through "Magic" intercepts that some in Japan were looking for a way out of the war, but one that would not relinquish all its gains and would retain its imperial institutions. Yet, while the Japanese navy knew it had lost, the army held out for the decisive battles on the beaches of the homeland, at worst to salvage its honor in defeat, at best to inflict such a cost in enemy casualties as to make the price of invasion too enormous for the invaders to want to pay. Defiance was the official Japanese response to Allied rigidity about unconditional surrender. The ruling elite was unwilling to spell out acceptable terms for peace either to Russia or the West although Japanese envoys in Moscow, Stockholm, and Bern, the chief listening posts for Tokyo in Europe, pleaded with Foreign Minister Togo for realistic overtures. The Americans were listening, but the Japanese General Staff was not.

# CHAPTER II

---

## · SUMMER GRASSES ·

---

With suicide ingrained in their culture, Japanese militarists spurned the lessons of Europe and the pleas of their diplomats abroad that they settle and save the homeland. A million and a half men of the army and navy had already died. The end had become inevitable, as Yamamoto had foreseen, once the possibility of a quick war had faded. Although written about internal dynastic conflicts nearly three hundred years before, the lines of Matsuo Bashō, Japan's greatest poet, had new resonance:

> *Summer grasses*
> *where soldiers dreamed.*

Wherever soldiers fought, the lush grasses of summer were all that survived of the dead.

Death required no uniform. The efficiency of war technology in 1945 ensured that civilians would perish in numbers eclipsing entire divisions. Hoarding their dwindling defensive capability for the inevitable invasion, the Japanese tried intimidating the B-29s by employing powerful searchlights and daunting ground fire. Some planes also fell because of mechanical failure or pilot error. Whatever the causes, crewmen bailing out sometimes reached the ground only to encounter the rage of the enemy, soldier and civilian.

The pistols and the pitchforks had to be hazarded because the B-29s had to fly at half the height and from longer distances than had been originally planned. Heavy bomber operations from China—"Operation Matterhorn"—had failed throughout 1944. The problems—political, operational, and logistic—thwarted Air Force strategists who had hoped to reduce Japan from thirty thousand feet, above enemy fighter levels and AA-fire, employing the graceful B-29s in precision bombing runs. The results were poor, and supplying fuel to China to feed the Superforts proved nearly impossible. But at the new island bases at Tinian, Saipan, Guam, and Iwo Jima (the latter largely a homeward-bound safety net),* tankers by the dozen could unload aircraft fuel. And the weather was better.

With spring the raids had increased, reaching a crescendo in May. The incendiary passes of May 23 and May 25 over Tokyo, each by more than five hundred bombers, and followed by wind-driven firestorms, devastated much of the city and even damaged the Imperial Palace. The cost was twenty-six planes. Eight survivors from one downed B-29 were turned over to the medical school of Kyushu Imperial University for vivisection; other crewmen were beaten to death or beheaded where they landed. Those kept for POW labor lived under the same hazards from air raids as Japanese workmen. Many suffered severe burns or died, allegedly, in bombings, often a lie for executions. On July 14, sixteen airmen were shot without any formalities at the headquarters of the Eastern Sea military district near Tokyo.

Susumu Ushioda, a middle school student drafted to work in the Hitachi factory at Katsuta, recalled watching from his hometown of Kasama the "orange night sky" over the factory complex as incendiary bombs torched the city. The next day the boys were enlisted to remove for cremation the bodies not pulverized in the firestorm. When the train that took them to work was attacked in daylight by two carrier planes Ushioda felt less fear than wonder at the "foreign, fat and

---

*From March 4, when the first crippled B-29 landed there safely, to the end of the war, 2,241 B-29s landed, unscheduled, at Iwo. Others, in July and August, would use Okinawa.

silvery things"—probably Grumman F6Fs. *Fat* was the key word. In the privation of 1945 nothing Japanese was fat.

When the factory at Omori where Shuji Nire (in *The House of Nire*) worked was firebombed, the students mobilized there cleared away the ruins before reporting to a labor battalion in Chiba prefecture, on the bay east of Tokyo. Although the school term had begun in April, those destined for the work force attached to the school were excused until August—but for brief home leave—to build fortifications to repel enemy landings. The orders meant the breakup of the factory group that had already studied nothing for more than a year. At farewell parties, friends got drunk on sake, linked arms, and sang the poignant "Farewell, Rabaul," a popular song of the moment. Withering and cut off from resupply except by an occasional cargo submarine, Rabaul in New Guinea had been one of the outermost colonial bases created by the victories of 1942.

Watching the May 25 night raid from a field near the Umegaoka Hospital, Nire heard a great roar overhead, and through the branches of the ginkgo tree under which he sheltered he saw the huge shape of a B-29, so low that he felt as if he could touch it. Its bomb bay was open, and it seemed no mere metallic creation "but rather the metamorphosis of some mythical bird. The wings and fuselage gave off dull reflections . . . a pale, strange beauty that made his skin creep." He forgot his danger and stood entranced until the field seemed "a sea of fire." He realized that he was not seeing flames "but billions and billions of flying sparks, driven onward by the wind, swirling about like a tornado." He had doused himself earlier with three bucketfuls of water and, in his youth, felt invulnerable—until a spark flew into his eyes. He trembled in pain and ripped his wet hood from his shaven skull.

Two days later the ashes everywhere, including the pile that had been his house, were still hot underfoot. He had home leave until June 1, but no home.

The aftermath entranced future playwright Juro Kara, who remembered playing in bomb craters near the Sumida River in Tokyo. So many buildings had burned to the ground that city dwellers used to rickety buildings fronting narrow alleys had a new sense of space. "You could see the horizon on every side. The skies were so bright that everything looked unnaturally sharp. It was wonderful to play in the ruins. It was like the landscape of dreams."

Yukio Mishima, later a novelist, remembered the sky over Tokyo turning red, yet that with each explosion "suddenly between the clouds we could see an eerie blue sky, as though it were midday. . . . The futile searchlights seemed more like beacons welcoming the enemy planes. They would catch the glittering wings of an enemy plane exactly in the middle of two beams that had crossed momentarily and would then beckon the plane courteously, handing it on from one baton of light to the next." He watched as "a chorus of cheers would rise from the crowd . . . whenever they spotted, against the crimson backdrop, the shadow of a plane that was falling. . . . It seemed to make no essential difference whether the falling plane was ours or the enemy's. Such is the nature of war."

The nearness of death excited Mishima. A melodramatic *seppuku* suicide in 1970, he was not yet ready to celebrate that gory ritual, although newspapers praised it as the supreme act of patriotism. Suicide tactics on the Pacific stepping-stones to Japan had demonstrated a willingness to die for the homeland that dwarfed anything in history. On Saipan not only had soldiers fought almost to the last man, but their dependents on the island, women and children, had hurled themselves from the high cliffs into the Pacific. Of the 2,843 prisoners of war, many were too seriously wounded to have been able to take their own lives; 27,040 bodies were tallied.

The *kamikaze* ("divine wind") mentality had resulted in hundreds of one-way flights into ships of the American armada off Okinawa, leaving nothing for family shrines but patriotic farewell letters, laconic poems, and locks of hair and fingernail clippings in envelopes left in Japan. Sometimes fortified by sake and the toast *"Tennoheika Banzai!"* ("Long live the Emperor!"), pilots flew obsolete planes, even trainers, loaded with explosives rather than return fuel, into the enemy as aimed missiles. Some even rode *bakas*, or flying bombs detached from mother planes and steered toward targets, just as others piloted manned *kaiten* torpedoes discharged from submarines on one-way missions. In Japan itself, awaiting an invasion fleet, were swarms of *shinyo*—exploding one-man motorboats. And in training were *fukuryu* ("hidden dragon") units of frogmen who were to detonate charges beneath enemy vessels.

The last mission of the giant battleship *Yamato* convinced even the most dubious among the Americans that the Japanese would not be starved into submission. Civilian rations were already reduced to fifteen hundred calories a day, and many dug for roots and grubs to supplement the thin diet. Boiled yams, and rice mixed with soybeans, made a memorably good meal, and fish (meat hardly existed) was a rare delicacy as few commercial fishermen risked their lives in inland waters. "I remember," Hiromi Tanaka's grandmother recalled, "being on a train so crowded that when it began to speed up on leaving the station, a man carrying a mackerel was thrown off." Clutching his precious fish, the man lost his head under the wheels of the train, yet the disembodied head, she claimed, kept crying out, "My mackerel! My mackerel!"

A few days later, Hiromi's grandmother added, recalling the Japanese tradition that the souls of the dead hover in a bluish fire, she passed the fateful section of track and saw a bluish phosphorescence floating in the air. "I was shocked," Miss Tanaka reflected, "at the horror of war and at the man's extreme desire for food."

The memory exaggerated the deprivation, but the quality of life, deteriorating badly in the home islands, could only get worse. It seemed better, some in the naval hierarchy contended, to die "admirably," as an example for the millions, civilian and military alike. "Sooner or later," Vice Admiral Seiichi Ito, commander of Task Force II at Kure, was instructed, "it will come to a special [suicide] attack by the entire nation, the hundred million of us." Combined Fleet headquarters intended that he demonstrate that resolve for Japan.

The "hundred million" were actually less than eighty million, but the larger figure (including colonies) was a more impressive image. Ito's force, ostensibly sailing to the aid of beleaguered forces in Okinawa, would have eight destroyers to screen the 73,590-ton *Yamato*, the largest warship afloat, with a complement of three thousand. But it would have no air cover. The requisite planes were being hoarded for defense of the homeland. Still, in defiance of orders, and the odds, some officers scrounged additional bunker fuel for a possible return to port. The sortie's planners never anticipated a return, intending a grand samurai gesture all the better if the battleship's huge guns could find the range of the gathering mass of U.S. troop transports off Okinawa. The *Yamato* could rifle a 3,320-pound projectile thirty-five miles and knock out a battalion—or a ship—with each of the thousand shells she carried.

A month before V-E Day in the West, when the *Yamato* had barely reached the open sea, it was discovered by carrier planes and became more target ship for torpedoes than divine wind. Less than halfway to Okinawa it went down with nearly all hands, the intended object lesson in sacrifice for the home front. On the island it-

self, troops and civilians alike, battered by offshore guns and thousands of tons of aerial bombs, holed up underground in caves and
tunnels, emerging only after dark to fight, and taking losses—as well
as inflicting them—on a scale beyond previous island-hopping en-
gagements. As the distance to Japan narrowed from thousands of
miles to hundreds, the resistance bore no resemblance to the odds.

The names of the suicide missions had, often, a delicate beauty that
belied actuality. A suicide attack often evoked to military devotees of
*haiku* the evanescence of cherry blossoms. On May 3 and May 4, the
Fifth Floating Chrysanthemum launched 125 *kamikazes* at the fleet off
Okinawa, sinking a destroyer and putting seventeen other ships out
of action. The chief targets were the broad expanses of carrier decks,
where a success meant a holocaust of aviation fuel and the disabling
of a takeoff-and-landing pad, but the withering armament arrayed
against the Japanese was overwhelming whatever their tactics. Even
if exaggeration affected the facts, the statistics were startling. On
May 4, well before the Okinawa occupation was declared a success,
the commander of Task Force 58 sent a message to his ships: "Today
this force have reached and well passed one thousand enemy aircraft
shot out of the air by aircraft and ships gunfire since 1 April." "The
enemy," he added hopefully, "cannot take it at such a murderous
rate much longer." Over Okinawan waters on April 6 alone, 200 *kamikazes* out of a swarm estimated at 355 got through a cordon of AA-
firing picket ships and clouds of fighter planes to do such severe
damage that Washington convened a study group to come up with
better countermeasures. The Japanese were banking upon American
unwillingness to take frightening casualties, and before the declared
close of the Okinawa operation, by U.S. count alone *kamikazes* would
have hit 200 ships (sinking 27) and damaged another 53 by near
misses. The awkward *bakas,* more deadly to the rider than the target,
hit another 11.

On May 6, American forces on Okinawa, regrouped after heavy
losses, resumed the offensive, the din increasing enormously when
news of V-E Day reached the island. Troops fired off everything at
hand, with fire-support ships offshore joining land-based artillery in
a celebratory noontime salvo at enemy positions.

Many on both sides had no idea why the tempo had escalated so
disproportionately, as the weather had made movement nearly impossible. What had happened in Europe had little immediate effect

on their war anyway. Although rain and mud mired Marine heavy equipment and kept planes grounded, other responses to incessant Japanese fire were found in the employment of a different kind of fire. Napalm and ten-gallon tins of gasoline reduced units of the Japanese 24th Division from battalions to companies to platoons.

The sector defended by Captain Tadashi Kojo's men, dominated by a height the Sixth Marines called Sugar Loaf, held out into May 10, when with few men left, Kojo put his pistol to his temple and found it blown from his hand by the concussion from a satchel charge thrown into his tunnel. The survivors used their bare hands to claw their way out. One was Kojo.

The *kamikaze* raids, frantic acts of self-destruction, continued into June. On May 9 two of them hit Admiral Marc Mitscher's flagship, the carrier *Bunker Hill*, starting huge fires. There were 343 dead and 43 missing, 243 wounded. Fighter pilots trapped in their ready room were asphyxiated. The ship remained afloat but was out of the war. On May 24, the Seventh Floating Chrysanthemum threw 165 suicide planes into the defense of what was left of the Thirty-second Army. A strong point, the walled Shuri Castle, built of coral block three hundred years earlier, was encircled by walls twenty feet thick at the base. On May 25, in one of the last significant employments of floating artillery, the battleships *Mississippi* and *Colorado* turned sixteen-inch guns on what was once the glory of Okinawan history. The city of Naha nearby was also destroyed.

There would be an Eighth Floating Chrysanthemum and a Ninth, in the waning days of May and the first week of June.

A second enemy was nearly as deadly. The typhoon season had begun, and task force commanders did not need standing orders to keep clear when possible; otherwise prudence required heading into the wind just enough to maintain stability. Admiral William Halsey had warning enough about the murderous weather but persisted in place at great cost. Damaged aircraft had to be pushed off carrier decks; destroyers unable to refuel became bobbing tin cans. The usually tough Chief of Naval Operations, Admiral Ernest J. King, radioed from Washington an "eyes only" message to Halsey with a copy to Admiral Chester W. Nimitz, Halsey's superior at Pearl Harbor: "When convenient and not to interfere with major current operations, I need to know the circumstances which caused operating units of the Third Fleet to encounter typhoon which resulted in the loss and crippling of so many combatant ships."

King understood that the reason was sheer stubbornness, but Halsey blamed faulty weather reports, the typhoon's unpredictable direction, and low fuel (to which he had contributed). A court of inquiry was convened, and while it met, Halsey early in June steamed into another killer typhoon, as did Admiral John McCain. The inquiry fixed blame on both men, but the time was not right to punish national heroes, and neither was reprimanded. It was more important to close with the enemy.

Draftees enjoying the good life in pacified Europe—privates and corporals were permitted to holiday in Paris, on the Riviera, in Switzerland—read the latest news from the Pacific in *Stars and Stripes* and most hoped that they would not be reassigned for the final assault on the Japanese home islands. No GI in the ETO knew that the ultimate weapon to make all combat reassignment unnecessary, the kind suggested in Buck Rogers comic strips, had already been discussed on December 6, 1941, the day before Pearl Harbor, and had been developed only a few months too late to be used in their theater of war, perhaps over Berlin. Manhattan Engineering District, as the two-billion-dollar effort was called, was readying its delivery system on a Pacific island taken from the enemy the year before. Although no connection with the top-secret project had been intended, Tinian, in the Marianas group one hundred miles north of Guam, was crisscrossed now by broad runways and streets named for those in Manhattan itself.

"Manhattan in the Pacific" had been the brainchild of an Engineers' officer who, in laying out the streets, thought that Tinian bore a geographical resemblance to home. The 509th Composite Group was given the "Columbia University District"—which was reasonable, given the coincidence that one of the purposes of Tinian's broad runways was to deliver the products of a secret army of professors. The *Cape Victory*, standing by at Seattle, had sailed on May 6 while the German surrender was being signed at Reims. Aboard were 1,200 509th support personnel. The advance air echelon for eighteen B-29s arrived on Tinian on May 18, eleven days before the *Cape Victory* docked.

By the end of May the "Interim Committee" of the Manhattan District, meeting in Oppenheimer's office in Los Alamos, had refined its target criteria. The urban area had to be big enough—at least three miles in diameter—to sustain extensive blast damage. It had to have significance to the Japanese war effort. And it could not have been substantially damaged by earlier conventional bombing. Secretary of

War Stimson added his personal limitation—that the target could not have profound cultural significance. While that ruled out temple-rich Kyoto and downtown Tokyo, which abutted upon the Imperial Palace grounds, pressure from Air Force brass to put both on the list exasperated Stimson well into July.

As June approached, A-Bomb planners were growing confident that they possessed a workable weapon, but they dismissed suggestions that an advertised atomic explosion might impress the Japanese. There was a chance that it wouldn't go off—a grotesque potential embarrassment. Truman and Churchill agreed, if a test of the device worked, to order a drop over Japan itself. Its dramatic force, taking the nation by surprise, might convince an enemy willing to try everything in its suicide arsenal that continuing the war was useless. After reviewing reports of soldiers detonating grenades strapped to their bodies, and recalling the ultimate *kamikaze*, the *Yamato*, the British embassy cabled from Washington to Whitehall on May 26: "The hard fighting on Okinawa has dispelled excessive optimism about a quick end to the Japanese war."

Given the fanaticism of Japanese resistance, the expected energy yields might not support the idea that the atomic devices were end-of-the-war bombs, but no one could be certain until an experimental detonation. Hans Bethe estimated that "Little Boy"—a U-235 device that used a gun-type mechanism—might set off an explosion equivalent to a maximum of fifteen thousand tons of TNT. It seemed more reliable than the alternative, a plutonium implosion bomb labeled "Fat Man" because the casing resembled an overinflated, oversized football. "Fat Man" had been reduced to fit within a B-29 fuselage. While "Little Boy"—there was sufficient refined uranium for only one of him—was being prepared for shipment to Tinian, a test was rushed for "Fat Man." The implosion mechanism had to be tried in a mock-up weapon, and its release of energy—if it worked—carefully calibrated. "Trinity" site, near Alamogordo, New Mexico, planned in March, was ready for the test by May 7, with firing scheduled for July 4.

The Bomb could have no effect on the outcome in Okinawa. Planners expected the island to be subdued by the time a "Little Boy" was ready. While Japanese suicide tactics created horror among Americans on the ground and offshore, there was no chance that the enemy could dislodge General Simon Buckner's Tenth Army, although resistance could delay operations to invade the home islands. Employing useless Western logic, Buckner airdropped a message to General Mitsuru Ushijima explaining that his case was hopeless and urging him to surrender. It would take seven days to reach him. Ushijima kept moving his command post as the ground he held diminished.

Sacrifice remained official policy, surrender the ultimate disgrace. Emphasizing that final duty to the Emperor, Admiral Minoru Ota, commander of the Okinawan naval base, now a shambles, radioed Ushijima on June 11 that although the base was now under direct tank attack, "Those at our positions will die honorably." Two days later, Marines found hundreds of suicides in the tunnels and caves. The admiral and five senior officers lay with their dress sabers and slit throats. Ota left, typically, a poem:

> How could we rejoice over our birth
> but to die an honorable death
> under the Emperor's flag.

The gravely wounded in Ikuo Ogiso's 2nd Field Hospital were given cyanide injections—but a few crawled away, preferring at least temporary life. Those who requested grenades were carried outdoors to pull the pin themselves. Ogiso slipped away to organize another hospital.

Ushijima would survive his opponent. On the eighteenth, Buckner was killed while with the 8th Marine Regiment by one of the last rounds fired from what was left of the Japanese 1st Heavy Field Artillery Regiment. No other accompanying officer was scratched.* When headquarters in Japan relayed overheard American broadcasts, Ushijima (so eyewitnesses claimed) said a prayer for Buckner. Then he sent an apology to Tokyo for failing to accomplish his mission, and planned his own death.

The next morning he radioed a general order to troops who could tune him in, urging them, "Resist to the very end, then live in the eternity of our noble cause." By then thousands of corpses lay rotting under a tropical sun or in the darkness of unmarked caves and underground passages. His own tunnel was under what Americans called Hill 89, two miles from the southern tip to which the defenders had been reduced. The 7th American Division was closing in with

---

*But the next day, Brigadier General Claudius M. Easely of the 96th Division was killed by enemy machine gun fire.

flamethrowing tanks, taking no chances from snipers, mortars, and machine guns. Every air shaft discovered was torched. On the evening of the twenty-first Ushijima donned his full-dress uniform and shared a last bottle of carefully hoarded Scotch with his aide and a few other surviving staff members, after which they sang "*Umi Yukaba,*" an ancient hymn about sacrificing one's life for the Emperor. A myth would surface that the general committed ritual *seppuku*, serving the samurai code, but the corpses of Ushijima and his second-in-command were later found with bullet holes in their temples. With his final message had been a poetic postscript:

> *Green grass dies in the islands without waiting for fall;*
> *But it will be reborn verdant in the springtime of the homeland.*
> *Weapons exhausted, our blood will bathe the earth, but the spirit*
>     *will survive;*
> *Our spirits will return to protect the motherland.*

Both commanding generals had died. It was a harrowing augury for the final land battles on the beaches of the home islands.


Behind all the preparations to defeat Japan loomed the Soviet Union. Russian manpower, and an Asian mainland diversion, had once seemed essential. Early in February at Yalta, as Americans were about to land on Iwo Jima, Roosevelt and Churchill secured Stalin's assurance that three months after the surrender of the Germans he would be ready to attack the Japanese in Manchuria. Now Germany was occupied, and with the Soviet record of rape, plunder, and murder, suspicion of and hostility to any sort of cooperation except on their terms was eroding the wary harmony between ostensible allies. Anything ending the war with Japan before the Russians joined in to claim their spoils, especially a role in occupying the home islands, began to seem to Truman and Churchill crucial to the postwar stability of Asia. Yet the Russians could not be kept out unless the conflict ended before they could come in.

An Imperial Conference in Tokyo on June 8 settled nothing. Few Cabinet veterans of Pearl Harbor were left, and those, like Lord Privy Seal Koichi Kido and Foreign Minister Shigenori Togo, were now eager for peace. The Foreign Office document under discussion, "The Present Condition of Our National Power," was titled to paper over

Japanese powerlessness. The possibility of Soviet mediation was raised, but General Korechika Anami, the War Minister and a realist, saw no chance that the Russians, at the height of their military power, could be kept out of the war. Desperate to avoid total collapse of what was termed the "national polity," Emperor Hirohito worried aloud that in too cautious an approach to the Russians "we might miss the chance." Still, the six members of the Supreme War Cabinet were hopelessly deadlocked, unable even to use words like *surrender terms* or *defeat*. As Anami explained, Japan still occupied most of the territory it had seized before 1943. Wasn't that worth anything in negotiating a settlement?

No one dared point out that what Japan held was useless, cut off from the homeland, with the imperial conquerors little more than their own prisoners of war. Even where B-29s were not omnipresent in the night skies it was clear that the Japanese presence would not last much longer. Taiwanese guards employed at POW stockades in Hong Kong would smile at roll calls and whisper, "Not long now. Hong Kong soon." And in Thailand, under Japanese military occupation since December 1941, a member of the National Assembly proposed on July 12 that Bangkok be made an open city to protect it from destruction. Such designations usually occurred shortly before a city fell to the enemy.

In the stifling imperial chamber the atmosphere of impending doom seemed to have no effect upon the proceedings. If former prime minister Prince Konoye or anyone else went to Moscow as intermediary, the ambassadors in Switzerland, Sweden, and Russia pleaded—and were overheard by Washington—he had to carry with him negotiable proposals. "I sincerely pray," Shunichi Kase pleaded from Bern, "that a Resolution be passed in the Cabinet Council to have the envoy carry a concrete plan for the termination of the war." But military dominance of the Council stifled such talk, and no one had the authority to carry alternatives of any sort directly to the West. Even Togo banked upon the Moscow route, as Russia was technically a neutral, yet that hope in itself was wishful thinking. The Japanese in Manchuria were well aware of the burgeoning Red Army presence across the border.

With diplomatic failure looming, one side or the other had to make the first move, and Japan's survival required it to take the initiative with a counterweight to the demand for unconditional surrender. Yet an "Ultra" intercept distributed to the top American leadership on June 16 reported that Premier Kantaro Suzuki had de-clared, "Unconditional surrender will only mean that our national structure and our people will be destroyed. Against such boastful talk, there is only one measure we must take—that is, to fight to the last." To underscore its resolve, the War Guidance Council ap-proved a resolution, in Hirohito's presence, calling for "supreme self-sacrifice" and "the honorable death of a hundred million." The patriotic slogan became policy at the highest level.

Dissent in Japan was unthinkable. Duty to the Emperor and Em-pire required laying down one's life for His Majesty if required, and the eighth of every month was Rescript Day, when the Emperor's pronouncement authorizing the Greater East Asia War was publicly re-read in schools, factories, and other gatherings. Opinions to the contrary brought swift punishment; nevertheless, a joke was whis-pered about that if the army leadership was driven by the enemy to the top of Mount Fuji, it would continue to insist that the war situa-tion was still favorable to Japan.

Tokyo's refusal to acknowledge imminent defeat paralleled Ameri-can reluctance to recognize anything less than utter defeat. Memories of Pearl Harbor had been reinforced by revelations of Japanese bru-tality and years of exposure to patriotic posters and slogans. Most Americans wanted to prosecute the war until the Emperor himself could be tried as a war criminal, and Truman's tough words, both public and private, had the obvious backing of the American people. A Gallup poll on June 1 asked, "Japan may offer to surrender and call her soldiers home provided we agree not to send an army of occupa-tion to her home islands. Do you think we should accept such a peace offer if we get the chance, or fight on until we have completely beaten her on the Japanese homeland?" Continuing the war to a decisive vic-tory received overwhelming approval, nine to one.

While the Americans continued to eavesdrop on Japanese code traffic, and learned additional information from Russia, now sending enormous numbers of troops by rail across Siberia, the Japanese en-voys abroad could read American newspapers and saw no easy solu-tion. But the American public was not being given realistic casualty figures about Okinawa as that would escalate fears of what could happen closer yet to Tokyo. Three days before the poll results were printed, Acting Secretary of State Joseph Grew, who had been ambas-sador to Japan at the time of Pearl Harbor, and Eugene Dooman,

Grew's Counselor at the State Department, who had also been interned in Tokyo in December 1941, had met with the American service chiefs. In the background, they realized, loomed the entry of Russia into the war and, at about the same time, possible atomic bombings of Japan. Would unconditional surrender, Dooman was asked, be more acceptable to Japan if it were interpreted as involving only its military forces and not its integrity as a nation?

"If the Japanese," he argued, "become imbued with the idea that the United States was set on the destruction of their philosophy of government and their religion [of the Emperor] we would be faced with a truly national suicidal defense." Grew reported the discussion to the President but it did not change Truman's blunt message on May 31, Memorial Day, that Japan faced "the kind of ruin which they have seen come to Germany." Even that warning was less than the truth. Although he had heard from Hopkins that the Soviets "will be properly deployed on the Manchuria[n] positions by August 8th," the additional factor of the Bomb amplified the potential ruin of Japan.

Unless the atomic bombs exploded Japan out of the war, the home islands might have to be invaded. Air Force proponents pressed instead for more massive incendiary raids, where firestorms generated in tinderbox neighborhoods might wipe out inhabitants by the hundred thousand. By December, bombers could destroy every major city. Navy strategists saw the end coming through submarine encirclement of the home islands and carrier-plane surveillance of inland waters, strangling Japan of raw materials, including vital oil. The lessons of Okinawa convinced the Army, however, that Japan itself would have to be occupied by force, and it would be costly.

Code names for wartime operations—"Desert Storm," "Sledgehammer," "Barbarossa," "Rolling Thunder," "Overlord," "Olympic," "Coronet"—range from the bloated to the banal. More specific was the collective signal for the planned landings on the Japanese home islands—"Downfall." Two vast undertakings had been worked out to the last paper clip. Late in May the Pentagon was refining its plans for "Olympic," which would put three quarters of a million troops ashore on southern Kyushu on or about November 1. A follow-up landing—"Coronet"—would storm ashore on Honshu, in the vicinity of Tokyo Bay, on March 1, 1946.

"Downfall" had been approved by the Joint Chiefs of Staff on July 11, 1944, even before the invasion of the Philippines, and refined through the early months of 1945. Late that January, Admirals Halsey, McCain, and Wilkinson—"Ping" Wilkinson had been the intelligence chief in Washington whose imperception before Pearl Harbor hardly slowed his climb from captain to vice admiral—had flown from Manila to Pearl Harbor to collaborate with a joint services group to outline "Olympic." In April and May, MacArthur's chief of staff, Richard K. Sutherland, who on the first day of the war had been responsible, with his boss, for the debacle at Clark Field, a second Pearl Harbor that left the air force in the Philippines in ruins, further refined the plans for what would be the most ambitious amphibious operation in history. Parts of the operation were already coming together, but at the White House were some who did not want to see it happen, notably Admiral William D. Leahy, the crusty adviser whom Truman had inherited from Roosevelt. Leahy also saw no need for the Bomb, which he characterized as un-Christian.

MacArthur pushed hard for the "Olympic" landing in Japan, having already won the battle of service rivals to lead it. For the President, General Marshall asked MacArthur for an estimate of probable casualties. Truman had let it be known that his approval would depend upon saving American lives; if a less costly war of attrition took longer, so be it. For Truman and the service secretaries, Marshall reviewed the alternatives at a White House session on June 18, describing the damage to the Japanese infrastructure and the state of the Imperial Navy and the Japanese air forces, both reduced largely to suicide tactics. Even so, Marshall emphasized, bombing and blockade would not appreciably diminish the strength of the Imperial Army, nor its resolve to fight to the death. Bolstering his contention, he quoted Eisenhower and his air chief in Europe, Ira Eaker, that air power alone had not been sufficient "to put the Germans out [of the war]."

In Truman's presence Leahy reminded Marshall that the troops in Okinawa "had lost 35% in casualties," and wondered how many men would be landed on Kyushu. A memo of the meeting quoted Marshall as estimating the "total assault troops" as 766,700—and Truman following with an "All right. . . . We can do this operation and decide as to the final action later." "Coronet," if it came off, would be even bigger. On the basis of the Okinawa percentages Leahy calculated 268,345 casualties for the first phase, a conservative figure, he thought, given knowledge of the *kamikaze* mentality and the fact that it was the Japanese homeland to be invaded. (An OSS planner in and out of the Pentagon with the Far East mapping team—

later a distinguished geographer—recalled estimates there of a quarter million.)

The White House had more optimistic estimates from General MacArthur. "Olympic," MacArthur had cabled, might cost 50,800 dead and wounded in the first thirty days. His estimate, he explained, was a "purely academic and routine" one but he did not really expect "such a high rate of loss." It was a substantial figure yet meant to reassure, but it would become much less credible two weeks later, once General "Vinegar Joe" Stilwell, who had taken over for the dead Simon Buckner, forwarded his preliminary casualty report for Okinawa. On July 2 a Stilwell communiqué would declare the campaign officially over. It had taken far longer than expected, and there were pockets of resistance that continued to hold out, but he saw the toll as not going much higher. In the eighty-two days of battle for Okinawa, about 2,500 Japanese troops died each day. American casualties— dead and wounded—on land alone amounted to more than 72,000. The Navy and Air Force casualties were also high—10,000 seamen, half of them dead, mostly from *kamikazes*.

No one at Truman's table was optimistic that such Japanese ferocity would subside through attrition, or that they would surrender without invasion. The casualty estimates were pronounced acceptable—Stilwell had not yet reported in—and Marshall observed, "It is a grim fact that there is not an easy, bloodless way to victory in war, and it is the thankless task of the leaders to maintain their firm outward front. . . . Any irresolution in the leaders may result in costly weakening and indecision in the subordinates." Truman approved, but clearly did not buy MacArthur's linkage of Luzon invasion casualties with likely resistance on the homeland. "I do not want another Okinawa," he said, "from one end of Japan to the other."

Stimson—a venerable cautionary voice like Leahy—expressed his hopes for "some fruitful accomplishment through other means," but Truman, despite misgivings, intended to try every means. A surrender short of invasion, a surrender eliminating need for the Bomb— these were desirable, but only the Japanese could make that decision. Some in the military establishment, for reasons of their own, wanted the investment in the Bomb paid off by its use, or an invasion eclipsing "Overlord"—and D-Day—that would cap, or enhance, careers. Buoyed by White House backing for "Olympic," MacArthur had his revised plan ready on June 21. He now estimated twelve divisions to carry out the initial assault, with eleven to follow and three in reserve, plus 22,300 airmen—a total assault force up to Marshall's projection, and backed up by many more support troops handling the logistics in the Marianas, the Ryukus, the Philippines, and Hawaii. The first phase of "Downfall" would begin on X-Day (November 1), with troops offshore at X-Day minus 4. On June 27 MacArthur added an intermediate landing three months after X-Day, in the north of Kyushu, if enemy resistance had contained the "Olympic" force.

Sutherland's summary of "Olympic" had observed that "the entry of Russia into the war . . . at some stage of the operation is not unlikely." With the prospect of "Downfall" as well as the test of the Manhattan Project's atomic device to precede it, Truman prepared to meet Churchill and Stalin at Potsdam. On the morning of July 7, as the cruiser *Augusta* left Newport News, the President penned a diary note about the last meeting he'd had at the White House. The day before he had seen his former Senatorial colleagues Burton K. Wheeler, Ernest McFarland, Albert Hawkes, and Homer Capehart, conservatives from both parties. Wheeler had been an outspoken prewar isolationist. The four had just returned from one of the many Congressional inspection trips to Europe—"and knew *all* the answers. Smart men, I'd say. Since Julius Caesar such men as Charlemagne, Richelieu, Charles V, Francis I, the great King Henry IV of France, Frederick Barbarossa, to name a few, and Woodrow Wilson and Frank Roosevelt have had remedies and still couldn't solve the problem."

The Senatorial solution, as Truman recorded it, was to pull out. There was no hope for Europe. "France would go Communistic, so would Germany, Italy and the Scandinavians, and there was grave doubt about England. . . . The Pope, they said, was blue." All except McFarland ("an optimist") "assured me that the European world is at an end and that Russia is a big bad wolf. Europe has passed out so often in the last 2000 years—and has come back, better or worse than ever . . . that I'm not impressed with cursory glances of oratorical members of the famous 'Cave of the Winds.' " And with that perspective, and Tennyson's hopeful lines about when

> . . . *the war-drum throbb'd no longer, and the battle flags were furl'd*
> *In the Parliament of Man, the Federation of the World*

on a slip of paper in his wallet, the self-taught historian who had been an artillery captain, haberdasher, county judge, and Senator looked forward to landfall at Antwerp.

# POTSDAM
## AND
# PLUTONIUM

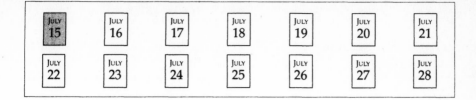

## CHAPTER III

# · JULY 15, 1945 ·

### *"a German solution"*

The *Augusta* moored at Antwerp at 10:04 on the morning of July 15. The voyage of 3,387 miles from Newport News had taken nine days. On board, Truman had a small library of preparatory papers to examine, wicker armchairs reminiscent of his Missouri front porch on deck, and the White House to run at long distance. The cruiser still operated, with its escort, under wartime precautions, and in the English Channel and the North Sea had to move cautiously around mine fields and buoys marking wrecked and sunken ships.

"It seems to take two warships to get your pa across the pond," Truman wrote to his daughter, Margaret, from the *Augusta*. The *Philadelphia* had preceded it, the two cruisers illuminated in peacetime fashion. No one expected a Japanese submarine. They were no longer plentiful even in the Pacific. The President had seen last-minute advisers and legislators until late on Saturday, having his secrecy blown by a visitor who boasted to a Washington reporter of his access. Truman's special train had hardly left Union Station when his departure was announced on Washington radio, and the news was in some Sunday papers before the *Augusta* lifted anchor.

One of the meetings on the final days before Potsdam had concerned the plans for "Olympic"—as if, Assistant Secretary of War John J. McCloy later wrote, the atomic option did not exist. For Truman it did not exist until proved. He had noted in his diary, "I have to decide Japanese strategy—shall we invade Japan proper or shall we bomb and blockade?" His decision had been to bomb and blockade—and ready an invasion in case nothing else, including the Bomb, worked. Not invading the home islands, General Thomas T. Handy, Marshall's closest assistant, had projected, might save half a million or more American lives. In anticipation that both phases of "Downfall" might have to be employed, the Pentagon would order so many Purple Heart medals—for the wounded-in-action—that the stocks outlasted the wars in Korea, Viet Nam, and American military involvements since. Nothing could demonstrate more dramatically what the anticipated costs of invading Japan appeared to be at the time for military planners.

With such alternatives in mind, Truman, through Stimson, had given the go-ahead to the additional, nuclear, option, but not quite as the Pentagon preferred. A Joint Chiefs of Staff top-secret memo had gone out, "eyes only," on July 3 to MacArthur, Nimitz, and Arnold:

> KYOTO, HIROSHIMA, KOKURA AND NIIGATA WILL NOT BE AT-
> TACKED BY AIR FORCES UNDER YOUR COMMAND UNLESS FURTHER
> INSTRUCTIONS ARE ISSUED

Contrary to Stimson's orders, all four were being held as atomic bomb targets. By his earlier proscription, Kyoto, a city of temples despite its war industries, was exempted from bombing of any kind. The top brass required tireless civilian oversight.

Truman's quarters aboard the *Augusta* included a map room counterpart to one in the White House and communication facilities comparable to those in Washington. Much of each day was spent reviewing memoranda or in conferences with Admiral Leahy and Secretary of State Byrnes. "I also ate a meal in every mess aboard the ship," Truman remembered, "taking my place in the 'chow lines' with my aluminum tray along with the men." One day at sea he watched, with Byrnes, from atop a three-gun turret while the *Augusta* practiced salvos. Two guns fired impressively; the third, according to

Charles E. Bohlen, who would be Truman's German interpreter as special assistant to Byrnes, "gave a sort of belch, and a shell eased out of the muzzle and fell into the water a hundred yards or so from the ship." The exercise gave the President an idea of the efficacy of even the best military hardware.

Through "Magic" intercepts transmitted to the cruiser Truman was kept current on what the Japanese were doing—and thinking. Listening posts were also picking up domestic radio in the home islands, including a broadcast to the nation by the Prime Minister, Baron Suzuki, in which he admitted the loss of Okinawa but boasted of the "damage" done the enemy in casualties and in "causing a miscarriage in the execution of his strategic plans." The enemy, he declared, had been dealt "a severe strategic blow." Even so he expected "further intensified" air raids and "an invasion of Japan proper." It was confessedly "the gravest crisis since the Mongol invasion," but he sought further sacrifice and mass enlistments in the National Volunteer Fighting Corps, for "How can we ever permit the sacred land to be outraged by a foreign foe?"

That a landing seemed inevitable to the Japanese was confirmed by "Magic" decrypts of messages from the legation in Sweden about American troop redeployments to the Pacific. Thirty divisions were to be moved from Europe. Awareness of Russian designs came in reports to Tokyo from the Manchurian border, where nervous observers expected the Soviets "to invade and occupy the entire country," and from Ambassador Sato in Moscow, to whom Foreign Affairs Minister Togo cabled that it was of the "utmost urgency" to keep Russia out of the war. Former Prime Minister Hirota appealed, so "Magic" heard, to Ambassador Malik in Tokyo for a new neutrality pact, Russia having abrogated the previous treaty on April 5. Russia and Japan together, Hirota cajoled, could be "a force unparalleled in the world."

Malik had replied, according to Diplomatic Intercept 1195, about ending the war in Asia: "Peace there did not depend on Russia." But Japan was making no concrete effort to buy off the Soviets other than to offer fishing rights and similarly token concessions.

To further Japanese frustration, American air raids late in June and early in July were disrupting communications—once for five continuous days—and "Magic" read that too. SRS Intercept 1723 on July 9, while Truman was at sea, reported that even the underground lines between the Central Telegraph Bureau and the Foreign Ministry "would not be repaired for another ten days." "Magic" also collected reports of civilian unrest in Thailand, Korea, Formosa, and other segments of the Empire. The fragility of Japanese control was clear. Seditious propaganda leaflets were being spread in Bangkok, while elsewhere in Southeast Asia Japanese authority barely stretched beyond military bases. Togo was forced to cable Sato in Moscow that he should inform Foreign Minister Molotov before the leadership left for Potsdam that Japan, "in preparation for the ending of the war, has absolutely no ideas of annexing or holding the territories occupied as a result of the war."

The cable was deliberately couched to protect Japan's northern empire—Korea, Manchuria, and the northern islands seized from Czarist Russia in the 1904 war—ironically, the areas in which the Soviets had the most interest. Both the Japanese civil and military hierarchies seemed to have had political and military realism pounded from their heads by the omnipresent B-29s.

As in the last months of the war in Europe, the emphasis on bombing military targets prefaced most American communiqués, but no one worried overmuch about the spillover onto areas of high-density population. The missions from the Marianas were now almost routine—or so they appeared. Actually it took twelve officers and seventy-three men on the ground to keep each B-29 flying, as well as a clandestine daily flight from Sacramento by a C-54 to bring General Curtis LeMay badly needed replacement parts. Each morning at 5:00 A.M. he would note the results of inspections—a daily average of fifty bombers out of service because of parts shortages, sometimes the result of strikes back home. With the end of the war in Europe there had been a relaxation of civilian effort that never had been as enthusiastic as certified in such songs as "Rosie the Riveter." Strikes for wages and job security and union jurisdictional rights anticipated the gearing down of war production. More planes failed for mechanical reasons than because of enemy action.

The runs to target were long, and bombs were released differently from the formation-and-pattern bombing typical of the B-17s and B-24s over Germany. A B-29 typically flew over a thousand miles of ocean before beginning its bombing run from a distance of seventy miles. Two or three lines of planes were strung out two miles apart and each flew, prudently, above or below the bomber ahead. Yet, in radio silence, each flew basically alone. If searchlights or AA-fire lit the sky a crewman would dispense aluminum foil, or "rope," to confuse Japanese radar, and once bombs were dropped, aircraft turned for home at the rate of two per minute. When reconnaissance photos showed that a populated area adjacent to the industrial or military target had been hit, the bombers would come back—as on the fifteenth, when Colonel Boyd Hubbard, Jr., commander of the 501st Bombardment Group, led his 315th Wing on a follow-up mission against the Kudamatzu plant of Nippon Company's oil refinery. Strong wind shifts along the Japanese coast sometimes caused bombs to drift and fanned firestorms in crowded housing districts. This time the follow-up mission put the plant out of production.

Ambassador Sato in Russia had some idea of what was happening at home from the American press as reported in Moscow's rigidly controlled newspapers and from the BBC world service. The lack of realism from Sato's own Foreign Office baffled him as he had no way of knowing how completely the direction of the Empire was captive to the military. "Japan," he responded, "is no longer in a position to be responsible for peace throughout East Asia. . . . The fact is that we have already lost Burma and the Philippines, and even Okinawa, which is at the very tip of our Empire." He followed his cable almost immediately with another, not decrypted until the day before Truman docked. "How much reserve strength does Japan have for continuing the war?" Sato challenged. "Is there any sense in continuing the war no matter how many thousands of our able-bodied men and no matter how many millions of our city populations are sacrificed? I am filled with thoughts of fear and heartbreak. . . . We must face the facts of the international situation without flinching. . . . My first responsibility is to prevent the harboring of illusions which are at variance with the reality."

The illusions, however, remained. Minister Shunichi Kase in Switzerland had already cabled that "a German solution" faced Japan—destruction from both east and west. Russia, he warned, would be joining the war "to accomplish her [own] plans." Realizing that the military was blocking a diplomatic solution, he appealed to Togo, hoping that his message would be overheard by the army die-hards: "At this juncture a truly great general would cast aside his arms in order to save his Emperor and his people. . . . I beseech you to mobilize all our organs of public opinion at this time to help prepare our people for the day. . . . I pray that the grave decision which you [must] make will not be delayed too long."

Kase's warning was already in hand when Togo, ignoring the imminence of Russian intervention, continued to press Sato in Moscow about mediation, yet offering little to satisfy the obvious Soviet appetite for spoils: "Since we are secretly giving consideration to termination of war, in view of the pressing situation . . . you are . . . to sound out the extent to which it is possible to make use of Russia with regard to ending that war. [We] will meet Russia's wishes on a broad scale." Yet Togo never offered details, hoping that the Soviets would fix their own price, although Sato had warned that "academical fine phrases" were useless. The next day Togo furnished language to confirm the Emperor's desire for peace. What Truman overheard as the *Augusta* was closing in on Europe was that "His Majesty, mindful of the fact that the present war daily brings greater and greater evil and sacrifice upon the peoples of all the belligerent powers, desires from his heart that it be quickly terminated. But as long as England and the United States insist upon unconditional surrender . . . the Japanese Empire has no alternative but to fight on with all its strength for the honor and the existence of the motherland."

Another message, relayed to Byrnes at sea, came from his Minister to Sweden, Herschel V. Johnson, who reported from Stockholm that at a dinner arranged by the Japanese military attaché, Major General Makoto Onodera, with Prince Carl, Onodera claimed that he had authorization from the Emperor to enter into peace negotiations, and that the Japanese Minister, Suemasa Okamoto, did not. It was clear that the Army and the Foreign Ministry were at odds, and that perhaps neither had Imperial approval. But Onodera wanted Prince Carl to ask King Gustav to intercede between the Allies and Emperor Hirohito. "He further stated," Johnson went on, "that the Emperor must be maintained in his position after the capitulation. No other conditions of surrender were specified." Presumably those acceptable to the army would be spelled out to Gustav were he willing—as he was not—to intervene. Who spoke for the Emperor?

Reading the intercepts, Secretary of the Navy Forrestal was coldly amused "that Russia would be impressed by Japanese willingness to give up territory which she had already lost." He saw Sato's message as warning Tokyo "that Japan was thoroughly and completely defeated and that the only course open was quick and definite action recognizing such fact." Word got about without "Magic" access. In the Philippines, white-scarved Air Force officers visiting from the Marianas intimated the existence of a new weapon that would end the war before Christmas. And Weldon E. Rhoades, MacArthur's personal pilot, predicted in his diary on the basis of overheard conversations that Russia would enter the war on August 15, leaving Japan without any further will to resist. But he worried over MacArthur's failure to perceive what four years of war in his personal style had taken out of his staff. "The General has his family with him and leads an entirely normal life."

It was not in Stalin's interest to lend Japan his good offices, and Togo was hearing that message from every quarter. The consul general in Harbin, Manchuria's largest city, had already informed Tokyo ominously, as American eavesdroppers knew, that a Russian officer on his way east had been sufficiently attracted to a Japanese woman in his carriage that "When he got off, he gave her a gold chain which he had inherited from his parents, and said, 'I'll look you up in Tokyo in a few months.' " Still, Sato was urged to rush off on July 13 to see Foreign Minister V. M. Molotov before offices closed for the day. He found only the Vice Minister, S. A. Lozovsky, who brushed Sato off with excuses that the Potsdam delegation was leaving "that very night." They would actually leave on the evening of the fourteenth, the ambassador would discover. Recognizing that he had been treated evasively, Sato pleaded by cable to Togo the next day: "In the long run, since Japan sincerely desires the termination of the war, I believe that she has indeed no choice but to accept unconditional surrender or terms closely approximating thereto." What he meant was clear enough. It would be far more costly if Japan stalled its surrender until Russia came in.

Because of "Magic," Truman was well aware of Japan's predicament, but he also realized that he could not keep Russia out of the war if Stalin wanted easy gains at Japan's expense. As the President landed in Antwerp he understood that it was up to Japan to evade that certainty. The Powers could only backtrack on unconditional surrender, which the Japanese rejected, if someone came up with semantic evasions that changed little or nothing. While the language of surrender seemed to be Truman's problem, it was Japan that was facing catastrophe.

The welcoming delegation led by General Eisenhower was sizable. A forty-seven-automobile caravan motored the thirty-five miles to the airport northwest of Brussels where the Presidential C-54 (DC-4), *The Sacred Cow,* was waiting with two other transports to ferry the entire party to Gatow Airfield in Berlin. Along the road was an honor guard from the 137th Infantry Regiment, 35th Division, in which Truman had served as a captain in France in 1918. An hour into the three-and-a-half-hour flight the C-54s picked up an escort of twenty P-47 Thunderbolt fighters.

From his window Truman saw the devastation of industrial Germany. Kassel and Magdeburg appeared completely shattered. Although the countryside "seemed to be under cultivation," he noted, "I could not see a single house that was left standing in either town." At Gatow another welcoming party was waiting, including Secretary of War Stimson and his chief deputy, John J. McCloy; Ambassadors Harriman, Pauley, and Murphy; Admiral King; and a Soviet group including Ambassador Gromyko. From there it was ten miles to the suburb of Babelsberg, where Truman's party was lodged in a large house beside Lake Griebnitz, three miles from Potsdam. Number 2 Kaiserstrasse, a three-story yellow-stuccoed house, they were told by the Russians, had been commandeered from a Nazi film producer since sent to Siberia. In reality it was the home of publisher Gustav Müller-Grote, no Hitlerite. In May the Russians had plundered it, raping Müller-Grote's daughters and destroying furniture, rare books, paintings, and furnishings. Evicted, they were told, for "a prominent purpose," they were given an hour's notice, after which a forklift filled a bomb crater with Müller-Grote's library and antiques. For Truman the Soviets refurbished the chateau with dark, oversized furniture looted elsewhere. There were no window screens, and in July the mosquitoes rising from the lake were voracious.

Churchill, who arrived with his party the same day, was given number 23 Ringstrasse, two blocks away. He had flown to Berlin from Biarritz, where he readied for the conference by painting landscapes. The Prime Minister had been a major presence in public life since his twenties; war-weary and in his seventieth year, he felt that his experience was his preparation. There was no sign of Stalin and his entourage, and the Russians professed not to know when he would arrive. It was assumed that, to emphasize his importance, he was being theatrically late.

With time to spare, Truman took a nap, then gathered with his advisers. Learning that Stalin might not even arrive the next day, the President asked to see what was left of Berlin, and plans were set in motion to make that a press event. Something had to be offered to reporters who had flocked to Potsdam and were kept at a distance by the Russians controlling the area.

There wasn't much left of Sunday, but Truman caught up with his information sources, from "Magic" intercepts to reports on what Russia was actually doing. Although no Anglo-American presence was wanted in the former German satrapies now becoming Soviet satellites, a flood of refugees reported what American listening posts could not. With the armed backing of the Russians, the Poles had been making good the Yalta promise of gains to their west to compensate for the Soviet seizures of 1939, when Poland had been divided with Hitler. On Russian orders, however, the Poles had slowed down their expulsion of Germans. During the Potsdam conference the terror and the dispossessions had to be moderated.

Silesia and Pomerania as far as the Oder and the Niesse were becoming Polish by fact of possession. As far west as Stettin and Breslau the Soviets had looted almost all undestroyed machinery and whatever crops could be harvested, stuffing everything into large trucks, many of them Lend-Lease vehicles. Counting on the historic hatred of Poles for Germans, the Soviets expected whatever was left on the land to be razed or looted, and the inhabitants whose forebears had lived there for centuries to be driven west into what had become the British and American zones. Hundreds of thousands had fled on foot with whatever they could carry, which wasn't much, as a Polish decree of March 2 had dispossessed all Germans in Poland of their property. Many fled by sea. Pomeranian ports counted 851,735 passing through by May 10. Some of the overcrowded ships were torpedoed by Russian subs. More than four thousand refugees went down with the *Wilhelm Gustloff*; the *General von Steuben*, a white-painted hospital ship, sank with 2,680 military wounded still aboard; the *Goya* took two torpedoes on April 16 and only 165 of the seven thousand civilians crowded below decks survived the chill Baltic. In early summer there were no more ships to hazard, and the numbers of refugees had overwhelmed the statisticians. Expellees from what was now de facto Poland had no way west but on foot.

The Japanese had become notorious for their own death marches of prisoners, trivial in number compared to the indiscriminate Polish expulsions. Of one group of 2,400 plodding west from Troppau, 1,000 died on the march. Luckier ones remained as forced labor. Frau Käthe von Normann wrote in her sketchy diary on July 15 that her wages were 250 grams of flour per day. A rare Polish Jew among the soldiers told her that she had pretty children (each was permitted 150 grams), that he had once had a wife and children also, but that the Nazis had killed them in a concentration camp. "He was saved because he had spent those four years in Russian prisons in Siberia."

The Japanese themselves had no land routes from the tattered Greater East Asia Co-Prosperity Sphere—their slogan of 1941 and 1942—back to the home islands. Troops from the Pacific atolls to Burma and the Dutch Indies, millions of them, more than half isolated in China and Manchuria, could do the Empire little good. The chief threat from the American standpoint seemed to be suicide aircraft, and debates were going on in Navy headquarters about how to cope with them. There seemed two alternatives on July 16—the fifteenth in Washington—more urgent installation of three-inch rapid-fire AA mounts on all ships, and the destruction of as many planes on the ground as were not hidden from view. Everything Japanese that flew was a potential *kamikaze*. Chichi Jima Airfield was left smoking by carrier planes, and at 0304, the Navy reported, the airfield on Moan, one of the eleven volcanic islands comprising Truk (now Chuuk) in the Carolines, "caught 75 tons of 500-pounders from 15 of LeMay's dreamboats"—B-29s. Carrier Task Force 38 moved in for strikes in the Tokyo area, then retired for refueling and replenishment: 379,157 barrels of oil, 6,369 tons of ammunition, 1,635 tons of provisions, 99 replacement aircraft, and 421 officers and men.

Other targets were the transport systems between the Japanese home islands. The coal trade between Hokkaido and Honshu was carried on largely by railway car ferries. On the fifteenth, eight of twelve ferries were sunk, two beached, and the remaining two damaged by carrier planes. Seventy out of 271 auxiliary colliers were sunk and eleven damaged; ten freighters were sunk and seven damaged. The Navy estimated that Japan's coal-carrying capacity had been halved in a single day. Coastal traffic by daylight had become so scant that Cruiser Division 17—four cruisers and six destroyers—made an antishipping sweep along the east coast of northern Honshu, above Tokyo Bay, without making a single contact. Another American task force made the first attack by naval gunfire on a home islands target, the ironworks at Kamaishi, on the northeast coast of Honshu. Beginning at ten minutes after noon the bombardment from three battleships and two heavy cruisers shook the coastline for two hours like a small earthquake, as from a range of five miles sixteen-inch, eight-inch, and five-inch shells, 2,355 in all, pounded the area. Six passes across the harbor mouth failed to draw a single defensive shot. Flames spread across paper partitions and straw matting from cooking fires upended by the concussion of the big shells.

Another strike force hit the Nihon Steel Company and the Wanishi Iron Works at Muroran on the southern tip of Hokkaido. Seaman Laird Shirk on the destroyer *McGowan* recorded his first sighting of the home islands at 0933 at twenty miles. When the ships moved closer, firing everything that would reach the shore, 860 sixteen-inch shells from five battleships pounded the target area. On the twentieth the *Iowa, Missouri, Wisconsin, Alabama,* and *North Carolina* returned. None reported any opposition from land, air, or sea. Still, there were almost always American losses, either from weather or malfunctions—and the Navy blamed weather for the collision off Honshu of two planes and the loss of Lieutenant Commander Richard G. Crommelin. He was one of five brothers in naval uniform. The lone pilot down off Hokkaido was picked up after ditching due to mechanical problems.

Docking in Okinawa, Seaman James J. Fahey of the light cruiser *Montpelier,* new to combat duty, was impressed by one of the three cruisers nearby in Naha harbor, the *Columbia,* like his ship, shifted north from the Philippines. "You could see the Jap flags painted on its bridge, for bombardments, planes [downed] and ships [sunk]. It shot down twenty-four Jap planes. It shot down quite a few in Lingayen Gulf before three Jap suicide planes crashed into them. They had 167 casualties." On the intercom his captain announced that their duty as part of the Ninth Fleet would be to patrol the coast of Shanghai and close off traffic to the home islands: "Our job is to sink all Jap ships, barges, small craft we come across. The Japs move a lot of troops around here from China to Japan and from Formosa to China." He was awed to see from the *Montpelier's* decks "the high cliffs from which the Japs jumped to their death[s]." He also noted in his diary that there were still enemy soldiers in hiding, and being flushed out and killed. Few were surrendering.

From the building in Tokyo next to a maternity hospital that was his POW barracks, Sergeant Frank Fujita, Jr., could hear the guns of American ships offshore, and he watched the B-29s that flew over day and night, sometimes only a "Photo Joe" reconnaissance plane. Earlier in the year Japanese fighters had risen to the city's defense, flying into their own AA-fire to get at the bombers, even ramming them *kamikaze*-fashion. Now there were no more Zeros. In the diary he secreted in the wall of his room Fujita called all Japanese fighters "Zeros." One of only two Nisei Japanese among the 26,000 Americans captured in the Pacific (nearly 11,000 of them would die), Fujita had been pulled from shipyard work as a POW in Fukuoka for a radio propaganda project at the Tokyo *Bunka Gakuin Kanda*, where an odd group of twenty-five would short-wave messages on programs like "Humanity Calls" and "Postman Calls" to undermine, the authorities hoped, Allied will to fight. Picked to seem representative, they surely were that, according to Fujita:

> We have traitors, confirmed, suspected, and potential; education from grammar school to university graduate; erotics, erratics[s], queers, mental cases, cowards, brave men, good men, no accounts, artists, writers, playwrights, actors, typists, journalists, newsmen, typesetters, farmers, cotton pickers, Americans, English, Australians, Scotch, Dutch, soldiers, sailors, marines, airmen, suck asses, dog robbers and civilians—Wow!

When he said on the air that POW life was generally monotonous "but now things are getting pretty lively at times," the broadcast, recorded for playback, passed the Japanese censor, but War Department monitors in San Francisco understood. Fujita had seen the action himself the day before when he was trucked to a Tokyo coalyard. The route "resembled a gigantic graveyard. . . . Every direction that we looked there was nothing as far as the eye could see except iron safes and brick smokestacks of all sizes. It was eerie to see them rise out of the ashes, looking for all the world like headstones, and truly that is exactly what they were, monuments to the hundreds of thousands of people who had perished there and were now part of the ashes that were piled silently everywhere." Somehow the hospital and the radio station remained standing, perhaps because they were close to the off-limits Imperial Palace grounds, hit occasionally but only by accident.

With so many American ships fanning out to blockade Japan, concern continued about the easy mark their very numbers were, not only to *kamikaze* planes but to *kaiten* torpedoes. Yet the Japanese were having little success with their submarines. From the beginning of the war, and the failure of their subs at Pearl Harbor, they seemed ineffective at undersea warfare. Importing U-boat technology from Germany, the Japanese began building huge subs capable of housing aircraft on deck, and even adding eager *kaitens*. The boats *I-400, I-401, I-13,* and *I-14* had German-style snorkels to extend their operations underwater, the latest radar, and antimagnetic devices to ward off mines. Each housed three *Seiran* bomb-carrying float planes. Under the operational control of Captain T. Arizumi in the *I-13,* two were to sail eastward to Hawaii and then southeast toward the Pacific entrance of the Panama Canal. Each plane aboard the subs, armed with a 1,700-pound bomb, would be launched on X-Day to cripple the canal and block reinforcements for the expected invasion of the homeland. The pilots, as before Pearl Harbor, had practiced runs over a facsimile of the target—in this case, models of Panama Canal locks towed to Nanao Bay on the remote west coast of Honshu directly across the island from Nagoya on the east. But before they sailed the plan was overruled in Tokyo. Rather than risk the valuable craft on a remote and hazardous operation, they were rerouted against forward American bases like Ulithi atoll, to operate out of Truk and Ponape (now Pohnpei), still in Japanese hands. It was a defeatist choice: the daring had gone out of the military, which was concentrating only on suicidal defense.

Adapting lessons learned in the Atlantic against the *Kriegsmarine* to Japanese waters, American hunter-killer forces built around escort carriers prowled for subs that might cause havoc among the huge gatherings of ships taking the war to the home islands. Off the east coast of Honshu at 7:47 on the sixteenth—still the fifteenth to the east—a plane from the carrier *Anzio* sighted a surfaced Japanese sub and crippled it with rocket fire. Trailing oil, the *I-13* plunged toward safety below, but its oil slick gave it away, and at 10:00 another plane hit it. Guided to the target by aircraft, two destroyers went after the *I-13,* and one of them, the *Lawrence C. Taylor,* gave it the coup de grace at 11:40 with a new weapon, the hedgehog—a device that threw multiple depth charges in a predetermined pattern. Debris from the sub floated to the surface.

From Kure Harbor in the south of Honshu the "Taimon" flotilla of submarines—the *I-47, I-53, I-58, I-363, I-366,* and *I-367*—had moved out a few hours earlier to hunt for the enemy. The mission was a shift in priorities, as the largest subs had been used to resupply troops isolated on bypassed Pacific islands. Outposts already living off the land on taro and coconuts were not being told that they were abandoned, but the Imperial Navy had decided that forestalling an invasion of the homeland was the only goal worth its remaining resources. One "Taimon" sub—the Japanese named task forces for their commanders—was the *I-58,* captained by Mochitsura Hashimoto, a 1931 graduate of the Japanese naval academy, now risen to commander. His newest ship, fifty-five feet longer than a football gridiron, was larger than any American sub and could fire simultaneously six 300-foot-long oxygen-driven torpedoes capable of forty-eight knots on the surface and a range of five miles. Some of Hashimoto's torpedoes were *kaiten* steered, and no *kaiten*—he had four aboard—was known to have resorted to the ejection mechanism at his right hand. *Kaitens* were an aspect of submarine warfare the Japanese had not learned from the Germans.

As the *Augusta* entered the Westerschelde and sailed upstream to Antwerp, American arrivals elsewhere would alter the direction of the war. On Tinian the 509th Composite Group, self-sufficient in support personnel, was settling in after its thirteen B-29s landed with their crews—sixty-five officers and fifty-two enlisted men. Their mission: to haul one explosive device of approximately ten thousand pounds on a round-trip (for the plane) of three thousand miles. The first bomb—"Little Boy"—was on its way. On Sunday morning at Los Alamos, New Mexico, Major Robert Furman, an engineer, had drawn from stores a bucket with a sturdy handle. No ordinary container, it was lined with two hundred pounds of lead surrounding a cylindrical mass of uranium 235, the refined, fissionable material derived from uranium 238. The core of the bomb would become explosive when a pistonlike slug of the same substance at the breech end of the bomb was fired into the larger mass, making the combination "critical." Future weapons were to use plutonium, derived from uranium and compressed in detonation by implosion lenses until it became critical, releasing its energy. The plutonium device required the more bulbous "Fat Man" shape.

To drop only one bomb, whatever its dramatic effects (if it worked), might suggest that it was only an experimental weapon. To impress the Japanese hierarchy that the United States was capable of a super-bomb offensive, another bomb, strategists thought, had to be delivered soon after. Since "Little Boy" was the only one of its kind in existence, the second would have to be a plutonium device like the prototype on a tower in the New Mexico desert.

Taking no chances with "Little Boy," scientists were delivering the two fissionable uranium 235 segments separately, the larger portion housed in the unusual bucket. Furman and his co-courier, Captain James F. Nolan, a radiologist in combat gear anonymity, needed help to get the bucket into an ordinary staff car, in which they proceeded down the mesa until they blew a tire. To their relief the uranium core failed to bounce from the bucket,* which was transferred to another car in their caravan and deposited into a waiting C-47 (DC-3) at Kirtland Air Base, near Albuquerque. Since both C-47s on the tarmac were listed as grounded for repairs, Furman rushed to the base commander's office with a letter signed by General Marshall authorizing the top-secret mission and requesting whatever assistance was necessary.

Suddenly both planes were reclassified as flyable, and the U-235 was airborne, the second C-47 accompanying the first in case of emergency. At Hamilton Field, near San Francisco, security officers surrounded the planes as they touched down. The bucket was transferred unseen to a waiting staff car for transfer to Hunter's Point Navy Yard, where the cruiser *Indianapolis* was waiting. Captain Charles McVay had learned only three days earlier that liberty was cancelled for his crew and that his ship was to sail on Sunday. He was to receive two Army officers and two top-secret pieces of cargo, one large and one small. The fifteen-foot crate was to be attached to the quarterdeck with eyebolts and guarded around the clock by the cruiser's Marine detachment.

A closed black truck and seven staff cars pulled up to the commandant's office, where the two pieces of cargo were guarded until moved dockside. After dark, under floodlights, a crane lifted the crate that carried the gun assembly to the deck, where it was bolted down. The bomb casing itself was already in Tinian, where Colonel Tibbets and his crews would soon be practicing loading and dropping facsimile bombs.

In his cabin McVay rechecked his top-secret orders. Via a refueling stop at Pearl Harbor he was to ferry his cargo to Tinian as fast as possible, then report at Guam for further assignment. A letter at-

*It was subcritical anyway. To make certain of that the remaining U-235 for the bomb was being sent to Tinian separately by air.

tached to his orders was not to be opened until he was at sea. A lifeboat was to be reserved for the cargo and its custodians in case of emergency, even if that deprived some of the crew.

Part of the fail-safe procedures involved shipping some of the parts, including the critical slug of U-235, on a C-54 to Tinian via Albuquerque and San Francisco. Groves asked for a second plane in case of emergency, so that if the first went down the other could spot the point with dye markings and circle it until help came. At Albuquerque the two C-54 crews, used to full loads, were astonished to discover a box the size of several orange crates loaded onto the first plane, and an even smaller shipment on the second. Still, they took off, refueled at Hamilton Field, and rose again over the Pacific.

Fifty-five minutes out, one C-54 returned with a malfunctioning engine, but contrary to instructions, the other continued on to Hawaii, where it waited for the second plane. And at Hickam Field, where the arrival was to be inconspicuous, the first C-54 was met by a group of senior officers, who, given the security laid on, expected an entourage of high brass. The only one to leave the plane was Second Lieutenant R. A. Taylor, Jr., who did not carry any written orders. They were in the second plane, in the possession of Lieutenant Colonel Peter de Silva, head of Los Alamos security.

At Kirtland Field, from which the cargo had come, another plane—a B-29—was being loaded on Sunday for departure before dawn. Physicist Luis Alvarez and engineer Deak Parsons stowed equipment throughout the evening—including radio and telemetry and camera devices and a myriad of sensors. Everything seemed to need delicate cathode-ray tubes. They were to fly over the Trinity desert site just before implosion and drop canisters with sensors by parachute. Once they radioed that the drop was made and that they were safely out of range, detonation would be triggered, and their monitoring devices would gather information about it. If the canisters made it to the ground without being incinerated, they were to be picked up by security personnel.

Arrivals and departures were plentiful on the fifteenth. The firing circuitry and detonators for the prototype "Fat Man" had been unloaded and installed at Trinity—the last pieces of the puzzle. (The plutonium core, in a case with a handle, had been delivered to the assembly shack by civilian-shirted Sergeant Herbert Lehr on July 12. It did not require a lead-lined bucket, and he carried it one-handed.) A few hours later, visitors began checking into the Trinity area, none as well known as the VIPs at Potsdam, but General Groves, the mission chief, preferred it that way. Buses and Army sedans from Santa Fe and Albuquerque were shuttling in scientists, including Vannevar Bush, James Bryant Conant, Ernest O. Lawrence and Sir James Chadwick, Klaus Fuchs ("Golia" to Soviet Intelligence), Edwin McMillan (one of the discoverers of the plutonium perched on Trinity tower), and a lone reporter, William L. Laurence, science correspondent for *The New York Times.*

A dramatic, if secret, arrival at Met[allurgical] Lab on the University of Chicago campus the same day emphasized the confidence of Groves and Oppenheimer in their test device. Working at the Lab was Leo Szilard, with Enrico Fermi credited with the world's first working reactor. Szilard, whose contrariness was the only thing predictable about him, was, with James Franck, another refugee physicist, circulating a petition among atomic scientists who had worked on the Bomb to prevent it, on moral grounds, from being dropped over Japan. Instead, they promoted the idea of a demonstration in an uninhabited area, with Japanese representatives present, and postwar international control of atomic energy. Considering the interference in military policy little more than mischief, and blaming Szilard as instigator, Groves was determined to defuse the campaign.

To convince Met Lab scientists that the decision was irreversible and politicking futile, Groves ordered a Manhattan District security officer to Chicago. He turned up without warning—Sunday was just another day—with two printed copies of a secret document strapped to his body. While armed guards stood at the door, the Army captain sat Szilard and others with appropriate clearance in a university classroom to examine galley proofs of a proposed report by Henry DeWolf Smyth, chair of physics at Princeton. "Atomic Energy for Military Purposes" described in as nontechnical a style as was possible, and with minimal risk to intelligence leakage, how the atomic devices were conceived, designed, and developed. The publication was to be released to the public if and when the A-Bomb was used successfully—possibly only after the war was over.

The lone uranium bomb, "Little Boy," was expected to work, and there were particulars about its release of energy to be filled in, but Smyth's details about "Fat Man" remained subject to its effectiveness. The test was now up to the Project meteorologist, Jack M. Hubbard. Rain in the desert? He predicted clear predawn skies.

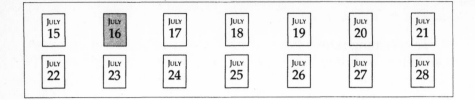

## CHAPTER IV

# · JULY 16, 1945 ·

*sunrise in the West*

Near Salmo, a village in British Columbia close to the border with Washington and Idaho, searchers found shroud lines and fragments of a balloon envelope. Several sightings had traced other incendiary balloons north to the Yukon, and a few days later one would be found as far south as Indian Springs, Nevada. As a last-resort weapon the Japanese effort was a far remove from the high-technology V-2 rocket of Nazi science, and an index to enemy war-making capacity. No one doubted the Japanese people's will to fight to the death, nor their realization, too, that the war was unwinnable. It seemed, then, to old Tokyo hands like Grew and Dooman that it was safe enough to leave the Emperor in nominal if regal state if that would insure a quick end to the war. Before Truman had left for Potsdam they had prepared a proclamation to be released there permitting a peaceful democratic government in postwar Japan that could be a "constitutional monarchy under the present dynasty." Dooman's text, with a preamble by Navy commander Douglas Fairbanks, Jr., who had left Hollywood for more prosaic duties, carefully omitted any promise to keep Hirohito himself enthroned.

Telephoning retired Secretary of State Cordell Hull at his apartment before boarding the *Augusta*, James Byrnes explained the proposed Potsdam declaration, and Hull, remembering receiving the Emperor's envoys as Pearl Harbor was under attack, would have none of it. Keeping the Emperor, he bridled, was appeasement. The feudal caste dominating Japan had to go.

Attempting to salvage some semblance of the power structure, not only were the official Japanese envoys abroad trying to get negotiations going but, to the dismay of Minister Kase, several other operatives were in Bern. The uncoordinated efforts evidenced diplomatic disarray. Two naval attachés, one formerly in Berlin, were in touch with Allen Dulles, who ran the American intelligence organization in Switzerland and had played a role in arranging the surrender of the Germans in Italy. The former military attaché in Berlin, a Japanese general, also approached Dulles in Bern, suggesting that the Japanese would be happy to give up everything but Korea and Formosa as long as the Imperial system was retained. A message from one of them went to Togo in Tokyo on the sixteenth and was intercepted by the United States. Dulles also reported the feelers to Stimson, explaining that he had given no encouragement to any other conditions but unconditional surrender, and that even surrender might not save anything if it occurred after Russian entry into the war. Perhaps because Dulles was talking too much, or had no business talking at all, he was suddenly transferred to Germany.

No one outside Stalin's closed circle knew that the reason for his delayed arrival at Potsdam was that he had suffered a mild heart attack a few days earlier. On the afternoon of the sixteenth both Churchill and Truman took advantage of the postponement by making separate tours of devastated Berlin. But first, Churchill paid a social visit to number 2 Kaiserstrasse. It was the first time the leaders had met. The Prime Minister looked more aged than in his jaunty photographs, and seemed gloomy about the future. Montgomery, his chief deputy in Germany, was concerned about Churchill, writing to General W. H. ("Simbo") Simpson at the War Office that morning,

Very hot here in Berlin and we live in shirt sleeves. The atmosphere is amazing. No one knows anything about the problem; the P.M. has been electioneering for weeks and has read nothing; Eden has been sick; there is no agreed Agenda; everyone is reading Foreign Office briefs madly. A curious show!!! Pug Ismay is very depressed about the whole thing; but I have no doubt something will emerge: if we can keep their feet on the floor.

The P.M. looks very old; I was shocked when I saw him; he has put on 10 years. . . .

Although Churchill (with daughter Mary in uniform as his chauffeur) brought with him his naval aide, Tommy Thompson, and his chief Foreign Office advisers, Anthony Eden and Alexander Cadogan, little business was discussed except for the latest news from the Pacific. Truman asked whether the Prime Minister had an agenda he wanted to present at the first meeting with Stalin. "No, I don't need one," Churchill said.

On the way back to the Ringstrasse, Churchill confided to Mary that he was sure he could work with Truman. To his physician, Charles Moran, whom he took everywhere with him, Churchill described Truman as "a man of immense determination. He takes no notice of delicate ground, he just plants his foot down firmly on it." And, by this time barefoot, he demonstrated on the wooden floor of number 23. Truman was more wary, writing in his diary that Churchill "gave me a lot of hooey about how great my country is and how he loved Roosevelt and how he intended to love me. . . . I am sure we can get along if he doesn't try to give me too much soft soap."

At 3:30—the sixteenth was almost over in the far Pacific—with Leahy and Byrnes sharing the back seat of an open Lincoln that had been flown over, Truman was given his first experience of a four-lane *Autobahn*, empty but for his motorcade. The United States had begun occupying its zone of Berlin, isolated from the Allied sectors of western Germany, on July 2. "About halfway to the city," he recalled, "we found the entire American 2nd Armored Division deployed along one side of the highway for my inspection. We stopped, honors were rendered by a band and honor guard, and I left the sedan in which I had been riding and entered an open half-track reconnaissance car." In his diary he described it as having "side seats and no top, just like a hoodlum wagon minus the top, or a fire truck with seats and no hose." Crawling along slowly so the troops could see the new President and so he could inspect "a mile and a half of good soldiers and some millions of dollars worth of equipment" took, Truman recorded, twenty-two minutes.

Beyond the soldiers on review in their spit-and-polish was the reverse image of war—miles of refugee Germans from the east, on foot and carrying all they still owned. Their faces were blank with fatigue and with shock. Marginally better off were the homeless of Berlin, scavenging in the ruins the Russians had bulldozed off the main streets. In the mid-July heat the city stank of open sewage and unburied corpses. "I never saw such destruction," Truman wrote. He recalled the names of destroyed cities in history—Carthage, Baalbek, Jerusalem, Rome, Peking, even fabled Atlantis, and saw no end to the cycle: "I fear that machines are ahead of morals by some centuries. . . . We are only termites on a planet and maybe when we bore too deeply into the planet there'll be a reckoning—who knows?"

The motorcade traveled down the rubble-flanked Wilhelmstrasse to the Reich Chancellery, beneath which Hitler had committed suicide in his bunker. Truman refused to leave his car to explore the site. He did not want the crowds of pathetic, threadbare survivors to think he was gloating over their catastrophe.

The Prime Minister's party traveled separately, Churchill in a jeep accompanied by nine other cars and jeeps, with the P.M.'s protection one officer with a service pistol. Churchill wore a tropical uniform with his 1915–16 Colonel's insignia and three rows of ribbons, all earned, and unregimental zip-up shoes. Riding with him, Dr. Moran was impressed by the placards on posts set along the road and emblazoned with quotations from Stalin's speeches bearing contradictory messages to the vanquished. One, in large red letters, declared: "The teaching of history tells us that Hitlers come and go, but the German people and the German State remain." Another, on a pillar of what had been a great museum, read: "For Stalingrad and Leningrad and all the ruined cities of Russia we bring back our hate to Germany." The wrecked and gutted homes Moran saw were still being looted by Russian soldiers, some peddling their haul, from mantelpiece clocks to every variety of garment, on the streets. "As I watched this evisceration of their homes," remembered the P.M.'s physician, "I felt a sense of nausea; it was like the first time I saw a surgeon open a belly and the intestines gushed out."

Churchill spent half an hour in the courtyard above the *Führerbunker*, observing that if England had lost, "We would have been the bunker"—presumably he meant in the condition of the bunker. One of the party was Eden's deputy, Alec Cadogan, who the day before bribed a Russian sentry with three cigarettes to be allowed to look for souvenirs. From behind a door the soldier pulled out an old boot. Cadogan explained that he didn't want boots, and came away instead with a beribboned Iron Cross, of which there were hundreds. From Hitler's study he removed a piece of the shattered marble top of the desk (for a paperweight), and in the Chancellery banquet hall a Russian sergeant obligingly "climbed into the crystal chandelier (astonishingly still intact) and wrenched off a little rosette for me."

While Eden and Mary Churchill descended the narrow stairs, Churchill sat on a battered cane chair plucked by a sentry from the Chancellery rubbish. "Slumped there," Australian war correspondent Ronald McKie wrote, "flushed, uncomfortable, tired, in a bad temper and now without even a cigar"—he had waved one earlier as he poked about the bombed-out buildings—"he was like an obese irritable child. . . . His one desperate need at the moment was a triple brandy." A British army photographer moved up and asked, "Mr. Churchill, would you mind standing where Hitler's body was burnt?" The fire-blackened patch, ten yards away, was still visible.

Churchill looked up into the swirling dust and heat and asked why, and the photographer explained the dramatic effect of "you and Hitler" on the same historic spot. "Oh, go to hell," said Churchill.

Although they did not encounter each other, also exploring the ruins was Andrei Gromyko, thirty-six, ambassador to Washington since 1943 and a comer in Soviet politics. In the advance party for Stalin, he had little to do but wait, and was taken by jeep past the tangled girders and collapsed concrete blocks that made Unter den Linden treacherous. Every step of the way, he recalled, was guarded by Red Army sentries, who handed him up and down the rubble to see the Chancellery, which once, he thought, "incorporated an aura of diabolical severity." He wanted to see the notorious *Führerbunker*. "Cylindrical in form, some nine meters high and five meters or so in diameter," he wrote, the entrance "appeared to have been carved out of solid rock. . . . [It] led down into a cellar filled with water. Shapeless lumps of reinforced concrete blocked the path from one part of the bunker to another. I had the feeling that our troops had done a good job in destroying the madman's last hiding place."

As for the *Führer* himself, an Associated Press dispatch from Montivideo, Uruguay, from the *Chicago Times*'s correspondent Vincent De Pascal, reported that it was "virtually certain" that Hitler and Eva Braun had landed in Argentina, Frau Hitler disguised in "masculine clothes," and were now hidden away "on an immense, German-owned estate in Patagonia." Stories of the *Führer's* survival and escape would surface for decades. The myth of the death and resurrection of the god was as old as history, and Nazi propagandists had suggested as much even before Hitler's immolation. Just two days before the event, the editor of the Lübeck *Anzeiger* had written fervidly of the besieged leader: "His heroic life at all times devoted to his people, achieves here amid an indescribable inferno a climax recalling the myths of far-off times; yes, a climax more brightly shining than the heroic battle in King Etzel's hall [in the *Nibelungenlied*]. The flames of Berlin represent no mere hopeless resistance to the inevitable, but the token of an iron will to save the future, a future assuring life to the European cultural community which this war has brought into consciousness."

Truman was content to forgo the ruined interiors of what had become the mausoleum of Naziism. His army chauffeur drove past the Tiergarten; the ruins of the Reichstag; the Sports Palace, notorious for Hitler's harangues there; and the Foreign Office. "Now they were nothing more than piles of stone and rubble. A more depressing sight ... was the long, never-ending procession of old men, women and children wandering aimlessly along ... carrying, pushing, or pulling what was left of their belongings."

The sampling of Berlin took two hours, Truman's return preceding by very little the news that he possessed at his command the capacity to outdo with a single bomb what had happened to Berlin. It was 3:30 that afternoon Berlin time when, at 5:30 A.M. from a remote desert area of the vast Alamogordo Air Base, earth and sky alighted and shook for miles with the unleashed energy of nuclear fission.

Since there was always the chance that in their single-mindedness to produce a working bomb the Manhattan District physicists might have miscalculated, and that the explosion might set off what Edward Teller called "a chain reaction that would encircle the globe in a sea of fire," he had offered to devise "controlled fantasies" to postulate every possibility he could within known physical phenomena. Before the device was armed, he claimed a "mathematical certainty" that the nuclear blast would be "limited." *Limited* did not mean "little," and Trinity, the area of hazard, embracing Ground Zero and Compania Hill, was 24 miles long and 18 miles across, 212 miles south of Santa Fe, just enough to maintain observers a safe 20 miles from the tower at Zero. There, men with Nobel Prizes and younger men who would earn them, men with knighthoods and some who would acquire them later, were ordered about by sergeants and corporals who warned them to lie down in the sand at blast time, turn their faces away, and bury their heads in their arms. Few intended to be that cautious, for everyone had been provided with welder's goggles, and many wore sunglasses beneath them. Each had protective clothing for the possible searing heat. But the night was dark with black clouds, and at 2:00 the desert was lashed by thunderstorms.

"It was raining cats and dogs, lightning and thunder," I. I. Rabi recalled unscientifically. They were "really scared that 'this object there in the tower' might be set off accidentally. So you can imagine the strain on Oppenheimer." The test had been scheduled for 4:00 but Jack Hubbard, the Project meteorologist, told his chief that while the original schedule would have to be scrubbed, they should be able to reset for sometime between 5:00 and 6:00. Groves demanded a fuller reading, receiving a learned explanation about the dynamics of desert storms at night, which almost always lost their energy by dawn. The general growled that he wanted a specific time, not a lecture, and Oppenheimer intervened to suggest 5:30. Army meteorologists with Hubbard agreed on the timing, but Groves, knowing what was expected of him, threatened, "You better be right on this, or I will hang you." At his order, Hubbard formally wrote out and signed his forecast. Although Teller had been assigned the mathematical fantasies about the extreme possibilities of the explosion, Enrico Fermi, looking up at the lightning, offered black-humoredly to wager anyone on the likelihood that the detonation would ignite the atmosphere. For Groves's benefit, apparently, he also offered to bet on whether the chain reaction would destroy the whole world or merely New Mexico. Groves, whose sense of humor seemed nonexistent, slipped off to a telephone and awakened the governor of New Mexico—it was just past 3:00—to warn him that if a test about to take place went awry, he might have to declare martial law.

At Zero the storm was lighter, yet at 3:30 gusts of wind threatened the austere guest facilities, collapsing Vannevar Bush's tent. Bush was unconcerned. He could manage until 5:30. And the wind had begun shifting toward the southwest.

George Kistiakowsky and his team made a final check at the tower, after which, at 5:08, the arming party arrived at the concrete control bunker, ten thousand yards (5.7 miles) away, and hidden under desert earth. Hubbard gave Kenneth Bainbridge his signed forecast for 5:30, and Bainbridge unlocked the master switches. At 5:09.45 Joseph Mc-Kibben, detailed to the countdown, began the timing sequence at minus twenty minutes. Oppenheimer remained at S-10,000 but Groves took a jeep back to the base camp, where the tension among the scientists and technicians was predictably high. In the chill darkness many rubbed last-minute suntan lotion on their faces and hands. Five minutes before contact a green flare went up from S-10,000, and then another at the one-minute mark. Groves hunkered down between Bush and Conant. With five seconds to go, Samuel K. Allison's radioed countdown to the base camp ceased. Another green flare flashed. Then he cried "Now!"

Many of the calculations of the device's likely release of energy had been made on IBM machine-readable punch cards—thousands of them—by twenty-seven-year-old Richard Feynman. He had been away as the test neared, recovering emotionally from the death of his wife. When the message came—"The baby is expected on July 16"— he flew back, arriving at the lab just as the buses were leaving for the test site. His post was frustratingly far off.

> Twenty miles away, you couldn't see a damn thing through dark glasses. So I figured the only thing that could really hurt your eyes (bright light can never hurt your eyes) is ultraviolet light. I got behind a truck windshield, because the ultraviolet can't go through glass, so that would be safe. . . .
>
> Time comes, and this *tremendous* flash out there is so bright that I duck, and I see this purple splotch on the floor of the truck. I said, "That's not it. That's an after-image." So I look back up, and I see this white light changing into yellow and then into orange.

Feynman did not confess it in his gleeful memoir of the day, but he had been temporarily blinded in one eye.

The power of the device was awesomely apparent. Despite all the high-tech gear to measure the energy yield, Enrico Fermi, who watched from S-10,000, waited for the 5:29 flare indicating a minute to go, then began tearing a sheet of paper into small pieces. Once he saw the flash through his welder's goggles, he dropped his bits of paper to be pushed by the blast wave. With his slide rule he calculated shock wave velocity based on a four-foot drop and estimated the release of energy as slightly under the equivalent of twenty thousand tons of TNT.

A brilliant yellow-white suffused the night sky, in which at the east appeared only the first faint grayness of dawn, and observers miles away felt the heat of the blast. The light coalesced into a half-risen sun, then a ball of red-orange fire. A roll of deep thunder shook the ground, reverberating and reverberating. As the blast hit the surface sixty-five thousandths of a second after fission, shock waves began raising thousands of tons of desert soil into the atmosphere. A flickering column of twisting smoke and fire curled upward into a mushroom shape, broad at the expanding top and cresting at forty-one thousand feet. Distant New Mexico counties trembled as if an earthquake had passed beneath them.

Leaning over from his prone position, Vannevar Bush reached out and shook Groves's hand. Relieved but excited, the general shouted through the noise that he was thinking of Charles Blondin's crossing Niagara Falls on a tightrope in 1859. Manhattan Engineering District—the formal name for the operation that had just peaked—had been, Groves confided, his tightrope. "I am sure," mused George Kistiakowsky, "that at the end of the world—in the last millisecond of the earth's existence—the last man will see what we have seen!" Watching the high desert winds work on the pillar of boiling energy, Edward Teller imagined the mushroom cloud being shaped "into a giant question mark." It was a vision that was as much metaphor as reality.

Turning toward his brother Frank, a fellow physicist in the Project, Robert Oppenheimer said, "It worked." Later, looking for more appropriate language, he went back to literature: "We waited until the blast had passed, walked out of the shelter and then it was extremely solemn. We knew that the world would not be the same." Returning to the base camp, his back ramrod straight in quiet pride, he saw only a few people with delight written on their faces. Most were solemn, some were in tears. "I remembered," he wrote, "the line from the Hindu scripture, the *Bhagavad-Gita:* Vishnu is trying to persuade the Prince that he should do his duty and to impress him he takes on his multi-armed form and says, 'Now I am become Death, the destroyer of worlds.' I suppose we all thought that, one way or another."

Once the first solemn wonder had passed, most scientists celebrated, but many who were awed by the display muted their elation quickly. Richard Feynman, who had been recruited in 1943 by his Princeton mentor, Robert Wilson, watched him "just sitting there moping." "It's a terrible thing we made," said Wilson. The Los Alamos scientists were not easily awed. They included more Nobel laureates, past and future, than would ever gather in a single place again, and such men could see past jubilation. The forces unleashed would win the war. If they hadn't found the formula, others would, somewhere and soon enough. As I. I. Rabi put it,

> At first I was thrilled. It was a vision. Then a few minutes afterward, I had goose flesh all over me when I realized what this meant for the future of humanity. Up until then, humanity was, after all, a limited factor in the evolution and process of nature. The vast oceans, lakes and rivers, the atmosphere, were not very much affected by the existence of mankind. The new powers represented a threat not only to mankind but to all forms of life: the seas and the air. One could foresee that nothing was immune from the tremendous powers of these new forces.

While Oppenheimer sat down with Groves to prepare a preliminary report for Henry Stimson in Potsdam, reduced to cablese in Washington, other scientists went—cautiously—to examine Ground Zero. The Army had provided two T-4 tanks, retrofitted with two-inch lead linings, increasing their weight by twelve tons. One was for Fermi, who declined the trip, fortunately, as the tank with an added winch broke down under its weight after half a mile and had to be abandoned. In the other, at 7:00 A.M., Herbert Anderson looked through a periscope at the blast center, discovering that the earth had fused into greenish, glassy scale. Radioactivity was intense, and they quickly turned around, past the site where the hundred-foot steel tower had vaporized. Using a mechanical external scoop he dug up a sample of soil to have the radioactivity analyzed, and clanked back.

The real sun had now come up. The desert heated quickly, but never as quickly or as fiercely as that morning. Exposed surfaces nearly a mile from the blast point had registered 750°F. Two scientists, Joseph Hirschfelder and John Magee, led a convoy of soldiers into the desert to monitor the radioactive fallout from low clouds and, if necessary, warn people living in the area to leave. At a small store at the crossing of two dirt roads the old proprietor came out to look at the sight—they were wearing white coveralls with gas masks hanging from their necks—and said to them with a laugh, "You boys must have been up to something this morning. The sun came up in the *west* and went on down again."

Someone else who had seen the phenomenon telephoned the *Albuquerque Journal* to find out what it was. A University of New Mexico music student was being driven to an early class by her brother-in-law. It was a very long drive and they had started early. "What was that?" she asked him as something far in the distance vaporized. It would not have taken much to notice the artificial dawn, but Georgia Green was blind.

As Anderson, Hirschfelder, Magee, and others were reconnoitering the blast environs, Harry Truman was returning from Berlin to dinner at number 2 Kaiserstrasse. The *Indianapolis,* on which Furman and Nolan knew nothing about whether the atomic device had worked, was casting off from Mare Island in the direction of the Golden Gate.

The recipient in Potsdam of the first news from Los Alamos had served his nation with distinction over five decades, but had not been invited as part of the conference party. Truman had just reviewed Secretary of War Stimson's troops without their boss. James Byrnes had only been sworn in at State on July 3, and wanted no competition from elder statesmen. Head of Roosevelt's Office of War Mobilization, in effect the domestic President while FDR ran the war, the crusty South Carolinian had expected the reward of the Vice Presidential nomination in 1944—the imprimatur to the succession. Instead, the opportunity went to a lesser-known senator from Missouri, a compromise between the too-liberal Justice William O. Douglas and the too-conservative Byrnes. Recognizing his disappointment and respecting his abilities, Truman had moved Byrnes up to replace the colorless Edward R. Stetinnius, Roosevelt's replacement for Cordell Hull. But Henry Stimson, as tactful as he was tenacious, had asked before the *Augusta* sailed whether the President was worried that his Secretary of War's health was not up to the rigors of Potsdam. "Top civilians in our Department," he said, "ought to be around to balance the opinions of the generals and admirals." Byrnes remarked to Truman that if the Secretary of the Navy were not present, why should Stimson go—but Stimson went, separately, via Marseilles, on the Army transport *Brazil.* (Secretary Forrestal would turn up also.)

Stimson didn't think the Bomb would be needed, and on the day before the investiture of the hawkish Byrnes had prepared a paper for Truman's use at Potsdam that began, bluntly, "Japan has no allies." He saw Japan as crumbling under bombing and blockade, while the United States had "inexhaustible . . . industrial resources to bring to bear against her diminishing potential." The "mad fanatics," he thought, were a minority, and the Japanese government was more "susceptible to reason . . . than is indicated by our current press." Yet he was the bearer of the news about the Bomb and would be the arbiter of its deployment.

No more experienced hand, with the sole exception of Churchill, was at Potsdam than Stimson, a protégé of Theodore Roosevelt who had held his first Cabinet seat under William Howard Taft and served as an artillery colonel in France when Truman was a captain. Although a conservative Republican, he had been pulled out of retirement by the second Roosevelt in 1940 to be Secretary of War. Without a seat in the Cecilienhof, he made his presence felt because he thought he had to. The shrewd but touchy Byrnes was as innocent of high-level diplomacy as was Truman. A veteran of international conferences, Stimson knew that his intrusions, always courtly with a small *c*, could not be brushed off. Looking ahead to the inevitable Japanese surrender, however it came about, he wrote a long memorandum to guide the President, dated that day from Babelsberg. The Yalta agreements signed by Stalin on February 11, he reminded Truman, did not give away Chinese sovereignty over Manchuria, nor did they give Russia any special rights in Korea, where Stimson hoped for an international trusteeship until the country could govern itself. Stalin, he understood, had once urged that no foreign troops be stationed in Korea. Yet the Russians, "I am also informed, have already trained one or two divisions of [expatriate] Koreans, and, I assume, intend to use them in Korea. If an international trusteeship is not set up . . . and perhaps even if it is, these Korean divisions will probably gain control, and influence the setting up of a Soviet dominated local government. . . . This is the Polish question transplanted to the Far East." With the Korean Communist forces, thirty-three, ambitious, and unknown to Stimson, was an officer named Kim Il Sung.

The Secretary also had suggestions about the occupation of Japan itself, and the need to limit the role of the Russians there:

> I would hope that our occupation of the Japanese islands would not involve the government of the country as a whole in any such manner as we are committed in Germany. I am afraid we would make a hash of it if we tried. The Japanese are an oriental people with an oriental mind and religion. Our occupation should be limited to that necessary to (a) impress the Japanese, and the orient as a whole, with the fact of Japanese defeat, (b) demilitarize the country, and (c) punish war criminals, including those responsible for the perfidy of Pearl Harbor.
>
> If the Russians seek joint occupation after a creditable

participation in the conquest of Japan, I do not see how we
could refuse at least a token occupation. I feel, however, that
no prolonged occupation by the Soviet should be approved. . . .
I would approve their occupation of the Kuriles or indeed
their cession to Russia, but I do not relish the main islands.
The conditions and terms must certainly be determined by us.

Two messages from Washington called for Truman's special attention that evening at Kaiserstrasse, one a long cable to Byrnes, the
other a laconic paragraph to Stimson. To Byrnes, Hull repeated his
earlier objections to any mention of the Emperor in a Potsdam declaration. There would be, he warned, recognizing the view of most
Americans that Hirohito was a war criminal, "terrible repercussions"
at home. In Japan, on the other hand, as Dooman and Grew warned,
there would be equivalent repercussions if their Emperor were not
spared as figurehead sovereign, for anything less would be seen as
threatening the entire fabric of Japanese life. From "Magic," Truman
and Byrnes had heard this argument before, but they had not yet
learned that while they were still at sea, Prince Konoye, whom the
Emperor hoped unrealistically could strike a deal with the Russians,
had told Hirohito frankly that the war was utterly lost and that the
Japanese, whatever the militarists claimed, were powerless to place
any conditions on the peace. The ultras, Konoye maintained, would
continue the war despite the costs. But he was willing to sacrifice his
own life to atone for his past errors as prime minister.

Weakening the Allied position on unconditional surrender,
Cordell Hull had warned in his cable, might suggest to the militarists
in Tokyo a weakening of resolve—that their *kamikaze* posture was
paying off. Hull preferred to hold off any ultimatum until the bombing of Japan had achieved further results, and also until "Russia's
entry into the war."

When Stimson arrived at Truman's quarters, leaning on his familiar cane, it was with a message from his special assistant, George L.
Harrison, on leave from the presidency of the New York Life Insurance Company. Harrison had a sense of humor about "Fat Man":

Operated on this morning. Diagnosis not complete but results
seem satisfactory and already exceed expectations. Local
press release necessary as interest extends great distance. Dr.
Groves pleased. He returns tomorrow. I will keep you posted.

The Secretary understood that the blast had been heard, seen, or felt over such a wide area that a cover story had been invented. It duly appeared in the *Albuquerque Tribune* later that morning, and was picked up by the wire services:

> Alamogordo, N.M., July 16—William O. Eareckson, commanding officer of the Alamogordo Army Air Base, made the following statement today:
>
> "Several inquiries have been received concerning a heavy explosion which occurred on the Alamogordo Air Base reservation this morning.
>
> "A remotely located ammunition magazine containing a considerable amount of high explosives and pyrotechnics exploded.
>
> "There was no loss of life or injury to anyone, and the property damage outside of the explosive magazine itself was negligible.
>
> "Weather conditions affecting the content of gas shells exploded by the blast may make it desirable for the Army to evacuate temporarily a few citizens from their homes."

With mock relief, Stimson told an aide that he no longer feared imprisonment at Fort Leavenworth for misuse of billions of dollars. But to Byrnes the news meant a different kind of reprieve. Until atomic bombs were dropped, no one had to decide anything about modifying unconditional surrender.

That evening Winston Churchill dined privately with Stimson's chief lieutenant, General Marshall, to whom Britain owed much. The next day the P.M. would tell Alexander Cadogan, "That is the noblest Roman of them all. Congress always did what he advised. His work in training the American armies has been wonderful. I will pay tribute to it one day when occasion offers." Churchill may have been recalling, also, the bleak day in 1941 when the austere Marshall appeared before a hostile House of Representatives committee to argue for passage of the bill extending the draft for another year. Without Marshall the United States would have been totally unprepared at the time of Pearl Harbor.

Although Truman had inspected an armored division at full strength, much of American military muscle was being diverted to the final offensives against Japan. Dated that day was the final movement order in the ETO—European Theater of Operations—by the Eighth Air Force, which was moving units the next day back across the Channel to High Wycombe. As the beginning of a longer move, its headquarters ("without personnel, equipment or combat elements") was to shift to Okinawa, to join the Twentieth Air Force in reducing Japan. Over ninety thousand of its personnel—more than half its strength at the time of the German surrender—had already been redeployed.

The Japanese were having difficulty moving their troops closer to the war. Cut off from resupply, soldiers in the Lesser Sundas—the Dutch Indies islands east of Java as far as Timor—were first moved by fast combat ships to evade American subs, but it took three months and the loss of two cruisers to evacuate the 46th Division as far as Java. On June 6 the Army had ordered a more desperate tactic to ferry the 48th Division (and leave the lower Indies virtually undefended). In violation of international law a hospital ship painted white would withdraw as many men as it could carry. "In order to keep secret the movement of the hospital ship *Tachibana Maru*," Second Army headquarters in Celebes radioed, "we should like from now on to call her *Sea Truk Hirose Maru*, thus preventing the appearance of her [actual] name in operational orders. . . ."

The ghost ship sailed from Java to Dilli on Timor. Troops boarded in hospital garments as if patients, and ordnance and ammunition were packed in boxes marked MEDICAL SUPPLIES. Loaded with 1,406 soldiers in hospital garb and 217 on stretchers identified as "seriously ill," and taking on 1,929 cases of "baggage" ostensibly belonging to the "patients," the *Sea Truk* raised anchor, and a message on July 16 confirmed safe arrival in Java.

It seemed a perfect ruse. With another load of hospital uniforms the ship began a second run, this time to Toeal in the Kai Islands, southwest of New Guinea, to evacuate the marooned 11th Infantry Regiment.

Efforts to carry the war to Japan from China had largely failed, but the slack was being picked up from the other side of the home islands. American forces in China were frustrated by the politics and the corruption that had drained whatever fighting spirit there was from Chiang's armies. Closest to the action among American brass was General Robert McClure, who was liaison chief to General Ho Ying-chin, commander of Chinese ground forces and provider of almost everything with which the soldiers were equipped. One example that day had been the planned move of six thousand troops of the 30th Division to a forward position. Ho's vice commander objected to relinquishing his peaceful perquisites. At nine in the evening, after a day of delays, units departed with half-empty trucks, one moving 2,717 men instead of a planned 4,000, the other moving 693 men instead of 1,050. McClure's aide on the scene was disgusted.

Perks for some American commanders were not to be sniffed at. General Albert C. Wedemeyer, who had replaced the crusty Stilwell, moved about in "Dade," his personal C-47. The "private ship," as Captain Richard D. Weigle, secretary to McClure's Chinese Combat Command—"Combat" was a clear misnomer—put it, was "a beautiful job finished in cream inside with brown curtains at the windows and a rug on the floor. The seats were just like a commercial transport back home, but more comfortable and elaborate. On the port side near the pilot's cockpit was a bed covered with a spread to match the curtains." In the rear was a stove and a row of closets for Wedemeyer's uniforms. (MacArthur had a more luxurious plane, a four-engined C-54.)

From the Marianas, only weather was keeping the Twentieth Air Force from daily poundings of Japan. Few planes rose to meet the American bombers, whose pilots were more concerned with AA-fire, their own fuel reserves, and mechanical failure. Piloting a B-29 over Japanese oil refineries on Honshu, Lieutenant Hays Gamble of the 315th Bomb Wing wondered in his diary, summing up the sixteenth, "Didn't see any fighters at all. Just a few scattered searchlights but no flak." He was puzzled why "they stand by while we blow hell out of them."[*]

Short on fuel to return to Guam, Gamble landed on Iwo Jima, where he also had a burned-out wing flap motor replaced. While waiting, he and his crew wandered on foot down to the shoreline. "What a stinking, horrid piece of land that is!" he wrote. "Grass and weeds just starting to cover the scars. Debris all over, Jap & Am, and barbed wire & bullets & shells & shrapnel lying all around. Many unburied Japs in holes & caves & trenches—skeletons all over. Place stinks to high heaven of rotten flesh still. Added to that are sulphur fumes and steam coming out of the ground. Picked up a Jap helmet. . . ." By 11:15 in the morning—before dawn in Potsdam—he was back in more antiseptic Harmon Field, Guam, from which that night 466 B-29s would drop incendiary bombs on Numazu, Oita, Kuwana, and Hiratsuka. War looked much different from 21,000 feet up.

---

[*]The military claimed that it was hoarding planes and fuel for the anticipated invasion of the homeland, but to Foreign Minister Togo—now a dove—"it was almost as if we sat with arms folded while attacked."

# CHAPTER V

# · July 17, 1945 ·

*"Terminal"*

As July 17 began, a typhoon bearing up the China coast kept all but the earliest naval and air strikes from hitting Japan, but the day was memorable for the addition of British warships to Halsey's Third Fleet as TF 37. At Potsdam the Admiralty would ask for more say about strategy but its role was seen as so small that the Americans were uninterested. Division of command and disagreement on strategy had lengthened the war in Europe and put the West at political disadvantage in dealing with Russia. Marshall would not repeat the mistake, although service rivalries, long tolerated as inevitable, had created much the same situation in the Pacific. On the seventeenth, British and American military chiefs met in Potsdam, Field Marshal Sir Alan Brooke minuted, "to reply to our desire to participate in the direct attack on Japan. . . . The offer is accepted in principle. The second [matter] was a question of Command in the Pacific. . . . We want a greater share in the control of strategy in the Pacific and they are apparently reluctant to provide this share." What Brooke did not add was that at one point General Marshall cleared the room except for the chiefs of staff themselves and announced the detonation of an atomic device in New Mexico.

Although British ground forces were operating in Southeast Asia, and were nowhere within the Pacific rim in which the invasion of Japan was developing, the guns and carrier planes of the Royal Navy had already begun participating in strikes against the home islands. "Back off Tokyo harbor with the bombardment group," wrote Laird Shirk on the destroyer *McGowan*, "joined by H.M.S. *King George VI.*" They shelled industrial targets just north of Tokyo in the Hitachi area. "We expected opposition but found none. The *McGowan* crew finds it difficult to believe that we could bombard close to Tokyo without suffering heavy losses."

The weather was a factor in both the offense and the lack of defense. Using as its heavy artillery not only the *King George VI* but the battleships *Alabama, North Carolina, Iowa, Wisconsin,* and *Missouri* (with Admiral Halsey aboard as observer), the task force commanded by Admiral Oscar Badger chanced the overcast weather, intermittent rain, and two-thousand-foot ceiling, and headed toward Hitachi. At eight in the evening they targeted the lengthy shoreline industrial complex entirely by radar, firing 1,238 sixteen-inch shells from seventeen miles out, and withdrawing by midnight. The damage to a string of Hitachi Engineering Works factories was extensive, but they had no idea if they had hit anything at all but the ground until later aerial reconnaissance. (After B-29s followed up the shelling two days later, production dropped to nearly zero.)

Shipping sweeps around Japan by Air Force bombers were hampered by heavy weather but other units striking from China, Burma, and the Philippines interdicted bridges, roads, railway yards, river traffic, and harbors from Celebes to Indochina to China itself. The aim was to cripple resupply efforts everywhere. An intelligence report from Shanghai noted that guests in hotels had to bring their own rice and that Japanese travelers were instructed to bring food for their needs on any journey whatever.

All defensive operations planned now had a *kamikaze* dimension. The Imperial Army and Navy, often rivals, had agreed to combine their remaining aircraft for use in suicide missions against the expected invasion fleet. Only 230 *Ohka* mother aircraft for manned bombs were available, but the Army was developing new turbojet models to be able to move in quickly and escape AA-fire. Even more urgent was the training of *kamikaze* pilots, no longer a volunteer oper-

ation. With that final American assault in mind, and the more immediate concern about Russia entering the war, Japanese intelligence
was riveted by a report on the seventeenth from its consul general in
Harbin (it maintained the pretense that Manchuria—"Manchukuo"—
was independent) that thirty trains a day from European Russia were
arriving in coastal Siberia and along the Manchurian border. In one
eight-day period alone, the report (intercepted by "Magic") went on,
2,932 railway cars carrying troops were counted. He estimated that
900,000 men and 4,000 planes were in place.

The High Command preferred a contrary report from an agent
in Shanghai who had talked to a *Tass* correspondent, although it was
bleak enough:

> Soviet Russia has not yet massed the strength to take part in
> the Pacific War, and is not expected to do so. This does not,
> however, take into account what Russia would do if the war
> situation should further deteriorate for Japan.

Shanghai itself offered no rosy picture of Japanese hopes. With
spring weather American bombers had begun hitting the Whangpoo
docks, flying very low over the crowded ghetto district just a few
streets inland that had been home to a refugee community of German
Jews since 1938. Ernest Heppner, twenty-four, formerly of Breslau
and night manager of the Dah Tung bakery on Dent Road, often
stood on his windowsill to cheer the B-24s on although he knew that
bombs would fall close by. The Japanese had a powerful radio transmitter near the Tongshan Road that directed naval activities in the
China Sea, and their wharves and warehouses shipped or stored synthetic fuel, munitions, and foodstuffs.

There had been a heavy raid on Sunday. Although the next day
was quiet, the English-language *Shanghai Evening Post & Mercury*,
which still published, enlivened it for readers by reporting from
Japanese sources that President Truman had arrived in Europe on the
*Augusta*, a cruiser well known to refugees because before the war it
had been the flagship of the Asian Fleet and had often been seen at
anchor in the Whangpoo. The Japanese had claimed its sinking; now
they were reporting it in Ostend harbor.

On the seventeenth Heppner had swapped shifts with the day
manager, but in the early afternoon he was dozing in his flat, having
brought a loaf of bread home to share with Illo, his bride of three

months—a refugee with her family from Berlin. For Illo, cooking rice for any meal seemed almost a full-time job. One had to take a pot of dry rice to a water shop and purchase a ladle of boiling water to pour over the rice. At home the next step was to fire and fan the coals (coal-mud fuel was toxic and the fumes deadly), afterward wrapping the pot in blankets or a pillow to complete the cooking. Safe hot water was a luxury.

At two, as Heppner rose to return, he heard the humming, then the roar, of bombers. The rickety building swayed in the explosions and both Illo and Heppner tumbled down their stairs in a crash of debris. Thirty-two refugees died, and many more Japanese. Uncounted Chinese were later piled into a putrefying mound of corpses. While refugee doctors worked to exhaustion at the hospital, Chinese doctors sat, indifferently, smoking cigarettes and playing mah-jongg. Their instruments were missing, they explained, but refugees thought the problem was that local laborers had no wherewithal for a fee. Such episodes were not new, and the penniless had become stoic about it.

Later in the afternoon Heppner decided to "look in" at the bakery. It was gone, along with nearby Japanese installations. He was out of a job. Two trucks came by, and soldiers of Wang Ching-wei's puppet government spilled out to carry off undamaged bags of flour. Later Heppner learned that the raid,* and others like it, had been directed from the ground by the caretaker of one of the ghetto synagogues, an agent trained by the OSS. "His portable transmitter was hidden behind the ark that held the Sefer Torah. . . ."

The Heppners had to begin queuing up for a meal a day from the Kitchen Fund. They placed an umbrella in the hole in their roof and hoped for a quick end to the war. It was no consolation to listen to a woman who had come from London just before the Pacific war and become marooned in Shanghai. She had endured, she claimed, 168 raids during the Blitz, and each was easier to cope with. London had solid cellars and deep underground stations, which offered a sense of security. Everything about Shanghai was flimsy.

The raids, which would continue, were as nothing compared to the firebombing of Japanese cities, which threatened to incinerate all of urban Japan. Foreign Minister Togo thought it was time to seek an-

---

*Far East Air Force records indicate that the raid on Whangpoo River shipping and the Shanghai area was on the eighteenth but Heppner recalls the episode as a day earlier.

other audience with the Emperor, to remind him that in Germany the Big Three were deciding Japan's fate. All three. He was as certain that Stalin was also involved, he told the Emperor, as he was that his plea for mediation had reached Molotov and Stalin.

"The Emperor said simply," he noted afterward, "that the fate of our proposal was now beyond our control; it depended on the response of the other party." On Russia, he concluded, depended "the destiny of Japan." It was a fatalism that left Togo with nothing more to say. He bowed his way out.

From the Foreign Office he rejected Ambassador Sato's conclusion that the Soviet reluctance to mediate left no choice but unconditional surrender. Unless Japan's "honor and existence" were guaranteed, Togo cabled Moscow, "then our country and His Majesty would unanimously resolve to fight a war of resistance to the bitter end." He knew that was no longer the Emperor's feeling, but that of those who still dictated policy to him. Almost certainly neither the Emperor nor his Cabinet had ever heard of a speech in 1895 by a onetime officer in the American Civil War, Oliver Wendell Holmes, Jr., in which he observed approvingly that only in war could men pursue "the divine folly of honor." They would have recognized the concept as Japanese.

When the "Magic" intercept arrived in Potsdam, Marshall would add it to what would become (for July alone) the seventy-eight-page SRH-0040 file, one of the bases for decision making. Marshall would also learn that the Scientific Panel of the Interim Committee [on uses of the Bomb]—Lawrence, Compton, Fermi, and Oppenheimer—had met on the evening of the sixteenth and into the early hours of the seventeenth, when it was already breakfast time in Berlin, to discuss the practicality of a demonstration explosion of sufficient persuasiveness to shock the Japanese into surrender. Fermi, Szilard, and others hoped to avoid a real drop on an enemy target, but "our obligation to our nation to use the weapons to help save American lives in the Japanese war," the panel concluded, after consulting scientific colleagues in the Manhattan District, left no other credible option:

> Those who advocate a purely technical demonstration would wish to outlaw the use of atomic weapons, and have feared that if we use the weapons now our position in future negotiations will be prejudiced. Others emphasize the op-

portunity of saving American lives by immediate military
use, and believe that such use will improve the international
prospects, in that they are more concerned with the prevention of war than with the elimination of this specific
weapon. We find ourselves closer to these latter views; we
can propose no technical demonstration likely to bring an
end to the war; we see no acceptable alternative to direct
military use.

Formal sessions at Potsdam were not to begin until late afternoon, but the news from Alamogordo had quickened the pace at
number 2 Kaiserstrasse. Stimson had spent much of the previous
evening after receipt of George Harrison's cable preparing a memorandum for Byrnes and Truman suggesting that the Japanese peace
feelers to Moscow and the validation of the atomic weapon ("the
power of new forces") made it possible to issue a stern warning to
Japan. Surrender would prevent national catastrophe; prolonging the
war might add to catastrophe a new adversary, the Soviet Union.
    When it had become known the night before that Stalin had ar-
rived, Truman sent former ambassador Davies to call on Ivan
Maisky, the Russian ambassador in London, to arrange an informal
meeting between their two leaders. It was set for noon.
    The U.S. Joint Chiefs of Staff had already met separately, before
joining their British counterparts, to review the military repercussions
of the warning to be issued to Tokyo. The suicidal fanaticism of the
Japanese had caused Marshall to reassess his position. He thought it
prudent to include no language that might imply removal of the Emperor, as his role in inducing the Japanese to lay down their arms
might be crucial—not only in the home islands but in the sprawling
territories which American forces had bypassed. The chiefs agreed to a
memorandum expressing misgivings about the paragraph promising
the Japanese "a peacefully inclined, responsible government of a character representing the Japanese people" because, it went on to elaborate, "This may include a constitutional monarchy under the present
dynasty." Might this be interpreted as a threat to depose, even execute,
Hirohito and install someone else? And, if democratic, even radical,
elements in Japan were to take over, might not any promise to retain a
culture of emperor worship make it difficult to get their support? To
the Chiefs, a noncommittal promise to let the Japanese choose "their
own form of government" might appeal to the broadest political base

in the nation. Although they were planning an invasion, they preferred a surrender without invasion. To that end they recommended more ambiguity than Dooman and Grew had written into the draft.

Interpreting the Japanese signal traffic and approaches to neutrals as "maneuvering," Stimson wanted "prompt delivery" of an unqualified message. Byrnes, so Stimson noted in his diary, "was opposed to a prompt and early warning to Japan," preferring to see an ultimatum emerge at the close of the conference if still needed. Rather than delay the deployment of "S-1" by having to wait for the outcome of repeated warnings, he would deploy it as soon as practicable. Although the Soviets at Yalta had been promised special status short of sovereignty in parts of Manchuria, according to Forrestal's diary "Byrnes said he was most anxious to get the Japanese affair over with before the Russians got in, with particular reference to Dairen and Port Arthur. Once in there, he felt, it would not be easy to get them out." Eisenhower, too, would urge Truman not to offer new inducements to the Russians to get them into the war, but the bargain had been made months before and had conceded only what the Soviets could seize without contributing to the defeat of Japan. Truman figured that Russia might as well earn its aggrandizements.

Byrnes would ask Stimson again several days later about the timing of the Bomb operation, which the Japanese appeared to be inviting by refusing to accept the two formulaic words, *unconditional surrender*. Stimson's newest proposal to Truman kept Byrnes's urgency in mind but combined it with his own view that a preliminary warning was needed, delivered "during the course of this Conference, and rather earlier than later? . . . In the meantime, our tactical plans should continue to operate without let up, and if the Japanese persist, the full force of our newer weapons should be brought to bear . . . backed by the power of new forces and possibly the actual entrance of the Russians in the war."

"Promptly a few minutes before twelve," Truman noted in his diary, "I looked up from the desk and there stood Stalin in the doorway." He had arrived in a long Packard with bulletproof glass obscuring the occupants. Truman's voluble sidekick and military aide, Harry Vaughan, rushed out to greet Stalin and escort the party—Molotov and an interpreter, Pavlov, accompanied Stalin—inside while the Soviet guards gaped at the materialization of the myth. Stalin apologized for arriving at Potsdam late. His health was not as good as it used to be, he explained, a point reinforced later when his toasts were taken in white wine rather than vodka.

Charles Bohlen, Truman's translator, long a Kremlinologist, thought that Stalin looked in poor health. His pockmarked face was pale, with a yellowish streak in his gray eyes. Still, Stalin carried his inevitable cigarette in his right hand, the one he always gestured with, as his left arm, crippled in childhood, was seldom seen. Despite his army khakis with a Hero of the Soviet Union star pinned over his breast pocket, and red seams down the trousers that might have suggested height, Truman was surprised at Stalin's smallness, something Russians used to heroic statues of the generalissimo never saw. He was only about five-feet-five. Truman appeared the symbol of the civilian president in his double-breasted gray suit and black-and-white summer shoes.

As they sat down in the bulky overstuffed chairs provided by the Russians, Harry Vaughan whispered to Truman something about inviting "these guys" to lunch. Truman wanted to know what was on the menu. Vaughan whispered it was liver and bacon. "If liver and bacon is good enough for us," said Truman, "it's good enough for them." Stalin protested politely that it would be impossible, he didn't need to add that he was under a doctor's care.

"You could if you wanted to," said Truman.

Stalin remained. There was more than liver and bacon—also creamed spinach soup, baked ham, julienne potatoes, green beans, pumpernickel, and fresh fruit—and California wine. "We had a real show drinking toasts to everyone," Truman wrote.

He was no diplomat who answered questions without really answering them, he told Stalin. He usually said yes or no after hearing all the arguments. Stalin said he liked that

> and that he had some more questions to present. I told him to fire away. He did and it is dynamite—but I have some dynamite too which I'm not exploding now. He wants to fire Franco, to which I wouldn't object, and divide up the Italian colonies and other mandates, some no doubt that the British have. Then he got on the Chinese situation, told us what agreements had been reached and what was in abeyance. Most of the big points are settled. He'll be in the Jap War on August 15th. Fini Japs when that comes about.

Truman wanted to like Stalin. "I can deal with Stalin," he concluded. "He is honest, but smart as hell."

"The truth is," Cadogan minuted to Churchill at much the same time, using "Russia" to refer to Stalin, "that on any and every point, Russia tries to seize all that she can and she uses these meetings to grab as much as she can get. . . . I am deeply concerned at the pattern of Russian policy, which becomes clearer as they become more brazen every day."

In time Truman's better impressions of Stalin would all be disproved, except that Stalin was smart as hell. The Russians were then bargaining with Chiang Kaishek's Chinese over border alignments in the north, and about the Soviet interest in Manchuria, which Stalin was willing to leave nominally Chinese as long as he acquired economic and military control. Mao Zedong and Chiang had been warring with each other as much as with the Japanese, and the Americans had been supplying only the Kuomintang forces with money and arms, much of it diverted by Chiang's corrupt family and lieutenants. Stalin was not yet ready to bet on his ideological counterpart, and wanted Chinese concessions before going to war. But Truman was happy: Stalin would march against the Japanese by the fifteenth, four weeks away. That was insurance if the Japanese didn't pack it in first when prodded with what the President called "dynamite." Truman's first priority was to end the Japanese war with American objectives met. He would tell Stalin about the Bomb when he figured out how to do it. It was not a matter of sharing the recipe, but that the Soviets learned of the Bomb openly before it was dropped.

For diplomatic reasons Truman did not note in his diary Stalin's wry skepticism that the British were unlikely to be very helpful in the Far East. Also that when Stalin hinted strongly that he would require vast American resources for his own efforts there, he was offered the equally wry observation that Russia was no longer in dire straits—as Britain had been in 1940 when facing the Germans alone. Then, before Stalin added something new to his Potsdam shopping list, Byrnes quickly recalled the Yalta agreements (since Stalin regularly brought them up to justify Polish annexations of Pomerania and Silesia) that limited Russia's gains at Japan's expense to the restoration of Czarist losses to the Japanese in 1904. Truman also recognized some demands raised at lunch as diplomatic poker. Stalin had no use for former Italian colonies in Africa, but would try to get something else as payoff for relinquishing the claim. And he also expected conservative pressure in the United States (as well as in the United Kingdom) to forestall the overthrow of Franco in Spain.

The formal business for Potsdam would commence at five that afternoon. After taking pictures with Stalin in what Truman called "the back yard," he agreed to a visit to Stalin's residence, then tucked in for an afternoon nap.

While Truman entertained Stalin, Stimson lunched at noon with Churchill and Attlee. For Churchill it was his usual breakfast hour; to the discomfort of everyone else, he worked through most nights until nearly dawn, telephoning anyone he cared to if his business required it. With the Secretary of War his business was less military than economic—the likely shortage of coal in Britain and Europe over the winter to come, and the disposition of the German merchant fleet, which Churchill knew the Russians coveted. He offered to walk Stimson to the gate afterward, and as they left the house the Secretary pulled a slip of paper from his pocket and held it up for Churchill to see. It read in large letters, BABIES SATISFACTORILY BORN.

Churchill was baffled. "It means," Stimson explained, "that the experiment in the New Mexican desert has come off. The atomic bomb is a reality."* Now Churchill was elated—or was until Stimson remarked that the Russians ought to know. Secretiveness, Stimson cautioned, would only feed Soviet suspicions about the West. He thought that Truman would want to tell Stalin something.

In England, where, according to Dorothy Bussy—Lytton Strachey's sister was writing to André Gide—London's bomb craters and ruins were "now a garden of grass and wild flowers green & pink and yellow, springing up on their own accord in the wastes," a small army of German generals was sequestered for debriefings in several large country estates untouched by war. At Grizedale Hall, near Windermere, the military journalist Basil Liddell Hart had, since July 9, been driving up in his 1937 Rolls-Royce to conduct interviews on German tactics and strategies. Some were cooperating because they felt flattered by the serious attention paid their professionalism; others saw getting their versions out as a means of escaping war crimes

---

*In volume 8 of Martin Gilbert's *Winston S. Churchill* (1988), the P.M. had asked Truman about the Alamogordo test: "Let me know if it is a plop or a flop." While still on holiday near Bordeaux (which he left for Potsdam early on July 15), Churchill allegedly received Truman's reply: "It's a plop." The device had not yet gone off, and Sir John Colville's recollections to Gilbert in 1987 are an invention. Churchill's source was Stimson.

trials. Some were elderly and others in poor condition, and at Wilton Park two generals had become ill. General Wilhelm Ritter von Thoma had been removed to a hospital and later had a leg amputated. On July 17, Field Marshal Ernst von Busch, who had commanded the fighting retreat through Belorussia and in 1940 had been assigned the planning of an invasion of England, died of a heart attack.

Lieutenant Colonel St. Clare Grondona, the Australian officer commanding Wilton Park, asked the War Office for instructions, and was told that the body was to be removed to Aldershot, to the south in Hampshire, for appropriate military honors. Burial would be the next day, July 17. In the morning the commandant accompanied the eight most senior generals, with guards, on a military bus. At War Office orders the blinds were drawn, but as the bus neared Windsor, Grondona permitted them to be raised for a view of the castle. Field Marshal Gerd von Rundstedt confided that the last time he had seen Windsor was as an official German representative at the coronation of George VI. Some of the eight had very likely visited Aldershot, one of the premier British military installations since Victoria's day, as young officers.

The conversation with Grondona gave von Rundstedt an opportunity to ask whether a firing party of the Brigade of Guards would be detailed to the gravesite, but the commandant evaded an answer by having the blinds pulled up again for a view of Eton and of the deer in Windsor Great Park. Soon after, they linked up with a hearse carrying the remains of von Busch, and when the bus began bumping over a very rough surface off the road, and shortly afterward came to a stop, the generals discovered on stepping down into the daylight that they were in what appeared to be an open field. It was, Grondona explained, the Aldershot cemetery "reserve ground."

Half a dozen scruffy German prisoners of war were standing by, and astonished by the sight of so much *Wehrmacht* brass—the generals were permitted their uniforms—they snapped to attention. The work party had just dug the grave, and, opening the hearse at a command in English, they bore the coffin to their handiwork and lowered it. The uniformed chaplain on duty raced through a burial service in English, turned his back on the generals, and walked away. The Guards, who had been put through their preparatory ceremonial paces at Wilton Park, had no orders to do anything. Astonished, but recovering his dignity, von Rundstedt raised his marshal's baton and the generals offered a last salute to von Busch. Then they returned to the bus, which had been moved conveniently close to a screened outdoor latrine.

No one spoke on the way back. That evening von Rundstedt asked whether Grondona could see him. The commandant came to von Rundstedt's room, where the general, trembling with emotion, asked why he and his colleagues had been subjected to such a bitter and dishonorable experience that was unworthy, too, of the dead von Busch.

As commandant, confided Grondona, he could make no comment other than that he was following orders. But off the record and man-to-man, he wondered whether von Rundstedt had seen the pictures recently reproduced in England of German concentration camp brutalities. Feeling against the Germans, as revelation followed revelation, was running high. Although the War Office did not believe that the man just buried had anything to do with such atrocities, had the field marshal observed at the cemetery a policeman in the distance to keep curious onlookers, and especially the press, away? In the present climate, Grondona went on, a simple ceremony was essential. Giving von Busch military honors due him would have caused embarrassing questions to be asked in the House of Commons. There would have been angry comments in the newspapers.

With his head down and his face in his hands, von Rundstedt said, agitatedly, "We do realize what you say, and have the utmost shame. But I give you my word of honor as a soldier that the revelations concerning the concentration camps have appalled the *Wehrmacht* even more than the people of Britain." Ironically, Wilton Park in Beaconsfield was only a few miles from Hughenden, remembered for its association with an English prime minister who, had he lived in Hitler's Germany, would have been sent to a Belsen or a Buchenwald—Benjamin Disraeli.

Two hundred reporters had been accredited to the Potsdam conference, from veteran bureau chiefs to Hearst's young John F. Kennedy. Kept from anything but carefully monitored sightseeing and handouts from government press officers, newspapermen, Churchill realized, were "in a state of furious indignation." But the Soviets would permit nothing else, and the sessions were in their zone.

The first plenary session of "Terminal"—an appropriate code name, as it was the final Big Three meeting of the war—opened at 5:10 P.M. in the oak-paneled reception hall, converted to a conference room, of the Cecilienhof Palace at Potsdam. Converted into a military hospital by the Germans, it had been, in Hohenzollern days, the summer home of the crown prince. The Russians had carpeted the inner courtyard with a red star, twenty-four feet wide, of red geraniums, and covered the circular conference table in burgundy cloth. Fifteen chairs surrounded the table, five for each nation.

With Truman were Byrnes, Leahy, Davies, and Bohlen as interpreter. Such conferences were new to the President. He knew of Churchill's command of the spoken word, and Stalin's no-nonsense bluntness. He had not had to deal with give-and-take in which translators interposed themselves, and was surprised at the ease with which the discussions went. "Bohlen would translate for me when I talked, Pavlov would translate while Stalin was speaking, and Major Birse would translate Churchill's words for the Russians. We would slow down from time to time so the interpreters could translate each sentence. If there was any disagreement among the interpreters as to the proper Russian word for the English equivalent, they would settle it right there while Stalin would sit back and grin. . . . I suspected he really understood English."

Stalin's chief aides were Molotov, Vyshinsky, and Gromyko; Churchill's were Eden, Cadogan and (representing Labour) Attlee. Speaking first as the convener, Stalin suggested that since Truman was the only head of state among the three, he be elected chairman. (Russia had a figurehead president, Mikhail Kalinin.) Churchill seconded the motion. Reading remarks he had prepared, Truman suggested as agenda items the establishment of a Council of Foreign Ministers to prepare for a European peace conference, and discussion of how the decisions made at Yalta were being implemented. There had not been free elections in most countries, he observed. The model, Truman proposed, was Italy, which was on its way toward democratic institutions and had helpfully even declared war on Germany and then Japan.

In almost every case, Churchill claimed not to have read the requisite documents and needed more time. The mention of Italy brought his interruption that Truman was moving too hastily. Mussolini, after all, had stabbed Britain in the back in 1940, and substantial resources had to be committed against Italy, with sometimes heavy losses. Churchill rambled on, with Stalin breaking in. He wanted a share of the German merchant fleet and navy. He wanted immense reparations from Germany, not only from the Russian zone (which he was already emptying), but from the Allied zones. He wanted trusteeship territories for Russia under the United Nations charter, not just from Italy's colonies, he implied, but from Japan. He wanted all former Axis states dealt with—meaning a share in the exploitation of Italy. He wanted the future of Poland settled: there was no official verbatim record kept but it was clear that meant ratification of Polish western borders and acceptance of its Communist government. Finally, he wanted to discuss the future of Franco's Spain.

When Churchill managed to get a word in he reminded Stalin that they were not settling issues but placing them on the agenda, which gave Stalin the opportunity to add new matters—what to do about Spanish-controlled Tangier, across the straits from Gibraltar; the problem of Syria and Lebanon, which Gaullist France was trying to retain against the wishes of their people; the liquidation of the London-based Polish government-in-exile and other exile governments representing old legitimacies rendered obsolete by new Soviet regimes. Churchill suggested that the foreign ministers prepare a list of the "least disagreeable" matters to take up first. Stalin warned that just the same, they would not escape the disagreeable ones, and brought up the matter of excluding China, not a party to the European war, from any parleys of foreign ministers. Truman explained that he was thinking in terms of the members of the new United Nations Security Council, but Stalin made it plain that he did not want China in discussions of non-Asian matters, and that its role would arise once the war with Japan was over. Churchill agreed that China had "only an intellectual interest" in Europe, and Truman dropped the subject. Besides, Stalin quipped, if they referred all difficult questions to the foreign ministers, "We shall have nothing to do."

France, the other permanent Council member, also peeved Stalin. He had already refused to permit France a German occupation zone of its own, feeling that France had cravenly submitted to Hitler in 1940 and become a Fascist puppet unworthy now of a victor's perquisites. Roosevelt and Churchill at Yalta had compromised by carving a French sector out of their zones, the French sector of Berlin being tentatively agreed upon that morning; but Stalin was adamant about French and Chinese participation in postwar decisions. Later, Byrnes explained the American position to Molotov privately, and a face-saving gesture was made to France and China.

Another problem Truman tried to confront quickly and preemptively was Stalin's known ambition, in the tradition of the Czars, to control the straits between the Mediterranean and the Black Sea. That the Bosporus and the Dardanelles belonged to a neutral nation was of no concern to Stalin, and Truman's attempt to make the expected demand moot was to propose as an agenda item the internationalization of all waterways, including the Panama Canal. Although he would bring the subject up several times, Churchill, thinking of Suez, was unhelpful, and Stalin each time merely brushed the idea aside. But while the proposal failed as an exercise in idealism, for the poker-playing President it succeeded in keeping Turkey from Soviet encroachment.

Still, they required a working agenda for the second session, and Truman was a pragmatist. "I told Stalin and Churchill," he recalled, "that we should discuss the next day . . . points on which we could come to a conclusion." Churchill asked whether he "wanted something in the bag each day," and Truman agreed, suggesting that they begin at an earlier hour, but as Truman was about to adjourn, Stalin again raised the question of the surviving German fleet. Britain had accepted the surrender of most German shipping, as it was in the North Sea.

Warships are weapons of war, Churchill remarked; the captured cruisers and destroyers and submarines all should be sunk.

"Let's divide it," said Stalin. "If Mr. Churchill wishes, he can sink his share."

Eden found Churchill's performance "very bad." Churchill, Eden added in his diary, "had read no brief & was confused & woolly & verbose. . . . We had an anti-Chinese tirade from him. Americans not a little exasperated." He had "never seen W. worse. Dined alone with him & again urged him not to give up our few cards without return. But he is again under Stalin's spell." During his campaigning at home, when his chief political card was that he had won the war, and his holiday in France after the polls had closed, the P.M. had not read the briefs painstakingly prepared for him. His responses, as was clear to the others around the table, were more personal than studied. To the quiet dismay of his aides Churchill announced about Stalin, "I like that man."

The first session closed with Truman feeling that it had gone as well as he could have expected. Byrnes and Leahy praised his performance, Truman wrote to Bess. "I was so scared I didn't know whether things were going according to Hoyle or not. Anyway a start has been made and I've gotten what I came for—Stalin goes to war August 15 with no strings on it. I'll say that we'll end the war a year sooner now, and think of the kids who won't be killed. That is the important thing."

Truman knew he had done well enough, and was confident that he could hold his own. He knew that he was not Franklin Delano Roosevelt, a nearly mythic figure known personally to the nearly mythic Stalin and Churchill, and admired as a grand improviser. Truman had been President for only as many weeks as FDR had years of high office. It was important to have done one's homework meticulously, to stick to positions worked out with advisers in advance, and to not permit the unyielding posture of the Soviets to create more giveaways than had been agreed upon earlier by Roosevelt at Tehran and Yalta.

Following the adjournment, the Soviets laid on a banquet at Cecilienhof, at "a tremendous table about twenty feet wide," Truman wrote in his memoirs, "and thirty feet long. The table was set with everything you could think of—goose liver, caviar, all sorts of meats, cheeses, chicken, turkey, duck, wines and spirits. The major-domo in charge was from Moscow's leading hotel." On the way back, Truman's car was stopped at a checkpoint by a Russian officer who insisted upon identification, and in a matter of minutes other Russian officers arrived and "scared the life out of the lieutenant," Truman recalled, "for making such a blunder." As they drove off toward Babelsberg, Leahy turned toward Truman and said, "I'll bet that lieutenant is shot in the morning."

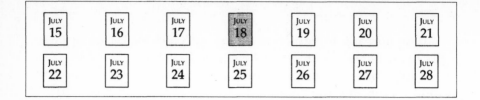

## CHAPTER VI

# · JULY 18, 1945 ·

### *"the Great New Fact"*

As the new day dawned in the Pacific, the Japanese intent to resist to the end came home in the Philippines to General Robert Eichelberger, tapped by MacArthur to lead one of the armies into Japan. Eichelberger had commanded troops for the man he described with mixed feelings, since New Guinea days, as the "Big Chief." One of his colonels, who had led the 21st Infantry in Mindanao, where there were still about fifteen thousand of the enemy who had not been killed or captured (as opposed to over twenty-five thousand on Luzon), had pulled a young company commander from combat in preparation for his reassignment to the States. The captain, Eichelberger wrote to his wife, whom he called "Miss Em," had more than his share of fighting time and was posted to a beach area to relax until his orders were cut to go home. "A Jap got in with a grenade and killed him. That leaves only three . . . original company commanders. There were a number of Japs and they killed and wounded a number of our men before they were killed. The undergrowth is so heavy down there that it is almost impossible to prevent infiltrators from getting in."

Those unready to fight to the death faced dishonor and prison. In the home islands, *kamikaze* pilot Ryuji Nagatsuka, released from prison July 2 after a sentence for failing to die, awaited another opportunity. From the Kanamaruhara camp near Utsunomiya, on the coast north of Tokyo, he had been ordered to make a suicide attack on June 29 as part of a *Kikusui* ("Floating Chrysanthemum") group to attack Task Force 38. At 5:30 A.M. the commandant had lined up the eighteen pilots before two rickety tables at the edge of the airfield and poured sake into small cups. Once they drank he said, "I have nothing more to ask of you but to die heroically for your country. I wish you success in this mission. Let us salute in the direction of the Imperial Palace."

Nagatsuka understood that his life was now "more fleeting than a humble blade of grass," but orders were to obey. One more part of the ritual remained before they received their flight instructions and targets. An officer instructed them to form a circle around him and, their voices bolstered by the flight crews, they sang "a solemn song with many verses" familiar to every schoolboy:

> *After the battle, our corpses will be strewn*
> *On the green mountain slopes,*
> *Our corpses will rest at the bottom of the sea.*
> *We shall give our lives for His Majesty,*
> *We shall die without regrets.*

At 6:00 they took off. "My plane is also my coffin," Nagatsuka thought as his plane flew low over the choppy sea with fuel only sufficient for a one-way mission. He fingered at his side a photograph of his family and two small volumes attesting to his passion at the Shizuoka high school for French literature, George Sand's *Les Maîtres sonneurs*. As they flew east, the weather worsened, and when there seemed no chance that they could find the enemy, Flight Lieutenant Norio Takagui, their leader, pointed back with his hand. In ten minutes they would have exceeded the fuel supply necessary for return. His pointless death, Nagatsuka realized, would be postponed.

At 8:05 the first two formations of six Kawanishi-43s began touching down on their rain-soaked airstrip. Saluting, Takagui reported the aborting of their flight and the failure of the third formation to return. "We are lined up, our heads hanging." Rain hammered on the roof of the briefing room as the commandant barked,

"The others pursued the mission to its conclusion, even though they were not lucky enough to sink any enemy ships. It is clear that they were ready for death. . . . But *you—you*—had not been able to prepare yourself for it." He railed at their "cowardly return on the pretext of bad weather conditions." They had dishonored the squadron and he was ashamed of them. The entire unit would very likely be punished by having to re-form as an infantry battalion, he predicted. "Why didn't you die like heroes? . . . I am putting you under arrest. You will copy out the sacred words of the Emperor until further orders!" His aide, Flight Lieutenant Uehara, stepped forward and slapped each of the pilots in the face.

In their cells they copied and recopied the Emperor's War Rescript of December 8, 1941, and after three days the disgraced pilots, most of them recent cadets, were released.

Through the early days of July there was no fuel at the Kanamaruhara airbase, and the airmen began infantry training with the ground crews. Since the defense of the homeland had to be undertaken by every adult, military and civilian, they had to learn how to repel enemy tanks. And on the eighteenth they learned to their disappointment that TF 38 was moving out of range. Other units closer to the action would be entrusted with suicide missions. "I had the impression," Nagatsuka recalled, "that the mechanics looked at us with limitless contempt."

At 1:00 P.M. TF 38 turned south toward the China coast west of Okinawa. Orders were to secure everything movable because of the heavy weather moving up from the Philippines. As there were carrier and battleship forces in a wide arc around Japan from north to south, when the weather began to improve, strikes were launched upon targets around Tokyo Bay, especially the shipyard at Yokosuka. With few scouting planes chancing the skies, Captain Masataka Chihaya, a naval officer for eighteen years, wrote after the war, "We had no means of knowing the approximate features of the American forces, even the symptoms of their approaches. The bombardments of Kamaishi, Hitachi, even of the Bohahu peninsula lying right in front of Yokohama Naval Station were to us a surprise attack." The presence of the battleship *Nagato* tempted the aircraft of the new (and second) carrier *Yorktown*. Moored close to shore and camouflaged, *Nagato* was of no use to anyone. There was no bunker fuel to move it out. But the *Nagato* had been Admiral Yamamoto's flagship, anchored in Hiroshima Bay on the day in December 1941 when Yamamoto oversaw

the attack on Hawaii by radio at long distance. The U.S. Navy was remembering Pearl Harbor.

AA-fire was fierce. Tokyo Bay was well defended. A submarine
and a destroyer as well as smaller vessels were sunk, and forty-three
planes were destroyed on the ground, yet the Americans and British
suffered surprising losses—fourteen planes and eighteen men. The
Japanese had not quit. And the *Nagato* had not gone down.

Despite the poor weather, American bombers could fly above
the low-hanging clouds and bomb by radar; and inland Asia was
clear. Over Indochina and southern China as well as Japanese targets,
nearly a thousand planes, ranging from hot P-47s to big B-29s,
bombed and strafed what they couldn't see as well as what was visible, twin-boom P-38s even finding and attacking a suicide boat hide-
out at Sandakan, on the north shore of Borneo.

The naval blockade and the attacks on shipping from the air were
having an impact in the occupied territories as well as the homeland.
In Hong Kong, itself supplied only by water, the chief of staff to the
military governor warned, "Those who have no means of earning a
living . . . as well as those whose stay is unnecessary should take the
first opportunity of leaving for their native villages. Hong Kong is no
place for idlers. Every resident is expected to earn his or her living and
contribute to the reconstruction of a new Hong Kong." The police
rounded up all undesirables they could find and shipped those who
worked on the land to the New Territories to grow food. The others
were deported to China.

The Japanese themselves would have left China if they could.
The vast colony, as much of it as was, had become a burden, a curse.
They needed no more mouths to feed, and needed their troops at
home, or at least in Manchuria, to shore up defenses against the Russians. At best the vast spaces were a buffer against American air
power. The United States had poured huge sums into putting some
fight into the Chinese, but the two opponents seemed to be engaged
in a Sumo contest more staged than fought. Colonel Lewis Leavel,
the chief liaison officer for the Chinese Combat Command in northern Burma, eager to have his troops affect the course of the war, had
to complain to his commanding general on the eighteenth that he
was never consulted about combat matters as the Army never fought,
although it used up immense amounts of supplies shipped in at great
cost. General Sun Li Gen, he complained, "has been absent throughout the entire move . . . and I feel that the crimes which have been

committed by the Army are attributable directly to the fact that he is absent [and] ... that the primary qualification for command in the Army is a demonstrated loyalty to the Army Commander." When he had complained about the failure to load heavy equipment (as it was heavy), he went on, "I was suddenly halted by a sentry who thrust a bayonet against my stomach." Even Chinese planes would "depart empty," and he lived, he reported, under "intimidations and threats." For the Chinese warlords, however, it remained a very good war.

"I've not yet gone to Berlin," Eisenhower wrote to Mamie from Frankfurt early on the eighteenth, suggesting that although he was "busier these days than the proverbial one-armed paperhanger," he was puzzled not to be in the Potsdam deliberations. "I *love you, only!"* he closed. Whether the letter passed across the desk of Kay Summersby in the adjacent office is unknown. She had traveled with him very openly to London and elsewhere, and Truman knew about her.

One of Ike's matters of business was a memorandum to all senior officers exercising courts-martial jurisdiction. The impromptu punishment of German prisoners of war as they had been taken in April and May, especially SS troops, was one thing; now it was mid-July and he was hearing stories of neglect and even brutality in the camps. "You will forthwith cause a thorough investigation to be made," he commanded, "into whether enemy prisoners of war have been killed or otherwise mistreated by members of your command and whether instructions have been given leading to such treatment or [whether] such practices have been condoned, and take disciplinary action where appropriate. Report will be made to this headquarters. ..." Decades later the question still simmered. It had not been easy to feed and clothe immediately on capture millions of prisoners, refugees from the east, and displaced persons on top of the normal civilian population. In some cases the difficulties were exacerbated by criminality, incompetence, and negligence. Of the seventy-five reports Eisenhower would receive, five were considered serious enough for corrective action from Frankfurt.

Eisenhower had already been asked by publishers across the Atlantic to write his memoirs—the sort of thing that had been done since General Grant's days, and in Ike's case a certain best-seller. He would not do such a thing yet, he replied to Simon and Schuster, Inc. Perhaps "when official duties are completed." But he had already thought about it, he confessed. (When his memoirs did appear, they would be under the imprint of the publishers of *Cartridge Carnival,* Doubleday—an irony he would not have noticed.)

With his role limited to Europe, Eisenhower was not part of the deliberations as the Joint Chiefs of Staff met at ten, although present were brass from five-star rank to a lone lieutenant colonel. The key agenda item was a memorandum for the President on an unconditional surrender formula for Japan, and the minutes recorded only that it was reviewed and amended after discussion. The JCS proposed a noncommittal sentence: "Subject to suitable guarantees against further acts of aggression, the Japanese will be free to choose their own form of government."

The last thing that Byrnes had done as he left his office in Washington was to put Dooman's draft ultimatum in his pocket. It had since received many airings as the conflicts in policy were fundamental. Old Japan hands like Grew and Dooman, even though lied to over their years in Tokyo and interned after Pearl Harbor, were sympathetic to Japanese aspirations and saw a dynamic, cultured race as compared to other Asians. They had not been as unhappy as their counterparts in Washington about the seizure and exploitation of Manchuria. However, public opinion was for a "hard peace" with trial and punishment of war criminals, not excluding the Emperor. Many in the military also considered disestablishment of the monarchy as essential to ridding Japan of its military caste. Truman's dilemma was to limit the obstacles to surrender while keeping domestic reaction in mind as well as longer-range goals for the Pacific rim. The peace could not be permitted to unravel after the high cost of attaining it.

The cost would go much higher if "Olympic" and "Coronet" were to become operative, and the preparations for "Olympic" were well along. MacArthur was already working on the March 1 landings in the Tokyo Bay area, to which the British wanted to contribute. His views about a British role were aired in the morning JCS meeting, which reviewed a MacArthur memorandum clearly intended to keep "Coronet" an American (and a MacArthur) show. There were good reasons, he claimed. Equipment had to be standardized and assault tactics had to be uniform. The JCS agreed to limit Empire "participation" to a corps of three divisions—one British, one Canadian, one Australian. They would be reequipped with American weapons and receive American logistic support. The Australian division would be one already fighting for MacArthur in Borneo, where the British division would train. The Canadian troops would be "lifted directly from the United States." The British element, MacArthur insisted (very likely in Richard K. Sutherland's words, as he was the key planner), should be "Anglo-Saxon." He wanted "homogeneity of language" to avoid communications problems in "a complex operation," and he explicitly ruled out Indian troops because of the problems of "acclimatization." Northern Honshu in early March could be a chilly place.

At 11:00 in number 2 Kaiserstrasse, Harry Truman and Harry Truman had breakfast together. Sergeant Truman, eldest son of the President's brother, Vivian, had arrived in Berlin the night before. In the President's greeting party in Antwerp had been General John C. H. ("Court House") Lee. Lee popped the usual question: "Is there anything I can do for you?" and Truman answered that his nephew was somewhere in the ETO and that he'd like to see him. He was found on board the *Queen Elizabeth,* still a troopship, in Glasgow harbor. Young Harry, the President wrote to his mother in Independence, Missouri, was offered "the choice of coming to the conference or going home. He elected to come and see me. I gave him a pass to Berlin signed by Stalin and me. Will send him home by plane and he'll get there almost as soon as if he'd gone on the *Elizabeth.* He sure is a fine looking soldier . . . and I'm proud of him."

After three days of meeting dignitaries and sightseeing, Sergeant Truman was put on the White House communications plane. He arrived at Norfolk in time to greet his outfit as it left the ship.

During Truman's late breakfast, Secretary of War Stimson arrived with news to share. Byrnes had wanted neither civilian service chief at Potsdam, yet not only was Stimson there but also Secretary Forrestal, who used the excuse of an inspection tour. From Bremerhaven to Berlin to Berchtesgaden his entourage included Navy men from admirals to an invalided-out lieutenant now a reporter, John F. Kennedy. His father had been a Forrestal associate in their stockbroker days. But the Secretary of the Navy had little entrée to the deliberations other than a courtesy dinner.

At the yellow-painted temporary White House Stimson could barely contain himself. He had a cable from Washington:

DOCTOR HAS JUST RETURNED MOST ENTHUSIASTIC AND CONFIDENT
THAT THE LITTLE BOY IS AS HUSKY AS HIS BIG BROTHER. THE LIGHT

IN HIS EYES DISCERNIBLE FROM HERE TO HIGHHOLD AND I COULD
HAVE HEARD HIS SCREAMS FROM HERE TO MY FARM.

Highhold was Stimson's Long Island estate, 250 miles from Washington; Harrison's farm, in Upperville, Virginia, was fifty miles from the War Department. The "doctor" was Groves. It was a graphic description of the power of the weapon in flash and in sound.

Truman was due at Churchill's house in Ringstrasse for lunch, and walked there to share Stimson's report on the Bomb. Half an hour earlier, fifty Scots Guards had taken up positions in the strip of garden in front of the house. Then came the blue-clad band of the Royal Marines. It would not be an ordinary *dejeuner*. Of immediate concern was how what Churchill called "the Great New Fact" should be communicated to Stalin without divulging any particulars of the weapon. Despite the Bomb, Churchill's mood was gloomy. His weary country had been bled economically by the war; it had overwhelming debts, little cash reserves, and was headed for decline as it inevitably shed its colonies and lost its international influence. Years later Charles de Gaulle would tell Richard Nixon, "All the countries of Europe lost the war, but only two were defeated." He had carefully left France out of the defeated category, but Churchill would have understood de Gaulle's paradox as it applied to Britain. Truman would learn—and the later "Marshall Plan" evidenced it. For the moment the two exchanged assurances of how much each nation owed the other. Britain could not have survived at all without the United States, said Churchill. But Britain, Truman insisted, "held the fort" against Hitler. "If you had gone down like France, we might be fighting the Germans on the American coast at the present time."

Truman raised the subject of airfields and other bases Americans had built on British territory at home and abroad at immense cost, and what postwar use the United States might anticipate from them. Churchill talked of reciprocal use of facilities, and Truman liked the idea, "fitted in, in some way, with the policy of the United Nations." It was, perhaps, a germ of NATO.

The President returned to the Bomb. Stalin could not be left in the dark until he learned it had been dropped. Churchill suggested that Truman merely tell Stalin about recent word from the United States that a new weapon of great potential had been tested—and that it had worked. The fact of the test would explain the timing. Truman said he would consider that approach.

Churchill also had something to share. The night before, Stalin had told him of the peace overtures by Ambassador Sato in Moscow. Sato had responded to the latest plea from Tokyo (as Truman would learn) that if he were able to get the Russians to mediate, he would stress the "absolute desire" of the Japanese to retain their form of government. If that were "taken care of," he added—a condition inserted into an otherwise unconditional surrender—"whether you call it unconditional surrender or whether you call it something close to this condition, in the final analysis it is a matter of degree."

When Churchill had suggested informing the President, Stalin said that he did not want Truman to think that he was trying to influence the United States to accept anything less than complete surrender—or that Russia was reluctant to go to war. Continuing his own line of thought, Churchill confided that he had been rethinking the ultimatum to Japan. Possibly they might find language that would suggest to the Japanese an honorable way out. The important thing was the surrender.

He was voicing the attitudes of an exhausted nation humiliated by the Japanese in Singapore and Hong Kong and Burma, but that no longer considered the Pacific basin very important in its priorities. Truman, who read American newspapers, and also saw how public opinion registered its views in the polls, recalled that at Pearl Harbor and elsewhere the Japanese had showed no sense of honor. Yet, he confessed, there was something like it in their willingness to fight to the death for country and emperor. His chief concern, as "Olympic" was being readied, was for the lives of American soldiers. Whatever was done had to secure real peace and punish Japanese treachery.

While it appeared to Churchill that some flexibility was emerging in the American definition of unconditional surrender, the State Department in Washington reiterated that no official or unofficial peace offers had come from Japan. In the Senate, however, Homer Capehart of Indiana, whose office had apparently secured some leak that he promptly exaggerated on the floor, claimed that the enemy had made "peace feelers of a definite nature. Peace is sought [by the Japanese] on our terms with a view to just punishment and future security, but without enslavement." What he may have seen was all or part of a draft of the proposed Potsdam ultimatum, versions of which had been circulating since Grew and Dooman first drew up a text.

The President and the Prime Minister were still discussing what surrender was to mean when Eden and Byrnes arrived to escort their chiefs to a courtesy call upon Stalin. On his way out, Truman noticed a piano in one of the rooms, stopped, pulled up a chair, and played something unknown to the P.M. Almost all music beyond "God Save the King" and "Rule Britannia" was unknown to Churchill.

It was three o'clock. The Russians had clustered around a buffet table for their own late luncheon, and Truman and Churchill diplomatically sampled the fare. Their arrival occasioned vodka toasts, which Stalin offered with white wine. Then he handed Truman a copy of a note from Ambassador Sato asking for the Kremlin's permission to receive Prince Konoye in the interests of peace. Should he respond?

Truman said that he did not trust Japanese expressions of good faith.

Still, suggested Stalin, since Russia had not yet entered the war, perhaps the Japanese should be lulled with a vague answer that was not quite a refusal. Truman liked that, and confided that Japanese peace activity wasn't confined to Moscow. He mentioned Minister Suemasa Okamoto in Sweden, but gave no particulars. "Magic" still had to be protected. Pleased thus far with Stalin's apparent openness—or inspired by the vodka—Truman proposed that Stalin visit the United States. The President promised to send the battleship *Missouri* to transport him in style. Then the party broke up to prepare for the second plenary session in Potsdam.

Stalin, Truman, and Churchill were quaffing toasts when the Combined Anglo-American Chiefs of Staff met at 2:30 in Potsdam. ("Stalin wants me to win the election!" Churchill told Dr. Moran.) Marshall again cleared the room of all but the principals and announced that the President had decided to drop the Bomb on Japan—that he had consulted his own JCS, and although no orders had yet been issued, he had received its agreement. Admiral King, a proponent of blockade and strangulation, later denied "any part of it." He "didn't like the atomic bomb." (But he was present at the session and had raised no qualms.) Admiral Leahy privately remained hostile because he felt that it would not work as anticipated and would be unnecessary anyway. On board the *Augusta* he had unburdened himself to Charles Bohlen about it, claiming that "longhairs" in the science establishment—apparently they all looked like Einstein—were cheating the Treasury of billions because the result would not be any better than cordite, the smokeless explosive that powered battleship armament.

Brooke reported for Britain that French and Dutch offers had been received to send troops to the Far East. No one had to point out that there were French and Dutch colonies ready to break away unless put down when the Japanese left. Also, Brooke formally requested "a one-quarter share" in control of Pacific operations, recognizing that he was "on thinner ice" than in the West. Politely, Marshall said no. His commanders would be prepared to discuss strategy but "to simplify the control and avoid delays" all final decisions had to rest with them. "It cleared the air," Brooke thought. He had not expected anything else. The bulk of the battle was being borne by Americans. One example was that although the British had their Task Force 37 operating off Japan with two battleships and four fleet carriers as its heavyweights, the American Task Force 38, fighting alongside, was itself larger than the entire Royal Navy.

The 2nd Armored Division was still in the Berlin area to protect the Presidential party, and Marshall invited the group to visit it. They had formed on an *Autobahn* facing inward, with all their tanks, armored vehicles, and self-propelled guns. "A most impressive sight," Brooke conceded. "The efficiency of their equipment left a greater mark on one than the physique or turn-out of the men."

Churchill opened the second meeting at the Cecilienhof with a plea for the press in Potsdam. The world was watching through them, he said, but they had little access to information, and complaints were heard in his country.

"Who let them in?" Stalin shouted.

They weren't in, said Churchill. That was the trouble. They were chafing back in Berlin. He was willing to talk to the journalists personally to explain why the delicate discussions required confidentiality. Truman gave in to reality. He knew that Stalin would not budge. Each delegation, he said, had a press officer, and his own people knew that there was still a war on.

The formal business began with discussion of a coordinated policy regarding Germany and the occupation of Germany. What did "Germany" mean, Churchill asked, implying the Soviet fait accompli of moving the Polish frontier west, in effect dismembering Germany. If Germany meant its prewar borders, he explained, he was in agreement. At Yalta no agreement had been reached on a Polish-German frontier because Roosevelt and Churchill had refused to accept the Oder–western Niesse line, but after the German surrender Stalin unilaterally put the captured territory under the Warsaw government.

Preferring to use Austria rather than newly Polish Silesia and

Pomerania as his example, Stalin said bluntly, "Germany is what she has become after the war. Austria is not a part of Germany [now]."

Truman proposed defining Germany as the nation of 1937, before the absorption of Austria.

"Minus what Germany lost in 1945," Stalin insisted. The Russians had sliced off a large portion of East Prussia, including Königsberg, for themselves.

Germany had lost everything in 1945, observed Truman, and Stalin agreed that the 1937 borders were adequate for discussion—once the western frontier of Poland was fixed—and why not do that now? Germany was a country with no frontiers and no government. All it had were occupation zones.

The Polish question was more than one of borders, and they turned to the question of its legitimate government. Stalin wanted it settled by asking all member states in the United Nations to withdraw recognition from the exile ministry in London in favor of the Soviet-installed regime in Warsaw. He also wanted all diplomatic property abroad, military equipment, and gold reserves held in England and Canada for Poland transferred to the puppet state.

Churchill spoke eloquently about the contribution of Polish exile troops and fliers to victory, never mentioning the Soviet accord with Hitler that had dismembered Poland in 1939. Britain, he said, owed a debt of honor to the Poles who had kept fighting. Any who wished to remain would be made British subjects: "We cannot cast adrift men who have been brothers in arms."

Stalin's response to such recognition of bleak facts was always, "We cannot get away from the result of the war." And he offered to put whatever diplomatic gloss was required on shutting down the Polish government in London—so long as it disappeared. He did not want to make the British position more complicated. As for the elections in Poland promised in the Yalta agreement, which Truman raised, Stalin offered what was obviously to be an empty expectation. "The Provisional Government," he said, "have never refused to hold free elections." The question might be left to the three foreign secretaries, he proposed.

While Churchill could move a House of Commons or an audience tuned to the BBC, his rhetoric was useless on Stalin, and much of it seemed improvised. In Cadogan's diary for the eighteenth, he was melancholy about the prospects for Russian compromise on anything. Reviewing the meeting, he deplored Churchill's having refused, since leaving London, "to do any work or read anything. . . . He can't have it both ways: if he knows nothing about the subject under discussion, he should keep quiet, or ask that his Foreign Secretary be heard. Instead of that, he butts in on every occasion and talks the most irrelevant rubbish, and risks giving away our case at every point." Cadogan was pleasantly surprised by the almost unknown and inexperienced Truman, who was "most quick and businesslike." But every topic mentioned "started Winston off on a wild rampage from which the combined efforts of Truman and Anthony [Eden] with difficulty restrained him."

As the discussions grew "useless," particularly over Poland, one of the unhappier outcomes of the war, Churchill and Truman suggested adjournment. The session had lasted less than two hours. It was only six in the evening—still morning across the Atlantic. For solace, Truman used a Signal Corps circuit to telephone Bess in Missouri.

That night Churchill dined alone—but for interpreters—with Stalin. "We conversed agreeably from half-past eight in the evening to half-past one next morning without reaching any crucial topic," Churchill wrote. Stalin offered optimism about the British election. All his information from Communist and other sources confirmed his belief, he said, that Churchill would be returned to office with a majority of about eighty seats. Cautiously, Churchill ventured that they had no idea how the armed services would vote, but Stalin seemed confident that the army would prefer strong government and would vote for the Conservatives.

They talked about Turkey and Greece, both grievances to Stalin. Turkey would not make territorial concessions, and Greece allegedly was stirring up trouble on the Albanian and Bulgarian frontiers. The Russians, he did not say, were abetting dissension in Greece, where Churchill had reinstalled the unpopular prewar monarchy. Piously, Stalin contended, as Churchill remembered it, "that in all countries liberated by the Red Army the Russian policy was to see a strong, independent, sovereign State. He was against Sovietisation of any of these countries, and all except Fascist parties would participate." (He would be true to his word—but all parties except the Communists would be eliminated in the early postwar years as Fascist.)

Yugoslavia, Churchill added, with its designs on Italian and Austrian territory, was a nagging problem. Britain had no ambitions there but it did not want the Balkans unsettled. Marshal Tito, said Stalin, "had the partisan mentality and had done several things he ought not to have done. The Soviet Government often did not know what Marshal Tito was about to do." Stalin did not know how bad that relationship would get.

"I then said," Churchill recalled, "how anxious people were about Russia's intentions. I drew a line from the North Cape to Albania, and named the capitals east of that line which were in Russian hands. It looked as if Russia were rolling on westward. Stalin said he had no such intention. On the contrary, he was withdrawing troops. . . . Two million men would be demobilised and sent home within the next four months." He had not satisfactorily thanked Britain for its wartime help, he added. Due acknowledgment would be made.

In Berlin itself, Ruth Andreas-Friedrich penned another note in her diary about the seemingly endless plight of German refugees from the Sovietized east. While bicycling from Steglitz to Charlottenberg she had seen a sign warning refugees away from Berlin: "Use detours. Avoid entering the city limits. Continue westward."

"A hospitable order," her bicycling companion remarked. "The West won't want them either."

The Germans evicted from the East, she thought, were "like pendulums" going back between towns that kept them briefly, then sent them away. "No settling, no admission, no accommodations, no ration cards. . . ." Someone from a refugee family of six told her, "Three times already we have walked back and forth between Fürstenburg and Genthin. Fifty-one times [in towns between] we've been rejected, seven times we've been told to wait until later, and twelve times we've been promised accommodations for three nights at most. What are we supposed to do?"

Some had been wandering back and forth so often and so long that they lost any sense of time other than it was summer, and a few dated movements by which side of the eclipse of the sun something had happened. Across Europe at midday on July 9 there had been a partial eclipse, an event also marked in an enigmatic novel about postwar Europe, *The English Patient* (1992), by Michael Ondaatje, in which a terminally burned husk of a pilot—who turns out to be German—is cared for by a Canadian nurse in an otherwise abandoned ruin in northern Italy.

The suffering of the German dispossessed, Ruth Andreas-Friedrich wrote, was "boundless." It was the reverse of Hitler's scheme to resettle Germans in the fertile basins of eastern Europe as far as the Ukraine, a relentless moving out of people who had lived on the land for millennia. Germans were being expelled in the "most gigantic depopulation of all times."

"Alsos" had moved the ten German physicists whom General Groves wanted kept apart from the "Dustbin" detention center in France to Farm Hall, Godmanchester, in the English countryside north of Cambridge. The spacious house belonged to the British Secret Service, which had bugged rooms liberally, the conversations recorded in pretape days on shellac-covered metal disks. When the Germans arrived, Kurt Diebner, a nuclear physicist, had asked Werner Heisenberg, "I wonder if there are microphones installed here?"

"Microphones installed?" scoffed Heisenberg, who had once studied atomic physics under Niels Bohr and was regarded as the leading younger physicist in Germany (he was forty-four). "Oh, no, they're not as cute as all that. I don't think they know the real Gestapo methods. They're a bit old-fashioned in that respect."

On July 18 the group discussed Potsdam and wondered how their fate might depend upon decisions made there. Karl Wirtz, who had worked on the molecular physics of liquids, worried over their inability to communicate with their families, and Heisenberg imagined a scenario to explain it. "Assume that it became known that we are here. Some clever journalist would turn up and, of course, he would not be allowed in. He would have a look at the place from outside. . . . The next day there would be a terrific article in a newspaper just like it was with Göring: 'German Nazi scientists enjoying life in England?' . . . It would of course be very awkward for everyone concerned."

He wondered whether Samuel Goudsmit could help them. He was a fellow physicist. "Of course," said Paul Harteck, a physical chemist, "Goudsmit can't forget that we [Germans] murdered his parents. That's true too and it doesn't make it easy for him."

At Mount Pitt, Oregon, a detonated incendiary balloon bomb was found. In almost the same place two days later an unexploded five-kilogram bomb was found. It was already night across the Pacific, where Rear Admiral Cary Jones's cruiser squadron was making a sweep around Cape Nojima, at the base of the long peninsula inside which was Tokyo Bay. Since the sea-lanes off the home islands were nearly empty by day, cleaned out by American planes and subs, were the Japanese venturing out after dark? There was nothing.

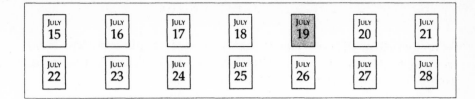
## CHAPTER VII

# · JULY 19, 1945 ·

*". . . letting the grass grow"*

Japan's most effective ally in a midsummer of political isolation was the weather. The American surplus of warplanes was nearly useless in stormy skies, and ships scrambled to keep out of the path of recurrent typhoons. On the *Montpelier*, Seaman Fahey noted fueling two destroyers before noon to help them ride out the rough seas south of Okinawa, midway in the chain of islands that curved from Kyushu to Taiwan. All vessels had been warned out of Okinawan waters, where gusts reached 140 miles an hour and anything on deck that was unsecured was washed or blown away. "The ships are pitching and tossing around like little balls," Fahey wrote. "It is very cloudy and dark. The destroyers are being swamped with huge waves as they go out of sight. . . . The ship rides up a big wave and then it comes down bow first and out of sight into the water." The experience was "like riding a wild horse."

Only deep in the interior of China could light bombers and fighter bombers operate, interdicting the rail system to keep troops from being moved north to Manchuria and east to coastal ports.

American strategy was to keep the Japanese from reinforcing areas where the Russians were expected to attack and from transferring troops to defend the home islands. Nor was there anything for *kamikaze* pilots to do but wait out the typhoons. Life hung heavy for most once they were mentally prepared to die, and their orders restricted them to their bases. Even the simplest map of Japan made it obvious that the American invasion path led up the arc of the Kuriles to southern Kyushu, the reason Hiroshima, close to the southern tip of Honshu, was the Imperial Army headquarters for the defense of lower Japan and why most *kamikaze* fields were located near the Kyushu coast, the sacrificial planes often concealed under straw to look from the air like peasant dwellings. At one base near Kanoya, on the southeast arm of Kagoshima Bay, the beaches of which were the projected but presumably top-secret landing sites for "Olympic," a pilot watched women and children beyond the bamboo groves bordering the base struggling to bring in the wheat harvest. He went back to his headquarters and asked the base commander, Tadashi Nakajima, for permission for airmen to work in the fields. It was granted and thirty volunteered to harvest wheat. But despite the weather, several planes were sent out toward Okinawa, their escort pilot returning to claim that two had crashed into a destroyer. It was more hopeful than accurate. No ship reported any damage, but the report was viewed with satisfaction.

From his Fifth Air Fleet headquarters at Kanoya, Admiral Ugaki was far less pleased with the deteriorating situation. On July 9 he had inspected the bombed ruins of Kanoya Base Number 2, and knew that few if any planes were rising to intercept the raiders. Orders higher than his own were that aircraft were to be hoarded—"preserving our strength," it was called—to repel the inevitable invasion, even if by then there was nothing on the surface of the home islands. Especially outrageous had been a flight of British carrier planes over the Kanto region, west of Tokyo, on the sixteenth, for their numbers were small enough to risk going after them. When he learned on the nineteenth from photo reconnaissance by the 9th Air Division on Formosa that there were already 307 troop transports massed at Okinawa, he penned angrily in his diary, "Come on, whether it's a task force or an invasion force, I don't care about them at all! We'll show them that we're quite different from those stationed in the Kanto district." And after lunch he asked his operations staff officers to restudy his *Ketsu Sakusen* (the latter word meant "Operation" or "Mission"), the suicide interdiction of the invasion armada, to see how much confidence they could place in their hoard of "5,300 navy planes and more than 4,000 army planes." Underestimating the huge logistical problems in landing hundreds of thousands on a home island as compared to tens of thousands on relatively small and remote Okinawa, he expected an invasion at almost any time.

Boasting to Yoshio Kodama, a Rightist politician who had worked for the military government in Shanghai, an army staff officer predicted that the "coming decisive battle" on home soil would shock Americans into negotiations:

> We will prepare 10,000 planes to meet the landing of the enemy. We will mobilize every aircraft possible, both training and "special attack" planes. We will smash one third of the enemy's war potential with this air force at sea. Another third will also be smashed at sea by our warships, human torpedoes and other special weapons. Furthermore, when the enemy actually lands, if we are ready to sacrifice a million men we will be able to inflict an equal number of casualties upon them. If the enemy loses a million men, then the public opinion in America will become inclined towards peace, and Japan will be able to gain peace with comparatively advantageous conditions.

*Ketsu*, Kodama claimed he replied, would not work. "The enemy is fully aware of such things. Before landing, they will thoroughly bomb the Japanese home islands and will not land until Japan is so completely destroyed as to be unable to raise a finger."

Ominously, *Ketsu* meant "finish." Plans to organize it had begun on April 8, after the Okinawa landing, and planners emphasized *Ketsu* 6 (Kyushu) and *Ketsu* 3 (the Kanto plain, inland from Tokyo Bay). It was almost as if they had been looking over the shoulders of their counterparts at the Pentagon. But skeptics at Imperial Navy headquarters reduced the mission privately to *Okatonbo Sakusen,* or "Operation Dragonfly," a recognition of how formidable they thought the stockpile of assorted *kamikazes,* piloted largely by cadets innocent of air combat, would be. Ugaki never learned of their defeatism.

Listening in to the American typhoon warnings, Ugaki prayed that the "divine wind" would "blow away enemy planes and sink enemy vessels." By supper hour his prayers appeared answered to some extent. Army reconnaissance reported observing only ten wakes of enemy ships, and those turning away, and only eight enemy fighters in the air. But he knew that the Americans would be back.

In Washington after an overnight flight from Albuquerque, General Groves called on George Harrison to discuss what information might be detailed to Stimson by courier. Then he pondered the question further with his deputy, Thomas F. Farrell. Their bosses in Potsdam required more than the guarded brevity of cablese. By evening they had separate drafts under way, which Groves and Farrell passed, page by page, to two secretaries cleared to type top-secret documents. A C-54 was to leave for Berlin at two in the morning on the twentieth. Groves set down vividly what he would have told Stimson in person—the massive energy released by the device, the brightness of several suns (one eyewitness miles away "was a blind woman who saw the light"), the monster mushroom cloud, the evaporated steel tower that had been the height of a six-story building, the crater a quarter-mile wide, windows shattered 125 miles away in El Paso, the sense of "profound awe."

In Groves's letter were the first-person comments of Farrell, who had been at the control shelter ten thousand yards from the blast point. As an enclosure Groves also added the first-person account of Ernest O. Lawrence, written while airborne and retyped without his seeing it again. Describing the scene as "unprecedented, magnificent, beautiful, stupendous and terrifying," Farrell wrote that "Dr. Kistiakowsky, the impulsive Russian,* threw his arms about Dr. Oppenheimer and embraced him with shouts of glee." Proofreading the typescript, Groves, always suspicious of Soviet intentions, left no ambiguity for Stimson. He added in his own hand a note after the description of Kistiakowsky: "an American and Harvard professor for many years." Ending the report Groves wrote cautiously, "We are all fully conscious that our real goal is still before us. The battle test [of the device] is what counts in the war with Japan."

Groves's courier, Colonel William M. Kyle, rushed to the airfield to carry the pages personally to Potsdam.

Recognizing that he had only one "Little Boy," Groves recommended to General LeMay in the Marianas that a protective cloud of B-29s should surround the aircraft carrying the precious Bomb and

*George Kistiakowsky would later be Science Adviser to President Eisenhower.

escort it to Japan. But Groves was a desk general and had no idea how the reduction of Japan was being accomplished. "That's not the way to do it," LeMay responded without defining "it." "We're running individual planes up there all the time and nobody pays much attention to them. We'll run yours up there like any other and all will be well."

The Manhattan Engineering District seldom failed to get its way, yet another response to Alamogordo was proceeding laboriously through channels despite Groves's roadblocks. While most physicists involved with the Manhattan District were elated at the vindication of their technology, some were also deeply disturbed by its implications. From the Metallurgical Laboratory at the University of Chicago the feisty Hungarian Leo Szilard had prepared a petition to the President deploring the use of the Bomb over populated places and suggesting other means of employing it as a deterrent or warning. On July 19 he sent six unsigned copies to Arthur Holly Compton, explaining that he had already secured the signatures of sixty-seven scientists. (He did not know that the Interim Committee had already recommended against a demonstration.) In any covering letter, he explained, attention should be drawn to the petition's concern "with the moral aspect of the issue only." Some who signed, he said, also feared that the use of atomic bombs would precipitate an armaments race with Russia. Even a "demonstration" ought to await, he urged, a thoughtfully prepared course of action for the years following.

Compton turned the awkward matter over to Groves. Whatever Szilard's moral anxieties, he risked compromising the colossal operation.

Each day at Potsdam the American chiefs of staff met at ten, and the three foreign ministers at eleven, to prepare for what would later be called "Summit" sessions. It was time, said Lieutenant General Hull, that the British position on furnishing joint intelligence to the Russians regarding Japan be adopted. Participants disagreed on what intelligence could be shared. Admiral King wanted only such operational intelligence as the Soviets needed given to them, with general intelligence offered as before, during the German war.

Eden, Molotov, and Byrnes met, with their aides, at eleven. Germany and Poland were the main agenda, with draft paragraphs for the leaders. Molotov wanted a clear understanding that the assets of the Polish exile government would be transferred to the regime the Soviets had set up. The matter proved too sticky and had to be carried over for another day, but they agreed on an afternoon agenda that included the political control of Germany, Poland, disposition of German vessels, and the problems of Spain—Stalin's pet subject after the German fleet—and the Russian satellites of Romania and Yugoslavia.

At the same time, an economic subcommittee met for the first time and agreed—it would be an empty decision—to treat Germany as an economic unit. Then at two, the Combined Anglo-American Chiefs of Staff met to discuss changes in strategic plans should the Russians enter the war, the possible participation of two French Colonial infantry divisions against Japan—the French were always quick to exploit non-French troops, and MacArthur didn't want them—and agreed not to pass on any intelligence information to the Soviets without mutual agreement. For production planning and the allocation of manpower they settled upon a terminal date for "the end of organized resistance by Japan" as November 15, 1946, and "that this date be adjusted periodically to conform to the course of the war."

At a quarter to five, McCloy, Bundy, and Stimson, none of whom sat in on the talks in the Cecilienhof, met to discuss gloomily what seemed the impossibility of good relations with an ally whose social fabric was predicated upon repression. "It exists everywhere," Stimson noted afterward in his diary entry for the day, and

> is felt by all who come in contact with the Russian rule in Germany. While the Russian soldiers and American soldiers seem to like each other individually when they meet, the people who have to deal with the Russian officials feel very differently, and it greatly impairs the cooperation between our two countries. Churchill is very rampant about it, and most of our people who have seen the Russians most intimately think we have been too easy and that they have taken advantage of it.
>
> It is a very difficult problem because they are crusaders for their own system and suspicious of everybody outside trying to interfere with it. At the same time it is becoming more and more evident to me that a nation whose system rests upon free speech and all the elements of freedom, as does ours, cannot be sure of getting on permanently with a nation where speech is strictly controlled and where the Government uses the iron hand of the secret police. The

question is very important just now, and the development of S-1 is bringing it into focus. . . .

The next day Stimson brought Harriman in on the discussions. Harriman's four years in Moscow as ambassador left him even more "despairing." The systems, Harriman thought, were incompatible yet they had to live with the fact somehow.

The third plenary session began at five. As soon as his turn came, Stalin raised the matter of German shipping, and Truman suggested a differentiation between war reparations and booty. Stalin saw no difference. He wanted German vessels, military and merchant, divided three ways—and if the Western Allies wanted to include France, they could give France ships from their allocation. It was his view about France in general. The French had earned no spoils. Truman observed that the United States needed shipping to transfer its troops and equipment to the United States and to the Pacific war zone. Further, Europe was in dire straits and would need shipments of food and fuel. "We will need every bomb and every ton of food," he said.

Stalin agreed that an accounting could await the end of hostilities with Japan. But he added, "Are not the Russians to wage war with Japan?" Churchill quipped that all vessels could be earmarked in advance, for transfer "if they had any ears when the Japanese war was over." Stalin, meanwhile, had followed through with his suggestion to stall the Japanese with vague responses, and Sato had to cable from Moscow to Togo, "The Soviet Government had declined to accept such an envoy [as Konoye] for the time being on the grounds that the mission is not specific." He begged for "a concrete proposal."

Stalin was less helpful on matters closer to Potsdam. When he charged that his representatives had been denied permission to see the German ships tied up in North Sea ports, Churchill brought up the forty-five subs the Russians had seized in the Baltic. "All we want is reciprocity," he said. Truman, too, raised the issue of mutual inspection. "In the Russian zone of Berlin, which was the industrial zone of the city, I had seen," he wrote later, "where the Russians had torn the plants up and taken everything out of them. They had loaded the industrial facilities on flatcars, and in many instances the cars were standing on a sidetrack. The material was rusting and disintegrating. Very soon it would be no use to anybody."

They went on to discuss Spain, where Stalin was eager to do

everything short of invasion to unseat Francisco Franco, who had sent his Blue Legion against Russia while dexterously staying out of the war. They agreed, finally, that Spain could be excluded from the new United Nations. But, said Churchill, "Breaking off relations breaks your influence." He had no love for Franco, said Truman, but "There have been enough wars in Europe." Yugoslavia was another East-West point of tension, as Marshal Tito was eager for slices of Austria and Italy as victor's spoils. The Yalta agreement made no provision for that, Truman insisted, and when the discussion moved to Tito and his rivals, he added, "I am here to discuss world affairs with the Soviet and British governments. I did not come here to hold a police court hearing. . . . I want to discuss matters on which the three heads of government can come to agreement." To settle every political difficulty, he explained, they would have to hold hearings for Tito, de Gaulle, Franco, and everyone else in Europe. "I want to see the Yalta agreement carried out."

Stalin insisted that Tito was "carrying out" the Yalta arrangements, but Truman responded, "Let's drop it."

Then it was Stalin's turn to brush a complaint aside. Churchill argued that British-owned oil-drilling equipment in Romania had been carried off to Russia as booty. Stalin suggested that it was a trifling matter for a lower level. "But since the question has been raised, I should like to correct an inaccuracy." And he went on to describe the seized drilling rigs as captured by the Germans before being taken by the Red Army. It was compensation. "Germany devastated our wells in the Caucasus."

It was not a trifling matter, expostulated Churchill. "Our people paid for them. We have made no progress through diplomatic channels."

Eager to close off the useless argument, although there were also American oil company complaints, Truman suggested, "Why not let the three foreign secretaries see what they could do?" And with that passing of the buck, the third session was adjourned.

At 8:30 the President entertained the eighteen participants at the session (himself included) at a state dinner at his "Little White House." Eighty Soviet soldiers from security units, with two security generals, preceded Stalin and surrounded the house almost shoulder to shoulder. There were the inevitable toasts, and Churchill, intimating his anxieties about the General Election at home, proposed, "The Leader of the Opposition—whoever he may be!" Stalin rose to say,

"There is one toast in particular I wish to propose. I drink to the American navy." He was almost certainly thinking of the Navy's recovery after Pearl Harbor to complete domination of the Pacific— now including Japanese home waters—but Churchill suspected an affront to the Royal Navy. Of the six hundred German subs sunk, he declared, interrupting the toast, the British had accounted for four to five times as many as the Americans had. He was clearly cranky, and earlier had complained privately to Truman about lack of support for British positions—that they were "in the same boat."

On the back porch overlooking the lake, Sergeant Eugene List played Chopin, Tchaikovsky and Shostakovich, beginning, apparently with no awareness of its political overtones, with Chopin's dramatic "Polonaise in A-flat." Churchill was bored by any kind of music but Stalin was so pleased that he sprang to the piano to shake the sergeant's hand, drank a toast to him and asked for an encore. List played again, and Stalin offered another toast to the sergeant. With violinist Stuart Canin, a private, List played other pieces, and Churchill, who had been grimly puffing at his cigar, ambled up to the piano and asked him to play "Missouri Waltz" as a compliment to the President. It was no favorite of the P.M.'s, but List had been assisted by a high-ranking page-turner. From his grand piano List had asked whether anyone in the audience could assist, and an Army captain in the security detail volunteered if List would tell him when to turn. Truman bounced up and waved the captain aside, remaining at the piano as Stalin and Churchill came forward. "The old man loves music," Truman wrote to Bess about Stalin.

Then it was the President's solo turn, and he played the Paderewski Minuet in G to enthusiastic applause, and without any pages to turn. He had known the piece for forty-five years. In his memoirs, Truman wrote, "The piano was not a good concert instrument, but List did a good job anyway."

The former men of power in Germany were having less exhilarating experiences. In Mondorf that day, Hermann Göring counted his paracodeine pills and found only sixteen. "Each day less and less," he complained. He complained unsuccessfully of headaches. No further pills of any kind arrived. But he found himself summoned for an interview. "Send up Fat Stuff!" his interrogators would order, and two guards would escort him to an interview room, this time a group of American Army historians led by George M. Schuster, later a college president. Göring was still angry with Hitler for replacing him in the succession by Dönitz, and offered litanies of the *Führer's* faults. "Once," he complained, "we had to make four thousand phone calls to answer one single question about an airplane engine." It was Hitler's chief aide, he thought, who had twisted the *Führer's* loyalties. "I can't conceal," he told the Americans, "that Bormann was the *Führer's* evil genius, and I couldn't wish anything sweeter than to shoot the dog myself."

Göring's name had just surfaced in the Netherlands, a country to which he had repaired, in better days, in his white-and-gold *Reichsmarschall's* uniform, only on art-buying excursions. In Amsterdam a little-known artist and connoisseur, Han van Meegeren, was being held on charges of collaboration with the enemy. In Göring's vast collections at Karinhall, legally looted in his unique manner, had been found a painting, *Christ and the Adulteress*, a brilliant work signed, and unmistakably by, the great Dutch master Jan Vermeer. The record of its sale, for what in *Reichsmarks* would then have amounted to half a million American dollars, traced it back to van Meegeren. Then another was found, also sold to Göring, *The Washing of the Feet of Christ*, which had brought nearly as much to Meegeren.

During the early days of the Nazi occupation, it appeared, van Meegeren had found in the possession of old and needy Dutch families six Vermeers and two canvases by Pieter de Hooch. With his millions gained from the sales, the ordinary little man whom no one in art circles had ever noticed before had bought fifty houses in Amsterdam and a country house in the south of France. But now that he was about to go on trial for his life as a traitor, he claimed that the *Christ and the Adulteress*, a magnificent work, although not as magisterial as another acclaimed canvas he had discovered, *Christ at Emmaus*, had actually been swapped by Göring for two hundred other Dutch pictures that van Meegeren had caused to be returned to the homeland. He was really a covert patriot.

But that did not explain a book of van Meegeren's own paintings found at Berchtesgaden with the inscription "To my beloved Führer—Han van Meegeren," or the fact that works by an artist venerated almost as much as Rembrandt van Rijn had been turned over to the Nazis. He had only signed his name in a pile of books, pleaded van Meegeren: someone else had forged the inscription. Further examination proved his innocence, but it did not account for the priceless art treasures sold to the enemy. And so in the Amsterdam police station, exhausted from the long interrogations, van Meegeren shouted, "Fools! You are fools like the rest of them! I sold no Vermeer to the Germans! I sold no treasure! I painted the picture myself. It is a valueless van Meegeren for which Göring paid this fortune."

It seemed clear that his bizarre confession was the result of sleeplessness or desperation. He was put back in his cell to sleep his madness off. Yet when he awakened, he called for pen and paper to write it all down. And a dispatch quoted an expert in The Hague as saying that if the paintings were indeed forgeries, van Meegeren was a genius. For the moment, however, he was incarcerated in far less comfort than the Nazi who had inadvertently brought him down.

A war crimes trial for Göring and others seemed far off, as the principal victors had yet to agree on procedures. Before Hitler removed himself from the justice system the British, concerned about making ex post facto law, proposed simply executing Nazi leaders without trial. Hellmut Becker, the German lawyer who would defend Ernst von Weizsäcker, called that the Italian solution: "You kill as many people as you can in the first six weeks, and then you forget about it: not very legal, but for purposes of purification, well . . ." Churchill had suggested as much to Stalin at Yalta, but the Generalissimo objected to summary shootings. "In the Soviet Union," he explained, "we never execute anyone without a trial."

"Of course, of course," Churchill agreed. "We should give them a trial first." But he meant a quick military dispatching of cases, not show trials that would feature war criminals and make martyrs of them, objects of victors' vengeance. If defendants were allowed to plead *Führerprinzip*, the concept that the leader has absolute authority to which all his minions were subject, only Adolf Hitler could be convicted, and he was dead. Justice Robert Jackson, appointed by Truman as principal American judge, was still trying to define the specific war crimes, including one of making aggressive war, and took himself to Potsdam, explaining to McCloy that the Russian attitude was "most discouraging." On the nineteenth he thought that his negotiations were finally working and that an international trial would take place. But he would go back to Washington and then to London before being satisfied.

Lesser fish than Göring were already paying for the crime of military service for the *Führer*. Voluntary and enthusiastic or passive and obedient, they were sometimes confined to the boredom of a stockade on minimal rations, more often put to work clearing the rubble of their war. The worst fear was to be turned over to the Russians. One prisoner, in civilian life a clerk, was pleased to get what he called "American marching rations" because they included cigarettes, but when he arrived at a camp near Le Mans in France, passing by Frenchmen who threw stones and made throat-slitting motions, he hoped, he wrote in his diary, "to be sent to a reasonable farmer where we would get enough to eat." Instead, on the nineteenth, guards took his group of ten by truck to "the most miserable work, in a quarry." It was, he wrote, "a very primitive operation, dynamiting a granite cliff, the rest of the work being done with hammers and crowbars. During the dynamiting everyone tries to find a boulder to hide behind." The war had been less risky.

Ex-soldiers had to share the limited food supplies with civilians, who, if they lived in the shattered cities, had a difficult time of it. Country folk in areas not occupied by the Russians lived almost normally; in Soviet or Polish areas, all the livestock was seized—cows, sheep, goats, chickens, pigs, geese. A farmwoman in East Prussia recalled being pushed off toward the Oder by the Poles, with only what she could carry. She put on her best clothes and hid them under "ragged stuff," and piled everything she could manage into rucksacks. Each time she was searched, soldiers took away what they wanted. Another war widow looked back into the evening sun at the farm in Pomerania where she was born and where generations of her family were buried, and wondered about the grazing cattle: "Who would milk them this evening and the following days?" Sometimes young girls were pulled out by randy soldiers while their mothers clung to them and wept. Rifle butts quickly separated them. "We had been driven out," Anna Kientopf remembered, "and were chased about, wandering along strange roads, without aim or hope, defenseless to every kind of danger. Only because foreign masters who had conquered us had made an agreement, according to which Poles and Russians were empowered to hunt millions of Germans out of their homes into the streets, while the crops had not been harvested, their fields were uncultivated, and the towns deserted." Few blamed their wretchedness on Hitler, who had been loyally supported to the nethermost village and farm in what had been the Third Reich.

In the cities there was more acknowledgment of the consequences of Naziism. Ruth Andreas-Friedrich's neighbor in Berlin, wife of a Party stalwart who had been arrested in May, had taken to her bed. She now weighed only eighty pounds, and inaction saved calories. "Housewives, unemployed people and Nazis," Andreas-Friedrich observed in her diary on July 19, "get food ration cards grade five. What does a mother do who gets only three hundred calories of bread per day. She divides it among her children and has to satisfy her own hunger by watching them. Nobody ever gained weight from watching. Not even if one's husband was a Party member." There was food somewhere, she knew, especially on the abandoned farms to the east of the city, in what was becoming Poland. "While the grass grows, the cow dies," was a saying she heard frequently now. "In Potsdam," she closed her daily entry, "the Big Three are holding a conference. The entire area is sealed off. No German is allowed to set foot on the sacred grounds where the negotiations are taking place. May they succeed in letting the grass grow. May it grow before the cows have died."

Yet living conditions had improved dramatically since her area had become the British zone on July 4. There were no more Russians cutting through apartment doors with bayonets to rob and rape. The water pump at her nearby *Schrebergarten* still worked, Rosemarie Hebek remembered, although the vegetable plot had long ceased to exist. The days when meat became available only when an artillery round hit a horse cart were only a memory now. With order had come ration cards which admittedly one still had to supplement by barter, but there was electricity for one hour during the day and another at night.

Schools slowly began to open and, given the need for teachers without a Nazi past, Fraulein Hebek and her friend, Ilse Baumgart, neither with any experience, applied. Rosemarie, a half-Jew whose gentile Silesian father had been permitted to serve only in the *Organisation Todt* construction battalions, had somehow survived in Berlin since 1941. She was immediately assigned a third-grade class with forty children in a half-destroyed building. Textbooks of the Nazi period were not permitted, and there were few others. There were no notebooks, pencils, or paper, "and new children appeared daily." But life was reviving.

One of the ironies of the occupation, at least in the West, was that Nazi civil law remained in force. On the nineteenth, for example, U.S. Army labor officers in Bavaria were reminded in a directive, "All workers are compelled by German law to participate in the Sickness Insurance Fund of the Social Insurance System." No one asked whether there were any funds left in the system by the expired government, or what they would be worth. It was the law. Meanwhile in Wiesbaden, ten former Party members were in jail for refusing orders from the city *Arbeitsamt* to report for work cleaning war debris. Here at least the law in question was Military Government Order Number 1, Article 2, Paragraph 21.

De-Nazification was having its impact in city jobs as the hated *Fragenbogen* were reviewed—and it was a criminal offense not to fill them out as instructed. A cynical *Burger* in the Prussian town of Sassnitz told an American soldier that his people were "naive on the subject of this old continent." The *Fragenbogen* got in the way of the future. After all, said Herr Neumann, claiming to quote an officer of his acquaintance, "We are now lunching the war backward, vomiting up our victories, and they don't taste as good as they did on the way down." The Hitler Youth, he dismissed, were "little more than Boy Scouts," not "dangerous animals." In the French zone, he pointed out, there was harshness, but no hypocrisy. "The French are free from any kind of false Puritanism in these matters, and waste little time in righteous indignation. Since they had to collaborate with Hitler, they understand why Germans also had to." His logic failed to explain why the Germans supported Naziism with enthusiasm long before they had to, but Neumann had an answer: "That when a course of events is started, there is not much chance to escape from the final conclusion." In most cases the consequences would be minimal and temporary, but 285 officials in the Augsburg city administration had been dismissed the day before, and in the Schluchtern district, all 46 mayors were removed. In Württemberg, where some areas had been carved out to be part of a French zone, all courts in the American sector reopened after judges with Party affiliations had been replaced. But in Straubing, an American military court acquitted the dismissed mayor of having concealed his SS membership on his testimony that his nominal dues had been paid by his wife only "to be left alone."

De-Nazification of another sort was spiriting former Nazis and their families not only out of the American zone but, secretly, even out of the Soviet-occupied areas. With even greater duplicity than the Vatican, all the former enemies of the Nazis occupying Germany were busy sheltering—sometimes kidnapping—German scientists who promised to give each a technological edge for the next war, or to deter it. With that excuse the American military even lured across the Atlantic medical researchers who had experimented on Allied prisoners, brought across for their expertise on human tolerance of high altitudes or immersion in cold seawater.*

Under pressure from high brass who claimed that keeping the Germans under wraps and over here prevented them from selling their services to the Soviets, the State Department and the Joint Chiefs agreed with some qualms on criteria that were at least nominally strict. Only an "essential minimum" of "indispensable" scientists, none deemed to be possible war criminals, would be recruited. As Major General Gladeon Barnes, an ordnance specialist, declared in the War Department study arguing for the undercover program, it was "a form of exploitation of chosen rare minds whose continuing intellectual productivity we wish to use." On July 19 it was officially if secretly approved by the Joint Chiefs of Staff as "Operation Overcast," allowing 350 German scientists to enter the United States on renewable six-month contracts. Ordnance was permitted an additional 100 rocket experts, including Wernher von Braun's entire team. With German help, the British were already building a new V-2 launching pad at Cuxhaven, on the North Sea, "for experimental purposes," a project Eisenhower had approved as "Operation Backfire." Before long, von Braun's Peenemünde team was expedited to Texas, no checks having been accomplished to see whether any were Nazis or war criminals. Rockets, too, arrived—the first hardware in the American space program.

While in some cases former Nazis were singled out for special coddling, the fate of former Russian prisoners—if they were hostile to Communism—was far more grim. For months they had been forcibly repatriated out of European camps from Italy to England. Not many were in the United States, but as they were captured in German uniforms after turning on the Soviet regime, a number of Russians were in POW camps for Germans in the United States. Post-Yalta surveys to identify them had been made, to turn them over to Russian authority. With difficulty, and some anguish, hundreds were shipped out of ports in the West to Vladivostock. Of those who had resisted, 154 tagged as Soviet citizens were taken to Fort Dix, New

---

*One, called afterward the "father of space medicine," was Dr. Hubertus Strughold, who had headed the *Luftwaffe* Institute for Aviation Medicine, which used inmates from Dachau who were locked in low-pressure chambers or tanks of ice water while pressure was altered to simulate extreme atmospheric conditions. They died agonizing deaths. He became chief scientist of the aerospace medical division at Brooke Air Force Base in San Antonio. The Justice Department had finally initiated proceedings to prosecute him and deport him—forty years later—when he died in 1986.

Jersey, for further examination of their status and transshipment via Germany to Russia.

When, on July 19, a party of four Soviet officers came to interview them, there were only 150. On June 29 they had barricaded themselves in their barracks block and were flushed out with tear gas. They emerged wielding knives from mess kits and clubs improvised from furniture parts. In real danger, guards opened fire, wounding seven Russians, one fatally. Three others were found hanging in the barracks, preferring death to repatriation. Although the survivors were taken to Camp Shanks in New York and the next day to Pier 51, where 280 armed soldiers and police were to force them aboard the former Italian liner *Monticello*, resistance flared again, even damaging the ship. Back went the prisoners to Fort Dix, guarded around the clock, and given nothing from which implements to put up a fight could be made.

The Soviet officers investigated the cases one by one in the presence of four American officers. No threats were permitted. Yet no prisoner believed the conciliatory promises or changed his mind. The few even willing to give their names said that they expected to be shot if returned and had organized the riot in hopes of being killed by the Americans instead.

The episode led to a review of American policy, but there was nothing that could be done other than to abrogate earlier agreements, which would put Soviet-American relations at risk during a delicate period. On August 9, Secretary Byrnes would reaffirm American commitments while refusing to return by force those who had not been Soviet citizens before seizure of their homelands in 1939 and 1940. Of the Fort Dix POWs, seven were judged to be Balts or Poles in that category. The rest were shipped under guard without incident on August 31, the last to be repatriated from the United States. By that date over two million Russians who had failed to escape the net had been handed over. Tens of thousands remained, having passed themselves off as non-Soviet with fabricated identification or the connivance of Allied officers. Some were deliberately overlooked by the Soviets, having been planted as agents in the West. Repatriations in Europe itself continued, but would trickle out. For the Americans it was a hard lesson, not to be repeated at the close of the Korean War in 1953, when Chinese and North Korean POWs were given a choice, and tens of thousands refused to return while the Communist bloc screamed vainly about violations of the Geneva Convention. International agreements made from the distance in time and geography of Geneva or The Hague that had once seemed humane and civilized were proving less so in an increasingly inhumane and uncivilized world.

On the same day the Russian POWs were being interrogated at Fort Dix, an editorial, "The Peace Rumors," appeared in *The New York Times*, critical toward trial balloons about a negotiated peace with Japan. Only an unconditional surrender, it argued, would render Japan "harmless for the future." The language seemed a response not only to feelers from Japan but to arguments in Henry Luce's magazines *Time* and *Life*, which were suggesting that unconditional surrender was too high a price to pay in terms of American lives. Further, the Navy was permitting Captain Zacharias's broadcasts to Japan to continue, as "Magic" intercepts made it obvious that he was getting through to a "peace party" of influential Japanese with his proposal that the only way to save the imperial house was to surrender before everything was lost. Few held office, but one who did was an old friend from the 1920s, Admiral Mitsumasa Yonai, now the Navy Minister. He understood Zacharias's retelling the story of a failed insurrection in southern Japan in 1872 when the rebel leader recognized the impossible, saying to the Emperor's emissary, "The bow and arrow and sword of my soldiers cannot compete with the rifle of the soldiers from the North."

A "peace party" did not imply a groundswell of public opinion. No such opportunity existed where the media were controlled and a police state apparatus existed. Although a German diplomat in Tokyo reported to Berlin, in a message intercepted by the United States, "Since the situation is recognized to be hopeless, large sections of the Japanese armed forces would not regard with disfavor an American request for capitulation even if the terms were hard," the message had to be read in context. Dated May 5, three days before the Nazi unconditional surrender took effect, the message mirrored German thinking, not Japanese. Not a single ranking general or admiral in the military hierarchy that ruled Japan would have subscribed to anything resembling capitulation, not even Admiral Yonai.

Public opinion did not exist in Japan, but a few elder statesmen, known as *jushin*, represented what little there was of moral authority. The *jushin*, or "important subjects" of the Emperor, were former prime ministers, former presidents of the Privy Council, and their like. Such elder statesmen might never be called in as an informal senate, but offered their counsel individually on imperial request. As early as the first months of 1945, Hirohito had called in seven *jushin,* and heard from each one that only an early peace would save the nation. One of the seven had been Prince Konoye; another had been the octogenarian Baron Suzuki, now prime minister. Now Suzuki was trying—vainly, it seemed—to send Konoye to Moscow to explore the chances of peace.

"Magic" had known as early as the Leyte landings in 1944 that the Imperial Navy saw the war as lost. After Okinawa there was almost no navy, but for die-hards in its air arm. The leadership had long scorned the hard terms and had planted suggestions through diplomatic third parties that if Japan could keep this conquest or that, and the Emperor and the old system, and possibly avoid occupation, that even the Army, the hard-line service, might accept a peace. The decrypts were only as credible as their sources, and as a chronicler of codebreaking has put it, "The historian has to shed hindsight, and consider what the situation looked like *at the time."* And at the time the army hierarchy dominating the government was suicidally belligerent. Perhaps the threat to turn the population into *kamikazes* was only that, meant to make the United States back away from a new and costlier Normandy, but American planners were taking nothing for granted.

Troops were already in serious training for the invasion of the home islands. On an inspection round, General Eichelberger flew from Manila to Davao City on Mindanao, and then to the lonely, torrid island of Morotai in the former Dutch Indies, one of the closest retaken points in the Indies to the Philippines. There General Harry Johnson had been training the "colored" (but for some higher-level officers) 93rd Division. Segregation and condescension were the way of the 1940s Army, which even at that was less rigid than the Navy. When Eichelberger wrote in such terms to his wife he almost certainly believed that he was being enthusiastically complimentary. "I have never seen so much snap in my life," he noted. "They had every vehicle polished, the engines were cleaned up fine, and every colored boy saluted as far as he could see you. . . . There are no disciplinary cases in the division and their kitchens are as clean and as neat as a pin. Johnson has certainly done a fine job. . . . It is apparent that he knows just how to handle these colored boys. . . ." They were being readied for the beaches of Kyushu.

| July 15 | July 16 | July 17 | July 18 | July 19 | July 20 | July 21 |
|---------|---------|---------|---------|---------|---------|---------|
| July 22 | July 23 | July 24 | July 25 | July 26 | July 27 | July 28 |

## CHAPTER VIII

# · JULY 20, 1945 ·

*". . . a vulture of uncertainty"*

At sea 430 miles southeast of Tokyo, a carrier plane, one of the few aloft on the rain-swept nineteenth, encountered a bomb-carrying balloon and shot it down. It sank before it could be recovered. But the primitive devices were still being recovered on the other side of the Pacific. On the twentieth, an unexploded incendiary bomb and deflated balloon were found on Mount Pitt, Oregon, and a balloon envelope and shroud lines, minus its explosives package, were located at Indian Springs, Nevada.

The Japanese were as short of materials as they were of technology. (It is possible, however, that the primitive technology of their balloon bombs had paid off in Oregon, where seventy square miles of forest were ablaze in the Wilson River area. "We're too busy to go to church for prayers," said a logger. "But we're praying inside.") As early as June 1944 Admiral Ugaki was despairing, "A country with no oil and a navy without fuel, how can we do [anything] with this [handicap]?" Now the economic strangulation was far worse. Ambassador Sato warned Minister Togo from Moscow on the twentieth that if the enemy began burning the fall harvest—the rice crop was beginning to dry—"we will be confronted with absolute famine." The Kremlin, he insisted, would not mediate. "Since we can assume that the enemy will one day attempt a landing, it is also clear that after our fighting strength is destroyed, the Soviet Union will [attack]. . . . There is no hope of achieving our aims. We must put a stop to continued resistance; the lives of hundreds of thousands are caught in a hopeless death trap. We are only a step away from total annihilation of our country. I pray that we may act now to save our 70 million compatriots, preserving at least our national existence." Sato was drawing a line between that and the sacred "national polity." "[We] will not save the Imperial House," he warned, "by dying a glorious death on the field of battle." Understanding his society, he went on, "It goes without saying that the Imperial Army and the populace as a whole will not surrender to the enemy as long as there is no Imperial command to do so; they will literally not throw away their spears until the last man. . . . Although it is possible to remain loyal to the great and just aims of the Greater East Asia War to the very end, it is meaningless to insist upon them to the extent of destroying the state."

Having made his patriotic gesture, Sato went on in a different vein, decrying "authoritarian rule" and "the domineering and self-righteous attitude of the bureaucrats," the "scorn for diplomacy and the indifference to international relations," and the "completely bankrupt" foreign policy that had brought Japan to its "present misfortune." In the "postwar dawn" Japan would have to "democratize" itself even if it retained the Imperial House. "I realize," he concluded, "that it is a great crime to dare to make such statements, knowing that they are contrary to the views of the government," but he was risking the tag of "defeatist" in "sincere concern for the country."

Responding the next day, Togo would acknowledge Sato's "opinion" but emphasized that the decision to play nothing but the Moscow card remained the will of the Cabinet. "Magic" transmitted both intercepts to Marshall in Potsdam.

A captured document made available to Pacific commanders on the twentieth exemplified exactly what Sato feared. His message to Togo had cited the futility of fighting—after the certain landing on the home islands—"as organized guerrillas . . . in the face of modern weapons." "Operation *Ketsu*" may have been activated only when precipitated by the landings on Okinawa, but as early as mid-1944 the Japanese had initiated staff exercises labeled "Hypothetical Defense of Kyushu." Now there was nothing hypothetical about it. The models were the suicidal defense of Tinian and Saipan in the summer of 1944, where local governments organized civilians, including women, children, and old men, into living bombs by arming them with explosives. It was a tragic business, Ugaki had confided to his diary, yet "No people but the Yamato nation could do a thing like this. I think that if one hundred million Japanese people could have the same resolution as these . . . it wouldn't be difficult to find a way to victory."

Marshall also had delivered to him, dated July 20 Far East time, an assessment of Japanese home island strength based upon photo reconnaissance, information from neutral nation observers in the diplomatic corps accredited to Japan, and decrypted signal traffic. The forty pages, "Estimated Unit Locations of Japanese Navy and Army Air Forces," noted about home defense, "Training of all kinds, other than suicide training in tactical units, is believed to have been abandoned in view of the expected imminent invasion." The pages on army deployment showed thirty-six divisions in eight headquarters areas, with 2,110,000 uniformed troops available. Kyushu defenses were overseen by the Second Army in Hiroshima, across the strait in lower Honshu. The top-secret estimates on navy dispositions, radioed from the Third Fleet in Okinawa waters, identified "remaining Japanese naval strength" concentrated at Kure, just east of Hiroshima. "Lesser concentrations" were in the Inland Sea, Tokyo Bay, and at Maizuru, directly across Honshu from Kobe, on the Japan Sea. Again the disquieting report noted, "The enemy is concentrating suicide airplanes throughout the home islands for use against BLUE [U.S.] shipping during the amphibious phase of the expected invasion."

Weather, the flagship *Shangri-La** reported, remained the major factor limiting operations, but the fleet had at least one of its four task forces, three carrier groups, and a bombardment group, pounding Japan every day. While the weather was marginally better in the seas north of Okinawa, the spray splashed gun mounts seventy feet above

*The carrier *Shangri-La,* almost certainly the only warship named for a place in a novel, recalled the Jimmy Doolittle–led raid on Tokyo, April 18, 1942. The B-25s had made their hazardous takeoffs from the carrier *Hornet,* but President Roosevelt, asked by reporters where the bombers had come from, joked that they had flown from Shangri-La, the mysterious Tibetan lamasery community in James Hilton's *Lost Horizon.* Now there was a real *Shangri-La* launching warplanes at Japan.

cruiser decks. Although sailors were soaked in the process, the remaining destroyers low on fuel were topped up. And waves of bombers pounded Japan again from Guam and Tinian, while fighters from Iwo Jima flew sorties against smaller targets.

The 509th Composite Group on Tinian had the most curious mission. With oversized and shielded bomb-loading pits constructed at North Field on Tinian ready, the 509th began what would be a series of sorties familiarizing crews with the areas of Japan expected to be "Special Bomb" targets, and dropping, one per mission, a ten-thousand-pound bright orange "pumpkin" approximating "Little Boy." Maneuvering tactics to evade blast and radiation were employed by groups of three planes flying widely apart. The Japanese were already accustomed to small formations flying at high altitudes to drop leaflets, take pictures, and sample weather, but these, Lieutenant Masataka Hakata of Central Communications Research realized, were different. B-29s with 400-range numbers flew from Saipan, 500-range from Guam, 700-range from Tinian. Hataka had figured that out from radio signals and downed planes. What were the 600-range planes doing, and where did they come from? Why had they begun dropping, with such curious maneuvers, such a curious-looking (but otherwise ordinary) bomb? No one had an answer.

P-38s, B-24s, and B-25s were over targets in the Dutch Indies, and to disrupt enemy withdrawals into China other fighter-bombers from Chinese bases raided power plant and railway targets in Indochina. Southeast Asia had become a crazy quilt of contradictions. Having failed to create an effective—if large—liberation army for India from prisoners held since 1941, and having never pacified the Burmese hinterland after occupying the major cities, all the Japanese wanted to do in mid-July 1945 was to extricate their own troops and hold on to negotiable territory. They had valuable commodities in British and Commonwealth prisoners of war, and they had Malaya and Singapore.

Elsewhere, too, they were losing control. Transferred to India, Prince Varanand of the Thai royal family, an RAF pilot who had flown missions over Normandy, was given the assignment of checking possible airdrop sites in his occupied homeland. Landing openly, complete to British uniform, he was greeted by officers of the Thai Air Force and shown eight abandoned Japanese airstrips. At the last strip he was met by an American OSS C-47, to the British a "Dakota," but the plane sank in the unpaved runway in mud up to the engine nacelles. It was the rainy season. The plane had to be burned to keep it from the Japanese, but the Thais got the prince and the OSS party away. The Japanese policed little beyond Bangkok.

The Allies were also all over Indochina, but Mountbatten's Southeast Asia Command had no way to direct the retaking of the former French colony from the inside because the Americans and the French were at odds over the country's future. Washington was then supporting the nationalist movement of the Viet Minh. As Lieutenant General F. A. M. Browning, Mountbatten's chief of staff, put it later, the Americans and the French "were the two at war in Indochina. The Japs were not in it."

Monsoon flying, recalled Flight Lieutenant Terence O'Brien, who had escaped from Singapore just before it fell, was "like cleaving through a seemingly endless Niagara" in support of clandestine operations that cost more than their contribution to victory. Planes, supplies, and men were being wasted in liberating territories that would free themselves easily when the Rising Sun was run down in Tokyo. However, when things go badly they go very badly indeed, and Japanese plans to swarm to safety across the floods fell into enemy hands. The orders were to withdraw "secretly" toward Bilin, "but in case of enemy hindrance the enemy will be destroyed." It was an order reminiscent of headier days. Now the Sittang was in monsoon flood, the few open land routes across lower Burma were covered by tanks and artillery "standing by, all waiting like a shooting party," and the guerrillas in their rear were battle-hardened men with machine guns, O'Brien wrote, "with bitter memories of friends and families wiped out in Japanese punitive expeditions over the past three years. . . . Now it was their turn to be executioners."

Every element of the retreating Japanese army, and even what was left of Chandra Bose's Indian National Army, was struggling to cross the flooded Sittang in the direction of Thailand. The fall of Rangoon in the spring had been decisive. Boats requisitioned for soldiers and dependents to get them to the docks at Moulmein, en route to Singapore or Bangkok or home, often raced away in the torrents, uncontrollably out to sea. But one boat had been reserved for the boxes of ashes of men killed in the failure to keep Burma, stored for shipment to the Yasukuni Shrine of military heroes in Tokyo. Thirty-seven large chests held forty thousand boxes, all of which reached Moulmein safely. It seemed easier to extricate Japanese soldiers from Burma if they were dead.

The Sittang usually went into such enormous flooding from late spring into early autumn that maps of the terrain posted areas with the warning "Usually flooded from June to October." X-Day, the day for "Breakout," to overwhelm British attempts to trap the Japanese and stage simultaneous crossings of the swollen Sittang, was to be July 20, regardless of the obstacles involved. Mud slides, pouring rain, tall elephant grass, waterlogged paddies, biting and stinging insects that multiplied in the stupefying heat, jungle sores, hostility of the Karen tribesmen, who hammered apart Japanese skulls for the gold in their teeth, all compounded to make the operation risky at best, perhaps impossible. Then, on July 2, a Japanese officer was captured with a monsoon-soaked leather bag that contained tissue paper plans pasted upon an old British map, and operations orders. It was taken to 17th Division headquarters, where a British intelligence officer and his American Nisei sergeant figured it out.

Alerted to the massive crossing intended by the Twenty-eighth Army, the British and Indians were waiting on X-Day. Japanese officers knew they would have to abandon most artillery and vehicles, and that boats hardly existed along the twisting Sittang from Pegu, north of Rangoon, all the way up to Toungoo. Yet hunger drove them to follow orders. They were starving as well as sodden. Little rice remained; they gnawed at raw yams and the maggoty carcasses of dead animals. South from Toungoo came Indians, while near Pyu were the British; everywhere it seemed were Burmese guerrillas. In many places the paddies were flooded chest-high. When British guns opened up, the nine thousand men left of the 54th Division broke ranks.

To the south the mud-slowed remnants of the 55th Division were horrified as they reached the river to see Japanese corpses bobbing by from upstream. Many men shed heavy equipment and retreated into the trees or slogged back toward dry land. One group found a field of tall grass that turned out to be sugarcane. Abandoning discipline, officers and ranks alike began breaking off pieces of cane and gorging themselves. Soon commanders, concerned about the price of delay, urged the men on. Elsewhere in the hills behind the Sittang could be heard the muffled explosions of grenades. Sick and seriously wounded men were sparing their comrades the burden of carrying them, and relieving themselves of bearing the burden of their own cholera-racked or broken bodies. A grenade to the belly would end their war.

Thirteen thousand men of the 54th Division would not make it across. The rest, scattered into small groups across the flooded rice paddies and into the foothills, were prey to Burmese tribesmen. Only a few surrendered. As of the day before the failed breakout Allied estimates were that the Japanese had lost 347,000 men in Burma, but in the rain and heat the traces of the dead disappeared quickly.

A survivor after four months on the run was Hiroshi Abe. In January 1941 he had been a Ministry of Railways surveyor. With the expansion of the war he went to Burma as an army officer to oversee construction of a Burma-Siam rail line through the dark, dense jungle. He had made his way from deep in Burma toward his familiar trackage, which ran across the enormous Songkrai Bridge, the wooden "bridge on the river Kwai" later famous in story but never, as in the film, destroyed. Engineered by the Japanese rather than by Hollywood, and built by tens of thousands of "contract" Burmese and sixty-one thousand British, Australian, and Dutch POWs, of whom perhaps a quarter died, it had outlasted the monsoon floods. Abe had helped get two divisions out by rail while their generals, to his disgust, flew home. Then he left by the last train, on March 8, getting as far as Mandalay before it fell. He had to limp on an injured leg all the way to Moulmein, where an army doctor ordered him to a hospital in Thailand, if he could get there.

From Moulmein "his" railway was still operative. He asked that the train taking him stop at Songkrai. "My orderly carried me on his back to where I could see the bridge for the first time in more than a year. It had been the target of heavy bombing, but had suffered no direct hits. The bridge spanned a gorge so closely surrounded by steep mountains that a bomber could not make a direct run at it. It was still there, exactly as I had built it. I was ecstatic. I went on to Thailand by train, arriving in Bangkok around July 20, 1945." Abe would get as far as Singapore, where he was picked up by British, identified, and tried for war crimes. (His death sentence was later reduced to fifteen years.)

July 20 was already memorable in Germany for a tactical failure more expensive than the failed breakout in Burma. "The day of Witzleben and Stauffenberg,"* a Berlin resident began his diary. "A year ago to-

*Field Marshal Erwin von Witzleben was the plotters' choice as chief of a post-Hitler *Wehrmacht*. He was strangled. Lieutenant Colonel Klaus Philip Schenk, Count von Stauffenberg, who carried the briefcase with the bomb, was hanged from a meat hook. Gestapo records list over 7,000 arrests relating to the plot; the death roll was reported to include 4,980 names, many of the accused tortured before execution.

day we thought that the terror would be over within a few hours. It wasn't over. That it didn't end that day cost the world millions of lives. . . ." The German officers who had bungled the assassination of Hitler at his East Prussian bunker, and miscalculated in Berlin the grip of Nazi officeholders, were martyred heroes in postwar Germany while somehow regarded as victims of the Allied enemy rather than of unshakable loyalties to Hitler. "Why didn't the world powers help us then? Why did they let slip this last of many chances to end Hitler's life?" For many Germans, however, active anti-Hitlerism came even later than that. A woman in Hohn ran up to an American soldier occupying her town to exclaim, "If you find Hitler, I want you to break every bone in his body!"

In Berlin, Germans now whispered of East-West hostility, of rumors that things were going badly at Potsdam. "Perhaps there will be war. They say it is possible." "War? We just had a war. Only eleven weeks ago. It's out of the question." But one survivor remembered a soldier telling his mother toward the end, "*Mutterlein,* enjoy the war; the peace will be horrible."

The secrecy of the deliberations and the few innocuous morsels of information fed the press were put together by Berliners with their awareness of shootouts between Americans and Russians "every night. They don't even greet each other on the street. . . . They don't seem to like each other, our Allied occupation powers."

The powers were even having difficulty agreeing upon the rank of the President of the Council of Peoples Commissars—whether it was *Marshal* Stalin or *Generalissimo* Stalin, as he employed whatever self-designated titles appealed to him. One paragraph for eventual release was already held up as no Soviet official would then sign a document referring to *Marshal* Stalin. (Despite the official *Generalissimo,* early in the conference Churchill had asked Stalin at dinner whether he preferred to be called *Premier, Marshal,* or *Generalissimo,* and, the P.M. recalled, Stalin replied that he hoped that Churchill "would call him Marshal as he always had done in the past.") Russian sensitivities plagued the conference. American planes could still fly to Moscow only circuitously via Tehran for reasons the Soviets would not explain, but it was clear to Air Force General H. H. Arnold that overflying territory they did not want Americans to examine closely had a lot to do with it. At the morning JCS meeting a memorandum was approved asking Truman to intervene with Stalin.

That morning, before the President had been driven to the headquarters of the U.S. sector to raise the American flag over Berlin, he had met with General Omar Bradley to ask him to become the new director of the Bureau of Veterans' Affairs. It was a thankless job certain of becoming one of the most onerous in the federal bureaucracy as twelve million Americans returned to civilian life. (One of the meetings on the twentieth, between Vice Admiral Emory S. Land and Lord Leathers, extended the time the United States would have for use of the *Queen Mary* and *Queen Elizabeth* for the movement of troops home and to the Pacific, arranged for the conversion by the British of one hundred vessels for troop carrying and for the use of captured German passenger ships for "trooplift.") Bradley, perhaps the most respected general among the men in the ranks, was also one of the most selfless, and agreed to take over on short notice— August 15. Then Truman and several high brass left for Berlin.

The flag, so the President noted in his diary, was the same one "raised in Rome, North Africa and Paris. Flag was on the White House when Pearl Harbor happened. Will be raised over Tokyo." Now it fluttered above the buildings that had housed the German capital's Air Defense Command. But Truman's brief address was much less triumphal than his private musings. The flag, he declared to the troops massed around him, was being raised to symbolize their nation's hopes "for a better world, a peaceful world, a world in which all the people will have an opportunity to enjoy the good things in life and not just a few at the top. . . . We are not fighting for conquest. There is not one piece of territory or one thing of a monetary nature that we want out of this war. We want peace and prosperity for the world as a whole. We want to see the time come when we can do the things in peace that we have been able to do in war. . . ."

As Raymond Daniell of *The New York Times* wrote, the event turned out to be more than "a routine patriotic display." Truman wrote his own words, and they were homely and eloquent, as were his gestures—hands in and out of pockets, sometimes chopping the air in emphasis. He was a pol from Missouri, and had never been to college. In the President's car on the ride back to Potsdam was Dwight Eisenhower. Full of the emotion of the occasion, and perhaps sensing his situation as accidental President, Truman leaned toward Ike and said, "General, there is nothing you may want that I won't try to help you get. That definitely and specifically includes the presidency in 1948."

Omar Bradley, in the third rear seat, sat quietly and tried to mask his surprise. Eisenhower had no idea what to say. Finally he answered, "Mr. President, I don't know who will be your opponent for the presidency, but it will not be I."

Domestic matters were inescapable for Truman at Potsdam, but invisible to reporters and to the record. Among them were strikes and threats of strikes that had erupted once the German war was over. Labor unions feared the factory layoffs that would come with victory, and the millions of servicemen the end of the war with Japan would add to the unemployed. Truman needed labor peace merely to end the Pacific war, and to show that urgency he proposed a sixty-day moratorium on walkouts while eight editors of major journals in the labor press got a firsthand look at the problems still confronting the armed services. He suggested representatives of the *CIO News*, the *United Automobile Worker*, the *Aero Mechanic*, the *Federated Press* of the AFL, and other key opinion makers. Service chiefs were asked for reactions. They would drag their feet.

While Truman was involving himself in an occasion the press could cover, the conference's Economic Subcommittee was meeting in Potsdam, its business dominated by the Soviet ambassador to Britain, Ivan Maisky. Maisky wanted the Ruhr, Germany's chief industrial sector, internationalized, an idea that had never worked with German territory in the past but was strongly supported by France, which saw the possibilities of a satellite state under its domination and an uncompetitive Germany. "Rhineland and Ruhr?" asked Will Clayton for the United States. Maisky had no specific boundaries in mind, and Mark Turner for Britain noted that Westphalia and the Rhineland had at least eleven million people. "25 × 50 miles," added Edwin Pauley for the United States, "all black coal and much industry."

For Britain, Walter Monckton asked whether the Soviets would leave the Germans there—a pointed reference to the expulsions in the East. "Yes," said Maisky.

"Leave them in ownership of properties?" asked Clayton.

"That is another question," said Maisky.

Since the area was in the zones of Western occupation, it suggested that what the Soviets wanted was another foothold in which to create instability, and another area from which to strip reparations. The proposal to prevent Germany from rebuilding its military potential was too obviously a mask for Communist encroachment into western Europe, a worry that even went beyond the proposal's recipe for Germany as beggar nation living on American largesse. The idea would die.

Russia, Maisky made clear nevertheless, wanted reparations regardless of the consequences to Germany. "The American people," Clayton responded, "will not again, as they did after the last war, finance Germany. That was President Roosevelt's position." It was also, he implied, that of the new President.

Germany before the war, Maisky insisted, had lived "on a very high scale compared with other European countries." He was prepared to "visualize quite another Germany"—on the bleak Russian level, was his implication. And when he took British and American objections as only "theoretical," Sir David Waley, for the British side, scoffed, "This is not a school debating society."

All they could agree upon was to report their disagreement to the Big Three.

Food supply in the Anglo-American zones of Germany (which included sectors given the French) was desperate. *Die Kornkammer Deutschland*—"the German granary"—was the territory east of the Oder and Elbe awarded by the Soviets to Poland, which had been shifted westward at Germany's expense. That the seizure had been accomplished, fleeing inhabitants protested, *"auf unrechtmässiger Weise,"* was an ironic reversal of a phony mid-1930s map concocted by the Nazis to prove that Poland planned an invasion as far as the Elbe.

However unlawful the means, the land would no longer produce crops for the industrialized West, and attempting to assess the urgency of the problem, the American Military Government canvassed each army *Bürgermeister* for a mind-boggling array of information. In the orders for July 20, paragraph 15 was

> State an estimate of the food situation within the area . . . types of food available, food surplus in seven days' requirements, type and amount, estimate days of food stock on hand, legal market prices for various food commodities, black market prices, if any. Under "black market" state importance as to major foods, food available, an estimate of local efforts made by Military Government detachments to eliminate [black marketeering].

There were other requests for data on individual bank balances; property holdings; vehicles licensed under the former regime; petroleum, coal, and coke on hand; railways operable; post and telegraph service; tax collections still ongoing under the Nazi regime's regulations; births and deaths; refugees and DPs in the area; and local requests for release of prisoners of war for farm and factory work. War, many officers sighed, was far easier and less stressful than peace.

Charles Moran's own first business of the day was a breakfast meeting with his special patient and charge, Churchill. "The Russians are being very difficult," the Prime Minister began. "'They talk about the same things as we do, freedom and justice and that sort of thing, but prominent people are removed and are not seen again. We are not even allowed to enter Vienna." With "brute cunning," Moran confided to his diary, Stalin had first stilled Churchill's suspicions, "and then, like a mule, with one vicious kick, he has demolished the structure so carefully built up, brick by brick. Perhaps he does not care. He must know that he holds all the trump cards." Although the cards in Stalin's hand were left for the imagination, Moran had enough of Churchill's confidences to have identified among them the Soviet domination of all of eastern and much of central Europe by the largest land army the world had ever seen, the reign of foreign and domestic brutality and terror that instilled absolute obedience, and the repercussions of promised military intervention against Japan.

"The P.M. stretched himself wearily," the physician wrote. Churchill was seventy and tired, and his relentless wartime pace and execrable care of himself—he seemed to live on brandy, cigars, and sleeplessness—had taken a toll. "I shall be glad," he confessed, "when this election business is over. It hovers over me like a vulture of uncertainty in the sky."

The foreign ministers met at 11:30, and again the Russians—Molotov this time—pressed for reparations, their agenda focused upon Italy. Byrnes responded as had Clayton. "In the best spirit," he declared, "I must say that the United States does not intend to make advances to any country in order that reparations may be paid by them." He had not suggested that, Molotov claimed, and pressed on to another of Stalin's objectives, Greece. The government had been imposed on the Greeks, he charged, and the British Army was still there. Byrnes proposed that free elections be held all over eastern Europe (the other governments, he did not need to say, were Communist-imposed) and that the press be invited to observe.

There were no excesses in Bulgaria and Romania like those in Greece, Molotov objected, but Byrnes noted that the press was able to report what was going on in Greece but nowhere else in the liberated countries. There was no reason to fear that elections in the rest of the region would not be free, Molotov insisted. Only in Greece was the situation "dangerous." And indeed it was, for a strong Communist effort was being made to subvert Greece, which if successful would force Turkey closer to the Communist camp. Britain and the United States had no intention of letting that happen. The "reign of terror" in Greece had to be ended, warned Molotov.

Instead of finding fault with each other, said Byrnes, an agreement should be drafted covering free elections in Italy, Romania, Greece, Bulgaria, and Hungary, with a provision for press coverage. Eden agreed. But according to minutes of the meeting, Molotov "saw no reason to supervise elections in Romania and Bulgaria. The press was now more free." It would never be so during the lifetime of Communism.

Eden had remained silent for most of the meeting, letting Byrnes do the talking for him. He had told no one but Churchill that a telegram had arrived reporting that his son, Pilot Officer Simon Eden, whose plane had crashed in Burma in June while flying supplies to forward troops in that region's terrible weather, had been found dead in the wreckage of his plane. Carrying on with his usual dignity, Eden would go through his day's schedule, sitting at the Prime Minister's right hand at the Cecilienhof.

At 2:20 the combined Anglo-American chiefs of staff met, the minutes noting only that a directive to the Supreme Commander Southeast Asia was approved and that it included a reallocation of zones of responsibility. Lord Louis Mountbatten had been pressing for activation of "Operation Zipper," which aimed at recovering Singapore, but the target date was forever being moved back as the crucial carriers and landing craft were being diverted elsewhere. The United States was not interested in Malaya and the Indies except as was necessary to protect British, Dutch, and Commonwealth prisoners of war there. Yet Mountbatten's new directive included "the opening of the Strait of Malacca at the earliest possible moment." The southern end of the strait, which separated Malaya and Sumatra, opened out upon Singapore. Mountbatten was also informed that British Commonwealth land forces he had counted on "should take part in the main operations against Japan which have been agreed as the supreme operations in the war." The boundaries of his command would be enlarged to include all of the Dutch Indies as of August 15 and he was to liberate, as soon as practicable, Malaya, Siam, Singapore, and the Indies, although he would have to wait for the resources with which to do it. There was no need to cable the ten-part directive to him. Mountbatten had been in Manila on the fourteenth and in Rangoon on the fifteenth. Now he was on his way to Potsdam via Delhi.

One of the differences of opinion in every meeting at Potsdam involving the Russians was semantic. When Churchill, Stalin, and Truman met at four, one of the first matters to come up was the supervision of elections in countries from Italy to Finland. It was Molotov's language, carried over from the earlier meeting. Churchill interrupted to say that he had no desire to control elections, if that was what *supervise* meant. Truman agreed, and Byrnes suggested *observe* as the operative word—which carried. Every operative word was crucial, as it had to mean the same in translation.

Italy remained a sticking point, with Stalin not only wanting a role there (on the ground that Italian forces had fought in Russia, however badly) but also a share of the Italian fleet. Worried that Stalin might also seek a share of Italy's former colonies, occupied for the time by British and Commonwealth forces, Churchill made a long speech intended to keep the Russians out. Truman later wrote amusingly about the interchanges between Churchill (long and florid) and Stalin (short and blunt):

> Churchill always found it necessary in cases of this kind, particularly where the Mediterranean was involved, to make long statements like this and then agree to what had already been done. The Mediterranean at that time was extremely vital to the British because it was the highway to India and Australia. He was apparently making a record for use later by the British when the peace treaties were really and actually negotiated. He did the same thing when we were talking about Franco and Spain. On several occasions when Churchill was discussing something at length, Stalin would lean on his elbow, pull on his mustache, and say, "Why don't you agree? The Americans agree, and we agree. You will agree eventually, so why don't you do it now?" Then the argument would stop. Churchill in the end would agree, but he had to make a speech about it first.

Truman pressed for settlements in individual countries rather than for an unworkable "final peace conference for the world as a whole." Stalin, he knew, would hold up any part of that to get something he wanted. The United States, he observed, was pouring nearly a billion dollars into Italy alone to feed the country through the following winter. Such prostrate nations needed to be made self-sufficient. (Truman's later Marshall Plan would have the goal of national self-sufficiency. In retrospect the seeds of the Marshall Plan seem sown at Potsdam.)

Neither East nor West expected to write peace treaties at Potsdam, but the wartime partners did agree to set up a Council of Foreign Ministers to draw up treaties with nations formerly at war, however reluctantly, with the Allies—Italy, Romania, Bulgaria, Hungary, and Finland. Austria did not count as it had been absorbed into the Reich in 1938. Now restored to independence, it remained a sticky problem, for the Russians were finding new technicalities daily to prevent the other Allies from taking up their zones of occupation, most crucially in Vienna itself. It seemed clear that until Soviet larceny in Vienna—the unilateral seizing of reparations—was completed, there would be no Anglo-American presence there. Stalin had also been hinting about concessions to the unruly Tito in Italy and Austria, but Truman and Churchill were not listening. "It is high time," contended Churchill, "that we were allowed to occupy our zone and move into Vienna." In Germany, he reminded Stalin, British and American troops "had retired long distances into the allotted zone, but we are still prevented from moving into ours in Austria." Recalling Stalin's urgency about German shipping—looted, he suggested, by the British—Churchill proposed reciprocity, Soviet visits to the fleet in exchange for relinquishing of zones in Vienna. And suddenly Stalin remembered that agreement on the zones had "only been reached yesterday."

As they broke up for the evening, Truman asked Stalin when the Soviet chiefs of staff would meet with their American counterparts. He did not need to add that the agenda would be Japan.

# "Magic"
# and
# Mediation

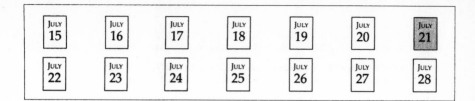

CHAPTER IX

## · JULY 21, 1945 ·

*". . . the Russians are coming"*

Although it seemed up to the Japanese to offer a concrete counterproposal, Togo had none to suggest because the military would not authorize any move that would concede defeat. The Japan hands in the State Department had campaigned through an Office of War Information study group for a declaration that the Emperor might remain, a policy statement that would have outraged the "hang Hirohito" American public. Stimson had listened to the OWI spokesman, George Taylor, and scoffed that from his own information the committee analysis was not worth the paper it was printed on. The Japanese had already demonstrated that they would fight to the end. "I have seen the island of Kyushu which we are to invade," he said, "and it is full of rocks and trees. They will fight behind every rock and tree." Privately, Taylor thought Stimson was "stupid," but it was the Secretary of War who was reading the "Magic" intercepts daily.

A dissenter with more authority, Undersecretary of the Navy Ralph Bard, a prewar Chicago industrialist whom Stimson had assigned to the Interim Committee on the Bomb, had been overruled in committee. "The Navy knew the Japanese were licked," he wrote later. The problem was to convince the Japanese before the Bomb did. He had written a memorandum to Stimson on June 27, nearly three weeks before the test in the desert, on the assumption that S-1 would work. The government of Japan, he urged, should be warned "two or three days in advance of use" both to safeguard the reputation of the United States "as a great humanitarian nation" and to utilize the threat of the Bomb as "some opportunity which they could use as a medium for surrender." He suggested offering to meet "representatives from Japan somewhere on the China coast." The stakes were "so tremendous" that every chance, he thought, ought to be taken: "The only way to find out is to try it out."

In his memo, Bard had mentioned American "fair play." Stimson and Truman saw, on the other side, whatever the diplomatic talk, nothing but continuing fanaticism. Feeling that he was "hammering on locked doors," Bard decided to resign.

The mission of Prince Konoye, so Sato was instructed to explain to Molotov according to Togo's final cable of July 21, at 9:30 P.M., was "to ask the Government of the USSR for its assistance in terminating the war and to explain our concrete intentions concerning the matter in accordance with the wishes of the Emperor." That Molotov's only interest in Konoye was to stall his visit until Russian troops were ready to go to war was obvious to Sato, but no one in Tokyo was listening.

As Togo pursued the forlorn hope of Russian mediation, his minister in Bern kept cabling his concerns that unauthorized Japanese meddlers in Switzerland were frantically exploring every avenue for peace, from seeking out Allen Dulles to pursuing Swedish banker Per Jacobssohn. Dulles, despite his understanding that Seigo Okamoto, Kojiro Kitamura, and Ken Yoshimura were offering only "local initiatives" rather than feelers from Tokyo, had arranged to see Jacobssohn in Wiesbaden on July 15, cautioning him that "dynastic and constitutional questions" were outside his authority. In truth, everything but information gathering lay outside his authority, as it did the Japanese, but Dulles considered General Okamoto a channel to Army Chief of Staff Yoshijiro Umezu, under whom he had once served in Manchuria.

Rumors of rifts between East and West in Potsdam raised fresh hopes in Tokyo, and Kase had to warn that no reliance could be placed on stories that "sooner or later" the United States and Russia would be at war. In Switzerland, meanwhile, the OSS had uncovered a correspondence between Hideki Tojo, prime minister at the time of Pearl Harbor, and a Japanese newspaperman in Zurich, Jiro Toguchi, in which the reporter observed that the Germans had miscalculated American determination much as had his own country. Captain Zacharias had been given the texts as grist for his radio talks, and he used them.

Zacharias's broadcast number twelve to Japan went on the air that morning. He urged immediate surrender, emphasizing that by holding out to the bitter end, Germany had lost everything. The Japanese, he noted, had the Atlantic Charter of 1941 to count upon as guarantee of their essential freedoms. It assured "certain definite benefits to victors and vanquished alike." American military law, Zacharias added, "clearly specifies that conquest or occupation does not affect the sovereignty of a defeated nation." In some ways he pre-empted the declaration being prepared for Churchill and Truman at Potsdam, for his gloss upon the meaning of unconditional surrender was that of an "official spokesman," as he was described in stepping up his authority. Although the broadcast intensified the debate in ruling circles in Tokyo, it could do nothing to accelerate a decision. Analyzing the radio traffic later that day, the Pacific Strategic Intelligence Section summed up to Fleet headquarters, "It may be said that Japan now, officially if not publicly, recognizes her defeat. Abandoning as unobtainable the long-cherished goal of victory, she has turned to the twin aims of reconciling national pride with defeat, and finding the best means of salvaging the wreckage of her ambitions."

As part of the psychological warfare campaign, Major General Allen Turnage, director of Marine Corps personnel, was heard on Columbia Broadcasting System radio a few hours after Zacharias on the first program of "Your Marine Corps," warning that "the greatest of amphibious operations" was "in the making in the Pacific." Nothing he said, "short of surrender" could stop it. And a few days later General Jacob L. Devers, who had led troops in France and was now in Washington as commander of all army ground forces, boasted that the United States, if it wanted to, could land seven million men on Japanese shores in a coordinated "single blow." He did not mean, he hastened to add, that he should be taken "too literally," as that many wouldn't be needed. It was an absurd exaggeration, but all the talk was to increase the political pressure in Tokyo.

Just north of Kyoto that morning, at a resort site on the edge of

Lake Biwa, a meeting of chemists and physicists from universities in Nagoya, Tokyo, Osaka, and Kyoto convened with two admirals present, one from the Naval Technical Research Laboratory, the other a centrifuge expert, Shigeharu Nitta. The subject was a wishful-thinking program to fashion an atomic bomb, and one physicist explained uranium and critical mass. Another raised the possibility of converting more accessible thorium 232 into fissionable material, noting that there was a thorium factory in Nihama on Shikoku, and "couldn't we do anything with the thorium?" When bombarded by neutrons, it could become uranium 233. But the meeting ended with no prospects for a Bomb, while not far away B-29s were now dropping leaflets with a picture of the dreaded bomber on one side, announcing targets in advance and urging the inhabitants to flee. Few fled, and civilians in their spare time from war work continued training for the invasion with implements from spears to awls. No one, as Hisako Yoshikawa put it, "wanted to be blamed for quitting."

Never quitting were the *kaitens*, all volunteers (as *kamikaze* pilots no longer were); yet many were doomed to riding a misfired torpedo to oblivion. But on the twenty-first in Sixth Fleet waters, a *kaiten* from the *I-53* sank the transport *Marathon*. So few Japanese subs were now operating that American crews were becoming careless. Near the coastlines they were more alert for mines, blowing them up with deck machine guns. Toward dusk a few enemy torpedo planes ventured out and were driven off—a rare sight now in the Yellow Sea.

At Kirchhorst, Ernst Jünger's home, near Goslar in the upper Harz Mountains, the veteran writer and soldier, author of the famed Great War novel *Storm of Steel*, now an unpublishable man of letters because he had refused to submit a *Fragenbogen*, was keeping a philosophical diary instead, and set down his thoughts on the topic of the day, unconditional surrender. However cynical he had been about Naziism, Jünger as a captain returned to duty had been enjoying the good life in Germanized Paris at the time of Pearl Harbor. Trying to affect distance from the realities, he once described in his diary an air raid as seen through a glass of wine with strawberries floating in it. On a visit to the Russian front he had written about the numbness of an infantryman ordered to shoot a group of captured partisans: "The automatic habit of killing things brings about the same physiognomic devastation as an automatically practiced sexuality."

On June 7, 1942, he had confided to his journal that his false front had been pierced when he saw for the first time—he contended—the newly imposed yellow star worn by French Jews. The encounter had "cut deeply . . . and immediately I felt embarrassed to be in uniform." But Jünger hung on in Paris on the staff of General Karl-Heinz von Stülpnagel (who ran the occupation) until the Normandy invasion.* Even after Jünger's eldest son's anti-Führer remarks earned him a sentence to a "punishment battalion" and death in Italy, Jünger had trouble coming to terms with his inner contradictions about war, heroism, and death. But indoors after cultivating his garden on July 21 he noted in his diary, "Unconditional Surrender. It is the counterpart of total war: that the most strenuous conflicts are followed by complete subjection." More practically, he felt, citing Karl von Clausewitz, "absolute war" led to a political settlement. It was in a "conservative spirit" to come to terms with an adversary.

What Jünger did not realize was that European ways of war and peace, developed over generations, were alien to America. There the central war experience remained the Civil War of 1861–1865, where total annihilation of the enemy's capacity to wage war preceded unconditional surrender. Americans were unsophisticated.

On conclusion of the Joint Chiefs of Staff meeting at Potsdam, a message was cabled to MacArthur and to Nimitz regarding business that appeared nowhere in the minutes of the session. It was expected that the Soviet entry into the war against Japan would occur on August 15. Further, Japanese capitulation might occur even earlier, and detailed plans had to be drawn up for the occupation and control of the home islands. The first event was the inevitable outcome of decisions made at Yalta. The second was the inevitable consequence of Alamogordo. The hardware for the Bomb was en route to Tinian. Given the test results, one or two bombs might push the Japanese to surrender. If they didn't, "Olympic" was still on, and the Russians were coming.

Only a month before, that would have been welcome news to MacArthur. While Roosevelt at Yalta had been extracting Stalin's pledge to go to war against Japan once Germany was finished, MacArthur was having a rough time extricating Tomoyuki Yamashita's troops from the Philippines. It would not be easier on home soil. There was almost no one in command in the West who was not willing to yield whatever spoils in the Far East the Russians

*Stülpnagel was ordered to take his own life in 1944 after the Hitler bomb plot failed.

wanted to pit them against Japan to end the war, especially since what the Russians were offered could have been plucked anyway.

In Manila, MacArthur's press spokesman told correspondents off the record that the Soviets were "essential" to victory and that "we must not invade Japan proper unless the Russian army is previously committed to action"—that the United States had to "make every effort to get Russia into the Japanese war." MacArthur himself had even sent a radiogram to Marshall, read at the June 18 meeting in Washington, on plans to achieve a Japanese surrender, in which MacArthur urged, "The hazard and loss will be greatly lessened if an attack is launched from Siberia sufficiently ahead of our target date to commit the enemy to major combat. I most earnestly recommend no change in OLYMPIC. Additional subsidiary attacks will simply build up our final total casualties." Later, as a conservative politician with aspirations for the Republican nomination for the presidency, he would lie that his views on Russian participation were "never solicited" and that the Yalta bargain was "fantastic." Now, in mid-July, with a million and a half troops already staged in the Philippines for "Olympic," he was less sure that he needed or wanted the Russians in—they would even want to share in the occupation of Japan, which risked communizing Dai Nippon.

The JCS met at 12:15, forty minutes after Colonel Kyle had placed Groves's report in Stimson's hands. They knew the basic details from Stimson's earlier messages. The Secretary took the long message to Truman, returning to find an insistent cable from Washington:

> TOP SECRET
> URGENT
>     WAR 35987. SECRETARY OF WAR EYES ONLY TOPSEC FROM HARRISON.
>     ALL YOUR LOCAL MILITARY ADVISORS ENGAGED IN PREPARATION DEFINITELY FAVOR YOUR PET CITY AND WOULD LIKE TO FEEL FREE TO USE IT AS FIRST CHOICE IF THOSE ON THE RIDE SELECT IT OUT OF FOUR POSSIBLE SPOTS IN THE LIGHT OF LOCAL CONDITIONS AT THE TIME.

Exasperated that Groves and the Air Force generals still pressed for Kyoto as their target of choice, Stimson did not wait for what he knew would be Truman's assent to fire back an even more concise message:

TOP SECRET
URGENT
    VICTORY 189. REFERENCE WAR 35987 FROM STIMSON TO PASCO
FOR HARRISON'S EYES ONLY. MESSAGE BEGINS: AWARE OF NO FAC-
TORS TO CHANGE MY DECISION. ON THE CONTRARY NEW FACTORS
HERE TEND TO CONFIRM IT. END.

Almost immediately came another cable from Washington:

TOP SECRET
URGENT
    WAR-35988. SECRETARY OF WAR EYES ONLY TOP SECRET FROM
HARRISON.
    PATIENT PROGRESSING RAPIDLY AND WILL BE READY FOR FI-
NAL OPERATION FIRST GOOD BREAK IN AUGUST. COMPLICATED
PREPARATIONS FOR USE ARE PROCEEDING SO FAST WE SHOULD
KNOW NOT LATER THAN JULY 25 IF ANY CHANGE IN PLANS.

Groves, so Harrison would report in a later message, had requested permission to brief MacArthur about the imminent use of the new weapon "in operations against Japan, 5 to 10 August." No one was eager to give the General the information any sooner than necessary, as he would predictably insert his ego into the mission and claim it as his own. Communiqués were still emanating from his headquarters crediting almost no one but himself. One he had issued that very date resulted in a *New York Times* headline: MACARTHUR FLIERS HIT 30 SHIPS. STRIKE OFF COAST OF MALAYA. Little had changed since 1941–42.

Churchill was to be informed right away, and when Truman had finished reading the report, Stimson carried it to number 23 Ringstrasse. As the plenary session was coming up and Churchill had to be briefed on the frustrations of the foreign ministers' preliminary meeting, there was little time for him to do more than begin reading. Stimson retrieved the papers, promising to return with them early the next day.

The foreign ministers had begun meeting at noon to go over the Big Three agenda, primarily questions related to Poland, the puppet government of which Molotov papered over as one of "national unity." It would have some non-Communist members certain to be both outvoted and powerless. Churchill had hoped that the conference might end in time for agreements to be announced and his return flight to be made to London in triumph. It appeared, however, Cadogan wrote to London, that if they didn't complete their business by the next Wednesday, "Winston and Anthony will fly back on that day and be back here on Friday."

Truman prepared for the meeting with Stalin in the only useful way, given American inability to influence the outcome about Poland. With or without the tier of Poland that the Soviets had seized in 1939, and with or without the segment of Germany sliced off to replace it in the West, Poland was Russia's doorstep. Across that flat slab of land that had been squeezed into yet another political shape was spread the largest land army in history. A State Department functionary with a paper for the President to sign arrived that afternoon at number 2 Kaiserstrasse and was shown into a room dominated by a grand piano and overlooking the lake behind the house. Seated at the keyboard, Emilio Collado saw, was "an alert small man in shirt sleeves with a drink on the corner of the piano." At the piano, also minus their jackets, were Byrnes and Leahy, singing. "The President played . . . quite well, in a rather old-time ragtime manner, and they were having a fine time. They weren't drunk or anything like that. They each had a drink. I have often thought of that picture: the five-star admiral, the Secretary of State and the President, together on a Saturday afternoon, having a little music. . . . They had a little free time and there they were."

The fifth plenary session at the Cecilienhof began at five with discussion of the Polish regimes, exiled and Sovietized. "We do not intend to assume the liabilities of the old Polish government," said Truman, "and give the new Polish government the assets." Stalin conceded it, having his way otherwise on Poland. Truman objected also to "another occupying government" having been given a zone in Germany "without consultation with us." When Stalin observed that at Yalta it had been decided that Poland would receive territory "in the west and north in compensation" for having lost lands in the east to Russia, Truman noted that Poland's assumed new borders had been claimed before any peace settlement. Unless this area counted as part of Germany, how could problems such as reparations be settled?

"We are concerned about reparations," said Stalin confidently, "but we will take this risk." It was "not accurate," he claimed, that Russia had given the Poles a zone of occupation in "the disputed western frontier area." He had an ingenious explanation. "The German population fled, and the Poles remained. Our armies needed local administrations. Our armies are not set up to fight and clear the country of the enemy.* We so informed our British and American friends. The more ready we were to let the Polish administration function, the more we were sure the Poles would receive territory in the west. I do not see the harm of permitting the Poles to set up an administration in territories in which they are to remain."

Not a single German was left in lower East Prussia, Pomerania, and Silesia, Stalin insisted, cheerfully, and leaning over toward Truman, Admiral Leahy whispered, "Of course not, the Bolshies have killed all of them!"

George Kennan, perhaps the shrewdest of Cold War diplomats out of Washington, would excoriate, in his memoirs, the "casual American acquiescence" in the land grab, "all the less forgivable because of the fact that it served, like other territorial concessions to the Russians, simply to extract great productive areas from the economy of Europe and to permit the Russians, for reasons of their own military and political convenience, to deny these areas and their resources to the general purposes of European reconstruction." The former German provinces, he said, having flown low over them in an American plane, were "a totally ruined and deserted country" with perhaps one hundred thousand Germans left of a population that had worked the land well for centuries. But the West had no vital interest in the shattered and looted areas of Germany appropriated by the Red Army, and their cession had not been accepted casually. The facts were on the ground.

The Russians would always claim that their occupation was benign—that the Germans had got what was coming to them after brutalizing a million square miles of Russia. A case in point that day could have been the memorandum from the commander of Soviet occupation forces in Berlin, Major General Nikolai Aleksandrovich Antipenko, to Comrade Anastas Mikoyan of the State Defense Committee, reporting that all known corpses had now been removed from the countryside and that farm production was being restored.

---

*Benjamin Cohen's notes of the exchange read "enemy agents"—but that makes less sense in a fluid combat situation than my emendation.

Five thousand cows had been "handed over" to German farmers—"handed back" might have been more accurate. Over a hundred civilian hospitals had reopened, with 31,780 available beds. Fifteen waterworks in the Soviet zone were working again, and fifty-one sewage disposal plants. Children were receiving 65,000 liters of milk daily, an amount that looked larger than it was until measured against the population, and 2,800,000 ration books had been issued in June. Shops and restaurants in Berlin were beginning to reopen "very slowly"; two theaters, a concert hall, forty-five cabarets, and 127 cinemas had returned to activity.

No one including Stalin was in any private doubt that the Germans were driven out literally by the millions, creating facts on the ground that Soviet interests required. "I have a good deal to say on the line," Churchill remarked, meaning the border between a revised Poland and a truncated Germany, "but I don't think from what the President has said that this is the time." In return Stalin contended that it would be "difficult" to restore any territory to the Germans from which their population fled. Then, more honestly, he added, "It is natural [for us] under these circumstances to set up a sympathetic administration."

Churchill went back to the urgent problem of feeding Germans when their breadbasket had been denied them. "There is no one but the Poles," said Stalin, "who will plow the land."

Moving from reality to legality, Truman interjected that the question was one of formal responsibility for the land. "I want it understood that the Soviet [Union] is occupying this zone and is responsible for it."

Amicably, since it changed nothing, Stalin was ready to accept the hairsplitting. "On paper it is German territory but in fact it is Polish territory. There are no Germans left. The Soviet Union is responsible for the territory."

"Where are the nine million Germans?" Truman asked.

"They have fled."

"How can they be fed?" asked Churchill. He was sure that two or three million remained, and he would be correct—but those who managed to stay would have to do so as Poles.

"France," Truman interjected, "wants the Saar and the Ruhr. What will be left?"

"As regards the claims of France," said Stalin, brushing de

Gaulle's greed aside, "we have made no decision. As to the Poles, we have."

Realizing that they were meaningless words, Churchill hoped that the departed Germans would be encouraged to return. "Germany," Stalin dismissed, "has never done without the import of grain. Let Germany buy more bread from Poland." And after more futile protests on legal, economic, and humanitarian grounds by both Truman and Churchill, Stalin said, not without some truth, "The Silesian mines have always been worked by a large number of Polish miners."

That was all right, said Churchill, as long as they mined the coal for the Russian occupiers of the zone.

"It is not possible," said Stalin. "It would disturb all normal relations between the two states. . . . Undoubtedly the Polish proposal creates difficulty for Germany, but Germany created this situation." Cajoling a little, he added, "The less industry we leave in Germany, the more markets there will be for your goods. We have destroyed for you a competitor with low living standards and low prices."

To the surprise of the others, the usually silent Clement Attlee came to Churchill's defense, observing that if Germany were left in chaos, destroyed as an economic unit, it placed a severe burden "on the occupying states in the west and south." And Truman added that he could not consent "to the removal of eastern Germany from contributing to the economy of the whole of Germany."

"Are we through today?" asked Stalin.

"Can't we sleep on it?" asked Churchill, weary of the business.

It was nearly time for Stalin's grand dinner for the others, and he had cause for satisfaction. In the east he held all the high cards.

The meeting was adjourned until 5:00 P.M. the next day, Sunday.

To his daughter, Margaret, Truman described the elaborate dinner as "a dandy." (To his mother and sister it was "a wow.") "Started with caviar and vodka and mare's milk butter, then smoked herring, then white fish and vegetables, then venison and vegetables, then duck and chicken, and finally two desserts, ice cream and strawberries, and a wind-up of sliced watermelon. White wine, red wine, champagne and cognac in liberal quantities, and a toast every five minutes to somebody or something—to the United States and its great, magnifique Presidente, to me individually, to the U.S. Army, the U.S. Navy, the U.S. working people, and the same procedure to the British & the Russians, to Molotov, Byrnes, Eden, the American Ambassador, to Russia, the Russian Ambassador to the U.S.A., ditto to the British, and to the interpreters, and finally Joe and I had to go shake hands with and toast the musicians." He confided that he cheated on the drinks and ate less, but "it was one grand and glorious evening." Seated next to Stalin, he remembered later, "I noticed that he drank from a tiny glass that held about a thimbleful. He emptied it frequently and replenished it from a bottle he kept handy. I assumed that it was vodka, which everyone else was being served, and I began to wonder how Stalin could drink so much of that powerful beverage. Finally I asked him, and he looked at me and grinned. Then he leaned over to his interpreter and said, 'Tell the President it is French wine, because since my heart attack I can't drink the way I used to.' "*

"Stalin sent to Moscow," Truman noted in his letter to his mother and sister of the musicians he had toasted, "and brought his two best pianists and two female violinists. They were excellent." According to Gromyko, Stalin "kissed the violinist Galina Barinov and the pianist Emil Gilels, who played beautifully." Gilels would become a world-class performer, and Charles Bohlen described the "two heavyweight lady violinists" as having, in Admiral Leahy's description, "made up in musical ability what they lacked in looks."

For Churchill it was a very long evening. At one in the morning he walked over to Truman's place and asked the President when he was going to leave. Truman confessed that he was enjoying himself, and, resigned to remaining, Churchill retired into a corner with the equally bored Leahy, where, Truman told his diary, the Prime Minister "glowered, growled and grumbled" for another half hour. For the President, the evening had another pleasant outcome. He had found it futile to oppose Stalin where the Red Army made the facts, but, Truman also noted in his diary, Stalin "talked to me confidently at the dinner, and I believe things will be all right in most instances. Some things we won't and can't agree on, but I already have what I came for." Stalin had apparently reiterated what the Joint Chiefs already knew—that Russia was going to help defeat Japan. The President's obvious satisfaction, even after receiving Groves's report on the Bomb, contrasts dramatically with charges that he was rushing use of the Bomb to keep the Soviets out of the war.

"I had gone to bed," Lord Moran wrote in his own diary, "when a messenger knocked at the door: the P.M. would like to see me."

---

*Andrei Gromyko, Stalin's never-trustworthy but always shrewd ambassador and later foreign minister, wrote in a memoir toward the end of his life that Stalin "did not drink spirits, but he liked dry wine and always opened the bottle himself."

Thinking his services as a physician were needed, he pulled on a dressing gown and went downstairs. There he found Churchill with Eden, each with a whisky in hand, which had already helped to improve the evening. "I thought the Russians were silent and not very forthcoming," the P.M. said.

"Oh, it went well," observed Eden, "considering the row over Poland in the afternoon. Anyway, I'm sure they were making an effort to be agreeable. This has been the President's best day so far."

"I thought the evening interminable," Churchill growled. But he would have his own turn to officiate and demonstrate what he thought a state dinner ought to be.

Truman would get up at six the next morning, as usual, without any aftereffects from Stalin's vodka. But before retiring he went through whatever of the day's news from the United States had come through couriers, cables, and the wire services. The House of Representatives had taken only thirty seconds to act upon a peacetime industrial conversion bill that made up to $5.5 billion available in corporate tax relief. For the first time in its history, Tammany Hall, the Democratic city organization in New York, announced support of a Communist candidate, Benjamin J. Davis, a Negro, who was running for reelection to City Council from a Harlem district. He was, a spokesman explained, "an enrolled Democrat." Two Marine officers were put on view at a press conference in Washington as the first escapees from a Japanese POW camp who had served on Wake Island, overrun in the early days of the war. They had been at Woosung, near Shanghai, and spoke of brutality as an everyday affair in the camps—one of the urgent reasons, no one needed to explain, to end the war quickly. In New York, seven troopships, including the *Queen Elizabeth*, had docked the day before, returning 31,955 troops, some of whom would be going on after home leave to the Pacific. (Newspapers on the twenty-first published photos of the first troops from Europe—from the Fifth Army in Italy—docking in the Philippines. Soon they would be "MacArthur's men.") And Joseph P. Kennedy, appearing to relinquish his political aspirations, had purchased, for $26 million, the world's second most spacious building, the Chicago Merchandise Mart. It looked like the beginning of a peacetime business boom before there was peace.

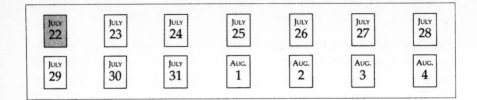

# CHAPTER X

# · JULY 22, 1945 ·

*". . . a piece of paper"*

Looking up from Groves's report at Stimson and Bundy, Churchill asked, exultantly, "Stimson, what was gunpowder? Trivial. What was electricity? Meaningless. This atomic bomb is the Second Coming in Wrath!" Now, he said, he could understand why Truman was so forceful in the Big Three meeting the day before: "He told the Russians just where they got on and off and generally bossed the meeting." Stalin's brazenness over Poland would have exasperated the President in any case, but the new card to play had stiffened his resolve. Acting supine in the face of accomplished facts had got them nowhere.

Now Churchill wondered aloud about how much information on the Bomb should be given the Russians—should it be used "as an argument in our favour" in the negotiations? The sentiment of the Americans was to offer the minimum for the present. It would make no difference as to Russia's going to war against Japan, for the Soviets would do what was in their interest. Bargaining positions would not change.

The P.M. was a late riser. Moran had seen him before breakfast to check on his indigestion after Stalin's banquet, but Churchill complained only that "this bloody election" was keeping his sleep restless. The estimates were all positive, said Moran helpfully, but did they have any substance?

"They are not guesses, Charles," insisted Churchill, "but the most careful estimates which come from each constituency—and you ought to know it doesn't help to tell me I can't attach any weight to these people's advice. Besides, they all agree I shall have a majority, Conservatives and Labour people alike."

Stimson and his assistant, Harvey Bundy, had gone to see Churchill at 10:40 after a postbreakfast meeting with Truman to confirm Bomb target priorities. Kyoto remained off the list, with Hiroshima, southern headquarters for home islands defense, put at the top of it. The likely dates for the first strike were the first days of August, and the decision to use the Bomb somewhere over Japan had already been made. Later, Truman would write to Air Force historian Curtis Cate that the day after the message about Alamogordo had reached him he had summoned his top military people, including Eisenhower, and asked them about the costs in lives of the planned landings in Japan, and on hearing the price he confirmed the use of the Bomb. No such meeting took place in Potsdam. All that had happened since the White House meetings in early July was that Japanese signal traffic picked up by "Magic" had confirmed earlier Japanese positions despite the increased pounding of the home islands. If either side had softened, it had been the United States, with Zacharias's official hints that what the Japanese called their "national polity" might be preserved even under unconditional surrender.

Rather than the formal meeting that Truman had misremembered, there was a smaller but significant one at number 2 Kaiserstrasse once the President had returned from the second of two Sunday services he had attended, the first a Protestant one in the Babelsberg area, the second a Mass conducted by his old friend of Battery D days in 1918, Father Curtis Tiernan, now Chief of Army Chaplains in Europe. After the Mass, at 11:30, Truman returned to talk with Churchill. The records are sparse, but it is possible that the P.M. had his science adviser, Lord Cherwell, with him, as he had earlier when Stimson had visited. With Truman were Marshall and Leahy. "I regarded the bomb as a military weapon and never had any doubt that it should be used," the President wrote in *Year of Decisions.*

"The top military advisers ... recommended its use, and when I talked to Churchill he unhesitatingly told me that he favored the use of the atomic bomb if it might aid to end the war."

In Potsdam, General Hap Arnold had been urging upon Stimson substantial flexibility for deployment of the Bomb by commanders in the field, in particular for Carl Spaatz, who was leaving his post as Arnold's deputy in Washington to take command of the Twentieth Air Force in the Pacific. A passion for secrecy had left even Colonel Tibbets, whose 509th Composite Group, a unit of the Twentieth Air Force, was to deliver the Bomb, without written orders even to do practice runs with their "pumpkin" facsimiles. It was left up to Spaatz, Arnold recalled, erroneously, "depending on weather, tactical situations, and any other factors that might influence his operations, which ones"—targets—"he should attack, that is, once it was determined that the atomic bomb was to be dropped at all." Spaatz's chief of staff, Curtis LeMay, already in Guam, knew of the Bomb from Tibbets and Groves. But, uneasy about responsibilities without instructions in hand, Spaatz asked General Thomas T. Handy, acting chief of staff while Marshall was in Germany, for written authorization. "Listen, Tom," he told Handy (according to Arnold), "if I'm going to kill 100,000 people, I'm not going to do it on verbal"—he meant "oral"—"orders. I want a piece of paper."

Handy conceded that the request was proper, but he had been waiting for word from Potsdam. "If a fellow thinks he might blow up the whole end of Japan, he ought to have a piece of paper." To get guidelines drafted, he suggested that Spaatz talk to Groves.

Arnold, meanwhile, had sent Colonel John Sloane back to Washington as courier with a piece of paper in hand recommending a fourth city to replace Kyoto. Nagasaki. Few major targets in the home islands were unscathed.

From Bern, the Japanese envoy, Kase, was employing his most persuasive strategies to get his side to stand down. The United States and Britain, he suggested in a cable intercepted by "Magic," would like to end the war quickly to prevent Russian participation, and it was also in Tokyo's interest. "Magic" had just decrypted his message of the twentieth to Togo, in which he had proposed surrendering "unconditionally" but with a "side reservation" that the Imperial Household be preserved. "It is meaningless," he argued, "to prove one's devotion by wrecking the state." Meanwhile the Navy was warning its attaché in Switzerland about his separate efforts to negotiate, that he should "take, at least outwardly, no further part in the matter."

The "side reservation" idea was gaining ground in the State Department even if Kase was getting nowhere with it in Tokyo. Assistant Secretary Archibald MacLeish, who had been involved in setting up the United Nations organization, broadcast from San Francisco something close to Kase's proposal. While nothing less than unconditional surrender would be acceptable, he declared, the Allies might be willing to indicate the measures that they would apply to postsurrender Japan. He was not suggesting, he pulled back, negotiations.

From Washington, Grew cabled a long message to Byrnes explaining Zacharias's—but not MacLeish's—broadcast to Japan in terms that suggested that the Japanese now had all the glosses on unconditional surrender they needed and that their freedom to retain the Emperor if they wanted him was equally clear. The implication was that the declaration for release at Potsdam needed to go no further in persuading Japan to quit.

Captain Zacharias began by reviewing points made in previous broadcasts. Japan, he stated, faced inevitable defeat. This situation resulted from bad leadership. Leaders continue to mislead people in stating that alternatives are victory or extermination. President Truman has made clear that this is not fact. Salvation of Japan lies in accepting unconditional surrender peace formula. The unconditional surrender formula is "humanitarian gesture of great constructive value." Broadcast then continues to state that time has arrived when Japanese leaders should face facts realistically and without shallow emotion. Surrender is a time honored formula provided for in Hague Convention. Moreover American policy is derived from Atlantic Charter and Cairo Declaration and "both begin with the categorical statement that we seek no territorial aggrandizement in our war against Japan." The leaders of the Japanese face two alternatives. "One is the virtual destruction of Japan followed by a dictated peace. The other is unconditional surrender with its attendant benefits as laid down by the Atlantic Charter." Japan's opportunity to think of these facts "is rapidly passing. As soon as our redeployment is complete, this opportunity will be lost to Japan: and as you know, it will be lost forever." Broadcast states that "at present there are still some influential people in the United States who would not like to see the destruction of Japan. But our patience, too, has its limits and it is rapidly running out."

[The] Zacharias speech was prominently featured with banner headlines in the entire metropolitan press: Washington Star—"U.S. Warns Japs to Surrender Immediately as Only Salvation; Enemy Looks for Easier Terms." Post—"U.S. Warns Japan to Quit Now, Escape Virtual Destruction." Baltimore Sun—"U.S. Again Calls for Japs' Unconditional Surrender." Herald Tribune—"Japan Told to Surrender Unconditionally or Face Inevitable Destruction: Official Broadcast Bids Enemy Leaders Yield Under Atlantic Charter." New York Times— "Japan Is Warned to Give Up Soon: U.S. Broadcast Says Speed Will Bring Peace Based on the Atlantic Charter."

OWI spokesman last night told the press that there was no significance in making this translation available; that it was just one of a series. Press speculating widely on this matter along lines that this broadcast made available for domestic use in order to tell U.S. public just what our terms of unconditional surrender are.

Particular importance is attached by U.S. press to statement in release that Captain Zacharias broadcast as "an official spokesman of the U.S. Government" and to the fact that the Atlantic Charter commits the signatory governments to permit peoples to select their own form of Government. This was interpreted as indicating formulation of American policy with reference to Emperor. Associated Press states that reports were circulating to effect that a statement clarifying Allied policy toward Japan would be issued within next few days by President and Churchill and possibly Stalin.

While the psychological pressure increased, military pressure continued to the extent weather permitted. In the north, strikes on the Kuriles had to be cancelled, but B-29s from Iwo Jima dropped mines in Korean waters to prevent reinforcement of the home islands from there. Minelaying from the air had become a sophisticated procedure, with the straits between the home islands mined and remined as the Japanese struggled to sweep them. Newly introduced pressure mines and others with counting and delayed arming devices frustrated the Japanese even after a series of aiming blunders dropped mines on land and exposed their mechanisms. At a POW camp furnishing labor for the port of Fukuoka a parachuted mine landed in the camp cookhouse rather than the harbor, and American prisoners were compelled to carry it to an open area and detonate it.

With Japanese imports of the oil for which, in part, they went to war now reduced to zero, the Air Force also stepped up its campaign to cut off synthetic fuel production. Seventy-two B-29s damaged the coal liquefaction plant at Ube, which supplied southern Japan. Other bombers from Pacific bases were hitting rail lines and docks, while planes from the Fourteenth Air Force in China and India continued the campaign to disrupt troop movements—almost all of them withdrawals—in China and Indochina. At sea, task forces were finding little to fire at but coastal shipping. Due to weather conditions, Admiral Ugaki claimed in his diary for the twenty-second, he called off a "general night attack against Okinawa" that may have been private bluster, and went to inspect Iwakawa Air Base, where *kamikazes* were being stockpiled for the expected invasion in the south. Concealment procedures satisfied him. Weeds almost covered the airstrip and planes were hidden under trees. There, Lieutenant Commander Tadashi Minobe suggested that night fighters be permitted to oppose American aircraft as "command of the air in the daytime" was impossible. Ugaki agreed and flew back to Kanoya. But he knew Japan had few night fighters.

Command of the air was impossible at any time, and no one understood that better than Jiro Horikoshi, the engineer who had designed the Zero and the planned *Reppu* fighter, which could only be built in underground factories remote from target areas. On July 22 he returned to the Mitsubishi plant in Matsumoto, west of Tokyo in central Honshu, to check on the progress of the dispersed workshops. The prospects seemed hopeless. Traveling across the island he had grown more depressed by each encounter with devastation and recalled a line from an ancient Chinese poem: "Mountains and rivers remain unchanged in this war-ruined land." The ruin he saw was more than debris from bombing and fire: it was inflation, corruption, exhaustion, hunger, desperation. At the factory in Matsumoto he added chaos to the list. The "unending confusion" because of damage to supply sources and communications, he noted in his diary on the twenty-second, "has become so great throughout the entire country that everybody realizes that the war cannot possibly be won. It is senseless to continue fighting, but the very momentum of our combat activities appears to carry us on."

In Japan as well as in the West, the press speculated about Potsdam but had little to feed upon. American and British briefings were not worth headlines, nor were the posed photos. Japan went unmentioned: the meetings were supposedly about the reconstruction of Europe. But redrawing the maps and the regimes was already raising hackles. Wherever there were substantial émigré Polish populations, outrage already existed about the inevitable jettisoning of the exile government in London.

A petition had been sent to the White House deploring a Soviet puppet state and urging free elections, release of non-Communists who had been jailed, the right of journalists to enter and report from Poland, and other matters, with the signatories including Republican stalwarts Herbert Hoover and Alfred Landon, labor union leader William Green, and prominent Catholic clerics. While Byrnes and Truman could do little about any of the objections, Acting Secretary Grew at home promised to try, at the least, to get American newspapermen into Poland.

Anthony Eden was in the chair for the foreign ministers' meeting at 11:10 A.M. The ministers argued at length over whether the Yalta declaration on liberated countries had been implemented, with each side suggesting bad faith on the part of the other. Then, as the afternoon grew hotter and more oppressive, a thunderstorm broke over Berlin while the Big Three were about to convene. High winds brought down trees; streets flooded. It was not a good augury for the sixth plenary session, which began at five.

In Malmö, a scrawny girl of twenty, Hedi Szmuk, and her sister Livi looked over the fence of the Swedish school where they had been shipped from Belsen to be cared for under medical quarantine, a ban loosely observed. A girl on the other side, Ingrid, invited Hedi home for hot chocolate. Their common language was a bit of English, which Hedi had learned in Sighet, then part of Hungary, before being put into her first concentration camp, Auschwitz. She had survived by luck and had kept her sanity by pretending that sleep was the reality and the terrible days a dream, remembering a little prayer by János Arany she had adapted into English:

*I thank Thee, God,*
*For night again.*
*One day less*
*Of earthly pain.*

Ingrid's mother was uneasy about the refugee girl's having left without permission ("One doesn't do such things in Sweden"), but her curiosity about what the sisters had been through overcame her disapproval.

"I am a Jew," Hedi began.

"But why did they send you to the concentration camp?" asked Ingrid's mother. "You must have done something."

"With mixed emotions," Hedi remembered forty-five years later, "I drank my chocolate and asked Ingrid to accompany me back to the school."

In the Cecilienhof in Potsdam, Stalin opened the sixth session with the announcement that Soviet troops in Vienna had begun withdrawing to their occupation zones. When Churchill and Truman expressed gratification, the Generalissimo shrugged that it had merely been an ally's duty. But the Russians had already dismantled as much as they could of Viennese industry, hauling it away to the east.

Poland came up quickly, and Truman, objecting again to a fourth occupying power unmentioned in the Yalta accords, drew the joint declaration from his papers and quoted the actual words:

> The three heads of Governments consider that the eastern frontier of Poland should follow the Curzon Line, with digressions from it in some regions of five to eight kilometres in favour of Poland. They recognise that Poland must receive substantial accessions of territory in the north and west. They feel that the opinion of the new Polish Provisional Government of National Unity should be sought in due course on the extent of these accessions, and that the final delimitation of the western frontier of Poland should thereafter await the Peace Conference.

There was nothing in Yalta, he said, to give Poland any legal rights to the land prior to a peace treaty. Both Churchill and Truman understood that they could change nothing, but Truman was groping for some Russian acknowledgment of indebtedness that might pay off elsewhere. Weary of the deadlock, Churchill tried to paper over differences by suggesting that Poles west of a "provisional line . . . would be working for the Soviet occupying authority" until a final peace settlement. "We should not despair of solutions. We should seek a half-way house."

The halfway solution proved to be an invitation to the Poles to explain their position—which was Stalin's—to a meeting of the foreign ministers.

Next came the issue of Italy's colonies, some of which Churchill suggested might be returned to Italy. "I have seen the excellent reclamation work done by the Italians in Libya and Cyrenaica," he observed. "At present we hold these colonies. Who wants them?"

"We do not want them," said Truman. "We do not want a trusteeship for them. We have enough poor Italians [in Italy] to feed. . . ."

"We considered them for Jewish settlement," Churchill added, "but the Jews are not attracted to them. Of course we have a great interest in them."

So, it turned out, did the Russians. The Soviet delegation at the San Francisco UN conference, Stalin noted, had declared in writing that "we were anxious to receive mandates for certain territories."

The last thing Churchill and Truman wanted, so Stalin knew, was a Soviet presence in the Mediterranean or in Africa at all. The fear itself gave Stalin bargaining opportunities elsewhere, and he was willing to have the matter held over for a Council of Foreign Ministers meeting in September. The issue of mandates was a delicate one for the West. Why weren't the Russians entitled to UN mandates wherever they might be? Harriman, Bundy, McCloy, and Stimson would discuss the "expanding demands" of the Soviets. "They are throwing aside all their previous restraint as to being only a Continental power," Stimson wrote in his diary the next day. Earlier the Russians had claimed no interest in further acquisitions—before San Francisco, he meant. Now they were seeking "to branch [out] in all directions. Thus they have not only been vigorously seeking to extend their influence in Poland, Austria, Rumania and Bulgaria, but they are seeking bases in Turkey and now are putting in demands for the Italian colonies. . . ." Harriman reported that Stalin was urging "an immediate trusteeship" for Russians in Korea, since Japan would be forced to relinquish its colony. "The British and French," he told the others, "are refusing to consider a trusteeship for Hong Kong and Indo-China, and I foresee that if that is continued the Russians will probably drop their proposal for trusteeship of Korea and ask for solitary control of it." That they were not bluffing would be seen when their surrogates attempted to communize all of Korea five years later.

Soviet claims on Turkey came next. Why, Stalin asked, should Russia, with a large shoreline on the Black Sea, have no more rights regarding the Dardanelles than the Emperor of Japan? Churchill and Truman were sympathetic, but claimed that until further study it was premature to "push" Turkey.

Among other issues raised by Stalin was the status of Ukrainians in a POW camp in Italy. They had fought with the Germans. The British, he said, had reported 150 POWs, but Russian representatives had visited and found 10,000. Only 665 of them had stated their willingness to return. He did not need to say that he wanted every one of them back.

"Perhaps," said Churchill, "some of these persons were Poles." He would order an investigation and report the results.

Returning to the Poles, Churchill noted that inviting them would be breaking the principle they had followed in Potsdam. "It is agreeable to me one way or the other," said Stalin, recognizing that he won the border issue more easily without the formal, plenary appearance of a Polish supplicant.

"We will drop it," said Truman. And so they adjourned.

Driving back, Sir Alexander Cadogan's British-beflagged car was halfway out of the Cecilienhof's park when he was stopped by Russian sentries. "From the road in the left," Cadogan wrote in his diary for the day, "emerged a platoon of Russian tommy-gunners in skirmishing order, then a number of guards and units of the NKVD. Finally appeared Uncle Joe on foot, with his usual thugs surrounding him, followed by another screen of skirmishers. The enormous officer who always sits behind Uncle at meetings was apparently in charge of operations, and was running about, directing tommy-gunners to cover all the alleys in the Park giving access to the main road. All this because Uncle wanted 5 minutes exercise and fresh air, and walked out to pick up his car 500 yards from the Palace!"

After a late and quiet dinner, Churchill sent for his economic expert, Sir Walter Monckton, the British delegate to the Reparations Commission, to solicit his views, which the P.M. then repeated over his nightcap whiskies to Charles Moran. Thirty-seven meetings of British and American representatives with their Russian counterparts in Moscow on economic issues, largely on German reparations, preparatory to Potsdam had yielded no agreements. Yet while the Western allies were finding no basis for sweeping Soviet claims, the Red Army was busy dismantling German industry wherever it controlled captured territory. Since the Soviet zone, but for a few major—but devastated—cities, was largely agricultural, and the area seized by Poland held the coal mines, the only reason left for the Russians to want to keep Germany as a single economic unit was to have access to more industrial machinery to haul east on flatcars and trucks. Stalin had left little reason for the West to keep to the Yalta formulas.

To Moran, hardly an economist, Churchill expostulated, "The idea of a single economic unit has vanished. Instead we have Russian Germany divided by British Germany by a line drawn by God knows whom, on no economic or historic grounds. . . . The Russians have stripped their zone and want a rake-off from the American and British zones as well. They will grind their zone; there will be unimaginable cruelties. It is indefensible, except on one ground: that there is no alternative."

Then, dipping deep into metaphor, as religion meant little to him, Churchill added, "I prayed the Americans on my knees not to hand over to the Russians such a great chunk of Germany, at least until after the Conference. It would have been a bargaining counter. But they would not listen. The President dug in. I shall ask Stalin, does he want the whole world?" It was a dramatic but inaccurate picture of the exchanges at the Cecilienhof. And as for the proposed question to Stalin, the P.M. knew the answer without asking.

In Paris, C. L. Sulzberger of *The New York Times* paid a call upon Yugoslav opposition leader Vladimir Maček, the Croatian Peasant Party spokesman who had fled Zagreb with his family on May 6. He was living in a boardinghouse and hoping for a British visa. Tito's intention, he told Sulzberger, was to establish "a complete Communist dictatorship." Then he went on with an image that struck the reporter: "I probably would have been arrested by the Partisans had I not left in a hurry. During the four years while I was interned by the Germans in Croatia I saw how the Partisans were lowering an iron curtain over Yugoslavia so that nobody could know what went on behind it." Sulzberger had never heard the term before but it represented to him vividly the reality with which the West now had to co-exist. He put it into his dispatch published the next morning.

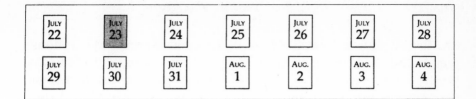

CHAPTER XI

# · JULY 23, 1945 ·

## *the momentum of "Olympic"*

The Joint Chiefs of Staff meeting at 9:30 A.M. in Potsdam recorded minutes beginning only with paragraph 4, an unimportant matter allocating responsibility for the southern half of Indochina to Mountbatten. More significant business about military alternatives for ending the war with Japan was omitted. The Russians were coming in. Another closing option also seemed to have a momentum of its own: the Bomb. Some planners wanted to use it because it now existed; others thought that it might make "Olympic"—even the Russians—unnecessary. But "Olympic" itself seemed to have a momentum difficult to arrest. Further surveys were being made about availability of LSM and LCI landing craft, and whether a crash program would be needed to get more into service. Long lists were being readied as to when, through August 15, each class of craft would be staged through Pearl Harbor. Yet a hitch had developed in supplying one piece of ordnance. Illuminating mortar shells being developed for the operation would not be available until December—too late. Minesweeping vessels needed for the assault stage but not already in the Pacific were to be at the Panama Canal by September 1. (The Allies were also bringing up minesweepers from as far off as Tel Aviv, where a shipyard employing refugee engineers was turning out all-wood vessels with pine hulls and eucalyptus interior trim.)

In Hawaii itself troops were in serious training for "Olympic." A private in his final exercise for an amphibious landing before shipping out to "Oki" remembered: "With 60 pound packs on our backs and a carbine we climbed down cargo nets from an 80 foot high wooden pier into bouncing Landing Craft Infantry—LCIs. When they were loaded with 80 people we left to circle with other boats. We became sick and nervous." The swells off Oahu were high, huge waves rushing in with a great roar. "At a signal," Martin Berkowitz went on, "the boats ran up to the beach, dropped their bow ramps and we all rushed out to a designated railroad track. We were to flop down and hold until other troops ran past us to forward positions. It was a fierce hot day and I almost lost my breakfast."

When he landed on Okinawa he saw disabled "tanks and landing craft rusting on the beach" and knew what was in store for his unit if the pounding of Japan didn't work. The next morning, waiting to board a truck to move his company up, he remembered: "I saw a guy I knew from the neighborhood. I asked where he was going. He asked me, 'Where have you been these last few years? *I'm* going home.' He was being rotated home after three years in a tank unit."

When the Combined Chiefs of Staff—British and American—met at 11:30, General Arnold leaned over to Air Marshal Portal, offering to bet him that the Army Air Force would end the war "nearer Christmas 1945 than Valentine's Day 1946." The agenda was largely lift capacity for "Olympic," the allocation of ships, including captured German troop transports, and whether any could make more than one round-trip before December 31, 1945. Arnold thought the calculations were unnecessary.

From the Marianas, the jumping-off area for the bombing of Japan, a flak officer for the 73rd Bombardment Wing reported a potential problem to Washington. Over Hitachi the night before, a tail gunner on a B-29 at 12,800 feet saw a barrage balloon about a thousand feet below. Common in Europe, they were rare over Japan. The gunner "had flown in the ETO, and had seen barrage balloons over there. He said that he could see the shroud lines on this one, that it was egg-shaped, and that it was about 25 feet in diameter. He could see it so plainly because the balloon was silhouetted in the fires underneath. This is the highest we have ever had a barrage balloon reported."

Few balloon sightings would follow, but "the altitude of attack," the report closed, "has been raised for these night burn jobs."

Whatever impact the "burn jobs" were having, the Air Force would press on with them although surveys of Germany had already shown that they had contributed little to unconditional surrender. The Germans had successfully camouflaged factories or put them underground, where they functioned until feeder rail lines were bombed, disrupting supply in and out. The Japanese, too, had their underground and concealed factories, especially for aircraft manufacture, but one of the later Air Force justifications for incinerating housing near war plants was not only that crucial workers would be disabled or dispossessed but that the industrious Japanese, to exploit home-bound labor, especially housewives, were redistributing machinery into residential areas. Unpretentious houses huddled close in narrow streets might hide, Air Force General John B. Montgomery later claimed, "a drill press or milling machine in the kitchen."

Cut off from external supplies of petroleum and heavily dependent upon coal liquefaction, Japan also required, to keep industry going, Hokkaido coal and synthetic oil plants on Kyushu and Honshu. Daylight aerial photographs had shown that the few interceptors going up after American heavy bombers were sometimes pushed to runways by teams of crewmen to save precious fuel. In the cities, the few buses still running used clumsy, inefficient charcoal burners. The evidences of shortages, and likely hoarding for *Ketsu-Go*, were everywhere.

While boats of every description were pressed into service as colliers on the Hokkaido run, and interdicted when they were visible—more and more ferrying was done by night—by sea and from the air, the 315th Bomb Wing was targeting the factories themselves. Early on the morning of the twenty-third it was flying its ninth coal liquefaction plant mission. Eighty-two B-29s had lifted off from Guam at nightfall, eight of them turning back frustratingly because of mechanical problems. Major Chuck Sweeney of the 509th puzzled Central Communications Research further by leading three B-29s over the rail marshaling yards at Kobe and dropping only one very large orange bomb that was no more powerful than ordinary bombs.

A complex on Kyushu housing a carbonization plant, hydrogenation plant, gas-generating plant, power plant, refinery, and storage area absorbed 636.8 tons of five-hundred-pound bombs, but thirteen reconnaissance photos showed only scattered damage to the target, built on low reclaimed land at the shoreline. Tinderbox housing, crowded yet spread over wide areas, flamed more easily, but industry and infrastructure were harder to hit the higher one flew.

Bombardment by sea was no more accurate, and was limited to accessible coastal areas that shells could reach from safe distances out. But the Navy and Air Force pressed their service loyalties on Washington. Submarine blockade and the mining from the air of inland waters seemed to have more disruptive effect on the home islands than the more visible and dramatic assaults, but no massive military bureaucracies backed them. Although it had taken eighty days and massive cost to occupy a sixty-mile-long island, Okinawa, there was no guarantee that with Russia in the war to distract the Japanese, it would be easier to effect landings on a bigger and better defended island, Kyushu, but the Army saw it as the way to win.

Everything could be tried, as the greatest industrial and technological mobilization in the history of war had produced nearly everything. It was all there, and nothing needed to be left to chance. One could not predict, either, the political motives of enemies—or allies. The Russians might enter the war in their own way, only to sweep up Manchuria, Korea, and the Kuriles and make their separate peace. There was no assurance that the only atomic weapon in the delivery process, "Little Boy," the lone uranium bomb in the arsenal, would work at all: it had never been tested; there wasn't enough material to waste. And much of the immediate supply of plutonium had been used in the Alamogordo experiment, which had not been an air drop. The schedule called for an air-delivered device to be ready and at Tinian by August 1.

Byrnes and Molotov met at 10:30 to come to some agreement about Russian reparations from Germany. Each occupying power, Byrnes suggested, might take all the reparations it wanted from its own zone, for 50 percent of the existing wealth of Germany was in the Soviet area (if one included the gift of territory to Poland). That would foreclose for the moment treating Germany as an economic unit, but each occupier could exchange goods or materials with another. That would not do for Stalin, who wanted to upgrade stodgy Russian industrial technology by modernizing with German machinery, and he would get, on paper at least, some of what he wanted. The U.S.S.R., the final protocol would read, "shall receive additionally from the Western Zones . . . 15 per cent of . . . usable and complete industrial capital equipment. . . ." But it would prove far easier to extract the words than to collect the spoils. The economic and political agreements—and disagreements—foreshadowed four decades of two Germanies.

Byrnes then met with Churchill, informing him that he had cabled T. V. Soong, second in authority to Chiang Kaishek, "not to give way on any point to the Russians," so the P.M. remembered, "but to return to Moscow and keep on negotiating pending further developments." Churchill minuted to Eden after seeing the Secretary of State, "It is quite clear that the United States do[es] not at the present time desire Russian participation in the war against Japan." Since Truman had privately revealed his pleasure and relief at imminent Russian entry into the war, the foxy Byrnes was speaking—more likely intimating—his own mind. If Chiang rejected Soviet prerequisites for intervention that would leave Manchuria a Russian zone under a token Chinese flag, Stalin might hold the Red Army back long enough for the Bomb to end the war without Russian intervention. Had Byrnes's strategy been to short-circuit the Sovietizing of East Asia by preventing an Oriental Potsdam, he was underestimating Stalin's variety of means.

At eleven, Secretary Stimson met with Truman, each to brief the other. "I am finding myself," Stimson wrote in his diary, "crippled by not knowing what happens in the meetings in the late afternoon and evening." Although the plenary sessions were more diplomatic than military in substance, and limited to very small working groups, he had been left out—and resented it, especially, he added, *"now that the program for S-1 is tying in with what we are doing in all fields."* Would the Russians come in before the Bomb fell? Would a clear warning to the Japanese be issued before the S-1 strike?

Truman told him that a draft ultimatum to Japan was in hand, with no date inserted. He wanted the warning in Churchill's as well as his own name, which meant getting it out before the P.M. returned to London for the election results. In preparation for that, Stimson said, he had cabled his deputy in Washington, Harrison, who conferred regularly with Groves,

WE ARE GREATLY PLEASED WITH APPARENT IMPROVEMENT IN TIMING OF PATIENT'S PROGRESS. <u>WE ASSUME OPERATION MAY BE ANY TIME AFTER THE FIRST OF AUGUST.</u> WHENEVER IT IS POSSIBLE TO

GIVE US A MORE DEFINITE DATE PLEASE ADVISE US HERE WHERE IN-
FORMATION IS GREATLY NEEDED.

If the Bomb were to be delivered at the first opportunity, the Allied
ultimatum had to precede it by a sufficient number of days to allow
for a Japanese surrender. Yet the atomic strike now had wider implications, for it had to happen before the Russians could seize more
Japanese spoils than they were entitled to in the Yalta accords. Since
his most recent discussions with Stimson, Byrnes, and Churchill, the
President seemed far less pleased about Soviet intervention, which
had been intended to reduce the cost of the "Olympic" landings.

Apparently the P.M. told his physician everything—doctors see
people at their most intimate and vulnerable moments—and that
morning had gone on about the Bomb and the Russians:

> "I am going to tell you something you must not tell to
> any human being. We have split the atom. The report of the
> great experiment has just come in. A bomb was let off in
> some wild spot in New Mexico. It was only a thirteen-
> pound bomb, but it made a crater half a mile across. People
> ten miles away lay with their feet towards the bomb; when
> it went off they rolled over and tried to look at the sky. But
> even with the darkest glasses it was impossible. It was
> the middle of the night, but it was as if seven suns had lit the
> earth; two hundred miles away the light could be seen. The
> bomb sent up smoke into the stratosphere."
>
> "It is H. G. Wells stuff," I put in.
>
> "Exactly," the P.M. agreed. "It is the Second Coming.
> The secret has been wrested from nature. The Americans
> spent £400 million on it. They built two cities. Not a soul
> knew what they were working at. . . . I have been very wor-
> ried. We put the Americans on the bomb. We fired them by
> suggesting that it could be used in this war. We have an
> agreement with them. It gives the Americans the power to
> mould the world. It may displace fuel; a fragment gives 800
> horse-power. If the Russians had got it, it would have been
> the end of civilization. Dropped on London, it would re-
> move the City. It is to be used in Japan, on cities, not on
> armies. We thought it would be indecent to use it in Japan

without telling the Russians, so they are to be told today. It has just come in time to save the world."

To save the world from Stalinism, Churchill meant. And while Truman and Byrnes apparently saw no way to rescue what had already become Soviet satellite states, they were looking for opportunities to apply the lessons of Europe to Asia. The continents, however, had different histories, and the Japanese had contributed the most recent chapter by encouraging, although with rays from the Rising Sun attached, independence movements in the Netherlands Indies, Indochina, and Burma. Chandra Bose's now-splintering Indian National Army, drawn from Indian Army POWs in Malaya and Burma, had also established new facts and states of mind. Whatever Chiang's aspirations, China was fractured by a civil war in which the other side had Russian assistance and popular support, both certain to burgeon if Russia drove the Japanese from the mainland. East Asia was already entering a postcolonial phase that the defeat of Japan would only accelerate and that the European colonial powers could slow down, at their own risk, but could not stop. Perhaps, though, Japan, the most advanced of Asian nations, could be saved from Communist revolution or occupation at the price of the obliteration of a city or two.

Such was the bleak vision offered to Truman that morning by Stimson, and repeated after lunch to Marshall and Arnold, and then to McCloy and Bundy. Byrnes had called Stimson at ten to ask "about the timing of the S-1 program," and had been told about the exchange of cables with Washington. To avoid talking on a possibly bugged phone—the Russians had renovated the house—the Secretary walked to the "Little White House" only to find Byrnes out. But Truman confided that he had the draft warning to the Japanese on his desk and was waiting only for a delivery schedule for the first bomb to "shoot it out." General Groves would call Truman privately "a little boy on a toboggan," as if a combat drop were inevitable, but until the bomb bay doors opened on a plane carrying an atomic bomb, it was in Tokyo's power to arrest the inevitable. Even to keep Russia out of the war.

Truman was "very anxious to know," Stimson told his colleague,

whether Marshall felt that we needed the Russians in the war or whether we could get along without them, and that was one of the subjects we talked over. Of course Marshall could not answer directly or explicitly. We had desired the Russians to come into the war originally for the sake of holding up ... the Japanese Manchurian Army. That now was being accomplished as the Russians have amassed their forces on that border, Marshall said, and were poised, and the Japanese were moving up positions in their Army. But he pointed out that even if we went ahead in the war without the Russians, and compelled the Japanese to surrender to our terms, that would not prevent the Russians from marching into Manchuria anyhow and striking, thus permitting them to get virtually what they wanted. . . . Marshall felt as I felt sure he would that now with our new weapon we would not need the assistance of the Russians to conquer Japan. . . .

In Washington, Groves arranged a morning meeting with Spaatz to go over a draft for Handy's signature (in Marshall's stead) over the orders to drop the Bomb.

To GENERAL CARL SPAATZ, CG, USASTAF:
1. The 509 Composite Group, 20th Air Force, will deliver its first special bomb as soon as weather will permit visual bombing after about 3 August 1945, on one of the targets: Hiroshima, Kokura, Niigata and Nagasaki. To carry military and civilian scientific personnel from the War Department to observe and record the effects of the explosion of the bomb, additional aircraft will accompany the airplane carrying the bomb. The observing planes will stay several miles distant from the point of impact of the bomb.
2. Additional bombs will be delivered on the above targets as soon as made ready by the project staff. Further instructions will be issued concerning targets other than those listed above.
3. Dissemination of any and all information concerning the use of the weapon against Japan is reserved to the Secretary of War and the President of the United States. No communiqués on the subject or releases of information will be issued by Commanders in the field without specific prior

authority. Any news stories will be sent to the War Department for special clearance.

4. The foregoing directive is issued to you by direction and with the approval of the Secretary of War and of the Chief of Staff, USA. It is desired that you personally deliver one copy of this directive to General MacArthur and one copy to Admiral Nimitz for their information.

T. T. Handy

The instructions were not for delivering a single bomb, but for dropping *bombs*, as soon as each became available, on specified targets. Only Washington could add or substitute targets. "Little Boy," the first and only uranium device, was en route and ready for assembly. An Alamogordo-type plutonium bomb would be delivered to Tinian, in parts, on or about August 6. Another "Fat Man" would be ready by August 24, with the time between deliveries then narrowing. Confirmation came later in the day from Harrison:

OPERATION MAY BE POSSIBLE ANY TIME FROM AUGUST 1 DEPENDING ON STATE OF PREPARATION OF PATIENT AND CONDITION OF ATMOSPHERE. FROM POINT OF VIEW OF PATIENT ONLY, SOME CHANCE AUGUST 1 TO 3, GOOD CHANCE AUGUST 4 TO 5 AND BARRING UNEXPECTED RELAPSE ALMOST CERTAIN BEFORE AUGUST 10.

The foreign ministers met at 11:30, with Molotov in the chair. The Combined Anglo-American chiefs of staff had met at the same time to work out allocations of captured shipping. Again reparations dominated the meeting, as Molotov had his instructions from Stalin, but in no way could he persuasively define matériel in other zones as war booty. Backed by Eden, Byrnes insisted that no matter how German exports and imports were defined, the United States would not permit itself to be left, however indirectly, with payments of reparations to Russia. Molotov then turned to the Italian colonies, proposing that they be placed under the joint trusteeship of the Big Three, rather than left, as they were, in the custody of the British Army. Again he was put off, the issue set aside for the eventual peace treaty with Italy. They turned to uniformity of directives to zonal commanders, and conceded that France should be involved. The Tangier question came up once more, and it was agreed that the territory should remain internationalized, with a meeting in Paris to work out details. The agenda proposed for the plenary session was Turkey, the Königsberg sector of East Prussia, Syria and Lebanon, and Persia.

With the military meetings over, Sir Alan Brooke noted in his diary, "We went round to lunch with the P.M. He had seen the American reports of results of the new Tube Alloys secret explosive which had just been carried out in the States." ("Tube Alloys" had been the British code name for the Manhattan Engineering District.) Brooke remained skeptical. Churchill "had absorbed all the minor American exaggerations and, as a result, was completely carried away. It was now no longer necessary for the Russians to come into the Japanese war; the new explosive alone was sufficient to settle the matter. Furthermore, we now had something in our hands which would redress the balance with the Russians. The explosive and the power to use it would completely alter the diplomatic equilibrium which was adrift since the defeat of Germany." The P.M., "pushing out his chin and scowling," suggested that the West could now say, "If you insist on doing this or that, well . . ."

An army man, Brooke understood that facts on the ground were created by large numbers of armed men. "I tried to crush this overoptimism, based on the result of one experiment," he wrote, "and was asked with contempt what reason I had for minimizing the results of these discoveries. I was trying to dispel his dreams and as usual he did not like it."

Stalin may have had little nostalgia for Czarist Russia, which, as a revolutionary fugitive using an alias he had since adopted as his name, he had helped undermine. Yet one of his goals had been to restore to Russia the territories lost to Japan under the Czars and to reabsorb the new states erected from Russia's eastern tier after 1917. Undoing the embarrassments of 1904 now seemed certain, and in the West he had lifted former Czarist provinces from Romania, Czechoslovakia, and Poland, seized portions of Finland, and reversed the independence of the Baltic states, to which he intended to annex a piece of East Prussia, German for nearly a millennium. At the seventh plenary meeting in the Cecilienhof he noted another territorial dish on his menu—"rectification" of Russia's borders with neutral Turkey.

Truman had gone to Potsdam with the hope that the appalling losses suffered by Russia—more than all other casualties by all sides combined, soldier and civilian—would cause Stalin to place his highest priorities on peaceably rebuilding the nation. Repairing the economy, reeducating the survivors, manufacturing consumer goods, restoring productive land, and making decent homes available would give citizens what they fought for. But Stalin seemed ready to restore the economy only by robbing the defeated. Otherwise, his interests focused upon aggrandizement. The West had accepted what Stalin had taken by force, but perhaps S-1 was stiffening Churchill and Truman. "Before I finished talking yesterday," Churchill began, "I made it clear that we could not support Russia's claim against Turkey for a military base in the Black Sea."

"Yesterday," answered Stalin through his interpreter, "Mr. Churchill asserted [that] Russia had frightened Turkey, particularly by concentrating troops in Bulgaria. Mr. Churchill's information is out of date. Russia has very few troops in Bulgaria, but the British have more in Greece."

Some argument followed about comparative troop strength in the region. "The Turks have nothing to be afraid of," Stalin continued. "The Turks have 23 divisions on the frontier. As to rectification of the frontier, I refer to the two provinces, Kars, formerly in Armenia, and Ardahan, formerly in Georgia." If Turkey agreed to a Soviet presence at the mouth of the Black Sea, he suggested, he would drop the claims. "Small states controlled by Britain," he charged, "have real control of the Straits. Turkey is not capable of keeping control of the Straits. The Straits must be defended by force, the same as the [Panama] Canal is defended by the American navy, the same as the British navy defends the Suez."

Piously, both Truman and Churchill agreed that the treaty affecting free navigation in and out of the Black Sea needed revision, but on the realities Stalin got nowhere, and they turned to the Königsberg area of East Prussia. "This was brought up at Yalta," Stalin said. "We stated that it was necessary to have at least one ice-free port [in the Baltic] at the expense of Germany. Neither the President nor the Prime Minister raised any objection." The ice-free claims for Königsberg were an excuse to acquire new territory and to prevent another exacerbating corridor between the two parts of Germany, as occurred after Versailles in 1919. (Poland would acquire the southern portion of East Prussia.) Then Stalin added frankly, "Too much blood has been spilled by the Soviet Union not to have some piece of German territory."

Neither Truman nor Churchill noted that there were ice-free

ports in the Russianized Baltic states, but they did have an objection to the draft language. The Soviet version, said Churchill, required Britain and the United States "to admit that East Prussia did not exist and . . . would commit us to the recognition of the incorporation of Lithuania into the Soviet Union." (The area was just south of Lithuania.) Stalin was happy to paper over the problem for the final protocol:

> The Conference examined a proposal by the Soviet Government to the effect that pending the final determination of territorial questions at the peace settlement, the section of the western frontier of the Union of Soviet Socialist Republics which is adjacent to the Baltic Sea should pass from a point on the eastern shore of the Bay of Danzig to the east, north of Braunsberg-Goldap, to the meeting point of the frontiers of Lithuania, the Polish Republic and East Prussia.
>
> The Conference has agreed in principle to the proposal of the Soviet Government concerning the ultimate transfer to the Soviet Union of the City of Königsberg and the area adjacent to it as described above subject to expert examination of the actual frontier.

A fortress town founded by the Teutonic Knights in 1255, Königsberg had once been the seat of the dukes of Prussia. With its inhabitants fled, dead, or expelled, the city and adjacent territory half the size of Belgium would become the Russian *oblast* of Kaliningrad, renamed for the ceremonial Soviet president. Lithuania would be unidentified in the Potsdam protocol as Russian property, and remained a part of the Soviet Union until the U.S.S.R. itself imploded.

There was even less disagreement among the Big Three about the independence of Syria and Lebanon. However hostile their populations, Charles de Gaulle was attempting to salvage both former colonies. If France secured any special privileges in either country, the leaders agreed, these would have to be freely offered by free governments. They turned to neighboring Iran, in which all three powers still had troops. Stalin agreed to get out in proper time. "The treaty says six months after all hostilities with Germany and her associates. That implies Japan."

The last agenda matter was Austria. Both Truman and Churchill declared that they would need Russian help to feed the 875,000 Viennese in their zones because of food shortages in Italy. "It would be a good thing," Stalin suggested for the provisional regime the Red Army had set up in Austria, "if the American and British governments would allow the Renner* government to extend its authority to their zones. This would not imply recognition. This will facilitate the distribution of food."

With the parties in agreement, the unusually businesslike session came to a close. Because of the General Election, Churchill added as they rose, "We must leave Wednesday [the twenty-fourth] at lunch-time, and will be back in the evening of the 26th; so we would suggest a morning session Wednesday, and we will be back for the Friday session." "Or," he amended, "some of us will be back." And they adjourned to await Churchill's state dinner later in the evening.

To the west in Luxembourg, Colonel Andrus recorded further reductions in Hermann Göring's paracodeine dosage. "He looks very good, is losing much weight [and], has apparently no other ill effects— except that he would like to get larger doses." He was trying to take charge of the Nazi contingent, and was busy advising Joachim von Ribbentrop how to file his long grievance about unfair treatment. "Dönitz," Göring complained to an American interviewer the same day, "just took command on the basis of a radio message that was never confirmed in writing."

The loss of seventeen pounds and the disappearance of his drug stupor had also returned Göring's proverbial jollity. When a Russian commission of law officers arrived he first shouted, "The Russians are coming!" and then disappeared into his cell, refusing to talk to them. But the next day he agreed to see them, and, a jailer remembered, "I couldn't distinguish what he was saying, but it was interrupted repeatedly by chuckles from the Russians. Soon Göring's voice rose, and the chuckles swelled to roars of laughter. For two hours the noise of guffaws echoed down the halls, and then the Russians came out slapping each other on the back."

Seeing the Americans afterward, he hitched up trousers that had become baggy with weight loss and complimented himself: "I really had those Russkies rolling in the aisles, didn't I?"

At number 23 Ringstrasse, Babelsberg, a banquet was in preparation on a scale that Göring would have appreciated. Although

---

*Karl Renner at seventy-five had been named by the Soviets in April as the chancellor of a reborn Austria although he had supported Hitler's *Anschluss* of 1938. A survivor, he had also been chancellor of the first Austrian republic in November 1918 after the fall of the monarchy.

Churchill expected to win the General Election and remain P.M., he oversaw the arrangements for *his* state dinner to Stalin and Truman as if it were his swan song. The military constructed a table seating twenty-eight, which meant cancelling invitations to Leathers, Monckton, and Cherwell, but salvaging a place for Moran, who was seated next to Admiral King—no friend of Britain, according to the loquacious physician: "His war is in the Pacific, and the conflict with Germany has been to him a irksome distraction." King, in fact, had to be ordered by Roosevelt to accept the Royal Navy in the Pacific, and could not have been pleased that its ships weathered *kamikazes* better than his own. Task Force 57,* all British, included five fast carriers with armored flight and hangar decks. They took hits that would have disabled American flattops for the duration.

Churchill had made it a point to include at his table the military commanders as well as the regulars at the plenary sessions. The dishes were as numerous as the speeches and toasts. The P.M. placed Truman to his right and Stalin to the left. The RAF band played—loudly. "Half an hour before the appointed hour," Moran wrote, "fifteen of the OGPU marched through the gate in single file, carrying their tommy-guns as if they were about to use them. They vanished to take up positions behind the house. And then came the three national leaders with their captains who had survived the miscalculations of six years of world war."

As it was his dinner, Churchill had the opportunity of the first toast, and drank to the President as head of state, but as the exchanges grew more numerous, he rose again and proposed a toast to the President "as a man." He had not met Mr. Truman before the conference, he confessed, but he was certain that everyone had been as impressed as he was by the firm, decisive, and businesslike tone Truman had brought to the proceedings. His sincerity and frankness reflected the best qualities of the great republic he represented so ably. He knew, Churchill said, that he also spoke for Stalin when he raised his glass "to a man who was sincere in purpose, clear in speech, and true in deed."

He was naturally a timid man, Truman said in response, and when he was made presiding officer he had been "literally overwhelmed." He would continue to do his utmost for the success of the conference, and he wished to say that it was a great pleasure and

*The numbering depended on which American admiral was in overall command.

privilege for him, "a country boy from Missouri," to be associated with such great figures as his two colleagues.

Stalin's own turn came and he praised Truman's modesty as a source of strength and an indication of character, coupled as it was with "honesty of purpose." He was glad, Stalin concluded, to welcome President Truman into their midst. "Watch the President," King told Moran. "This is all new to him, but he can take it. He is a more typical American than Roosevelt, and he will do a good job, not only for the United States, but for the world."

Warmed by wine and the genial atmosphere—and perhaps by the fact that he had already gotten his way on most matters—Stalin continued on, "without even assuring," Churchill recalled, "that all the waiters and orderlies had left the room," proposing "that our next meeting be in Tokyo." It would not be right, Stalin went on, to allow America and Britain to shed their blood in putting down Japanese aggression without help from their brothers in the Soviet Union. Russian involvement seemed only weeks away.

Stalin "spoke with enthusiasm," Churchill would write, "about the Russian intervention ... and seemed to expect a good many months of war, which Russia would wage on an ever-increasing scale, governed only by [limitations of] the Trans-Siberian railway."

To lighten the proceedings, the P.M., moving about in a light blue summer Air Force uniform, arranged to have his guests change places from time to time, and on one occasion Stalin walked among the guests getting his menu signed and listening to the RAF band. "Could they play something light?" he asked. Churchill had long watched the exchanges of toasts by the Russians out of tiny glasses, but as Stalin returned to his seat he found Churchill waiting for him with two claret glasses filled with brandy. They examined each other's faces, then lifted their glasses and drained them. After a pause, Stalin said, referring to the discussions about Turkey, "If you find it impossible to give us a fortified position in the Marmara, could we not have a base at Dedéagatch?"*

"I will always support Russia," said Churchill, "in her claim to the freedom of the seas all the year round."

*Dividing European from Asian Turkey, the Sea of Marmara lies between the Bosporus and the Dardanelles. Once Turkish, Alexandroúpolis (Stalin used its old name, Dedéagatch) was a Greek port in eastern Thrace near the border with European Turkey. Harsh and continual pressure on Turkey would lead in 1947 to the "Truman Doctrine" of supporting such nations threatened by the Soviets. Demands on Turkey ended with Stalin's death in 1953.

The toasts continued, and Truman proposed the healths of the British and Russian generals, Brooke and Antonov. Brooke took the response, and reminded Stalin of his toast at Yalta to "those men who are always wanted in war and forgotten in peace." And rising yet again in closing the evening, and mindful of the General Election, the P.M. raised a final glass to "the Leader of the Opposition, whoever he may be!" Everyone looked in the direction of Mr. Attlee, whose presence had hardly been noticed.

When everyone had left, Churchill went to a telephone and put through a call to Lord Beaverbrook in London. Did he still think the Conservatives would win? He had predicted, earlier, a hundred-seat majority. The estimate was not sacrosanct, said Max Beaverbrook, but he still saw a "comfortable" majority. Churchill invited him to lunch at Downing Street on Thursday the twenty-sixth, to watch the first results come in.

Bumped from the dinner for lack of seating, Sir Alexander Cadogan spent some time bringing his diary up to date. He would be taking Eden's place at the Council of Foreign Ministers, as Eden was returning with Churchill. "Winston says he will be back on Friday. That, of course, depends on the election. If he has a comfortable majority over all the parties, I have no doubt he will be back. If the Conservatives are the largest party, but with no clear majority over the others, I don't know what he'll do. I suppose he would come back with Attlee. If Labour get a clear majority, I don't know what will happen. . . . But I doubt if [Churchill] could come back here. . . . Well, all this uncertainty is a great bore."

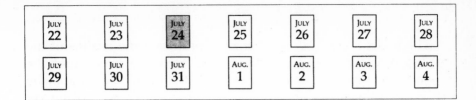

| July 22 | July 23 | July 24 | July 25 | July 26 | July 27 | July 28 |
| July 29 | July 30 | July 31 | Aug. 1 | Aug. 2 | Aug. 3 | Aug. 4 |

## CHAPTER XII

# · JULY 24, 1945 ·

### *". . . a new bomb far more destructive"*

As the weather improved around the home islands, the Japanese were punished hard by air and by sea. By air from the Marianas and offshore carriers there were 1,363 combat sorties alone over the Kure-Kobe-Osaka area region, with 32 planes and twenty crewmen lost. Through the twenty-eighth over 133 aircraft would go down, with over one hundred air crew. To be downed alive was a harrowing experience, as it was known that the Japanese were brutal, even sadistic, captors. Picket ships, submarines, and float planes stood by to pick up survivors at sea. "This grew into a large effort," Commander Bill Leonard, then aboard a fast carrier in TF 38, remembered. "Each submarine operated at periscope depth but was protected during daylight by a fighter plane. Similarly, rescue stations for float and sea planes to pick up victims were fighter patrolled and opposition fought off as necessary. . . . Submarines developed rescue swimmers and equipment and were truly dedicated friends. They were not asked to enter mined or confined waters, but they sometimes went to heroic extremes."

"Evergreen" was the code word for a downed airman who had deployed his dye marker to show his position and attract rescuers. "Unfortunately," Leonard wrote, "this could attract unwanted attention and was a gamble." The "lingering, greenish tint" had to be manually deployed to indicate that the airman was "vital, survivable, and worth the old college try." Sometimes the try was more hazardous than the original mission, as when pilots after the derelict *Nagato* found, too late, that the *Nagato* crew had removed the AA guns from the ship and emplaced them in the hills overlooking Yokosuka, coordinated into a radar system. Aircraft and airmen losses were painful, especially so when incurred over a battleship hulk that had nowhere to go.

In some ways the war above and around Japan was a technologically updated war of attrition, a 1945 version of the trench warfare of 1918. The United States now had a seemingly endless supply of ships and planes, and so many trained men that it was releasing thousands daily, returned from the Pacific or the ETO, into civilian employment. Farm production was burgeoning, and cutbacks were already being made in war industry as the two-front war resolved into a single front. The Japanese were starved of resources. Civilian life was stark and urban homelessness was increasing with every fire raid, while the armed forces were increasingly dependent upon hastily trained men and obsolete weapons. Some of the best equipment lay rusting on abandoned islands. Seasoned troops sat restlessly and uselessly in conquered territories now cut off from the home islands. Combatwise pilots and seamen were largely dead, used up in the good years of expansion and the bad years of fighting withdrawal. Yet another example was an air encounter over the Bungo Strait on the twenty-fourth. *Bungo suido,* between Kyushu and Shikoku, led into the inland sea that ran up the southeastern coast of Honshu. Even that had become unsafe for coastal shipping, and Captain Minoru Genda, who commanded Naval Air Group 343 at Kanoya, appealed for experienced fliers.

Genda himself had been one of the planners of the Pearl Harbor attack, and but for untimely appendicitis, which kept him on his carrier, he would have led a flight. To defend the strait, Genda was offered Lieutenant Takashi Oshibuchi and Kaneyoshi Muto, who had fought in China, the Indies, and the Philippines and was credited with twenty-eight downed enemy aircraft. Over the *suido* the Japanese claimed, exaggeratedly, sixteen enemy kills to four losses of their own. Two were their veterans.

Admiral Halsey had sent his Third Fleet close to southern Japan to have his planes concentrated on coastal shipping and, at Kure, on what remained of the Japanese navy. Claims were high—twenty-two warships damaged, including a battleship and two cruisers, and more than fifty small merchant ships. Also, in sweeps of airfields, 74 planes destroyed and 135 damaged.

Admiral Ugaki's planes suffered the most. In that and a follow-up raid on the twenty-ninth the battleships *Haruna, Ise,* and *Hyuga,* as well as the heavy cruisers *Tone and Aoba,* were badly hit. Several settled on the bottom of Kure harbor. Other ships were damaged, but the symbolic effect was even greater. The *Tone* had been one of the lead ships in *Kido Butai,* the Pearl Harbor strike force. And the *Haruna* had been the battleship erroneously reported sunk off the Philippines by B-17 pilot Colin Kelly, posthumously made a hero when the United States badly needed one in the first days of the war.

Later that evening, Ugaki wrote, "the full moon hung in the middle sky," and he placed "great expectations" on finding Halsey's force, but the *Saiun* reconnaissance plane that located the Americans was having trouble with its radio transmitter and the report never reached the mainland until the pilot landed. Three planes from the carrier *Yorktown* had been shot down, two of them over the Bungo Strait, and another collided, at fourteen thousand feet, with a plane from the *Shangri-La.* In war the other side's losses were always high and often included overlapping or unverifiable claims. One's own losses were always lower than the truth, for a variety of reasons, valid and invalid. One did not want to give the enemy any idea of its efficiency—or inefficiency. Downed fliers might still be rescued. Also, one seldom tallied—for the public at home, at any rate—planes lost to mechanical or operational failures. Newspapers, however, played up the official statistics in large type, and any cumulative score would suggest that each side had sunk or damaged more ships and downed or damaged more planes than existed.

Nothing else more personally brought home—literally—to the population of Japan the defensive plight of the nation than the People's Volunteer Corps. On June 13 the moribund Imperial Rule Assistance Associations, neighborhood patriotic organizations, had been officially dissolved so that their members could join what the Tokyo police referred to as "the final people's movement." Civilian men under sixty-five and women under forty-five were qualified for what were described as volunteer fighting corps, but in practice the army would not let them use precious rifles and ammunition and at first they were put to work clearing air raid debris or digging shelters. Following the expected landings, the government intended them to be home front *kamikazes*, prepared to die using makeshift weapons.

One example of "makeshift" was that scabbards for bayonets were made of bamboo. Yet there were so few rifles for overage army recruits—draftees over forty—that there was only one bayonet for every ten soldiers, and seventy rounds of ammunition for every rifle. For new draftees, rifles were unnecessary as the "special attack" strategy for infantrymen was to train with a thirty-five-pound weight—earth or rocks—strapped to the back and practice digging a foxhole. Once the enemy landed, the recruit was able to hide in his foxhole with a few days' supply of food. By then the weight would be a bomb the army intended to rush into production. When the soldier saw an enemy tank approaching he was to leave his foxhole, run toward the tank or other armored vehicle, release the safety device, which operated like a large grenade, and hurl the bomb. The time between release and detonation was three seconds, which left little chance to perform the operation again another day. But men accepted the *kamikaze* drill stoically.

At thirty-two, with a husband in the Army in China, a brother in the Air Force, and another brother in the Navy "special attack" *kaiten* unit, Toki Tanaka worked in the hills near Inami gathering and bundling thatch, which she hauled on her back. She was also a reservist. "We practiced with bamboo spears on the schoolground under the blazing sun," she remembered. "Some fainted because of the heat. Men made the spears for us and hung up dolls made of straw, shaped like men. We wrapped our heads with *hachimaki* and wore the sash of the National Defense Women's Association across our chest. We did our best. If you opposed anything about war, of course, you were a traitor. You had to say, 'Yes, yes,' whatever the subject. But when I thought of my husband's hardship at the front, doing that much seemed natural."

Many "volunteers" trained in predawn darkness before going to work, often a long walk in the absence of buses and private cars. At 3:00 A.M. members of the *Kokumin Giyūtai* would assemble for worship at local shrines, then drill with bamboo staves. A skeptical recruit, Isoko Hatano, wrote about her unit on July 24: "The enemy will attack with bombs and guns; it is absurd to meet them with such weapons." Shuhei Hayama, later an author but then a seventeen-year-old student drafted into a munitions plant, wrote in his diary that workers "were severely punished because we uttered among ourselves such seditious and unpatriotic statements as 'There is no longer any hope for Japan now that Okinawa has fallen' and 'How are we to fight the battle for the homeland with bamboo spears?' Along with five of our roommates, we were taken to a nearby meadow and made to sit down. Then we were pummeled until far into the night. This was for the good of the country."

Drill, prayer, and punishment were recognizably insufficient preparation to repel an invasion. Civilian "volunteers"—often before or after a long day's work—were set to constructing pillboxes, barbed wire, and tank traps along the shoreline. A student corps was organized to root out pine stumps from trees already cut down for lumber. The pine resin was to be turned into aviation fuel, as was the alcohol from fermented sweet potatoes, once only a staple food ration. A drillmaster told his student group, "Two hundred pine stumps will keep one airplane flying for an hour."

The People's Volunteer Corps had already caused Colonel Harry F. Cunningham, intelligence officer of the Fifth Air Force in China, to declare in his report on July 21, "The entire population of Japan is [now] a proper Military Target. . . . THERE ARE NO CIVILIANS IN JAPAN. We are making War and making it in the all-out fashion which saves American lives, shortens the agony which War is, and seeks to bring about an enduring Peace. We intend to seek out the enemy wherever he or she is, in the greatest possible numbers, in the shortest possible time." Perhaps the key word in his manifesto was *she*. It suggested the total resistance many expected when the final pushes came.

In remote Shimane prefecture in southern Hokkaido, high school girls trained with carpenter's awls to guard their honor, "like samurai without shame," against the Americans. Yikiko Kasai was warned by her teacher, "When they do [assault], we must be ready to settle the war by drawing on our Japanese spirit and killing them. Even killing just one American soldier will do. You must prepare to use the awls for self-defense. You must aim at the enemy's abdomen. Understand? The abdomen! If you don't kill at least one American soldier, you don't deserve to die!" The honor lay not in living, but in dying.

Trainees in the army-sponsored programs kept prudent silence

about practicing to die for nothing. One did not question the inevitable. On Luzon there were thousands in the north of the island
still fighting while living off the land, and equally isolated on some
of the other five thousand Philippine islands were other holdouts.
(In Shōhei Ōka's graphic 1957 novel, *Fire on the Plain,* hungry Japanese soldiers on the run in Leyte even resort to cannibalism rather
than capitulation.)* A report for the week covering outlying islands
would also list four killed on Iwo Jima and nine surprisingly taken
prisoner, five dead on Saipan and two POWs, fifteen killed on Guam
and three prisoners, and two killed on Tinian. Few Japanese surrendered unless they were too wounded or ill for suicide. A few would
hold out for decades.

Anchoring at 4:30 A.M. in Buckner Bay, Okinawa (renamed to
memorialize the general), Seaman Fahey on the *Montpelier* saw in
the early dawn what looked like "any peaceful countryside in the
States," but while the crew took on fuel and supplies they could hear
"spasmodic gunfire." There were still thousands of Japanese holed
up on the far side of the island. With radar detecting unidentified
planes, possibly *kamikazes,* toward evening, ships in the bay signaled
General Quarters, and all of them with fog screen machines set them
going. Small fog-laying craft added a blanket of white smoke. "It
would put the thick London fog to shame," Fahey noted in his diary.

No enemy aircraft appeared overhead, but below the surface the
Japanese scored a rare success off Okinawa. *I-53* and *I-58* had sortied
out together and via a tip from a reconnaissance plane located a small
convoy in the Philippine Sea en route from Okinawa to Leyte. Leading the way for a "reefer"—a refrigerator ship—and several LSTs was
the destroyer *Underhill.* Spotting a floating mine, it attempted to sink
it by gunfire. It was 2:15 P.M. That was all the *I-53* needed to home in,
and at 2:51 the convoy reported sound contact. Two minutes later
*Underhill* dropped depth charges, but then its skipper, Lieutenant
Commander R. W. Newcomb, reported that he had sighted torpedoes and was about to ram either the sub or a *kaiten.* At 3:07 the *Underhill* blew up, the entire bow of the ship up to the forward fireroom
separating from the stern. The fore section, with the skipper, 9 other
officers, and 102 men, sank within seconds. The after section floated

*In "The Last Supper," a short story by Shusaku Endo collected in his *The Final Martyrs* (1994), a
corporate executive who has become an alcoholic confesses to a psychiatrist the source of the
torment he blots out with drink: as a starving soldier in the war he ate a dead comrade's flesh.

for four hours, and more *kaitens* were sighted and fired on as the PC-803 was ferrying a surgeon to an LST picking up the 116 survivors.

It was a rare loss. Few enemy subs were still known to be operating so far from home except as supply vessels to ferry rations to isolated stations unreachable now by surface craft. It raised no special alarms in the commands that should have been concerned.

While Spaatz flew west toward his new Pacific command, messages about delivery of the Bomb went back and forth between Stimson and Groves. On the twenty-fourth Groves sent a two-page memorandum to which he attached, in case there were no maps at Potsdam, a small map of Japan scissored from the *National Geographic*. With it were one-page descriptions of the four targets—the three reserved cities and Nagasaki, which had never been excluded from bombings. It was understood that, barring a Japanese surrender, the first device would be dropped on or about August 3, the date depending upon the fickle weather over Japan.

At 9:30 that morning, when the day was nearly over in the Pacific, Stimson walked to the "Little White House," where he found Truman alone with his work. The President had just finished a brief courtesy meeting with Admiral Mountbatten, whom he congratulated on his successes in Burma. Truman was at his desk drafting a letter to Churchill on a subject he cared more about than had his predecessor. One British government after another had reneged on the 1917 "Balfour Declaration" promising a homeland for oppressed Jews in what was then Turkish Palestine. Up until mid-1941, when American consulates in Germany were closed, it might have been possible to assist persecuted Jews in Hitlerian Europe to emigrate. Most countries, including the United States, had refused help, or admission, to refugees. Roosevelt's administration blamed restrictive immigration legislation, widespread joblessness, concern over admission of subversives, or other excuses—anything but the actual reason, indifference. Worse than indifferent were career State Department officials, some openly anti-Semitic. During the German war itself, opportunities to interdict the death camp rail and power networks and make mass exterminations, already known, difficult if not impossible, were ruled out by the War Department on false grounds. Stimson's deputy, John J. McCloy, had argued in 1944, when it was still possible to save hundreds of thousands from the Holocaust, that targeting Auschwitz would require "diversion of considerable air support essential to the success of our forces."

Truman was not then in the decision process; the shame and dishonor were not his. But he wanted something done now, and wanted to plant the idea with Churchill before he left for London:

MEMORANDUM

Subject: Palestine

There is great interest in America in the Palestine Problem. The drastic restrictions imposed on Jewish immigration by the British White Paper of May, 1939, continue to provoke passionate protest from Americans most interested in Palestine and in the Jewish problem. They fervently urge the lifting of these restrictions which deny to Jews, who have been so cruelly uprooted by ruthless Nazi persecutions, entrance into the land which represents for so many of them their only hope of survival.

Knowing your deep and sympathetic interest in Jewish settlement in Palestine, I venture to express to you the hope that the British government may find it possible without delay to take steps to lift the restrictions of the White Paper on Jewish immigration into Palestine.

While I realize the difficulties of reaching a definite and satisfactory settlement of the Palestine problem, and that we cannot expect to discuss these difficulties at any length at our present meeting, I have some doubt whether these difficulties will be lessened by prolonged delay. I hope, therefore, that you can arrange at your early convenience to let me have your ideas on the settlement of the Palestine problem, so that we can at a later but not too distant date discuss the problem in concrete terms.*

Once Truman put aside his correspondence, Stimson told him "of my conference with Marshall, and the implication that could be inferred as to his feeling that the Russians were not needed to subdue Japan." (Stimson's diary makes no reference to the fact both he and Marshall conceded that the issue had been beyond debate since Yalta.) "I also told the President of the question which Marshall had suggested might be put to Stalin as to the Americans going home,

*In May 1948, despite the strong disapproval of his own State Department, Truman would instantly recognize the new State of Israel, established in the face of British opposition and the invading armies of Arab nations.

and he said that he would do that this afternoon at the end of the hearing, but he told me that there had been a meeting called by Leahy of the Ministry Staffs to meet either this afternoon or I think tomorrow morning. . . ."

The "hearing" and much else is unclear. No threat had been made by the American delegation. The Poles, whom Truman and Churchill did not want to hear out as their territorial gains were beyond agreement, were coming after all to talk to them. "I'm sick of the bloody Poles," Churchill told Moran that morning before Admiral Leahy arrived. "I don't want to see them. Why can't Anthony talk to them? If I have to see them I shall tell them there is no support in western Europe for a puppet Polish state, the tool of Russia."

It had been Eden's job to see the Polish group—also that of Byrnes. At 11:15 they convened with Molotov to listen to President Boleslav Beirut and his delegation, most of them Communists in fact or name. It was a long session, lengthened by translations into both Russian and English. Poland, Beirut claimed, would lose more territory in the east than it would gain in the west, but no one questioned the history of the relinquished eastern lands, seized by the Poles during the weakest moments of the new Russian revolutionary government from both Lithuania and Russia. Much of it at the time was ethnically non-Polish. Poland had ceded territory to the Soviets for the sake of peace, Foreign Minister Rzymowski declared: it was right that Germany should also lose land for peace. As for the purely German Baltic harbor of Stettin, it had been an outlet for the produce of Silesia. Most of Silesia would be in Polish hands—why not its principal port?

Further ministerial business involved Allied recognition of other eastern European governments, at which Eden and Byrnes balked. Eden told Molotov bluntly that Romania and Bulgaria were run by "minority governments mainly composed of Communists." Adding Hungary to that list, Byrnes observed that the United States "did not regard them as governments having broad representation of all democratic parties." Molotov asked that the matter be referred to the leaders: "The Big Three are more reasonable people than we and will find a way out."

While the foreign ministers argued, the Combined Chiefs of Staff conferred at British headquarters with Truman and Churchill to review a final draft of war plans and objectives. Marshall had already asked the British chiefs their views on dividing Indochina into two operations segments, the northern part—above 15 degrees—to be left in the China Theater and the southern in Mountbatten's Southeast Asia Command. For the British, Admiral Cunningham pointed out that the assignment of forces would depend upon operations from Burma into Thailand, and Admiral King ventured that any boundary would be arbitrary and could be altered to suit requirements. When the Chiefs met again on the twenty-fourth with Mountbatten present, Marshall raised the matter again and asked whether Mountbatten would accept two French divisions—of white men, he added—for service in Indochina, which he now proposed dividing at 16 degrees north. The French, said Mountbatten, thinking that the division might harden into something difficult to readjust, might be dissatisfied, but he was favorably disposed. The sixteenth parallel ran almost through Da Nang, not much below the future political division of North Vietnam and South Vietnam.

A more difficult matter for Marshall was a British proposal that would commit the United States to "maintain the security and war-making capacity of the Western Hemisphere and the British Commonwealth as necessary for the fulfillment of the strategic concept." The Americans wanted the draft limited to the prosecution of the war against Japan, and while the British claimed the language dealt largely with the occupation of Germany it seemed obvious that maintenance of the Empire was the covert objective. Ultimately they agreed to "bring about at the earliest possible date the defeat of Japan" by air, land, and sea, including "invading and seizing objectives in the Japanese home islands." The invasion "and operations directly connected therewith" would have "supreme" priority, and would remain "in the hands of the United States Chiefs of Staff." Further, "Russian entry into the war against Japan should be encouraged. Such aid to her war-making capacity as might be necessary should be provided."

After a break for lunch, the first and only joint meeting of the three chiefs of staff took place. General A. I. Antonov, the Red Army chief of staff, and his deputy, Lieutenant General N. V. Slavin, were accompanied by Admiral N. G. Kuznetsov and Air Marshal F. Y. Falaleyev. Leahy presided, and opened bluntly by asking about Russian plans against the Japanese. Antonov confirmed that his troops were being deployed in the Far East and would be ready to begin operations "in the last half of August." Although the Soviets were stalling on a firm date in order to coerce Chiang's Chinese into political concessions, Stalin was actually eager to strike as soon as possible, concerned that if the Japanese surrendered before Russia was in the war, the Yalta concessions made as the price of his intervention would be invalid. He had even telephoned his Far East General Army on the sixteenth to ask whether the invasion could be moved up ten days, but was told that the buildup required more time. Operational plans were for thrusts into Manchuria and its Liaotung Peninsula, which stretched out into the Yellow Sea just above the northern boundary of Korea. At its tip was Port Arthur, a Czarist stronghold until the embarrassments of 1904. After the defeat of Japan, Antonov contended, Russia would withdraw its troops from Manchuria. By his language separating the peninsula from the rest of Manchuria he left the implication that Russia might try to keep it militarily if not politically—one of the points of dispute with the Chinese government. Since the only reinforcements the Japanese could secure would be from the China interior, he went on, he expected Allied interdiction of such routes.

Antonov asked Marshall about Japanese manpower. Marshall estimated a million troops in China, noting that some had been withdrawn from Manchuria and Korea to the homeland, especially to Kyushu, for the expected American invasion. But the ferry service from Korea to Japan had now been "terminated" by air strikes and submarine patrols. Minelaying operations all along the western coast of Japan had reduced convoy traffic from China and Indochina to "none whatever at the present time." Most troop movements in China itself, Marshall conceded, were toward Manchuria, except for about 150,000 men establishing a "fortress garrison" around Canton and Hong Kong. Other troops were gathering about Hankow and Shanghai. The Japanese were readying last stands.

Redeployment of American troops for the invasion, he continued, was "well under way." The principal difficulty other than to secure enough shipping to ferry them all was to "find ground room for troops and aircraft we wish to deploy." Six divisions withdrawn from Germany were in the United States awaiting transportation, and the divisions already in the Pacific were "now being reconditioned and trained for the next operation."

Admiral King described the preparations for "the next move against the Japanese homeland." He overestimated the enemy navy available as a third of its former strength, and saw its value as largely "for suicide purposes." General Arnold offered to follow up Marshall as well, explaining that B-29s from new airfields on Okinawa could now support Russian ground operations to the north of Port Arthur and Harbin. When more strips were completed he would be able to fly as many as 3,500 planes out of Okinawa alone. Underestimating Japanese strength, he thought there were not enough suicide pilots being trained for all the planes remaining in the homeland—that about 1,500 aircraft might be expected to be used that way, against ground targets, shipping, and even planes.

When Antonov expressed concern about Japanese ability to reinforce its Manchurian garrison, Marshall said that there was no chance of movement from Japan, while "it would be a slow process" to bring troops northward in China. Antonov asked whether the United States would open a sea route through the Kuriles in order to open a line of communications to Siberia, and whether the United States might attempt an amphibious landing in Korea. King offered to open a communications route, but preferred to avoid engaging the island chain itself. As for Korea, Marshall observed that all assault shipping was being reserved for Japan itself and that Korea was so deep in Japanese waters that the risk of suicide attacks on shipping was too great.

The review of the East Asian situation continued at length, from Japan to Singapore and Burma, before the Chiefs adjourned. He would want another meeting, said Antonov—just with Marshall.

While the Soviet military talked war, the Suzuki government remained blind to the clearest signal yet that Russian neutrality was near its end. On July 24, female employees of the Soviet embassy in Tokyo, and diplomatic wives and children, sailed for home from Sakata, a port on the Sea of Japan across northern Honshu from Sendai. To the government it was only to secure safety for Russian women and children from American air raids, yet these had been intense since March 9. No one wanted to consider alternative reasons.

Before the military planners adjourned, a luncheon meeting of the foreign ministers had begun, with Eden excusing himself early. A great many formalities were being talked of, Byrnes said, for ratification or disposition at a general peace conference attended by "fifty-odd nations." He saw nothing useful in it—only "endless discussions and no satisfactory results." Churchill and Eden thought differently, Byrnes conceded, but they could be persuaded otherwise. Molotov agreed about the undesirability of a broad peace conference; and without Eden they concluded their business early.

Byrnes's staff (with Truman present) was meeting at number 2 Kaiserstrasse with the Polish delegation. It was a brief session. Truman hadn't wanted to see them at all. He wanted justice for Poland, he told them, but not in the arbitrary manner in which the boundary question had been arranged with the Soviets. The title to the absorbed land might not be valid. Boleslav Beirut said he understood, but there were homeless Poles who had to be resettled. Apparently Byrnes had been speaking for himself with Molotov, for Truman's parting words to the Poles were that their western frontier would have to be formalized at a peace conference.

The eighth plenary session began at five with some of the principals at earlier meetings returned to the large table in the Cecilienhof, including Field Marshal Alexander and Fleet Admiral Leahy. First business was the admission of Italy and the east European states into the United Nations. Every mention of Italy was an opportunity for Stalin or Molotov to point to Italy's odious past as an Axis partner. Truman saw the odious present of the eastern satellites as a more immediate blot. Their governments had not been reorganized along democratic lines, as had been agreed upon at Yalta. He wished to assure the President, said Stalin, that "the Governments in these countries are more democratic than in Italy, and that they are closer to the people than the Italian government." The argument then turned upon deleting for all countries the American language "responsible and democratic governments," as, Stalin argued, "it served to discredit these countries."

It was important, said Truman, to support for admission those nations that had "democratic governments."

They were not "Fascist" governments, Stalin objected; the United States had argued in San Francisco for the admission of pro-Nazi Argentina, which was. "If a government is not Fascist, a government is democratic."

"Our mission in Bucharest," said Churchill, "has been practically confined." An "iron fence"—which he meant literally as well as metaphorically—had come down around them in Romania, he charged. "I am sure the Marshal would be astonished to read the long list of incidents which have occurred."

"They are all fairy tales."

"Statesmen may call one another's statements fairy tales, if they wish."

"Our missions," Truman broke in, "have encountered great difficulties in the satellite states."

Whether each of their nations recognized any other nation, said Stalin, ignoring the charged word *satellite*, had nothing to do with preparing, at the least, a peace accord for the country.

"Then," said Churchill, seizing upon the semantic distinction, "we should provide for the conclusion of treaties *for*, not *with*, these countries."

"That will be more satisfactory."

"Thank you, Marshal."

"Don't mention it."

Stalin then brought up, in order to dismiss it, Truman's ideal of internationalizing all great waterways that coursed through and were used by many nations. Stalin had no interest in more freedom of movement, especially in areas so dominated by the Soviets as the Danube basin. Truman's paper, he said, "refers to the Danube and the Rhine, not in particular to the [Black Sea] Straits. We would like a reply to our statements on the Straits and a base."

A naval base that would give Stalin control of the Dardanelles would also give him leverage upon Greece and Turkey. They were the only Balkan countries, Churchill and Truman well knew, not yet Sovietized. If the Black Sea straits were guaranteed free for passage, said Truman—he wanted additional guarantees for other waterways promulgated—there need be no "control" by anyone.

The mood was increasingly rancorous. In his memoirs Truman would call the afternoon "the bitterest debate of the conference." Getting nowhere about Turkey, Molotov asked whether the Suez Canal operated under the same international rules as were being proposed for the Black Sea straits.

Since his question was inappropriate, said Churchill, that matter had not been raised.

"I'm raising it," said Molotov.

"We have a treaty," said Churchill.

"We want a treaty with Turkey," shouted Stalin.

There was more argument, and Truman interjected that he was for freedom of navigation "for all of us, without fortifications by anyone."

"It becomes evident," said Stalin finally, "that we differ in our views. We have more urgent questions than the Straits, so this question can be passed."

What Stalin saw as urgent business was the sticky matter of the remaining Red Army prisoners of war in German garb, most of them in sectors under Field Marshal Alexander's stewardship. Many had worn *Waffen SS* uniforms while flying the prerevolutionary colors of their claimed countries—Ukraine, Georgia, and others.* Since these were all Soviet citizens under the 1939 borders—the Yalta distinction—Stalin reminded Alexander "not to raise obstacles in the way of returning Soviet nationals to their own country."

The Russian Mission in Rome, said Churchill, had full access. "The personnel in the camp were said to be mainly non-Soviet Ukrainians and included numbers of Poles who, so far as we could find out, had not been domiciled within the 1939 frontiers of Russia." However, Stalin could send the Soviet general "who was concerned with these matters" to Alexander's headquarters and he could inspect the camp. "All right," said Stalin.

It was 7:30. The Anglo-American Combined Chiefs of Staff had already been meeting for two hours to discuss, with Mountbatten present, operations against Japan. It was time, Truman determined, to inform his increasingly difficult Russian ally about the Bomb, and to do so in the least hostile manner possible, yet suggest American strength within the adversarial climate. He had received a lot of advice on how to do it. As early as June 21, at an Interim [Bomb] Committee session, Conant, Bush, and Bohr urged that "if suitable opportunity arose," the President at Potsdam should "advise the Russians that we were working on this weapon with every prospect of success and that we expected to use it against Japan." If Stalin pressed for details, Bohr suggested, Truman should promise future discussions in the hope that after the war this "new means of warfare will become an aid in preserving peace." Now, at the close of the meeting, Truman walked around the huge circular table past Churchill to share a few words with Stalin. "I have something to tell you in confidence," he began—"casually," in the President's recollection. "We have," he said, "a new weapon of unusual destructive force." Stalin's interpreter, V. N. Pavlov, translated.

Stalin "showed no special interest. All he said was that he was glad to hear it and hoped we would make 'good use of it against the Japanese.' "

*One from Soviet Georgia was Dmitri Shalikashvili, father of an eight-year-old son, John, who would become a four-star American general and chairman of the Joint Chiefs of Staff in 1993. The elder Shalikashvili was among those for whom pretexts were found for release in 1946 rather than return to Russia.

Byrnes recalled Truman's words as being slightly more detailed. As they rode together in the President's car back to the "Little White House"—according to the Secretary—"he said he had told Stalin that, after long experimentation, we had developed a new bomb far more destructive than any other known bomb, and that we planned to use it very soon unless Japan surrendered. Stalin's only reply was to say that he was glad to hear of the bomb and hoped we would use it."

Churchill remembered watching "with the closest attention." From his vantage, only five yards off, Stalin "seemed delighted." As they waited for their cars, the P.M. asked, "How did it go?"

"He never asked a question," said Truman. Later, Churchill interpreted the scene as evidence that Stalin had no idea of the implications of Truman's vaguely informative revelation. "Nothing would have been easier than for him to say, 'Thank you for telling me about your new bomb. I of course have no technical knowledge. May I send my expert in these nuclear sciences to see your expert the next morning.' " Standing with Churchill, Eden saw—he remembered—Stalin respond only with a laconic "Thank you," while Pavlov later claimed to Gromyko that Stalin had only nodded his head in acknowledgment and said nothing. All the recollections represent the political agendas of the participants—and Churchill had misunderstood the deviousness of Stalin as much as had Truman. The Generalissimo knew exactly what the President had withheld. To be congratulatory would admit the success of Soviet espionage. To act concerned might confess weakness in arms capability.

A few days afterward, Gromyko and F. T. Gusev, the ambassador to Britain, arrived at the Marshal's residence to find Stalin and Molotov already in deep discussion. Gromyko thought that the principal subject had come up when Stalin barked, "Well, what about German reparations to the Soviet Union?"

Molotov, as Gromyko remembered it, "jumped in" to speak harshly of Churchill's unwillingness to give Russia "a realistic level of compensation from the Western zones 'for the appalling damage done to our economy.' "

Stalin allegedly agreed. "It is not the way allies should behave. The USSR is being cheated, cheated because the Americans have already shipped out the best equipment, complete with all its documentation, from* the various technical laboratories in the sector

*Gromyko's translator used "for"—but the implication is that German advanced technology as sought by the "Alsos" mission was being spirited out.

occupied by the Anglo-American forces. I don't know what Roosevelt's attitude would have been ... but Truman doesn't know the meaning of justice."

Then Stalin raised the unexpected new issue: "Our allies have told us that the USA has a new weapon, the atom bomb. I spoke with our own physicist, Kurchatov,* as soon as Truman told me that it had been tested successfully. We will no doubt have our own bomb before long. But its possession places a huge responsibility on any state." And Stalin went on, if we are to believe Gromyko, talking about how atomic energy should be reserved for peaceful uses only. It remains unknown how imaginative and political is Gromyko's reconstructed discussion, but he goes on to quote Molotov as complaining, "And the Americans have done all this work on the atomic bomb without telling us."

By early 1942, Russian as well as German physicists had begun to realize that articles on nuclear physics in the English language had disappeared from scientific journals—even the names of leading investigators. By then, Kurchatov had been forced by the German invasion to move his facilities to Kazan, where he had a cyclotron constructed and chafed about the slow pace of his weapons research, more concerned about the Americans than the Nazis. The Soviets, of course, communicated nothing about their Bomb program to the West.

"Roosevelt clearly felt no need to put us in the picture," Gromyko reports Stalin as saying. "He could have done it at Yalta. He could simply have told me the atom bomb was going through its experimental stages. We were supposed to be allies. No doubt Washington and London are hoping we won't be able to develop the bomb ourselves for some time. And meanwhile, using America's monopoly, in fact America's and Britain's, they want to force us to accept their plans on questions affecting Europe and the world. Well, that's not going to happen!" And he cursed, in Gromyko's recollection, "in ripe language."

According to Gromyko, Stalin "contacted Moscow several times" while at Potsdam "to give instructions to the experts in the matter." Yet Truman had never identified the new weapon as an atomic bomb. Unless Gromyko invented the scene and the dialogue

*Igor Kurchatov was considered later by the Soviets as the "father" of their atomic bomb. In his memoirs, Marshal Zhukov also discloses that the very night of Truman's revelation Stalin had a telegram sent to Russian scientists working on the Bomb to hurry their work, but it was not until November 6, 1947, that Molotov announced that the Soviets knew "the secret of the atom bomb."

almost completely—all, perhaps, but Stalin's wrath at hearing of a momentous mystery weapon for the first time—the knowledge about the Bomb had to have come from Soviet spies. The first to inform Stalin's regime of the Manhattan Project had been one of the "Cambridge Five" (with Guy Burgess, Donald Maclean, Kim Philby and Anthony Blunt), John Cairncross, who had been private secretary to Lord Hankey, who chaired the Cabinet Scientific Advisory Committee. Cairncross's KGB desk officer in Moscow in 1944–45, Yuri Modin, sent the information on to the Kremlin. A direct British contribution to Bomb development, émigré physicist Klaus Fuchs, also explains Gromyko's identification of the project as Anglo-American, for Fuchs had already delivered to his courier, Harry Gold, detailed plans of the plutonium bomb and the gaseous diffusion separation process. The Russians even had information to expect a test blast as early as July 10. Stalin may have had no need to ask Truman any questions.

Triggered by reports from informants that the explosion involved plutonium and Truman's confirmation that a working bomb existed, the Russians would hurry construction deep in the industrial Urals south of Sverdlosk, near the marshes and lakes that are the source of the river Tyecha, one of the world's largest military complexes. One of several secret atomic districts given the name of a nearby city and a special postal code, Chelyabinsk-40 would begin producing weapons-grade plutonium by 1949, dumping radioactive pollutants into the Tyecha that would contaminate a vast area inhabited by Tatars innocent of the reasons why so many villagers died so agonizingly and so young. (Pursuing their own nuclear agendas, the United States would publicly pollute Pacific atolls by atomic testing and secretly conducted tests exposing humans that were revealed only in the 1990s; France would conduct its own tests in the South Pacific, condoning murder—the blowing up of a "Greenpeace" vessel—to keep onlookers away. The Soviet level of "dirty" manufacturing and testing, however, was on a scale apart.)

Two other matters concerning the Bomb occurred on the eventful twenty-fourth. From the Metallurgical Laboratory in Chicago, Arthur Holly Compton, having held the James Franck–Leo Szilard petition to the President, with its signatures of sixty-seven scientists, for five days, sent it on to Colonel Kenneth D. Nichols, a young West Point–educated engineer close to both Oppenheimer and Groves, as it was both a security and a scientific matter. The signed draft, he noted, was in a second sealed envelope, with only a carbon copy of the text attached to his letter. "The question of the use of atomic weapons," he observed, "has been considered by the Scientific panel of the Secretary of War's Interim Advisory Committee. The opinion which they expressed was that military use of such weapons should be made in the Japanese War. There was not sufficient agreement among the members of the panel to unite upon a statement as to how or under what conditions such use was to be made."

An independent opinion poll, Compton went on, had been conducted among a group of 150 scientists and evaluated by Farrington Daniels, director of the Metallurgical Laboratory. "You will note that the strongly favored procedure is to 'give a military demonstration in Japan, to be followed by a renewed opportunity for surrender before full use of the weapon is employed.' This coincides with my own preference, and is, as nearly as I can judge, the procedure that has found most favor in all informal groups where the subject has been discussed." Compton and Daniels were scrupulous patriots, but when an opinion poll had been conducted among 150 scientists, and a petition signed by 67 scientists, many of them addicted to technological talk, with some idealistic enough to feel that knowledge was gained only to be shared—spies on Soviet assignment like Fuchs were almost superfluous.

That any secrecy remained after the moral qualms and loose talk may be a greater mystery than how Stalin learned about the Bomb, but pragmatic military considerations at the top eclipsed overwrought consciences. There was only one uranium bomb, never tested. Whether it worked or not under combat conditions, there was no other. Only one plutonium bomb could be made ready immediately, and its tactical efficacy was unknown. The first and only other device had been fixed in a stationary tower and ignited electrically. Would Japanese intransigence escalate if a much-touted weapon was a public dud?

When "Tooey" Spaatz arrived in Guam he handed over to Curtis LeMay—without comment—the letter dated July 24 over General Handy's signature formally authorizing the use of the atomic bombs yet to arrive and be assembled on-site. Little but the dates in it was news to LeMay. The Twentieth Air Force had long been the instrument chosen to deliver the package.

At the close of the plenary session, after the ritual good-byes, Churchill dined alone with Admiral Mountbatten to fill him in on what had not been covered since his arrival earlier in the day. The

Southeast Asia commander learned about the Bomb and plans for its delivery over Japan. Churchill felt certain that if it worked, it would awe the Japanese out of the war. "He advised me," Mountbatten told his diary, "to complete the capitulation[s] as soon after that date as possible." When it was all over, said Churchill, Mountbatten should call on him in Downing Street: "We will talk about your future, as I have great plans in store."

"It was a mournful and eerie feeling," the admiral wrote that night, "to sit there talking plans with a man who seemed so confident that they would come off, and I felt equally confident that he would be out of office within 24 hours."

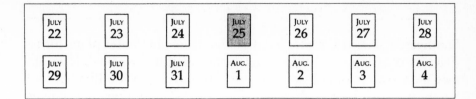

# CHAPTER XIII

# · JULY 25, 1945 ·

*". . . to hold out until complete collapse"*

Awakening earlier than usual, Churchill called for Dr. Moran. "An unpleasant dream" had left the P.M. shaken. "I dreamed that my life was over. I saw—it was very vivid—my dead body under a white sheet on a table in an empty room. I recognized my bare feet projecting from under the sheet. It was very lifelike. Perhaps this is the end."

Moran assured him that undue concerns about the election were responsible. Churchill had long worried about what he viewed as the difference between his personal popularity and that of the Conservative Party, which had symbolized to much of the electorate all the wrong things. He had made it clear in the campaign, he said, that he could only be Prime Minister with a Tory majority.

From Potsdam that morning General Marshall cabled MacArthur in Manila that it appeared likely that decisions would be reached soon on the occupation, control, and treatment of Japan. MacArthur had been informed a few days earlier to begin planning for Japanese capitulation. Russia was not yet a co-belligerent, and again it was clear that Russia had not, at least yet, been informed.

MacArthur's ideas were to be considered by the Combined Chiefs. The Navy had already anticipated the occupation, and by the twenty-fifth Admiral Nimitz had his scenario ready for landings in the Tokyo Bay area and other strategic points by Third Fleet and Marine forces, pending the arrival of MacArthur's command.

With other matters on the agenda, MacArthur's planning staff in Manila was juggling priorities. Since late in May General Sutherland's minions had been working to flesh out the plans for "Olympic" and to begin implementing them.* There were troops galore gathering on various islands in the Philippines and Marianas. All through July "casuals"—supplementary troops—for the Fleet Marine Force, as well as additional pilots for the Third Marine Aircraft Wing, were being shipped to Guam, Saipan, and Tinian from the Marine Training and Replacement Command in San Diego. Nimitz and MacArthur remained rivals as usual, but both had their hands in "Olympic." On the twenty-fifth the refraction diagrams for beaches in southern Kyushu were being prepared in Manila, outlined in red on Part B of the secret intelligence study delivered the month before. Little had changed in the planners' view to modify the operations document, which defined the task as: "By joint overseas expeditionary operations, [to] seize and occupy Southern Kyushu as far north as the general line Tsuno-Sendai and establish air and naval forces for support of Operation CORONET."

The "Olympic" brief assumed levels of opposition that had not diminished with the end of the Okinawa campaign. The Japanese "will continue to resist to the maximum with Army and civilian population." The landings would be met by at least three divisions, with three more moving down from northern Kyushu and four more from Honshu. The Japanese Air Force, but for planes—perhaps thousands of them—intended for suicide missions, might withdraw to Honshu or to the near mainland of China. Sixty airfields had been identified on Kyushu, with five more under construction. In southeast Kyushu the 86th Division was working around the clock to fortify the coastline around Shibushi Wan, east of Kanoya and separated from the much larger Kagoshima Wan by the Ōsumi Peninsula. Planners guessed that the first landings would be made there, and they would

*But Sutherland himself was about to exit the command briefly, not only because of personal conflicts with MacArthur but because even Harry Truman had learned of Sutherland's Australian mistress, who had received an American army commission. She would be sent back to her husband. Sutherland would be reunited in the United States with his wife.

not have been far from wrong. After the war, Lieutenant General Tomatoro Yoshinaka, the division commander, claimed, "We were confident that we could wholly destroy the first-wave landing of five American divisions at the water's edge." However, his troops may have had more courage than confidence. Rations—there was not enough food on Kyushu for the enormous buildup of forces—were a bowl of rice mixed with tofu once a day. Malnutrition and debility were enemies more immediate than the Americans, but intelligence gathering to learn such things was almost impossible. Even knowledge gleaned from the heavily censored Japanese press was hard to come by except when smuggled out through neutrals, and their movements were now heavily restricted. Had American intelligence had access to the Tokyo *Yomiuri-Hochi* for the day before, the matter of meager rations, at least for civilians, would have emerged dramatically. With rice, the national staple, in short supply, people in the cities depended upon a flour made from sweet potato vines, mulberry leaves, pumpkins, and horse chestnuts. A letter to the editor (escaping the censor) mourned, "The number of emaciated men and women . . . is conspicuous. Everyone is suffering from diarrhea. . . . No one can work properly, and production will inevitably. decline. The problem is the flour. . . . If we are to win the war, we must be supplied with food that will not make us sick."

The Navy, once the pride of the Empire, suffered from malnutrition of a different kind. "Olympic" assumed that the Navy, starved of fuel and larger warships, would be "limited to possible suicide attack[s] . . . submarine[s], small suicide craft and mine[laying] activities." As long as Russia remained on the sidelines, war production in Manchuria, northern China, and Korea was expected to continue.

"Amphibious lift" would land twelve divisions for the initial assault and follow-up service and support troops equal in numbers to the fighting divisions. Before they were delivered, "maximum neutralization of enemy ground, naval and air forces" was to be accomplished. The Okinawa experience, built into the operational plans, was that the Japanese would not defend the beaches because naval gunfire, despite waves of *kamikazes*, would pulverize beach defenses. Instead, they would defend inland, giving up as little maneuvering room as possible.

Someone on the planning staff was clearly an automobile aficionado. While the "Overlord" landings in June 1944 had their *Utah Beach* and *Omaha Beach*, "Olympic" had a showroom—and museum—of automobiles new and historic. The beach zones around the two claws of lower Kyushu, separated by Kagoshima Bay, were *Taxicab, Roadster, Limousine, Station Wagon,* and *Town Car.* The two zones in the bay itself were *Delivery Wagon* and *Convertible.* The eastern beaches (each three thousand to four thousand yards) included *Austin, Buick, Cadillac, Chevrolet, Chrysler,* and *Cord.* The southeast beaches were *DeSoto, Dusenberg, Essex, Ford,* and *Franklin.* The western beaches were *Zephyr, Winton, Stutz, Studebaker, Saxon, Rolls-Royce, Reo, Pontiac, Mercedes,* and *Maxwell.* To their south were *Plymouth, Packard, Overland,* and *Oldsmobile.* Beaches in the bay were *Locomobile, Lincoln, LaSalle, Hupmobile, Graham-Paige,* and *Hudson.* Beach subdivisions of the small islands to the west of Kyushu—to be invaded on X-5, and collectively called Koshiki Retto—were *Brakedrum, Windshield, Cylinder, Dashboard, Gearshift, Headlight, Hubcap, Mudguard, Rumbleseat, Sparkplug,* and *Toolbox.* (Taking Kerama Retto prior to the Okinawa landings had proved the value of occupying a lightly defended location offshore of the primary target.)

Troops to be landed in the first assault—Army, Navy, and Marines—would total 436,486. Follow-up forces would number 356,902. With air support personnel of 22,160, the numbers topped 800,000. For the assault on the beaches in Normandy the year before, Eisenhower had employed 150,000 men and 1,500 tanks. "Olympic" would be, by far, the largest amphibious operation in history.

During two early occupation months in Japan, future *Washington Post* journalist Chalmers M. Roberts (he had worked for the *Times-Herald* until 1942) was chief of an eight-man team deputed by the Strategic Bombing Survey to reconstruct what the defensive situation on southern Kyushu had been when the war ended. On Captain Roberts's team were Captain John C. West, later the governor of South Carolina; Lieutenant John G. Palfrey, later a Columbia dean and a member of the Atomic Energy Commission; and Lieutenant Richard Sneider, later a Foreign Service officer who negotiated the return of Okinawa to Japan. They explored caves where *kamikaze* aircraft were still hidden, went over captured documents, and flew low, in a light plane, over some of the "Olympic" beaches.

By chance they were over the beach at Miyazaki on November 1, X-Day for the operation. On the "Olympic" charts these were *Chevrolet, Chrysler,* and *Cord* beaches, on the southeast coast, assigned to units of General Walter Krueger's Sixth Army. The stretch, a small fraction of the landing sites, "was perhaps 40 miles long and at first glance appeared to be an ideal landing spot, long and gently sloping into the sea, the biggest beach on a rugged island where the mountains looked like hiked-up rugs. But the beach was terribly shallow, and behind it rose a range from which murderous fire could have been poured down upon the men debouching from landing craft." His notes from interviews with officers running the defense at Miyazaki "say that the estimate we got at the time was that there were 56,000 troops dug in nearby, with another 70,000 in reserve. The Japanese told us they had figured we would land on Miyazaki beach; where else? they asked."

"I want to explain something to you," Lieutenant General Torashiro Kawabe told them. "This is a very difficult thing which you may not be able to understand." And he went on to describe how "our spiritual conviction in victory would balance any scientific advantages, and we had no intention of giving up the fight. . . . We knew you would do everything in your power to destroy all our airfields but we believed the airfields for launching *kamikaze* planes were such simple affairs that they could be mended very quickly. We believed that by taking advantage of weather intervals, heavy or overcast, between your bombing raids, we could repair the airfields enough to keep them serviceable. Also we could use stretches of beaches along the coast." They realized, Kawabe added, that they might not be able to throw the Americans off Kyushu, "but we planned to do everything possible and thought probably we would be able if we exerted ourselves to the utmost."

"Olympic," the army team concluded, "would have been a very rugged operation" if beaches could be defended like Miyazaki.

Units being redeployed to "Olympic" were often veteran outfits that had seen a lot of action against the Germans and could be counted upon to bolster untested troops. But Eisenhower had been quoted in *Stars and Stripes* as saying that no one who had served both in North Africa and the ETO would have to go to the Pacific, and Corporal D. E. Jarvis of the 4378th Quartermaster Truck Company figured he had nothing to lose by complaining directly to the top that the assurances had been ignored. Marshall had warned Eisenhower to keep the human dimension in mind in reassignments, and Ike had responded to him on May 10 in a letter released by his office to the press. Now his staff, worried by potential bad publicity, wrote and rewrote a letter to Jarvis for Eisenhower's signature that hedged the promise by defining it as applicable only to combat troops:

*Dear Corporal Jarvis:* I have read with sympathy and interest the letter you addressed me telling me of your feelings and those of your friends and fellow-soldiers in the 4378th Truck Company regarding your new assignment to the Pacific. Because you have taken the trouble to write me and because, as you indicate, your morale and the morale of the men serving with you may be affected by what seems to be a troop movement in contradiction to my orders, I want to assure you that this is not the case and at the same time to give you my full views on the subject. . . .

I had, with you, served in both North Africa and Europe, and I understood the very deep desires of each man who had served long overseas to return home. The urgent need in the Pacific for service units made it impossible for me to include service personnel in this order, but forced me to limit it to soldiers who had fought in actual combat in both Theaters. In this category were included enlisted men who were assigned or attached to any organizational unit of an Infantry or Armored Division, or to any of nine other types of units while such units were assigned or attached to a Corps or Division during actual combat. Antiaircraft units, but not truck companies, were included in the above mentioned nine.

You must realize that it was my desire to include every possible man who had served in both Theaters under this order, but you must also realize that of necessity the needs of the war in the Pacific come first. I am sorry that the statement which appears in the *Stars and Stripes* on this subject was somewhat incomplete and perhaps subject to misinterpretation.

I want, finally, to assure you and all the men of your unit through you that far from being forgotten, you are more in my thoughts than some men whose assignments may seen to you at the moment to be more fortunate. By the time you arrive . . . American divisions will be gathering in their full and final strength for the assault against Japan. Your mission there is important. As your Commander-in-Chief in North Africa and later here in Europe, I wish you and your comrades God-speed and a safe return home after the final victory has been won.

Corporal Jarvis had not changed the orders of his commander-in-chief, but he might have consoled himself that few men wearing two stripes on their sleeves had ever received at mail call a letter from a general with five stars on his epaulets.

Jarvis would have the dubious honor of serving under still another five-star general, Douglas MacArthur. Since MacArthur wanted Robert Eichelberger, who had led effectively in Luzon, close at hand to direct operations, the actual landings were assigned to General Walter Krueger, who had taken the 161,000 men of his Sixth Army ashore at Leyte to run an undistinguished campaign. But he had been in the vanguard of MacArthur's oft-promised return to the Philippines. This time he would have with him I Corps, V Amphibious Corps, IX Corps, XI Corps, 40th Infantry Division, 11th Airborne Division, 158th Regimental Combat Team, and Army Service Command troops. Most troops would rehearse, stage, and assault from the Philippines, with three amphibious attack forces, Marines and Navy, mounting from the Marianas following an advance force commanded by Admiral Richmond Kelly Turner, the boastful, hard-drinking coordinator of bungled planning in Washington at the time of Pearl Harbor. One of the attack forces from the Marianas was to be led by the smug and sophisticated Vice Admiral Theodore S. Wilkinson, a failure as intelligence chief in Washington in December 1941 but, like Turner, a favorite of Admiral King and a planner of "Olympic." The other two commands were entrusted to Vice Admiral Daniel E. Barbey, who had run the last amphibious operation for MacArthur, hitting the beach at Balikpapan in Borneo with a combined Aussie-American force. More press-conscious than ever, MacArthur had literally barged in while the bullets still flew, bringing with him war correspondents and a camera crew. (He had done the same thing not far away at Brunei Bay, prompting an Aussie's remark: "Christ! It's the fucking messiah!") For the west coast landings on Kyushu, to be a Marine operation, an outsider was chosen, Major General Harry Schmidt, who had been training the Marine V Amphibious Corps on Maui for what his orders described as "landings on hostile shores."

Air Force and Navy units received their orders for the grinding down of shore and airfield defenses on July 28. Admiral Spruance's huge Fifth Fleet, with two fast carrier groups and an escort carrier group, was to be the covering force for the landings and for advance mining operations. Halsey's Third Fleet, with the U.S. Second Carrier Task Force and the British Carrier Task Force, was to initiate the softening up, making widespread attacks on home island communications, especially between Kyushu and Honshu, and shifting at X-14 to create diversions near Shikoku and Honshu while isolating Kyushu. At X-10 the British task force would spin off to create a diversion around Hong Kong and Canton.

The "all-out" preliminaries involving Kyushu itself—prolonged bombardment by sea and from the air—would last from X-10 to X-Day, with an "advance attack force" landing for "preliminary [ground] operations" on X-4. A "floating reserve" force would make a feint off the home island of Shikoku, to the northeast of Kyushu, about X-4 and then withdraw in the direction of the Ryukyus, returning on or after X-Day to land on the southwest "claw" of Kagoshima Bay, or—if necessary—"reinforce any of the previous landings as developments may dictate."

The phased requirements for construction of "Olympic" bases at Kagoshima, Shibushi, and Miyazaki alone, beginning at X-120, which had passed in the first week of July, were 290,461 tons of matériel. The Navy was bringing in everything from portable piers to oxygen; acetylene and carbon dioxide plants to dispensaries; a prosthetic lab and a typewriter repair unit. Prefabricated hospitals complete to beds were already piled up near the runways of the 315th Bombardment Wing on Guam, a tremendous temptation to the Air Force personnel who slept in two-man tents on cots and had no electricity. Someone discovered that the stock included Coleman lanterns—something to read and write by on the long nights. Lieutenant Hays Gamble and friends made, by jeep, several moonlight requisitions, trading a supply officer two bottles of whiskey for a lantern, and one bottle each for mattresses. Prudently they had flown over with several cases of the golden liquid, having been warned by returnees that money was of no use in the Marianas but that "Black Death"—a reference to the label—could buy nearly anything.

Near another runway sat a hundred P-51 Mustang fighters, removed from their crates, bolted into shape, and test-flown once—to make sure they were operative for "Olympic." The stockpiling of resources for the operation was repeated elsewhere—on Tinian, Saipan, Leyte, Samar, Luzon, and points east as far as Hawaii and the

West Coast. The logistics were mind-boggling. The basic tactic was to employ overwhelming force in the face of what was expected to be a "fanatically hostile population." The mission of the assault troops, who were to land 61,190 vehicles of all descriptions as well as nearly a million men, using at least the 1,371 landing craft already available, with many more in the pipeline, was to "destroy hostile garrisons," "advance inland," and "block movement of hostile reinforcements from the north." The 2nd, 3rd, and 5th Marine Divisions would secure the western shore of Kagoshima Wan; other troops would be Army divisions. During the amphibious phase of the operation, the Pacific Fleet commander (Nimitz) would exercise control; authority over units ashore would pass to the Commanding General, Sixth Army. One of the new generals attached to Krueger's Sixth Army, John Dudley, arrived in Manila to help plan his outfit's landing and was annoyed to find that he was scheduled only as a second echelon. His indignation faded when he found the reason. The second landing force was to be given the same assignment as the first. "It was clear to me then," Dudley recalled thirty-five years later. "They expected the first echelon to be wiped out in the invasion. The second echelon would get the thing done."

Writing to his wife, Eichelberger confessed reluctance to take home leave at such a delicate point. Although Emily knew he was going to oversee new offensive operations, she could not be let in on the targets, however obvious they were. All he could do was worry aloud about being out of the picture when and if Japan sued for peace and occupation troops went in. He phrased his doubts in those terms, observing that "a great many people, probably 50%, feel that Japan is about to fold up." The next day, the twenty-fifth, he added that "many believe that the Japs will quit if Russia comes in, and I hope they do." It was not the cliché attitude of the professional militarist who wants his operation to come off to add to his glory. Eichelberger recognized the potential casualties in "Olympic," and also knew that the glory would go to "the Big Chief [who] writes his own communiqués." While Eichelberger was indebted to MacArthur's patronage, he also recognized "the centralization of publicity around one man. . . . It hasn't been exactly fair for the many brave men who have died in winning those victories."

In preparation for occupation rather than for "Olympic" the Navy Department radioed all ships on Pacific stations to have on board anchorage charts covering key home island ports other than

Kagoshima—Tokyo Bay, Nagoya (Ise Bay), Osaka-Kobe-Kyoto, Hi-roshima-Kure-Matsuyama, Shimonoseki, Fukuoka, and Hakodate. Yet there was no letup in bombarding those harbors. During the night that stretched into the morning of the twenty-fifth, Admiral Cary Jones's cruiser force boldly entered the Kii Suido and shelled the seaplane base at Shimonoseki, at the southern tip of Honshu, but bad weather limited sea and air strikes. Admiral Ugaki confided to his diary that a *Saiun* reconnaissance plane out of Kisarazu had esti-mated fifteen carriers in Task Force 38, but they were three hundred miles offshore—"a little bit too far to do anything about." By evening he had changed his mind and sent ten *Ryuseis* from the Third Air Fleet to do what they could, "but most of them seem to have been discovered and shot down." Even an attempt to shadow TF 38 at night, by eight *Gingas* sortied from Taisha, was "a complete failure." However much the low clouds and rain hampered the other side, in-experienced pilots, poor weather, and aircraft no longer competitive with American technology were formidable handicaps.

Even suicide pilots needed some training, as did the pilots of manned torpedoes. Wakana Wada remembered her brother's return on leave for what her family knew was the last time. Too young to be told, she wrote, thirty years later,

> Unaware my elder brother's departure in his kaiten was immi-nent,
> I played with him, skipping stones on the sea.

Submarine *I-363* carried him off for a month, but there were few targets, and he returned to Kure, one of the "ghosts" who remained among the living dead until they were launched, a skipping stone on the sea. On July 25, during training in Kure harbor, his *kaiten*, the family learned, "porpoised" to the bottom—a mechanical failure. "They searched desperately for him, but, unfortunately, a large-scale American air attack came in. . . . Kure was the target of regular car-rier attacks."

Although B-29s flying well above the weather hit Nagoya* and Osaka by daylight, targeting aircraft factories, they had to bomb by

---

*Fifty years after Boeing B-29s bombed the Mitsubishi Heavy Industries plants at Nagoya, where most Zero fighters had been made, ultramodern equipment at the same plant site was building fuselages for Boeing's newest generation of jet passenger aircraft to be assembled in Seattle.

radar, which despite Twentieth Air Force claims, was often valueless. Sixteen planes hit "targets of opportunity," which meant jettisoning their bombs over something or other. Over Osaka the AA-fire was admittedly "very accurate." The Kobe-Osaka corridor was labeled "Flak Alley" by B-29 pilots. "Unlike most alleys," Harold F. Atkins of the 501st Bombardment Group wrote, "it was very well lighted. In fact, too well lighted." Four B-29s were lost. "Flak was so heavy," Atkins exaggerated, "that Jap infantrymen were marching up on it and firing on the planes with small arms. Pappy Baldwin lost six feet of a wing. . . . Paul Mason's *Dottie's Baby* had some instruments shot out." The Japanese were not giving up easily. Nor were American crews seemingly remote from the action. Two heavy bombers from Adak, far out in the Aleutians chain, bombed an airfield in northern Hokkaido "with unobserved results."

Only a few B-29 wings had advanced radar permitting more precise bombing with visual sighting of the target. The state-of-the-art instrument was the AN/APQ-7 "Eagle" radar, designed at the MIT Radiation Laboratory and tried out in the last weeks of the war in Europe on twenty B-24s. Planes equipped with "Eagle" had what looked like a small wing attached to the underside of the fuselage—it was an antenna that narrowed the radar beam to a better defined sixty-degree downward scan. In compensation for the drag, all turrets and guns but those in the rear were removed, the retrofitted B-29s gaining speed and bombload and higher altitude capability. Gamble's 315th Bomb Wing, targeting refineries, owed the technology to the first postwar studies of bombing in the ETO, which suggested that the mobility of the *Wehrmacht* and *Luftwaffe* had been severely handicapped by lack of fuel.

By nightfall, Hays Gamble reported in his diary, there was "no weather at all over Japan and full moon out." At nineteen minutes before midnight he unloaded his five-hundred-pound bombs from a prudent 16,200 feet. Over the Chinese mainland, hundreds of planes ranging from P-38s and P-51s to big B-24 Liberators had bombed and strafed river, road, and rail traffic, still trying to prevent troop movement to the home islands or to Manchuria. A lone plane flew over Stanley Camp in Hong Kong, where British captives—those who survived—had languished since Christmas Day 1941. According to the Japanese account, "The internees were taking their tiffins at the time of the bombing . . . altogether nine bombs were released of which three scored direct hits, and of the three bombs, only one exploded, which testifies to the inferior quality of the bombs recently used." Seven British prisoners were "severely injured."

In some ways the survivors at Stanley Camp, where Japanese internees had been taken on December 8, 1941, for what turned out to be an abbreviated stay, were better off than the Emperor himself, who lived now in what amounted to a large air raid shelter. American bombers had been ordered to keep clear of the palace grounds, but stray incendiary bombs, carried by firestorm winds, had damaged the low, graceful buildings. The Imperial Library remained, and it was there that Hirohito received his Lord Privy Seal, the Marquis Koichi Kido, at 10:20 A.M. At the time of Pearl Harbor, Kido only warily supported the war; now he was trying to put an end to it, and a crucial step was to dissuade the peace faction that there was any hope left for a Konoye mission to Moscow. "His Majesty," Kido noted in his diary after an hour's effort to get the Emperor to intervene, "on this occasion earnestly urged steps to conclude peace with the Allies, disapproving the Army's proposal for a war of decision." But Hirohito would not personally order the Army to do anything: it was beyond his constitutional powers. He was still banking on Konoye and Russia.

So was Togo, who telegraphed again from the Foreign Office to Ambassador Sato in Moscow. He was to knock once more on Molotov's door and see his deputy, Solomon Lozovsky. It was now seven in the evening, Tokyo time—1:00 P.M. in Moscow. Clearly, Togo had also been talking with Kido. The message, decrypted by "Magic" but not instantly available in Potsdam, may have been the most important yet in the series between the Foreign Minister and his frustrated emissary, however much it failed to take into account the intransigence of the Army hierarchy. "Special attention should be paid to the fact," Togo urged, referring to Captain Zacharias's broadcast several days earlier, "that at this time the United States referred to the Atlantic Charter. As for Japan, it is impossible to accept unconditional surrender under any circumstances, but we should like to communicate to the other party through appropriate channels that we have no objection to a peace based on the Atlantic Charter. The difficult point is the attitude of the enemy, who continues to insist on the formality of unconditional surrender." Under such conditions, he insisted, there was no recourse "other than for us to hold out until complete collapse because of this point alone." And Sato was to declare to the Russians that his was not a "peace feeler" but "obedience to the Imperial command."

"Also," Togo added, "it is necessary to have them understand that we are trying to end hostilities by asking for very reasonable terms in order to secure and maintain our nation's existence and honor." Here Togo broadened the gulf between unconditional surrender and surrender under, as a face-saving gloss, the Atlantic Charter. "Reasonable terms" were almost certainly out. Dutifully, Sato went to the Kremlin as soon as Lozovsky would see him, explaining that the Emperor had ordered Konoye to Moscow "to put an end to the tragedy of additional bloodshed."

Although "Magic" was listening, Lozovsky's orders from Stalin—as he had already told Truman—were to string Sato along. At 11:53 P.M. Sato cabled from Moscow the actual dialogue in the Foreign Ministry, which demonstrated how well the loyal Lozovsky had conducted his charade:

> SATO: As you have already understood from my proposal, the Japanese Government is asking the Soviet Government to mediate in a friendly manner relative to the termination of the war, and at the same time will have Prince Konoye explain directly to you the concrete intentions of our Government.
>
> L: Could you give me the text of the proposal which you have just made? Its content is really important. If you could prepare a written text for me, I should be able to understand it more correctly. It is difficult to expect real accuracy from an oral presentation. It would also be convenient for me to make a report to my Government if I have a written text. I should like to ask one or two questions: (1) I understand that the Japanese Government is asking the Soviet Government to mediate in order to terminate the war, and (2) concerning the above problem Prince Konoye is going to bring up some concrete proposals. Now, are these concrete proposals for the termination of the war or for strengthening Russo-Japanese relations? As this point was not made clear, I should like to have you explain it to me so that I can make a report to my Government.

Konoye's mission, Sato painfully explained, would encompass "a vast area." That was exactly what Lozovsky hoped, as it would take longer to set down in writing. But Molotov's deputy listened,

Sato cabled to Tokyo, "with an earnest and attentive attitude, promising to contact Potsdam as soon as he had a full text in hand. It had to be, Sato explained, kept Top Secret.

That Japan was losing the war and had no capacity now to win it was apparent from the highest echelons of the Foreign Office and the Army to the most desperately deprived prisoners of the Japanese. At a camp for British and Anzac POWs north of Bangkok, the survivors of the Indies and Singapore who had stayed alive through the building of the Burma-Thailand railway kept deviously abreast of the war news. Through Chinese laborers they had acquired a radio they built into a chair. Leader of the POWs was Lieutenant Colonel Edward "Weary" Dunlop, a combat surgeon in his late thirties who had served in Greece, Crete, Tobruk, and Java. He expected, he confided to his diary on the twenty-fifth, a "death march" of "fit men" to the east as the Japanese retreated. "The rest to be bumped off."

His men talked hopefully of "Red Cross amelioration" but Dunlop scoffed privately that it took "little account of the deadly earnestness of the Japanese, and the Götterdämmerung darkness as the Gods desert them." To defend themselves against an enemy final solution he had chosen "10 NCOs of high courage and discretion, each to select 10 men not otherwise chosen. Each man to devise a weapon such as a stone. . . . My own armoury, carefully hidden, consists of two 'Molotov Cocktails' devised from saki bottles and petrol stolen from trucks. I have plotted our desperate breakout as frontally towards a machine gun post in the wall which can be approached with visual cover to either side." His aim was to "pre-empt" a "massacre." If nothing else, he felt, he wanted "to get some men out to tell the story if they survive, but I am not going over the wall myself. My proper fate must be here with my patients. . . ."

Some of the discussion at Potsdam that morning would deal with expediting the defeat of the Japanese, but it would not appear that way. The conferences began early, in order for Churchill's party to leave for London and the polling results. First order of business was the posing for photographs in the garden of the misnamed "palace"—a low, sprawling, stone residence—by press and newsreel cameramen. Then came photographs at the table inside. Truman posed shaking hands with Stalin and Churchill at the same time, and with arms crossed like the county politician he once was. As everyone filed in, Stalin handed Truman a response to a JCS request for "weather liaison groups" in eastern Siberia to coordinate air strikes when Russia entered the war. The Soviets appeared accommodating only on paper, as "detailed arrangements on entry of personnel" were always arduous and frustrating, preserving the Russian passion for secrecy.

Prior to the meeting, Maisky had circulated a memo slyly defining "war booty"—which the Russians were freely seizing—as all German equipment and supplies used in prosecution of the war. Nothing could be more all encompassing—"You have a right to take them," he had earlier told Edwin Pauley, "but of course you may yield your right here and there." Maisky had no idea that his description could be interpreted as meaning the German Navy and merchant fleet until Churchill hinted as much. Realizing that he might not be back, although he affected optimism, Churchill, with Truman following his feisty lead, made the brief session, as recorded in Benjamin Cohen's probably condensed transcript, memorable:

TRUMAN: Shall we discuss the Polish western frontier? I think the Prime Minister had something to say.

CHURCHILL: I saw Mr. Beirut this morning. The Foreign Secretary saw the Polish delegation last night. They all agree that there are about one and a half million Germans in this area. The issue is all mixed up with the reparations issue, and the four power zones of occupation.

TRUMAN: Secretary of State Byrnes expects to have further conversations with the Poles also. In view of the British and American conversations with the Poles, it might go over to Friday. The German fleet and merchant marine are also on the agenda. I thought we had agreed on that.

CHURCHILL: Obviously, we must have some concrete proposals.

TRUMAN: Secretary Byrnes tells me that [Assistant] Secretary Clayton and Admiral Land are working on such proposals.

STALIN: Let us postpone it.

CHURCHILL: We must at some time discuss the question of the transfer of populations. There are a large number [of Germans] to be moved from Czechoslovakia. We must consider where they are to go.

STALIN: The Czechs have already evicted them.

CHURCHILL: The two and a half million of them? Then

there are the Germans from the new Poland. Will they go to the Russian zones? We don't want them. There are large numbers still to come from Sudetenland.

STALIN: So far as the Poles are concerned, the Poles have retained one and a half million Germans to help as laborers. As soon as the harvest is over, the Poles will evict them. The Poles do not ask us. They are doing what they like, just as the Czechs are.

CHURCHILL: That is the difficulty. The Poles are driving the Germans out of the Russian zone. That should not be done without considering its effect on the food supply and reparations. We are getting into a position where the Poles have food and coal, and we have the mass of the population thrown on us.

STALIN: We must appreciate the position of the Poles. The Poles are taking revenge for centuries of injuries.

CHURCHILL: That consists in throwing them on us, and the United States?

TRUMAN: We don't want to pay for Polish revenge. If Poland is to have an occupation zone, that should be clearly defined, but at the present time there are only four zones of occupation. If the Poles have an occupation zone they should be responsible for it. The boundary cannot be fixed before the peace conference. I want to be helpful, but Germany is occupied by four powers, and the boundary cannot be changed [now]; only at the peace conference.

I must make clear at this point my constitutional powers. . . . Peace treaties must be confirmed by our Senate. When I indicate my support of a proposal, I will use my best efforts to secure its acceptance. That does not guarantee its acceptance, nor does it preclude my coming back and informing you that my continuing to press it might endanger our common interests in the peace.

I make this statement, not to change the basis of our discussions, but to make clear beyond misunderstanding my constitutional authority. This is particularly important with reference to the Polish question. I want a treaty of peace which can be ratified by the Senate.

STALIN: May I ask a few questions? Does your statement refer to peace treaties only, or to other questions?

TRUMAN: Only matters which must go to the Senate. I have large war powers, as have the rest of you, but I do not wish to use them to the point that they may endanger the final conclusion of peace.

CHURCHILL: If the conference ends in ten days without agreement on the present state of affairs in Poland, and with the Poles practically admitted as a fifth occupation power, and no arrangement for the spreading of food over the whole of Germany, it will mark the breakdown of the conference. I suppose we will have to fall back on the proposal of the Secretary of State, and each of us fall back on our own zones. Maisky's definition of booty is a very wise one. I do hope that we will reach a broad agreement. We must recognize that we have made no progress so far on this point.

STALIN: Coal and metal from the Ruhr is more important than the food supply.

CHURCHILL: Coal will have to be paid for by food. We could not agree that Russia could dispose of everything in her zone and still claim supplies and reparations from our zone.

STALIN: Supplies will have to be drawn from the whole of Germany.

CHURCHILL: Why not food?

STALIN: That should be discussed. The question is under discussion. Germany had always had to import foodstuff.

CHURCHILL: How will she pay reparations?

STALIN: There is much fat in Germany.

CHURCHILL: I am not going to consent to arrangements which will lead to starvation in the Ruhr, when the Poles have all the feeding grounds.

STALIN: Only recently the Poles requested help by the way of bread from us until their new harvest.

CHURCHILL: We in England are going to have the most fireless winter since the war.

STALIN: How is this? England has always exported her coal. Let the prisoners of war work. They work in the mines in Russia. You have 400 thousand German soldiers in Norway who have not been disarmed.

CHURCHILL: It is our intention to disarm them. I thought that they were disarmed. I will inquire about it. We are short of coal because we export coal to France, Holland and Belgium. We find it odd, when we need coal, that the Poles should be selling coal from lands which we do not regard as Polish, to Sweden and other countries.

STALIN: The Poles are selling their own coal, not the coal from the former German territories. I am not accustomed to complaining. We have lost five million men in this war. We are short of coal and many other things. If I described our situation and our needs, I might make the Prime Minister weep.

CHURCHILL: We will sell coal from the Ruhr for food.

STALIN: This question must be discussed, or thought over.

CHURCHILL: We were only exchanging views. I am finished.

STALIN: What a pity.

TRUMAN: We shall adjourn until Friday at five p.m.

CHURCHILL: I hope to be back.

STALIN: Judging from the expression on Mr. Attlee's face, I do not think he looks forward avidly to taking over your authority. We have tackled the problems of the war successfully. We should be able to tackle the problems of the peace as well.

EDEN: The Prime Minister referred to the transfer of populations. President Beneš has sent some communication to us. May the Foreign Secretaries look at it?

STALIN: Yes. May we not have to summon the Czechs?

CHURCHILL: I shall be glad to see Beneš. He is an old friend.

STALIN: But is this not serving mustard after supper? The Germans have already been driven out.

CHURCHILL: They have some agreement for gradual transfer.

STALIN: No such agreement exists.

CHURCHILL: There is still the problem how this is to be done. May the Foreign Secretaries look into it?

STALIN: Yes.

TRUMAN: I should like my suggestion on the waterways, the Rhine, the Danube, the Kiel Canal and the Bosporus considered by the Foreign Secretaries.

STALIN: All right.

MOLOTOV: May I circulate a memorandum on the obstacles in the way of return of Soviet citizens from Austria and

Germany, and also a memorandum on the presence of German troops in Norway.

TRUMAN: Yes.

CHURCHILL: I wish to assure the Marshal that I intend to disarm the troops in Norway. I am not keeping them up my sleeve for use, if any misunderstanding arises in the north. Perhaps the Marshal will let me make a report.

STALIN: I promise in advance, and I shall not criticise.

It was 12:15. At 1:23—not yet noon in London—Churchill's plane was in the air, with the wrangles and the near deadlock put aside by the counting of ballots. Those who remained in Potsdam could not put the problems aside. At 12:25 Stimson paid a courtesy call on Stalin, going over some of the key episodes in the war that they had seen from opposite sides of the German frontiers. It was Russian pressure on the Germans that helped make the Normandy landing successful, Stimson observed. "I distinctly remembered the Generalissimo's [answering] language," Stimson noted in his diary, "—it was terse and clear—that he distinguished between a supporting action and an action that was a mere diversion."

Between the lines lay hints of two years of Russian desperation, until the greatest battle of the war, at Kursk late in 1943, that ended *Wehrmacht* hopes for victory in the East. Appeals for a realistic Second Front in the West had led only to landings in North Africa, Sicily, and Italy, with Churchill even pressing for a useless invasion of Greek islands in the Aegean. He would try anything but the cross-Channel operation urged by Stalin and pressed vainly by Roosevelt, until American military preponderance was too overwhelming for the British to dictate policy any further. Were the British, by letting Russia and Germany exhaust each other, bent upon their centuries-old policy of attempting to keep any Continental nation from establishing European supremacy? Or was Churchill's strategy of fighting on the margins one of protecting British interests in the Mediterranean while keeping casualties down until America could bear the brunt of the fighting? Britain, after all, had been bled nearly to death in France from 1914 to 1918, and had never really recovered. Whatever the reasons, although Hitler had, against all military logic, drawn substantial forces from Russia to bolster Rommel in Tunisia, Stalin suspected Churchill's motives and was grateful for the American dimension in the war. The Channel operations, he told Stimson,

were unparalleled in history. Now he expected, because of the magnitude of the Pacific fronts, to see an even more massive attack on
Japan. "We would all operate on the same field of battle—it was high
time for this."

As Stimson knew from memos he had been receiving, even that
morning, the comradely talk did not disguise the Russian economic
rape of what was left of Germany, the land-grabbing on Germany's
eastern boundaries, the forced communizing of central Europe, and
the inroads, by every means not excluding terror, into the West. One
thuggish Belorussian major involved in the forced repatriation of Soviet nationals, after showing some unexpected signs of remorse and
"contamination" to the British, was abducted that morning in the
Norwegian harbor of Tromsō by two NKVD agents who boarded the
hospital ship *Alba*. (In Russia the major recanted his bourgeois senti-
mentality and was put back into the operation in Cairo. Meanwhile,
other repatriates from Norway were on their way to Murmansk by
sea and across Sweden by rail.)

The seizure of people was only slightly less important to the
Soviets than the seizure of usable industrial property. A report of
the twenty-fifth to the Secretary of War by two representatives of the
Commission on Reparations described what the Allied presence in
Berlin, because of the Three-Power Conference, enabled them to see.
The loading docks along the Spree in Berlin were bustling, with most
of the work being accomplished by Russian soldiers. The freight-
loading platforms of the Schliesser Railway Station were crowded
with outgoing boxes, bales, and wrapped (but identifiable) machine
tools. Flatcars were filled with forging and pressing equipment, dynamos, boilers, turbines, and office furniture. "When machinery is removed," the report to Stimson summarized, "everything in the plant
is taken with it. The process is wholesale, not retail." Soviet authorities were hardly waiting for a reparations agreement. While the Potsdam proceedings were in partial recess, the infrastructure of
Soviet-occupied Germany was being removed to Russia.

What had been going on had been obvious to Charles Lindbergh, just back from Germany, where high American brass of Rightist leanings—and most were—recognized him warmly as the
isolationist Cassandra of pre–Pearl Harbor days who supported Nazi
Germany as a bulwark against Communism. He was still warning of
the chicanery of the Soviets and the contagion of Communism, both
of which suggested the usefulness of blurring his pro-German past.

Generals from Patton down had been filling him in with particulars of the Russian peril, and in comments meant to be heard at Potsdam he told a luncheon group of editors and writers at Robert R. Mc-Cormick's *Chicago Tribune*, rigidly isolationist until Pearl Harbor, "We have not established peace or liberty there [in Europe]. A third world war worse than the present one may occur. I have always believed that America's destiny should be kept independent of the endless wars between European nations. But to make ourselves independent of Europe's welfare [now] is impossible."

Without naming Russia he was obviously referring to the Soviet impact on the Continent, east and west. "The civilization that is falling to pieces in Europe is our civilization. . . . We have taken a leading part in this war and we are responsible for its outcome. We cannot retire now and leave Europe to the destructive forces which it has let loose. Honor, self-respect, and our own national interests prevent doing that." Should another war come, he predicted, referring to Germany's abortive lead in jet and rocket research, "New weapons will be used; these are already invented but are not developed enough to put into this war with their full effectiveness."

Although Stalinism or its local equivalent was as real a possibility in shattered, underdeveloped, and postcolonial parts of the world as Cold Warriors would visualize it, the playing upon fears that Britain or the United States could be undermined substituted Red rhetoric for reality. While the Soviet Union needed a period of postwar stability to absorb the demobilizing millions needed back in industrial and food production, the paradox that played to Rightist paranoia was that the Russians also cultivated instability everywhere outside their own borders except where the Soviet brand of "guided" government had already been imposed.

One unfinished matter of business not part of the Three-Power discussions, yet relevant to them, was the Potsdam ultimatum to Japan, cabled to Chiang Kaishek for approval to include his signature. A failure in transmission at Honolulu and again at Guam had delayed receipt until late in the evening Chungking time. It took until midnight for Patrick Hurley, the American ambassador, to get it translated for delivery to Chiang's residence. "We then had difficulty procuring a ferry across the Yangtze," Hurley cabled to Truman. "The prime minister declined to go out to Yellow Mountain with me in the night." The message would have to wait for morning on that side of the world.

In London the joint war crimes trials were still under discussion. Justice Jackson had taken the delegates to Nuremberg to examine the physical setting, feeling that the birthplace of Naziism was a usefully symbolic place to legally dispose of it. General I. T. Nikitchenko said that his side had no objection to conducting the "first trial" there but that the "permanent headquarters" of the tribunal should be in Berlin. Jackson accepted the empty language of "permanent seat" in Berlin, with trials at such venues as the tribunal might determine. Yet they could not agree upon binding language describing what war crimes were. It was easy to talk about atrocities, but the American side, frustrated by French and Russian disapproval, wanted to make initiating aggressive war a crime. Jackson threatened that "whether we got an agreement or not we would go ahead and try those people that are in our captivity." And he had Göring and Dönitz and Hess and Ribbentrop and similar luminaries for the dock. But since British representatives had no idea what government would have to approve their actions, the meetings were adjourned for a long weekend.

At 2:45 P.M. Churchill's plane from Gatow Airport in Berlin landed at the Northolt Aerodrome, between Uxbridge and Wembley. He was driven, with his daughter Mary, to Number 10 Annex at Storey's Gate, which had been his principal residence since the Blitz in 1940 had forced him out of more vulnerable Downing Street. There, waiting, were senior Conservative Party officials, who dampened his homecoming by a disquieting new estimate of a Tory majority of only thirty seats. Even Stalin had estimated eighty seats, but in Russia Stalin could have arranged any majority he pleased.

Before a late dinner, Churchill went to Buckingham Palace to report to George VI on the Potsdam proceedings and to discuss arrangements for the King to meet Truman when the *Augusta* was in English waters en route home. Back at Storey's Gate he discussed election prospects with Beaverbrook, dined with his family, then listened to his son-in-law Duncan Sandys, who was gloomy about retaining his own seat in Norwood. After everyone else left, Churchill worked on past midnight, then went to bed "in the belief," he recalled, "that the British people would wish me to continue my work."

Attlee had also returned to London, leaving the leading representative of the United Kingdom to be a civil servant, Sir Alexander Cadogan, who stood in for Eden at a brief foreign ministers' meeting. "Then, for the first time in days," Cadogan wrote later, "I walked out about 5:45 for an hour. One has to walk rather like a tiger, round and round one's cage, as, if one goes outside the British Sector, one is challenged at every yard by Russian sentries with tommy-guns." It was ten before he returned for a late dinner in the delegation mess. An RAF pianist was playing for whoever would listen. Then Cadogan returned to fill in his diary.

More fortunate than some in nearby Berlin, he had electric light to write by. Ruth Andreas-Friedrich had more difficulty with her diary. "The Committee for the Rehabilitation of National Socialists," she began, "has been temporarily suspended by the city council." It was a well-meaning organization with questionable jurisdiction and a glacial pace. If it went on at its current leisureliness, she wrote, "the last Party members will have their rehabilitation documents put on their graves by our grandchildren and great-grandchildren." Communist exiles who had spent the war years in Russia had returned, and "believe they're the best anti-Nazis and they, more than anyone else, are therefore entitled to shape our future. Those who've stayed believe the contrary. Anti-Nazis versus anti-Nazis." The "Muscovites"—she used a polite term in case her diary was seized—were clearly in a position to dictate the future.

It was a struggle, she added, "for every minute of electricity. It comes and it goes, capricious as the weather in April." She and other Berliners already suspected that the Russians were stripping the city of coal to run the dynamos, and of the dynamos themselves. She scoffed at the excuse of "broken cables." Others had told her that when the Russians left her sector to the West, "they took the coal reserves with them." Perhaps neither answer was correct, she shrugged. "Only one thing is for sure: whether we like it or not, we have to go back to our brick stove."

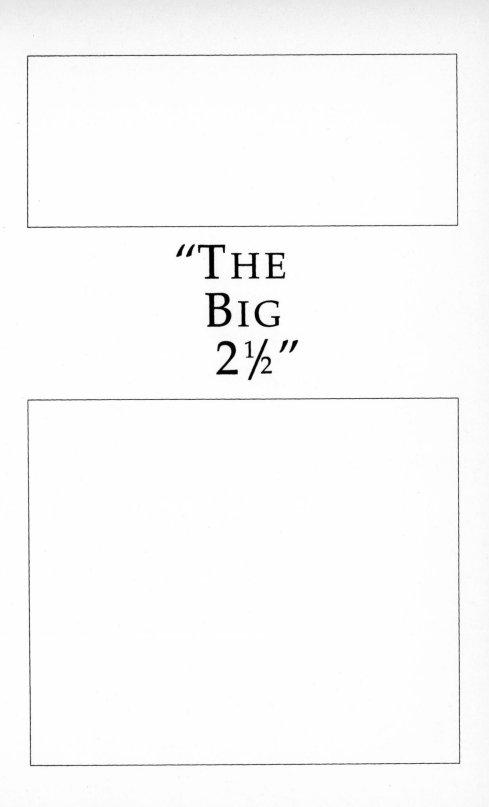

# "THE
# BIG
# 2½"

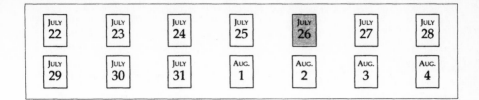

| July 22 | July 23 | July 24 | July 25 | July 26 | July 27 | July 28 |
| July 29 | July 30 | July 31 | Aug. 1 | Aug. 2 | Aug. 3 | Aug. 4 |

CHAPTER XIV

# · JULY 26, 1945 ·

*". . . a field of thistles"*

In London, Churchill woke just before dawn "with a sharp stab of almost physical pain. A hitherto subconscious conviction that we were beaten broke forth and dominated my mind. All the pressure of great events, on and against which I had mentally so long maintained my 'flying speed' would cease and I should fall. The power to shape the future would be denied me. The knowledge and experience I had gathered, the authority and goodwill I had gained in so many countries, would vanish. I was discontented at the prospect, and turned over at once to sleep again."

The P.M. often worked from his bed in the morning hours, but reawakening at about nine he rushed through the dictation of several telegrams in order to clear his decks for the tallying. The first went to Truman, who was to fly to Plymouth, where he would rejoin the *Augusta* for the voyage home. "The King feels," Churchill advised, "[that] he would not like you to touch our shores without having an opportunity of meeting you. He would therefore be in a British cruiser in Plymouth Sound, and would be very glad if you would lunch with him. He would then pay a return visit to *Augusta* before she sailed."

With the British and Commonwealth contribution to "Olympic" settled at Potsdam, Churchill sent a telegram to the new prime minister of Australia, Joseph Chifley (John Curtin had died on July 5), informing him that a Commonwealth Land Force, and—tentatively—a largely symbolic Commonwealth Tactical Air Force, had been invited to "take part in the main operations against Japan." The British had agreed with American service chiefs that salvaging some modicum of the Emperor's authority would enable enemy armies to surrender in his name. The last sentence of the declaration that would be the final wartime act under Churchill's signature warned that the alternative to surrender would be "prompt and utter destruction." If Chiang would sign promptly, the ultimatum could go out on the day that the means had arrived within delivery range of Japan.

"Little Boy"—at least the most lethal part of him—had been removed from the deck of the *Indianapolis* earlier on the morning of the twenty-sixth. Among the scientists greeting it—there were more scientists there to arm the bombs than there were bombs—was Navy commander Francis Birch, an MIT geophysicist at the Radiation Laboratory on leave to Los Alamos. He had helped design the device and joked that his job on Tinian was "screwing the nozzle."

The *Indianapolis* itself could not wait for the show and its crewmen had no idea what the fuss and the security at the dock were all about. Captain McVay's orders were to proceed via Guam to Leyte, where the crew was to undergo two weeks' training before joining Vice Admiral Oldendorf's TF 95 off Okinawa. The cruiser weighed anchor without ceremony the same day, just as Seaman Fahey's *Montpelier* was leaving Okinawa. A storm was approaching from the southwest; ships were safer riding weather out in the open. The two battleships, four cruisers, and nine destroyers of the task force were to enter the Yellow Sea just above Shanghai and move up the Chinese coast to within a thousand miles of Vladivostock.

As the ships pulled out, twenty LSTs were coming in—more landing craft for "Olympic." Preparations for the big push were visible almost everywhere in the western Pacific. On the twenty-sixth, also, Lieutenant Philip Habermann's Construction Battalion 29 on Samar, near Leyte, was formally assigned to "Olympic," his Seabees to sail in late October for Kyushu. Priority after the landing forces was going to dock and airfield construction units, with new assignments being made daily. From as far away as Hawaii, Washington, and California, 300,000 tons of construction material designated for Kyushu were to be offloaded beginning fifteen days after the landings. Included was equipment for a tank farm more extensive than anything west of Pearl Harbor. The infrastructure was going in for a long stay.

On completing minelaying missions in Japanese waters, the 40th Bomb Group returned to incendiary raids, thirty-four B-29s dropping five-hundred-pound clusters over Tokuyama, on the coast of lower Honshu, and twenty-nine (four missing the city) raiding Uji-Yamada, south of Nagoya. Over Tokuyama one *Baka* was sighted and shot down by a tail gunner. *Baka* interceptions of bombers were rare: bigger targets improved their limited effectiveness. An intelligence report to Admiral King's office dated from Okinawa on the twenty-sixth tallied only eleven *Baka* hits on ships since the beginning of the operation, but in the *kamikaze* attacks, 173 ships were hit and 53 damaged by near misses, with 27 vessels actually sunk. Much more had to be done to keep *kamikazes* away from the "Olympic" armada.

Although the 40th reported only "negligible" opposition, the 315th reported that a combination of moonlit night, searchlights, and a bursting yellow parachute flare left the Superforts highly vulnerable. "Muzzle flashes of guns," Hays Gamble noted in his diary, "stood out very plain[ly] and were constant and numerous." Two minutes before bombs-away, "plane 2nd position behind me caught direct hit in #2 engine and caught fire and exploded and fell to the ground in pieces." Not all losses were due to mechanical failure.

Compared to the delivery system for "Little Boy," the wherewithal for "Fat Man" was being shipped by express. "Fat Man" casings for the plutonium bomb had already arrived in Tinian. Raemer Schreiber, a young physicist with the "pit team" to assemble "Fat Man," had been assigned to escort the *Pu* core of the bomb to Tinian on its own C-54. With the uranium core for "Little Boy" safely in the Marianas it seemed less risky to send the second device by air. Carrying what looked like an oversized portable typewriter case, Schreiber left Los Alamos for Albuquerque at 4:30 A.M. in the middle of a convoy of staff cars. It was still dark. A glowing desert sun was up when his plane took off at 9:15 for Hamilton Field. The manifest listed him as "technical courier."

•     •     •

It was afternoon in fetid eastern Burma when U Nu, "Thakin" Nu to his followers, was deposited with his family in a hut on the far side of the Sittang where he was to stay if the retreat could be stabilized. The Japanese had forced their puppet Burmese regime to follow them, and Nu, a nationalist imprisoned, at thirty-three, by the British in 1940 and freed by the invaders in 1942, had long been devoid of choices. Military discipline had collapsed, but soldiers around him were each allotted one grenade. If one were wounded and in unbearable pain or unable to follow his unit, he was expected to blow himself up.

In the first light of the new dawn, Nu was awakened by explosions, and soon troops were at his door to urge his family into the seeming safety of the nearby jungle. In Burmese heat and humidity lush vegetation grew quickly, often right up to occupied areas. A village trolley station was only three hundred yards away, and British planes were bombing and strafing it even as the Japanese were trying to start the engine of a car that had come up from Moulmein. In an hour, once the area was again quiet, a lieutenant came to tell Nu that the trolley in which they were to have ridden south had been disabled. Space was made for Nu's family instead in a truck full of wounded troops, and the reluctant refugees continued on, apprehensive that some soldier in pain might pull a grenade pin and clap it to his body, spattering all of them, at best, with his guts.

While Raemer Schreiber and his nondescript black case were en route to the Pacific, in Manila at MacArthur's headquarters, Weldon Rhoades, his pilot, was noting how each new day was likely to become more interesting than the one he was recording. He had been to Nichols Field to make arrangements for his boss's trip, on "Olympic" business, to Okinawa. And the boss had been receiving messages outlining "the boundary between ourselves and Russia[n military zones] when and if Russia enters the war." "Certainly," Rhoades went on, "no one would have wasted time in meeting with the Russians to determine our zones of operation, unless the Russians had committed themselves on entering the war."

The American and Soviet military chiefs were meeting as he wrote, but the atmosphere was the typical Russian mixture of friendly protestations and rigidly limited cooperation. What was later called the Cold War had begun in Russian suspicions of the West and ambitions to extend Communism—and Western recognition of both—long before. In his warmest Potsdam manner, General Antonov opened by asking General Marshall to preside. But then he read a copy of a cool letter that Stalin had already handed to Truman. The American military had wanted to set up weather stations at Petropavlovsk in central Siberia and Khabarovsk, north of Vladivostock, to transmit weather data to American air crews flying toward Japan or in support of Russian troops. The sites would monitor weather patterns that the Air Force should anticipate. "The Soviet Command," Stalin offered, "is ready to accept and use the radio stations and equipment." But Russia considered it "wiser to use Soviet personnel which already had a great deal of experience in working with American radio. . . ."

Whether or not the Soviet-supplied data would be accurate was only one aspect of the response. The other, it was clear, was that Americans were unwelcome on Russian soil. Every Westerner was a potential spy. Further, each brought with him a standard of living and a freedom in behavior out of keeping with what the Soviets preferred their people to encounter and expect. Even the upscale experience of defeated and demolished Nazified Germany had already caused culture shock to Russian troops unused to civilized amenities taken for granted elsewhere. Recognizing both, Truman would note after a talk with Ambassador to France Jefferson Caffery, who worried that the Communist Party was already the largest and most aggressive political force in such liberated nations as Italy and France: "He is scared stiff of Communism, the Russian variety which isn't Communism at all but just police government pure and simple. A few top hands just take clubs, pistols, and concentration camps and rule the people on the lower levels." Stalin and his leadership, Truman observed, were "no different" in method than "the Czars and the Russian Noblemen (so-called: they were anything but noble). . . ." Caffery also had a down-to-earth warning that Truman did not record in his diary. Unless the French got coal from the United States to help them get through the coming winter, "there would inevitably be Communism and possibly anarchy."

In the military chiefs' sessions at Potsdam the boundaries for coordinating attacks on Japan created few political problems. Each offensive was confirmed as proposed, even to permitting (no doubt carefully insulated) American "liaison groups" in Khabarovsk and Vladivostock—as long as Russian observers could be posted in the headquarters of Admiral Nimitz and General MacArthur. In approval, Marshall "hoped that there would develop such an intimacy in liaison that we would find later that the commanders in the field would develop an even greater intimacy." This was hardly what Antonov had in mind.

Marshall and Arnold wondered whether any coordination could take place before Russia entered the war, and Antonov was coy, suggesting only that "preliminary" arrangements could be made. But when, he asked, would the invasion of Kyushu take place?

The "occupation," said Marshall frankly, "depended upon three factors: The first was the movement of troops from Europe. This was being done as rapidly as possible, and engineering troops were being moved first in order to prepare the way for the full application of air power. The movement involved two oceans and one continent, and although we could not be certain of carrying out the entire movement on schedule, and were now somewhat behind on both personnel and cargo, he hoped that all difficulties would be overcome. The second factor was the movement of large amounts of supplies from the Solomons, New Guinea, Halmahera* north to the Philippines and Okinawa, to be loaded on assault ships for the tremendous amphibious effort against Kyushu. The third factor is the recent withdrawal of our divisions engaged in the Philippines and Okinawa from heavy fighting, and the problem of rehabilitation and training for the next operation."

Finally, Marshall said, weather conditions made landings in September and early October too hazardous to undertake, although this was not a controlling factor. "At the present time the landing on Kyushu [is expected] to take place the last part of October."

He also expected, said Marshall, to extend attacks to Korea and to the Liaotung Peninsula in Manchuria, at the southern tip of which were Port Arthur (Lüshun) and Dairen (Talien)—long coveted by the Russians. This made the exact operational limits on the mainland crucial. The United States proposed a line for naval activity in Korean waters "beginning at latitude 38° north," then on the other side of the peninsula as far as "45° 45' north." Antonov offered a counterproposal shortening American lines to much less of Korea, beginning at 40 degrees north, but the actual demarcation would be overtaken by events.

---

*The largest island in the Moluccas, then part of the Dutch Indies, south of Mindanao and east of Celebes.

As the meeting ended, Marshall promised copies of minutes to his counterparts and was given a Russian-drawn map of Soviet understandings.

Despite the absence of British representatives, other consultations went on, including that of the group preparing the Potsdam protocol, chaired by Andrei Gromyko, and an Americans-only meeting, led by James Byrnes, dealing with the trials of war criminals and reviewing Justice Jackson's negotiations. One of the more sensitive matters concerned requests by other nations for custody and trial of alleged offenders surrendered to the United States but not to be tried jointly. "Renegades and Quislings," the Byrnes committee decided, could be turned over once regulations were written to indicate how the charges of war crimes were to be described.

War crimes were also on the minds of the throngs of reporters and the six hundred spectators permitted seats in the Paris courtroom where, resembling his wax effigy in the Grévin Museum, Marshal Henri Philippe Pétain, frail and eighty-nine, and former head of the Vichy puppet state, was on trial for treason. Not really a trial, cabled Janet Flanner to New York, but a lesson in history. The lesson was being taught, she wrote, by expert witnesses like ex-premiers Paul Reynaud and Edouard Daladier and ex-president Albert Lebrun, and "next morning the French newspapers are giving the text to ignorant citizens." *Paris-Presse* had headlined, "AUDIENCE INSTRUCTED," explaining that "the disastrous events of the year '40 are still not fully known except by a small number of initiates."

The French public was learning about its government's "lack of interest in those military modernities like tanks and anti-tank guns," and Pétain's prewar domination of the military. Newspapers played up the revelation that in June 1940

> Pétain had ready in his pocket, like an extra handkerchief, a tentative list of names for his prospective autocratic cabinet. The collaboration policy arranged at the Montoire meeting between Hitler and Pétain also got a big front-page play. . . . And, finally, the French armistice of 1940 hit the front page, after the Marshal's unattractive, sour, stammering, black-robed chief defense advocate, the *bâtonnier* [Fernand] Payen, angrily inquired if anyone present in court so much as knew the armistice terms, and after the charming, smiling Presiding Judge Mongibeaux leaned down from his bench, rather

like an elegant host catering to his guest's whims, to ask if
perchance there was a copy of the armistice in the house. At
that point, the terrifying old Prosecutor of the Republic [An-
dré] Mornet, who wants Pétain's head and has said so,
leaped up from his box to recite by heart those armistice
clauses that gave to the Nazis the right to occupy two-thirds
of France. "That's unfair!" the defense screamed. "You've
no right to begin with the worst part." "I have a right to begin where I choose and my good memory dictates," the
prosecution snarled back. The red and black robes recalled
the face cards in the trial scene of "Alice in Wonderland,"
but in the Paris trial scene there was no gentle humor, no
awakening from a dream.

The hiatus in plenary meetings gave Truman the opportunity to
visit the posh American occupation headquarters in Frankfurt, where
Eisenhower had a military band play "The Missouri Waltz" and commanding officers of units the President inspected managed to find
Missourians for him to meet. So many had been presented that he
told Secretary Byrnes that Missouri had won the war and that
Byrnes's home state of South Carolina had apparently not participated in it. After several jests at the paucity of South Carolinians the
84th Infantry Division driver of Truman's car, Pfc. Warren E. Baker,
swung around in his seat and said, "Mr. President, I would like to say
that I am from South Carolina and I live just around the corner from
the Secretary of State." Major General A. G. Bolling, Baker's commanding officer, was sharing the back seat with Truman and Byrnes,
but the young soldier was an ex-civilian with no sense of awe
for rank.

At Hamilton Field in California, a civilian in nondescript service
uniform—it was Raemer Schreiber—was briefed about ditching procedures over the Pacific in case his C-54 had difficulties. He had no
idea, Schreiber cautioned, how plutonium interacted with seawater.
"Well, nothing will happen anyway," said the briefing officer. "Don't
worry about it." (It was found later that a heavy insoluble material
forms when plutonium is exposed to seawater.) Schreiber tied a stout
cord between himself and his carrying case and lugged it aboard. A
crewman followed with box lunches for the overnight flight to
Hawaii, and they were airborne at 3:04 P.M. Pacific Time.

The C-54 was still gaining altitude when an engine stalled. Fortunately the other three were working, and they turned around and headed back for Sacramento, landing safely at 3:50. By 5:10 they were aloft again on a replacement plane, another aircraft in the 509th's "Green Hornet" cargo fleet, Schreiber still attached to the core of "Fat Man."

Churchill was in his bedroom at ten when the first results were delivered to the Map Room at the Annexe in the Office of Works Building. Captain Pim, the P.M.'s map expert, had fitted up the room so that the tally for each seat in the Commons could be flashed on a screen. There were, already, ten Labour gains over the Conservatives. Pim brought the news to the bedroom and found Churchill in the bathtub, clad only in a cigar. He was, Pim recalled, "surprised if not shocked. He asked me to get him a towel and in a few minutes clad in his blue siren suit and with cigar he was in his chair in the Map Room—where he remained all day."

With Churchill were his daughter Sarah and his brother Jack, and Conservative stalwarts Brendan Bracken, Max Beaverbrook, David Margesson, and the P.M.'s private secretary, Jock Colville. Every time Pim posted a Conservative gain, Churchill "offered me a brandy. I think there were only three during the day." Colville realized after half an hour that "there was going to be a landslide to the left."

Evelyn Waugh went to his club, White's, at eleven to follow the results on ticker tape, "and in an hour and a half it was plainly an overwhelming defeat. Practically all my friends are out. . . . 10,000 votes against Winston in his own constituency for an obvious lunatic. At 12.30 . . . I went to Rothermere's party—a larger, despondent crowd joined later by a handful of the defeated candidates. Watered vodka and exiguous champagne, rude servants, a facetious loudspeaker. Back to White's."

Just after one o'clock Clementine Churchill, with Mary, arrived after attending the declaration of results at Woodford, where her husband had been announced as reelected with a majority of seventeen thousand votes over a nonparty independent. The P.M.'s son Randolph and son-in-law Duncan Sandys were both out. On their way to the Map Room they met Colville, who was leaving. "It is a complete debacle," he told them, "like 1906." Everyone, Mary wrote, "looked dazed and grave," and when lunch was served the inhabitants of the room where the screen kept flashing appalling new losses sat "in Stygian gloom [as] Papa struggled to accept this terrible blow." Clementine offered the lame suggestion, "It may be a blessing in disguise."

"At the moment," said Winston, "it seems quite effectively disguised."

Walking along Pall Mall toward the College of Physicians, where he was to lunch, Dr. Moran encountered Colville, who repeated his "like 1906" remark, referring to the landslide for the Liberals, who gained a majority over all the other parties combined in a more multiparty era. Bracken, Macmillan, and other Ministers, Colville said, "were out." At three Moran was given a radio update, and another at four. It was a "rout." He walked to the Annexe, where he saw Churchill conferring with Sir Alan Lascelles, Private Secretary to George VI, to arrange for the P.M.'s audience with the King to formally resign. Moran sent in a note, and Churchill sent for him. Seated in a small room used by the secretaries, he was "doing nothing," lost in gloom. He looked up at Moran. "Well, you know what has happened?" Churchill asked. Moran assured him that he did, and spoke of the ingratitude of the people. "Oh, no," said Churchill. "I wouldn't call it that. They have had a very hard time."

"My dear Attlee," Churchill wrote that afternoon, "In consequence of the electoral decision recorded today, I propose to tender my resignation to the King at seven o'clock this evening. On personal grounds I wish you all success in the heavy burden you are about to assume." Then he wrote a message "to the Nation" that he released to the press and in which he "laid down the charge which was placed upon me in darker times" and regretted that "I have not been permitted to finish the work against Japan." It remained to him, he concluded, "to express to the British people, for whom I have acted in these perilous years, my profound gratitude for the unflinching, unswerving support which they have given me during my task. . . ." But they had swerved, and his words did not conceal that. Then he ordered his Humber automobile—"my carriage," he described it to Pim—to take him to Buckingham Palace, where he offered his resignation and formally recommended that his office go to Attlee.

George VI offered a title, the Garter, other rewards. Churchill refused them all. English political transitions were brief. He was expected to be out of Downing Street by the weekend. At 8:45 when his statement was read on the BBC he was back at the Annexe having supper with his family, joined by Eden and Bracken. "Inevitably mournful enough," Eden noted afterward in his diary, "though all tried to put [a] brave face on it."

Although the German physicists kept at Farm Hall by "Alsos" were permitted newspapers, they had not yet heard the election results. Some had speculated that they were held incommunicado to keep them from being useful to the Russians. Heisenberg, who had an opinion about everything, thought that the connection might be a French one. "It looks as though the Americans fear nothing so much as the possibility of the French getting even an inkling of the Uranium business. . . . The Americans know that [Pierre] Joliot is interested . . . and they are afraid that Joliot, who is a Communist, will do something with the Russians." The West's "position with Russia," he suggested, might hinge not only upon Potsdam but upon "the outcome of this election. It is obvious that if Attlee becomes Prime Minister—"

"We will be handed over to Russia," worried Horst Korsching, whose specialty was electrochemistry. "That's just it."

Erich Bagge, who had experimented with isotope separation, was more concerned about his family in Germany. The French had sent Moroccans into Hechingen who "raped the women one after the other. . . . The day I had to leave, three Moroccans were billeted in my house . . . and I'm supposed to look happy here. I shall go mad."

The talk moved to atrocities, and Bagge added, "If during the war, we [put] people in concentration camps—I didn't do it. I knew nothing about it and I always condemned it when I heard about it. If Hitler ordered a few atrocities in concentration camps during the last few years, one can always say that these incidents occurred under the stress of war. But now we have peace and Germany has surrendered unconditionally and they can't do the same things to us now."

At sea en route home on leave, Lord Halifax heard the news of the Labour landslide. He had never really liked Churchill but had served him loyally as ambassador in Washington. "It must be a cruel and bitter blow for him," Halifax wrote in his diary, and predicted that "this must be the effective end of his political life, and of his power, which has been food and drink to him for the last four years. It remains a terrible act of ingratitude." A few days later he put the ingratitude into horse-and-rider metaphor: "It is rather like being carried by your best hunter over very stiff country without a fall, and when you get home instead of taking him into a nice stable with a good mash and making him comfortable, giving him a clip on the backside and turning him into a field of thistles."

General Bernard Freyberg, a hero of both world wars, agreed with press and radio opinion that the "Services' vote" had produced the Labour turnout, and saw the sweep as emerging from dissatisfaction in the ranks—the "failure to have a fair system of replacement of battle-weary fighting troops. . . . When formations had been two years overseas there was a sharp increase of sickness and crime, particularly absence without leave and desertion on the eve of a battle." Further, he found, those British troops who came into close contact with American and Commonwealth soldiers "found by comparison that their conditions of service were appreciably better than his own. This was apparent not only in the matter of replacements but also those of pay, medical services and particularly of welfare." To Freyberg that had projected as well into the feeling that the same governmental attitudes would again prevail in postwar life unless the majority party were turned out.

The Labour leadership crowded Transport House to review the results. Herbert Morrison had won overwhelmingly, turning a 6,449 Tory majority at the previous poll into a Labour majority of 15,219. Promoted by economist Harold Laski, who considered himself the brains of the landslide, Morrison even had ideas of challenging Attlee for the top job, although Buckingham Palace had no doubts that it would be Attlee who would form the government. Ernest Bevin had also won big. After being unopposed before, he kept Central Wandsworth by a majority of 5,174 over a Brigadier who had won a Victoria Cross. Attlee considered himself, upon the King's summons, as Prime Minister, and told a press conference, "The people of Britain are facing [a] new era with the same courage as they faced the long years of war." Driven by his wife, a traffic hazard when behind the wheel, to the Palace, Attlee survived the experience and accepted the King's commission.

A jubilant rally for the faithful followed at the Central Hall, Westminster, where Harold Laski, claiming to be "the temporary head of the party," spoke in Stalinist vein. "At long last," he declared, "we have made possible full friendship with the Soviet Union. . . . We shall give no help either to decaying monarchs or to obsolete social systems."

In Potsdam, Sir Alexander Cadogan, minding the shop for the government, described the returns as "a terrible blow for old Winston, and I am awfully sorry for the old boy. It certainly is a display of base ingratitude, and rather humiliating for our country." Cadogan would be present that evening for the last major proclamation to be issued under Churchill's name, the Potsdam ultimatum to Japan.

The other message Truman found on returning from Frankfurt (the first confirmed Churchill's defeat) was Chiang's conditional approval of the declaration. Ambassador Hurley had cabled: "This morning, K. C. Wu, Assistant Minister of Foreign Relations, accompanied me to the Generalissimo's residence at Yellow Mountain. The Generalissimo read the translation carefully, and then K. C. Wu interpreted my explanation of the necessity for immediate concurrence." Explanation followed explanation, including a separate conversation with the Minister of Information, Wang Shih-chieh, who was about to become the Chinese Minister for Foreign Relations. Chiang and his advisers had only one reservation. He wanted to change the order in which the three heads of governments were listed, putting him ahead of the British prime minister, saying that his position second among the signatures would "help at home."

"When Chiang Kai-Shek had approved the message of concurrence," Hurley concluded, "we found the telephone out of order. It was necessary for me to return to Chungking to contact facilities to make transmission to you."

At 9:20 that evening, Truman released the proclamation, which would be broadcast to Japan in every way that the Office of War Information could devise. In thirteen brief paragraphs the heads of government announced that they were "poised to strike the final blows upon Japan" but would give Japan, before that happened, "an opportunity to end the war." Otherwise the war would be prosecuted "until she ceases to resist." Germany's costly resistance after its war had become "senseless" would "in awful clarity be an example." The terms followed, with a warning that the Allies "shall brook no delay." Those responsible for Japan's militaristic ways had to be eliminated from "authority and influence." Until Japan was judged to be peaceable, it would be occupied. Sovereignty for Japan would be limited to the home islands "and such minor islands as we determine." After disarming, military forces would be permitted to return home. Japan would not be "enslaved as a race nor destroyed as a nation"; however, war criminals, "including those who have visited cruelties upon our prisoners," would have to be punished. Fundamental human rights and freedoms would be established. Japanese industries needed "to sustain her economy" would be permitted, but "industries which would enable her to rearm for war" would be abolished. "We call upon the Government of Japan," the thirteenth point declared, "to proclaim now the unconditional surrender of all the Japanese armed forces, and to provide proper and adequate assurances of their good faith in such action. The alternative for Japan is complete and utter destruction."

The intent was clear between the lines as well as in the text of the declaration. The Allies—in effect, the Americans—showed that they were aware of Japanese feelings regarding the institution of the Emperor, but only by indirection. Nowhere was specific language about the future of Hirohito or the imperial institution he represented. There was neither call for his dethronement nor his punishment. If that question had been an obstacle to surrender, it had been blunted. Japan's adversaries had implicitly recognized that only the Emperor could proclaim and ensure surrender.

A messenger was dispatched to Foreign Commissar Molotov with a text of the document, and he telephoned Byrnes on reading it to ask that it be held up for "two or three days." When Byrnes explained that it had already been released, Molotov "seemed disturbed." Byrnes would explain that his intent was to avoid any embarrassment to the still-neutral Soviet Union by implying that it was a partner in the war, but Molotov insisted that he should have been consulted anyway. What he and Stalin wanted was an opportunity to delay the release of the ultimatum as long as possible, as they worried that the war might end before Russia was ready to seize its spoils. Truman and Byrnes wanted the declaration out so that Japan would have its opportunity to surrender before "S-1" went up. If Russia was not in the war by then, so much the better.

It was now up to the Japanese government, and in Tokyo it was already morning of the next day. The radio-monitoring service picked the text up at 6:00 A.M. The Cabinet would meet later that morning.

At Hyde Park, Eleanor Roosevelt took her husband's beloved Scottie, Fala, for a walk among the low, young pines, planted for sale as Christmas trees. When listing his occupation, FDR used to amuse Americans who hardly knew another president by identifying himself on voter registration forms as "tree farmer." Millions of housewives read Mrs. Roosevelt's "My Day" column in newspapers across the nation, where she would describe losing her dog temporarily as he pursued a scent, and quickly moving on anyway before the mosquitoes settled on her. "So I walk on just as fast as possible, meanwhile singing in unmusical fashion and as loudly as possible all the hymns I can remember from my childhood days. That seems to bring Fala back more quickly than calling him by name."

She went on to check her kitchen garden—it was important to set an example—and counted on putting up "many things for the winter months. My freezer, which is a new acquisition, makes it possible to plan for the future and use one's surplus." But guests were still due and there would be no surplus yet. Postmaster General Robert Hannegan and others were coming up to New York to spend the night under her roof. "Tomorrow we attend the ceremonies at the post office when the stamp issued in memory of my husband, showing the Hyde Park house, is first put on sale."

That afternoon itself there was another ceremony in memory of a war casualty. At the Fore River shipyard in Massachusetts, the Navy's newest destroyer was being launched, named for a pilot lost on August 2, 1944. He had been flying an explosives-laden B-24 from which he and a co-pilot were to bail out before reaching France. The bomber, radio-controlled from a nearby plane, was then to plunge into its target near Calais. Still over Suffolk, he switched on his radio guidance system. Shortly afterward the ten tons of TNT blew up. Behind him, a Mosquito photo-reconnaissance fighter flown by the eldest Roosevelt son, Elliott, was nearly flipped over but survived. At Fore River nearly a year later hundreds of dignitaries had gathered. Even *The New York Times* was covering the event, for the honoree's father was the multimillionaire Democratic political power Joseph P. Kennedy. He had hoped for a great political career for Joe Jr. Now there would be only a 2,200-ton destroyer by which to remember him, a ship launched too late to see any redemptive action. The torch would have to be passed to the next son, who was inconspicuously absent, traveling still as a Hearst reporter in Forrestal's entourage in Germany. No one in the audience but Joseph Sr. could have been thinking of torches being passed, for the very public paterfamilias overshadowed the surviving sons. Bobby and Ted were both still schoolboys, and Jack, however much a war hero, was a near invalid. The elder Kennedy, tears in his eyes for the vanished dream as well as the vanished son, stood rigidly at attention as a band boomed out "The Star-Spangled Banner" and the *Joseph P. Kennedy, Jr.* slipped into the water.

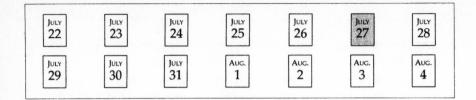

CHAPTER XV

# · JULY 27, 1945 ·

*". . . so heed this warning"*

Even before the *Indianapolis* joined the traffic jam of ships in Apra Harbor, Guam, early in the morning of the twenty-seventh, the Potsdam ultimatum filled the airwaves to Japan. Washington left almost no means untried, as a cable from the Office of War Information described to Truman:

> PROCLAMATION ON JAPAN HANDLED AS FOLLOWS (ALL TIMES EWT):
>
> TEXT RECEIVED AT 3:10 P.M. AT 3:32 P.M. GIVEN TO PRESS THROUGH OWI PRESS ROOM, WHITE HOUSE AND STATE DEPARTMENT SIMULTANEOUSLY.
>
> AT 4:00 P.M. (5 A.M. TOKYO TIME) OUR WEST COAST SHORT-WAVE TRANSMITTERS BEGAN BROADCASTING TEXT IN ENGLISH. HIGHLIGHTS BROADCAST IN JAPANESE AT 4:05 P.M. FULL TEXT IN JAPANESE NOT BROADCAST UNTIL TRANSLATION MADE BY OWI'S SAN FRANCISCO OFFICE HAD BEEN CHECKED BY TELEPHONE WITH STATE DEPT LANGUAGE EXPERTS IN WASHINGTON. FIRST

BROADCAST FROM SAN FRANCISCO AT 6:00 P.M. (7 A.M. TO-
KYO TIME).

THEREAFTER, JAPANESE TEXT BROADCAST REPEATEDLY ON
OUR ELEVEN WEST COAST SHORTWAVE TRANSMITTERS, SHORTWAVE
TRANSMITTER AT HONOLULU AND ON OUR MEDIUM WAVE SAIPAN
TRANSMITTER. CARRIED IN TWENTY LANGUAGES FROM WEST
COAST. ALL REGULAR PROGRAMS WERE CANCELLED TO PERMIT
FULL AND REPEATED BROADCASTS OF THE PROCLAMATION.

TEXT TRANSMITTED IN TELEGRAPHIC JAPANESE TO PACIFIC
AND CHINA OUTPOSTS SO ONE OFFICIAL JAPANESE VERSION WOULD
BE USED ON OUTPOST RADIO PROGRAMS AND IN LEAFLETS.

URGENT TELEGRAMS ORDERED PSYCHOLOGICAL WARFARE
OUTPOSTS IN HONOLULU, MANILA, CHUNGKING, AND KUNMING TO
USE FULL TEXT WITHOUT COMMENT OR SPECULATION UNTIL FUR-
THER NOTICE.

OUR NEW YORK OFFICE MADE PROCLAMATION HIGHLIGHTS
AND TEXT LEAD STORY FOR PROGRAMS IN 24 LANGUAGES BROAD-
CAST OVER 26 TRANSMITTERS.

CURRENT INSTRUCTIONS TO ALL OFFICES AND OUTPOSTS ARE
NO EDITORIAL COMMENT OR OTHER REACTION TO BE USED. THIS
WILL NOT BE MODIFIED WITHOUT CONSULTATION WITH STATE.
FULLEST PLAY WILL BE CONTINUED ON ALL PACIFIC TRANSMITTERS
THROUGH FRIDAY. FOR SEVERAL DAYS THEREAFTER THE PROCLA-
MATION WILL BE REPEATED AT REGULAR INTERVALS.

The efficiency of the operation was complete, yet there was one
matter overlooked even by old Tokyo hands. A concept alien in the
extreme to Japanese military tradition, the word *kōfuku*—"surrender"—did not appear in Army regulations.

A monitoring station in Chōfu, a Tokyo suburb, picked up the
San Francisco broadcast at 7:00 A.M. Listening to its repetitions, Sei-
ichiro Katsuyama made six recordings of it, typed it out from the
clearest one, jumped on his motorcycle, and rushed to the Foreign
Ministry in the hot early morning sun.

The ultimatum was also added to the paper war. During June
and July, B-29s dropped millions of leaflets aimed at the ordinary
Japanese citizen, as if he had some role in influencing his government. The first campaign urged the Japanese to surrender before they
were bombed and blockaded into starvation. However miserable
their lot, country dwellers had greater access to food, and carried on.

Exhausted from long working hours, air raid–punctuated nights, and malnutrition, city dwellers by government decree now received a portion of their rations at their places of work—a sure incentive for them to turn up, even if bombing and blockade left them with little or no work but the sweeping away of debris.

Leaflets directed at destroying public confidence in the Japanese leadership, complete to a montage of familiar faces, began, "Military leaders of Japan. Can you convince the people that you are able to defend the soil, the waters, and the sky of Japan?" And the messages concluded on the other side with an appeal by Truman that the Japanese choose a "peace with honor" over the "predestined end" of a "wasteful unclean death." The leaflets would exasperate the leadership, but subjects of the Emperor could only shrug them off, relieved that the M-26 bomb cases contained no explosives.

For weeks the Office of War Information, still misunderstanding its inability to move the Japanese, had also been raining warnings that the devastating bombings of the home islands were not directed against the people but against the military leaders who had "enslaved" them. Peace, the messages promised, would free people from military domination and ensure "the emergence of a new and better Japan."

"You can restore peace," the leaflet went on, "by demanding new and good leaders who will end the war." On the reverse side was a sketch of a B-29 dropping bombs, with the names of ten or twelve cities, enclosed in circles. "We cannot promise that only these cities will be among the attacked, but at least four will be. So heed this warning and evacuate those cities."

The texts, including the newest one, quoting the Potsdam ultimatum, were translated into idiomatic Japanese not by academically trained Americans but by several Japanese prisoners in a Quonset hut on Guam who had been clever enough to avoid *gyokusai* or *jisatsu* or one of the many other terms for dying with honor rather than surrendering with dishonor. College-educated POWs, their reading and writing knowledge of English exceeded their ability to speak it. One was a talented calligrapher whose graceful *kanji* could be photographed to good effect in Saipan. Another was a *kamikaze* pilot who survived a suicide dive and was taken to a stockade. When he refused to talk, one of the onlookers who had crowded into the Psychological Warfare Office quipped, "Why don't you tell him that if he doesn't talk you won't let him commit suicide!" Lieutenant Paul F. Boller, Jr., who knew enough Japanese to work with the POWs, would have their handiwork flown to Saipan, where the messages would be printed, wrapped in rolls, and packed in five-hundred-pound bomb casings to be dropped by the 73rd Bomb Wing, which made regular weather runs over Japan. Millions of leaflets warned thirty-one cities of raids to come. The new one threatened consequences even more dire.

In Hiroshima, the evacuation to the countryside of twenty-five thousand children above the third grade, begun in April, was completed. The construction of fire prevention zones, begun the previous November, was still continuing. Eight thousand dwellings had been demolished to leave firebreaks; now municipal authorities decided that a further twenty-five hundred had to be destroyed. Stoically, designated householders removed their possessions and watched the frail dwellings crumble into debris. Without any bombing, Hiroshima had lost ten thousand homes to the air war.

Many residents wondered at the fuss. Rumor had it (repeated in Makoto Oda's 1984 documentary novel *Hiroshima*, translated as *The Bomb*) that since many of the Japanese living in America were originally from Hiroshima prefecture, the city would not be bombed.

On that hot and humid summer morning in Tokyo, the Emperor, accompanied by Marquis Kido, inspected the bombed-out areas at a safe 9:00 A.M. However hungry and dispirited, people emerged from the rubble to greet the God-Emperor loyally, and he remarked to Kido that he was reminded of the great Kanto earthquake of 1923, when three quarters of Tokyo had been leveled. As Crown Prince he had toured the devastation to an enthusiasm no more loyal than he was now experiencing. And then 140,000 people had died, as many as had been victims of the first March fire raid.

Within hours of Tokyo's interception of the text of the Potsdam proclamation—at 10:30 A.M. Japan time—the Supreme Council for the Direction of the War met at Premier Suzuki's request. To his "inner Cabinet" he explained the very positive shift he saw from the unconditional surrender *of Japan* called for earlier to the unconditional surrender *of the armed forces*. The imperial structure, as Suzuki saw it, had been rescued, and it would be "extremely impolitic" to reject what amounted to an offer to preserve the key political institution of the Empire.

The military representatives among the six—the Ministers of War and Navy and the chiefs of staff of the Army and Navy—could only be persuaded to withhold a no until further word from Moscow. There would be "watchful waiting"—at least until after lunch, when the entire Cabinet would assemble.

When the Ministers reconvened, Togo took the floor. The Potsdam text, he emphasized, was now the only basis for a formal peace settlement. He thought that no dissemination of the ultimatum should be made until the government took a stand it could announce. Dissenting, the Welfare Minister, Tadahiko Okada, observed that the proclamation had been broadcast on domestic radio frequencies. The people could not have failed to learn of it. The Director of the Information Bureau, Hiroshi Shimomura, agreed. Withholding known news would be seen as a sign of weakness.

Everyone turned to the most forceful member of the Cabinet, fifty-seven-year-old General Korechika Anami, the War Minister. Since the fall of Hideki Tojo he had been the most powerful man in the country. He was not opposed to release of a partial text, he said—as long as the government's objections to it were also stated. The two chiefs of staff seconded him—but no one was ready to spell out the official objections for the Japanese public, for whom the government line was one of unlimited sacrifice until ultimate victory. The Foreign Office compromise prevailed: publication but without the Allied assurances that might make peace palatable to the people. Censored out was the guarantee that disarmed troops "shall be permitted to return to their homes with the opportunity to lead peaceful and productive lives," and the assurance, "We do not intend that the Japanese shall be enslaved as a race or destroyed as a nation." However, even the text that was assumed would frighten people into denouncing the proclamation caused many to feel that peace was suddenly attractive. Exhausted by privation and loss, a few citizens of some political and economic status stopped in at the Foreign Office to murmur cautious approval to Togo. According to his deputy, Toshikazu Kase (who had been with Togo even before Pearl Harbor), with the publication of the ultimatum, despite its omissions, "the last ounce of [bellicose] energy was sapped from the people at large." But no such impact was outwardly discernible.

While the Potsdam ultimatum was seeping into Japanese consciousnesses without a government gloss, an official Foreign Office translation was brought to the Imperial Presence by Togo himself as soon as it was ready, but Hirohito was an avid radio listener—he had a powerful shortwave receiver in his library—and had followed the war news that way since Pearl Harbor. Looking over the document that he already knew about, he wondered to Togo why the text had come to Japan by broadcast and not through diplomatic messages. Why hadn't the Allies handed it to a Japanese diplomat through third parties in Stockholm or Bern or Lisbon or Moscow?

Togo explained the means of delivery as discouraging for Japan. It was not so much a communication but a declaration of policy beyond negotiation. The terms were hard, the Emperor agreed, but they specifically ruled out making the Japanese a subject race. They were acceptable, as the war had to be stopped.

Since he had nothing more to offer, His Imperial Highness grew silent, and Togo understood that his audience was over. He stood. The Emperor rose and left the room, Togo bowing after him.

If the Emperor assumed that his communicating a desire to his Foreign Minister that the war be stopped would indeed stop the war, he was more naive than the record of his bellicose statements indicated. As late as April, and the *Yamato* fiasco, he may have been posturing for the military hierarchy, dancing to their tune. Yet if he wanted the war to end he had to talk to the generals who kept it going, not the harassed and impotent civil servants who did their bidding. He had not attempted that, preferring the elaborate indirection of the Court. The idea had long surfaced that the imperial system might be preserved through asking for a modification of unconditional surrender to guarantee that, but he could not specifically ask to save his own neck if surrender turned his military leadership into indicted war criminals. The dilemma continued to leave the onus of retreating on surrender conditions to the imminent victors, who owed the enemy nothing. That hadn't bothered Assistant Secretary of War McCloy when, at the White House meeting on "Olympic" prior to Potsdam, participants rose to leave and Truman turned to him to ask, "McCloy, you didn't express yourself and nobody gets out of this room without standing up and being counted. Do you think I have any reasonable alternative to the decision that has just been made?"

McCloy had heard the casualty estimates and was shocked into silence. Now asked for his opinion, the former Wall Street lawyer tossed aside the Gallup polls and the niceties about who should sue for peace. "We ought to have our heads examined," he said, "if we don't seek a political solution in preference to invasion. We should threaten Japan with the Bomb while offering to let them keep the Emperor." Truman thanked him for his "interesting ideas" and suggested he offer them to Secretary of State Byrnes. But Byrnes, McCloy knew, was opposed to "deals" with the enemy. In Tokyo, so were the real rulers, men like General Anami.

At 3:00 P.M. Tokyo time, the Emperor received Prince Konoye, who was responding to an imperial summons. On leaving, Konoye looked in at Marquis Kido's office in the palace. "Asked my opinion by the Throne regarding the termination of the present situation," Kido noted the Prince as saying, "I reported to His Majesty that I believed it necessary at the present moment to speedily put a close to the situation. His Majesty intimated to me that I should be prepared as I might be sent to Soviet Russia, and I respectfully accepted the assignment."

The elaborate indirection was typical courtier language. Konoye had long known of his potential peacemaking mission, although not directly from the Emperor. But there were now added concerns for Kido in setting anything down. His diary might be read by military informers. Nothing in the Imperial Palace, not even the Emperor himself, was safe from the militants bent upon continuing the war.

From Sato in Moscow would come what would seem later a haunting interpretation of the Potsdam ultimatum. Cabled to Togo at 4:30 P.M. Moscow time—late in the evening in Tokyo—it described the declaration as "a big scare-bomb directed at us." It was, he judged, a "counteroffensive" against the Japanese peace efforts directed at Moscow, and he worried about reports that "Stalin has for the first time participated in a discussion of the war in the Far East." Molotov's evasiveness in responding to the Konoye initiative seemed "designed to compel Japan to come out with a concrete proposal." Cautiously, Sato conceded, he had referred only to an ambiguous "concrete aim," which had not been enough. "I believe," he urged, "we must pay special attention to this point."

The hope that Russia could be bought as mediator (with concessions reversing only some of Japan's 1904 gains) had kept the Foreign Office from employing any other neutral nation as intermediary. It was a wish-fulfillment fantasy shared fervently in Tokyo, where Kido had already been called in, as he expected to be, for an audience with the Emperor soon after Konoye had left the palace. Konoye's authority, Hirohito explained, "was imperative to bring a close to the war at this juncture." Konoye had agreed to go to Moscow, the Emperor went on, to "endeavor his utmost at the risk of his life, were it the Imperial command."

While Baron Suzuki wrangled inconclusively with his Cabinet, B-29s began dropping over Tokyo and ten other cities millions of leaflets offering the reassurances censored from the Potsdam text in the Japanese press. Although suspicions of disloyalty could be attached to anyone picking up a leaflet, they were retrieved and read. A common ploy was to read one and then, holding it at arm's length, as if it emitted a bad odor, turn it in at a police station. Yukio Mishima, attending law school lectures again as well as working in a naval arsenal (which had replaced the destroyed airplane factory as his work site), found that "views favoring surrender had become fashionable among the students." Although Mishima "despised the fanatics who still believed in victory," he rejected, too, the turncoat disloyalty of his surrender-now lecturer, thinking, "Don't you try to fool me!" But neither students nor professors made government policy.

Unheard in Potsdam or in Washington, but still the official line in Japan, was Admiral Ugaki's boast, at a farewell party at the Navy Club for officers of the new Kyushu Air Group: "We should be the ones calling for the unconditional surrender of the United States, Great Britain, and China!" In his diary Ugaki was more realistic. "With the clearing of the weather in the south," he wrote, "enemy air raids from that district increased remarkably."

The intensity of the attacks was to emphasize the Potsdam ultimatum as well as to reduce Japanese capacity to repel "Olympic." And by the twenty-seventh what the Joint Chiefs had called "the pressing necessity" to have an occupation plan in place had been accomplished by MacArthur—devised, actually, by Eichelberger, who had taken over some of General Sutherland's duties on top of his own. It was strange, Eichelberger wrote home to his wife as he juggled "Olympic" and occupation, that one of his other concerns was the readjustment of the "point system" to send more long-term veterans home. "If the figure is lowered it will mean that the rest of the non-coms and . . . veterans will go. I do not suppose that there is an army in the history of the world that discharged its veterans just before a big battle."*

Although he would not take the "Olympic" force ashore, Eichel-

---

*The ruling in force as of July 23 required thirty months overseas before reassignment home—unless the draftee were over forty, which entitled him to discharge within 90 days. Eighty-five "points" made one eligible otherwise for discharge—one for each month in service, another for each month in a combat zone. Children at home earned a draftee twelve points; service stars for combat campaigns earned five points each.

berger had MacArthur's assurance that if victory came before he was to lead "Coronet" on the Kanto plain, he would go into Tokyo Bay with the first occupation forces. Eighth Army, carried and supported by Halsey's Third Fleet, was assigned eastern Honshu. The Sixth Army under Krueger and the Fifth Fleet would occupy western Honshu, Kyushu, and Shikoku. The XXIV Corps and Admiral Kinkaid's Seventh Fleet would occupy Korea south of the thirty-eighth parallel; and Hokkaido would go to Admiral Frank Fletcher's North Pacific Force, using troops of the Eighth Army. The contingency of surrender required lists of ships and units to be readied, some of the forces the same as those tagged for "Olympic."

A key to the operation would be the big naval base in Tokyo Bay at Yokosuka, which was to be occupied by a provisional regiment of Third Fleet Marines augmented by Marines from Guam. Three U.S. Navy landing battalions of four hundred men each—bluejackets—and a Royal Navy landing battalion from Task Force 37 would also be involved, the entire Yokosuka operation to be commanded by Rear Admiral Oscar C. Badger. But none of the plans would take effect as enumerated unless an invasion could be avoided.

Each day brought new evidence from the shifting attitudes of the colonized that the Japanese empire was crumbling. Syngman Rhee, exiled self-styled leader of the Korean opposition, urged action by the American military to encourage an uprising and to keep Korea from being seized and occupied, as he feared, by the Russians. No U.S. force, he felt, could get to Korea ahead of the Red Army, but the Koreans needed encouragement and assistance. In 1919 émigré dissidents had elected Rhee (originally Lee Sung Man) President of a Korean Provisional Government. He was seventy in 1945 but had held on to his empty title, living largely in Washington, where he could cajole American governments. "We the hereditary enemies of Japan," he wrote, "have been fighting the Japanese for forty years." He had cautioned Koreans by radio as early as July 1942, he went on, not to rise, but to wait for instructions. "Information reaches me through various sources that they are waiting for my message. I want to tell them when to rise."

Chester Nimitz responded that Rhee's cable of July 27 should be addressed to the Joint Chiefs of Staff, "under whose orders I exercise my command in the Pacific Ocean. I am of course sympathetic with your desire to fight the Japanese."

In Hong Kong, the internees at Stanley Camp, however gaunt and hungry, were no longer dispirited. According to John Luff it was no hardship after the mistaken Allied bombing two days earlier to sleep in the open. Hong Kong was hot in July, and the raid signified Allied proximity. When a Japanese disposal squad came to examine the damage and an unexploded bomb, they found that it had come through the roof and passed through Luff's bed. "Had I not turned in my bed at that moment," he wrote, "I should not have lived to tell the tale."

On the twenty-seventh Colonel Nomura called for Luff and asked, "Was that an American plane which dropped the bomb on your roof?"

"No," he said. "It must have been a Japanese plane because the Japanese had vowed that no American bomber would reach Hong Kong."

It was a remark that earlier would have been made at the risk of one's life, but the military governor's office was becoming aware of the likelihood of postwar trials for misconduct. Next, Nomura called in Noel Croucher, another internee, and was given the same impudent answer. Frustrated, the colonel gave Croucher a bomb fragment and asked him to identify the markings. He couldn't, Croucher explained. His glasses had been broken. Nomura put his own milk-bottle-bottom glasses in Croucher's hands and shouted, "Read! Read!" Croucher looked again and said, "I don't know. It must have been captured from the Americans."

In the city itself the Japanese-run *Hong Kong News*, now down to a single sheet, published the censored text of the Potsdam proclamation with the headline "DON'T SCARE US." The ultimatum, it declared, was a piece of unqualified impudence. To most Hong Kong Chinese it seemed a very confident document.

In Burma, when the astonishing news arrived by radio that Labour had unseated Churchill's government, George MacDonald Fraser remembered his exchanges in the jungle west of the Sittang when barely literate troops tried to fill out their ballots:

> " 'Ey, Grandarse—'oo d'ye spell Iredell?"
> " 'Oo the hell dae Ah knaw? W'ee's Iredell?"
> "Liberal candidate in Carel.* Ah's writin' yam tae see w'at 'e's on aboot."
> "Weel, Ah doan't belang bloody Carel. Ah belang

*Carlisle.

Peerith,* an' Ah doan't ken w'at constituency it's in, an' Ah doan't care 'cos Ah's nut votin', neether."

"Ye ought to vote, man."

"W'at for? The Labour man doesn't stand a fookin' chance, an' Ah'm boogered if Ah'll vote Tory. Them boogers 'es bin in ower lang."

"Weel, vote Liberal, then. . . ."

"Ah want Choorchill oot, an' his whole fookin' gang. Ah remember the 'thirties, marra, if thoo doesn't. Ah want rid of the bloody Tories, see, an' the lah-di-dahs, an' the lot o' them. They got us into this fookin' war, didn't they?"

For Evelyn Waugh, a dedicated Tory, the results of the election were devastating. He had finished with his war—liaison with the Partisans in Yugoslavia, where he had served with Randolph Churchill—but was finding the unheroic aftermath distasteful. At 7:30 A.M. he was awakened in his room at the Hyde Park Hotel by the younger Churchill, "dazed by adversity" but hoping to find another parliamentary seat. His father, he told Waugh, was "trying to get used to being a private citizen, fretting about [ration] coupons for curtains and petrol, [and] homeless without his despatch boxes and aeroplanes. Max Beaverbrook giving ill advice to the last, urging on him the joys of opposition. Nothing could be more unfortunate to his reputation. . . ."

Dr. Moran was at the Annexe by 9:15, finding it "strangely quiet," almost "deserted." The loyal Frank Sawyers, the P.M.'s valet, told Moran before he went to Churchill's bedroom that Churchill had complained of feeling giddy before retiring, but when Moran checked, Churchill said at once, "I'm very well." He had been "stunned," he confessed, and saw "some disgrace in the size of the majority." Moran suggested a holiday. "There is no difficulty about holidays now," said Churchill wistfully. "The rest of my life will be holidays. It will be worse in three days, like a wound; I shall then realize what it means. What I shall miss"—he pointed toward the traditional red box of official papers—"is this. It is a strange feeling, all power gone. I had made all my plans. I feel I could have dealt with things better than anyone else. This is Labour's opportunity to bring in socialism, and they will take it. They will go very far."

*Perth.

John Colville discovered how quickly things had changed when he walked into No. 10 Downing Street and found himself Private Secretary to Clement Attlee. Colville congratulated Hugh Dalton on having engineered the victory, and Dalton explained that the Tories "had left the constituencies untended, the agents being for the most part away fighting." Colville was privately surprised that burly Ernest Bevin had been named Foreign Secretary rather than Dalton, but learned that on advice of Sir Alan Lascelles, the King had persuaded Attlee to change his mind. A trade unionist, Bevin was likely to be more conservative than Dalton, an intellectual with a doctorate.

At the Annexe, Churchill said good-bye to his service chiefs, Brooke, Portal, and Cunningham, and then to one of his private secretaries, Paul Beards. "Mr. Attlee," Churchill said, "is a very nice man and you will be well with him. The Private Office is a most important mechanism in the machinery of the State and it is a little known and most useful experience to serve in it." Then he rose from his chair, put his hand on Beards's shoulder, and said good-bye.

At noon came a final farewell Cabinet meeting in Downing Street. "It was a pretty grim affair," Eden noted in his diary. When it was over, and he was on his way out, Churchill called him back and they had a half hour alone. He couldn't help feeling that his treatment by the electorate had been "scurvy," Churchill said. "Thirty years of my life have been passed in this room. I shall never sit in it again. You will, but I shall not."

His place in history was secure, Eden assured him. Nothing in the postwar years could change that. "This he accepted and at length we parted."

That night, Paul Beards recalled, Churchill's last in the Annexe, once the ex-P.M. went to bed, "I counted several half-finished glasses of whisky and half-smoked cigars." As he was about to retire he called for Captain Pim. Churchill had turned ashen and looked about to faint. Then he recovered himself. "They are perfectly entitled to vote as they please," he told Pim, who hadn't asked. "This is democracy. This is what we've been fighting for."

There was another requiem in London that day, a memorial service in Holy Trinity Church, Kingsway, for a German, and broadcast by the BBC. Philosopher and theologian Dietrich Bonhoeffer, one of the few great humanists in Germany in the grim 1930s, had been murdered at the Clossburg concentration camp by the Nazis just before the Neustadt area was liberated by the Americans. He was,

Bishop Bell eulogized, "one of a noble company of martyrs of differing traditions," and exemplified "the moral and political revolt of
the human conscience against injustice and cruelty. He and his fellows are indeed built upon the foundation of the Apostles and the
Prophets." Bonhoeffer had lost both his sons and both his sons-
in-law to Nazi execution squads. It was, said Bishop Bell, "a death
for Germany."

Germany itself was still a country of the dying. Many could not flee
fast enough from the de-Germanized East. In the Sudeten town of
Aussig (now Ústí nad Labem) more than two thousand had been killed
by revenge-bent Czechs, who threw women, and even children in
baby carriages, according to the Red Cross, into the Elbe. (One death
camp survivor, Ben Helfgott, remembered seeing Hungarian women
beating up a German woman with a small boy and a baby in a carriage.
The boy watched, crying. "What do you think you are doing?" Helfgott asked one of the women. "Paying them back," she said.)
    On the day of Bonhoeffer's memorial service a boat arrived at the
docks on the Spree in Berlin with a cargo of nearly five hundred children, the Red Cross reported, "half dead with hunger," who had
come from Finkenwalde in Pomerania: "Children from two to 14
years old lay in the bottom of the boat, motionless, their faces drawn
with hunger, suffering from the itch and eaten up by starvation." But
too many people were absorbed in their own survival to offer any aid.
    Other victims of the chaos of identities and borders, "displaced
persons"—DPs—were in some cases becoming out of desperation a
new criminal class. Armed robberies, black marketeering, and pilferage, often brazenly from military stocks, were burgeoning out of the
disorder. Returning to Lübeck from Hamburg, where a curfew had to
be imposed by British occupation authorities, Arthur Dickens noted
in his diary the "flourishing Black Market" in both areas. "Most of the
sellers are . . . foreign D.P.s who began business not only with the
proceeds of theft but with the coffee and cigarettes which they receive in the American Red Cross parcels. A favourite trick is to offer,
at exorbitant price, a tin of coffee with a thin topping of genuine coffee and an interior of *ersatz*. Consequently when buying coffee on the
Black Market, the normal procedure is to pour out the tin first upon
a newspaper."
    In Potsdam, Alexander Cadogan learned from a telegram from
Attlee that the Labour delegation could not return that day as he was

still forming his government. He included messages on the postponement of plenary sessions for both Stalin and Truman. Other meetings would go on with nonpolitical British representatives. Cadogan hurried a packet of papers for Attlee to study aboard a fast Mosquito bomber for London.

After what Truman had heard from Jefferson Caffery about France the day before, he drafted a memorandum to Stalin on the "acute coal famine" that threatened Europe as the heating season approached. With the "large commitment of industrial and military resources" the United States had to make for the coming offensive against Japan in mind, Truman asked for a common four-power policy with respect to coal, including "the portions of Germany occupied by Soviet forces." Realizing that it was useful for Communist parties in Western Europe to have unhappiness to exploit, Truman had little hope for any help from the East.

Then he drafted a memo to Eisenhower asking him to look into ways to extract as much as ten million tons of German coal for use elsewhere in the West, and to attempt to secure more from the Soviet zone. (In the United States, coal miners would become eligible on August 1 for increased meat rations and an extra pound of sugar per month as an inducement for them to extract more coal.) He realized, Truman added, that carrying out such policies "may cause unemployment, unrest, and dissatisfaction among Germans of a magnitude which may necessitate firm and vigorous action. Any action required to control the situation will be fully supported." He could not let the West go Communist by default.

It was no coincidence that the foreign ministers' meeting, in which Cadogan sat for Britain, was preoccupied with economic matters—and Molotov insisted, as they convened at four that afternoon, that he would discuss nothing other than reparations until that matter had been settled to Soviet satisfaction. Although everyone recognized that Germany had to remain the chief industrial engine for Europe if the Continent were to revive, Molotov was not interested in its prospering. He was fixed upon Russia's industrial rehabilitation, and more, at the expense of German potential. Byrnes understood, and used blunt Americanese to make his position clear to Molotov. "When you ask for 20 billion [in reparations]," Byrnes said, "and I say I will discuss it, it does not mean I will write a check for it."

Twenty billion dollars, he went on, had been a figure suggested at Yalta for the whole of Germany, including what was becoming

Polish Silesia and Pomerania. And the Russians were also excluding what they had already seized as war booty. "Mr. Pauley and Mr. Clayton tell me that in the American zone in Berlin they saw a plant of the I.T. and T. stripped of all machinery and four other plants were stripped, a rayon plant, Zeiss plant, and others. . . . It is impossible under these conditions to tell what reparations are available in Germany." He wanted an agreement, Byrnes said, but he did not see how they could reach one. "We do not want a plan that will cause constant friction between us."

"Neither the United States nor Great Britain was occupied," Molotov insisted. "Our plants were laid waste. . . . The right of occupied and invaded countries to reparations is inalienable. . . . It is high time that we have our answer."

Cadogan suggested waiting until Attlee was present and could contribute to a solution, but even as they postponed the subject of Germany, Molotov brought up reparations once more as they turned to the problems of Austria. "Why should Romania pay," Molotov asked, "and not Austria?"

When the formal session ended as rancorously as it had begun, Byrnes and Molotov sat down privately at six. Molotov began with a new protest at the issuance of the ultimatum to Japan before he could stall it, and Byrnes could not tell him that the machinery of the ultimatum had to operate in coordination with the planned atomic bomb strike. Instead, he reminded Molotov that Russia was not at war with Japan. Between the lines it seemed clear that the Russians did not want Japan to surrender prematurely. Stalin, Molotov suggested, might offer his personal objections to Truman.

Since it had become obvious to Molotov that without compromise the Soviets would only be able to pillage their own zone, he returned to the reparations question on a less adversarial note. The United States, said Byrnes, now more softly, was sympathetic to the distress caused in Russia by the Germans, but conditions in Germany had changed since Yalta. Germany's prolonged resistance had left much of its infrastructure in ruins: "war booty" had been removed wholesale; and a large and productive part of Germany had been "alienated" to Poland.

Molotov was ready with a rejoinder. In February at Yalta the Soviets assumed greater destruction than in fact had occurred. (Allied saturation bombing had failed more often than it had succeeded, despite boastful communiqués.) There was still much that could be removed. But the Ruhr was in the British zone. They would have to wait for the return of Attlee without Churchill.

What might be in store for Europe if economic chaos led to its political equivalent could be seen, in Moscow, by those privileged to experience the many celebrations of victory and parades of returning military units almost every day since early May from Butyrki Prison, where the jubilation could be heard but not seen. Since V-E Day, the huge block had echoed with rumors of peace amnesties. Someone had even soaped high on the wall of the baths "Hurray! Amnesty on July 17!" The amnesty had come even ten days earlier than that, but applicable only to criminals—not to deserters and political prisoners—sentenced to three years or more. On the twenty-seventh Aleksandr Solzhenitsyn and a cellmate named Vallentin were summoned by guards. From nearby cells other prisoners exhorted them to take messages out and to send in food parcels. "Perhaps," Solzhenitsyn remembered, "you honestly didn't believe it, you tried to brush it aside with jokes, but flaming pincers hotter than anything else on earth suddenly seized your heart. What if it were true?"

With twenty other inmates they were led through the palace's once-grand interior courtyard with its unbearably bright little stand of trees, usually encountered only by prison officials: "Never had my eyes seen the green of the leaves with such intensity. . . . And never in my life had I seen anything closer to God's paradise than that little Butyrki garden, which took no more than thirty seconds to cross on the asphalt path." On the other side they were locked into a holding cell known as "the station."

Three hours later the first prisoner, a former bookkeeper, was called forward. He returned crushed. He had been awarded five more years. A second was called. Fifteen years, he reported with a hysterical giggle.

When Solzhenitsyn was summoned he was taken to the "frisking box," where new prisoners were searched. An NKVD major sat at the far end of a rough-hewn table on which there were some papers and a lamp. He gestured to Solzhenitsyn to sit down, then leafed through the typed documents and pulled out a single sheet. It contained the bureaucratic formula of the prisoner's sentence, which the major read out in a bored voice. Then he turned the paper over and wrote down his attestation that the text had been read to the defendant. The sentence was for eight years. It was the defendant's entire trial proceeding.

The neat, black-haired bureaucrat pushed the paper across the table to Solzhenitsyn to sign. "No," said the beneficiary of Soviet due process. "I have to read it for myself."

"Do you really think I would deceive you?" said the major.

Solzhenitsyn saw that the sheet was actually a carbon copy, dated the seventh, the day of the peace amnesty, which was described as the day of his official "trial." His crime was listed as "Anti-Soviet agitation and attempting to found an anti-Soviet organization. 8 years in corrective labor camps."

Uselessly he said, "But this is terrible. Eight years! What for?"

"Sign there," said the major, trying to speed the formalities.

"In that case," said Solzhenitsyn, "allow me to write an appeal here and now. The sentence is unjust."

"When the time comes, you can," said the major. The warden standing by hurried Solzhenitsyn out.

On the way to the gloom of the former Butyrki church, now crowded to its high ceilings with three tiers of cells, Vallentin reassured his friend. "Well, never mind, we're still young and we'll survive. The main thing is not to make any more mistakes. When we get to the camp we'll keep mum with everybody, so they don't slap another sentence on us. We'll work honestly and keep our mouths shut."

For hundreds of thousands of Russians similarly circumstanced it was their outcome of what Soviet propaganda called "The Great Patriotic War."

At Hickam Field on Oahu, Raemer Schreiber arrived, carried his tethered plutonium core into a fresh C-54, and lifted off for Kwajalein Atoll, where, on Wake Island time across the International Date Line, it was already the next day.

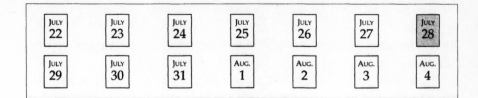

| July 22 | July 23 | July 24 | July 25 | July 26 | July 27 | July 28 |
| July 29 | July 30 | July 31 | Aug. 1 | Aug. 2 | Aug. 3 | Aug. 4 |

# CHAPTER XVI

# · JULY 28, 1945 ·

### *". . . to kill with silence"*

The *Indianapolis* weighed anchor at Apra Harbor, Guam, at 9:00 A.M. It was still the previous day in Potsdam. Her estimated time of arrival at Leyte Gulf in the Philippines was 11:00 A.M. on July 31, which meant that an unhurried cruising speed of sixteen knots was indicated. Three hours and thirty-five minutes later Raemer Schreiber's C-54 landed in Kwajalein, refueled and took off again for Tinian, where he delivered the core of "Fat Man" at 10:10 P.M. The cruise of the departed *Indianapolis* by then had long been routine. Captain Mc-Vay had been informed of two possible submarine contacts within one hundred miles of his likely route, but not of the sinking of the *Underhill*. Expected arrival time was radioed to the battleship *Idaho*, flagship of Admiral Lynde D. McCormick, who commanded the Leyte training unit at Tacloban, but it was received in such a garbled form that it could not be deciphered. The *Idaho*'s communications officer failed to signal for a repeat.

Although McVay had requested an escort, headquarters at Guam replied that none was available or needed. All escort vessels in the Marianas were convoying reinforcements and supply vessels for "Olympic" or were patrolling "up the ladder of the Bonins" for B-29 crews who might have to ditch. An older vessel, although refitted, *Indianapolis* had no sonar gear, although it had radar. McVay's instructions were to zigzag "at discretion," which he did during daylight. Cruisers like McVay's had no air-conditioning. To make sleep possible during the tropical nights, he intended to keep hatches and ventilation ducts open.

In the path of *Indianapolis* was Lieutenant Commander Mochitsura Hashimoto's *I-58*, twelve days out of Kure. On the eighth day, having encountered no targets, he went to his sub's shrine—every ship had one—to pray off his depression. On the twenty-eighth his supplications seem to have been answered as he was able to launch two *kaitens* at what appeared to be enemy ships, one a suspected tanker. Yet the war had turned sour for Hashimoto. He had been an officer aboard one of the mother ships to the two-man midget subs launched on December 7, 1941, off Pearl Harbor; and submariners, in the face of contrary evidence, still believed that at least one of the midgets that had slipped past the submarine nets had torpedoed the *Arizona* in the most spectacular and costly American loss of the war. Now they were crowded against their own home islands and the Imperial Navy had almost nothing to fight with but the obsessively eager suicide pilots of their manned torpedoes. If the *I-58*'s fuel ran out, *kaitens* would have to return to Kure alive and shamed.

Japanese offensive operations were at as low a point as they had been in the war. Morning and evening, carrier planes and heavy bombers raided the length of Honshu, while warships moved in close to land and bombarded coastal cities. On the northernmost coast, opposite the lowest point of Hokkaido, was the bustling city of Aomori. A hub of ninety thousand people then, it was the northern terminus of the Honshu main railway line, and the terminus of the much-interdicted rail ferry from Hokkaido, domestic source of Japan's coal. Colliers and coal barges accounted for its sawmills, lumber yards, and shipbuilding trade, making it, Homer Bigart reported, a "sawdust city" ripe for conflagration. Bigart, of the New York *Herald-Tribune*, was over the city riding a B-29 in the last group of raiders early on the twenty-ninth. The Superforts had refueled en route on Iwo Jima in order to make a 3,050-mile round-trip—a break in the "desperately tedious" overwater flight.

When his plane reached its aiming point there was nothing left to incinerate, and the pilot, Captain Wyatt J. Gay of Milton, West Virginia, altered course to bomb a row of buildings adjacent to a marshaling yard. Directly ahead a pillar of smoke arose more than six thousand feet above the plane. Gay flew through it and out.

"It is no use pretending," Bigart understated, "that B-29 raids on smaller empire cities are exceptionally thrilling. Apart from the slight uneasiness that always comes with landfall on an enemy shore, and another moment of tension when the ship goes on her bomb run, there is seldom anything to alter the brutal monotony.... A conflagration seen from 14,000 feet has the same fascination as a pile of burning leaves to a small boy. It is of course different for the Japanese."

As they turned back toward Guam he saw, far across Mutsu Bay toward the Ominato naval base, flashes that might have been antiaircraft fire, harmless from that distance. Sixty-five miles out the fires were still visible. "It was a beautifully clear night. We picked up Moscow radio perfectly."

From Okinawa, where MacArthur had flown for a brief conference about "Olympic," Weldon Rhoades noted Japanese offensive capacity—an air raid before dawn in which a single plane dropped one bomb "about 100 yards from an airplane." The airstrip just missed had "500 airplanes parked." Admiral Ugaki reported nevertheless that four torpedo-carrying *Tenzans* "either sank or destroyed three cruisers and others at Okinawa." The claims he received—or boasted of—were often imaginative. What his diary did make clear was that Kyushu, Shikoku, and Honshu were all under severe bombardment by air and sea. Carrier planes ranged about Japan, augmented by P-51 Mustangs from Okinawa, 146 of which struck around Tokyo, strafing communications and the power grid—locomotives, electric cable towers, radar stations, patrol boats, even a floating dredge.

Five planes were lost to enemy ground fire; three pilots were rescued. One ditched pilot from the *Yorktown*, Lieutenant Donald E. Penn, radioed for a rescue seaplane, and four were dispatched to Tokyo Bay. Just before dark a PBY5A "Catalina" piloted by Air Force Lieutenant John Rairich splashed alongside Penn's life raft. Unfortunately, plowing toward them was a Japanese destroyer escort. Zooming down almost to wavetop altitude, Rairich's P-51 fighter escort strafed the ship and drove it off. But just as Rairich struggled into the air with Penn aboard, while shots from enemy small craft exploded about him, a fighter from the escort group ditched in the bay.

Returning through the fire, Rairich picked up the second pilot,

Lieutenant (j.g.) Henry Camara. The overloaded plane lifted off the water amid even heavier fire. Rairich flew toward the safety of TF 38, 150 miles to the south, but low on fuel, shot up, and lumbering, his "Dumbo" needed help itself. Soon below he saw two American destroyers. One turned on a searchlight into the wind; the other took up a position a half mile upwind. Landing nearby, Rairich, with his crew and the two rescued pilots, clambered up the net lowered by the destroyer, which then turned its guns on the disabled float plane and sank it.

The log of the TF 38 carrier *Bonhomme Richard* reported a similar, although less hazardous, incident two days earlier. Lieutenant W. F. Smith and Ensign J. G. Selway had been launched in a rescue operation off Jizo Saki. "En route to area they were advised that the rescue . . . had been effected and were directed to escort a PBM Dumbo to the scene of some downed pilots off Shikoku. They covered the Dumbo while the rescue was effected and later ditched when their fuel was exhausted. They were picked up in good condition by the Dumbo and returned to the Dumbo base." The rescue had required the ditching of two operational, late-model fighters and the hazarding of their pilots in addition to the PBM and its crew. Such feats were valiant but costly, with planes, ships, and men risked to save a single life. Few episodes demonstrated better the difference between the philosophies of the combatants.

American flight crews forced down in the home islands faced terrors already well understood, although not less feared for that. To the Japanese, particularly in remote, unsophisticated villages, airmen from the mighty planes were mysterious figures, a conception fantasized in Kenzaburo Ōe's dreamlike story "Prize Stock" (1964). Ten years old in 1945, Ōe lived in a remote mountain village on Shikoku, where he imagines a black airman has been taken prisoner, so exotic as to be "an animal of genius." In the segregated American army there were no such crewmen on B-29s, but Ōe mythicizes the muscular black giant much as he does the rural area, which is medieval and romantic. The child narrator's ecstatic relationship with the almost childlike prisoner is a moment of bliss aborted by the violence that erupts when soldiers come to take the "wonderful domestic animal" away. In the wartime summer the event is a rite of passage, yet "Prize Stock" also encapsulates the airman's nightmare.

The fantasy prisoner survives—for a while—because he hadn't been greeted by farmers with pitchforks or military police in burned-out cities. The firebombings had almost made the propaganda characterization of aircrews as devils unnecessary. Some were killed on capture; others were given sketchy trials and then executed, often by beheading. Yet however unpleasant the prospect of having to parachute from a disabled plane, pilots and crews continued to take their aircraft up, and the bombings continued to escalate. The day before, the 494th Bombardment Group, flying B-24s from Yonton Airfield on Okinawa, had been briefed about a mission the next morning to bomb the *Haruna* in Kure Harbor. High-level reconnaissance photos had not revealed that the *Haruna*, its plates unsealed by near misses, had already settled into the harbor mud. Its continued existence had an almost mystical resonance for military planners, although it was already crippled. It was, a briefing officer claimed, the "last symbol of the strength of the Japanese Navy."

Listening, Lieutenant Tom Cartwright took in the warning that Kure was "an amphitheater" of antiaircraft firepower. He did not need to have the maxim repeated that one should "never fly over an enemy battleship." How else, he wondered, do you drop bombs on a battleship? Crews were also reminded, as before each mission, that name, rank, and serial number were no longer the only data to be revealed if captured. They knew as individuals little of intelligence value and were to cooperate fully with their captors in order to mitigate possible abuse. Also, they were to avoid civilians if possible and seek out military personnel to whom to surrender. Escaping or finding friendly people on the ground was out of the question.

Such concerns had never occurred to Cartwright as an aircraft-happy junior college freshman in Amarillo when the Sunday movie he had been watching had been interrupted by news of Pearl Harbor. Nearly four years later his *Lonesome Lady* was in one of six flights of B-24s taking off from Okinawa at dawn on the twenty-eighth. Flying at about ten thousand feet through broken clouds, he found the target area amid a flurry of black smoke puffs. Several B-24s were hit; two were badly damaged. *Lonesome Lady* was struck in the critical join of fuselage and right wing.

Cartwright hoped to be able to reach the comparative safety of the sea before ordering a bailout, but the plane was aflame and the hydraulic controls no longer worked. Out of intercom contact, the tail gunner bailed out. With the fire spreading, Cartwright ordered the rest of his crew out. Then he scrambled through the gyrating plane to the bomb bay and saw the ground "coming up so fast" that he popped his chute almost immediately and hit the ground only seconds later.

Admiral Halsey was far more jubilant than the airmen of the *Lonesome Lady* and the *Taloa*—those, at least, who had survived. With instructions to concentrate on the *Haruna*, he had ordered the Kure strikes. At the very least he now considered the *Aoba*, the *Ise*, and the carrier *Amagi* as destroyed, and the carrier *Katsuragi* badly damaged. Yet the big ships left to the Imperial Navy were impotent anyway, grounded on the home islands' doorstep. "Mark well this day the 28th of July," Halsey congratulated all ships. "To the Dumbos and lifeguards, to combat air patrol and men of the surface team, to the valiant British force on the right flank. Well done. For the flying fighters who fought it out over Japan for a smashing victory, I have no words that can add to the record with their courage, their blood, and their lives."

Two United Press correspondents with the Third Fleet reported that every major enemy warship was believed to have been rendered inoperational, probably for the duration of the war, which, one added, "means forever." Another report, datelined "Aboard Admiral McCain's Flagship off Japan" on the twenty-eighth, reported a pilot as awed by the heavy flak. "Today they waited until we got well over the shipping and then gave it to us."

The *Lonesome Lady*'s momentum had taken it inland over a pine forest. Cartwright plunged into the trees and climbed down, gathering and concealing his chute. Encountering a puzzled farmer walking along a path, he explained in sign language that he wanted to be taken to the military. Failing that, he pulled out his unloaded .45 (he had discarded his ammunition) and pointed along the path; understanding, finally, the farmer led him to a police station in the village nearby, where Cartwright found a group of excited police and local peasantry—and his co-pilot, Durden Looper, also cut and bruised from his hard landing.

Although they had pocket first aid kits, they were forbidden to use them. Instead their hands were tied behind their backs. Blindfolded, they sat on the ground before the police station. "We were hit and pinched but only by women I think. We were very lucky."

That Saturday morning on Guam, Hays Gamble had sat through a target briefing at 9:00 A.M. Since his group specialized in oil-related installations it was no surprise to him when his target was identified as the Shimotzu Refinery, sixty miles southwest of Nagoya. It would be a milk run, they were told: few flak units were known to be in the area and few planes were rising to challenge B-29s. Shimotzu was one of the few refineries left still processing crude petroleum. Reconnaissance had estimated its tank capacity at about 600,000 barrels.

Of the eighty-four planes of the 315th Bombardment Wing that were airborne at 2:30, seventy-eight found the primary target through the turbulence, dropping by radar from 10,400 feet 658.3 tons of five-hundred-pound bombs. It *was* a milk run. Photos showed the plant so "thoroughly saturated with bombs and obliterated beyond repair" that a return to the site was written off.

Despite Imperial Army intransigence, commanders in Tokyo had no idea how low their fortunes were because communications from places like Shimotzu were now so poor. Antennae and wires were down almost everywhere in Tokyo, and news that came by radio often was from Allied sources, disbelieved as propaganda exaggerations. The Allied press was reporting the enemy debacle in Burma, which was actually worse than was known because weather there interfered with all communications. On the twenty-eighth a Japanese engineer colonel reconnoitering the rushing Sittang warned that what was left of the Twenty-eighth Army would be trapped by ambushes if crossings were attempted as planned. Pushing northeast along the riverbank instead, they met British artillery anyway. In the half-light before dawn, Lieutenant General Shōzō Sakurai stood near the spreading Sittang with Lieutenant Colonel Eiichi Tsuchiya. To Tsuchiya the situation seemed hopeless. His feet had blistered and swelled. Wearing boots was agony. Large leeches clung to his bare skin. The river looked angry and impassable.

Sakurai later remembered feeling, as the Sittang roared on, how he had defeated the British in the same area three and a half years before, when in dry seasons the land was pleasant and the dark jungle cool. Now over Tsuchiya's groans he heard the screams of men hurtling by in the water, black forms like uprooted trees. He could make out *"Tsuwamono da! Tasukete kure!"* ("54th Division here! Help!") and *"Tasukete kure! Oretachi wo misuteru ki ka!"* ("Help, for God's sake! Don't let us go!"). There was nothing he could do for the men who chanced swimming across.

The Sittang in better times, Sakurai remembered, had been eighty yards wide at its narrowest, twice that where it broadened out, and there were fordable points. Now it was three hundred yards across, flooding imperceptibly into swamps on both sides and taking everything with it. Some of his men had been trying to cross on crude rafts since the evening before. The lucky ones were washed back by the current. To get the general to the other side Sakurai's men found what he called a "country boat," in which they struggled across. "When I looked back, I could see that some of my men had made it, but others had been swallowed up by the river, and their tired bodies were whipped away downstream. I kept praying and praying for the gods and the Buddhas to protect us."

The precious boat went back and forth to pick up the trapped survivors before daylight exposed them, even Japanese officers' mess waitresses and Korean and Japanese "comfort girls" who had straggled with the headquarters unit. Soaked, mud-stained, and baggy-uniformed, with their hair cropped like the men, the women were indistinguishable from Sakurai's troops. Now the remnants had to form into a column, evade the enemy, and slip south through the foothills into Thailand. Since Sakurai's horse had drowned, his men went off in search of the closest equivalent likely to be available, an ox.

For the *ianfu*—"comfort girls"—who were employed in an *ianjo* wherever the army went, there seemed no hope of going home again, whatever they had been promised by army-financed entrepreneurs who supplied prostitutes for overseas garrisons. Denied in Japan for decades afterward, the system used willing Japanese women and impressed Koreans and Chinese, each promised untruthfully two yen per three-minute service (condom included), and freedom after earning real riches of one thousand yen. (A sergeant earned thirty yen a month in 1945, a private first class ten and a half, with higher pay overseas.) Freedom was largely a fiction. When one beleaguered unit in Burma, down to eighty men, decided to commit suicide, the Japanese *ianfu* urged the Koreans to escape. They slipped out with improvised white flags; the Japanese prostitutes stubbornly swallowed potassium cyanide.

In isolated areas the collapse of Japanese occupation authority remained unknown because people were remote from the war. Villages in parts of upper Burma, Thailand, and southern China now seldom saw a soldier. Shelling unseen targets above Shanghai along the Yellow Sea, American fleet units encountered no opposition whatever. Seaman Fahey on the *Montpelier* wondered whether the Japanese were "saving everything for the homeland." A few months before "the Japs would have been swarming around us day and night with bombers and warships. Today we could land on the coast of China with little opposition."

For the landings on the home islands, American planners were filling the air on the twenty-eighth with radio messages about troop "lift"—the number and nature of vessels needed all over the Pacific. All "troopers" of every variety not essential elsewhere were directed to the West Coast and forward areas at the assembly times of August 23, September 19, October 12, November 14, and December 15. Battle-damaged ships requiring extensive repair were to have reduced priorities over conversion of freighters to troopships. Orders for troop-carrying vessels delayed by strikes at home—jurisdictional strikes had erupted as labor unions began to gear up for postwar struggles with management—were to be reassigned to other yards. "Congestion" at Pearl Harbor because of the buildup for "Olympic" was to be relieved by direct routings to the Marianas and to Kwajalein in the Carolines "if capable of through voyage." All Army tugs and Navy tows and tugs "towing from mainland to destination west of Marshalls" were also to be routed via Kwajalein, which was to be a crucial "Olympic" staging area. A further indication of the numbers of landing craft still considered vital for "Olympic" and "Coronet" was a top-secret memo from the Undersecretary of the Navy that the Navy was "undertaking a secret project to be called Dagwood. The Production Executive Committee had accorded the project an urgency rating of 1 to rank with, but after, the Manhattan Project but superior to all other activities.... Dagwood is Navy production of the utmost urgency...."

Very likely because of the *wood* in his name, the hero of the "Blondie" cartoon strip seemed in the process of acquiring a new fame akin to the code for the Bomb. Such was the urgency gathering about "Olympic."

The Japanese were anticipating a landing on the home islands no less seriously. Plans for *Ketsu-Go* assumed the arming in some way of the entire nation, and local inhabitants were to remain to fight it out and then become a guerrilla force. Evacuating them would congest roads, cost valuable resources, and bring to a standstill industry that had to run until the last moment. Further, warehousing food for the population in inland areas, or building shelter for evacuees, was out of the question. For the Army's 3,800 hoarded (inactive) aircraft, mostly *kamikazes*, 13 million gallons of fuel were stockpiled. By August 1 the Navy expected to have hoarded and largely hidden 5,145 planes for *kamikaze* use, but it had only 2 million gallons of aircraft-quality fuel for them. Most flights were expected to be one-way. Aside from major vessels not immobilized in port, the new Naval General Command would have a fleet of 3,294 secondary vessels, consisting of suicide boats (*Shinyo*), midget subs (*Kairyu* and *Koryu*), and 38 Home Fleet submarines that would employ *kaitens*. Nineteen additional army divisions would be raised, exhausting all reserves of manpower outside the primitive civilian home defense force. The aim of *Ketsu-Go* was less to drive the Americans from the beaches than to inflict such opening losses as to create a new mood for renegotiating the surrender.

As far as Premier Suzuki's government was concerned, the Potsdam insistence on unconditional surrender was impossible for Japan to take seriously. Supporting Sato's contention that Potsdam was the only avenue to peace, and that the Zacharias gloss on its terms was a crucial "divergence" from the utter surrender forced upon Germany, Minister Kase cabled Togo from Bern that he saw real guarantees offered. The "Imperial House" was unmentioned, and thus sanctioned by implication. Further, "a Japanese domain is recognized in which Japanese sovereignty holds sway." ("It seems to me," Kase added in a parenthesis, "that this Proclamation provides a basis on which we [can] carry on our national structure which the Japanese race is now protecting with its very life's blood.") As Sato did, Kase also observed that unconditional surrender applied only to the military and not to the government or the people, and he pleaded that it should be understood that the careful language of Potsdam appeared "to have occasioned a great deal of thought" on the part of the signatory governments—"*they seem to have taken pains to save face for us on various other points.*" And he pointed out in particular the promise that the Japanese people would "be given an opportunity to lead a peaceful and productive life."

"Magic" intercepted the cable as H-199392, possibly before Suzuki saw it in Tokyo, but the Premier felt stronger pressure closer to home—the Army hierarchy that dominated his Cabinet and the leaflets putting Potsdam into Japanese that were almost as ubiquitous as newspapers. To make his point amid the rain of leaflets over Honshu, he held a press conference at his official residence at 4:00 P.M. A reporter was prompted to ask, "What is the Premier's view regarding the Joint Proclamation by the three countries?"

"I believe," Suzuki said, in a transmission quoted by the Domei agency, "the Joint Proclamation by the three countries is nothing but a rehash of the Cairo Declaration. As for the Government, it does not find any important value in it, and there is no other recourse but to ignore it entirely, and resolutely fight for the successful conclusion of this war."

Much controversy would focus upon the word *mokusatsu*, which could be translated as "ignore entirely" or "regard as unworthy of notice." *Moku* means "to be silent"; *satsu* means "to kill." Taken together it meant, according to a dictionary of the time, "kill with silence" or "treat with silent contempt." These were distinctions without a difference, for Japanese and Western newspapers alike interpreted the statement as a rejection of Potsdam. Suzuki's truculent choice of words actually was intended to be ambiguous and to postpone judgment while awaiting a reply from the Soviets, but no one outside the Cabinet knew that, and Togo was helplessly furious. Tokyo's largest newspaper, *Asahi Shimbun*, would take the language as a finding of unacceptability and elsewhere it was viewed as Japan's resolve to continue the war.

With no overtures to the United States through neutral governments explaining that all the Japanese wanted was an explicitly favorable construction of Potsdam language with respect to the Emperor, Suzuki's statement, even to watchers of "Magic" intercepts, appeared inescapably to be a victory of the all-or-nothing military over the moderates. If the press conference language was only for domestic consumption, there was nothing evidenced in Japanese diplomatic activity elsewhere than in Moscow to confirm Japanese interest in giving up the war. Explaining his single-mindedness to Sato, Togo cabled unconvincingly, "No matter how hard I may try to persuade the military to hold direct negotiations with the Americans or the British, I have no doubt whatsoever that they will refuse to listen. Therefore we must attempt to negotiate through the Soviet Union because there seems no other way to terminate the war."

As far as General Anami and his circle were concerned, the Soviet Union had still another role to play on Japan's behalf as a potential postwar adversary of the United States. If Americans sufficiently feared Communist domination of Asia they might settle with Japan and terminate the war before the Russians and their ideology overwhelmed the continent—even the Japanese islands. It was as much an Army fantasy as Soviet mediation was a Foreign Office one.

More than five hours after the *mokusatsu* dismissal of Potsdam,

Sato, cabling from Moscow at 3:25 P.M. local time, reported no progress on the mediation plea and reminded the frustrated Togo that "in reality the terms may be mollified." Potsdam was political rhetoric. Zacharias's gloss was the reality. "In the meantime," Sato added, "Attlee, the newly appointed Prime Minister . . . is reported to have joined the conference immediately." Sato still awaited, he repeated to Togo, a "concrete and definite proposal" to put to Molotov, who would learn soon enough of Suzuki's rejection of Potsdam. So would Truman, for whom *mokusatsu* meant the inevitability of the Bomb.

On the same day as Suzuki's conference, General Maxwell D. Taylor, back in Washington after relinquishing the 101st Airborne Division in the ETO, had a surprising visit from George C. Marshall, who had returned from Potsdam. "In the course of the afternoon . . . he told General Patton and me"—Patton was on leave and would return to Bavaria—"about the recent explosion of the experimental atom bomb at Alamogordo and the plans for its use against the Japanese. . . ." To Patton and Taylor he guessed that two such bombs would convince the Japanese to end the war, "however this estimate was not shared by the War Department because a few days later the [101st Airborne] Division was ordered to withdraw to the Auxerre region in France as the first leg of its movement to the Far East." All options remained open.

Fissionable material and bomb parts were still in the pipeline to Tinian. Three B-29s from the 509th support group left Mather Field at Sacramento at about the time that Marshall was conferring with Patton and Taylor. One, the *Laggin' Dragon*, justified its name when airborne only fifty feet. The life raft hatch blew open and blocked the right elevator flap. Realizing that the plane was shuddering violently because an elevator was stuck, the pilot and co-pilot began tugging desperately at the lever that operated it, forcing the elevator upward. At three hundred feet the jammed raft blew loose, but the hatch was still open, and the tower advised *Laggin' Dragon* to land after burning off fuel to soften its impact on the runway.

The B-29 came in for a crash landing. Its tail section was fluttering. The tail gunner reported that elevator panels had torn away and more surface was fragmenting off. *Laggin' Dragon* could not afford a fuel-lightening exercise. Reversible pitch propellers still new to aircraft made the difference and, under control, the plane came in safely. Two days later, after ground crews cannibalized an elevator from an older model returned from the wars, *Laggin' Dragon* would take off again, at 12:30 A.M. on the thirtieth.

On the morning of the *Laggin' Dragon*'s abortive flight in California, it was evening in Potsdam, where, back in puzzled triumph, Attlee and Bevin visited with Truman and Byrnes prior to the late-scheduled plenary session. Bevin, to whom Attlee deferred, appeared, in Leahy's terms, "gruff and tough," objecting to Stalin's various demands, including the accomplished fact of the Oder-Neisse border. Byrnes nevertheless outlined a series of compromises, largely concessions, which he proposed to put to the Russians the next day to end the meetings before they became too divisive for agreement. Cadogan thought they were "quite sensible" when he had met earlier with Byrnes, but noted in his diary, "I must try to sell it to Attlee between the time of his arrival and this evening's meeting." The problem he saw was that Bevin was "the heavyweight of the Cabinet and will get his own way with them."

Bevin, so Truman agreed (in his memoirs), "appeared to me to be a tough person to deal with, but after I became better acquainted with him I found that he was a reasonable man with a good mind and a clear head." At the time, however, he wrote to his daughter, Margaret, about Churchill's and Eden's replacements: "these two are sourpusses." Minister of Labour in the former coalition government, Bevin had bargained on a very different level. "These people, Stalin and Truman," he remarked, "are just the same as all Russians and Americans, and dealing with them over foreign affairs is just the same as trying to come to a settlement about unloading a ship."

As the session opened, Attlee, with more wit than anticipated, expressed regret that "domestic occurrences in Great Britain had interfered with the work of the conference." Stalin pressed him for an explanation of Churchill's unanticipated defeat. "Labour enthusiasts," Attlee explained, "sometimes acted in a strange way. During meetings they would cheer and applaud a Labour candidate, but when it came to voting they would vote against him. The reverse happened in this case."

The problems of encouraging German economic recovery while coping with refugees, rebuilding infrastructure, finding enough fuel to run industry, and enough food to prevent illness and hunger worried the new British government. Its own situation at home was precarious. The United States worried more about coping with liberated Europe.

With Stalin less interested because hardship helped Communist parties in the West, the Americans focused first on Germany, where occupation authorities were often mired in a maze of bureaucratic regulations, some from the Nazi era, some new. Military government authorities often had little background for their responsibilities, and Germans in the U.S. zone wanted to continue their occupations in a maze of *Fragenbogen*, identity cards, and fears of losing factories and equipment to reparations. An appeal from Wolfgang Reichau on July 28 handled in Bavaria requested the return of confiscated equipment that would be used to make photos for identity cards. Another from Christian Kerscher sought approval to send twenty thousand liters of his wine to Mainz in the French zone. Josef Daburger wanted permission to purchase cement to repair his war-damaged flour mill. (He was given urgent certification.) Michael Troger wanted the confiscated blacksmith machinery he had used to repair *Wehrmacht* vehicles returned so that he could fix farm tractors and motorcycles. He would even accept his own equipment back "on loan." Paul Aicher asked for return of his power saws and planing machine so that he could return to cabinetmaking. He was willing to buy back his seized lathes and circular saw.

Another plea—which would be denied—was from the Maxmilianbrauerei in Traunstein for "sufficient malt for producing strong beer for about one month" in order to supply American occupation troops. The response was that "no more grain, malts or coal supplies will be diverted from food channels for the production of beer"—not even for the victors. The shortage of foodstuffs was too acute. Only on December 1 would the prohibition be relaxed.

Even such small rulings—made by sergeants and lieutenants who in civilian life may have never balanced a checkbook—were now actions determining, as much as Potsdam, the direction of Europe.

Since the meeting had begun almost at Truman's usual bedtime, it was not expected to be more than a formality to introduce Attlee and his party, but Stalin had an announcement to make before the official business began. The Soviet government had received another proposal from Japan that it send an envoy to Moscow to discuss bringing the war to an end. An interpreter read the complete memorandum from Sato, after which Stalin scoffed that there was nothing new in it. "Our answer, of course, will be negative." The last thing Stalin wanted was peace before he could secure all he wanted in East Asia.

Although "Magic" had read whatever had passed between Sato

and his boss in Tokyo, Truman thanked Stalin for being open about the message. Then the Soviet delegation brought up the first of two matters it had held for the session, the recognition of the governments of Italy and the satellite states of Bulgaria, Romania, and Hungary. With no agreement on the legitimacy of the regimes, the matter was again put off. Truman used the discussion to move to the second agenda question, Italian reparations. All this would mean, he said, was that the United States would pay them indirectly, as it was already keeping Italy from starvation. Austria, Stalin countered, a captive country under Hitler, should not be expected to pay reparations (which he had in fact already confiscated as booty and removed), but the Soviet people felt that Italy, which had sent its army as far as the Volga to devastate Russia, had a moral obligation to materially recognize its guilt.

Attlee expressed sympathy with Russia for its suffering at the hands of Italy and reminded Stalin that Britain had also suffered. He had no objection to Soviet seizure of Italian "war plants" or military equipment as reparations. Otherwise, Italy needed its infrastructure in order to survive.

Stalin agreed to accept equipment as reparations. "I do not ask much."

"*Military* equipment?" Bevin shot back. There was no more militant anti-Communist than a hard-nosed trade unionist.

"Yes," said Stalin. "Military equipment."

Attlee asked whether Stalin had one-time-only removals in mind, and not levies on production.

"Yes," said Stalin, "once-for-all removals."

Bevin pressed further, inquiring whether the Soviets meant military equipment having no peacetime utility.

"War equipment," said Stalin, "can be adjusted for peacetime production. There is no equipment which has no peacetime utility. Ammunition plants are producing motor cars."

"It is so difficult to define," Bevin cautioned, "what you can take away without affecting the economic life of a nation."

"We want," Stalin insisted, "recognition of the principle. . . . We can't let aggressors inflict damage without holding them responsible for some compensation."

"I agree with that," acknowledged Truman, and at five minutes past midnight they adjourned.

Returning to his house in Babelsberg, Truman found a message from Washington that the Senate had just ratified, by a vote of 89 to 2, the United Nations Charter. He wrote out a message for the press: "It is deeply gratifying that the Senate has ratified the Charter by a nearly unanimous vote. The action of the Senate substantially advances the cause of world peace."

The other news from across the Atlantic was more startling. What war might have been like to Americans had enemy technology a little more time to develop came home to New Yorkers when, at 9:49 A.M. on a misty Saturday morning, the equivalent of an unguided missile struck the Empire State Building, tallest in the world, 915 feet above street level. A B-25 "Mitchell" bomber, the type of twin-engine plane used for the Doolittle raid on Tokyo in April 1942, lost in blinding fog as it flew west from Squantum Army Air Force Base in Massachusetts, crashed into the seventy-ninth floor and engulfed two stricken floors in fire from its fuel tanks. Sheared off by the impact, its wings fell as fiery debris while the fuselage and motors ripped a hole eighteen feet wide and twenty feet high in the brick wall, and the building swayed momentarily in a two-foot arc. One motor hurtled across the seventy-ninth floor, tore through the south wall, and fell to the roof of a twelve-story office building on Thirty-third Street, demolishing a penthouse apartment; the other, along with part of the landing gear, crashed into an elevator shaft, plummeting down a thousand feet to the subcellar.

The pilot, Lieutenant Colonel William F. Smith, Jr., had completed thirty-four bombing missions over Germany safely, but he and two others on board perished high over Manhattan, while ten people in the building, many fewer than would have been at risk on an ordinary working day, died. One man, panicked by the flames, leaped from a window, striking a ledge on the seventy-second floor. Empty elevators dropped eighty stories. Fire trucks materialized by the dozens, choking miles of streets.

Mayor Fiorello LaGuardia's car radio, always tuned to the police band, alerted him to the disaster. He rushed off, siren sounding, to Thirty-fourth Street, announced himself, and climbed to the nearest safe floor to supervise operations. It was almost like the old days, when he was Franklin Roosevelt's bumbling first Director of Civilian Defense—an appointment many took as reassurance to Americans that its cities would never be bombed. "If the pilot had been up there where he belonged," said the Mayor, "there would have been no trouble."

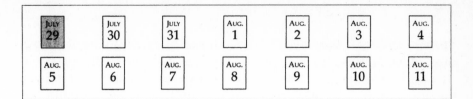

| JULY 29 | JULY 30 | JULY 31 | AUG. 1 | AUG. 2 | AUG. 3 | AUG. 4 |
| AUG. 5 | AUG. 6 | AUG. 7 | AUG. 8 | AUG. 9 | AUG. 10 | AUG. 11 |

# CHAPTER XVII

# · JULY 29, 1945 ·

## *". . . destroying the instrument"*

While "Olympic" planners worried that the beach layouts for each landing force were too narrow and requested a re-charting, and reconnaissance sorties over Kyushu from Okinawa continued, the Japanese tested the possibilities of their *kamikaze* equipment. Technologically superior planes were unnecessary. The Pacific Fleet's "Blue Summary" for the twenty-ninth reported the destroyer *Callaghan* sunk just outside Buckner Bay with 120 dead, and the *Pritchett* badly damaged, both hit by wave-skimming aircraft that the Red Baron might have rejected. "Japs," the report went, "used several planes simultaneously. Very bright moonlight. Planes were flimsy construction using wood and fabric with some plywood. Biplanes with wheels. Very maneuverable with expert pilots. Maximum speed tracked 90 knots but generally less. . . . Not picked up by any ship until planes closed to 13 miles although altitude estimated at about 1,000 feet."

Seaman Fahey explained the tactical problem from his vantage on the nearby *Montpelier*: "If the Jap planes maneuvered between us, and we attempted to knock them out of the skies, our shells would land among the cruisers and theirs among us. We could have done more damage to ourselves than the Japs would do."

Embarrassing as was the Navy's helplessness, worse would come before the day was over. With the weather poor during daylight hours, Lieutenant Commander Hashimoto's *I-58* remained submerged until 11:05 P.M., rising then to break the waves with her periscope. Seeing the moon up and the overcast thin, he ordered the sub to surface and almost immediately saw, ninety degrees off on the eastern horizon, a ship silhouetted just over five miles distant. As he dived, the ship approached, its watch unaware. Hashimoto's *kaitens* clamored to be used. "Why can't we be launched?" they appealed, but Hashimoto wanted to save them for a target harder to hit. The "battleship," as he thought it was, seemed too easy. It was approaching fast across his bow. He ordered six torpedoes set for forty-two knots and six yards depth, firing from tubes in fanwise sequence at fifteen hundred yards. It was 11:32. In little more than a minute they could see geysers from two hits, and flashes of flame.

Surges of pressure against the sub led to shouts of "Depth charge!" but the stricken cruiser was in no condition to respond. Cautiously, Hashimoto ordered his helmsman to dive to seventy yards and reload torpedoes for another salvo. In the intermittent darkness, as clouds covered the moon, then floated off, he could not tell how wounded the ship was. And he did not want to leave too soon in case he could pick up a survivor or two who might identify what he had hit.

Aboard the *Indianapolis*, Captain McVay had no idea what had happened. Many of his 1,196 men were off duty and in their bunks. No sub had been detected; the explosions that flung him from his own bunk suggested another *kamikaze*—his bad luck off Okinawa months earlier. Then he realized that he was too far from land for that: it might have been a mine. Yet mines, from what he knew, caused no such shocks. Without warning, he had been torpedoed. Groping his way through acrid smoke to the bridge, McVay discovered that all communications were inoperative—control room, loudspeaker systems, telephone, telegraph. Breathlessly, Kyle C. "Casey" Moore, a lieutenant commander and the damage control officer, reported the chaos below. While McVay had sensed only a few degrees of list, the compartments below were filling up rapidly with seawater; the never-closed watertight doors could not be shut; many sailors were already trapped or dead; fires were uncontrollable and spreading.

"Do you want the abandon-ship order given?" Moore asked. There was no way to reach the control room to order the engines stopped; metal decks were becoming too hot to touch. McVay hesitated. He had to do the unthinkable. It was even too late for formalities. Shouted orders were unheard above the sounds of explosions and falling debris, the cries of burned seamen, and the crashing of the sea. As the ship tilted precariously, men continued clambering up ladders from below and jumping into the water. Below, a ship's surgeon clad only in pajama bottoms, assisted by a pharmacist's mate, jabbed screaming men with morphine just before the sick bay began to flood. It was automatic. He realized as he went from one to another that if they made it out into the night the salt water would eat into their burns and his patients would die anyway. Still, he sent the mate to fetch life jackets.

Until forced by smoke and fire to flee, a radioman punched out a coded message: "WE HAVE BEEN HIT BY TWO TORPEDOES, NEED IMMEDIATE ASSISTANCE." He added the ship's position. For good measure he keyed in several SOS messages, but all the distress signals would emerge garbled at best. There had been some waning transmitting power but the antennas may have been dislodged. No systems were operative. With the ship still moving forward, enormous quantities of seawater pushed through the rents in its hull; its bow section was, within minutes, deep in the water. Men dragged lifelines and nets to the port side and tried to get clear of the hull before being sucked under. Far aft, having chewed up men thrashing near the stern, the number three screw still turned, although now high in the air. Within, the fire mains had been ruptured with the first blasts, and there was no hope of hosing down the hot steel decks, walls, and escape ladders.

Men behaved in some cases mechanically if irrationally. McVay himself got fully dressed before overseeing what he could of damage control and abandoning ship. A seaman combed his hair by flashlight. Many filled bags with treasures almost certain to be lost at sea even if their owners weren't. One grabbed the paperback edition of the novel he'd been reading. Another finished the letter he'd been writing and tucked it into his shirt pocket. Still another searched for his list of seamen who owed him money.

Within minutes the ship was virtually on its side, bow down. Most crew off duty and sleeping below were already trapped and drowned. By the intermittent moonlight that somehow filtered through the smoke surrounding the hulk of the *Indianapolis,* hundreds found their way into the water, some onto rafts and floating debris. Suddenly Hashimoto saw his target vanish from his periscope. The stern had just plunged below the surface. He noted his position as 134 degrees 48 minutes East, 12 degrees 2 minutes North. It was thirteen minutes before midnight on the twenty-ninth, local time. He was the only one who knew the whereabouts of the struggling survivors of the *Indianapolis*. He had no idea what he had sunk, nor could he safely radio Tokyo of his victory. He broke the surface to look out from his bridge. Scanning the twelve-foot swells with his binoculars, Hashimoto saw nothing.

Landing on Guam, General "Tooey" Spaatz hand-carried the directive from Washington authorizing the deployment of "Little Boy," "Fat Man," and additional bombs when ready. After conferring with Curtis LeMay, Spaatz telexed Marshall's office: "Hiroshima according to prisoner of war reports is the only one of [the] four target cities . . . that does not have Allied prisoner of war camps."

In the village inland from Kure where Tom Cartwright and Durden Looper had spent the night trussed and blindfolded on the ground in front of the police station, a small army truck with an officer and an armed guard arrived and hauled them away. They had no idea until they were pulled out and their blindfolds were removed that they were now in Hiroshima. It appeared to be a building close to Hiroshima Castle. In the foul-smelling cell lit by a single dim bulb were the others from their crew except for tail gunner Bill Abel, who had been taken elsewhere, and the navigator, Troy Pedersen, who had apparently ripped his chute on the bomb bay door and fallen to his death. Forbidden to talk, the prisoners could only make eye contact with each other.

Each was interrogated individually in a small second-floor room by a colonel with a swagger stick, Cartwright's session interrupted by diarrhea, possibly from tension—or the village water. Blindfolded, but badly, when taken out to relieve himself, he got a glimpse of a bridge and a river. Back under questioning he was rapped on the knuckles by the colonel's stick when answers failed to come readily enough, but he had few answers. How many troops were in Okinawa? What was next in American plans? Then he was returned to the stinking cell where, but for visits to the honey bucket that was their latrine, they had to sit silently and Buddha-like, legs crossed. Their muscles screamed.

While the quiet—the freedom from air raids—was almost unearthly in the area around Hiroshima, elsewhere in the home islands and in occupied China, American planes continued to hit the dwindling number of useful targets. Roads and railways in China, river shipping, bridges, oil tanks, and docks were bombed and strafed. Af-

ter dark twenty-four B-29s of the 313th Wing again mined the Shimonoseki Strait and the waters around Fukuoka and other southern
ports. The nearly twelve thousand airdropped mines sown since
spring had clogged navigable waters so dangerously that the few
functioning home island shipyards had nowhere to send new or repaired coastal vessels. From Guam, Hays Gamble's 315th Wing of
B-29s made another "oil" run and watched the fires develop from
10,400 feet. "No searchlights and no fighters," he reported, "but moderate flak. Saw fires at Nagoya area from other wing."

With pressure on the Suzuki government increasing to end the
war while some Japanese cities remained, the Army command understood that peace talk was coming from officials who had no divisions.
Togo deplored the *mokusatsu* response as "most disadvantageous for
Japan" but Anami preferred to see it as "rejection by ignoring"—a
proper demonstration of contempt.

For Anami the divisions outside the home islands no longer had
meaning except as bargaining chips or as buffers against the Soviets.
Some on outlying islands (and cut off from home) had no meaning
whatever. In Burma what was left of the Twenty-eighth Army east of
the Sittang hid in the rain and high reeds from RAF reconnaissance
planes until nightfall, when they hoped to close at least some of the
thirteen miles between them and the Shan foothills. Now in friendly
territory, they began encountering elements of the 53rd Division,
who offered them red bean soup with rice cake. *Shiruko* would have
been a delicacy even had they not been famished. But the Burmese
were aware that the days of the Japanese conqueror were numbered,
and villagers were claiming they had no rice.

When early on Sunday morning from Potsdam, Harry Truman wrote
to his daughter, Margaret, he had not yet been given a message from
Stalin's interpreter, Pavlov, to Byrnes that the Generalissimo was ill
"and will not be able to go out tomorrow." Otherwise he could not
have written, "Marshal Stalin"—Truman could not get used to the
"Generalissimo" tag—"and Molotov are coming to see me this morning. I am hoping that we can get things in shape so we can quit about
Tuesday." Stalin's request that Molotov substitute for him was unacceptable for agreements at the highest level, but Truman and Byrnes
agreed to meet informally with Molotov without the British contingent. Bevin was already unhappy about the cavalier manner (in his
view) in which Byrnes was working out compromises that he and At-

tlee considered more as appeasement. "Attlee," the President told his daughter, "is an Oxford graduate and talks with that deep-throated swallowing enunciation, same as Eden does. But I understand him reasonably well. Bevin is a tough guy. He doesn't know, of course, that your dad has been dealing with that sort all his life, from building trades to coal miners."

Privately, Bevin's deputy, Cadogan, agreed, writing the same day, "Bevin has always taken an interest in foreign affairs and knows something about them. He has a tendency, of course, to take the lead over Attlee, who recedes into the background by his very insignificance." But with Stalin unavailable and no Big Three meeting on the twenty-ninth—and the thirtieth, too, it would turn out—the bilateral American-Soviet meetings would be crucial to the outcome of Potsdam, although Attlee and Bevin would dispute them when the plenary sessions resumed.

While physically unavailable, Stalin kept his hand in through messages to Truman. One that morning agreed to routing American planes to Moscow via Berlin rather than Tehran, a significant gesture, although its execution would be delayed by "technical questions." A second memorandum dealt with the supply of coal to all of Germany, a matter Truman took very seriously. If Poland were to keep what it had already taken, the area between the eastern and western branches of the Niesse, rich with the coal of Silesia, what happened to that coal was crucial to how Europe survived the next winter. A third matter was the exacerbating one of Soviet reparations. Stalin and Molotov had insisted on a huge German bill; to back it up they displayed a report from Marshal Zhukov that the United States and Britain had removed considerable equipment in advance of a reparations agreement.

In a memorandum to Truman, the American representative to the Committee on Reparations, Edwin Pauley, conceded that Zhukov was correct in that the Allies had taken as war booty military equipment representing "recent German technical advances." Compared to what the Russians had seized, Pauley explained, these removals were "trivial." "Some areas, such as our sector of Berlin, have, as you know, been stripped of virtually all peace-time industrial employment possibilities, in violation of principles agreed to with us and the British in Moscow." Still, facts had to be recognized, and Will Clayton, the shrewd Assistant Secretary of State, observed in a memo to Byrnes that reliable estimates placed about 40 percent of the "removable industrial capital equipment" of Germany in the Russian zone, most of that light industry, with half of the remaining industry in the Ruhr. His suggestion was that Russian and Polish claims should be satisfied "from the Russian Zone plus 25% of such industrial capital equipment as we decide should be removed from the Ruhr . . . on condition that an additional like amount of such equipment would be exchanged for an equivalent value in food, coal, zinc, potash, timber and oil to be made available to us by the Russians from their zone."

When, at noon, Truman and Byrnes sat down with Molotov at number 2 Kaiserstrasse, Byrnes offered Clayton's proposal. Molotov balked at "25% of an undetermined figure." Inflating Clayton's figures, Byrnes maintained that half of the national wealth of Germany lay in the Soviet zone, and Molotov countered that according to their calculations it was only 42 percent—which made Clayton's estimate look good. Actual amounts were never fixed at Yalta, said Byrnes, and Truman added that all the United States was trying to do was create a workable plan that would award Russia 50 percent of German reparations. Molotov expressed appreciation, but returned to his demand of a fixed sum—in 1938 prices, he said—of German removals. That would be impossible to calculate, Byrnes insisted—thus the percentage basis. And he went back to the Yalta discussions, which he clearly had studied to the letter.

Molotov changed the subject. Stalin wanted him to take up another matter, he said—Japan. The Generalissimo wanted the warring parties to address a formal request to the Soviets that they enter the war. The rationale might be, he proposed, the refusal of Japan to accept the Potsdam proposal and the need to shorten the war and thereby save lives. Of course, Molotov added, Russia's entry remained predicated upon an agreement on postwar arrangements with China.

Truman was quietly furious. Beg Russia? The Soviets had agreed at Yalta and now at Potsdam to enter the war, and had just held military discussions on Japan.

Keeping his exasperation to himself, Truman agreed to examine Stalin's proposal carefully and to consult with his allies—meaning Great Britain. Had he not wanted Russian intervention, it was an opportune moment to discourage it. Yet nothing, he knew, could keep Stalin from taking what he could seize from Japan, even if the Red Army did not fire a shot. Good terms with Russia seemed always to mean Stalin's terms.

While the bilateral talks went on, Secretary of the Navy Forrestal, back in Berlin, was lunching with General Lucius Clay, the recently appointed American military governor in Germany. Ambassador Averell Harriman was also at the table. "Averell," Forrestal noted in his diary, "was very gloomy about the influx of Russia into Europe. He said Russia was a vacuum into which all movable goods would be sucked. He said the greatest crime of Hitler was that his actions had resulted in opening the gates of Eastern Europe to Asia."

Afterward, at the house in the Babelsberg compound where Harriman was living, Forrestal was introduced to Edwin Pauley. The three discussed Soviet reparations, which seemed to them more like rape. "They are stripping every area they are in of all movable goods, and at the same time asking reparations and designating the goods they take as war booty." They were also forcing their way into the American zone, Pauley added, to shoot some Germans and kidnap others, and from what he had heard from Commander Henry Schade, head of an American technical mission, the Russians had shot one woman near his house for refusing to give up her jewelry and another for running away. "Averell said this did not represent persecutions particularly, but rather reflected the Russians' indifference to life."

Forrestal went on to meet Ernest Bevin, who told him of Labour's plans in Britain to nationalize "power, railroads, mines and textiles up to the spinning mills." Dealing with Communists, he added, was not new to him. He had years of that in contending with Communists in British labor unions.

Forrestal asked him about the policy of insisting upon "destruction of the Emperor concept along with the surrender." Bevin hesitated, saying that the question required some thought, "but he was inclined to feel that there was no sense in destroying the instrument through which one might have to deal in order to effectively control Japan." Then Bevin surprised Forrestal, so much so that Forrestal put the statement down in quotes: "It might have been far better for all of us not to have destroyed the institution of the Kaiser after the last war; we might not have had this one if we hadn't done so. It might have been far better to have guided the Germans to a constitutional monarchy rather than leaving them without a symbol and therefore opening the psychological doors to a man like Hitler."

Bevin had to go on to a meeting, joining Attlee, with Truman and Byrnes, and at 4:30 P.M. was at number 2 Kaiserstrasse. The discussion, although officially unrecorded, was recalled by Truman in his memoirs. "I did not like this [Stalin] proposal for one important reason," he wrote. "I saw in it a cynical diplomatic move to make Russia's entry at this time appear to be the decisive factor to bring about victory. At Yalta, Russia had agreed, and here at Potsdam she reaffirmed her commitment, to enter the war against Japan three months after V-E Day, provided that Russia and China had previously concluded a treaty of mutual assistance. There were no other conditions. . . ." He was "not willing," he added, "to let Russia reap the fruits of a long and bitter and gallant effort in which she had no part." Attlee agreed that Truman should prepare a letter in which there was no plea whatever that Stalin could later exploit.

Even while the Potsdam conference was going on, the Russians were demonstrating their cynicism on almost every issue. In former Königsberg, Russians removed manhole covers from the streets because the German emblem of the once-Prussian city had to be expunged from history. On the very day that Molotov had reminded Byrnes of the policy of treating all of Germany as an economic unit— apparently so the Soviets could better extract what they could from beyond their zone—General Zhukov ordered all industries in the Soviet zone to resume production. Heavy penalties were threatened for noncompliance. Yet four days earlier he had made most legal business transactions almost impossible, ordering all German institutions, organizations, firms, and private citizens to hand over valuables to the new state bank—gold, silver, coins, foreign money, bank notes, and all documents relating to property and valuables. Money deposited in banks before May 9—the Soviet V-E Day—was irrecoverable. Looting and robbery now were state policy.

It was open season on Germans everywhere in Europe in the summer of 1945. For generations beyond memory, German-speaking people had lived in the Danube basin. Saxon farmers had tilled the Transylvanian soil and lived in villages with Romanians, Hungarians, and Gypsies, but as the Russians had moved in during the autumn of 1944, Germans had begun to flee, traveling in horse-drawn wagons as far as Austria. But they could never outpace the Red Army, and men and women alike were herded into forced labor for the Russians. Then they were forced to return to their old homes, where in mid-July they were met by Romanian farmers, so Mathilde Maurer, then thirty-one, once a teacher in Sachsisch-Sankt Georgen (Sangeorzul-Nou) in northern Transylvania, remembered.

"Not one of you shall set foot in the village," a farmer threatened.

"We have got nothing for you here." Gypsies who had been farm workers for the Germans piled on further abuse, and the "colonists" who had seized the German farms behaved "like a pack of animals."

The Germans slept on straw in what remained of a barn dismantled by the Russians, and were guarded by the local Romanian militia until a mass interrogation by the clerk of the local council—clearly the power in the community—on the twenty-eighth. Those who had served the *Wehrmacht* were asked to identify themselves. No one did. Nevertheless they were declared unwanted, told to pack their belongings before evening and to be prepared for deportation. To Russia, they assumed.

As they were to leave, the clerk announced that deportation had been postponed until 5:00 A.M. the next morning. This time there was no reprieve. At dawn, "Gendarmes appeared and immediately began to look through our small bundles. Horses and wagons had to stay behind. It was only after a great deal of begging and entreaty that we obtained two teams of horses for our very old people—there were some in their nineties among us—and invalids would be exempted."

The militia began driving the Germans out of the village, Frau Maurer testified in 1956. "Our belongings on our shoulders, holding our weeping and terrified children by the hand, mothers carrying their infant babies in their arms, and supporting the aged and the infirm, we walked along the dusty road. Where were we going? Nobody knew. . . . This time we said goodbye to our homes forever, but we did not let our torturers see this. Once more, of course, the colonists and gypsies came to look on, grinning scornfully behind us and making it clear how eagerly they were looking forward to plundering what we had left behind."

The current was strong and the destroyed bridge at the first stream they encountered was unrepaired. "Many of us waded through the deep water, while others tried to reach the further bank over the ruins of the bridge." There was little choice. Abusing them as "Hitlerites," the gendarmes employed "awful curses and blows from rifle butts." The Romanians and Gypsies were not the only revenge seekers, Mathilde Maurer would write. There were also "Jews, Hungarians and Communists," a poignant irony, for the tragedy would be reenacted all over central Europe, especially by displaced persons and concentration camp victims who attempted to return to their old homes. In Poland—and other places—Jews who had survived years in Auschwitz or Belsen were murdered to prevent their reclaiming the places where they had lived their pre-Hitler lives.

The cruelties of the postwar realignment of power came in all sizes and shapes. In southern Germany, DPs in a camp at Minden broke out and battered down barns, removing the doors and fences for firewood. In the town of Höxter 4,768 DPs in a former barracks overwhelmed guards and plundered the shops. In Fürstenau the villagers defended themselves and killed a Polish DP, but on the twenty-ninth nearly 200 Poles broke out again and threw hand grenades into shops and homes. Gun and grenades could be found nearly everywhere, abandoned by troops and picked up as toys by small boys and almost anyone bent upon robbery or revenge. Seven townspeople were murdered before troops restored order. Fifty Poles were arrested; four were sentenced to death and twenty-seven received long sentences. Karl Jünger noted in his diary on the twenty-ninth a letter from a pastor in Pomerania whose wife had been killed. He had placed a large candle by her coffin when a soldier entered the house, exclaimed, "Oh, your wife is dead!"—and seized the candle, leaving the grieving man in darkness. "When people do such things," Jünger wondered, "how can we restrain the abuse of power?"

In Augsburg, Ursula von Kardorff and her friend Bärchen cycled to the office of the American military government to fill out the "fantastic" 131-question *Fragenbogen*, which she took as a petty misuse of power. Among other things it asked

> how much we weighed, what scars we had, the color of hair and eyes, whether our forebears had ever had any titles of nobility, and if so which, whether we had left the Church, what salary we had earned, whether we had ever filled any post in German-occupied territory and whether we had ever been arrested. It seemed to me particularly asinine to ask how we had voted in 1933, in the first place because it would have been so easy to have lied and in the second because I had always imagined that the secret ballot was one of the cornerstones of democracy. Altogether the whole thing seemed so utterly ridiculous that we got a fit of the giggles while we were filling the questions in. In the old days a Jewish grandmother was the thing not to have had, but now the same applies to an aristocratic one. And what on earth has the color of my eyes to do with my political

opinions? Afterward we had a long talk with the major. He was very understanding.

Bärchen is extremely brave. She is terrified of the Russians but she is going to see her sister in the Russian zone.

Staying clear of the Russian zone, James Krüss continued to trek northeast toward the North Sea ports and home. At Aschersleben, on the road to Braunschweig, he was taken in by a family that had escaped misfortune. He was offered pound cake and coffee, and sat on a balcony "with the quiet park under my feet." He could even pick from the bulging bookshelves and read. "Everything became confused: Dresden beleaguered, people digging in garbage, Dresden burning, an old woman pushing a baby carriage away from the fire zone, stubbornly straight ahead and stupefied. . . ." He emptied the thermos and ate half the cake. "I had no idea what was going on in Europe as I was sitting on the balcony. I knew nothing of a conference in Potsdam,* nothing about agreements, treaties, or new rules. I was no longer registered anywhere. And that suited me just fine. I had no identification card, no passports, only a knapsack, a blanket, and the clothes I wore. The world was a chaos for me but one in which a person could live as long as he was alert. Hitler was dead, I was free, and I decided to keep it that way."

He finished the story by [Wilhelm] von Kügelgen he was reading, penciled a thank-you rhyme on the back of a scrap of paper, pinned it to the blanket he had picked up in Hartmannsdorf—Krüss preferred traveling light—and slipped away.

In Rome, people read that the famous Eighth Army, which had bested Rommel's Afrika Korps and crossed the Mediterranean into Italy, was being disbanded. In Paris the trial of Pétain, which was really a trial of wartime France, mesmerized newspaper readers. In New York, although the headlines were of B-29s and Japan, people were more curious about the lone, lost B-25 that had lodged in the world's tallest structure. The men who, daily, set up their telescopes on Forty-second Street to sell customers a close look at the top of the Empire State Building were out early on Sunday. Long lines of Manhattanites with quarters queued up. "There's nothing to see but a hole in the building," said veteran telescope hawker Edward Blod to a reporter. "Well, it's good business anyway."

---

*Krüss clearly meant Potsdam, but wrote "Yalta."

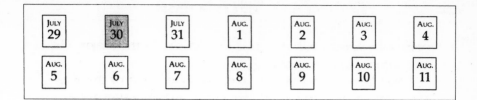

## CHAPTER XVIII

# · JULY 30, 1945 ·

### *"[pushing] forward like raftsmen"*

Only a dozen life rafts and six floater nets were released from the *Indianapolis* before the cruiser began sinking, bow first, into 1,200 fathoms about 450 miles from Leyte. Not all of the eight hundred men who got into the midnight sea alive had kapok life jackets. Some had leaky inflatable rubber life belts; others had nothing. As Captain McVay bobbed to the surface he saw overhead one of the screws still turning, a meat grinder once it dropped into the water. Several seamen, he saw in the pale moonlight, stood, as if safe, on the stilled propeller. If he remained where he was, he knew there would be no court-martial for possible negligence. "It would be much easier," he thought, "if I go down. I won't have to face what I know is coming after this."

He began swimming away from the ship, the instinct to survive taking hold. With suction drawing men under with it and a tidal wave of hot water and bunker fuel vented out by its plunge, the *Indianapolis* went down, pushing the lucky crewmen away. McVay kept swimming until he chanced on a floating potato crate. He put an arm around it. Soon, in the light of the half-moon, he saw two empty life rafts lifted by the swells. He climbed aboard one. Hearing voices nearby he saw Quartermaster Vincent J. Allard struggling with two seamen. He helped them aboard. On the other side of where the ship had sunk, the night was quiet. McVay saw and heard no one else.

Giles McCoy, a Marine, thrashed about and vomited some oily salt water. Then he saw a cluster of what appeared to be about a hundred survivors. Struggling toward them he encountered a floating ammunition can and used it for support while he twisted himself into his life jacket. Then he saw a raft about fifty yards away. Removing his kapok jacket, he gave it to someone treading water nearby, dived under the blanket of oil and scum, and pushed out toward the raft. As it drifted farther from him he thrashed on, getting weaker with each stroke. He reached for one of its trailing ropes and missed, but someone aboard grabbed him by his hair and pulled him up onto the latticed framework. Vomiting more scum helped revive him. McCoy counted sixteen men on the raft or hanging to its ropes.

In the moonlight he thought he saw, silhouetted, something shaped like a submarine, with a conning tower, and running no lights. "Look, a ship!" someone cried. It may have been the *I-58*, looking for evidence of what it had torpedoed, but the shape vanished silently into the darkness. Left to his imagination, Commander Hashimoto guessed at an *Idaho*-class battleship, an unlikely vessel to be traveling without companions. If there were such ships, he wanted to be clear of the area.

Once they were safely below, Hashimoto ordered a celebratory meal for everyone, and the crew feasted on canned beans, corned beef, boiled eel, and sake. The fresh but rotten scallions could wait. Also the crew's staple—tasteless, deteriorating sweet potatoes.

Another *Indianapolis* survivor who crooked an arm about a floating ammunition can was Chief Engineering Officer Richard Redmayne. Near the can was a more valuable object, a kapok jacket. He wriggled into it. Hearing voices, he swam toward them and found a dozen men clinging to a life raft that kept bobbing under at the edges because of excess weight. The group reflected a new democracy of rank—Ensigns Harlan Twible and Donald Blum, Chief Firecontrolman Clarence Benton, Gunner Duward Horner, and other crewmen.

McCoy's raft included a cluster of seamen, with the highest rank Ship's Cook Third Class David Kemp. He claimed later to have fired a shot from his probably waterlogged Marine pistol to signal the outline of a ship that might have been the *I-58*. If it worked, the hope raised would have faded with the flash.

With the first light of morning came the realization that the clusters of survivors were thinning as those seriously burned awakened from pain and exposure and went under. The largest group of seamen included two physicians, Lieutenant Commander Lewis L. Haynes and Lieutenant Melvin Modisher, with more than a hundred men for whom the tumbling of debris from the decks had provided no rafts or floater nets, but at least something to clutch. The men began to fragment into subgroups as the swells broke them apart, but from each came shouts of "Doc! Doc!" Haynes or Modisher would struggle over toward the voices in what became an arduous routine.

"These two guys: can you do anything for them?"

The physician would place his finger over the pupil of an eye to feel for a reflex. If there was none he would help to remove the kapok jacket for those who had only the inflatable kind—or none. The bodies would be pushed off toward the waiting sharks. Haynes and Modisher had no medicines or ointments for their clientele, a dwindling band of oil-blackened bodies with whites of eyes and little more to differentiate them than size. The only medical advice of any use was their warning not to drink the salt water, which would aggravate thirst and bring on diarrhea. The most severely injured were kept in the center of each group, but their ordeal only added to the despondency of the others.

A cork life ring floated by in the growing light. It had a long rope attached to it. Haynes had a dying sailor placed across the ring, and dozens of the others began supporting themselves on kapok and the line. They began seeing planes flying over at very high altitude, but even the cork ring with its long tail of seamen was imperceptible from above—and no one was looking for them.

With the dawn, Redmayne's cluster discovered dozens of other survivors around them, two groups with rafts. Through the night, some of the swimmers had hung on to a large floating object that they discovered with daylight was an unrolled floater net. Spread out, its canvas-covered floaters held up a square of knotted-together manila line. Clinging to it, sailors also clung to hopes that the *Indianapolis*'s radio messages would bring a rescue effort their way, or that CA-35 (their ship's navy number) would soon be missed and searched for. Meanwhile the sun's heat was becoming intense, and its glare seared eyes searching the sea and sky for friendly ships and planes, even for floating flotsam that could hold someone up, or stray edibles—drifting onions or potatoes from the ship's stores. There seemed no other hope of food.

McVay's group of about thirty men was all he could see or hear. Although he could not imagine that out of twelve hundred aboard these were all that had not gone down with the ship, he was the only officer. Rafts were supposed to have stored food, he knew, and he located biscuits, malted milk tablets, and Spam. It was enough to sustain his few for about ten days—if they could manage without water. There was even some fishing gear. Someone still had a soggy wallet, and McVay asked for a scrap of paper from it to keep a log. He had the sun to judge time and position. He even set up two-hour watches to look for passing ships or planes. An experienced angler, he decided to try out the line, and soon caught a fish—but it was recognizably poisonous. He cut it up for bait and hooked a far bigger specimen—a thrashing shark. The men were horrified. Obviously there were others nearby. McVay realized that he would never be able to bring in an edible fish before the sharks got to it.

The largest group of seamen had been formed after first light when three rafts and two floater nets were lashed together. Even the men who had struggled to create the life-sustaining apparatus had difficulty climbing back. Others kicked and fought for a handhold—which itself was not enough to keep one's dangling body safe from the prowling sharks. Screams of men who interpreted any sensation beyond numbness as a shark attack terrorized the others, especially once the sun sank again and darkness became more demoralizing than the day.

Given the air and sea strikes across the central and western Pacific on the thirtieth it seemed almost impossible that the *Indianapolis*'s survivors would not be spotted, but no one had missed them. The port director's operations officer at Tacloban had lists of expected arrivals in Leyte Gulf, and *Indianapolis* was on it for 11:00 A.M. Tuesday the thirty-first. Lieutenant Stuart B. Gibson had duly noted the message from Guam about it in his log. But port regulations did not require arrival reports for combatant ships, and since the *Indianapolis* had been Admiral Spruance's flagship, it was considered possible that Spruance himself would redirect it away from Leyte.

In the Marshall Islands, to the *Indianapolis*'s east, the Navy was busy clearing some islands of inhabitants in order to bomb and shell the areas. The object was to close off food supplies to Japanese holding out on nearby atolls like Maloelap, Wotja, Jaluit, and even Wake, without endangering native populations. Helldivers hit Taroa Island and the surrounding atolls, targeting storage sheds; Wake was shelled by the *Pennsylvania* and six destroyers—overkill, but revenge, perhaps, for its invasion in the first weeks of the war and the imprisonment of its Marine detachment. Prisoners were very much on the American government's mind, as reports were being leaked that POWs were becoming hostages to Japanese security by being placed in small prison camps in known or anticipated "bombardment areas." General LeMay's headquarters on Guam had inadvertently made that strategy easier by releasing lists of targeted cities, identified to the press and encircled on the warning leaflets. On the thirtieth one of the leaflet targets was Hiroshima. "If the war goes on," the warning began, "Japan will be destroyed. This is certain. The longer the war goes on, the more Japan will be crippled and the harder will be the task of postwar reconstruction. It is not difficult for a man to give up his life for his country, but true loyalty now means the termination of the war and the concentration of the national effort on the rehabilitation of the country." But what could a reader of a leaflet in Hiroshima do?

While the stocky, cigar-chewing "Ironpants" LeMay was, at thirty-eight, the youngest major general in the Army, and ruthless as a combat commander of B-17 groups over Europe, he had little comprehension of the Japanese. The leaflet war made headlines in American newspapers and added few casualties in the air as the enemy seldom rose to interdict a B-29. But the Japanese would not flee their cities on the forewarning of a leaflet, and some American prisoners would die.

Looking for fleeing Japanese from the islands in the central Pacific, one of the destroyers in the carrier group off Wake, the *Murray*, held its fire as it intercepted a marked hospital ship off the atoll, the *Tagasago Maru*. A boarding party found 974 evacuees, most apparently in such weak condition that it was doubtful that many would make it back alive. No prisoners were taken off, and the ship was allowed to proceed.

It took considerable effort to bring a carrier strike force close to outlying atolls no longer of much military value, yet some islets were shelled and strafed daily until a Helldiver crashed, unhit, into the lagoon at Taroa, and the crew was lost. Few such missions were worth the cost, as Japanese units on the atolls were withering without replenishment, and senior commanders knew it.

Navy planes from carriers struck as far west as a lonely lighthouse on Sakishima Gunto, northeast of Formosa, but hitting that group of islets, as distant as the home islands were considered to extend, could at least be explained as a diversionary thrust hinting at a possible invasion of Formosa itself. And all around the Inland Sea carrier planes looked for coastal shipping and anything else in the transportation network to bomb and strafe. On the east coast of Honshu the Japanese Musical Instrument Company factory was attacked, as it was reported to be manufacturing airplane propellers, and the Third Fleet looked for other targets, from railroad repair yards to dock facilities, eliciting, because of its low-altitude attacks, ferocious flak. Of 1,602 combat sorties, 35 planes were lost to ground fire and 9 others were labeled as operational losses. Picket ships and Dumbos rescued some airmen, but twenty-two pilots and twenty-one crew were listed as lost. All the missions would have been explained as necessary, to keep the pressure on the enemy.

Not having been sufficiently forthcoming with information, Tom Cartwright and the two naval pilots shot down over Kure were being shipped out to a more sophisticated interrogation center. Separated from his crew, with whom he had been unable to communicate, he recalled feeling "a little sorry for myself." Blindfolded and forbidden to talk to his two companions on the train, he could only wonder what else they wanted him to say about "rather routine military operations." He knew nothing about a possible invasion and had no secrets to hide. And he had no idea where he was going other than that he was on a train.

For an American POW in Japan—although Cartwright didn't know that—conditions were almost idyllic compared to that of Chinese slave workers, some of whom had been captured draftees, others dragooned laborers. Many worked in the mines, without shoes and with thin rags for clothing, winter and summer, on a diet of watery rice gruel and little else. Visiting Hanaoka, an inspector from the Health Ministry claimed to Dowa Mining Company officials that treatment of the Chinese was too soft. "They should be squeezed like a damp towel," he ordered, "until not one drop remains."

After dark on July 30, about 800 brutalized survivors of the 986 that had been shipped to work the copper mines at Hanaoka, in the far northwest of Honshu near Akita, tried to flee. They had heard of a camp of American and Australian POWs nearby, and hoped to join forces and seize fishing boats that might get them north to Hokkaido, which they thought had already been invaded and liberated. If they failed, and drowned in the sea, that was preferable to dying by degrees.

Rumors spread that they had killed and cannibalized a Japanese, and the local militia—farmers and shopkeepers armed with bamboo spears and clubs—hunted them down. "Rabbit hunting," it was called. There was nowhere to go in the barren hills. Seized, they were forced to kneel with hands tied behind their backs in the yard of the community hall while their captors took turns torturing those dragged inside. It was the hottest time of the year, and the prisoners were given neither food nor water. Those retaken alive wished they had not been, but for the militia, chasing down the hapless slave laborers seemed good practice for resisting invasion.

Cartwright's captors knew nothing about an invasion of Hokkaido, but had all the evidence they needed that an enormous buildup was under way for a landing on Kyushu. American preparations were far too massive to hide, and there were abandoned Japanese with radio apparatus everywhere in the western Pacific, unable to do more than inform. American listening posts were even more active, but seldom via informants on the ground. Headquarters in Manila had access to "Ultra" and cryptanalysts could bring in and decode radio traffic on Kyushu. They knew on the twenty-ninth that the 40th, 56th, and 57th divisions were already awaiting an invasion of southern Kyushu and that another was in the process of formation. They knew that the 216th and 303rd—two new divisions—were supplementing the 40th. On the thirtieth it seemed likely that the 145th Division was also moving from Hiroshima across the strait to Kyushu, and that the 7th Division was deploying south from upper Honshu. By August 2 it would appear that troop strength on Kyushu was up to 545,000 and was still being augmented. Address routings on another message picked up on the thirtieth located three additional armored brigades with 480 tanks in southern Kyushu. No feints toward Formosa or Hong Kong or anywhere else were likely to divert the Home Army. Nevertheless, deception was an integral part of "Olympic" strategy, so much so that MacArthur's command distributed, on July 30, with a sloppy secrecy intended to inveigle the Japanese, "Pastel Two," which set October 1 for landings on the Chinese coast to set up airfields from which to attack the home islands, and December 1 for an invasion on the home island of Shikoku. On September 7 the China phase was to be just as secretly postponed in favor of the Shikoku operation.

Washington had other alternatives before the switch was thrown

on "Olympic." From Henry Stimson, back in his War Department office, came a message to Truman in Potsdam: "The time schedule on
Groves' project is progressing so rapidly that it is now essential that
[the] statement for release by you be available not later than Wednesday, 1 August." Stimson had revised an earlier draft because of "your
recent ultimatum" and "dramatic results of test." The original version
prepared by Groves and his staff celebrated the triumph of American
technology more than the expected success over the Japanese.

Stimson cabled that a courier was bringing a new text, as it could
not be entrusted to the airwaves, and urged that Truman authorize
its release even if the courier failed to reach the President on time. As
Truman knew, the window of opportunity for the Japanese between
the issuing of the ultimatum and the projected delivery of "Little
Boy" was closing fast. The orders to Tinian had specified the first appropriate day after August 1, and the Japanese rejection of Potsdam
had already made delivery inevitable.

Despite Brynes's absence, a State Department memorandum
prepared by the Office of Far Eastern Affairs for a meeting of the Secretary's Staff Committee was being considered that morning in Washington to provide guidance on the Potsdam declaration. It focused on the
modifications. Unconditional surrender, it emphasized, applied only to
"all Japanese armed forces," softening earlier understandings that it
also applied to "the emperor, the government and the people." The language "might also mean that the emperor will accept the terms proposed in the proclamation and will continue to function, but will at
once dismiss all his militaristic advisers, democratize the constitution of
Japan, arrange an election, appoint a government in accordance with its
results, and direct that government to carry out the terms of the proclamation." The Allied military authorities, however, "would have full
powers of government in Japan until their objectives were carried out."

Byrnes was too busy to be concerned about a document the
Japanese had already scorned, although his staff understood that in
due course the Japanese would have to live or die by it. The Secretary
was trying to wind up the conference before "Little Boy" complicated
arrangements. The well-informed Cadogan would complain, "Jimmy B. is a bit too active and has already gone and submitted various
proposals to Molotov which go a bit beyond what we want at the moment." An authentic career public servant, Cadogan was already
speaking in the voice of his new Labour masters—in particular, Ernest
Bevin, who was inclined to hold out for tougher solutions than Byrnes

knew either could get from the Russians. Byrnes and his men had been working for weeks in advance of Potsdam on a settlement for postwar Europe, and he knew how far he could go with Stalin and Molotov, who possessed the facts on the ground. Bevin had brought to Berlin his long-standing foreign policy interests and his longer-standing anti-Communism, but had not yet recognized that he and Attlee were essentially powerless. The United States wanted to get on with the war in the Pacific and to get out of Europe with whatever it was possible to salvage from the Soviets. With the American armies withdrawing and Communist parties burgeoning, Byrnes was willing to draw the line at what the Russians had already seized.

The State Department had yet another sensitive matter to present to the new Labour government—Palestine. In Washington, Loy W. Henderson, the Director of Near Eastern and African Affairs, min-uted Acting Secretary of State Grew, following up Truman's memo of July 24 to Churchill in Potsdam, to remind him that the Labourites had been more positive toward Jewish aspirations than the Tories. In 1939, Henderson noted, Labour members of the House of Commons voted overwhelmingly against then–Prime Minister Neville Chamberlain's White Paper repudiating the 1917 Balfour Declaration, which had promised a "homeland" in Palestine for the Jews. But, Henderson cautioned, "While the Labour Party is definitely committed to a pro-Zionist policy, there is some question as to the extent to which it will find it feasible to put this policy into operation." In 1939, he observed, Herbert Morrison, now a power in the Cabinet, had told the House that Labour wanted to raise "the economic, social and political status of the Arab masses in Palestine, Trans-Jordan and the other Arabian countries without prejudicing the development of the Jewish National Home," and he had charged that the Conservative regime had been guilty of a "breach of faith" toward the Jews. As late as December 1944, Henderson went on, the annual conference of the Labour Party had passed a resolution recognizing "an irresistible case now, after the unspeakable atrocities of the cold and calculated German Nazi plan to kill all the Jews in Europe," to resettle the remnants "on humane grounds" in Palestine "and to promote a stable settlement [by] transfer of population. Let the Arabs be encouraged to move out, as the Jews move in. Let them be compensated handsomely for their land and let their settlement elsewhere be carefully organized and generously financed."

With the opening of the German death camps, the revelation of the extent of the genocide, and the enormity of the displaced persons dilemma, the situation could not be ignored, and Truman would remind Attlee of the memo to Churchill. Yet Attlee needed no reminding, as more than two hundred newly elected and reelected Labourites recalled to their government the 1944 resolution, and the Arab Office in London rushed out a warning that Arabs would "never acquiesce" to Jewish settlement even if it became Big Three policy emanating from Potsdam: "The Zionists are using the refugees as the cloak for their political aims in Palestine." The U.S. interest, the statement went on, was "imperialist desire" to insure sources of oil in the Middle East.

For Secretary of the Navy Forrestal, whose ships ran on oil, Jewish aspirations in Palestine were at odds with the political realities. At breakfast with Truman that morning in Potsdam, Forrestal told the President that it was "a matter of the first importance" to placate Saudi Arabia and to get "the benefit of it." He told Truman, Forrestal noted in his diary, "that, roughly speaking, Saudi Arabia, according to oil people in whom I had confidence, is one of the three great puddles left in the world, the other two being the Russian Caucasus and the Caribbean." (A few days later in London, Forrestal talked with the retiring First Lord of the Admiralty, the Conservative Brendan Bracken, who expressed concern about the Labour M.P. "pledge" to support the Jewish national home: "He said this could touch off a most explosive situation in the Middle East; that many millions of Arabs would be willing to fight immediately if such a program were set in motion.") Forrestal would not have to worry about the Labour attitude toward Palestine, as Ernest Bevin preferred stability in the Middle East to the immigration of Jewish refugees, and his attitude could be read into Attlee's cautious response to Truman that he could not make any statement on Palestine policy "until we have had time to consider the matter." That his party had considered the matter the previous December meant nothing. It was one thing to be in Opposition; it was another to execute policy.

Forrestal's breakfast for Truman on the thirtieth brought the Secretary of the Navy's young traveling companion to Potsdam, but John Kennedy did not have the clout to sit at the table with Truman, Eisenhower, and senior American powers then in Germany. It did mean, however, that the two succeeding presidents were in Potsdam with the current one—Eisenhower, who would succeed Truman, and, most improbable at the time, Kennedy, who would succeed Eisenhower.

Once the breakfast meeting ended, Forrestal flew off at 10:30 with his party for an inspection tour of North Sea ports, visiting what was left of Bremen and Bremerhaven, and the Frogge shipyard where the Germans had operated an assembly line that produced a submarine every twenty-four days. Traveling through the Soviet zone before flying north, Forrestal observed the Russian rape of German industry and pondered in his diary, "I wonder if the Russians' objective is now to reduce the German standard of living so that it compares more nearly with their own and keep it at that level."

From breakfast, Byrnes went back to his homework, the preparation of documents to end the Soviet-American deadlock on the issues that kept the conference from closing. He knew that if he secured Molotov's blessing the British would have to go along. The first matter disposed of Italy and the former German satellites in eastern Europe, now Russian satellites. The new Council of Foreign Ministers was to prepare a peace treaty for Italy that would create the conditions for its admission into the United Nations. The Council would also draft treaties for Bulgaria, Romania, and Hungary, but these would be held for signatures until they possessed "recognized democratic governments." The formula stalled formal recognition by the United States and Britain but offered legitimacy of a sort.

On the Polish border issue Byrnes conceded the western Niesse, "pending the final determination . . . which should await the peace settlement." The exposed finger of Silesia was indefensible and lost anyway, but Byrnes linked his concession to Soviet acceptance of the American reparations formula, which evaded fixed monetary equivalents and established the principle that each power would meet its reparations claims from its own zone, although Russia would additionally be entitled to a percentage of industrial equipment from the Ruhr as a quid pro quo for produce from its zone. There would also be side agreements on the war crimes trials.

Truman and Byrnes were acknowledging the realities and recognizing, too, that further agreements would be harder and harder to get and that some of the promises made might therefore never have to be implemented. And the parties might sign and depart from Potsdam before events in the Far East overtook the accords.

Byrnes arranged to meet bilaterally with Molotov at 4:30, and handed his proposals to the Foreign Commissar while pointing out that one paper conceded the western Niesse boundary. Molotov expressed his "gratification," but Byrnes emphasized that the suggestions were his own.

At five the Ministers met for the tenth such session at Potsdam. Whatever limitations his proposals put upon Soviet claims, said Byrnes, they were much less than the concessions required of "our British friends." And he referred, too, to "my friend," Commissar Molotov. It was not South Carolina courtesy, but an attempt to keep rancor out of the meeting. Bevin circulated a paper on "stopping all private wars," which meant, he said, "that until peace was established, the *status quo* should be maintained and that frontiers should not be altered by force." The nine officials and three translators present all understood that Bevin was referring to Tito and Yugoslavia. Molotov said that he would "need time to examine the draft," but it was in any case an indirect message to Tito about his ambitions at the expense of Austria and Italy.

Molotov followed with his series of complaints. There were "Fascist agents" operating with British and American connivance in their zones of Austria and Germany. And he contended once more that many German troops captured in Norway had not been disarmed. Bevin replied that a complete response would be forthcoming in writing. (It was handed to Molotov the same day. The British had taken the surrender of 365,000 Germans in Norway. All were disarmed but officers and 2 percent of the ranks who were deputed to maintain order. No German was permitted to bear arms outside his "reservation." Bevin also offered to return to the Russian zone the 108,000 troops whose homes of origin were there.) Molotov also objected to British and American refusal to "permit" the repatriation of citizens of Soviet republics held in camps for German war prisoners. It was now an old story. The POWs themselves did not want to go back. No prisoners from territory seized by the Soviets after 1939, such as the Baltic states, would be returned. Since there was now so much slave labor in Russia, the Soviets had no need to import people they would either imprison or execute, but leaving them in the West left a cadre of anti-Communists, some of whom would work at their anti-Communism. Truman's diary for the day would observe about such negotiations with the Soviets: "It is a sick situation at best." To his mother and sister in Missouri he wrote, "You never saw such pigheaded people as the Russians. I hope I never have to hold another conference with them—but of course I will."

The German POWs already freed and returned home were better

off than the millions in labor camps in Russia, but not nearly as well
off as the disarmed troops in Norway or even those doing forced labor
in France. "Sometimes, walking through the streets," Ruth Andreas-
Friedrich noted in her Berlin diary on the thirtieth, "one can barely
stand to look at all the misery. Among the smart American uniforms,
the well-fed figures in the occupying forces, the first German soldiers
[back] appear ragged and haggard, sheepishly looking around like
caught offenders. Prisoners of war from who knows where. . . . Seeing
them one wants to look away because one feels so ashamed of their
shame, of their wretched, pitiful looks. Are these the glorious victors
whom Adolf Hitler years ago sent into the war so well equipped?"

The scene she described seemed like a vision by Hieronymus
Bosch, or, closer to her time, a vision of December 1918 and the survivors of the trenches. The returned troops, sent back perhaps because
they were too sick or disabled to work, shambled about "like walking
ruins. Limbless, invalid, ill, deserted and lost. A grey-bearded man in
a tattered uniform leans against a wall. With his arms about his head
he is quietly weeping. People pass by, stop and shyly form a circle
around him. . . . It is terrible to see grey-bearded men cry, unable to
stop crying. . . . Sometimes all that's left is the trunk. Amputated up to
their hips, they sit in an old box supported by wheels. With their arms
they push themselves forward like raftsmen, maneuvering their pitiful vehicles through the stream of cars and trucks. 'Heil Hitler!' one
feels like cursing out of angry compassion when one sees them."

In the American zone, at least, the concrete, if not the fleshly,
vestiges of Hitlerism were being expunged. An Eisenhower order
framed a week earlier was being distributed with a July 30 date.
"Any park, street or public way, institution, building (public or privately owned), or industrial concern in the U.S. Zone of Occupation,"
it declared, "which was named for any person or thing associated
with either Naziism or German militarism as herein defined, shall
have its name removed from public display and use." Each was to be
replaced by a more sanitary name. "All movable monuments or statues associated with either Naziism or German militarism," the order
went on, "should be removed immediately and transported to a place
of storage." (These were to be disposed of by the theater commander.) Further, "All emblems, insignia, or symbols of Naziism or German militarism shall be removed from those statues, monuments,
and edifices which are not amenable to removal or storage."

Fortunately the directive did not mandate removal of statues of

Frederick the Great or Bismarck, or the wholesale effacing of European history, much of which was a history of wars. Nazi-style "German militarism" was defined by date as beginning on January 1, 1933. It made the policing easier.

The French were doing their own ideological housecleaning, but obliterating the vestiges of Vichy was more than a matter of statues and squares. While the trial of Marshal Henri Philippe Pétain mesmerized Frenchmen, and some homegrown Nazis were already in prison or shot, the infamous Pierre Laval, once chief of the Vichy government and four times Premier of France, had been tantalizingly free across the border in Barcelona. He had flown there with his wife, but to a cool welcome, just after Hitler's suicide. Franco, he was told, had decided that it was not in Spain's interest to accept high-ranking war criminals. Perhaps he should fly to Ireland. "Me?" he exclaimed. "I'm not a war criminal—I'm a peace criminal."

He was temporarily interned until the Franco regime could figure a way out, and for weeks the issue simmered, Laval hoping to hang on until what he saw as postliberation excesses waned. On July 30 the governor of Catalonia, Antonio Correa Vegleson, informed him that his presence could no longer be tolerated and that the Junkers transport in which he had arrived would take him wherever its German pilots could fly. At 3:00 P.M. he boarded the plane wearing his customary white tie and chain-smoking as usual, but instead of flying to France to surrender he ordered the pilot to Austria, where Laval was arrested in Linz by the American military—who handed him over to the French. He was still wearing his white tie when, in Fresnes Prison, he was executed for treason at 12:32 P.M. on October 15.

It was eight o'clock in the evening in Moscow when Ambassador Sato wearily sent off the first of two cables to Tokyo. "There is no reason to believe," he began, "that Stalin was not informed beforehand on the Potsdam joint declaration." If one accepted that, Sato went on, Stalin understood the situation and "it would mean that our request to send a special envoy cannot be accepted and will be futile." He felt certain that if Japan surrendered, "Stalin will exert heavy pressure on the United States, Great Britain and China regarding Manchuria, China, Korea, etc." Further, Sato explained, Stalin "actually holds the power to do so" and had "no necessity for making a voluntary agreement with Japan." It took no tea leaf reading for him to see, he warned

Togo, "a serious discrepancy between your view and the actual state of affairs."

What had happened, he explained in a further cable at 10:31 P.M., also decrypted by "Magic," was that he had met once more with Vice Commissar Lozovsky. Again, Sato had appealed for a response from Molotov in Potsdam, reiterating that unconditional surrender was "out of the question" but any formal end to the war that would guarantee Japan's "honor and existence" would be acceptable. "I promise again to convey your request," Lozovsky had said, ushering Sato out. But Sato knew that nothing would come of it.

Now out of the line of political fire, Churchill in London could only guess what was happening in Potsdam, Moscow, and Tokyo. He could, however, read the London newspapers, where it was reported that in an unusual display of independence, the *Asahi Shimbun* in Tokyo had just asked, in a strong editorial, for increased aircraft production and higher-angle AA guns, and had entreated the government to place telegraph and telephone lines underground. "Air raids against our medium and small-sized cities are gaining in intensity each day," the plea went on, "and what we are worried about is the destruction of our means of communication and traffic system as well as our electrical, gas, and water supplies." It was a remarkable admission for what it conceded between the lines as well as for what was actually printed. Smaller cities were now being targeted because most large conurbations had already been torched. Inhabitants who had fled to smaller cities were again homeless. Toshikazu Kase, Togo's deputy, reported to his chief that 75 percent of the telephones in Tokyo—and most of the lines—were destroyed, and as in Morio Kita's epic novel about the period, *The House of Nire,* newspaper boasts of ever-increasing numbers of American planes downed and ships sunk began to imply that even if true, the enemy military was inexhaustible. The infrastructure of urban Japan was not. Few planes rose to interdict the omnipresent B-29s,* even after pamphlet warnings of targets that turned out to be accurate. Japan was coming apart.

What did not reach either the Western press or newspapers in what American airmen liked to call "the Empire" was that a new bomb shelter for the Emperor within the palace grounds had been

---

*It was no immediate help to Japanese city dwellers that a jurisdictional strike between two unions at the U. S. Rubber plant in Detroit had cost seventy thousand B-29 tires in lost production before, at the request of General Curtis LeMay, the Army, on July 30, took over the factory.

completed. Hirohito had made a half hour inspection tour at three in the afternoon on July 11 as the work went on. The army had also finished what was described to him as an impregnable shelter at Matsushiro, in Nagano Prefecture, but His Majesty had refused to go there, possibly realizing that he would have no control whatever over events if he left Tokyo. The new underground structure was designed to take a ten-ton bomb and was only a hundred yards from the *Gobunko,* where he was living, and camouflaged from the air by green netting meant to look like foliage. Before withdrawing outside the wide moats that gave the palace compound its traditional privacy, officers and men who had worked on the project were given presents by the Emperor—cigarettes with the emblem of the imperial chrysanthemum for private soldiers, chrysanthemum-embossed porcelain cuff links for the officers. The ceremony was brief: Tokyo was in the process of being raided by 180 B-29s.

Churchill had left 10 Downing Street on the thirtieth for his home at Chartwell, but not before opening a letter from the President. Messages by the thousands had begun arriving (including, a count later confirmed, 268 hostile ones and 217 from "cranks or lunatics"). One on White House letterhead had been sent by courier from Berlin. "My dear Mr. Churchill," Harry Truman began, "I could hardly refrain from saying as my predecessor used to say, 'Winston.' In the short time we were associated here I became a great admirer of yours. It was a shock to me when I returned from Frankfurt and learned the result of the English elections. We miss you very much here, the Secretary of State, Admiral Leahy and I, but we wish you the happiest possible existence from now to the last call and we shall always remember that you held the barbarians until we could prepare."

"I am sorry indeed," Churchill replied, "that our work together has been nipped in the bud, but I cherish the hope that our friendship will continue to ripen, and that there may be occasions when it may be of service to both our countries and to the common causes they pursue."

Little about defeat could be amusing, but a letter from William Deakin, who had been Churchill's research assistant on writing projects before the war and was on a mission in Yugoslavia, was the exception. He had been in Croatia when the election results were broadcast, Deakin wrote from the British embassy in Belgrade. "The comment of one old lady in Zagreb," he wrote, was: " 'Poor Mr.

Churchill, I suppose he now will be shot!' " On his own, Deakin added, "At first I felt very saddened and shocked, but now realise that this political decision can never in any way reflect upon the greatness of your leadership during our darkest moments."

The German physicists held at Farm Hall had lost their fears that the new Socialist government would turn them over to the Communists, and worried instead about possible allegations that they had served Nazi science. Reading the English papers, Otto Hahn, at sixty-six the senior scientist of the ten, worried over press speculation, which must have also given the secrecy-obsessed General Groves in Washington fits, that the Nazis had been defeated just short of development of a superbomb. Since German technology had come up with the V-1 "buzz bomb" (the first cruise missile), a potential ICBM in the V-2 rocket that terrified England until its launch sites were seized, and the first operational jet fighter, the suggestion seemed reasonable, but the lid on atomic bomb talk had largely been successful through the war.

"I read an article in the *Picture Post* about the uranium bomb," Hahn, the co-discoverer in 1938 of nuclear fission, observed to Kurt Diebner, a younger nuclear physicist. "It said that the newspapers had mentioned that such a bomb was being built in Germany. Now you can understand that we are being *detained*"—he emphasized the word—"because we are such men. They will not let us go until they are absolutely certain that no harm can be done or that we will not fall into Russian hands or anything like that."

Early in the war, German physicists had determined that the critical mass of U-235 necessary for an explosion—Heisenberg overestimated it as between two and six tons—meant that it was practical to think only in terms of creating usable energy through the slower process of a nuclear reactor. Experimentation toward that goal, they hoped, would also preserve German science and technology through the war. Nazi policy on military exploitation of atomic power had followed from the erroneous feasibility values projected by Heisenberg and other Germans in the first years after Otto Hahn's breakthrough. Resources were diverted toward more practical weaponry.

Confident as the physicists were that a uranium bomb was impossible to manufacture and deploy, they understood the fear in the less knowledgeable West. "It would have been just the same in

Germany," said Diebner. The day before he was captured, he confessed, he suggested to his wife that they both commit suicide.

The outlook for misuse of nuclear physics was "dark" for all of them, said Hahn, but at his age he assumed he did not have a long future to worry about. Walther Gerlach, another of the Farm Hall ten, Hahn noted, wanted to go back to the University of Munich to build a "uranium machine"—a nuclear reactor: "Men are not idealists and everyone will not agree not to work on such a dangerous thing. Every country will work on it in secret. Especially as they will assume that it can be used as a weapon of war."

Later in the day Gerlach and Bagge wondered what punishment their Nazi pasts might bring. Party membership was compulsory, Gerlach claimed; it also enabled him to keep a "half-Jew" on his staff until 1944. He had fended off attempts to place a picture of Hitler in his institute: "I always said, 'No, I already have one.' I had a very small picture I had bought for 5 pfennig. The Nazis treated me badly. They reduced my salary and withdrew my allowances." Diebner and Hahn came in and Gerlach left, but the conversation continued about Nazi connections. "Wirtz knows my views," said Diebner. "I told him, 'I am a Party member. We'll see what happens. If the Nazis win, I shall still be a Party member and that will help us; and if things go the other way, you will have to help me.' That's what we arranged at the time."

Heisenberg joined the group, and talked of the "calls for help" to which he tried to respond "where people"—Belgian and Polish and Jewish mathematicians, philosophers, physicists—"were being murdered by our people." He could do nothing, not even through a contact in Himmler's office.

"We have done things which are unique in the world," Wirtz conceded. "We went to Poland and not only murdered the Jews . . . but, for instance, the SS drove up to a girls' school, fetched out the top class and shot them simply because . . . the intelligentsia were to be wiped out. Just imagine if they arrived in Hechingen, drove up to the girls' school and shot all the girls! That's what we did."

Among the lesser folk shocked by the British election results was a youngish writer in Wales who had managed to keep out of the war. Dylan Thomas had been working intermittently on a radio script he called "Quite Early One Morning"—later expanded into *Under Milk Wood*—but he spent at least as much time in the pubs, where he shared concerns about rampaging socialism. He was just back from the Edwinsford Arms, he wrote to American poet Oscar Williams. The pub was a "sabbath-dark bar with a stag's head over the Gents and a stuffed salmon caught by Shem and a mildewed advertisement for pre-1914 tobacco and a stain on the wall, just above my head, that I hoped was beer." He drank with a man who claimed he was shot in the groin in the 1914 war and had not been able to bed a woman since. He blamed it on "the dirty Jews. Look what they did, the moochin"— his Welsh for *mochyn*, or "pig." And he showed Thomas the scar on his calf. Politely, the poet said he thought his chum had been shot in the groin. "And the calf, the bloody yids," said the swiller.

Unlike Thomas, he had a regular job in a government agency that investigated the authenticity of discharged soldiers' pension claims, especially those labeled "psycho-neurosis." They exchanged gross stories; then Thomas bicycled home "through the justice-must-be-done-let's-rain-on-sinners rain." Back at his card table he turned to a BBC script for the Children's Hour that he was calling "Memories of Christmas"—it would become *A Child's Christmas in Wales*— and wrote his letter thanking Williams for an anthology of war poetry, asking him also to help find an escape to America from the "Socialists-in-power." Although Thomas had not been to war and had composed no combat poetry, he pontificated, "War can't produce poetry, only poets can, and war can't produce poets either because they bring themselves up in such a [way] that this outward bang-bang of men against men is something they have passed a long time ago on their poems' way toward peace. A poet writing a poem is at peace with everything except words. . . ." Between paragraphs Thomas added to his jam jar of cigarette butts.

The writer's life in Oscar Williams's New York was sometimes more colorful and no less inane than in Cardiganshire. At about the same time—it was 4:00 P.M. in Manhattan—the Stage Door Canteen, for servicemen, run by the American Theatre Wing, began its move from 234 West Forty-fourth Street two blocks away to the Hotel Diplomat. Actors, actresses, and writers from sixteen Broadway shows led by husky-voiced Jane Cowl carried equipment and supplies. First in the line was Mayor LaGuardia, who puffed along with a canteen chair cradled in both arms. "You're not really tired?" he twitted the volunteers. The press cameras clicked.

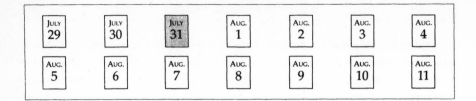

| July 29 | July 30 | July 31 | Aug. 1 | Aug. 2 | Aug. 3 | Aug. 4 |
| Aug. 5 | Aug. 6 | Aug. 7 | Aug. 8 | Aug. 9 | Aug. 10 | Aug. 11 |

# CHAPTER XIX

## . JULY 31, 1945 .

*"Release when ready . . ."*

Lost in the red tape of expected arrivals and departures in the port director's office in Tacloban was any evidence that the *Indianapolis* was overdue. Its mission to Tinian had been top secret; its routing from Guam had
been reported and forgotten. Many ships checked in and out of Leyte
Gulf. The day before, the *West Virginia* had arrived from Okinawa, as
good as new although it had been raised from the mud of Pearl Harbor.
On the last day of July the very battleship for which Commander Hashimoto had mistook the much smaller *Indianapolis*, the *Idaho*, sailed out of
San Pedro Bay, the innermost pocket of the gulf, for exercises offshore.*
The older battleships *Arkansas*, *Texas*, *New Mexico*, *Mississippi*, and *Col-
orado* were also assembled there. The Navy had a surfeit of big guns.

---

*Since Commander Hashimoto had radioed Japan that he had sunk an "*Idaho*-class" warship,
a message intercepted as usual by U.S. Intelligence, the Navy, within sixteen hours of the
cruiser's sinking, knew on Guam that something big in the *Indianapolis*'s likely position might
have been torpedoed. The Navy also knew that the *Idaho* itself was afloat, but it later dismissed
the "failure to evaluate accurately a report made by a Japanese submarine" as "of only local significance" as there was a great deal of signal traffic to evaluate.

The Navy seemed to have a surfeit of everything, although it was rushing the construction and delivery of more landing craft. Ensign Charles Hosler, assigned to a reconnaissance plane for typhoon spotting, recalled, "It is difficult to imagine the magnitude of the buildup. Power generators lined up for miles. Warehouses full of binoculars, blankets, carbines, etc. Jeeps in packing cases piled six high for *miles*. The breakwater for Apra Harbor on Guam was built after the war by driving new trucks full of coral into the harbor along with tanks and half-tracks. Millions of bags of cement falling apart in the tropical rains. . . ." The Associated Press released photographs of the buildup in the Philippines for the invasion of Japan, showing what appeared to be an immense, even endless, parking lot of "weasels"—light amphibious troop carriers—and "ducks"—another variety of small personnel carrier. Hundreds of them, row on row. Clearly the photos were no breach of security but a salvo in the campaign of psychological warfare. Yet on Samar, one of the assembly points, a Seabee supply officer, Lieutenant Phil Habermann, was writing to his wife in Wisconsin about the boredom of waiting. He was reading a Charlie Chan mystery, and had just sat through a "drippy" movie about the Brontë sisters, *Devotion*. He couldn't tell his wife about "Olympic" but rattled on about the new "point" entitlement system for getting home. At the new rate he would be out, he estimated, in about three and a half years. "Oh, well, something is bound to happen before then, don't you think?"

Not missed by anyone, and 550 miles to the east, Captain McVay, as sodden and oil-blackened as the lowest-ranking sailor scrambling in the swells with him, was still trying to organize his raft group. He estimated its size optimistically as seventy-five feet across, large enough to be spotted from the air. Contents of some rafts had been lost in their violent upheaval from the decks, but he found a sealed can of Very flares—four each of green, red, and white—and a small pistol for firing them. Also an emergency signaling mirror. A fish line trailing in the water indicated direction of drift. Underneath the rafts were paddles, useless in the circumstances except to drive sharks a few feet farther away.

The second night out McVay used his flares. A C-54 flying east toward Guam rumbled overhead, and every raft with a Very pistol sent up distress signals. Out of his starboard window Captain Richard G. LeFrancis of the Army Air Force saw flashes that he took to be a minor firefight below. The Japanese had been trying to slip small craft by American picket ships to provision stranded outposts. He made a note of the location and reported it on arrival in Guam. It was no concern of the Air Force, he was told. Forget it.

The raft in which Ensign Ross Rogers and ten other men drifted had lost some occupants overnight, dead of injuries or burns and a meal for sharks. Rogers thought that their best bet was to paddle toward the Palau Island group, perhaps 30 miles to the south. Had his men realized that the Palaus, the nearest land, lay nearly 250 miles away, their sense of despair would have been overwhelming.

The supervisor of the last watch, to whom Richard Redmayne had reported to the bridge for the 8:00 P.M. to midnight duty, had been Commander Stanley Lipski, once a naval attaché in Finland and an intelligence expert fluent in Russian. He knew that promotions came far more quickly at sea than in Washington, and had pulled strings to get into action before it was too late. Somehow in the darkness he had been thrown clear from the plunging ship, burned and blinded beyond a prayer of survival. But he had been pulled onto Haynes's raft, held up out of the searing salt water by Aviation Machinist's Mate Anthony Maday and Machinist's Mate Granville Crane, each of them injured but taking turns nevertheless to cradle him between visits from the doctors. Haynes, a buddy of his aboard ship, talked to him when he could throughout the day; when night came again, although Lipski could not sense the difference, he knew who was with him and managed the words, "I'm going, Lew." There were no eyelids for Haynes to close.

Despite the circling sharks, the men on the raft had no choice but to remove the precious kapok jacket and lower the body into the swells, where it quickly disappeared in the darkness.

Lipski was the last of the horribly injured in Redmayne's group to remain alive; after him there were only seamen miserable from lesser burns or fractures, but men kept dying—of drinking deadly salt water, of heat-and-thirst exhaustion and delirium, of the desolation of hopelessness that made one do suicidal things like swimming away.

Although the *Indianapolis* had been on a well-traveled track, its survivors were drifting off it. Army transports redeploying divisions from Europe were streaming through the Panama Canal to the west, and on the last day of July the Army requested the Navy to employ greater security on other ships passing through to support "Olympic" because "high-octane tankers and vessels carrying explosives as cargo" could endanger the troops if an accident occurred. An explosion could also close the Canal.

There was also regular air traffic overhead, although most of it passed to the north. Colonel Tibbets encountered a cloud of B-29s going in the other direction as he returned from Iwo Jima. With "Little Boy" nearly ready, he was flying a mock mission with a weather plane and an instrument plane as planned for the real thing. Crews had already flown test runs as actual combat strikes over Japan, three-plane formations dropping one "pumpkin" each (to likely local puzzlement) over Koriyama, Nagaoka, Toyama, Kobe, Yokkaichi, Ube, Wakayama, Maizuru, Fukushima, and Niihama. Each bomb had four sections of cordite charge, enough to blow up the evidence. Three of the 509th's bombers flew the final test run with a facsimile bomb, taking off from Tinian, rendezvousing over Iwo Jima, and returning to Tinian, dropping pumpkin L-6 into the sea and making the hard turn that would be necessary to evade the blast effect. The Bomb with the active components was labeled L-11, its casing on hand since late in 1944.

Despite the activity of the Twelfth, Fourteenth, Twentieth, and Philippines-based Far East Air Force, their targets a gazeteer of sites in China, Korea, and Japan and their planes a catalog of equipment from B-25s and P-38s to B-29s and P-51s, the flights were only a prelude to August 1. As Hays Gamble on Guam noted in his diary, "Mission was called off for tonight—will be held tomorrow night in conjunction with Air Force Day. A maximum effort by all Air Forces & Navy over Japan and it should be a real good show." Arnold in Washington (out of most day-to-day decisions because of heart trouble) and Spaatz and LeMay on Guam assumed that with Japan beaten (the ultimate means not yet clear), the strategic priority was now an independent postwar Air Force. Talks had already begun in Washington, and were continued in Potsdam, about a unification of the armed services in a "Department of Defense." The Army Air Force, practically autonomous under Hap Arnold, wanted coordinate status with the Army and Navy, and intended to put on a "show" that would be less to stagger Japan than to upstage the rival services. The likely costs in people and planes were incidental.

Another typhoon was approaching the home islands. While the weather front was still a day or two away, and Admiral Halsey's carrier planes had been scouting it, he did not want to risk another embarrassment, and ordered a mass retirement to deep water for re-provisioning and refueling from the logistic support group. Much of the fleet began skirting the swells after some last hits at Honshu. One force of destroyers boldly entered Suruga Gulf, shelling port installations only seventy-five miles southwest of Tokyo, while carrier planes claimed 136 planes destroyed or damaged on the ground. One fighter rose in defense and was shot down. The Third Fleet claimed the sinking or damaging of a variety of small craft, from midget submarines to gunboats, suicide vehicles stockpiled for the future invasion. But there was fierce flak. Dumbos searching with a sub rescued seven pilots and crewmen and dropped a boat to nine other survivors. There were also downed aircraft with no survivors.

"Ultra" decrypts revealed that two more divisions and two additional armored brigades had reached Kyushu in the last days of July, very likely through night crossings of the Shimonoseki Suido from Honshu and the Bungo Suido from Shikoku. In Washington, as part of Special Branch—the "Army Chair Corps" unit decrypting "Magic" messages—former Harvard professor Edwin Reischauer, a wartime major, discovered that telegraph offices were beginning to send uncoded military messages within the home islands. It was another indication of bombing damage to the communications system, yet seemingly safe to the Japanese because they relied on code names and numbers for units. With no spy network within the islands, Reischauer's crew relied instead on low-level messages informing a private in "Kuma 7112" in southern Kyushu of the death of a relative, or requesting a corporal in "Akatsuki 3657" to return from Kyushu to Hokkaido for the funeral of his father. "It was not difficult to piece messages of this sort into a fairly clear picture of the massing of a great number of newly created divisions on the coast of Miyazaki Prefecture in southeastern Kyushu, just where American forces were in fact planning to land."

The number of newly identified divisions was so considerable that top brass in G2 called Reischauer in to question the reliability of his information. "I assured them it was quite accurate though I had no idea how young, ill-armed, or poorly trained these divisions might be." The Imperial Army was calling up every available body it could find, from workers freed from assembly lines by bombings or materials shortages to whatever university students remained out of uniform. On Tokyo Radio, Home Minister Genki Abe urged volunteers and conscripts to be ready to sacrifice themselves for defense of the homeland and occupied China—some as young as fourteen were in training—"until fire belches forth and blood is drawn."

Momo Iida got away. He remembered the morning of Pearl Harbor, when, on his way to school by train, he heard an old soldier warn that the war would be like none before. Drafted now, and in a camp at Kashiwa, just northeast of Tokyo, he gambled that a "little place" like his barracks would not have X-ray equipment and claimed severe tuberculosis. It was "a war of nerves between me and the doctor. . . . As he tapped me, he asked questions, and I described to him every symptom of TB that I could think of: my temperature went up in the evening; I had diarrhoea all the time; I coughed phlegm and sometimes it had flecks of blood in it. . . ."

Of all the conscripts who had faked symptoms he was the only one whose bundle of civilian clothes was not returned to anxiously waiting parents. As he walked out the gate he thought, "I've done it! Perhaps I am going to survive this war after all!" But he knew that he couldn't smile or walk jauntily, and tried to look "as miserable and downcast" as he could. He could sense that his father was doing the same thing, and when they were far enough down the long flat path between the rice paddies as to be out of sight, they both relaxed into smiles. For several days Iida was afraid to show his face outside. "But in the end I went round to all the neighbors and told them that I was ill and had been sent home and now I was heartbroken not to be able to fight for my country."

"In those days," Yukio Mishima wrote in *Confessions of a Mask* (1949), "one had to have either medals or illness." And he recalled his own fakery about tuberculosis, which kept him from being drafted, at twenty, out of the vast aircraft plant that took thirty minutes to walk from one end to the other, into "a rough rural unit." After the "stripling of an army doctor" had rejected him for a wheezing chest,

> Once I had put the barracks gate behind me, I broke into a run down the bleak . . . slope that descended to the village. Just as at the airplane factory, my legs carried me running toward something that in any case was not Death— whatever it was, it was not Death.

What was in store for Japan was still being worked out in Potsdam as well as across the Pacific. On the thirty-first, Tinian time, an update went to Stimson in Washington: "LeMay needs eleven hours more which would be August 1, 1000 hours EWT." Stimson's message to Truman on approving the revised text of an announcement had arrived in Berlin late on the night before, and was delivered to the President in Babelsberg at 7:48 A.M. Truman turned over the pink message form and wrote on the back with a pencil, "Suggestion approved. Release when ready but no sooner than August 2." He handed the paper back to the courier, Lieutenant George M. Elsey, with a comment that he didn't want "anything happening" until he got away from Stalin and away from Potsdam.

In Washington, Marshall fielded a request from Spaatz on Guam that Nagasaki be replaced on the target list for the Bomb. Its contours were wrong for optimal blast effect; besides, he had a report—unverified—that a prisoner-of-war camp had been located close to the center of the city. After consulting Groves, Marshall reaffirmed the four designated cities, as "practically every major Japanese city" had such camps. But he did suggest alternative targets to consider for later strikes—Osaka, Amagasaki, and Omuta. On Tinian, Air Force brass was hoping to replace Nagasaki with Tokyo, but there was no chance that Marshall or Truman would accept that. There was some merit in hitting Omuta, at the head of Kagoshima Bay on Kyushu, as the strike would support "Olympic." Amagasaki, just west of Osaka, a bigger target, was a large suburb of Osaka, and weather conditions that might rule out one would also eliminate the other.

With alternative targets for the first atomic strikes denied, LeMay had to focus upon delivery of a bomb as soon as weather permitted a daylight drop. He had already been refused a waiver for a night mission. Truman had amended his directive with "no sooner than August 2"—to give him time to exit Potsdam. LeMay could interpret that as Marianas time—August 1 in Washington.

Whether or not the Bomb would alter Japan's will to resist further, Truman was unwilling to prepare a begging letter to Stalin, as requested, to furnish an excuse for Soviet intervention and American indebtedness. The message Truman had delivered to the Generalissimo's residence by courier, prepared by Byrnes's shrewd assistant, Benjamin Cohen, was coldly courteous, referred only to the "Far Eastern situation" rather than to Japan, and to a "form of letter" he proposed to sign and send as soon as Stalin had "reached an agreement" with China. If its language was acceptable, Truman would furnish the original, "to be used as you see fit." If, however, Stalin decided to issue a statement on entering the war "basing your action on other grounds or for any other reason prefer not to use this letter it will be satisfactory to me. I leave it to your good judgment."

Truman's accompanying draft referred to paragraph 5 of the October 30, 1943, Moscow Declaration of the four powers, including China, that the signatories confer "as occasion requires . . . with a view to joint action on behalf of the community of nations." He quoted Article 106 of the UN Charter on such joint action, and Article 103: "in the event of a conflict between obligations under the Charter and 'any other international agreement.' " In such cases—Truman had in mind the nonaggression pact of the Soviets with Japan, which had not been renewed but would be in force until early in 1946—the Charter was to prevail. Then the President went on blandly: "It seems to me that under the terms of the Moscow Declaration and the provisions of the Charter . . . it would be proper for the Soviet Union to indicate its willingness to consult and cooperate with other powers now at war with Japan with a view to joint action on behalf of the community of nations to maintain peace and security."

Stalin would never respond. But the day before, Colonel Suenari Shiraki, an army intelligence officer, had spoken to the operations section of General Staff Headquarters in Tokyo about the transportation of Soviet troops to the Manchurian frontier. Stalin already had a million and a half men concentrated there, he warned, as well as five thousand planes and three thousand tanks. The depleted Kwantung Army could not cope with the threat. Shiraki predicted an attack in ten days. There was little question in his mind that if Japan were still in the war then, it would have to contend with a new enemy.

At ten, Truman met with Leslie Rowan, Attlee's Principal Private Secretary, to brief him on the upcoming Big Three session, which would, Truman hoped, wind up the conference. The only way to bring Potsdam to a close, he and Byrnes realized, was with an agreement that, however unpalatable to Bevin, who was fresh to his post and eager to argue, he would have to accept as de facto junior partner. Soon after Rowan left, Byrnes went off with his and Truman's initiatives, which he described as the only further concessions the United States was willing to make—on reparations, on what he called (as a face-saving gesture for the West) Polish administration of a part of the Soviet zone of occupation in Germany, and on admission of Italy and the Soviet satellites in the Balkans to the United Nations. He and Truman would leave for the United States the next day, he said, with or without a settlement of the issues. Molotov agreed to take the proposals to Stalin.

When the eleventh plenary meeting began at four, Stalin immediately rejected the idea of a package deal: "The questions are not connected."

"The subjects are different," said Byrnes with exasperation, "but they have been before the Conference for two weeks. The United States is making concessions which it would not make except to obtain an all-around settlement." He went on over Stalin's objections to explain how each concession would be "advantageous to our Soviet friends." The United States was not willing to accept one without the others. "Our British friends have not been pleased but have agreed to accept this proposal in principle."

Not entirely satisfied, Bevin insisted that reparations percentages should be determined by what was necessary to remain in place to support a "peace economy." What he had agreed to earlier, he said, was "very liberal."

"Just the opposite," said Stalin.

"It was generous," said Bevin, uncowed.

"We have a different point of view."

They agreed to halve their differences, and Truman turned to Poland, where Bevin again raised objections. The sticking point was Stettin. Losing it restricted Germany to less adequate harbors on the Baltic. Furthermore, the city had been German for centuries.

Germany lost the war, said Stalin.

Truman offered language he knew was a facade—that the final borders were "subject to the peace treaty. It is only for administration."

"The Polish state must have a border," Stalin agreed readily, "but it is subject to the final decision of the Peace Conference."

"This settles the Polish question," said Truman from the chair.

Stalin: "Stettin is in the Polish territory."

Bevin: "Yes."

Stalin: "Yes."

Truman: "Next question. Mr. Byrnes will speak."

So they agreed on the remaining issues, from Romania to the Ruhr. Earlier ideas floated about separating the Ruhr from the rest of Germany had faded, and both Truman and Bevin (Attlee said almost nothing about anything) wanted the matter dropped. Agreement on disposal of German shipping was reached, and the final agenda item was Stalin's desire to specifically name the war criminals to be tried by the international tribunal.

"It is not wise to put in names," said Attlee, surprising everyone by actually speaking.

"We merely suggest that such people as Göring and Ribbentrop be tried," said Stalin. "If we remain silent it will cast a shadow on our prestige. If we name persons as an example we do not leave out the others. . . . It will be helpful politically." He also wanted Alfred Krupp charged.

"Every country has its favorite criminal," said Byrnes.

The matter of names was held over for a final meeting the next afternoon, when they would go over a draft of a joint memorandum to be released to the press.

With the agreement on Poland and the zones dividing Germany, the political map of Europe was redrawn. Although there was pious talk of a future peace conference, what seemed more likely was a series of separate agreements involving individual states. No one mentioned Versailles and 1919, but its disastrous results could not have been far from the Potsdam conferees' minds. What was suggested as provisional in the Potsdam accords was destined in practice to be— so it would then seem—permanent.

"We have not done too badly, I think," Cadogan noted in his diary. "Joe had got most of what he wants, but then the cards were mostly in his hands." Bevin, he thought, was proving both prepared and tough—"I think he is the best we could have had. He effaces Attlee, and . . . does all the talking while Attlee nods his head conclusively and smokes his pipe."

In Lübeck, a young *Oberleutnant* named Walter applied at the military government office to begin publishing a literary magazine. "What is your ultimate intention?" Arthur Dickens asked.

"Giving the people spiritual direction," Walter explained. He wanted to get away from the "sterile Fascist-Communist controversy." The group he represented considered Goethe its "patron saint." He proposed a "genuinely humanistic" paper.

What future, Dickens asked, did Walter see for Germany?

"I am entirely pessimistic about the political future of Germany: it can never again rise to be a great power in central Europe. We are utterly divided and ruined. I admit, our natural hope of reshaping a reasonable German state lies in British and American help. As regards the possibility of our becoming a great democracy in Europe, we are now too biologically weak; we have lost too heavily in Europe." He was thinking, he said, of the next thirty or forty years— "That is perpetuity so far as we are concerned."

Licensing of newspapers and magazines was essential to provide the public with information and to return communities to a semblance of normality. In the American zone, the *Frankfurter Rundschau* began publishing on the thirty-first with its circulation of 400,000 limited only by newsprint shortages. Radio stations were broadcasting. Civil courts were operating. Schools were reorganizing. The Stuttgart Symphony and the Munich Philharmonic were performing, and the open-air theater in Berlin's Schöneberger City Park had scheduled *The Taming of the Shrew*. Shakespeare seemed politically safe.

That picture of restoration of ordinary life was the surface of what remained for many a grim reality. Although the Russians had claimed that, at least while the Potsdam conference was going on, the expulsions of Germans from the satellite countries would be slowed or even halted, the actuality was that the defeated and displaced of every sort were being brutalized by a cold bureaucracy as well as by what would later be described as "ethnic cleansing," a savagery that did not end with the end of the war.

Much of the violence by Russians had no political or ethnic motive. It was mindless barbarism in the disappearance of discipline. Witold Sagajllo, a Pole who had done prisoner-of-war time in Russia and had been released to teach in a newly opened agricultural college in a former castle on the outskirts of Tarnobrzeg, halfway between Cracow and Lublin, went fishing on a free day. The town was full of Russian troops going home. Dozens of soldiers who had been bathing in the stream were listening to a young man who was sitting naked on the stump of a tree. On the grass near him was the uniform of an officer in the 117th Armored Guards Brigade. The captain, who appeared to be leading the unit back, was boasting of his exploits in Germany, all of which seemed triumphs over the opposite sex: "The immense penis between his thighs had tell-tale syphilitic boils on it."

Anti-Communist from experience as well as conviction, Sagajllo may have exaggerated, yet what he remembered hearing on the last day of July had happened to Germans whom he detested almost as much as he despised the Russians. "I am glad I am going home," the captain admitted. ". . . I have fucked old women and young but what I liked most was fucking small girls in front of their mothers, when the girls were crying, 'Mutti! Mutti!' ... I had gonorrhea but I did not bother about it. But now I have syphilis. I have had enough of fucking."

Sickened, Sagajllo recalled the hair at the back of his neck "tingling" at the recital, which went from horrifying to revolting. It reminded him of the commandant of Sandomierz, a general who dismissed a delegation of townspeople protesting the rape of a small girl: "I do not understand your complaint. The cunt is for fucking, is it not?" That time it had been a German. "The tortures, the inhuman treatment of the inmates of the concentration camps, the mass gassings of the Jews and other ethnic minorities, the genocide perpetrated by the SS and the Gestapo—was all known to me," Sagajllo wrote. "With all this the Germans were just degenerate Europeans. But that captain seemed inhuman, someone from a different planet."

Yet his own compatriots, he must have known, were displaying stomach-turning savagery not only to Germans guilty only of living in space now allocated to Poland, but to survivors of Nazi bestiality guilty only of returning to the Polish homes from which they had been dispossessed. With DP camps in the American zone overflowing, U.S. desk officers and imported civilian bureaucrats were ordering Czech and Hungarian and Romanian and Polish Jews back to their countries of origin. Illegal refugees, frail and frightened, penniless and powerless, they had lived through Nazi death camps but were in danger of not surviving their return to their native towns and villages. "My job was sickening," said a Jewish private from Chicago who had been posted to Munich to assist in the loading of refugees on trucks destined for the railway station and repatriation. "Men threw themselves on their knees in front of me, tore open their shirts, and screamed, 'You might just as well kill me now! I am dead anyway if I go back to Poland!' They kept jumping off the trucks. And we had to use force."

A woman from Poland would tell a *New York Post* reporter a few weeks later that although she and her husband had survived a camp near Lublin, on liberation they had returned to Cracow. The synagogue they were attending on their first Sabbath at home was attacked by troops of General Wladyslaw Anders's army. A nationalist, anti-Semitic, anti-Communist force backed by the exile government in London, it would disappear only to be replaced by Communist thugs, leaving things no better for Jews trying to reclaim their homes. Anders's men were shouting, Luba Zindel told the reporter, Pat Frank, "that we had committed ritual murders. They began firing at us and beating us up. My husband was sitting beside me. He fell down, his face full of bullets." Luba Zindel fled with her baby for the West. The *Post* printed the story under the headline PATTON TURNED BACK 600 JEWS FLEEING TERROR IN POLAND. The Army explained that refugees had indeed fled into the American zone and as illegals they had been returned—but to a Czechoslovak DP camp rather than to Poland.

Even before Potsdam, wrenching incidents like that of the Zindels had been causing a stir in the United States, and Truman had appointed Earl Harrison to investigate on the scene. Three months after V-E Day, Harrison reported,

> Many Jewish displaced persons and other possibly non-repatriables are living under guard behind barbed-wire fences, in camps of several descriptions (built by the Germans for slave-laborers and Jews), including some of the most notorious of the concentration camps, amidst crowded, frequently unsanitary and generally grim conditions, in complete idleness, with no opportunity, except surreptitiously, to communicate with the outside world, waiting, hoping for some word of encouragement and action in their behalf.

They had to be recognized, he argued, as a group with special needs and identity, with resettlement made possible where they wished to go and where persecution would not be possible. That implied Palestine. "Beyond knowing that they are no longer in danger of the gas chambers . . . they see—and there is—little change." Yet, Harrison continued, in many cases they were "able to look from their crowded and bare quarters and see the German civilian population, particularly in the rural areas, to all appearances living normal lives in their own homes."

Not all Germans, however, were in the Western zones of the occupation. Germans in the Sudeten areas of Czechoslovakia were being banished with a barbarity reminiscent of the Nazi excesses, which continued into the last days of the Potsdam proceedings and beyond. In the Sudeten district of Aussig in June, paramilitary Revolutionary Guard groups rounded up German families for expulsion, confiscating valuables and even searching female genitals for concealed jewelry. Then the expellees were taken by truck and tram to Tellniitz, from which they had to walk, whatever their age or frailty, across the mountains of the Erzgebirge to Germany. The expulsions continued through July, on the last day of which Czechs found a new cause for reprisal against the Germans who still remained.

At 3:45 P.M. the confiscated arms and ammunition stored helter-skelter in the warehouses of the former sugar refinery at Schönpriesen blew up. All windows within a two-mile radius were shattered. The explosion had resulted from carelessness, but militia seeking suspects surrounded the renamed Beneš Bridge over the Elbe, which ran northwest across the border toward Dresden. Germans by then were required to wear white armbands or an "N" patch (Czech, for *Nemec*, or German)—an ironic reversal of Nazi practice. By 4:10 people returning from work were crossing the bridge on foot. Hundreds were herded into the town square. Any Germans were shot. In three hours, according to a report in 1947 by a former Czech administrative official in Aussig, two thousand Germans were murdered. "The dead were robbed; interned Germans had to load them on lorries and drive them to the crematorium in Theresienstadt. Those who accompanied the dead never returned. After this massacre, the Minister of the Interior [Vaclav] Nosek, and the Minister of National Defence, General [Ludvik] Svoboda, visited the town. It came to a severe difference of opinion in the council of the Administrative Commission. But it did not alter the fact that the explosion had occurred as a result of negligence. . . ."

As some previously German areas were forcibly rendered *deutschrein* and alleged Nazi persecutors and collaborators were picked up and imprisoned, sometimes in camps that had previously incarcerated Jews, the new jailers often turned out to be the former captives. A phenomenon of a few months—until the new ethnic power structure filled the gap—it created such paradoxes as the red-brick prison at Gleiwitz in Silesia, a town soon to be Polonized as Gliwice. At her confiscated house near the prison, Lola (once Leah) Potok, formerly of the Polish border town of Bedzin, where Jews had lived for seven hundred years, and then of Auschwitz (later Oświecim), lit a row of seven remembrance candles on the evening of July 31. It was the anniversary of the death at Auschwitz in 1943 of her fifteen-month-old daughter Itu—and of Lola's sister, mother, two nephews, and two nieces. "May they rest in the Garden of Eden," she prayed, and placed the candles on the broad dinner table with those of her temporary boarders in the house—like her, survivors from vanished families.

The candles would still be flickering the next dawn as she motorcycled off to oversee the Gleiwitz jail, her blonde hair, now grown out from its Auschwitz crop, streaming in the wind. At twenty-four she was the acting commandant. The candles and the memories would not permit any humanity toward her thousand prisoners, some unrepentant SS veterans, others guilty of nothing but being German. Even as she had escaped from a labor camp supplied by Auschwitz in January, half frozen and starved to sixty-six pounds, and an old German let her thaw at his potbelly stove, a woman in the house into which she stumbled had growled, "No, don't let her in! She's a Jew!"

Walking farther west in the snow and cold, painfully, in two left shoes, only led to more rebuffs. It was Sunday, and for warmth she wandered into a German church at Mass, only to be frightened off by stares as cold as the minus-ten-degrees morning. There was no alternative but to trudge into the east wind toward the likely path of the Red Army, evading SS watchtowers and a railroad crossing where Jews being herded from Russian-threatened Auschwitz were dying in open coal cars.

At Königschütte (now Chorzow) near Kattowitz (Katowice), she knocked on a door and passed out in the entryway of the German dairyman with whom her sister Cyrla, sixteen when Lola was born, had—to the distress of the Potok family—eloped. Her brothers had come and dragged his weeping wife away, yet during the war the dairyman had hidden six local Jewish families in the bomb shelter in his back garden. Lola joined them until the Russians came.

"What do you do [now]?" a prewar friend had asked her.

In a black hatred that was hardly uncommon she snapped, forgetting people like her badly used former brother-in-law, "The same things the Germans did to us!"

Her revengeful, often Jewish guards were survivors, too: like Lola employed by the Polish Office of State Security for the Minister of Repossessed Territories. Repossession was in part accurate. Some areas had been Polish in 1772 and others in 1335. In 1939 there had been 27,500 Jews in Bedzin. More than that number of Germans died of brutality and neglect in the Office's prisons before most of its Jewish employees found it prudent, as did Lola, to flee to the West. Poland would behave like Poland.

Over eight million Germans had lived in the "repossessed" territories. Nearly that many were forced out of Lithuania, East Prussia,

Czechoslovakia, Hungary, Poland, Romania, Yugoslavia, and the Ukraine, few in the "orderly and humane manner" prescribed in the Potsdam protocol. Revenge was routine, but it also masked a rapaciousness that would take an ending of the anarchy to run its course. By then the new facts on the land had been legalized.

Victors' justice worked in many ways. In the French zone, far to the west, the military governor, Jean Lattre de Tassigny, was a Gaullist stalwart. Possessing a theatrical bisexuality and, locally, what amounted to a blank check, the general lived magnificently. He had his villa at Lindau, just above the Swiss border, sumptuously landscaped, and the National Opera brought from Paris to perform for him. He imported painters to decorate barracks, and musicians to compose military airs. Although he also established rest camps and sanatoriums for former concentration camp inmates, he became notorious for extravagance, for the indiscipline of his troops and for harshness toward the civilian population. When anti-French posters mysteriously appeared in Lindau, he expelled the population; after two days he permitted the people back except for men under fifty, whom he ordered to a camp for "political examination."

Local administration was anarchic: it made no difference whether a Gaullist or a Vichyite was in power. As military governor he did not care. Since Paris did, on the thirty-first he was dismissed. As a critic of Lattre commented, "Perhaps the Gaullist movement did not have enough room for two de Gaulles."

Lattre's successor, General Pierre Koenig, had been military governor of Paris just after the Liberation. His job would be one of establishing and implementing an occupation policy that went beyond revenge and greed, yet he made Baden-Baden his headquarters, a spa like Pétain's capital, which would become known as "a little Vichy filled with Vichyites." The administrative and officer fiefdoms might put a Pétain or a Laval in the dock, but on less visible levels old professional loyalties prevailed. And whether Gaullist or Vichyite, the professionals were interested in the good life and in keeping Germany divided and weak.

Even more divided and weak was neighboring Austria, the safest haven in the former Reich for Nazis on the run. In Althausee, in the American zone, Anton Berger, who had worked with Adolf Eichmann before becoming deputy commander of the Theresienstadt (Terezin) concentration camp, was arrested by chance on July 31 for possession of a pistol. Also in Althausee, Eichmann got away, but the Austrian police turned Berger over to the Americans, who took him to the internment camp for Nazis in Glasenbach, near Salzburg, which became more porous as the months passed. He would escape, was assisted in false identities, and died in Essen in December 1991 as "Willi" Bauer. Most Nazis did not have to flee to Paraguay or Syria. The zonal divisions made bureaucratic evasions easier, and where war had wiped out records, reinventing one's past was not uncommon.

Provisional President Karl Renner complained to the occupation authorities about the partition of his little nation into four zones, and Vienna itself into more zones: "Let us have one rule and one government." More immediately serious was the zonal impact on the supply situation in Austria and Germany, and equivalent shortages in other liberated countries. Winter was coming, and most German coal was in the East. The United States itself would be cold in the approaching winter if existing and predicted supplies had to be shared with western Europe, and Secretary of the Interior Harold Ickes, who doubled as wartime Solid Fuels Administrator, warned in Washington that unless thirty thousand experienced miners were furloughed from military units, six million tons of coal needed for Europe would not be shipped. "We must expect rioting, bloodshed and the destruction of nearly all semblance of orderly government," he told a press conference. Truman had already warned as much in the secrecy of Potsdam.

With no such concerns to keep him occupied, Winston Churchill felt his new powerlessness most as he realized that in a day or two the post-Potsdam meeting of President and King he had arranged would happen, and he would be nowhere in sight. Recognizing that, George VI wrote a letter early on the thirty-first to reveal to Churchill that when he came to Buckingham Palace to formally resign, "I was shocked at the result & I thought it most ungrateful to you personally after all your hard work for the people." Later in the day he sent Churchill a longer message, also handwritten, to tell him once more "how very sad I am that you are no longer my Prime Minister." During the course of the war, the King went on,

> we have met on dozens, I may say on hundreds of occasions, when we have discussed the most vital questions concerning the security & welfare of this Country & the British Empire in their hours of trial. I shall always remember our talks with the greatest pleasure & I only wish they could have continued longer.

You often told me what you thought of people & matters of real interest which I could never have learnt from anyone else. Your breadth of vision & your grasp of the essential things were a great comfort to me in the darkest days of the War, & I like to think that we have never disagreed on any really important matter. For all these things I thank you most sincerely. I feel that your conduct as Prime Minister & Minister of Defence has never been surpassed. You have had many difficulties to deal with, both as a politician & as a strategist of war, but you have always surmounted them with supreme courage.

Addressed to "My dear Winston," the letter closed with the King's confession that he regretted, personally, what had happened more than anyone else, and that he would miss Churchill's counsel "more than I can say." He hoped that as friends they would be able to meet again.

Churchill responded in his own hand that he had read the letter "w[ith] emotion," and would treasure it all his life:

It was always a relief to me to lay before my Sovereign all the dread secrets and perils wh oppressed my mind, & the plans wh I was forming, & to receive on crucial occasions so much encouragement. Yr Majesty's grasp of all matters of State & war was always based upon the most thorough & attentive study of the whole mass of current documents, and this enabled us to view & measure everything in due proportion.

It is with feelings of the warmest personal gratitude to you, Sir, & devotion to the Crown that I have relinquished my Offices & my cares. . . .

Nine years earlier, Churchill had been one of the "King's party" when the king was George's brother David (Edward VIII), who was trying to hang on to his throne as well as to the twice-divorced American woman he loved. The present king, whom Churchill had then been trying to keep from the crown, knew it, but that was a world now gone.

U.S.S.R.

MANCHURIA

CHINA

HOKKAIDO

JAPAN

KOREA

HONSHU

Hiroshima

Tokyo

Nagasaki

Kyushu

SHIKOKU

Ryukyu Is

OKINAWA

Bonin Islands

THE
JAPANESE
HOME
ISLANDS

0 miles     200     400

Mariana Islands

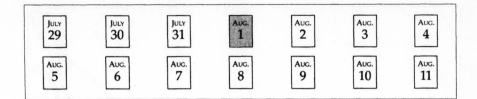

## CHAPTER XX

# · AUGUST 1, 1945 ·

*"Seventeen whole days . . ."*

As dawn seeped through the sky on Wednesday hallucinations were common among the *Indianapolis* survivors. The nearly sleepless men imagined beds, docks, ships, barrels of fresh water. Resignation competed with incoherence as the scorching sun reflected off the sea. Some carefully removed their kapok jackets and swam away to die quietly. Madmen screamed about sharks and threatened other survivors. On his group of three rafts, Ensign Donald Blum saw about thirty-five men remaining where the day before there had been more than a hundred. Feeling safer apart from the unstable men rather than with them, he proposed to a few others that they separate a raft and their portion of the rations that remained and strike out for themselves. Richard Redmayne, a lieutenant and Blum's superior, saw no good in splitting up but gave the group a raft, one fourth of the food, and two paddles, and they pushed off.

As a reward for his own loyalists, Redmayne distributed biscuits and fresh water from their own stock. The water was brackish and the biscuits too hard and dry for thirst-swollen tongues. Each settled instead for a taste of Spam and a malted milk tablet, no less dry than the biscuit. Unhappily they bobbed on the swells and watched to see who would be the next to disappear.

The long seawater-and-sun exposure was now proving too much for even the hardiest of the injured. Radioman Elwin Sturtevant had not known when a burn victim was brought aboard his raft that he was an officer, Lieutenant J. L. Freese. "He was somewhat hysterical from the burns he had received and his hands were burned very badly. His face was also burned and he had lost one of his front teeth." In calming him the other survivors tried to find out who he was and where he bunked. Room JJ, he said, which was officers' quarters.

> He then asked for some water, but we had none and we could not find any. In the morning he crawled out of the raft into another raft where they had some water, and he drank a lot all day Monday. Tuesday evening he went to sleep, and when they tried to awaken him, he was dead. Because there were sharks following the raft, we decided to keep him aboard till Wednesday morning. On Wednesday morning, just before dawn we buried him without services because half the men were still asleep and we thought it better to get it over with.

On the raft-and-net configuration with the two medical officers, there were more and more vacated life jackets. Lieutenant Thomas Michael Conway—Father Conway, the chaplain—had blessed dozens of bodies consigned to the sharks, become irrational, and died in Dr. Haynes's arms, making another kapok jacket available.

Captain McVay had put his faith into fishing, as no planes were spotted through the blazing sunlight, but the only fish he caught, however fresh and white their flesh, looked poisonous—again. He tossed them back. In the distance, bonito played, but the clustering sharks kept them away.

Some sailors preferred the cool water to the torrid sun, despite their fear of sharks and of saltwater skin ulcers from the rubbing kapok. Some quietly took off for imaginary islands they had seen, but the islands kept moving farther away until they disappeared, leaving more empty life jackets. On Giles McCoy's raft, the seventeen men were now five, and only he and Seaman First Class Felton Outland were still conscious. Before darkness set in, McCoy prepared himself for death. He had already prayed his sins away, but needed to meet his maker with a clean body. Pulling his shirt over his head, he lowered himself into the water to scrub off the fuel oil that still blackened all of them. Outland screamed at him, "Get your ass back up here! You'll wear yourself out—or those goddam sharks'll get you!" Stubbornly McCoy persisted; then, almost too exhausted to make it back, he climbed up on the raft.

Outland watched curiously. "I'll outlive you sure as hell," he predicted.

Wednesday was a night of dementia and decline on the rafts, now bobbing farther apart. In a stupor from dehydration and exhaustion, more men vanished through the night.

Early on August 1, Combined Fleet Headquarters ordered Commander Hashimoto, who had encountered no shipping since the *Indianapolis,* to move north, closer to American supply routes around Okinawa. Traveling alternately under water and on the surface, the *I-58* sighted nothing until about 3:00 P.M. Lookouts identified a *Liberty*-class ship by its hull and funnels, and Hashimoto headed toward it, but his angle was wrong and the freighter pulled away. After that there was nothing to be seen. Weather to the north grew increasingly ominous, where Admiral Halsey was beginning several days of circling his fleet slowly to the east of Okinawa to wait out another typhoon. The sea and air strikes he had planned were put on hold. Although big planes from island bases farther from the storm's path would take off and fly over the typhoon, planes on carrier decks shuddered in the gales and remained in place. Only surface ships well to the east could remain active, hitting enemy atolls again and again with shellfire and with strafing by carrier planes that dropped napalm as well as bombs.

On Guam, Lieutenant Paul Boller, Jr., working on the B-29 leaflet campaign, had contacted, as usual, his Air Force liaison, Lieutenant Ardath Burke, to ask, "Well, what are the cities for next week?" Burke "would then reel off the names of cities (almost like listing movies, I thought, for the outdoor theater's coming week) and I would head for the stockade and see to it that the leaflets were modified accordingly." Now "Ardie" had no cities for him. "There seems to be a special deal of some kind planned for next week," Burke explained. "I really don't know what's going on."

Later, Boller connected the hiatus with "Little Boy," yet nearly two dozen cities had already been warned—eleven on July 27 and twelve on July 31. A million and a half leaflets had been dropped daily, including three million of the Potsdam ultimatum. "This will be," Hays Gamble noted in his diary, "an Air Force Day of maximum effort by all wings in the Pacific."

When General Arnold called for maximum effort, he meant that worldwide. The sleek new C-69, the four-engine Lockheed Constellation, was already airborne before the day had begun in the United States, flying 3,600 miles from New York to Paris to set a new transatlantic record. Piloted by Brigadier General Lawrence G. Fritz, it landed at 6:50 A.M. on Air Force Day, covering the distance in fourteen hours, twelve minutes. Also part of Arnold's show was the public unveiling of the Air Force's first operational jet plane, the Lockheed P-80 Shooting Star, a trim gray plane with nacelles near the tips of its long wings. Several flew for airfield audiences. One made it from Dayton to New York—544 miles—in sixty-two minutes. Another gave demonstrations at Mitchell Field on Long Island, and a third flew from Niagara Falls to Boston. When one crashed on a return trip a day later the news was reported in smaller type.

Arnold had specified a thousand planes over Japan, and he got nearly that from the Twentieth Air Force alone, which put up 836 B-29s and 79 long-range fighters, all immune to the ten-foot swells in Japanese waters. From runways in the Marianas, two B-29s took off abreast every forty-five seconds, beginning in the late afternoon, to reach Japan as darkness was setting in.*

Wilbur Morrison, a veteran of the early B-29 raids from China, was barely back on Tinian from a raid on Aomori, where air turbulence from the firestorms had boiled up at later planes in the flight, when his group was called in for another briefing, and learned about Air Force Day. "What cities are we going after?" he asked.

"The 58th Wing is going to bomb Hachioji, near Tokyo."

"The whole wing going to one city? . . . That's wasteful. Why send the whole wing? Only a normal effort has been needed to wipe out a city that size in the past."

---

*Differing counts of planes exist but final postwar figures show that while 836 B-29s were dispatched by the Twentieth Air Force, 52 returned because of mechanical failures. Although 79 P-51s went up from Iwo Jima, only "30-plus" actually reached their targets because of the onset of bad weather. The FEAF's strikes put the total well over a thousand as 50 B-24s hit the Nagasaki Harbor area, "80-plus" P-47s struck Sendai, and other B-25s, B-24s, and P-38s (as well as Marine aircraft) hit targets in China and Southeast Asia.

"There aren't enough cities left. As I said before, the Air Force wants to put on a show of strength."

"I'm not impressed with such logic. It's ridiculous to send men and planes when they are not needed."

"We're not making the decisions."

"Are the targets going to be announced in advance?" another pilot broke in.

"Yes," said Colonel Alfred F. Kalberer. "They will be announced. As a matter of fact, they have been broadcasting the news all day." A loud shout of disapproval arose from the crews. "There's nothing to worry about," the colonel shouted above the uproar. "The Japanese don't have the fuel to send planes against us."

Briefings had taken place at noon, followed by preflight lunch. The Sixth Bombardment Group of the 313th Wing was typical, sending up forty-seven B-29s from two runways on Tinian beginning at 6:40. Two returned after takeoff with mechanical trouble. Forty-four hit Nagaoka, a machine tool manufacturing center of seventy-five thousand people on northern Honshu, by one in the morning. (One plane, navigated badly, had to bomb a "target of opportunity.") The last crews over Nagaoka reported smoke rising to twenty thousand feet, and later reconnaissance showed that two thirds of the city had been burned out. Six night fighters went up but none approached closely, and all bombers made it back. Gamble's "oil group" took off from Guam at 4:30 for the refinery at Kawasaki, near Tokyo, and dropped its bombs at 11:26. At sixteen thousand feet he was fourth over the target. "Searchlights picked us up just before bomb run and we were held in 20-20 beams for 11 minutes. Used much rope and took violent evasive action. Only thing that saved us from flak. Flak was intense and accurate and we could hear shells bursting around us."

Japanese AA-fire and searchlight probes were both worrisome, especially under twenty thousand feet, but many more planes failed to complete their missions because of operational problems than from the intensity of the opposition. Design flaws left in the haste of getting the planes into action supplemented the parts shortages caused by strikes and delivery foul-ups at home. Grounded planes were often cannibalized for parts, especially engines—which often overheated. Imperial Headquarters would claim 29 B-29s shot down and 70 damaged. Actually, one plane was lost and its crew seen bailing out. It was one of the 180 B-29s that had hit Hachioji. The others in the 58th Wing hoped the crew had made it down safely, but they had parachuted over land, out of the reach of Dumbo rescuers.

To the Twentieth Air Force the statistics looked good. Japanese claims were as imaginative as their announced tally of 1,021 planes downed during the month of July. Imperial Headquarters wanted its own thousand-plane score.

In central Tokyo, POW Frank Fujita was kept awake wondering whether he'd survive to make it home. "What surely must be the biggest raid yet, started at 8:00 P.M. last night and lasted until 3:00 this morning," he wrote the next day in the diary he had extracted from its hiding place. "The air in every direction was filled with the droning of hundreds and hundreds of bombers. They seemed to be everywhere except over Tokyo. All the surrounding areas were being obliterated. Chiba Peninsula, Ibaraki, Izu, Boso and Shikoku were heavily pounded and Kawasaki, fifteen miles south of us, was bombed from 10:00 P.M.* until 3:00 A.M. There were ten POWs killed on the last raid there."

In Hiroshima, spared from the raids, a rumor spread, according to Kōichi Okitsu, a bank clerk, that "the Americans were planning to bomb the great dam that had been built in one of the northern mountains in the prefecture, releasing a flood of water that would inundate the whole city and carry all its inhabitants to a watery death in the Inland Sea." The rumor gained such credence that municipal authorities distributed improvised life rafts to 200,000 applicants. Only four bamboo stems tied together by straw ropes, the rafts were to be tied to one's back much like a crude life jacket.

Those who failed to receive a raft were urged to make "lifesavers" for themselves. Okitsu got one. So did Mrs. Shinobu Hizume, but she had children and a husband, and trudged into the mountains to cut down enough bamboo to make additional rafts. They inspired confidence.

The first big raid on Nagasaki had come on July 22. The next one, on August 1, was, according to Aussie POW Richard Downie in Camp 14, "a beaut." Prisoners crowded into a concrete shelter little more than a tunnel—a yard wide and high and thirty feet long. "Built for midgets," Downie recalled. Not everyone could squeeze in, and one POW was killed and six injured as the carpet of bombs spread along the industrial area, including the foundry for which the camp

*There was a one-hour time difference between Tokyo and Guam.

supplied labor. Looking up at the distant, silvery B-29s, the prisoners "used to say that those lucky bastards will be back at their base in a couple of hours, sitting down in their mess eating bloody big steaks and eggs and drinking beer, and then retiring to a nice clean bed without the bugs, lice and fleas."

The raid finished off the foundry, and the Aussies and Dutch who shared the camp were put to work in two shifts, day and night, digging a tunnel in a nearby hill just inland from the Urakami River. "There was plenty of talk and speculation on the purpose of the tunnel. The main theory was we were digging our own tomb in the event of an invasion; all they would have to do would be to herd us inside and blast the two entrances."

The Japanese were suddenly concerned about an invasion. Earlier they had predicted it would come only after the typhoon season. The evening before, Admiral Ugaki, who had been planning to move his flag from Kanoya to Oita, had been held up by gales and rain. Packed and having cleared his quarters, he put up at the officers' club. On Wednesday morning the typhoon kept him at Kanoya, which left him uneasy. Oita, on a small bay opposite Beppu on the northeast coast of Kyushu, was across the Bungo Suido from lower Honshu and the smaller home island of Shikoku, and a good location for overseeing the defense of the Inland Sea as well as all of Kyushu. While Kanoya seemed ideally situated for the protection of Kagoshima Wan, it was much too close to the anticipated landing sites, likely to be overwhelmed if not obliterated on—or by—the first day of an invasion. But all that Ugaki could do as gales battered Kanoya was to practice his calligraphy, in which he took much pride, and then join a group drinking "to forget unpleasant things in the past." But while they were forgetting, "an urgent telegram" sent them scurrying to their underground headquarters. At 10:30 P.M. "an enemy convoy of thirty vessels in three columns was sighted sailing northeast in the east of Izu-Ō Shima." The island was the largest in the Izu chain at the mouth of the Sagami Wan, into which Tokyo Bay emptied. The Grand Naval Command—the new name for the depleted "Combined Fleet"—had ordered a Section 3 *Ketsu-Go* alert.

The Yokosuka Naval Station, the principal base defending Tokyo, was equally unprepared, but jumpy desk admirals in Tokyo had been watching the largest B-29 raids of the war materialize and apparently had put the convoy and the clouds of planes together as an orchestrated event. "The whole navy was taken by surprise," Ugaki noted afterward in his diary. "As to ourselves, we should move to the new position as soon as possible to take the necessary steps for the decisive homeland battle. But a night search plane soon discovered that phosphorescent microbes had been mistaken for an enemy convoy, and everything was restored to the former condition." Ugaki understood the "constant fear of an enemy attack" and the lack of "good confidence in the defense," but hoped for more caution and calm when the real thing occurred.

The defense was far from ready despite the stockpiles of suicide craft of all varieties. Since the best defense was sometimes to take to the offensive, the Army Flying Corps had also devised *Ken-Go*. "Operation Ken" was to be executed from the Chitose base, just below Sapporo in Hokkaido, safe so far from attack. Suicide troops— airborne army companies and sailors trained for land combat—had begun night exercises for a one-way mission to American airfields in the Marianas, where the *kamikaze* troops would crash-land their "Betty" (Mitsubishi) twin-engine bombers if necessary, destroy as many B-29s on the ground as they could reach, and set fire to fuel storage tanks and ammunition dumps. The operation was scheduled for a night between August 19 and August 23, when the moon would be at its brightest.

Other suicide operations were in the experimental stages. Tests on the manned *Okha* Type 22 flying bomb were plagued by mechanical problems. The first aerial test was aborted even before the mother plane became airborne. The *Okha* came loose from a retrofitted "Frances" (*Yokosuka Ginga*) night bomber while it was taxiing down the runway and was seriously damaged. The plane, remodeled to use an Italian Campini jet engine, vibrated so badly that it could not be controlled, and the jet engine stalled when speed was reduced. By August 1, six unsuccessful tests had been carried out, but the enemy threat required desperate measures and the *Okha* force was ordered to be ready for its first drop test by August 12 even though the vibration problem had not yet been solved. A special unit—the euphemism for "suicide unit"—was ordered to Mount Hieizan to test launching *Okhas* from a catapult. Pilots were ordered to the temple on the mountain, where they would be billeted in the priests' quarters.

Also in training in a special unit near Matsue, on the northern coast of Honshu above Hiroshima, was Yasuo Kuwahara. Unlike many *kamikazes*, he was no novice pilot. His new squadron was rejoicing in the "good fortune" of the death of one of their number in a claimed ramming of a B-29 in flight, and in the damaging of another, forcing its crew to bail out over the Inland Sea. "How I wanted to verify that kill," he wrote, "to see her hit the water!"

Kuwahara had been in Japan only a month, recalled from Formosa, which he now considered a "lost island," via China because more direct routes were unsafe. He had not been able to see his family, who understood why he was back, and when he returned from a reconnaissance flight he found an envelope and a tiny parcel left by his sister. "How proud of you we are, Yasuo-chan!" she wrote. "We know that you are bringing great honor to the Emperor, your country, your family. I love you for this, my brother, for your courage— but, always, more for what you have been to me, what we have been to each other. I speak now not only for myself but for your father, your mother, and your brothers as well. Wherever you may go, whatever you may be doing, our love goes with you. Each day I pray for you at the shrine, and in my heart—many, many times. . . . Your sister, Tomika." He opened the little parcel. It was a lock of her hair.

Since even travel by train was now hazardous, Masuo Kato worried whenever he traveled between Tokyo and Chiba, to the east across the top of Tokyo Bay. His family had gone there for safety. Kato had been in Washington at the time of Pearl Harbor, then exchanged home in 1942 when Japan was at its apex of success. Now, although B-29s did not bother with moving trains, he feared the P-51s and other fighters from Okinawa and Iwo Jima that dropped small bombs and strafed rail lines while passengers crawled under the seats. So many people were killed when a commuter train was hit at Hiratsuka, he wrote, that the event was beyond censorship. "Newspapers were permitted to publish an account of it."

He recalled that after the May fire raids a young woman who had been working as a secretary to the head of his news agency, Domei, had said to him on the train, "What a pity that Germany surrendered! Why did they not fight on to the end?"

"They did," he had explained. "What else could they have done?"

When she insisted that they should have continued the fight to the last parcel of the homeland, he told her sharply, "The same thing will be happening soon in Japan as well."

"I would rather die an honorable death," she said, "than to surrender to the enemy."

"Young girls," he assured her, "know nothing of reality."

Neither did the military, he recalled, as "old men, women and children" trained with bamboo spears, "even though they could see that the skies over Japan were already ruled by the enemy." People, so Kato thought, were able to cling to some hope of victory because "Japan had never lost a war; therefore, she could not be beaten." Some divine but unpredictable chance would intervene. The "fatalistic and frenzied desire to die heroic deaths," encapsulated in slogans like "Better to die than to seek ignominious safety" and "One hundred million people die in honor," Kato took seriously although he did not believe in them himself: "To the average Oriental mind there was nothing insincere in this theme." But he had lived for years in the West.

On a train plodding north despite interruptions from air raids, Tom Cartwright wondered where he was being taken, and why. There was a one-night layover in a bare room, which he assumed was guarded. His destination was what he took to be a military base in the Tokyo-Yokohama area. There he was held and periodically interrogated, then returned to a solitary cell. He began looking forward to his daily rice ball.

There were no rice balls for the recaptured Chinese slave laborers in Hanaoka. Tsuneo Yachita, a village boy, heard that desperate prisoners tried to drink their own urine. Older schoolboys from the local youth association were brought in and given sticks to club the prisoners, and were encouraged to spit on them. Three days after their recapture a variety of tortures far more gross ended the lives of some who had survived the heat and hunger and thirst, yet 568 of the original 986 were still alive in September, *after* the Japanese surrender, when a court in Akita tried the Chinese for rioting during wartime. They were sentenced to life imprisonment—until the evidence of a mass grave came to the attention of occupation authorities. At an Allied tribunal in Yokohama, eight employees of Kajima Gumi, the construction company for whom the Chinese had been contract labor, were sentenced to death by hanging, but the sentences were not carried out and they were released in 1956. The official formally responsible for all wartime slave labor, Nobusuke Kishi, would become prime minister. Kajima Kensetsu, as the corporation was renamed, burgeoned into one of the largest construction companies in the world, with major interests in China. In 1972 Chou Enlai signed, for Communist China, an agreement with Japan, from which it was seeking large commercial credits, absolving its former enemy from any responsibility for wartime outrages and of any obligation to compensate victims. One of the survivors of Hanaoka committed suicide. Decades later, according to Yachita, elder villagers still remembered the "pata pata, pata pata," of the barefoot escapers, memorialized by a stone erected to recall "the martyrdom of the Chinese heroes." A companion stone commemorated the "loyal spirits" of dead Japanese soldiers.

While Spaatz's planes marked Air Force Day over Japan, he was in Manila to consult with MacArthur on the two major contingencies in which they would have to work together—an early surrender and occupation of Japan or, if that failed to happen, Air Force support for the invasion of Kyushu. Since the directive of July 25 to Spaatz ordering the delivery of the "special bomb" specified that he was to "personally deliver one copy" to MacArthur, it must be assumed that it was done at this time, although accounts vaguely ascribe the information to a "special courier" on August 5—so late in the game as to be insulting. By the fifth, if all went well with the weather and the arming of the Bomb, "Little Boy" could have been deployed.

MacArthur's own news was far less momentous. Early that morning his forces had invaded tiny Fuga Island, across the Babuyan Channel from Aparri, on the northern coast of Luzon. The entire garrison of two Japanese was captured.

Also in the Philippines, but not privy to Spaatz's top-secret directive, was General Frank U. Greer of the War Department Public Relations Office in Washington, fielding press gripes. "Before he left," Robert Eichelberger wrote to his wife, "he made some very interesting remarks about the publicity from out here. He said the newspapermen out here are very outspoken in their complaints . . . and he found out that the Big Chief writes his own communiqués."

Another general who was always a problem both to the army and to the press left the war on August 1. Claire Chennault of the former "Flying Tigers" got on with almost no one, but the China front in any case was expendable—a morass of service and political rivalries that saw Chiang making deals with the Japanese enemy to keep Mao's troops, ostensible allies in freeing China, weak and distant. (After the war, in fact, Chiang would make Yasuji Okamura, the Japanese commander-in-chief in China, his unacknowledged military adviser at the price of suppressing war crimes charges against him.)

Chennault, recalled once and future *Herald-Tribune* columnist Joseph W. Alsop, then on his staff, was "very nearly stone deaf" although only "pushing sixty." He insisted on returning home via India by flying his own almost unusable C-47 over the Himalayas "hump" himself. "To please their chief," Alsop remembered, "the air-service command had glued this dreadful vehicle together to the best of their ability, although they could not prevent its wings from flapping—or so it seemed to me." The plane was visibly overloaded with "General Chennault's loot, my loot from Sian"—dealers in antiquities continued to get rich throughout the war—"and everybody else's loot, along with a fair number of the general's closest junior staff advisers." Even as they arrived over New Delhi the passengers remained alarmed, "since the general, who flew this ramshackle C-47 as though it were a 1920s fighter plane, insisted on diving down to inspect every significant building in the city, including the viceroy's house and the other grand old palaces of the Anglo-Indian bureaucracy."

As August began, Burmese guerrillas who had been expending generous quantities of airdropped ammunition to massacre the Japanese relaxed by using their guns, Terence O'Brien observed, "to vary their diet." A Karen leader ticked off the bag of his group as "two buffalo, three sambhur, seven wild pigs, twelve barking deer, and 'many dozens' of birds." The remaining Japanese, with two further rivers to cross, both swollen by rains, were hacking down bamboo for rafts. Each soldier had to cut and carry two poles to the river. But the rafts were impossible to direct across the raging floods, and the men trapped on them were easy targets for the Karens on the far bank.

Still preparing to cross, the soldiers shifted strategy, covering their rafts with branches of broad leaves, camouflaging the surface to look like river debris. Carrying short bamboo pipes, the men hung underneath, swimming with their improvised breathing tubes. Some got across until the guerrillas saw through the trick and lobbed mortar shells on the plantain-covered rafts.

It was appropriate that among the Japanese forces in the watery Burmese approaches to the Sittang was the Fukami unit of land-based sailors. When they crossed the soggy Mandalay Road at 3:00 A.M., much to their surprise not a shot was fired. Suddenly, green and yellow signal flares illuminated them and the British opened up with heavy machine guns. The sailors returned fire with grenade launchers, rifles, and machine guns, then struggled across the twenty yards of a small swollen stream. In a grove of trees that concealed them from the dawn and an observation plane, they crouched to await the next darkness. In the ambush they had lost over 400 men, including 14 officers and petty officers. Only 148 remained.

Still pushing east among the civilian refugees was U Nu and his family, who had fled from a train that the British were strafing. Five minutes distant from the railway line they heard a loud explosion. The RAF had demolished the train. Nu would have liked to have been free from the Japanese, but not that way. As he recalled his escape, jolting along now in a bullock cart,

> We arrived at the house of Thakin Kyan about midnight. He immediately recognized me, but we did not explain who we were and made as if we were just weary and unfortunate travellers. While the others were talking about the withdrawal of the Japanese, Thakin Kyan called me aside to ask why we had come; 'Thakin Nu,' he said, 'what is it all about? Have these blighters tried to arrest you? If you want to hide I can manage it for you quite safely without fear of anyone splitting.' I was astonished that he should know me, and after chatting about various matters we rested that night in his house.

As the victors were reconvening in Potsdam late on August 1, Truman had no idea whether Stalin would make good on his Yalta bargain about Japan. Along the route of the railway across Siberia, the buildup of forces in East Asia was apparent to American internees along the line—crews, largely, of planes forced to land on Russian territory, which in any case was better than being a POW under the Japanese. Yet even POWs knew that something was up. Brigadier General W. E. Brougher, in a camp in Mukden almost since surviving Bataan in 1942, noted in his diary on August 1, during the incessant typhoon wind and rain: "Reports of much Red Cross food here but we get none of it. The report has been confirmed"—it *was* true—"and denied now so we don't know what to expect. We know that Russia is not at war with Japan so there is no reason why trainloads of Red Cross [parcels] and mail could not be delivered at the border." But few supplies were crossing the border now and the Japanese in Manchuria were feeling the strain.

There was much talk among the POWs about an imminent Japanese surrender. All that was preventing the inevitable—news got around and B-29s had overflown with impunity—was, they thought, the shift in status from conquerors to "fugitives at the mercy of [other] Orientals who have no mercy. The Government must carry on until arrangements can be made for some guarantee of security on surrender. . . . In the meantime, they invite destruction of the Homeland."

In Potsdam, the Russians no longer appeared interested in Japan. No more messages had been intercepted by "Magic" from Moscow to Tokyo since the thirtieth, when Sato had appealed again to Lozovsky at the Foreign Office. He had not received, either directly or indirectly, any response from Molotov, and—on the subject of the Konoye mission—none would come.

In Berlin itself, the Russians seemed more concerned about setting up the "Four-Power Kommandatura" (it included France) to run the former capital, which they expected to dominate. The French were not much interested in Berlin other than in flying their flag and, with no representation at Potsdam, sent only a low-level administrative team dominated by Communists who had fought in the Resistance. Attlee and Bevin had a government at home to reconstruct and wanted to return as quickly as possible, although without earning any suspicion of a sellout, and Russians and reporters alike were given samples of Bevin's truculence. Field Marshal Montgomery, however, was impressed. Bevin, he wrote General W. H. Simpson, "will be the power behind the throne in the new set-up." Truman wanted to be back in Washington before "Little Boy" was delivered. The war against Japan was coming to a climax, and communications, however elaborate at Babelsberg and on the *Augusta*, were inadequate for a President. He might literally be at sea at the wrong time.

Truman had just informed Attlee about the Bomb. Churchill had not told him although he was technically the Prime Minister's deputy until he became Prime Minister himself. Attlee, impressed, immediately responded, "Thank you so much for your letter of today about the new weapon to be used on Japan. If it is quite convenient to you, I will come to see you for a few minutes after the Plenary Session this afternoon." The foreign ministers had met at 11:25 that morning to deal with the draft paragraphs their staffs had prepared, about which there were still differences. Some were on small issues, like the Romanian oil equipment, which would not go away. Another matter that would not vanish was the Russian passion to retrieve holdouts who might form "hostile organizations." This question, declared Molotov, was a "burning one," although Byrnes assured him, "We have enough people to feed without encouraging other people to remain."

"There were many complications," said Molotov. But Byrnes would not be pinned down further.

The Russians also remained eager to keep more of the German submarine fleet than had been agreed to earlier. Churchill, Bevin pointed out, having done his homework, laid down the British position that only token submarines be preserved "for experimental purposes only." Bevin claimed to be "very sensitive" on that point. If the Soviets insisted on acquiring a fleet of Nazi subs after U-boat warfare had cost the lives of thirty thousand British seamen and nearly strangled Britain, his government could not survive a vote of confidence. Molotov tried again, asking for a small increase to the thirty to be saved, then, for each nation. Getting nowhere, he gave in. Bevin thanked him.

Not yet finished, Molotov asked that claims against German merchant shipping by satellite nations be satisfied. The merchant fleet was war booty, said Bevin; Britain and the United States had agreed to an equal division with the Soviets after such ships as necessary were used in the war with Japan. He was willing, with the United States, to meet the claims of Norway, France, and the Dutch out of their share. Even the Greeks. But the Poles would have to take their small claim to Moscow. "What about the Yugoslavs?" Molotov asked.

He would leave the Yugoslavs, said Bevin, to the "generosity" of the Soviet Union. But every mention of Tito's regime made it obvious that the Soviets, even then, could not control their unruly ideological neighbor.

Yet Stalin was not the only leader at Potsdam vexed by unruly allies. Charles de Gaulle would have annexed to France the Val d'Aosta, the Alpine Italian province just below the southwestern corner of Switzerland, had Harry Truman not intervened. In many ways de Gaulle was the West's Tito.

The twelfth plenary session failed to solve all remaining Big Three differences. They argued over foreign assets in Germany, and Stalin agreed that gold was booty beyond his claim. As for seized investments, he said, why not apply the demarcation line between their zones of occupation, each taking what was found. Truman inquired whether Stalin meant a line continuing south of the German border—

running, that is, from the Baltic to the Adriatic. Attlee was ready to argue until Bevin interrupted, "Greece belongs to the British."

"Austria is divided into parts," said Stalin. "How shall we deal with these?"

"You better give it to us," Bevin suggested.

"You want all of Austria? You can have part of Austria—and Yugoslavia."

Stalin's concessions were few, and Yugoslavia was not really one of them, but Tito had become a thorny joke to the Soviets. When pressed on some issues, Truman recalled, Stalin would say, "What can I do if I am not ready to make a decision?" On the war criminal issue, Stalin still wanted Alfred Krupp indicted. "The people should know that we are going to try some industrialists."

"I don't like any of it," said Truman. "If you name some, others will think they have escaped."

"People will wonder about Rudolf Hess living comfortably in England," remarked Stalin.

"You need not worry about that," said Attlee with a bluntness that must have surprised Bevin.

The remaining differences were on minor points and nuances of phraseology. As Truman put it, "Prolonged and petty bickering continued on the final wording of the protocol. I was getting very impatient, as I had many times before in these sessions, with all the repetition and the beating around the bush, but I restrained myself because I saw that we were slowly making progress in the right direction." Molotov's way of putting it before their temporary adjournment at 5:50 was that he saw "no difficulty in substance, but the wording must be exact." Equally fussy about exactitude was Bevin. "At one point," Truman recalled, when Bevin criticized the English phraseology of the communiqué, "Stalin said that whatever English was acceptable to the Americans was acceptable to the Russians."

One matter remained totally unacceptable although pressed hard by the American side. Truman had begun the sessions with a plea for the openness of European international waterways. "I should like a mention in the communiqué," he said, "of the matter of inland waterways which I brought up."

"We did not discuss it," objected Stalin. "It was not mentioned in the lists of subjects to be covered by the conference. We should not be in a hurry."

Truman disagreed: "We discussed it several times. Marshal

Stalin," he added, "I have accepted a number of compromises during this conference to conform with your views, and I make a personal request now that you yield on this point."

Even before Pavlov had finished translating, Stalin shouted *"Nyet!"* And in English, which he had never used before, he emphasized, "No! I say no!" He had wanted some control over what he called the Turkish Straits, and was headed off on grounds that Turkey was a neutral nonparticipant. But he wanted no Western intrusion via the waterways issue into what he had carved out of Europe for the Soviets. The authentic Stalin had emerged.

Shouted down and embarrassed, a red-faced Truman turned away toward Byrnes and said, deliberately loudly enough for Stalin and his interpreter to hear, "I cannot understand that man! Jimmy, do you realize that we have been here seventeen whole days? Why, in seventeen days you can decide anything!"

"I like Stalin—he is straightforward," Truman had written to Bess. Yet Stalin's relentless pursuit of his own agenda, and his brushing aside of anything in its way, would not be forgotten and became a key to post-Potsdam policy. At Potsdam, Truman said of himself after he had left the presidency, he had been "an innocent idealist." He even confessed, "I liked the son-of-a-bitch." But after Potsdam they would never meet again.

While the principals dined separately with their staffs, the Protocol Committee returned to work on the unresolved language. All that would be said about international inland waterways in the Protocol was that the matter would be referred to the Council of Foreign Ministers—where it would be buried.

Cadogan dined with Bevin to go over details for the final hours. "Byrnes talks too much and wastes too much time," Cadogan noted in his diary, sharing the peevishness of his new boss. "But we polished off quite a lot." The principals, he noted, having observed the lightweight qualities of Bevin's ostensible superior, Attlee, were now the "2½" rather than the Big Three.

At 10:40 P.M. the plenary session continued. Where the Polish-German frontier at the Baltic would begin was settled by changing "to the town of Swinemunde" to "immediately west" of it, costing Germany another port, now Polonized as Swinoujście. There was more bickering over the differences between full diplomatic relations with a country and what Attlee called "necessarily incomplete" relations. "We are still at war with Finland," Bevin explained.

Section by section the protocol was approved, including the language on war criminals, where it was agreed that a list of major defendants would be released by September 1. Even the order of signature was debated. "In our previous conferences," Molotov reminded the newcomers, "it was agreed that the signatures should be rotated. According to this procedure the Russians would sign the present communiqué first."

Truman had no objections, but Attlee, in a rare attempt at humor, said, "I favor alphabetical order; that is where I would score over Marshal Zhukov."

After agreement on a release time that would make what Bevin called "the Friday morning press," exchanges of compliments followed. Attlee thanked Stalin for his "excellent arrangements" and Truman for his willingness "to come so great a distance." Stalin added his thanks to Truman and continued, "I should also like to express our thanks to Secretary Byrnes, who has worked harder than any one of us to make this conference a success. He has worked hard and he has worked very well. These sentiments, Secretary Byrnes, come from my heart."

Thanking all the foreign secretaries, and announcing the close of business, Truman formally adjourned the sessions with the pious hope that their next meeting might be in Washington.

"God willing!" exclaimed the militantly atheist Stalin.

A round of hand shaking and good-byes followed. It was already 12:30 A.M. Truman had wanted to leave Potsdam on August 1. It was still August 1 in Washington, which was small consolation.

The President remembered the adjournment as being at 3:00 A.M. with departures from Cecilienhof an hour after that, but it only seemed that late after a long and exhausting day. The last "summit" conference (the term had not yet been invented) until Eisenhower and Nikita Khrushchev met at Camp David in 1959 had finally ended. Until then, and even after, the superpowers talked in a language of threat and counterthreat, gesture and countergesture, buildup and reciprocal buildup. But the Potsdam bargains held.

Byrnes later referred to Potsdam as "the success that failed." Britain and the United States had conceded much to establish a workable balance of power in postwar Europe and to bring Russia into the war against Japan. But the Soviets had every intention of undermining any aspect of the agreements when and if Western weakness or divisiveness could be exploited. If Stalin looked with suspicion upon

Truman's failure to inform him more frankly about the Bomb, he also knew that he would have acted no differently, and had in fact been spying on the Manhattan District in every possible way. The Americans had hardly become tougher in their bargaining after news of the Bomb, except in the refusal to pander to Stalin's request for a plea to intervene in a war he had promised to join the previous February. On Poland, on Germany, on the other Soviet satellites, on booty and reparations, Stalin got just about all he wanted, and more. If Byrnes's reparations plan helped lead to a forty-year division of Germany, it may have saved the Western zones from more severe plundering, and the Ruhr from an internationalization that would have given the Soviets a foot in the West. Potsdam was the best bargain possible at a time when the facts on the ground heavily favored the Russians.

It was not only in retrospect that Truman felt the implications of Potsdam for East Asia. It was obvious that the Russians would be just as relentlessly aggrandizing there. "Anxious as we were to have Russia in the war against Japan," Truman recalled in his memoirs, "the experience at Potsdam now made me determined that I would not allow the Russians any part in the control of Japan. Our experience with them in Germany, and in Bulgaria, Romania, Hungary and Poland was such that I decided to take no chances with a joint setup with the Russians. As I reflected on the situation during my trip home, I made up my mind that General MacArthur would be given complete command and control after victory in Japan. . . . I knew that the Russians should not be allowed to get into any control of Japan."

While the conference in Potsdam was concluding, the new Parliament was assembling at Westminster without Attlee and Bevin. "Churchill didn't disguise at all that it was a bitter blow to him," Lord Halifax recalled, but it would not prevent him from taking his rewon seat. "He said it was almost impossible to believe that a week ago he had been at Potsdam; the measurement of time seemed to have no relevance. He had for five years had everything through his hands day and night, and it was hard to realise that this had suddenly evaporated." But he "staged his entry well," Tory M.P. Henry Channon noted in his diary, "and was given the most rousing cheer of his career, as the Conservatives sang 'For He's a Jolly Good Fellow.' Perhaps this was an error in taste, though the Socialists went one further, and burst into 'The Red Flag,' singing it lustily; I thought that Herbert Morrison and one or two others looked uncomfortable." Old Commons hands were shocked at the lack of decorum.

Few of Churchill's close parliamentary allies had survived the Labour landslide. Robert Boothby had seemed unlikely to regain his East Aberdeenshire constituency, especially as he had been enjoying the good life in California during the early days of the campaign, the *Daily Mirror* giving precious newsprint space to his affair there—he denied it—with a onetime admirer of Hitler, Inga Arvad, a Danish beauty who had met the leading Nazis before the war and considered the *Führer* "an idealist."* Boothby blamed disenchantment with the Conservative Party for the hostility of his audiences at political meetings, yet won one of the twenty-four Scottish seats (of seventy-one) the Tories retained. His clubby friends at White's had telegraphed him, "We all congratulate you most heartily, and are thankful that in the midst of the Red Ruin that remains, you erect one pillar of sound Conservative Principle, of Prosperity, of Temperance, and of Morality." Another friend, Colin Coote, wrote to him, "You are a bloody marvel, aren't you? The saviour of England gets thrown out on his neck, but the Peter Pan of Hollywood gets triumphantly returned!"

Sir Robert Bruce Lockhart found Boothby at a party in London "looking very fat and opulent in a new purple-blue suit. He tackled me afterwards on the election, and informed me in a loud voice that he was the only Tory who had sung 'The Red Flag' in the House of Commons that day."

Anthony Eden had discussed Churchill's future, and his own, with Halifax, who "apparently thought," Eden wrote in his diary that night, "that W[inston] would retire to write books, make occasional great speeches & hand over leadership of the opposition to me. I told him this was not W[inston]'s idea at all. . . ." Eden had just returned from dinner at Claridge's with Churchill, who had moved temporarily to a penthouse on the sixth floor. "It is a staggering change of fortune," Eden added, suggesting the parallel to his own in the phrase. Perhaps, he mused, it was better for Churchill's place in history, however hurt his pride. "For he would not have been happy handling those tangled peace questions, especially at home. History will dub the British people ungrateful, whereas perhaps they were only wise."

That peace would indeed be tangled was apparent from the reception of the U.S. Army–made "Belsen" film, which was ordered to be shown to German prisoners of war as part of the denazification process. Even as the gaunt and dazed survivors of the death camps

*Boothby had succeeded a young Navy officer, Ensign John F. Kennedy, who had bedded Mrs. Fejos—she was, at least technically, married—in Washington before going off to the Pacific wars.

struggled back into life, unbelievers in their catastrophe burgeoned. Although it was compulsory viewing, German officers in Canadian camps turned their backs and refused to watch. There was such resistance elsewhere that in the Dhurringile camp in Australia, machine guns were set up outside the compound as the POWs were marched out to see the film. One prisoner recalled the fakery of bayoneted Belgian babies in 1914, and another scoffed at the ingenuity, now, of misusing air raid casualties. A third found an old copy of *Life* with pictures of famine victims in India and claimed that the Belsen film had used them. Even if true, most said, "What did that have to do with us? We didn't do it. We weren't even there." And in the diary of Horst Wolff, in a prison camp in the north of England, is this entry for August 1: "Yesterday we all had to see a film about the atrocities in the concentration camps. It was very clumsy, cheap propaganda. (Lampshades from human skin!) Much hooting and catcalling."

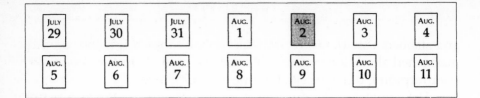

| July 29 | July 30 | July 31 | Aug. 1 | Aug. 2 | Aug. 3 | Aug. 4 |

| Aug. 5 | Aug. 6 | Aug. 7 | Aug. 8 | Aug. 9 | Aug. 10 | Aug. 11 |

CHAPTER XXI

· AUGUST 2, 1945 ·

*survivors and expellees*

In the light of Thursday morning, Richard Redmayne saw bodies on his rafts either too weak to move or already expired. Near the rafts, corpses floated facedown. Less than a hundred men remained more or less alive. He began hallucinating. A ship was nearby; he had to jump off the raft and swim to it. He raved about having to get to the engine room, and Ensign Harlan Twible pulled him back. A biscuit can floated by. Twible reached for it and struck Redmayne unconscious.

The dwindling group with the ship's doctors was breaking up. Some were determined to swim to Leyte. It was 550 miles to the west; even if it had been only 5 miles distant none of them had the stamina for the ordeal. It was suicide, Haynes insisted. No, said one of the fantasists. They could do it in a day and a half. Before noon they swam off. Haynes watched silently.

McVay's group was in the best shape—floating on an expanse of rafts and supplied with malted milk tablets and Spam, more than enough for the ones still alive. But their failure to pull in an edible fish had driven one sailor berserk. With a tiny knife he reached out and stabbed a shark between the eyes, then toppled into the sea. The maddened shark went after him, and the men aboard, roused from their torpidity, pulled the fisherman back on the raft.

The sun was still mounting toward noon when a Ventura patrol plane out of Guam, searching for ships or subs supplying the isolated Palau Islands, ventured over the scattered rafts. To Lieutenant Wilbur C. Gwinn it looked like a narrow oil slick—the signs of a likely enemy sub. On the intercom he ordered depth charges armed, and throttled down.

Closer to the surface, Gwinn thought he saw men bobbing on rafts. Pulling up, he shouted, "Secure from bomb run!" Circling for another and lower pass, he ordered survival gear dropped—a raft, kegs of water, life jackets, a radio buoy from which they could talk to the plane. He was still too high. The kegs ruptured on impact with the sea, and the dazed men below had no idea what the buoy was for other than to mark the location. Gwinn nosed up to gain altitude for radio transmission and signaled Guam: "SIGHTED 30 SURVIVORS 011-30 NORTH 133-30 EAST. DROPPED TRANSMITTER AND LIFEBOAT EMERGENCY IFF ON 133-30." Swinging around again, Gwinn counted seventy-five heads, then twice that many. His radioman kept keying in supplementary reports, one of which was heard on Peleliu, where Lieutenant Robert Marks, in civilian life an Indiana lawyer, assembled the crew of his Dumbo—a Catalina flying boat—and loaded the plane, fueled it, and took off at 12:40. Another message from Gwinn had warned that his Ventura had only enough fuel to remain in the area until 3:30.

The crew on the Ventura kept dropping supplies. Gwinn radioed another message: "SEND RESCUE SHIP 11-15N 133-47E. 150 SURVIVORS IN LIFEBOATS AND JACKETS." Not a float plane, the Ventura could only circle above to be visible, and was spotted by an Army Air Force PBM patrol plane heading west. Altering course, the pilot dropped three rafts—and flew on. Gwinn was dumbfounded. Yet radio messages were now getting through from Guam and Peleliu, and at the port director's office at Tacloban the Leyte command happened to discover that the *Indianapolis* was overdue. So were two other ships, however. All of them could have been rerouted elsewhere.

More concern was manifested at the Western Carolines Sub-Area headquarters of Rear Admiral Elliott Buckmaster on Peleliu. Seven vessels in the area were diverted to the search. And off the runway just after Marks was Lieutenant Commander George C. Attebury in a Ventura intended to relieve Gwinn. His plane was faster than Marks's lumbering PBY5A.

At 2:10 Marks picked up a message from Attebury. He was overhead and counted at least 150 heads below. Thirty minutes later Marks was in contact with three ships heading for the rafts, one of them the fast new destroyer escort *Cecil J. Doyle.* Its skipper, Lieutenant Commander W. Graham Claytor, Jr., a prewar lawyer whom Marks had known back home,* had been on picket duty off Babelthuap, the largest of the Palau group, where forty thousand bypassed Japanese were being blocked from resupply. Claytor had reached the PBY on voice radio only to relieve the boredom, and Marks explained that he was vectoring in on a survivor scene, following the signal of a Ventura that had preceded him. Not awaiting orders, Claytor turned the *Doyle* around and made for the fix he was given.

Sighting Attebury's plane just as he was spotted, Marks picked up another voice message, this one from the Ventura. "There are a great many survivors scattered about a large area. You shouldn't drop any survival equipment until I can show you the whole area, and you can form a judgment of where the equipment can be dropped to best advantage." Marks followed and dropped three rafts near groups with only nets and debris. Circling farther, he noticed that one raft had torn apart on hitting the water. The emergency rations kit had disintegrated; the shipwreck kit drifted unused because the men were too weak to reach it. Only the dye markers had some effect.

Soon another plane from Peleliu circled overhead and dropped supplies, but the exhausted survivors were in no condition to use anything. At 4:25 P.M. Marks's radioman sent a message in clear to Peleliu: "BETWEEN ONE AND TWO HUNDRED SURVIVORS AT POSITION REPORTED. NEED ALL SURVIVAL EQUIPMENT AVAILABLE WHILE DAYLIGHT HOLDS. MANY SURVIVORS WITHOUT RAFTS." Radioman France remembered watching the bobbing of the oil-blackened bodies: "It wasn't the best sight I have ever seen when . . . you watch a shark swim off with a man." The victim was floating next to Seaman Second Class Loel Dene Cox, who heard the screams, saw the thrashing, and watched the bleeding body drift away. Soon after, two hallucinating survivors swam over and told Cox that there was a special island for

---

*Postwar, Claytor left law in 1963 for the Southern Railway, retiring as chairman in 1977 to be Secretary of the Navy, then Acting Secretary of Transportation and finally Deputy Secretary of Defense from 1979 to 1981. Following the Carter presidency he was president and chairman of Amtrak until 1993. He died at eighty-two in 1994.

officers close by; if he would help guide them there, they'd talk the authorities into letting Cox ashore.

His mind also fuzzy, Cox dutifully paddled with them for about five hundred yards, then realized that he had no idea where they were going. He didn't know how to guide them, he confessed; he was turning back. "O.K.," one of the men said; "If you want to, you can go back, but we're going on."

Like Cox, not all the men had been in a position to see and hear the circling planes, now down to two after Gwinn's fuel-short Ventura headed home. Some in the water who watched the airdrops were too dazed to understand what was happening. Fire Controlman Third Class Cleatus Lebow heard someone explain that the crates contained B-29 parts; they were to assemble the plane and fly off. Dr. Haynes watched the objects fall and saw one of his group swim over to a package and pull at the toggle on what proved to be a $CO_2$ bottle. Too weak to make it operate, he called for help, and Haynes and several others tugged to break the seal. A raft blossomed out, and boldly labeled in its survival box was something called FRESH WATER KIT.

For Marks the shark attack was as much as he could take. Yet he was forced to circle helplessly. Marks knew that landing on the twelve-foot swells was beyond dangerous. It was also forbidden. The PBY could break up and sink, which would accomplish nothing. He polled his crew, and all agreed to chance it anyway.

Radioman France messaged Peleliu: "WILL ATTEMPT OPEN SEA LANDING." The crew stowed loose gear and belted themselves into ditching positions. Marks slowed the PBY to a stall and smacked the water nose-high, bounced, and came down again near the single swimmers. With Attebury still aloft acting as their eyes, Marks threw out a lifeline with a ring and drew in the first emaciated survivors. "What ship are you from?" he asked.

When he learned that the men were from the *Indianapolis*, which he knew had a complement of more than a thousand, Marks realized that his Dumbo had landed in the middle of the worst American catastrophe at sea during the entire war. Yet even the remnant who survived could not all fit in, or on, his Catalina, which in any case was no longer flyable. Marks was counting on the arrival of other support before his own crew was added to the casualties.

One by one, Ensign Morgan Hensley, the navigator, and Aviation Ordnanceman Earl Duxbury pulled oil-blackened survivors aboard, squeezing them into the cramped hull. Marks supervised; at the controls his co-pilot, Ensign Irving Lefkovits, flicked one engine off and on to move the plane closer to men too weak to swim. The interior became a steamy confusion of skeletonlike bodies grimy with grease, ulcerated with saltwater sores. The smell of vomit, urine, excrement, and oil reeked through the cabin. Some men slept instantly, but groans, cries, and hallucinatory shouts kept the PBY crew on edge.

Haynes had moved his worst cases to two rafts for pickup, but with the plane full, Marks arranged the men on the wingtops, securing them with parachute shroud line. Other planes were overhead now, and one parachuted a lifeboat. Harlan Twible managed to swim to it, along with Redmayne. Another PBY circling overhead, piloted by Army Lieutenant Richard Alcorn, began a landing approach. Marks's derelict plane could take no more; darkness was closing in. Taking his chances, Alcorn landed cleanly near a lone swimmer, whom his crew picked up. Switching on his lights, he taxied toward others in the water, then realized that search planes might confuse his beam with a beacon on a buoy and drop survival gear on them. He cut his engines and lights.

Moving at twenty-two knots, his fastest time, Commander Claytor was getting close, as he knew from radio communications between the PBYs. He turned on the *Doyle*'s searchlights, whatever the chances of a sub in the area, hoping to find, and not collide with, men in the water. As midnight approached, another plane overhead dropped a parachute flare. The *Doyle* edged toward it.

From other directions, alerted by radioed orders across the expanse of the Marianas and as far west as the waters off Leyte, six other ships were steaming toward the PBYs and rafts. The *Madison, Talbot, Bassett, Ringness, Register,* and *Dufilho* were destroyers and destroyer escorts on routine patrols, some given correct fixes, others fixes as much as twenty miles off. The *Bassett* would pick up 151 survivors early on Friday morning, but the *Doyle* had closed in before the darkness lifted. To Haynes its lights seemed blinding— another apparition.

Claytor lowered his whaleboats to pick up survivors so weak that they had to be lifted up the ladders to the deck of the *Doyle*. Haynes drained a glass of water in one swallow. "What ship are you off?" asked Claytor.

"You're looking," Haynes croaked, "at what's left of the *Indianapolis.*"

At 1:30 A.M. a searchlight from the *Bassett* picked out Ensign

Blum's raft. A whaleboat was lowered, captained by Ensign Jack Broser. He drew his .45 in case he was being lured into an enemy ambush. The Japs had good American speakers, and it was dark. He turned his searchlight on the men. They appeared to be about a dozen, all blackened with oil and scum. "We don't know who you are or where you've come from," he shouted, "but we want to get you out of this water."*

The *Dufilho* plowed toward the rafts by picking out the *Doyle*'s searchlights. Ordering his speed cut and all men not otherwise engaged to act as lookouts, Lieutenant Commander Albert Nienau cautiously closed in. At about eight thousand yards from the *Doyle* the *Dufilho* pulled in one sailor. Seaman Second Class Francis N. Rineay, Jr., had been without food or drink for four days. Using life jackets detached from floating bodies, he had made a small raft that had kept him clear of the sharks. As far as he knew he was the only man from the *Indianapolis* still alive.

Surfacing the *I-58* sufficiently to radio home, Commander Hashimoto learned that Imperial Navy communications had picked up heavy radio traffic from ships and planes searching for survivors of a major enemy loss. He assumed that it was his victim, but he was now too far off its route to go back after the rescue craft.

Although General LeMay, eager chief of staff of the Twentieth Air Force, wanted to be ready to deliver "Little Boy" as early as August 1, Captain Costello's repaired B-29—with the last of the parts for the Bomb—did not arrive at Tinian until 12:15 P.M. Marianas time on August 2. While the mission awaited better weather over Japan for a visual drop, Field Order number 13 for the 509th Group was signed that morning by Lieutenant General Nathan Twining, who had taken command of the Twentieth that day, specifying Hiroshima as the target of choice. The secondary target was Kokura, with Nagasaki to follow if neither Kokura nor Hiroshima were visible from thirty thousand feet. Before 1945 Hiroshima had been, with 365,000 people, Japan's eighth largest city. Civilian evacuations had shrunk its population. War industry had been its main activity until the mining of the bay had cut off coastal shipping, but it was the headquarters of the Second Army Group, with responsibility for the defense of Kyushu,

---

*Probably apocryphal is the story that Broser asked suspiciously, "Where do the Dodgers play?" "In Brooklyn," said Blum. But even the baseball-happy Japanese would have known that.

just to the southwest. Since the city sprawled across the flat Ota River delta, the area was ideal for observation of blast effect. Further, Hiroshima had been spared for months to preserve it as a target. And it appeared to have no POW camp nearby.

All of Colonel Tibbets's fifteen B-29s were ready. He would need several as advance weather reconnaissance, with three on the actual mission. He chose himself to lead the strike and drop the Bomb. In Washington that Thursday, Secretary of War Stimson concluded preparations for whatever public announcements would be made. He had no idea that the "pumpkin" missions had been watched carefully by the Japanese, who observed that the big practice bombs detonated only a small charge—to mark the accuracy of the aim—relative to their large size. Tokyo Rose scoffed in her regular propaganda broadcasts, "You are now reduced to small missions of three planes, and the bombs they drop are just duds."

On the evidence of Alamogordo, Stimson did not expect a dud, and had, through Groves, commissioned a scientific report in accessible language for the media by Henry D. Smyth, an eminent Princeton physicist. James Conant thought it would provide the basis for rational public discussion of atomic energy without releasing any military secrets. The British, as partners in the development of the Bomb, were reluctant to have any such document published, while the Americans saw it as essential—not only to have an informed public but also to foreclose any reckless or irresponsible outbursts from scientists outside the project and thus not under any obligation to withhold data. Besides, there was Leo Szilard and his petition, still gathering momentum.

Conant joined Stimson's advisers on Thursday for a meeting with British physicists James Chadwick and Roger Makins, arguing that the explosion itself would corroborate enough known theory that any nation—he did not need to specify Russia—could supply the data, if not the technology and the hardware, in three months. Smyth's report, Conant contended, would preserve essential secrecy with little sacrifice, and was in the public interest. Chadwick and Makins conceded that press policy was different in the United States. Stimson confessed his own misgivings. The experience of Potsdam had convinced him that the Soviets could never be part of any peaceable international control system about anything, let alone atomic power. The Communist system relied on repression, and the Russians had no compunctions about exporting Communism.

Even the conservative and secrecy-obsessed Groves came to Conant's defense, assuring Stimson that although Soviet industrial mobilization to build a Bomb was inevitable, there was nothing helpful in Smyth's text. A magazine like *Time,* Conant added, could put enough snoopers on the technological trail to produce a report far more informative than Smyth's. And then there was Congress, which was certain to demand information and postwar control. The scientific cat would be out of the bag. No one raised the possibility that Stalin's intelligence network had already found its way into the Manhattan District through the project's own personnel.

Contingent upon British concurrence, Stimson gave his reluctant approval—if the scientists could assure him that nothing Smyth had written would assist a Russian effort to manufacture a Bomb. Chadwick agreed. Makins would not accept personal responsibility, but offered to recommend clearance to the new government. Stimson's judgment, he felt, would be the deciding factor in London. What would become known as *The Smyth Report* could go to the printer.

Throughout the early hours of the morning a procession of returning planes that had belied Tokyo Rose's gibe touched down on Guam, Tinian, and Saipan. The extravagant Air Force Day strikes had dropped about six thousand tons of explosives on Japan. Hays Gamble landed his B-29 at 6:40. Since his had been the "target ship" over Kawasaki and had "caught all hell," he noted in his diary, once they were out again over the open sea, "We all said the Lord's Prayer in unison over [the] intercom and were the luckiest bunch ever." On the tarmac he inspected his plane, finding a flak hole in one engine cowling and another gash—four inches by two inches, and more threatening—in the fuselage.

At sea off Japan, crews up early battened everything down. The waves were rough, the winds fierce. Hundreds of ships moved south and east to lie as much out of the heavy swells as possible. The rain squalls were heavy on Japan itself, but Admiral Ugaki and his staff left by slow train—all rail travel was now slow—for the north anyway. Bad weather was good cover for the transfer of his headquarters. Stopping at a military hospital en route for baths and supper, they found that the patients had been removed to underground shelters and the hospital office hidden in a bamboo grove. At 6:50 P.M. they continued on through the night and into Oita station.

On August 2 the Japanese Air Force spotted only twenty enemy planes over Kyushu. Reconnaissance for home defense now went on whatever the weather and with whatever aircraft and hoarded fuel the services still had. To save precious fuel for the final battle, training flights were kept to the essentials, although the testing of new models that might fight off a Superfortress went on as if the aircraft might go into instant production. One had the advantage of an alternative fuel. To prepare for *Ketsu-Go* the Navy air arm was resting its hopes upon the rocket-powered *Shusui* ("Shining Blade"), a copy of the Messerschmidt 163 based on blueprints brought from Germany by submarine. A tailless aircraft that ran on hydrogen peroxide, it could, on paper, outfly anything the United States possessed, and could pump thirty-millimeter cannon shells into a B-29 formation. The manufacturing was entrusted to Mitsubishi, which had the first fuselages delivered on July 7 to Air Group 512 at Yokosuka, where the first rocket engine was installed. Lieutenant Toyohiko Inuzuka took it up for its first test flight. Sixteen seconds after it became airborne it lost speed and crashed, severely injuring Inuzuka, who died the next day. A valve malfunction was found and immediate modifications were begun with a planned flight in early August. If successful, it would go into production in underground factories in September, with 3,600 to be delivered by March 1946.

At Oppama, an airfield adjacent to Yokosuka, another new fighter was being tested and was closer to production. The *Reppu* was not as daring as a rocket plane, but it was equipped with a four-bladed propeller and superchargers that might enable it to contest the P-47 and P-51 and rise to attack B-29s. Yet Mitsubishi was running out of materials and above-ground factories. The few aircraft manufactured would be almost hand-made.

All missions from Okinawa had been scratched because of the weather, but the Fourteenth Air Force in China sent its B-25s, P-47s, and P-51s over transportation and communications targets. In the Philippines, General MacArthur issued a routine communiqué announcing that thirteen P-38s had attacked enemy ground forces in northern Luzon, hitting "pockets of resistance" near Kiangan and Bontoc. Months earlier he had announced the capture of Luzon, but tens of thousands of Japanese were not cooperating.

At 7:15 A.M., after little sleep, Truman left Babelsberg in a motorcade that was the only parting fuss he would permit. At 8:05 his plane, *The Sacred Cow*, took off from Gatow Airport for a scheduled landing at

Saint Mawgen's Field near Plymouth. Ground fog obscured the runways and the C-54 had to touch down instead at Harrowber, a U.S. Navy air base. The greeting party and security personnel rushed from one base to another through the morning haze, leaving the President to spend forty-five minutes of his one hour and twenty-five minutes on British soil in a stripped-down waiting room. By then the fog had given way to bright sunshine, but the disarray of his schedule left thousands waiting in vain along the streets near Princess Jetty.

Having left Antwerp two days earlier, the *Augusta* and *Philadelphia* were already anchored in Plymouth Roads, where they joined the cruiser *Renown*, on which Truman was to lunch with George VI, who had come to Plymouth by train. "Welcome to my country," said the King, looking around for guests who hadn't arrived. Ambassador John Winant and Admiral Harold Stark had traveled from London to the wrong airport and had missed the launch to the *Renown*. At the table the President and King ("a good man," Truman noted) discussed Potsdam ("Talked of everything and nothing," Truman wrote) and dined on soup, fish, lamb chops, peas, potatoes, and ice cream with chocolate sauce. Winant, the American ambassador to London, was still missing, but the British ambassador to Washington, Lord Halifax, was present, along with the King's private secretary, Alan Lascelles, and Leahy and Byrnes.

Winant and Stark caught up with the party on the *Augusta*, to which Truman and the King transferred after the formalities of departing the *Renown*. After the required inspection of the guard, the pair went down to Truman's quarters, where he offered the King "a snort of Haig & Haig." What he really wanted, said His Majesty, while accepting the drink, was Truman's autograph—three of them, in fact. He had promised one each for the Queen and the two princesses. Truman obliged; soon after, the King was piped off the cruiser. At 3:49 P.M. the *Augusta* began the voyage back.

Eager for sea air after being below decks, Truman told his staff that he wanted to go out on "the front porch for a while." Observing the scene, correspondent Merriman Smith watched regular Navy officers arch their eyebrows at the unnautical term, and the President explained to Smith, "The only time I was at sea before was going to France and back in the last war. Now, wouldn't it be silly for me to try to ape the language of men whose business is ships?" As for front porches, Truman knew all about them. His unpretentious old house in Independence, Missouri, had one.

•   •   •

While Truman traveled on his first leg back, deputies remained behind in Potsdam, polishing the protocol and communiqué. The detailed text released to the press made it obvious that Germany was the big loser and Russia the gainer. "In politics," Cadogan recalled Stalin as saying during the conference, "one should be guided by the calculation of forces." Yet the communiqué seemed to go a long way toward settlement of issues that a comprehensive peace treaty could only confirm and suggested a solidarity that was only a facade when it claimed that Potsdam had "strengthened the ties between the Three Governments and extended the scope of their collaboration and understanding." In reality, Potsdam had exposed areas where there would be little or no collaboration or understanding over decades to come.

As an earnest of good faith, however, the Navy Munitions Assignment Board in Washington transferred, as the conference closed, thirteen seventy-foot PT boats to the Soviet Union for use in the far Pacific. Whatever games Stalin had played about how he was going to go to war with Japan, it would happen.

Potsdam was, but for that reconfirmation of Yalta, a verdict on what Germany in defeat would be, and it accepted, more than determined, a settlement of central Europe largely laid out at Yalta before *Mitteleuropa* had been overrun. In a less than ideal fashion Potsdam began the reconstruction of the Continent and avoided some of the pitfalls of Versailles. Writing from New York after the document was made public, William L. Shirer, who had reported from prewar and early wartime Berlin, saw the results as a sentence of death upon Germany, pronounced ironically at Potsdam, the intellectual and military center of Frederick the Great.

Article XIII of the protocol dealt with "orderly transfer of German populations" remaining in Poland, Czechoslovakia, and Hungary— Romania went unmentioned—"in an orderly and humane manner." The three nations were ordered "to suspend further expulsions" pending an examination of the situation by the Control Council. The panic, fear, and desperation among the remaining Germans dissipated only briefly as the West had no effective way of securing information or monitoring events in rural areas well outside the capital cities. "Humane" proceedings in Sudeten Czechoslovakia often involved twenty minutes' notice for the expellees to pack two suitcases each for a trip by horse and cart to an evacuation camp where Germans were gathered for transport over the Bavarian frontier into the American zone.

A typical order, addressed to the entire family at a particular address, read:

> I order you to make ready to leave the territory of Czechoslovak Republic before 7 A.M. today.
>
> You are allowed to take with you luggage of a maximum weight of 30 kilograms per person.
>
> Food supplies for five days. You may take all your German bank notes with you.
>
> The keys of your flat and of the house, furnished with a piece of paper giving your address, are to be handed over by you to the security authorities.

By August 24 the Czech Ministry of the Interior had promulgated regulations stripping Germans of citizenship, even wives who were ethnically Czech or Slovak and their children. ("She remains a foreigner in the eyes of the Czechoslovak Republic as do lawful or legitimized issue of her marriage.") Even earlier, on August 2, a presidential decree had declared that citizens "of German or Magyar nationality who became German or Magyar subjects in accordance with the regulations of a foreign occupying power"—southern tier areas had been seized by Hungary in the prewar dismemberment of Czechoslovakia—"shall be deemed to have lost their citizenship on the day they became subjects of those states." But pending expulsion, an earlier decree, of June 27, 1945, requiring compulsory labor of "all persons of German nationality, irrespective of sex, who have passed their tenth and not yet had their sixtieth birthday," remained in effect, for a working day of twelve hours.

The situation was little different in Hungary. In Poland and Romania the level of brutality in carrying out expulsions was greater, and seldom was there any pretense of legality.

Still walking home from the war, James Krüss got as far as the road to Lüneburg and Hamburg when he first heard about the post-Potsdam division of Germany into formal occupation zones. He had been told about the Poles "who had been held captive on the estates of the Lüneburg Heath with little bread and almost without pay, slaving over the farmland for many years." Now, he was warned, Poles "had become dangerous," and the Germans were in for it. It was crucial to get across the Elbe into the British zone, although German refugees from his side were being turned back. He now had a bicycle, and biked up to the bridge, where a soldier asked him for his permit. Krüss dug out his travel pass in English, signed weeks ago "by a far-off mayor" and of questionable validity. "I fingered it, pointed at the word *Helgoland*, tried out my limited school English, waved the permit without letting it leave my hand, simply mounted my bike, stepped down on the pedals, and accomplished with little effort what had become an insurmountable obstacle for many citizens: the crossing of the Elbe."

He wheeled to Pier 4 at the harbor in Bremerhaven and asked for a ticket for the boat to Helgoland. "Helgoland? Helgoland is no more. A dead piece of rock. The houses are no more. The people are dead. There are no tickets to Helgoland."

Too confused to be shocked—he had no knowledge of the ferocity of the bombing of submarine pens and missile launching sites on the periphery of the North Sea—he headed for the Hohenzollern Allee, where an aunt lived. The house still stood and her name was on the door. It was as close to home as he could get.

Also getting as far away as he could from the Soviet zone was Ursula von Kardorff's friend Bürklin, like Krüss an ex-soldier prudently minus uniform. "He now has a first-class forged pass and walked all the way here to dig up his uniform. He waited until it was dark before doing so but only took his Iron Crosses with him. The rest was rotten with mold."

In the American zone, having completed an inspection of North Sea ports from Kiel to Bremerhaven and flown to Frankfurt to visit Eisenhower's vast headquarters in the I. G. Farben complex, Secretary Forrestal's party flew south to Salzburg. From there, Forrestal, still with Jack Kennedy in tow, motored to Hitler's mountain retreat at Berchtesgaden. One was not legitimized as a VIP unless given a tour of the Bavarian redoubt in which the Nazis had failed to make their expected last stand. To Forrestal's group Eisenhower confided that at Potsdam he had urged Truman not to "give anything away" to induce the Russians into the Pacific war—if true, an indication that the Supreme Commander in the West had never been informed about decisions at Yalta concerning the Far East.

Returning to Frankfurt via Salzburg, the Forrestal group went on to London, where young Kennedy was to part company and cover, for the Hearst papers, the new Labour government. The London press had no idea what to make of Cabinet ministers new to such office, but one paper published a cartoon of Attlee in Parliament being observed with alarm by "the past rulers of England" from Victoria to William the Conqueror under the caption, "Thumbs Up! After All, He IS An Oxford Man!" The point was made in reality as well. John Colville—formerly Churchill's private secretary—noted in his diary for August 2 about Attlee: "He thought he should acquire a sober 'Anthony Eden' black Homburg hat and asked me where to buy one. With deliberate irony I took him to Lock's in St. James's Street, the most aristocratic hat-maker in London. He bought a hat that suited him well."

Churchill had a different sort of transition to make. Lord Moran went to see him at Claridge's. The sun streamed into the sixth-floor penthouse but the ex-P.M. was not as cheerful as the day. "I don't like sleeping near a precipice like that," he said, pointing to the window and balcony. "I have no desire to quit the world, but"—and he grinned—"thoughts, desperate thoughts, come into the head."

Churchill worried aloud to Moran about Socialist Britain. "Attlee and Bevin and those who worked with me in the war will not allow chaos if they can help it; they are strong men. But there are grave dangers threatening our poor country." He also worried about maintaining his lifestyle. Although he had "dazzling" offers, including twenty thousand pounds from *Time* and *Life* for four articles— literally a pound a word—he questioned whether he could keep enough of it from taxation to make it worthwhile: "The Government would take it all. I'm not going to work when they take nineteen and six out of every pound I earn." (It had been *his* wartime supertax.) He worried, too, about the cost and the regimentation of Labour-promised social services. "If Aneurin Bevan becomes Minister of Health, will there be private practice? Will you be able to look after me?"

While, in London, the World Zionist Congress was meeting under the chairmanship of Chaim Weizmann—the addressee in 1918 of the unforgotten Balfour Declaration, which promised a homeland in the Holy Land for the Jewish people—Arab leaders were convening at Emir Abdullah's palace in Amman to oppose it. Jews, warned David Ben-Gurion at the London conference, had only two alternatives— "the establishment of a Jewish State or prolonged resistance to a regime of injustice." In the dusty capital of Trans-Jordan, Abdullah proposed a joint committee of Arab unity under the exiled pro-Nazi Haj Amin el Hussein, the former Grand Mufti of Jerusalem, and demanded a complete stoppage of Jewish immigration into Palestine as well as a ban on land sales to Jews. The British could be intimidated, the Emir said; the important thing was to intimidate the new United Nations before the Jews could make their case there.

Late in the day, newspapers were out with the Potsdam communiqué, which generated headlines worldwide except where Japan still ruled. In government circles two matters arose from the Potsdam text or its inferences that created serious foreboding. An "Ultra" intercept picked up a report from General Miyakawa in Manchuria that a source in the Russian consulate in Harbin had reported that the Soviets were preparing to invade southern Sakhalin, which the Japanese called Karafuto, with American help—on the pretext of "preserving order." The other bleak matter emerged from Article X of the Potsdam document itself. "Italy," it began, "was the first of the Axis powers to break with Germany, to whose defeat she has made a material contribution, and has now joined with the Allies in the struggle against Japan." The "Three Governments," it went on, would soon support Italian membership in the United Nations. Stalin had signed the document—first of the three. The reference to Japan was ominous. No intervention with Ambassador Jacob Malik in Tokyo or Commissar Molotov in Moscow was likely to change what now seemed inevitable.

In the consternation that followed in Tokyo, Foreign Minister Togo thought he had the vague sanction of the military to press for a quick end to the war. Yet no one with authority seemed willing to offer conditions or to employ any other avenue than the hopeless one of Moscow. "Magic" intercepted an August 2 cable to Sato declaring that there was now "unanimous determination to seek the good offices of the Russians in ending this war." Yet despite Sato's ceaseless warnings, Togo continued as if the time available were endless: "Although it is difficult to decide on concrete peace conditions here at home all at once . . . we are exerting ourselves to collect the views of all quarters." There was "a disposition," given the circumstances, to make the rejected Potsdam ultimatum "the basis of our study concerning terms." But the foot-dragging Togo still wanted to persuade the Soviet government "to accept the mission of our Special Envoy. His Majesty, the Emperor, is most profoundly concerned about the matter and has been following developments with the keenest interest. The Premier and the leaders of the Army are now concentrating all their attention on this one point."

Whether the "one point" was the frustrated mission of Prince Konoye or Soviet mediation in general, the fantasy world that survived in the ruins of Tokyo puzzled and exasperated Sato. As soon as he received the message he cabled back, "There is no alternative but immediate unconditional surrender if we are to try to make American and English [conditions] moderate and to prevent Russia's participation in the war." But the Emperor's ministers were listening only to themselves.

# "LITTLE BOY"
## AND
# "FAT MAN"

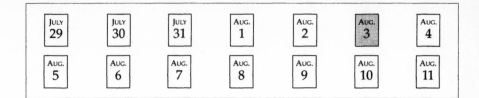

CHAPTER XXII

# · AUGUST 3, 1945 ·

*new lives for old*

Moving in behind the *Bassett,* the *Ringness* by mid-morning had plucked survivors from far off to port. Lieutenant Commander William C. Meyer was on the bridge when his whaleboat returned with nineteen men, all that were left from McVay's rafts. One of them, once he was cleaned up, reported to Meyer and saluted. The gaunt, badly sunburned man identified himself as Captain Charles Butler McVay III, commander of the former *Indianapolis.*

Transferring the casualties aboard Lieutenant Marks's PBY to the *Doyle* took two hours. Fifty-six were still alive, all burned and blackened. With its motor whaleboat the *Doyle* had retrieved thirty-seven more, including the only one Alcorn had been able to rescue. Once Marks and his crew took off all the gear they could salvage from their crippled plane and returned in the whaleboat, the *Doyle* trained its guns on the Dumbo and sent it down. Alcorn watched the sinking and radioed to the *Doyle* that he would try to get airborne; his plane had not suffered the stress of the other PBY.

The *Ringness* rendezvoused with 39 survivors; the *Talbot* with 24.

The *Bassett* had 151; the *Register* 12; the *Dufilho* 1; the *Doyle* 93. Of nearly 1,200 aboard the cruiser, 320 had lived to be gathered up; four of those were too far gone to make it back to hospitals on Peleliu and Leyte. Although the remnants of the *Indianapolis*'s crew had spent more than four days in the water without anyone missing the ship, and for most of that time without anyone noticing hundreds of men in rafts or in the water, the facts remained known only to those who heard the radio signals from the rescuers or who were receiving the victims. The Navy was keeping it that way.

To the north, the sea was still too rough after passage of the typhoon for normal operations against Japan. Destroyers could not be refueled because waves could sweep a sailor overboard. By afternoon the weather cleared, and ships and planes were on the move again. On the *Montpelier*, Seaman Fahey noted that they were 140 miles from Shanghai and would be sailing to the north of the mouth of the Yangtze, an area so full of reefs that the heavier cruisers *Guam* and *Alaska* had to remain behind. To be grounded in Japanese-held territory was a gloomy prospect: "I wonder what Fleet Admiral Nimitz had in mind when he made plans to send us up here."

Nimitz, an ordinary seaman did not need to know, had a surfeit of fighting ships and wanted to employ them. Naval strategy was to interdict all Japanese maritime traffic and choke off the home islands. The tentacles of the imperial octopus would fall away. The occupied areas would then surrender, or be subject to revolution. The latter prospect worried the former colonial masters—the French, Dutch, and British. Each was eager to have a role in the reconquest of Southeast Asia, to set Humpty Dumpty back upon his wall. But decisions at Potsdam had lowered the priorities for those sectors even further.

The priority now was the delivery of "Fat Man," in hopes that its power would impress the Japanese into taking the Potsdam ultimatum seriously. On Tinian the 509th was watching the weather—in particular, the long-range forecast. With prospects looking brighter all the time, Colonel Tibbets scheduled for 4:00 P.M. the next day a preflight briefing for the seven crews who would fly the advance weather planes and the bombing mission itself.

At 7:40 A.M. Japan time, Admiral Ugaki finally arrived, three and a half hours late, at his new base at Oita. His quarters, a small house dispossessed from a farmer, were lively with mosquitoes and fleas. While he settled in, aided by the quiet afforded by bad weather, the commanders of two depleted air flotillas visited to discuss "pertinent matters." At 5:30 the chief of staff of the Grand Naval Command telephoned to inform Ugaki that a Combined Air Fleet would be established soon, with the admiral as commander concurrently with the Third Air Fleet (at Kanoya he had been commanding the Fifth Air Fleet). What naval air units would be combined was unclear, but so many had lost pilots and planes that Ugaki must have understood the implication.

Although weather had curtailed missions from the Marianas, almost one hundred Mustangs from Iwo Jima flew sorties in the Tokyo area, bombing and strafing rail installations and trains. "The radio said," Frank Fujita wrote from his downtown Tokyo POW billet, "that there were large flights of P-51s roaming the area. We could see them off in the distance looking like a swarm of flies. At 12:30 P.M. a lone B-29 came over and dropped leaflets. The AA guns opened up on him, which was unusual, for they had not been firing on a single plane." Japanese intelligence might have begun pondering the purposes of B-29s that came in alone, or accompanied by only one or two others, and dropped only a single large bomb that went off with little more force than was necessary to destroy the bomb. What was even more peculiar to monitors of radio messages from the Marianas is that such flights were never reported in an Air Force communiqué—as if they never happened.

While weather near Japan limited strikes from Guam, Tinian, and Saipan, airmen on the islands spent some hours outdoors after dark watching Hollywood's contributions to the war. Combat simulations or even the real thing had lower priorities than Van Johnson in *Between Two Women*, Lana Turner in *Keep Your Powder Dry*, Veronica Lake and Sonny Tufts in *Bring on the Girls*, Claire Trevor and Dick Powell in *Murder My Sweet*, Judy Garland in *Meet Me in St. Louis*, a new teenager named Elizabeth Taylor in *National Velvet* (horses were popular, too), or—more horses—Roy Rogers in *Lights of Old Santa Fe*. Even Japanese soldiers still hiding out were attracted to the big lighted screens, sometimes to see (if seldom to understand) the likes of Bob Hope in *The Princess and the Pirate*, sometimes to pilfer food from garbage cans, unattended messes, and open tents while air crews watched Anne Baxter and John Hodiak in *Sunday Dinner for a Soldier*. One evening on Guam two Japanese who found the lights turned on and the screen darkened too soon were spotted on a slope to the rear and chased down.

In a prison camp on Hainan Island, over which his B-25 had been shot down on April 3, Lieutenant Gene Lawlis had been watching the men around him deteriorate. He knew the Americans were winning—they had been winning before his plane took AA-fire into its open bomb bay over the big Chinese island east of Hanoi. Realizing that he very likely had less than a hundred pounds on his own six-foot frame, he wondered whether any of his fellow POWs would survive into victory. Two rice balls and a bottle of boiled water three times a day left them constantly hungry. "One day something moved in my rice bowl," Lawlis remembered. "My first reaction was revulsion. I made some derogatory remark about worms. Then it occurred to us that worms must have protein in them. We didn't savor them, but we ate them gratefully."

As conditions, even the food, deteriorated further, they realized that the Japanese were losing the war "while we were losing our lives." Malaria, tropical ulcers, beriberi, and dysentery were weakening them relentlessly. The beriberi-caused edema that each POW had to some degree had affected one of his companions, Eugene Harviell, so grotesquely that he had to carry his scrotum when he stood. It was soon the size of a volleyball, Lawlis guessed. His last image of him in the camp at Sanya remained with Lawlis indelibly. It was in the first days of August—he never knew which day. "I suggested," he remembered, "that we all do some exercises; and I led the way, calling the cadence for knee bends and the like (push-ups were beyond our capacity). But Gene had no strength even to stand up. What he did was to remain sitting, but he turned so that he could see me through the bamboo bars that separated our cells. Then as we exercised in cadence, he bent his right forefinger up and down, keeping perfect time with our movements. At first I thought he was joking; but then I realized that he was quite serious. The finger-bending was the external manifestation of an inward empathy: in his mind he was doing the exercises right along with us." Harviell's war ended a week later.

In Kunming, in southern China, once the rackety focus of American "Flying Tiger" activity and still a supply center from which U.S. aid disappeared into the hinterland, a meeting took place between the head of the Gaullist military mission in southern China and an Indochinese nationalist leader. On the first floor of a restaurant in an obscure alley, Jean Sainteny made the acquaintance of Nguyen Tong Tam, a Vietnamese intellectual who would become known to history as a Vietnamese foreign minister. Tam's purpose was to let Paris know that the nationalists filling the vacuum being left by the Japanese would not react kindly to any French effort to recolonize the country. Sainteny could not have been less sympathetic. He had just returned from France, where his government had informed him that it had no intention of relinquishing its legitimate rights in Indochina—although it was prepared to make some domestic compromises. Even in remembering the exchange fifteen hard years later, Sainteny's arrogance on behalf of the discredited old regime came through: "I had not hesitated to tell Nguyen Tong Tam that although we would not let ourselves be forced to give concessions . . . France was ready to work out with the Indochinese themselves reasonable land leases and other agreements warranted by the circumstances and the political maturity of its protégés."

Tam agreed that bloodshed was the wrong path to independence, but insisted that the Vietnamese wanted the French to be better enlightened about the realities. He suggested that Sainteny meet with Tam's more radical brother in Hanoi.

As improbable as a meeting in Hanoi between a Gaullist official and a Vietnamese nationalist sounded, given the Japanese occupation, it was quite possible, although it would not happen. The Japanese had a presence in Indochina but were no longer in control except on paper. The same anomaly existed in Thailand, and in Burma they were in full flight. Although they had a considerable military presence in Malaya—especially in Singapore—and in the Dutch Indies, the Japanese were there largely because they could not get out. The sea-lanes to the home islands were blocked by British and American fleets almost everywhere. Few aircraft made it safely to Japan, except by a hazardous journey via China, and the only safe physical connections with Tokyo were by submarine.

Sainteny's chief contacts with the Vietnamese occurred through the good offices of the American OSS in Kunming, which viewed France's "protectorate" days as sponsor of puppet regional kings as effectively ended. The Americans backed and supplied an anti-Japanese revolutionary named Nguyen Ai Quoc, later known as Ho Chi Minh, who as an exile worked in the Communist movement in Canton but saw Marxism as less than useful for an exploited peasantry. Ho wanted political independence and recognized that support from the West would not go to doctrinaire Communism, which in any case better fit the needs of an industrial proletariat. But as the general secretary of a Viet Minh party on Chinese soil, Ho was arrested on orders of Chiang Kaishek, who did not want yet another Communist threat nearby. After fifteen months, Ho had been released in hopes that he could be turned to Chiang's use on his southern border. With American aid, Ho began to wrest the northern provinces from Japanese control, his military chief a bitterly anti-French young lawyer and historian, Vo Nguyen Giap. His wife had died in a French prison.

The OSS knew Sainteny's group as Mission 5, and offered it the Viet Minh League's conciliatory offer—that a postwar parliament be elected by universal suffrage, that France grant full independence after a transition period of five to ten years, that the resources of the country revert to its inhabitants after equitable compensation, and that the sale of opium be forbidden. The document was even written in English for OSS purposes, and a mixed French-American mission had been flown into Indochina on July 16 to work with the Viet Minh resistance. But the Gaullist goal of restoring the glory of prewar France required restoration of the French colonial empire. As Japanese authority in Indochina eroded, there was still no agreement on what would replace it. The Potsdam division of authority in the area between two commanders, Wedemeyer in China above sixteen degrees north, and Mountbatten below that line, may have served projected operations but not a postwar settlement. It meant that after enduring Japanese occupation, the peoples of Indochina, who had always feared designs on them by China, would have to suffer at least temporary Chinese occupation of Tonkin and parts of Annam and Laos. It was a military decision meant to speed the disarmament of the Japanese, but it excluded the Vietnamese as well as the French.

In Southeast Asia the series of Japanese retreats and evacuations evidenced a domino effect. The loss of most of Burma created changes in Thailand that in turn impacted upon Indochina. The military command structure in Thailand had become an Area Army because it was absorbing the remnants of divisions fleeing Burma; and what had been considered a Siam occupation force was now nearly on the front line and could no longer be a garrison army enjoying the good life. Bangkok, the utopia of brothels and beer, was being bombed daily. The country could no longer be run in a leisurely fashion from the ambassador's residence, which sent instructions to the General Headquarters Building. As far as the Japanese were concerned, the country had largely been Bangkok, plus a few air bases. Through the one-sided Japan-Thai alliance that had ended the half-day war of December 8, 1941, the rest was left much as before, even by the Kempeitai, the secret police.

Newspapers on the third were filled with Potsdam-related stories, including reports from London that Anglo-American talks involving Lord Louis Mountbatten had charted the future course of the war in East Asia. The disclosure emphasized that Russia, not a party to the war with Japan, did not participate. From the *Augusta*, departing British waters, Harry Truman insisted that he had made "no secret agreements of any kind" with Stalin. And it was true that he had made no new deal to have the Red Army go to war with Japan, as that had been concluded at Tehran in 1944 and confirmed at Yalta.

It would take a few days before the results were clear to those closest to Potsdam and who had the most to lose. Newspapers under Allied control had limited circulation, and few Germans who had experienced the Russian occupation now had radios. To her friend Frank, Ruth Andreas-Friedrich predicted that "sooner or later all borders between the zones will become superfluous. I already see the dove of peace."

"Don't see it too soon," warned Frank; ". . . I shudder to think of the consequences. My politically untrained mind doesn't quite grasp it." And he counted on his fingers the territorial and economic losses to Germany; the Polonization of areas east of the Oder, and the forced expatriation of millions of Germans. "What if this madness is carried through?"

Suddenly depressed, she fell silent. "That is not how I imagined it. The Potsdam agreement begins to make me feel uncomfortable."

Not all Berliners even knew of it. Rosemarie Hebek remembered that in radio-starved Berlin, where newspapers were still rare and prized, "We were being kept informed by news posters glued against walls and trees."

From London the Baltimore *Sun*'s bureau chief called home a report that the Big Three meeting had been hailed there as "a triumph of collaboration." While papers like the New York *Herald-Tribune*, not particularly friendly to the Truman administration, praised the protocol for helping to develop "concrete organs" like the Council of Foreign Ministers to perform international tasks, it found the Carthaginian treatment of Germany breathtaking: "Here, section by section, are blueprinted the principles and machinery for the liquidation of a great modern nation-state, its resolution into its elements and its gradual rebuilding along very different and deliberately conceived ideas. Nothing of the kind has ever before been attempted in modern times. Always in the past, wars have ended in a formal peace which, however severe, accepted the existence and continuity of the defeated nation-state organism. Here the organism is dissolved. . . ." But the editorial did not go on to speculate whether the same bankruptcy judgment might soon apply equally to Japan.

On his first full day at sea, Truman called to his cabin the few members of the press corps fortunate enough to be traveling with him on the *Augusta*. Since he realized that they were still likely to be on board and out of reach of their telephones when the Bomb went off, he offered them a surprise scoop. Sitting at a small table on which he had placed, open, a looseleaf notebook, he spoke of his thankfulness that the United States had now, ready to employ, a weapon that might speed the end of the war. He knew that its use would bring with it new problems. For the moment the United States would be its "exclusive producer" but that would not be forever. And from his notebook he read from the statement prepared for the occasion of the atomic weapon's use.

White House correspondent Merriman Smith, who had rushed to his beat on the Sunday when the bombs fell on Pearl Harbor, had nowhere to go. "Here was the greatest news story since the invention of gunpowder. And what could we do about it? Nothing. Just sit and wait."

It was not important enough to be news in London that a twenty-eight-year-old invalided American naval lieutenant was sick and in the U.S. Naval Dispensary. "Patient flew in from Germany yesterday where he has been eating Army rations and drinking Army certified water," Commander Weddell, the senior physician on duty, wrote on John Kennedy's chart. ". . . No other member of his party is ill." Weddell went on to note that his patient's nausea, fever, and abdominal discomfort were repetitions of an illness of 1942, and that he had also had service-connected malaria and a ruptured lumbar disc ("PT boat rammed"). The chart described coolly what was a high fever and would be a siege of four days in wringing wet bedclothes—probably a recurrence of malaria. Kennedy's prognosis for an active life seemed poor. He suffered permanent lower back pain and apparently chronic malaria, and was susceptible to a variety of ailments and allergies. Whether in deference to Kennedy's condition or to his father, Forrestal kept his plane in London until his young friend was able to fly home.

In Marseilles, at one of many war crimes trials going on involving both Frenchmen and Germans, Captain Karl Staubacker responded to the charges, in fluent French, with a line that would become more and more familiar: "Those were my orders." Similar trials were going on in Norway, Holland, Belgium, Italy, and the former Nazi satellites, now Soviet vassal states. In Russia most of the many being sentenced daily had committed misdemeanors hardly worth a passing thought outside a police state. One prisoner of no importance, Aleksandr Solzhenitsyn, was being transferred from his cell at Butyrki, where his sentencing had taken place, to the Krasnaya Presnya transit prison in another part of Moscow, itself a city of prisons.

    Vast and overcrowded, Krasnaya Presnya was the hub of the widespread prison system that Solzhenitsyn would christen the "Gulag Archipelago," his acronym for *Glavnoye upravleniye lagerei,* or "Main Administration of the Camps." Butyrki had at least immured political prisoners charged with disloyalty to the regime, which gave them a sense of respect for, and solidarity with, one another, even if the offenses were minimal or nonexistent. Those on the other side of the bars were the enemy—wardens, interrogators, officials. Krasnaya Presnya housed authentic criminals with long terms behind them and ahead of them. They ran the place. "From your very first steps in the transit prison you notice that you are not in the hands of the wardens . . . with stars on their shoulders, who at least minimally observe some kind of written law. Here you are in the hands of the prison trusties."

    The war was over but he was in a new and more terrifying kind of war. While it was no less unpleasant, it was more unpredictable. And there was no way to defend oneself. On arrival they were robbed of "everything loose, like tea and tobacco." Being a "political" was now a grave handicap. It meant the insulting address of "Mister Fascist." To be called "Comrade" meant a linkage with the Soviet revolution; a "Mister" was a class enemy, a throwback to the prerevolutionary bourgeois. A "Fascist" in Gulag terms was even worse—a reference to the alleged collaborators with Nazi occupiers, or to the returned prisoners of war who were enemies of the state because they had surrendered or been captured and had lived (or survived) in non-Communist circumstances, however horrific, thereby becoming tainted by suspect values. Criminal convicts were encouraged by Soviet prison authorities to believe that they were the more favored class, having not been judged guilty of political nonconformity.

Solzhenitsyn and his Butyrki companion Valentin were pushed into a cell crowded with over a hundred prisoners but far fewer bunks. They crawled on their bellies under two low bunks where the concrete floor was free. All they had with them were knapsacks with their small treasures of bread, sugar, and lard from parcels sent by their families, but soon their hoard was gone. "In the semi-darkness, with a wordless rustling, some 'juveniles' started to creep up on us from all sides and on all fours, like big rats. They were still boys, some no more than twelve years old, but the criminal code accepted them too. They had already been 'processed' under the thieves' law.... They leapt on us from all sides, and six pairs of hands ... stripped us of all our wealth. And all this took place in total silence. . . . We had given up our food without a fight."

The young robbers had been sent by their gang leader, an arrogant professional thug who ran the cell from his top bunk next to the only window. Humiliated but not quite cowed, Solzhenitsyn wormed out on his backside and saved face by demanding that if their food was to be seized, the least they should get in exchange was a bunk.

From his eyrie at the window, the cell chieftain ordered two defenseless politicals out of their bunks and onto the concrete. Solzhenitsyn felt ashamed, but the episode was another dimension in his continuing political education. In the army in the snows of East Prussia, thanks to Potsdam (but he did not know this) now part of the Soviet Union, he had thought that life held nothing more cruel for him than huddling four abreast in a freezing concrete cellar—or marching for two days through icy winds and sleet. In Lubyanka he had learned about solitary confinement and the mental torture of interrogation. In Butyrki he had been teased by rumors of amnesty, slept with two hundred others on the floor of a rat-infested cell, and learned of his sentence in a trial that had never taken place. At each stage he had deceived himself about the limits to which the system could dehumanize its victims. The Great Patriotic War (as the Soviets called it) had been won, but his wounds were being inflicted in the peace that had preserved Communism.

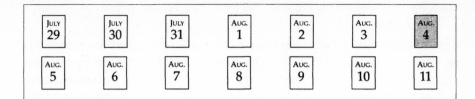

| July 29 | July 30 | July 31 | Aug. 1 | Aug. 2 | Aug. 3 | Aug. 4 |
|---|---|---|---|---|---|---|
| Aug. 5 | Aug. 6 | Aug. 7 | Aug. 8 | Aug. 9 | Aug. 10 | Aug. 11 |

## CHAPTER XXIII

# · AUGUST 4, 1945 ·

*eastbound trains, westbound planes*

At dawn on Saturday, five and a half days after the *Indianapolis* went down, destroyers from Palau and Ulithi arrived over its watery grave to try to identify what a Navy message to Washington called the "floating dead." Sailors in motor whaleboats scoured the swells for identifying marks or gear—rings, watches, dog tags, tattoos, dental work. Bodies and body parts still on the surface were weighted down and sunk with five-inch shells. Each encountered was the subject of a report: "Body clad in dungaree trousers only. Badly mangled by sharks." "Fully clothed with dungaree shirt and trousers, skivvy drawers, shoe and sock on left foot (right foot missing)."

In Hawaii, Admiral Nimitz pondered the line of judicial inquiry necessary. A hearing had to be held. The news had to be released to the press. It would appall the public and embarrass the Navy. But it had to be done before the survivors came home and told their stories.

The *Indianapolis* disaster was only the latest Navy embarrassment, and possibly the hardest to hide. As early as the day after Pearl Harbor its shocking losses were known in Washington, but on grounds of patriotism Secretary of the Navy Frank Knox, a former newspaper publisher drawn into the Cabinet from the opposition party, had talked the press into keeping the extent of the catastrophe from the public. In the summer of 1945, as Halsey's fleet pounded Japan, a joke going the rounds of reporters was that seven of the two battleships sunk at Pearl Harbor were in action off the home islands. For the armed services, especially the Navy, public relations was a combat arm. In the first year of the war—November 1942—the Japanese had torpedoed the cruiser *Juneau*, then supporting the invasion of Guadalcanal. Of the complement of more than 700, only 150 escaped the sinking ship, yet the task force commander, Captain Gilbert C. Hoover, anxious about the safety of his other vessels, ordered them off without rescuing the survivors. (Eight days later, after gross negligence and communications confusion had left only 10 crewmen uneaten by sharks or dead from exposure, hunger, and thirst, rescuers arrived.)

The findings of a secret inquiry were quashed, and the sinking was recycled into patriotic sentiment because five brothers had perished. "Let the *Juneau* be remembered simply," the Navy determined in burying the truth, "as the ill-fated ship on which the celebrated Sullivan brothers courageously died fighting when it went down, bringing new glory on the U.S. Navy." Dramatically, a new destroyer would be christened U.S.S. *Sullivans*.

Quashing the *Indianapolis* story would be less easy. The news would emerge as the survivors came home. And censorship would end with the war.

Well before 3:00 P.M. on Tinian, seventy men comprising the crews of the seven B-29s of the 509th who would fly the "Little Boy" mission arrived at their briefing hut to discover it guarded for the first time by Military Police carrying carbines. They had been warned to keep no notes, but Sergeant Abe Spitzer, a radio operator, kept an unauthorized diary in his footlocker. Tibbets stepped up to the briefing platform followed by Captain William S. ("Deak") Parsons, the Navy ordnance expert who had headed the engineering division at Los Alamos. The Parsons team designed the combat versions of the nuclear bombs, first called "Franklin Roosevelt" (the "Thin Man," later "Little Boy") and "Winston Churchill" ("Fat Man," the plutonium bomb).

Parsons had seen four B-29s crash and burn at the end of one of Tinian's runways. Mechanical failures were not uncommon, and he was worried. He confided his qualms to General Thomas Farrell, Groves's deputy, who had been on Tinian since the thirty-first to observe the mission: "You know, if we crack up at the end of the runway . . . and the plane gets on fire, there is the danger of an atomic explosion, and we may lose this end of the island, if not the whole of Tinian with every blessed thing and person on it."

"We will just have to pray that doesn't happen," said Farrell.

"If I made the final assembly of that bomb after we left the island, it couldn't happen."

"You mean, if the plane cracks up and burns, we just lose the airplane and the bomb and the crew and you—but we don't lose the island. Is that right?"

"Yes."

"Isn't that nice? Have you ever assembled a bomb like this before?"

"No," said Parsons, who knew more about how it was engineered—by a committee—than anyone else, "but I've got all day to try it."

"Go ahead and try," said Farrell.

Aside from his role in the briefings, Parsons worked on a way to arm the otherwise completed Bomb when airborne. He had the entire heavily guarded hangar in which the Bomb was stored, ready to go. There he could disassemble whatever was necessary to study the problem.

In the Quonset hut with the aircrews, Tibbets and Parsons had a blackboard and a movie screen. Tibbets began with the blackboard, on which he had aides display aerial photographs of Hiroshima, Kokura, and Nagasaki. (Niigata, the other alternative target, had been scratched because it was not in the same flight path as the other cities; the bomb-carrying plane could not be rerouted that far after landfall.) Hiroshima, the primary target, had only been hit twice— once, on May 7, by seven B-29s that had missed their aiming point and lodged bombs in the shallow waters of the Ota, then again on June 2 when planes passed over the city and apparently dumped bombs intended for another site on islands in the delta. Otherwise, Hiroshima had experienced only leaflet drops.

The moment for which they had been training, Tibbets told his men, had arrived. The special Bomb they were to deliver had been tested successfully back home; now they were to deliver it to the enemy on one of the targets on the board. Three crews—and he named them—would fly ahead of the plane with the Bomb to check the weather, especially the cloud cover. To analyze the results with cameras and sensors, two other planes would accompany them. The seventh plane would stand by at a loading pit on Iwo Jima as a spare in case the Bomb-carrying plane malfunctioned and had to make an emergency landing.

Tibbets introduced Parsons. He explained the device they would escort as the most destructive weapon ever made. It would probably obliterate an area three miles across. The Bomb would be detonated in the air, close to the ground. Since its power could only be guessed at, aircraft flying near the explosion would have to be careful to avoid the cloud rising from the burst, as the effect of its radioactivity was unknown. He did not use the word *atomic*.

He and Tibbets had a motion picture of the Trinity explosion to show them, said Parsons. He ordered the projector turned on. It balked, and began chewing up film. The projectionist switched it off and began rewinding, but Parsons went on without the newsreel. "The film you are *not* about to see," he said to some nervous laughter, "was made of the only test we have performed." And he went on to describe the explosion, the fireball, the magnesium-bright light, the mushroom cloud formed atop a twisting pillar of fire and smoke, the thundery noise, the energy release, the destruction. The crews who had been practicing steep turns after releasing their peculiar "pumpkins" understood.

Tibbets took over again. Anything they had done in their lives before, he said, was small potatoes. He praised them for their dedication and morale while they did not know what they were training to do. The Bomb was no gimmick but the real thing now, no pumpkin. It might shorten the war by six months. They were not to write home about it. If the weather cooperated they would ready themselves for the flight through the next day—the fifth—and take off that night for a morning drop.

In the Philippines, General Eichelberger, who, unlike his superior, MacArthur, still knew nothing about the Bomb, speculated in a letter home about Russia. He had just received his first orders "concerning what we are able to do if Japan quits." He expected from the Potsdam meetings "either an early entrance of Russia into the war or a threat to Japan by Russia that she will enter the war if Japan does not quit." Even when in better shape, he wrote, Japan could not "fight the world." Now her industries were being destroyed from the air and she was losing the ability to wage modern war. "If it were any other country but Japan I would say that early surrender would be in sight, but the very traits of character that make them fight to the death in a hopeless fight might make them continue to fight as a nation, particularly as the public mind in Japan has hardly been prepared for a defeat."

As had occurred in Germany, wholesale bombings of cities often intensified hatred of the enemy and hardened resolve. Also as in Germany, many industries and installations were safely underground. But the expenditure of matériel, power, and people to rebuild and relocate factories and bases also used up irreplaceable resources—oil, steel, coal. And the manufacture of synthetics often cut into the shrinking food supply. Yet each day relatively free from air attack renewed hope among the people that the bombers could be driven off, even when the only factor in their favor was rain, wind, or a blinding overcast. On the fourth there were no B-29s over Japan, and only a few B-25s from Luzon over Kyushu. Even without aircraft as eyes over Kyushu, "Ultra" decrypts in the Philippines continued to track new units deploying there to defend against the expected invasion, some even from Manchuria, as if the Japanese still did not believe that the Soviets had any designs upon them. On the fourth, "Ultra" traced the 206th Division on the western coast as part of the Fortieth Army, and the arrival of the 216th and 303rd divisions. There was also a new 4th Artillery Command in Kyushu, and a new estimate of 560,000 troops on the island.

From Washington on the fourth, via the Joint Logistics Plans Committee, came a directive ordering the coordination of plans to supply the invasion of Kyushu, with a deadline to all commands to supply recommendations by August 10. The conquest of all of Kyushu, it emphasized, was not necessary to an operation intended to establish a forward base for staging and mounting "Coronet." If the Japanese moved into the central or northern hills, they could be kept useless without taking them prisoner. The goal was Kagoshima Wan and sufficient land around it for air bases. On July 31, General Stilwell's forces on Okinawa had come under MacArthur's command for "Olympic" as part of the coordinating effort. Army Air Force units were included—and both captured and new airfields on Okinawa were already overflowing with planes, as were those on smaller Iwo Jima.

•   •   •

Ambassador Sato, in Moscow, needed no decrypts to recognize that if the war were not already lost it would be over within days of the imminent Russian intervention. In his "Purple" code, which U.S. cryptanalysts using "Magic" read, he had been sending a constant flow of military intelligence to Tokyo. As early as mid-June he had been reporting on the hundreds of eastbound military trains seen traveling through Siberia carrying troops, self-propelled guns, Soviet and American tanks, heavy trucks, and loaded tank cars.

On August 4 he pleaded to Togo once more that the good offices of Russia were irrelevant: "The fact is undeniable that the 3-Power Declaration of July 26 already provides a basis for ending the Greater East Asia War. . . . If there is dillydallying by government and military in bringing this [Potsdam] resolution to fruition, then all Japan will be reduced to ashes. . . . It is already clear in advance as to what the peace terms will be, even without looking at the example of Germany, and we must resign ourselves beforehand to giving up a considerable number of war criminals." It was even necessary, Sato urged, "that these war criminals make the necessary sacrifice to save their country as truly patriotic warriors." One can guess that the Foreign Minister never showed Sato's cable to colleagues in the Cabinet.

As early as July 25, Togo had urged Sato to proceed, if necessary, "to a place of the Russians' choosing in order to obtain an interview with Molotov," and to suggest that Soviet mediation "would permit Stalin to acquire the reputation of an advocate of world peace." Further, if Japan's willingness "to meet fully the Russian demands in the Far East" still left the Soviets "indifferent to our request, we will have no choice but to consider other courses of action." Togo's message had not reached Sato for three days, long after "Magic" had intercepted it, but even so, another week had passed and the Japanese Foreign Ministry, despite its ambassador's nearly daily warnings, had considered no "other course of action." Paralysis had set in. There were other embassies and other neutral avenues by which to respond to the Potsdam ultimatum of the twenty-sixth. Minister Kase, in Switzerland, had tried his best on the twenty-ninth to turn Togo elsewhere. Ken Harada, at the Vatican, had also tried, unsuccessfully. Sato had even warned of the possibility of popular revolt at home—an empty threat. An American intelligence summary put the situation much as had all of Togo's advisers *outside* Japan: "Although Togo continues poised to follow what Sato once counseled as a course of desperation—'to fly into the arms of Russia,' he blindly refuses to accept the possibility that Russia might not be there to catch him."

An index to Japan's woes on a day when the home islands were spared the usual fire raids was the fate of the 11th Infantry Regiment, which was to be smuggled to Java from the Kai Islands, off southwestern New Guinea. There were more than 200,000 troops living precariously on bypassed islands. Since the hospital ship *Sea Truk* had completed a similar run successfully, evacuating 1,623 men of the 48th Division as patients, and even bringing along 1,929 cases of weapons and ammunition as "baggage," it had gone out again in humanitarian white, with medical markings and the same instructions for deception as before. But regimental officers were concerned about carrying the unit's flags aboard, and radioed before sailing, "Since it is not fitting to keep the regimental colors on the ship, please give your consideration to transporting them by air . . . to Surabaya."

The United States Navy, however, was also listening, and the next day, August 4, the *Sea Truk Hirose Maru* was boarded near Timor and all 1,500 hands, some wearing fake bandages, were taken into custody. That left 28,000 Japanese on the Lesser Sunda group still stranded. There were no longer enough subs for evacuation and supply missions. And in the vast Dutch Indies, from top to bottom, the Japanese had all of eighty planes left.

Both the U.S. Navy and the Army Air Force were chafing at the weather-induced inactivity. Service rivalries required that each demonstrate a maximum contribution to the defeat of Japan, as a surrender might come at any time. As if to handicap Halsey further, Nimitz ordered his task forces to concentrate on northern Honshu and Hokkaido, the unspoken intention to distract the Japanese home forces from the Russian buildup and to keep the fleet away from the 509th's projected B-29 activity to the south. It would take a day or two to turn the ships around. There were still some as close as the mouth of the Yangtze.

For Japanese defenders the seeming cessation of enemy activity was equally puzzling and frustrating. On the *I-58*, Commander Hashimoto's *kaitens* were pleading to be permitted to die honorably, but there were no targets to be found. On lower Kyushu, not far from Hiroshima, Corporal Yasuo Kuwahara waited impatiently for his culminating *kamikaze* mission. "Death was no longer my greatest fear. Waiting was my greatest fear. No hope now. I estimated that . . . surrender would still not take place for many months." He thought of suicide—"a painless little cut across the wrists"—as he found "nothing honorable in dying for a lost cause." But that, he rationalized, would be taking "the easy way—to escape the hard way." He prayed through the night and into the morning for a way out of dishonor, as there was no longer the means to "humiliate" the enemy. "God, send me an enemy plane. Don't make me wait here! Don't make me wait!"

For the ordinary Japanese villager or city dweller, news of the war still came by street corner radio loudspeaker—unless an air raid created instant facts or a lone B-29 dropped leaflets that citizens were urged not to read. There was little other newsprint—newspapers were skimpy, or had ceased publication—and the temptation was great. The government felt it necessary to literally answer the leaflets and, over NHK radio, broadcast a challenge that again suggested that someone in Tokyo had been reading MacArthur's plans for "Olympic."* Suicide pilots with wooden planes "would play a vital part in the forthcoming showdown battle of the Japanese mainland," NHK warned. "Calculation brings to light the fact that an army of 800,000 troops might be employed in the first wave of the enemy's proposed landing operations. . . . Japan is waiting for the enemy to come to her shores and when the enemy does come, Japan will unleash her full power, the power she is conserving now."

Flattering the Soviet Union, the broadcast predicted another Stalingrad, in which the formidable invader was held, then driven back, at great cost to both sides. The Russians, Tokyo Radio explained, had Asian blood. "Japan simply will not submit. The severe pounding which Germany received is no criterion as far as Japan is concerned. Orientals are made of sterner stuff." Yet the reality belied the boasts. As Iwane Kawanami expressed it wearily in a *tanka,*

> In a room streaked by faint morning light,
> I am dead tired with Tokyo still aflame in my eyes.

For the retreating troops in Burma, there was no waiting for evacuation or waiting for the enemy to strike. The enemy remained the in-

*Kagoshima Wan was arrived at by the Japanese in the same way as it had been chosen by the Americans—by eliminating the less satisfactory alternatives.

cessant downpours and swollen rivers, first the Sittang and its tribu-
taries and now, for Lieutenant Colonel Tetsujiro Tanaka of the Twenty-
eighth Army, the Shwegyin Chaung, north of Pegu. Even that wasn't
the last river he had to cross before reaching the comparative safety
of the Thai border. As he waited for his headquarters unit to catch
up, the dead arrived first, by the hundreds, hurtling down the river
like logs in a millstream. Eventually small bedraggled groups of survivors from the west bank emerged. One was Major Tatsumi Yamaguchi, who despite the lack of a uniform—he was in a loincloth, with
his bayonet scabbard swinging from his naked hips—looked like the
fellow officer who had helped find a boat days earlier to get their
commander across. Tanaka shouted across the roaring Shwegyin
Chaung. Yamaguchi waved recognition, plunged into the water, and
swam across to join the motley army Tanaka was collecting for the
next stage of the retreat. According to Louis Allen, chronicler of the
war, who pored through accounts of what the defeated realized was
the tragedy of the Japanese army in Burma,

> Tanaka thought he had already seen the extremes of suffer-
> ing in what was left of 53[rd] Division, but nothing like
> these tatterdemalions with rotting feet, calves swollen to
> elephantine size with beri-beri, eyes burning with fever,
> thighs dripping with the excrement of dysentery—some of
> them were still carrying rifles and ammunition hung from
> their belts. The thought of being near the end, of course,
> spurred them on. The alternative was to become like those
> white bones by the side of the path, with flies and bluebot-
> tles by the thousand swarming over them, and the vultures
> hovering over the fields, waiting to complete the task. Some
> of them had been wrapped in the Rising Sun flags, as a last
> tribute. But many simply lay there in putrefying uniforms,
> in such numbers that it was intolerable to go into the edge of
> the forest to rest or eat.

Farther north toward Toungoo, Colonel Tomotoki Koba tried to
keep his men moving west. They were sick, hungry, and nearly
naked. To remain was to die. He broke off a switch of green bamboo,
and each time he saw a soldier falter and drop out of the march he
chased after him shouting *"Aruke! Aruke!"*—"Keep moving! Keep
moving!" And Koba thrashed each straggler until the bamboo shred-

ded and he had to reach down for a sturdier stick. The Japanese had conducted death marches of Americans in the Philippines and of British and Commonwealth prisoners in Malaya. Now they had to turn on themselves to keep as many as possible alive.

As the *Augusta* plowed west across the Atlantic, Harry Truman was up at 5:30 to pace the decks for exercise, a seaman's cap on his head. His energy renewed, he was at his desk early to go over radioed reports and to prepare a speech he was planning to deliver about Potsdam on his return. He had done "practically a full day's work" by nine, said Charlie Ross, his secretary. At any moment, too, a message from Tinian might trigger in Washington his statement on the Bomb. That kept Truman near his telephone. He chafed at not being at hand in the White House.

In New York, on the twenty-ninth floor of the Time-Life Building at Forty-eighth Street and Rockefeller Plaza, Robert Sherrod, war correspondent with the Marines in the Pacific and author of the grim *Tarawa*, was pounding a typewriter for Henry Luce and writing more *(On to Westward)* about the cost of retaking coral atolls. He was impatient to get back, as he was on the approved press list for covering the invasion of Kyushu. Sherrod was pulling his draft of a cover story for *Time* on General LeMay from his typewriter "when we got word from Washington that a very big bomb was to be dropped on Japan two days later. My story was ditched and the project was turned over to the science writers."* Washington had always been as leaky as an old sieve. Now *Time* had a leak to match any in the war.

---

*The cover remained LeMay, but the story, titled "V.L.R. Man" (for "Very Long Range"), was moved several pages farther into the issue dated August 13 to furnish space for a "Birth of an Era" story illustrated by the "Atomic Bomb Plant" at Pasco, Washington.

# "SUFFERING THE INSUFFERABLE"

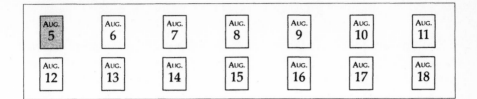

| AUG. 5 | AUG. 6 | AUG. 7 | AUG. 8 | AUG. 9 | AUG. 10 | AUG. 11 |
| AUG. 12 | AUG. 13 | AUG. 14 | AUG. 15 | AUG. 16 | AUG. 17 | AUG. 18 |

## CHAPTER XXIV

# · AUGUST 5, 1945 ·

*". . . not before the end of this war."*

An editorial page cartoon showed a caricature Japanese civilian with buck teeth reading the best-selling book about Jimmy Doolittle's April 18, 1942, raid, *Thirty Seconds Over Tokyo*, in the firebombed ruins of his neighborhood. He moans, hand to bandaged forehead, "Ah! Those were the good old days!" Doolittle now commanded the Eighth Air Force, based on Okinawa—a far more spacious and solid launching platform for his bombers than the carrier *Hornet* had been, and closer to Japan. With the typhoons now spent, B-29s were over the home islands again, 580 of them blasting—among other targets— four more of the thirty-one cities on the condemned list. Fourteen of the forewarned cities, some of them rather small, already had been struck. Saga, hit by the 468th Bombardment Wing, was only a prefectural capital on Kyushu. Ube, at the southern tip of Honshu, was even smaller, yet was targeted by 108 B-29s of the 315th Bombardment Wing because it was the site of a coal liquefaction plant that was one of the few sources of fuel still operating in Japan.

Ube had been hit by seventy-four aircraft on July 22 with only scattered damage. Hays Gamble's B-29 did not make the first raid but he was first to take off for the follow-up mission, his wing's thirteenth. This time, radar-bombing from 10,200 feet after dark, the B-29s lit up the sky with flaming oil. Dikes holding back the sea from the reclaimed land on which the installation was built were breached by five-hundred-pound bombs. The area flooded and the sprawling plant and storage tanks slipped into the Sua Sea. Photo-interpreters sent a reconnaissance photograph to Admiral Nimitz with a caption: "This target destroyed and sunk."

Sunday was just another day for planes and ships blasting and blockading Japan. Nimitz's ships held church services, and gunners worked afterward at target practice off the China coast until a few Japanese fighters appeared, dropped their bombs short when attacked, and ran for cover. Three were shot down. "It must have burned the Japs up," Seaman Fahey wrote, "to see us having practice in their own back yard." Some amateur strategists in the fleet saw the lack of aggressiveness as stockpiling for the invasion, others as clear shortages of combat craft. Respecting Japanese tenacity, no one ventured that the enemy had no fight left.

On Kyushu, Admiral Ugaki left at 4:00 P.M. from Oita to inspect the air base at Saeki, a twenty-minute flight south. To the admiral's surprise, the base on the shoreline overlooking the Bungo Suido had been attacked only twice. All its facilities but a barracks remained intact. "It was an extraordinary case in these days," he noted, "that they were still using regular buildings." He credited their good luck to the "bad air currents" over that part of the strait, but the relative freedom from attack made Saeki an excellent location, he thought, for stockpiling now-surplus training planes to be used as *kamikazes*. There were already suicide craft stationed there—one-man submarines. Tenth Special Attack Squadron commander Noboru Owada, a rear admiral, had one of the midget *Koryus* brought to a wharf to show Ugaki. "I wished him further efforts and success," Ugaki wrote; then he took off for Oita at 6:45. Skirting the Bungo, so much overflown by American aircraft, left him uneasy. "We couldn't relax at all and I acted as a lookout."

Worried that the United States could attack from almost any direction, as its naval forces were roaming the China Sea and could now operate as easily in the Japan Sea to the north—between Korea, the home islands, and the Vladivostok thumb of Siberia—the Japanese Naval General Staff altered its plans for *Okha* launch sites. Construction was hurriedly begun on the western coasts overlooking Tsushima Strait, between Korea and Kyushu, and the Tsugaru Strait, between upper Honshu and Hokkaido. Two of the three main entrances to the Japan Sea could be covered this way. The third, the Soya Strait, between northern Hokkaido and Sakhalin, overlooking Siberia, had to be left unfortified lest Russia construe a buildup there as a provocation. But the desperate program to set catapults in place was no evidence that the manned suicide bombs would really work.

The ordinary *kamikaze* also awaited deployment. Yasuo Kuwahara rose early on the fifth. He had been brooding over dying for nothing. Now, he remembered, "I wiped the sweat from my body, and began to pace the floor. I was seeing things in a different perspective. What did it matter how I died, just so I got it over with?" He walked around in the cool of the gray morning, then went back to bed barely in time to be awakened by reveille.

Kuwahara's orders came. He was to fly for the last time on August 8. Early on the sixth—the next morning—he would use a two-day pass to see his family in Hiroshima.

That afternoon, to a group of six hundred Army officers assigned to the Hiroshima garrison, Professor Yoshitaka Mimura of Hiroshima Bunri University, a theoretical physicist, was explaining the scientific possibilities of new weapons which might reverse what seemed inevitable. "Could you tell us, sir," a young lieutenant colonel asked, "what an atomic bomb is? Is there any possibility that the bomb will be developed by the end of this war?"

Mimura chalked a rough sketch on the blackboard to illustrate the chemical reactions required. Scientists at Tokyo University, he explained, have "theoretically penetrated" the secrets of nuclear fission. If they could apply their theories practically, an atomic bomb "could be even smaller than a piece of caramel candy, but, if exploded five hundred meters above a populated city, it could possibly destroy 200,000 lives."

"When can we have that bomb?"

"Well, it is difficult to say," Mimura answered, knowing nothing of any Japanese enterprise to apply fission theory to bomb-making. "But I can tell you this much: not before the end of this war."

Also in Hiroshima that afternoon, Captain Mitsuo Fuchida was involved in planning discussions for the defense of Kyushu. Fuchida, who had led the first wave over Pearl Harbor, would have been an admiral had his exploits since 1941 taken place in the United States Navy, but the Imperial Navy was rigid about seniority. Still, he was the service's ideas man, and while at Second Area Army headquarters he fielded a telephone call from the Navy chief of staff, Admiral Shinkazo Yano. Urgent business had arisen regarding the new underground naval headquarters being built at Nara to consolidate commands for *Ketsu-Go*. Admiral Jisaburo Ozawa was coming with engineering consultants.

Fuchida looked at his watch. It was only two. There was time to return to Yamato by dark. He preferred to get back to the organization of "Operation *Ken*," the planned suicide strike at the B-29 bases in the Marianas, which seemed more pressing, but he had, at the least, an excuse to leave Hiroshima. Fuchida asked his assistant, Lieutenant Toshio Hashizume, to remain, paid a courtesy call on Field Marshal Shinroku Hata, retrieved his gear at the hotel that housed the Navy delegation, and at 5:00 P.M. flew off alone in a three-seater plane. That privilege was itself a tribute to his prestige and perceived value.

Wherever Fuchida went, higher brass were struggling with the options, all of them unattractive, on how to fight the last battle. Fuel shortages were sinking the country into paralysis. Factories that had survived bombing were shutting down, and few planes were permitted to fly in order to preserve fuel for *Ketsu*. Japan had lost 90 percent of the freighter and tanker tonnage with which it had begun the war, as well as most ships turned out by its yards since.

One of the Allied commanders now registering victories after years of failure was being frustrated by similar shortages. From London, Lord Louis Mountbatten was trying to cope with the expanded mandate he had brought with him from Potsdam. Whether or not the Japanese would surrender, his forces were ordered to reoccupy much of Southeast Asia. From the Philippines, MacArthur's troops had jumped to Borneo, but were now to concentrate upon "Olympic" and Japan. Mountbatten's "Operation Zipper" had been planned to land troops in the lower Malayan harbors of Port Swettenham and Port Dickson in order to cut off the peninsula from Singapore. Yet diversion of resources to "Olympic" had starved Mountbatten's command of carriers and landing craft, putting off his landings until September 9. What Mountbatten had learned in Berlin required that his service chiefs convene in his absence to plan for the emergency occupation of Singapore and the acceleration of the takeover of POW camps—and to do so without additional resources. Whether the Japanese Southern Army would abide by a distant Tokyo surrender was anybody's guess.

On August 5 Mountbatten's deputies met at his forward headquarters at Kandy in the highlands of central Ceylon. If the war continued, they agreed, their D-Day could not be advanced. Only if the Japanese accepted surrender would landings have to be carried out to reoccupy the territories—and the risks even then required arrival in sufficient force. Once the necessary ships were available for that contingency, the loading of ammunition and stores would have to begin. If a surrender in Singapore had to be accepted in haste, a preliminary landing would be necessary at Penang, off northern Malaya, to furnish a naval and air staging area between Rangoon and Singapore. The distances were vast.

Mountbatten's deputies chose the 3rd Commando Brigade to land on Penang Island on August 26 as a preparatory move for D-Day if the war continued. But if Japan capitulated earlier than that, a force of Royal Marines would land on August 21—nothing could be put together any sooner—to conduct negotiations for surrender of the Japanese occupation garrison. Other Royal Marines would protect sealanes to Singapore by occupying Sabang Island, off the northern tip of Sumatra, at the top of the Strait of Malacca. A fleet would sail on to Singapore itself, if all went well, to negotiate its surrender on the twenty-seventh, landing two brigades of the 5th Division the next day.

Despite the complexities of the contingency plans and the increasing tension, Mountbatten was busy ingratiating himself with the new Labour government and enjoying London society. He had no plans to return to Kandy until August 14.

In London, too, another of the by-products of Potsdam was being played out. Although Justice Robert Jackson was in Washington, some of his staff had remained in England to negotiate with the British, French, and Russians a list of primary criminals to be put on trial that would satisfy each nation. Given Jackson's inadequacies as a diplomat and the special agendas of each nation—the Soviets were still insisting that industrialist Alfred Krupp be charged—it had been for the best that Jackson had only planned on returning to London on the ninth. His staff sent a list to SHAEF headquarters in Frankfurt on Sunday, August 5. The prisoners would need to be transferred to Nuremberg, where the once-grand Palace of Justice and its adjoining detention block were being refitted for the trials.

Chief criminal listed, to his satisfaction in Luxembourg, was Hermann Göring. He had insisted since his capture that Admiral Dönitz was only a Johnny-come-lately. But the trip to Nuremberg would have a price. His doctors were ordered to take him off paracodeine permanently before his departure.

If the war crimes proceedings were not a sign of return to normality, other aspects of German life were coming into place. In Berlin, mail service was restored in the American zone of Berlin—"Real mail, delivered by a real, official-looking mailman carrying a mailbag," Ruth Andreas-Friedrich wrote. "Also here and there, a mailwoman. The return of civilization continues." The challenge of obtaining an occupation postage stamp, however, remained acute. One could not affix the ubiquitous visage of Adolf Hitler to an envelope without an Allied overprint, although Rosemarie Hebek would receive a letter as late as November 26 with an unmarked *Führer* on a forty-two-mark stamp. It was her own. She had mailed the envelope to her mother on April 10, as Germany crumbled, and it was returned to her—Rosemarie's mother had fled to Hamburg—marked only *"zuruck"* ("return"). Hitler had traveled unscathed, however, through the efficient postal bureaucracy.

In Lübeck, Arthur Dickens assisted the return of civilization by confiscating "a particularly damnable book" by one of the *Führer*'s surrogates that he found planted in the display room of the British Information Office. It was, he noted,

> entitled *Vater aller Dinge, ein Buch des Krieges* ("Father of All Things, a Book of War"), by Kurt Eggers, and issued by the central publishing agency of the Nazi party. With this issue (1943) 360,000 copies had been printed. Even in Germany I believe no more impudent glorification of war as an end in itself has ever been published. The reader is throughout peppered with small, hard pellets of maxims, each one a gem of perverted imbecility.
>
> "The cannon thunder of war tears down the delusion of peace and the dream of beauty, and human beings who have proscribed war with their will, experience through war their conversion to a conscious existence."
>
> "The savagery of warlike reality has also its beauty! But not on account of this beauty alone should it be beloved, but

rather on account of its great educational possibilities for the soul."

"The more civilised and sluggish man becomes, the more the warrior-ideal loses its validity and attraction. In mere bourgeois times the warrior counts as barbaric, uncultured and destructive."

"The barbarians always enter into the inheritance of peoples collapsing under their tired civilisation."

At Farm Hall in England, the physicists still held incommunicado worried about the effect of their having dealt with alleged scientists whom "Hitler made" professors, and about the Potsdam communiqué, which caused alarm and then despondency. The loss of the war now meant the loss to Poland and Russia of provinces historically German. "At any rate," said Heisenberg, "it would have been infinitely worse if we had won the war."* Bagge was convinced that they were being held until British and American scientists could "imitate our experiments." In particular the physicists thought the West wanted to go through their "secret papers" on nuclear reactor research in order to develop the "uranium machine" the Germans claimed to have been on the edge of achieving when the war turned badly. The wartime possibility of both Nazi and British spies had worried Gerlach and Heisenberg. A former Hitler Youth leader with a doctorate had created anxiety at Hechingen. "I mistrusted him," said Gerlach, "and didn't let him see anything." Heisenberg "understood" Gerlach's suspicion of another scientist suspected of being a British Secret Service contact. They had agreed then that the man "be told nothing about the uranium business."

"Little Boy," its U-235 sphere in a cordite charge, was loaded into the bomb bay of B-29 number 82 on the afternoon of August 5, Marianas time. Its uranium content in a cylinder weighing over 9,000 pounds was about 50 kilograms, or 110 pounds. It was no twin of the Trinity—a prototype "Fat Man"—device exploded at Alamogordo, which used an almost-critical uranium-tamped sphere of plutonium that was to

*In 1947, however, at the Oxford home of a German-Jewish physicist, Heisenberg reportedly said, "If only the Nazis had been left to go on for just fifty years, then they too would have become decent." (N. Kurti, *TLS*, June 18, 1993)

be compressed by spherically converging shock waves produced by a cordite explosive. Nothing like "Little Boy" had ever been tested.

When Captain Robert A. Lewis went out to look at the historic activity going on about *his* plane, he found a GI putting the finishing touches to foot-high letters painted beneath the pilot's window: ENOLA GAY.

"What the hell is *that* doing on *my* plane?" he yelled. The painter explained that the orders came from Colonel Tibbets, and Lewis went off to complain. But Lewis was to be aboard only as co-pilot. Tibbets commanded the 509th and he had chosen himself for the mission. He had rank, and history, on his side, having flown what was claimed as the first plane to bomb North Africa for Eisenhower in support of "Torch," and the first B-17 to cross the Channel to bomb Germany. The only other person on the flight who could give orders was "Deak" Parsons, who commanded the scientific team on Tinian.

Parsons was busy. He had checked out the arming problem in the assembly hangar. Once "Little Boy" was winched into the bomb bay and before the B-29 was gassed up, he wanted to make sure he could perform the same operation with the plane in flight. He squeezed in behind the bomb and practiced alone, with hand tools and a flashlight. The heat was oppressive. Farrell came by to check, and found Parsons happy with the result but nursing hands black from graphite lubricant and bleeding from the sharp-edged parts. Farrell offered to lend him a pair of pigskin gloves.

"I wouldn't dare," said Parsons. "I've got to feel the touch." And he joked, perhaps with an edge of guilt in his choice of words, that he would have to bomb Japan with "dirty hands."

At 7:17 P.M. Farrell cabled Groves, in Washington, "Judge"—the code name for Parsons—"to load bomb after takeoff."

The loading crew in the bomb hangar winched "Little Boy" onto a transport dolly made for "pumpkin" casings and covered it with a tarpaulin. Army Signal Corps photographers followed each step. On tracks, the dolly was wheeled to a loading pit thirteen feet by sixteen feet across and nine feet deep. A hydraulic lift rose to take the uranium bomb, and the crew wheeled the dolly away, rotated the cylinder of dull, blackened steel on the lift, and lowered it into the pit to remain until it was hoisted aboard. The bomb—a trash can with fins, one of the crew called it—was ten and a half feet long and twenty-nine inches in diameter, with a boxy tail and a flat, rounded nose. It weighed 9,700 pounds.

While Parsons had tinkered in the bomb bay, plutonium casing F33 was being prepared in the assembly hangar. For a test drop of "Fat Man" it would pack explosives similar to the real thing but with a concrete rather than a nuclear core. If all went well, F31 would be loaded with a plutonium core once "Dimples eight-two"—the radio designation for the *Enola Gay* had not changed with its new name— had deployed its bomb. Scientists on Tinian watched the dry run just offshore through binoculars, awaiting the explosion just about two thousand feet above the water. Nothing happened. Wires had pulled out of their sockets on the aircraft. Parsons would have more work to do. There was only one plutonium core available.

Few if any of the crews could nap, as recommended, after dinner. Major Thomas Ferebee, who had been bombardier for Tibbets from the start and was to drop the Bomb, played poker with Theodore "Dutch" Van Kirk, the navigator, who had taken two sleeping pills that hadn't worked. According to the 509th's Operations Order 35, the weather crews' briefing would be at 11:00 and the "Special Briefings" at 11:30, with "General Briefing" at midnight. Crews were reminded to pack pistols and survival gear. The Twentieth Air Force would have no other missions scheduled for the same time period but would provide a limited air-sea rescue service. Because of the expected hazards, no planes except those on the mission were to approach within fifty miles of the possible targets from four hours before the strike to six hours after its completion, even for rescue purposes. At 12:15—a new day now—Parsons introduced a Lutheran chaplain who offered a prayer on behalf of all the crews that "armed with Thy strength may they bring this war to a rapid end."

The preflight supper was sausage and eggs. At 1:37 the three weather planes and the Iwo Jima standby, *Straight Flush* (Hiroshima), *Jabbit III* (Kokura), *Full House* (Nagasaki), and *Top Secret* (Iwo), began taking off from North Field, missing the historical fuss that began at two. The runway on which the *Enola Gay* sat was suddenly floodlit. Motion picture and still cameramen poised to record the crews in their flight coveralls, as if they were returning from a triumph rather than anticipating one. It was General Groves who had ordered the Hollywood premiere setting. A civilian scientist looking on called it a drugstore opening. The only thing not photographed was the Bomb.

The group shot of the *Enola Gay*'s crew included only the ten regulars from the 509th, officers standing behind the kneeling enlisted men. Parsons refused to be photographed, and his ordnance expert,

First Lieutenant Morris R. Jeppson, loyally stood with him on the sidelines. In front of the nosewheel stood Tibbets, Lewis, Ferebee, and Van Kirk, with Sergeant Robert Caron, the tail gunner; First Lieutenant Jacob Beser, the electronics technician; Private Richard R. Nelson, the radio operator; Staff Sergeant Wyatt Duzenbury, the flight engineer, elderly at thirty-two (Tibbets was only thirty); Sergeant Robert H. Shumard, the assistant engineer; and Sergeant Joseph Stiborik, the radar operator.

In twenty minutes the photographers were gone, and by 2:27 Duzenbury had started all four engines. Crews clambered aboard the three planes, scheduled to leave two minutes apart. At 2:45 Tibbets began to roll, gathering speed. He needed to reach 180 miles an hour, and used almost every yard of the 2 miles of oiled and crushed coral on Runway A. All of it was necessary. While Number 82, with the Bomb, carried only 7,000 gallons of fuel, 400 less than the others because of its 9,700 pounds of bomb and a twelve-man crew, it was flying overweight at sixty-five tons. Every mile of its northwest-by-north course would lighten it, but *Enola Gay*'s range was shortened by the undersupply.

By 2:52 they were flying at a steady 4,700 feet to keep the temperature tolerable in the unpressurized and unheated bomb bay. Parsons felt confident now about arming the Bomb and tapped Tibbets on the shoulder to announce, "We're starting." Then he crawled into the frigid bay with Jeppson, who shouted over the engine roar, "Put on your gloves!" Parsons shook his head. For the balding, forty-four-year-old "weaponeer," as he called his trade, his concession to the cold was a baseball cap.

Jeppson held a flashlight and handed Parsons, one by one, his tools. First he checked that the three three-inch-long plugs that blocked the firing signal to prevent accidental detonation were secure. Then he unscrewed the rear plate that concealed the armor covering the cannon breech and wrenched out the breech plug. He inserted the four sections of cordite that would fire the U-235 home, and replaced the breech plug and the plates after connecting the firing line. Both men rechecked the external circuitry, retrieved their tools, and returned to their monitor box in the forward cabin. Until landfall neared they had no duties except to watch the monitor for possible malfunction.

Leaving the controls to Lewis, who put down the letter he was writing to his mother, Tibbets crawled through the narrow, padded tunnel to the crew compartment in the waist of the plane and tried to nap, but his brain refused. When he gave up and headed back, Sergeant Robert Caron moved down to chat, and Tibbets asked if any of them knew what they were really carrying. "A chemist's nightmare," Caron suggested.

"Not exactly," said Tibbets.

"A physicist's nightmare," Caron tried.

Tibbets gave him the same answer, and got up to return to his cabin. Caron had been teased too much, however, and tugged at the pilot's foot as it was disappearing down the thirty-foot crawl space. "Colonel," Caron asked, in a last try, "are we splitting atoms today?"

"That's about it," said Tibbets. He decided to go back to his intercom and end the suspense.

Lewis, in his co-pilot's seat, was continuing his letter to his mother and letting "George"—the automatic pilot—fly the plane at five thousand feet, which conserved fuel by not permitting the B-29 to lift its weight of fuel and bomb higher. The "letter to mother" was actually a journal that William L. Laurence, *The New York Times* science writer, had asked Lewis to keep. Laurence's presence aboard had been scratched because of alleged weight limitations. But Lewis, while concealing his journal as something else, cautiously began by omitting any reference to Parsons and Jeppson.

The run over the waves and through the brightening sky was routine, and a reporter for *Yank*, Yeoman Second Class Robert Schwartz, who had a look inside the plane later, wrote that the crew "read, ate, talked a little, and said little more historic than 'Move over, you bastard, and give me some room.' " He also noted the souvenirs aboard from their training base at Wendover Field, Utah:

> Occasionally they consulted various charms and talismans, of which the *Enola Gay* had an inordinate number. These included the following items: Three pairs of silk panties from Omaha, stowed in one corner with a booklet on VD. One picture of Wendover Mary, a group companion during training in Utah—Wendover Mary had on [nothing but] a pair of high-heeled shoes. One Good Conduct ribbon, fastened on the radio set. . . . Six prophylactic kits, presented by the ground crew in case of forced landing in territory "where the natives are friendly." One ski cap, purchased in Salt Lake City and worn by [Sergeant] Stiborik. One picture of the lobby of the Hotel Utah at Salt Lake. One lipstick kiss

print on the [plane's] nose, signed "Dottie" and bearing a
dateline, "Omaha, one time," placed there by a civilian girl
who worked at an Omaha air base; it had been shellacked
over promptly for permanence and was the source of the
crew's common prayer, "Omaha, one more time."

These things were a binding force to the men of the *Enola
Gay*. A series of good drunks together in the States had helped
weld them into a unit, and they were all very close friends.

At 4:55 Japan time, an hour earlier than they had set their watches
on Tinian, they rendezvoused at 9,300 feet over Iwo Jima with the
laboratory and photo planes, the *Enola Gay* taking the lead at the angle in the *V*. Major Charles W. Sweeney flew *The Great Artiste*, with
three scientists aboard, as the instrument ship; Captain George Marquardt's unchristened Number 91 was equipped with a battery of
cameras. At 3:30 there had been a late moon in the east; now the sun
was up and brightening. The weather looked good for any target
in Japan.

At 6:30 Jeppson slipped back into the bomb bay and exchanged the
green plugs for live red ones, activating the Bomb's internal batteries.
At the console box, Parsons confirmed that the arming was complete
and told Tibbets that it was "final." Overhearing the conversation,
Lewis jotted down in his letter to Mother: "The bomb was now independent of the plane. It was a peculiar sensation. I had a feeling the
bomb had a life of its own now that had nothing to do with us."

Over the intercom as they approached landfall Tibbets warned
the crew that all talk on the communication systems would be
recorded: "This is for history, so watch your language. We're carrying the first atomic bomb."

At 7:15, as the three B-29s were climbing from a cruising altitude
(since Iwo) of 26,000 feet to the planned drop altitude of 31,600 feet,
the weather planes began reporting in. From Major Claude Eatherly's*
*Straight Flush*, over Hiroshima, came "Cloud cover less than three-
tenths and at all altitudes. Advice: bomb primary [target]."

Five minutes later they sighted the coastline. At 8:09 Japan time
Tibbets signaled Sweeney, "Chuck, it's Hiroshima."

• • •

---

*A postwar alcoholic and drifter, Eatherly misidentified himself as "the Hiroshima pilot" who
dropped the Bomb, and blamed his problems, which preceded his service in the 509th, on a
prolonged guilt trip.

Early on the morning of August 6, Corporal Kuwahara burst into the orderly room at his air base to pick up his two-day pass. He had applied to visit his family in Hiroshima for the last time but the night before had decided that it would be too emotionally wrenching. He changed his mind.

Since he had been expected to sign for his pass the evening before, he had to date his signature August 5. He thanked the sergeant and left. "Moments later I had hooked a ride in an army truck headed for Hiroshima. . . . I should have known that the pull of home would be too great. . . . I had almost forgotten the magic of early mornings. Suddenly I was very happy. . . . Two golden days. Perhaps when they ended I could accept death."

He jumped from the truck on the outskirts of Hiroshima at about 7:30 and took a streetcar. Before leaving for the suburb of Onomichi he wanted to visit a friend at Second Army headquarters, and after a short ride he hopped off and began walking along Shiratori Street. Vendors had already opened for business and he stopped to buy an orange. Farther on, noting his Air Force uniform, a wrinkled old woman stopped him. Her voice was raspy. "Please tell me the truth," she asked. "Why is it that I no longer see Japanese planes in the sky? Tell me the truth, young man."

Her face, Kuwahara thought, was like a dried apple. He could not be evasive. He laid his hand on her shoulder and looked away from her blinking eyes. "Old mother," he said, "there are few planes left. Before long it will be all over and we won't have to hide from the bombs anymore." Her bony hand closed on his, and they parted.

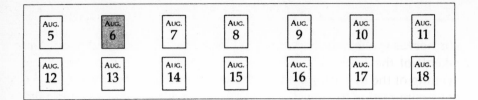

| Aug. 5 | Aug. 6 | Aug. 7 | Aug. 8 | Aug. 9 | Aug. 10 | Aug. 11 |
|---|---|---|---|---|---|---|
| Aug. 12 | Aug. 13 | Aug. 14 | Aug. 15 | Aug. 16 | Aug. 17 | Aug. 18 |

## CHAPTER XXV

# . AUGUST 6, 1945 .

*". . . the greatest thing in history."*

Just before his fourth day at sea, President Truman left the sunny "front porch" of the *Augusta,* cruising southwest just below Newfoundland, to lunch with some of the crew. He was seated in the after mess and just tucking into his tray when Captain Frank Graham slipped in and handed him a message from Secretary Stimson together with a map of Japan. A red circle was drawn around Hiroshima. "Big bomb dropped on Hiroshima August 5 at 7:15 P.M. Washington time," Truman read. "First reports indicate complete success which was even more conspicuous than earlier test."*

"I was greatly moved," Truman recalled. "I telephoned Byrnes aboard ship to give him the news and then said to the group of sailors around me, 'This is the greatest thing in history. It's time for us to get home.'"

•　•　•

*Stimson's hasty radiogram included a significant technical error. The uranium bomb had not been tested earlier. (The Alamogordo device employed plutonium.)

His nerves frayed from waiting once he had been informed about the takeoff of the *Enola Gay*, General Groves, in Washington, spent the evening of the fifth pacing up and down in the vicinity of his desk, finally committing the unprecedented act of rolling up his sleeves, taking off his tie, and loosening his collar. Groves was not the unbuttoned type. At 11:30 the strike message had arrived under the signature of Deak Parsons. Waiting for details, Groves settled into a restless sleep on a cot in his office, until a long coded cable came in at 4:30 A.M. At 6:58, having finished a two-page report for General Marshall, he was waiting in Marshall's Pentagon office when the Chief of Staff arrived, and the pair rang up Secretary Stimson at Highhold on a secure scrambler telephone. Stimson ordered release of the presidential statement and asked them to radio the *Augusta*.

Marshall cautioned Groves to look over the Bomb statement again before release, to make sure that there was no element of gloating in it, given the certainty of large Japanese casualties. "I replied," Groves recalled in his memoirs, "that I was not thinking so much of those casualties as I was about the men who had made the Bataan death march."

Ten minutes after Truman read the first radiogram from Washington, Captain Graham returned with a follow-up message:

Following info regarding Manhattan received. "Hiroshima bombed visually with only one tenth [cloud] cover at 052315A. There was no fighter opposition and no flak. Parsons reports 15 minutes after drop as follows: 'Results clear cut and successful in all respects. Visible effects greater than in any test. Conditions normal in airplane following delivery.' "

Truman understood that the crew in the mess hall knew that something big had happened. Tapping a glass with a fork, he signaled for silence, then told them that a powerful new bomb, using an explosive charge "twenty thousand times as powerful as a ton of TNT," had been dropped on Japan. Abandoning his tray, he hurried off clutching his two messages and with the cheers of the sailors ringing, to the ship's wardroom, where he told officers at lunch about the Bomb. "Mr. Truman almost ran as he walked about the ship spreading the news," Merriman Smith wrote, observing "the broad, proud smile on his face." Waving the two pieces of paper, "he saw the quick end of the war between the lines."

The *Augusta* was one day out of Newport News, Virginia. Truman listened to the reading of his own message on the ship's radio, broadcast at 11:00 A.M. from Washington:

> Sixteen hours ago an American airplane dropped one bomb on Hiroshima, an important Japanese Army base. That bomb had more power than 20,000 tons of T.N.T. . . . The Japanese began the war from the air at Pearl Harbor. They have been repaid many fold. And the end is not yet. . . .
>
> It is an atomic bomb. It is a harnessing of the basic power of the universe. The force from which the sun draws its power has been loosed against those who brought war to the Far East. . . .
>
> We are now prepared to obliterate more rapidly and completely every productive enterprise the Japanese have above ground in any city. We shall destroy their docks, their factories, and their communications. Let there be no mistake; we shall completely destroy Japan's power to make war.
>
> It was to spare the Japanese people from utter destruction that the ultimatum of July 26 was issued at Potsdam. Their leaders promptly rejected that ultimatum. If they do not now accept our terms they may expect a rain of ruin from the air, the like of which has never been seen on this earth. Behind this air attack will follow sea and land forces in such numbers and power as they have not yet seen and with the fighting skill of which they are already well aware.

The message was tough and in no manner exaggerated. Yet such was the Bomb's awesome impact that the warning was heard in Japan before anyone left alive in Hiroshima was really certain what had happened. And no one, in the shock of the Bomb, would have thought of the irony of the choice of Hiroshima as target, despite Truman's reference to Pearl Harbor. It was from Admiral Isoroku Yamamoto's flagship *Nagato*,* anchored in Hiroshima Bay, that Yamamoto had overseen by radio the attack on Pearl Harbor, and it was in Hiroshima Bay that the Hawaii strike force dropped anchor on homecoming, on December 23, 1941. When Paul Tibbets, now pilot of the *Enola Gay* over Hiroshima, had heard the news of Pearl Harbor on

---

*Yamamoto was now dead, ambushed and shot down in 1943; his battleship was a grounded hulk in Tokyo Bay.

his A-20's radio, flying back to Savannah from maneuvers in North Carolina, his B-29 Superfortress had been only a design on a drawing board. "Little Boy," his sole cargo, had been only a concept of a committee of scientists on a Saturday morning in Washington the day before Pearl Harbor. Like Tibbets, Curtis LeMay, then a captain, had first heard of Pearl Harbor on his radio when returning from a training exercise. No one had planned it that way, but the bill presented at Pearl Harbor was being paid in full at Hiroshima.

At 8:15.17 on Tibbets's watch the aiming point came up—the slender branches of the Ota River and the Aioi Bridge. With Ferebee's "Bombs away!" signal the bay opened. Forty-three seconds later, with the *Enola Gay* at 31,600 feet and racing away from the impact point in a 155-degree turn to the right, "Little Boy" erupted 1,890 feet above Hiroshima like a thousand rising suns. The plane had lurched upward with the lightening of its load; it shuddered again in the shock wave, then trembled in the echo effect. "I think this is the end of the war," said Tibbets to Lewis. "Bingo!" Private Nelson radioed to Tinian. "Flash followed by two slaps on plane. Huge cloud," Parsons noted in his terse log.

The two observer B-29s had been laying back so far that few on the ground realized that more than a single aircraft flew overhead. Some saw only two. From *The Great Artiste* an instrument package drifted down, suspended from a parachute. Monitoring the sensors was Luis Alvarez, later a Nobel laureate in physics. On December 7, 1941, he had been working at MIT on radar research. "I decided not to wear a parachute," Alvarez remembered; "If we were shot down, I didn't want to be captured." For half of the time the Bomb was falling, his plane was in its two-G turn, but he kept his eyes on the calibration pulses that indicated that his plummeting equipment was working. "Suddenly a bright flash lit the compartment, the light from the explosion reflecting off the clouds in front of us. . . . A few moments later two sharp shocks slammed the plane. . . . We left our cramped quarters and looked out the window for the first time over Japan. . . . I looked in vain for the city that had been our target. The cloud seemed to be rising out of a wooded area devoid of population. My friend and teacher Ernest Lawrence* had expended great energy . . . building the machines that separated the

*Lawrence, with Lyman J. Briggs, Arthur Holly Compton, Vannevar Bush, and James Bryant Conant, had been on the Washington committee that had met the day before Pearl Harbor on President Roosevelt's injunction that if atomic bombs could be made, the United States could not afford to be second.

U235 for the Little Boy bomb. I thought the bombardier had missed the city by miles—had dumped Ernest's precious bomb out in the empty countryside. . . . Sweeney shortly dispelled my doubts. The aiming had been excellent, he reported; Hiroshima was destroyed."

Van Kirk, in the *Enola Gay*, saw "a pot of boiling black oil" below the turbulent, fiery pillar and bubbling expanding mushroom; to Caron, watching the target recede from the plane's tail, "it looked like lava or molasses covering the whole city." They would discover later that the aiming point was missed by only eight hundred feet. The shaft of fire and smoke seemed to push the mushroom violently higher, reaching fifty thousand feet. Only when they were 363 miles away, racing home, did they lose sight of it.

For the journal that Robert Lewis pretended was a letter home, the *Enola Gay*'s co-pilot looked away from the destruction and wrote, "My God, what have we done?"

Fifteen minutes after the flash, Captain Masatake Okumiya received a telephone call from Kure. Okumiya, in charge of homeland air defense, was deep in the second underground level of Navy headquarters at Kasumigazki, Koji-machi, Tokyo. It had become the communications center after the firestorm of May 27 destroyed the Navy Department. Air Defense Command at Kure was reporting "a terrible flash* over Hiroshima," which was twelve miles away. "Immediately afterward a terrible mushroomlike cloud rose into the sky over the city. Many of the people here heard a heavy roar, something like distant thunder." It must have been "something big," Commander Hiroki said, but he had been unable to reach Second Army Group headquarters by phone.

"Do you know if it was an air raid," Okumiya asked, "or some other explosion on the ground?"

"I don't know what it was. Only a few B-29s were seen, that is all."

Okumiya queried members of the Naval General Staff, but no one had any answers. Then he telephoned Captain Yasukado Yasui of the Naval Bureau of Aeronautics and repeated the few details he had learned from Kure. Yasui's reply was "staggering," Okumiya remembered clearly: "It may be an atomic bomb, but I can't tell until I actually look at the city."

---

*The "flash" of the explosion would go into the language as *pika,* the Japanese term thereafter for "atomic burst."

There was no way to get near Hiroshima until the next day. Until then Okumiya gleaned whatever information he could. Just before noon he heard again from Kure. An eyewitness had reported that just after two B-29s had passed over Hiroshima at high altitude "there was a searing flash, like a fantastic burst of lightning. It was followed by a sudden, roaring sound. In the next instant houses collapsed all across the city. . . . Fires broke out everywhere. Everything is all confused. The raging flames and the streams of refugees have made it impossible to get in touch with any place closer than Kaidaichi [five miles southeast]."

It took longer for a report to reach Tokyo from Satoshi Nakamura, a reporter for the Dōmei Agency. He had been eating breakfast with a friend in Rakurakuen, eight miles from the city, when all the windows to the east, facing Hiroshima, shattered. He was thrown to the floor. Recovering, he ran outside and saw a pillar of smoke rising, at the top of which was a ball of red flame. He thought of the blossoming of a giant flower.

With his reporter's instincts he jumped on a bicycle, but as he reached the town of Itsukaichi he was buffeted by a strong wind and a downpour of heavy rain mixed with what seemed to be sand and dust. His fingers, gripping the handlebars, were stained black. Abandoning the bicycle he began to walk, and after half an hour of black rain the storm ceased suddenly and the sky turned summery blue. At the village of Hara, on the outskirts of Hiroshima, the Japan Broadcasting Company had a transmitter surrounded by rice paddies. As he approached it he encountered thousands of people staggering north, away from the city, bleeding, burned, blackened, nearly naked. Another throng, clothed and uninjured, was rushing toward the city, shouting names of relatives and friends they were seeking.

Inside the station he found everything dead but a single telephone line to the Okayama transmitter, ninety miles west of Kobe. He pleaded as a Dōmei representative to use the telephone and dictated what he thought had happened from the devastation he had seen across the flat, nearly featureless land. "At about 8:16 A.M., 6 August, one or two enemy planes flew over Hiroshima and dropped one or two special bombs (they may have been atomic), completely destroying the city. Casualties are estimated at one hundred seventy thousand dead." It was 11:20 A.M.

Nakamura's assumptions were accurate, although he had overestimated the dead, guessing that half the population, including military personnel (about ninety thousand), had been killed. The Second Army, responsible for all of western and southern Japan, had its operations section close to the epicenter. Many of its officers died in the blast. Soldiers in the garrison at Mount Futaba were largely spared, but Second Army headquarters was no longer in any position to oversee the defense of lower Japan. Although Harry Truman had written in his diary in Potsdam that the Bomb would be dropped against a "purely military target," it would have been hard to find another in Japan that was not already hit. As in most Japanese cities, war-related activities went on adjacent to residential neighborhoods. In Hiroshima the aiming point of the Aioi Bridge was flanked by the Fukuya department store and the purely military Hiroshima Castle. Not only was the city now a military headquarters second only to Tokyo (which was responsible for upper Japan through the First Army), an assembly area for troops, a communications center, and a commercial harbor, it was the main port of embarkation for China. Yet because it lacked heavy industry it was never high in priority for advanced antiaircraft weapons and its old-fashioned guns had little cause to be fired. To the three hundred thousand civilians in the area the few silvery bombers that appeared overhead were *B-sans*, the *san* a respectful suffix for the awesome, high-flying bird.

For Honolulu-born Tosh Kano, the war had begun when he was drafted out of engineering school in Tokyo to fight in China. A third of his unit had died, but he had returned for officers' training and was in Tokyo, on his way to the Army Engineering Academy, when he saw the first bulletins posted about Pearl Harbor. Released in March 1945 because of ill health, he was back in Hiroshima, where he had a wife, a daughter, and an infant son. Walking to the barracks of the local Fire Protection Brigade, where he now worked, he was quick to warn a group of giggling girls on their way to high school that an air raid alarm had sounded at twenty-five minutes after midnight and another (triggered by Claude Eatherly's weather plane) less than an hour before. It was still in effect. "We are very sorry," they chorused. *"Gomen-nasai."* Looking up as he heard the hum of a plane, he saw a high-flying B-29 release "something shining like a parachute." It appeared to be a leaflet drop: he had not seen "Little Boy" fall from another plane. "Be careful, girls," Kano admonished. Late now for duty, he hurried through an underpass toward the barracks.

Hiroko Nakamoto had heard the news of Pearl Harbor at

school in Hiroshima, connecting America only with a song she had learned about a celluloid doll. In sixth grade then, she was now, under war conditions, a working girl, hurrying to a factory job. Alerts through the nights had kept her awake; she was groggy from lack of sleep. From beneath half-closed lids she saw a blinding light—"as if someone had taken a flashbulb picture a few inches from my eyes. There was no pain. Only a stinging sensation, as if I had been slapped hard in the face. I tried to open my eyes. But I could not. Then I lost consciousness."

Tosh Kano "felt" the flash as he emerged from the underpass; then a pressure wave pushed through the tunnel that had shielded him. Jolted forward—"just like a strong wind coming out of a narrow passage"—he was blown into a drainage ditch. His cap, glasses, and briefcase scattered. Instinctively he lay low and covered his face with his hands. Raising his head to look around, he saw a whirlwind of debris. A "ball of pinkish fire" sizzled through the underpass, and again he flattened himself into the ditch. As it passed he smelled a strong, gassy odor. He could see nothing through the black cloud that crawled along the ground. In the darkness he heard people crying in pain, calling for help.

Just after Corporal Yasuo Kuwahara had parted from the old woman with the dried-apple face, he heard air raid sirens and saw a single B-29. It could, he thought, "meander at will like a grazing animal." When he was less than half a mile from Second Army headquarters he saw a tiny speck separate itself from the plane, and a minute later "a monstrous, multi-colored flash bulb" went off in his face. A "fierce flood of heat" struck him, slamming him to the ground. The pressure and the roar had "the fantastic power of earthquakes, avalanches, winds and floods." He awoke pinned under debris and tried to wriggle out. In "a frog's croak," he cried for help. The situation for him, he realized, was an irony: "A suicide pilot dying on the ground, only a short distance from his home."

Six hours later voices wearing white, he thought, lifted the boards and broken tiles to let him out, then vanished. "Don't go," he cried. "We must," came the answer. "Hiroshima is in ruins—everyone dead or dying." The blurred figures faded.

Kuwahara stood, swaying, until his vision cleared. A black rain was settling. Shiratori Street was buried under the debris of houses that looked like "trampled strawberry boxes." Bodies were scattered everywhere. Fires burned. Nearby he saw a concrete water trough "about the size of an office desk." The water had evaporated and it was full of ash, but he had fallen at its base, protected from the searing blast that carbonized many in the street. He listened to the wailing of the blistered and burned living. Bodies turned hideous were falling apart. A woman it turned his stomach to see mumbled in a "dry buzz" he could make out as "Kill me! Kill me!"

An hour later he had stumbled as far as the Yamanaka Girls' High School. Wailing hysterically, a few parents who had survived were examining bodies charred beyond recognition for pendants or other identification. He held his stomach and vomited. Going on, he spotted an army truck that had brought men to assess the damage. He called, but his remnants of uniform were unrecognizable. A second truck passed, went on, then backed up for him. They crossed the Ota, where he watched a mass of "throbbing blotches" sprawled along the riverbank to cool themselves. Many had collapsed, face down, and floated downstream. What was left of Hiroshima faded in a crimson haze as he was borne away.

Novelist Yōko Ōta, whose wartime writings, such as *Daughter of Battle*, pulsated with patriotic enthusiasm, was asleep under her mosquito netting. The air raid alert had been lifted at seven; she had returned groggily to bed in the northeast suburb of Hakushima Kuken-cho. On the day of Pearl Harbor she had felt like "a fresh new flame"; now she thought she was dreaming of being "enveloped by a blue flash, like lightning at the bottom of the sea. . . . With an indescribable sound, almost like a roll of thunder, like a huge boulder tumbling down a mountain, the roof of the house came crashing down. When I came to, I was standing there, dazed, in a cloud of dust. . . . Yet there was no flame, no smoke. And I was alive. . . . I looked about dazedly, half expecting to see my dead body stretched out."

All her furniture and belongings, from the twelve pieces of luggage packed for the countryside to the three thousand books in the library, were gone; there was only a small mound of broken roof tiles. "Of the mosquito net and even of the bed, there was not the slightest trace. . . . Outside, as far as the eye could see—which was much farther than usual—there stretched ruined house after ruined house." Her sister Nakagawa materialized, white dress covered with blood and face swollen like a pumpkin. Yōko looked at her own kimono. It was drenched in blood from shoulder to waist.

They stumbled to the cemetery just past the board fence beyond the garden. The fence was gone, as were the shrines. A lone *torii* stood gauntly, and blood-soaked survivors sat expressionless on grave-stones. Thin wisps of smoke began to issue from the flattened buildings. Yōko's mother handed her Nakagawa's baby. It was still asleep.

Fleeing Hiroshima, Ōta, who had taken her pen name from the area's most striking feature, its river and delta, made her way back to Kushima, the village in the hinterlands to the west where she was born Hatsuko Fuchida in 1903, and where now she would write *City of Corpses*.

Closer to the blast center, Hiroko Nakamoto lay inside a shattered house; she had no idea how she had got there. Dazed and in shock, she began stumbling down a ruined street. The air was heavy "with a sickening odor." She saw bodies everywhere. A stalled streetcar was filled with dead people. She passed a miraculously unscathed woman. "She looked at me, then turned away with a gasp of horror. I wondered why. I felt as if one side of my face was detached, and did not belong to me. I was afraid to touch it with my hand."

People who could walk through the nightmare were moving toward the river—"burned people with clothes in shreds or no clothes at all, men and women covered with blood, crying children." The wooden bridge she crossed every day to her factory was afire. Hiroko stopped. For the first time she looked at her body. It was a mass of burns from the ankles up. "I realized that the left side of my face must be burned, too. . . . Not pink, but yellow. The flesh was hanging loose. I went down to the water's edge and tried to put the skin back with salt water from the river, as I saw others doing."

In the Minami-machi district, Mrs. Shinobu Hizume was hanging the family laundry to dry on her wooden balcony when a blinding flash—on a clear, hot morning—seemed to sear her eyeballs. Her body felt as if an electric current was running through it. Suddenly she was intensely hot, and her hair crackled with fire. She ran inside and rolled on a tatami mat to smother the flames, imbedding bits of glass from her shattered windows into her flesh. Her house was roofless; the walls had collapsed. Outside it had turned dark; dust swirled. Her emergency collection of bamboo rafts for her family was gone, and although she did not know it yet, so was her scattered family. The more fortunate ones—her husband and sons—had died, somewhere in the city, instantly. Kazuko would linger for a month; fourteen-year-old Masumi—who had seemed uninjured—for six painful years. Mrs. Hizume would be discovered and taken to Kyosai

Hospital, ashamed to be found only in her underclothes. The blast had removed her *mompe*.

Badly injured in his collapsed house, Dr. Michihiko Hachiya, with his wife, Yaeko, rushed, although cut and bleeding, toward his hospital, a few hundred yards away. All his clothes blown off, Hachiya stumbled in the street over bodies and debris. "The sky filled with black smoke and glowing sparks. . . . Updrafts became so violent that sheets of zinc roofing were hurled aloft and released, humming and twirling in erratic flight. Pieces of flaming wood soared and fell. . . . Scorching winds howled around us, whipping dust and ashes into our eyes and up our noses." He collapsed and was carried to the main gate, where people were being drenched by a fire hose from one of the few undestroyed mains. *"Kurushii,"* he murmured—"I am done."

Before the hospital blazed he was painted with iodine that seared his body. He fainted. When Hachiya found himself outside with those who had fled the building he watched large raindrops falling—large, dirty drops of radioactive dust, memorably described in Masuji Ibuse's documentary novel *Black Rain* (1969), where Yasuko, who would suffer from radiation sickness, writes in her diary for August 6, "I found that I was spotted all over. . . . However many times I went to the ornamental spring to wash myself, the stains from the black rain wouldn't come off." To Dr. Hachiya, fleeing again despite his injuries, "The streets were deserted except for the dead. Some looked as if they had been frozen to death while in the full action of flight; others lay sprawled as though some giant had flung them to their death from a great height. Hiroshima was no longer a city, but a burnt-over prairie. To the east and west everything was flattened. The distant mountains seemed nearer than I could ever remember. . . . How small Hiroshima looked with its houses gone."

At the badly damaged but functioning Red Cross Hospital, the deputy director, Fumio Shigetō, was puzzled by the unusual nature of the burns he treated. When an X-ray technician showed him some undeveloped film that had turned as black as if exposed to light, although it had been stored in a lead container, he knew what the Dōmei reporter had guessed. The blast had emitted radioactivity: the city had been flattened by an atomic bomb.

The catastrophe of Hiroshima has become one of the most minutely recorded events in history, yet "all the thousands of stories," Masatake Okumiya summed up, "do not reproduce the shud-

dering limbs and screaming cries of the victims who already were beyond all possible help; they do not show you the dust and ash
swirling about the burned bodies which groveled and writhed in indescribable agony; the twitching and spasmodic jerking of fingers
which were the only [remaining] expressions of agony; the seeking of
water by *things* which only a short while before had been human beings." The human impact was beyond statistics. Japanese authorities
would put the dead and missing at 71,379 with 68,023 injured. A
third of the injured would die; many others were disfigured or
maimed. Nearly 98 percent of the buildings in the city proper were
destroyed (81.1 percent) or severely damaged (16.7 percent). Yet
more deaths and damage had occurred in the March 9 firebombing of
Tokyo. Ironically, Second Army Group headquarters, on the lower
slope of Mount Futaba, was high enough above the blast to be
wrecked but not incinerated.

Japanese Home Service first broadcast a bulletin that "a small
number of B-29s" had penetrated into Hiroshima and "reduced to
ashes . . . a considerable number of homes." The unidentified explosives, it reported, were attached to parachutes, and their effectiveness
"should not be regarded as slight." It would be necessary to "formu-
late strong steel-like measures to cope with this type of bomb."

The news came to Marquis Kido in devastated Tokyo through
military chiefs who spoke of a "new type of bomb" that they had
once been assured could not be made during the likely span of the
war. Kido reported to the Emperor, who confessed to being "overwhelmed with grief" at the catastrophe. Although he realized that
the army hierarchy might resist, Hirohito said, the dread new circumstances required that Japan "bow to the inevitable." However
unconstitutional it was for him to place his imperial self in the decision process, he requested an emergency session of the Cabinet. "I
thought," Hirohito later told Hidenari Terasaki, who had been press
officer for the embassy in Washington at the time of Pearl Harbor,
"that the Japanese race would be destroyed if the war continued."

A teacher at a Christian school in Yokohama when the war began, Takaaki Aikawa was working reluctantly at Nippon Hikoki, an
airplane factory. The radio news at noon had mentioned "considerable damage" at Hiroshima "by a small group of enemy planes." It
took two days, however, before newspapers were permitted to print
anything about the atomic bomb. "Most unforgettable" to Aikawa
was a photograph of the streetcar Hiroko Nakamoto had encountered,

frozen by the blast. "As it stopped, it suddenly changed into a car of the dead, skeletons still hanging on the straps just as they had hung on them as living persons a few moments before." Another picture became famous as the "Thinking Man." Sitting on the stone steps of a bank, waiting for it to open, a man had been obliterated. "The flash printed his shadow on the stone wall of the bank, a shadow in the posture of the *Thinker* of Rodin. And there it has remained."

Like all Japanese cities, Hiroshima had been home to a host of household Buddhas, impassive and friendly, large and small. Like the city's flesh-and-blood inhabitants, Buddhas by the tens of thousands—wood, stone, ceramic, bronze—were incinerated, imploded, glassified, pulverized, blistered, liquefied, fused. At Pearl Harbor a thousand men had died instantly on the exploding *Arizona*. Four years later the technology of war had reached a decisive new level of efficiency.

Momo Iida remembered as a schoolboy on the first day of the war hearing an old soldier on a train declaring that the war would be like none before. When the news of the Bomb came, Iida recalled the prophecy, and also his father's forecast—the elder Iida was an inventor and manufacturer of small household appliances—that with nuclear power "a bomb the size of a matchbox could burn up the whole of the world." Now Japanese radio warned that more attacks "of this new type of bomb" might occur, and citizens were urged "to wear white clothes as a protective measure." The wearer of white might, perhaps, not become a shadow.

On the night after the Bomb, *kamikaze* pilots training at Kumigaya Air Base to fly to their deaths heard the whine of an air raid siren. They ran to shelters carrying white sheets over their heads. The *kamikaze* hopefuls did not want to lose their opportunities for heroic suicide. Among them was Mutsuo Saitō, who had run about on the morning of Pearl Harbor protecting his family's house with pasted-up rice paper, which had approximately the same value against incendiary raids as white sheets against an atomic bomb.

A White Russian émigré who had joined the British Army as a medic, Constantine Petrovsky had gone into action on the night of the first raid on Singapore, in the first hours of the Pacific war. When the garrison surrendered, he began nightmarish months of prison camps in Malaya, Thailand, the Philippines, and finally Japan. His lot of sick and starved prisoners worked twelve-hour shifts in a coal mine near Hiroshima. Petrovsky and an American POW doctor cared for the sick without medicines. No appeals had worked. "Look, we don't have [medicines] now, Captain," he was told. "It's Americans bombing us all the time."

With no newspapers, no radio, no news other than overheard conversation among guards, they understood nevertheless that the war had turned around. Seeing the first B-29s confirmed it: "Americans were coming to Japan day and night. . . . When the planes attacked, they put down red flag, alert, and on loudspeaker [warn] that Americans are coming, and everybody is to go out to the shelter. We saw this red flag and [heard an] alarm. But only high up was zzzzzzzzzzzzzhhhh going—[one] plane. . . . I went out where I was looking after the sick room, looked at the sky and suddenly phew! Like earthquake." A column of smoke arose "like a mushroom, spreading out, black. . . . I said, 'My God! They shot one plane, one bomb, they got oil tanks.' "

He saw the Japanese officers shuddering. One exclaimed, "That's a lucky shot." But later a Japanese doctor came in and announced that he was leaving—that the war was, in effect, over. He was needed in the city. "Americans no good," he said.

"Why?" Petrovsky said.

"They dropped bomb. Hiroshima finished. Everybody dead."

"Can't be one bomb," said Petrovsky.

"Oh yes, we don't know. But that happened."

As the Army and Navy searched for antidotes and answers, the military learned more of the shocking details than did the civilian population. In a prison camp at Hakodate, near Sapporo, the onetime telegraphist of the *Peterel*, sunk in Shanghai harbor on the first morning of the war, was working in the coal mines. Life was stark and Jack Honywill remembered with gratitude the meal he had been given en route from an even worse camp, a bowl of rice and pickled grasshoppers, first described as prawns. On fire watch, he was approached by one of the sentries who spoke a little English. "Hiroshima," he said. "One bomb. Finish." Honywill thought that the guard must have awakened from a nightmare, but then all work stopped.

The "great hordes" of B-29s conducting daylight raids had "looked beautiful" to "Pappy" Boyington from his prison camp, from which he was marched daily to dig bomb-proof tunnels deep below the surface of Honshu. A Flying Tiger in Burma on the first day of the war, and a fighter ace in the South Pacific later, he could not imagine from his combat experience "what kinds of bombs were going to be dropped to necessitate a tunnel two hundred feet underground." Then a Japanese guard "tried to tell me about the atomic bomb. He could speak no English . . . and I couldn't fathom at first that it was only one bomb he was talking about."

Squadron Leader Tom Lamb had flown a torpedo bomber into the Malayan chaos. Feeble after years of malnutrition and exposure, he was at a prison camp at Palembang, Sumatra, when Flight Sergeant "Mel" Melville brought the news "in great excitement." Their radio, concealed in the screw-leg of a stool, had picked up a bulletin that a bomb had "blown half of Japan into the bloody sea." It seemed true. Guards began bowing and the food improved.

At a camp on Java the news reached the POW population after another secret radio, built into a wooden shoe, picked up a broadcast from Delhi. The Dutch and British prisoners, captives in one of the richest rice-producing areas in the world, were so near starvation that the report seemed merely the product of hunger and hallucination. The "listening officer"—a New Zealander—had missed the opening of the broadcast, but he was able, Colonel Laurens van der Post, who had been in Singapore at the beginning, remembered, to relate "that something tremendous had happened. He wasn't quite certain precisely what it was, but in the course of the morning of the day which was now ended, something more like an act of God than of man had been inflicted on Japan at a place called Hiroshima. Exactly how and what had been done he couldn't explain. All he knew was that it was something new and terrible in human experience, more terrible even than earthquakes, tidal waves or volcanic eruptions."

Van der Post wondered whether they had picked up some dramatized radio fiction like Orson Welles's *War of the Worlds*, which once had caused a panic in America. When the New Zealander again twisted his contraband coils and picked up Perth and San Francisco, the awesome event was confirmed. They returned to their ragged blankets on the stone floor with a certainty that the unexplained, but manmade, cataclysm would end the war. All they had to do was survive a little longer, not an easy thing given the Japanese contempt for prisoners of war and their likely refusal to similarly degrade themselves.

The *Enola Gay* touched down at Tinian at 2:58 P.M. The accompanying B-29s, which had lingered to sample and photograph, landed within forty minutes afterward. General Spaatz was at the runway to present Tibbets with the Distinguished Service Cross; the others received lesser medals although Parsons (a Navy man, however) might have been better recognized. Their reports had gone around the world before they had returned. The official Japanese report, echoing the confusion of eyewitnesses, referred to a bomb of a new type dropped by parachute. Because of Truman's announcement, broadcast from Washington, the authorities in Tokyo knew what had hit them, but they intended to see for themselves. The Twentieth Air Force would make certain that ordinary Japanese knew. Lieutenant Boller flew back from Saipan to Guam to work with his POWs on the leaflet, but felt "a wave of depression" about the "frightful new weapon." He would write home: "The prospects for the future look a little terrifying. I hope no more use of it is made in this war."

Boller was struck by the businesslike way his Japanese assistants turned "atomic bomb" into *genshi bakudan,* as if there was nothing special about Truman's statement, and he couldn't help remarking, "It's really awful, isn't it, this *genshi bakudan*?"

"You mean it's real?" said one POW in surprise. They had merely translated something that they took for granted was propaganda.

Groves telephoned Oppenheimer from Washington with the news. "I'm very proud of you and all of your people," he began.

"It went all right?"

"Apparently it went with a tremendous bang."

"When was this, after sundown?"

"No, unfortunately; it had to be in the daytime on account of security of the plane. . . . It has been a long road and I think one of the wisest things I ever did was when I selected the director of Los Alamos."

Oppenheimer convened colleagues and staff in the Los Alamos auditorium, striding down the aisle barely ahead of the throng. As he mounted the podium he clasped his hands above his head like a victorious prizefighter. After that he hardly needed to announce anything but the target.

In Chicago, Leo Szilard claimed to a colleague that using the Bomb against Japan was "one of the greatest blunders in history." Dozens of other scientists who had worked on the Bomb had co-signed Szilard's petition, yet the military realities remained that an untried piece of ordnance could not have been employed in a demonstration. And only one uranium device existed.

With global politics more in mind than the war, Albert

Einstein—whose first response was *"Oy veh!"*—told a *New York Times* reporter who had called at his home in Princeton, "The world is not yet ready [for an atomic bomb]." Yet it had been his influence that had committed President Roosevelt to the project and made possible the crucial meeting of physicists in Washington the day before Pearl Harbor. Now the Bomb's implications had taken precedence over its results. Whether the world would ever be "ready" for an atomic bomb was no longer the point. The world had reached the point where any number of nations would eventually find the wherewithal to develop atomic weapons, whatever the ethical scruples of those scientists who had signed petitions. The laws of physics might unfold a little more slowly elsewhere, but unfold they would.

"All of us in Special Branch," Edwin Reischauer wrote—these were largely Japanese experts in the War Department—"were stunned and dismayed at the news. Through [decrypted] military and diplomatic messages we knew how near to defeat Japan already was and how eager some elements in the government were to bring an end to the fighting.* We were aware that the economy was grinding to a halt. . . . We looked dazedly at one another, and said something about hitting below the belt when the opponent was already on the ropes."

On December 7, 1941, *Time* correspondent Theodore White had thrown slips of paper down twenty-nine floors to the street at Rockefeller Center to let Christmas shoppers in Manhattan know that Japan had attacked Pearl Harbor. Now, interviewing General MacArthur in Manila, who had been shocked when his air force was destroyed on the ground at Clark Field nine hours after Pearl Harbor, and lied to Washington about it, White listened to the general, whose blunders had been buried under victories, blame the Bomb as likely to end the days of heroic warfare. "Scholars and scientists" had stolen future wars from military professionals and made "men like me" obsolete. There would be "no more wars" of the kind he knew, MacArthur mourned.

For the troops who were going to storm the beaches of Kyushu and Honshu for him, the news came like a reprieve to a condemned man facing execution. "When I thought about what that would be like," Lieutenant Sam Hynes, a young Marine pilot based on Oki-

*Only the nonmilitary elements, however. Japanese diplomats, the people best known to old Tokyo hands, were not running the war.

nawa, remembered, "I felt doomed, with a Japanese fatalism." He knew the cost of taking Okinawa, on Japan's doorstep. "I imagined the desperate defense of the homeland, the suicide attacks, the fierce concentrations of AA fire. The whole population would fight against us. In my imagination farmers attacked with pitchforks, crying 'Banzai!' and geisha girls held grenades between their inscrutable thighs; every object was a booby-trap, and all the roads were mined. We would all be killed, I thought, by fanatics who had already lost their war." "I felt," wrote Sy Kahn, whose 244th Port Company in Luzon was tagged for early duty in Kagoshima Bay, "my life had been spared, and that I would live to be twenty-one after all."

Perhaps they would live to come home. Perhaps they would be privileged to grow old. Yet not all of them. Confined in Hiroshima's Chugoku Police Headquarters, six of Tom Cartwright's crew were killed by the blast. One, Sergeant Ralph J. Neal, and a Navy flier, Norman R. Brissette, survived because they had been emptying "honey buckets" into the cesspool and had leaped into the filth, but they died afterward of radiation sickness. Several other POWs also died there, and another outside Hiroshima Castle. A Japanese witness saw an old woman throwing chunks of concrete at a young man wearing only undershorts as he sagged from a pole to which he was bound. He may have already been battered to death by survivors retaliating for the Bomb.

Cartwright was still in Tokyo, grilled almost daily. Suddenly the questions changed. What was the "new kind of bomb" that could end the war? Cartwright didn't know, and wasn't told why he was being asked. But to loosen his tongue, a huge soldier, brandishing a samurai sword, was motioned in, and Cartwright was blindfolded and marched out with him. "This is your last chance to keep your head," the interrogator warned.

Despite his terror, Cartwright convinced both captors that he knew nothing. Led back to his cell, he was unaware that his crewmen had been killed by the blast of the first atomic bomb. Later the Japanese identified twenty Americans among the Hiroshima dead, including some apparently executed elsewhere in the city and concealed in the nuclear toll. Eight alleged casualties had been murdered in medical experiments at Kyushu University.

The news came to Nine-Section in Burma from a garbled radio transmission. It was a quiet sunny morning; there was no shooting heard.

The men bandied talk about superbombs, and whether the Japanese opposite them knew:

> " 'Ey, Grandarse, 'ear w'at they're sayin' on't wireless? The Yanks 'ave dropped a bomb the size of a pencil on Tokyo an' it's blown the whole fookin' place tae bits!"
>
> "Oh, aye. W'at were they aimin' at—'Ong Kong?"
>
> "Ah'm tellin' ye! Joost one lal bomb, an' they reckon 'alf Japan's in fookin' flames. That's w'at they're sayin'!"
>
> "W'ee's sayin'?"
>
> "Ivverybody, man! Ah'm tellin' ye, it's on't wireless! 'Ey, they reckon Jap'll pack in. It'll be th' end o' the war!"
>
> "Girraway? Do them yeller-skinned boogers oot theer knaw that?"
>
> "Aw, bloody 'ell! 'Oo can they, ye daft booger! They 'evn't got the fookin' wireless, 'ev they?"
>
> "Awreet, then. Ah's keepin' me 'eid doon until the Yanks've dropped a few more pencils on Tokyo. An' w'en them boogers oot theer 'ev packed in, Ah'll believe ye."

"Packed in" said it all for troops with their lives still on the line, and for prisoners of war for whom every day meant more of them dying of starvation and abuse. Even on the home front the war's toll escalated, as when Major Richard Bong, twenty-five, testing the new P-80 "Shooting Star" jet, crashed at Lockheed's airport at Burbank. He may not yet have heard the news from Hiroshima. Bong had flown at least 146 combat missions in the Philippines and downed more than forty enemy planes with his P-38. But the real enemy had been Time. The longer the war went on . . .

For most readers of newspapers and listeners to radio the revelation that a new kind of weapon had been employed was at least as riveting as the possibility of a rapid end to the war. In what was referred to in pressrooms as "Second Coming" type, often four inches and very black, was the adjective *atomic* or *atom*—even in Paris, although the French had not made the Bomb. In Germany, a former *Wehrmacht* soldier who, forty-five years after, still thought that Hitler was "quite a guy" and had "the right ideas" and "the best of intentions," recalled hearing the news while a POW at a former concentration camp, Flossenburg—"that's how I know that all the gassing of the Jews is true. We saw the gas chambers. I remember the sixth of August 1945. A sergeant from Oklahoma came in and said, 'We just dropped the atomic bomb.' " The POW's moral outrage rose at the thought, but his memory of the gas chambers had been matter-of-fact. He had company, even in America, where from San Francisco poet Kenneth Rexroth penned an anti-Negro, anti-Semitic diatribe to his publisher, James Laughlin: "America has turned into the Inferno of organized irresponsibility where bright young Stalinist college professors named Oppenheimer and such, can turn the spigot of the Apocalypse and no one can stop them. I for one am hardly proud of being geographically, at least, an American."

In Berlin, novice teacher Rosemarie Hebek remembered August 6 only as her twenty-third birthday, marked by her schoolchildren's bringing her "presents: scraps of paper with cakes and candles drawn on them, old picture postcards, one little flower." ("It was most moving. . . .") While eschewing sanctimony, Ruth Andreas-Friedrich marveled at the news of the Bomb:

> It has happened. He who chooses war will be destroyed by war. Not invasion, but the atomic bomb. What if Hitler had succeeded in creating such a powerful weapon of destruction. Retaliation weapon X. Unimaginable! However, the grotesque thing about it is that three of the scientists who invented it are German emigrants. So he might have played the murderous trump if his racial hatred—oh what a vengeful nemesis—hadn't blocked his way. Another proof that dictators at the decisive moment destroy themselves by their own measures. Hiroshima lies in ruins. Tomorrow perhaps it will be all of Japan.

Shortly before dinner hour at Farm Hall, Major T. H. Rittner took the stairs to Otto Hahn's room to inform him in advance of the others, as Hahn had been co-discoverer of atomic fission—that the BBC had reported the explosion of a nuclear bomb over Japan. Hahn was shattered. He felt responsible, he explained to Rittner, for the thousands of deaths. In fact, he confided, when he first realized the terrible potential of fission, he had contemplated suicide. "With the help of considerable alcoholic stimulant," Rittner reported to his superiors, "he was calmed down and we went down to dinner where he announced the news to the assembled guests."

The announcement, the Major added, "was greeted with incredulity." And he furnished extracts from the bugged exchanges.

Since the group had only the scanty information Rittner had picked off the radio, Hahn added as his gloss, "They can only have done that if they have uranium isotope separation."

Gerlach offered a guess that at least a ton of uranium would have been necessary, and Hahn agreed that the effort had to have been complicated and lengthy. "If the Americans have a uranium bomb then you're all second-raters. Poor old Heisenberg!"

The scoffing, very likely alcohol induced, at the colleague whom the others had long deified led to a chorus of "No!"—and Heisenberg insisted that as the word *uranium* had not appeared in the BBC report, "Then it's got nothing to do with atoms."

Since the announcement had referred to a blast equivalent of twenty thousand tons of TNT, Carl von Weizsäcker disagreed: "It corresponds exactly to the factor $10^4$." The thirty-five-year-old Carl Friedrich Freiherr von Weizsäcker, son of an aristocratic career diplomat* who had drafted the Munich pact that dismembered Czechoslovakia in 1938, had worked on the structure of the atomic nucleus and the evolution of stars.

"At any rate, Heisenberg," Hahn repeated, "you're just second-raters and you may as well pack up. . . . They are fifty years further advanced than we are."

They argued over whether uranium was really involved, or whether the Bomb could have been a clever bit of chemistry, but nothing else fit the announced results. Kurt Diebner observed ruefully, "We always thought we would need two years for one bomb."

"I'm glad we didn't have it," said Wirtz; and Weizsäcker added, "I think it is dreadful for the Americans to have done it. I think it is madness on their part."

Heisenberg remained dubious about the Bomb's reality, as "ten tons of pure U-235," he guessed, would have been necessary. Hahn agreed: "I always thought that one could only make a bomb of such a size that a whole province would be blown up." Heisenberg suggested that given the use of uranium and the energy released, they ought to

*Ernst Freiherr von Weizsäcker, Foreign Office State Secretary in 1938, had eased himself out of Berlin during the war and become Minister to the Vatican. His second son, Richard, brother of the physicist, would become President of Germany in 1984.

be able to work out "properly" how much fissionable material was utilized. Still it was "a bit odd," he confessed, to be so surprised. They had all been working on fission theory through the war years.

The nine o'clock BBC news was anxiously awaited. Major Rittner made certain that it was tuned in before he left the room. They would converse more freely, he felt, without him.

The scale of the project awed them. They understood that the news was genuine. Their government would not have allocated 120,000 men as the United States had done, Heisenberg said, on the chance that something would come of it. He didn't have "the moral courage" to make such demands. Weizsäcker agreed that moral courage had been involved. "I believe the reason we didn't do it was because all the physicists didn't want to do it, on principle. If we had all wanted Germany to win the war we would have succeeded."

"I don't believe that," Hahn scoffed, "but I am thankful we didn't succeed."

However it was done, Heisenberg ventured, "It is possible that the war will be over tomorrow."

The ten had been at it long enough after the radio had been switched off that some implications about Nazi sympathies began to emerge. If some of them had been permitted the resources, Diebner claimed, "Professor Gerlach would be an *Obergruppenführer* and would [now] be sitting in Luxembourg as a war criminal."

"If one hasn't got the courage," Korsching charged, "it is better to give up straightaway."

"The point is," said Heisenberg, "that ... although we were not 100 percent anxious to do it, on the other hand we were [as scientists] so little trusted by the State that even if we had wanted to do it, it would not have been easy to get [a bomb project] through."

"Because," Diebner explained, "the official people were only interested in immediate results. They didn't want to work on a long-term policy as America did."

He had been convinced, said Heisenberg, that a reactor for producing energy was possible, but not a bomb, "and at the bottom of my heart I was really glad. . . ."

Once Hahn had left the room, Weizsäcker suggested that if they had begun soon enough, they might have been able to build one bomb by the winter of 1944–1945—the period, he did not need to say, of Hitler's last-ditch Battle of the Bulge counteroffensive in the Ardennes. "The result would have been," Wirtz countered, "that we would have obliterated London but still not have conquered the world—and then they would have dropped them on us." Conventional bombing, Weizsäcker observed, might have "smashed up the factories" even before a device had been completed. In any case, he confessed, "It might have been a much greater tragedy for the world if Germany had possessed the uranium bomb." It was that fear that propelled the American atomic effort, and, ironically, it was during the "Bulge" crisis in December 1944 that President Roosevelt had called in General Groves to ask whether a bomb could be rushed to completion and used against the *Wehrmacht*. Later revisionist speculation that a "white bias" would have kept the Bomb from being employed in Europe was nonsense.

The news from Hiroshima dramatically exposed the inner contradictions of the physicists who had worked in Germany throughout the Nazi period. (Weizsäcker's father had been Hitler's Deputy Foreign Minister almost to the end of the war, not because he was a Nazi but because he was a career diplomat and a German.) Their patriotism as Germans made most of them loyal scientific soldiers—all, perhaps, but the distinguished and untouchable anti-Nazi von Laue, who had won a Nobel Prize as early as 1912 and was remote from work that could have led to a superweapon. For the others, Hiroshima was spurring what has been called "the moral renegotiation of each scientist's relation with Naziism." For some, Hitlerism had been less a crime than an inconvenience; few would have confessed that it was an opportunity at which they had failed. Even at dinner that evening the courtly Otto Hahn had referred to one of the most brilliant atomic theorists of the era, who had graced his institute until racial laws forced her to flee Germany in 1938, as "the non-Aryan Fraulein [Lise] Meitner." It was a reflex he could not suppress.

When Gerlach fled to his room and could be heard sobbing, the gentle Max von Laue, only a few months younger than Hahn, and once Max Planck's assistant, and Paul Harteck, who had worked with Lord Rutherford at Cambridge, went up to comfort him. Rittner's diagnosis was that Gerlach felt "like a defeated general" and wanted to commit suicide. After Harteck and von Laue left, Hahn came in. "Are you upset," he asked, "because we did not make the uranium bomb? I thank God on my bended knees that we did not make a uranium bomb. Or are you depressed because the Americans could do it better than we could?"

"Yes," said Gerlach. ". . . You cannot prevent its development. I was afraid to think of the bomb, but I did think of it as a thing of the future, and the man who could threaten the use of the bomb would be able to achieve anything. That is what I told Geist,* Sauckel and Murr. Heisenberg was there at Stuttgart at the time." Fritz Sauckel had become Nazi manpower chief in March 1942; Wilhelm Murr was then *Gauleiter* of Württemberg.

"I must honestly say," Hahn told Gerlach as he left the room, "that *I* would have sabotaged the war if I had been in a position to do so." Then Hahn went to see Heisenberg. Distancing himself from Gerlach, Heisenberg charged that their colleague was the only one of them who had wanted the Nazis to win—not because he approved of their criminality but because of his loyalty to Germany.

Because he loved Germany, Hahn confided, he had hoped for her defeat. And he went on to speculate about the feelings of British and American scientists who may have felt that whatever the ethics of building the Bomb, nothing else mattered but the defeat of Hitler.

Heisenberg continued to insist that it would have taken an impossible ton of uranium to pack into a bomb, and Hahn questioned, "How can they take it in an aircraft and make sure that it explodes at the right moment?" Possibly he was too much of a theoretician to imagine the technology, but Heisenberg had the answer—to separate the critical component "in[to] two halves, each one of which would be too small to produce the explosion because of the mean free path. The two halves would be joined together at the moment of dropping [the bomb], when the reaction would start. They have probably done something like that."

Hahn could recall no publication about uranium fission in British or American sources after 1940. However, munitions czar Albert Speer would remember meeting early in June 1942 with Hahn, Heisenberg, and others at the Berlin center of the Kaiser Wilhelm Institute, Harnack House, to question Heisenberg in particular about German atomic research. With Speer were Erhard Milch, armaments chief of the *Luftwaffe,* and Friedrich Fromm, his *Wehrmacht* counterpart. Heisenberg had reported on the progress of the "uranium machine"—the reactor that was still more theory than reality—and complained about the lack of technical and financial support.

After Heisenberg's presentation, Speer recalled, "I asked him

---

*The transcriber of the bugged audio disks apparently misheard the name. Geist is very likely Paul Giesler, the *Gauleiter* of Munich and Upper Bavaria.

how nuclear physics could be applied to the manufacture of atom bombs. He declared that . . . theoretically nothing stood in the way of building such a bomb. But the technical prerequisites for production would take years to develop, two years at the earliest." General Fromm offered to release "several hundred" scientists from the services to help, and Speer asked for a cost estimate. When the request came from Heisenberg's staff, "I suggested that they take one or two million [additional] marks and correspondingly larger quantities of materials. But apparently more could not be utilized for the present, and in any case I had been given the impression that the atom bomb could no longer have any bearing on the course of the war."

While technical publications on the possibilities for fission had vanished, as early as May 6, 1940, a report had appeared in the London *Daily Telegraph* describing "a new substance, and a potential source of vast power" with implications upon "the outcome of the war." In the *Sunday Dispatch* on January 11, 1943, appeared a speculative article headlined ONE LITTLE BOMB THAT WOULD DESTROY THE WHOLE OF BERLIN. It forecast a device "that would blast a hole twenty-five miles in diameter and wreck every structure within a hundred miles. . . . The explosive in this bomb would be the energy contained in the uranium atom."

The Nazis were not unaware of the concept, but Speer found no way to realize it in wartime hardware. As late as December 1944 Speer had still been trying, writing on December 19 to Walther Gerlach, who after Heisenberg's lack of enthusiasm had been put in charge of the uranium project, that the government would meet whatever needs he had. But Gerlach was going nowhere.

The Americans had known that since Pash and Goudsmit had descended for "Alsos" upon the town of Celle, northeast of Hannover, and Hechingen. At Celle, concealed in a spinning mill, was an experimental centrifuge for separating uranium isotopes. Also hidden were supplies of heavy water, one and a half tons of metallic uranium cubes, ten tons of carbon, and other materials for nuclear research. Much of the work was still theoretical, on paper. At Hechingen, Goudsmit recalled, "was the central group of laboratories, and all it amounted to was a little underground cave, a wing of a small textile factory, a few rooms in an old brewery. . . . Sometimes we wondered if our government had spent more on our intelligence mission than the Germans had spent on their entire project."

•          •          •

Hahn got up to go to bed, but had a last word for Heisenberg—that the Americans "must prevent the Russians from doing it."

"I would like to know what Stalin is thinking this evening," said Heisenberg.

On that note Wirtz and Weizsäcker, who had continued discussing the bomb with the others downstairs, went up to the bedroom they shared, wondering how the political situation had changed, if at all, for Russia. "Stalin certainly has not got it yet," said Weizsäcker. "If the Americans and the British were good Imperialists they would attack Stalin with the thing tomorrow, but they won't do that. They will use it as a political weapon. Of course that is good, but the result will be a peace which will last until the Russians have it, and then there is bound to be war."

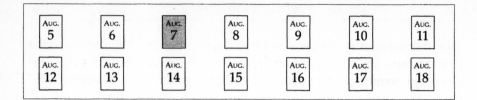

| Aug. 5 | Aug. 6 | Aug. 7 | Aug. 8 | Aug. 9 | Aug. 10 | Aug. 11 |
| Aug. 12 | Aug. 13 | Aug. 14 | Aug. 15 | Aug. 16 | Aug. 17 | Aug. 18 |

CHAPTER XXVI

---

## · AUGUST 7, 1945 ·

---

*". . . this awful fact"*

The second Bomb and first "Fat Man" had been scheduled for delivery on August 11, then moved up to August 10. When bad weather over Japan was forecast for five continuous days beginning August 10, Deak Parsons and Harvard physicist Norman Ramsey proposed readying the Bomb for August 9. "The pressure to be ready with the much more complex implosion device," Ensign Bernard J. O'Keefe, who was with the assembly team, wrote, "became excruciating. . . . Everyone felt that the sooner we could get off another mission, the more likely it was that the Japanese would feel that we had large quantities of the devices and would surrender sooner." Every day the war went on meant more deaths, he added, and "the *Indianapolis* sinking also had a strong effect on us."

While the working parts for the plutonium bomb were checked over for the last time prior to their being set into casing F-31, General Hap Arnold was cabling Guam to rush a pamphlet drop that might make the delivery of the second bomb unnecessary. Washington had been baffled that the Japanese government had not made any move after Hiroshima to surrender immediately. "What we did not take into account," General George C. Marshall wrote, ". . . was that destruction would be so complete that it would take an appreciable time before the actual facts of the case would get to Tokyo."

The facts picked up in Tokyo from American radio and the first reports from Hiroshima should have been enough. Nevertheless, Generals Spaatz and Farrell, on Guam, ordered stepped-up broadcasts on Japanese domestic frequencies from Saipan and the printing of six million leaflets to be dropped over forty-seven cities with prewar populations exceeding one hundred thousand. It proved to be easier to enlist the usual leaflet teams, and make use of a printing press that had produced a Japanese newspaper dropped regularly over the home islands, than to convince Air Force wing commanders that the leaflet war was safe. The enemy, they worried, would now be looking for flights of one to three planes as potential atomic bomb carriers. Further, there was a shortage of T-3 leaflet bomb casings.

That Farrell—Groves's deputy—oversaw and edited the text of the post-Hiroshima leaflet makes clear that immediate surrender remained a higher priority than the wartime deployment of the first plutonium bomb. The Alamogordo test was evidence enough of the energy yield and blast effect. If the second $Pu$ device was dropped, it would be because the Japanese had failed to signal an end to the war.

It took until early evening to ready the text, in five brief and blunt paragraphs:

TO THE JAPANESE PEOPLE:
America asks that you take immediate heed of what we say on this leaflet.
We are in possession of the most destructive explosive ever devised by man. A single one of our newly developed atomic bombs is actually the equivalent in explosive power to what 2000 of our giant B-29s can carry on a single mission. This awful fact is one for you to ponder and we solemnly assure you it is grimly accurate.
We have just begun to use this weapon against your homeland. If you still have any doubt, make inquiry as to what happened to Hiroshima when just one atomic bomb fell on that city.
Before using this bomb to destroy every resource of the military by which they are prolonging this useless war, we ask

that you petition the Emperor to end the war. Our President has outlined for you the thirteen consequences of an honorable surrender: We urge that you accept these consequences and begin the work of a new, better, and peace-loving Japan.

You should take steps now to cease military resistance. Otherwise, we shall resolutely employ this bomb and all other superior weapons to promptly and forcefully end the war.

    EVACUATE YOUR CITIES

It did not take long before pundits on editorial pages and prophets in the streets began reflecting upon the implications of the Bomb. Kingsley Martin, editor of the *New Statesman*, deplored the "solemn jubilation" of the BBC over the "vaporising" of Hiroshima, and Albert Camus in *Combat* called it "organized murder." Georges Bernanos considered Hiroshima "a triumph of technique over reason." Thinking about it when remote in miles and time from the Burmese jungles, George MacDonald Fraser agreed that the use of the Bomb seemed "a hideous thing" when considered out of perspective. "Now take Nine-Section as representing those Allied soldiers who would certainly have died if the bombs had not been dropped. . . . Could I say, yes, Grandarse or Nick or Forster were expendable, and should have died rather than the victims of Hiroshima? No, never. And that goes for every Indian, American, Australian, African, Chinese and other soldier whose life was on the line in August, 1945. So drop the bomb."

Like many others, Eleanor Roosevelt hoped that the Bomb meant "the end of war." The "ever-increasing price for indulging ourselves in this uncivilized way of settling our difficulties" would now be "too high" and paid "by whole populations." Visiting Lord Camrose at his *Daily Telegraph* office in Fleet Street, Winston Churchill confided off-the-record that he thought America could, if it wished, dominate the world for five years, and at the least it could use the new weapon to restrain the Russians. Out of office, he could oversimplify solutions. Karl Compton, in Manila, told MacArthur's pilot, Weldon Rhoades, that the United States could soon settle into the manufacture of three superbombs a month at a cost of thirty million dollars each, but that the consequences—moral, constitutional, and practical—were a separate issue from the fabricating of atomic bombs.

Given the strides of physics, there was an inevitability about the Bomb. If there hadn't been an Anglo-American bomb, that would not have precluded an eventual Russian or German or Japanese or French bomb, and the possibilities for even more powerful and efficient bombs. "A single demand of you, comrades," Stalin exhorted his technological and weapons chiefs after Potsdam and Hiroshima: "provide us with atomic weapons in the shortest possible time. You know Hiroshima has shaken the whole world. The equilibrium has been destroyed. Provide the bomb—it will remove a great danger from us."

James Bryant Conant's impression of the Alamogordo bomb had been one of "a cosmic phenomenon like an eclipse. The whole sky suddenly full of white light like the end of the world." After Hiroshima he startled Harvard Librarian Keyes D. Metcalf with a letter as university president asking him secretly to research the possibility of preserving and sequestering in a safe place microfilm copies of the world's printed record—the achievements of humankind—so that something might be left for some successor culture after the end of contemporary civilization. The estimate Conant was given was 2.5 billion pages—and he would do nothing to follow up on it. Even if the funding were found, the project itself could not be kept secret—and it would alarm Americans, possibly the world.

When no surrender offer came from Tokyo in the aftermath of the Bomb, Washington ordered not only mass leaflet drops but the continuation of planned operations. Spaatz sent up 170 B-29s on the seventh, attacking targets on Kyushu and Honshu. The FEAF in the Philippines pounded Kyushu with B-24s, A-26s, B-25s, and P-38s, and also hit Formosa, Java, and targets in enemy-held northern Luzon. Of the Twentieth's B-29s, 131 were sent over the Toyakawa arsenal near Tokyo and the nearby Nakajima aircraft plant. Another raid had been scheduled—over the big steel center of Yawata, reputed, still, to be the best-defended industrial site in the home islands. Briefing the Yawata and Toyakawa groups, Colonel Kalberer told them to firebomb Yawata itself and to stay away from the AA-fire at the factory. "The war is not over yet," he said. "I believe it will be very soon. We can't expect the Japs to quit suddenly. Such things take time. Meanwhile, we've got to keep hitting them so they won't have a moment's peace. Go out and let them see we're still pitching."

Few B-29s took off for Yawata. Two planes, one on each runway, cracked up on takeoff, aborting the mission. Those already airborne were radioed to join other formations. Yawata was put off until the next day.

●   ●   ●

On August 7 there were more Japanese planes than usual aloft over the home islands as authorities struggled to find out what had happened in Hiroshima and how to get help there. Lieutenant General Seizō Arisue, chief of the Army Intelligence Bureau, assumed charge of one team, which took off without physicist Yoshio Nishina, whose flight was aborted by engine trouble. Landing at Hiroshima Airport in an American DC-3, distant from the blast center, he discovered, Arisue reported, "every single blade of grass at the airport had turned brown and bent in one direction. I looked toward the town and found nothing obstructing my view except a solitary tree scorched totally black. Nobody came to meet us. We waited until a man came tottering out of a nearby shelter. It turned out to be the commander of the airport defense unit, a lieutenant colonel. His face was charred." After Arisue traveled through the flattened city in a truck, he reported to Tokyo on the enormity of the calamity and recommended only that soldiers and civilians wear white clothing to protect themselves against flash burns.

Rescue work went on. Lieutenant Colonel Shigeo Tamura of the Akatsuki Corps had worked all night, rested for an hour at four, then with fifty men resumed digging in ruins where voices were heard. At Asano Park, a charred wasteland, they found blackened victims less than half alive and begging for help. The air was foul with the stench of rotting flesh; the burned and baffled children seemed to him to have gone mad.

Prince Yi, of a Korean noble family co-opted by the Japanese after the occupation, had been attached to the Army headquarters at the time of the blast. In the naval hospital at Ninoshima, attended by his adjutant, who had been elsewhere at the moment of the Bomb, the prince died. It was four in the morning, not yet light. Lieutenant Colonel Hiroshi Yoshinari went out on the hospital lawn and expiated his guilt with his service pistol.

At dawn new teams of rescuers found little to recognize, even in the ruins of Hiroshima Castle. Survivors claimed unbearable thirst, but the metallic-tasting water did little good. Hiroshima Station, distant from the blast center, had remained erect, and trains ran to it with medical supplies that were largely useless. Tents were set up around it as emergency quarters, but treatment was primitive—mercurochrome and, for burns, a mixture of flour and oil.

Somehow Dr. Michihiko Hachiya, hospitalized with injuries in his own hospital, managed to make light of the chaos, where "in the space of one night patients had become packed, like the rice in *sushi*, into every nook and cranny...." They were under the stairways, in the toilets, in the front garden, in the corridors—most with severe burns. An emergency operating light had been rigged by an ambulance driver from a car battery and headlight, and had lasted through much of the darkness. In the new day patients were without traditional services—possibly the reason for Hachiya's *sushi* metaphor. It was customary for patients to provide bedding, cooking utensils, and a charcoal stove, and for food to be prepared by a friend or family member who also did the bedside nursing.

In the disorder, patients unable to move urinated or defecated where they lay, or vomited, and such attendants and physicians as there were wallowed, barefoot or in open clogs, through a sea of filth. In and out of the hospitals, survivors with burns wandered dazedly as sheets of skin peeled away from bodies to hang, one of the doctors told Hachiya, "like rags on a scarecrow. They moved like a line of ants." By morning the procession of injured had stopped. "I found them lying on both sides of the road so that it was impossible to pass without stepping on them."

Hachiya "lay with my eyes shut while Dr. Tabuchi was talking, picturing in my mind the horror he was describing." As a result he neither saw nor heard when a friend, Mr. Kasutani, a retired army officer, arrived looking for him. Uninjured, Kasutani had been in Jigozen, a village on the Inland Sea, ten miles distant, at the time of the Bomb. He could not suppress his tears at what he saw as he hurried on foot toward Hiroshima. "There was a man, stone dead, sitting on his bicycle as it leaned against the bridge railing.... I saw a few live people still in the water, knocking against the dead as they floated down the river." Many of the dead and dying were soldiers, "burned from the hips up; and where the skin had peeled, their flesh was wet and mushy.... And they had no faces! Their eyes, noses and mouths had been burned away, and it looked like their ears had melted off. It was hard to tell front from back." One soldier still alive who had nothing left of his face but his white teeth was mumbling for water. "I didn't have any. I clasped my hands and prayed for him." As Kasutani stared in disbelief the soldier fell dead.

On his way to Hiroshima, he recalled, he had run to the military post at Hatsukaichi to warn the officer in charge that something terrible must have happened in the city. "There isn't much to worry about," he said. "One or two bombs won't hurt Hiroshima." The

complacent dismissal reflected officialdom's continued propagandiz-
ing of the home islands with vague, unrealistic optimism. At 6:00 A.M.
Japanese Home Service radio issued its first countrywide report on
the Bomb, picked up by an American monitoring station in the Pacific and in translation teletyped to Washington:

> A SMALL NUMBER OF B-TWENTY-NINES PENETRATED INTO HI-
> ROSHIMA CITY A LITTLE AFTER EIGHT AM YESTERDAY MORNING
> AND DROPPED A SMALL NUMBER OF BOMBS. AS A RESULT A CON-
> SIDERABLE NUMBER OF HOMES WERE REDUCED TO ASHES AND FIRES
> BROKE OUT IN VARIOUS PARTS OF THE CITY.
>
> TO THIS NEW TYPE OF BOMB ARE ATTACHED PARACHUTES, AND
> IT APPEARS AS IF THESE NEW BOMBS EXPLODED IN THE AIR. INVESTI-
> GATIONS ARE NOW BEING MADE WITH REGARD TO THE EFFECTIVE-
> NESS OF THIS BOMB, WHICH SHOULD NOT BE REGARDED AS SLIGHT.
>
> THE ENEMY HAS EXPOSED HIS COLD-BLOODEDNESS AND
> ATROCIOUS NATURE MORE AND MORE IN KILLING INNOCENT PEO-
> PLE BY THE USE OF THIS NEW-TYPE BOMB. IT IS BELIEVED THAT THE
> ENEMY, BEING FACED WITH DIFFICULT CONDITIONS, IS FEELING
> RUSHED TO TURN THE WAR INTO ONE OF SHORT DURATION. HENCE
> HE HAS BEGUN TO USE THIS NEW TYPE OF BOMB.
>
> THE USE OF THIS NEW TYPE OF BOMB BY THE ENEMY IN THE
> FUTURE CAN BE EXPECTED. AS FOR MEASURES TO COPE WITH THIS
> BOMB, IT IS ANTICIPATED THAT THEY WILL BE DISCLOSED AS SOON
> AS POSSIBLE. UNTIL THESE MEASURES ARE DISCLOSED BY THE GOV-
> ERNMENT AUTHORITIES, IT IS NECESSARY FOR THE GENERAL PUBLIC
> TO STRENGTHEN THE PRESENT AIR DEFENSE SYSTEM.
>
> AS FREQUENTLY POINTED OUT IN THE PAST, THE PEOPLE MUST
> WATCH THEMSELVES AGAINST UNDERRATING THE ENEMY SIMPLY
> BECAUSE HE HAS CARRIED OUT RAIDS WITH A SMALL NUMBER OF
> PLANES. THE ENEMY HAS BEEN CARRYING OUT LARGE-SCALE PRO-
> PAGANDA ON THE EFFECTIVENESS OF THIS NEW-TYPE BOMB SINCE
> USING THESE BOMBS, BUT AS LONG AS WE FORMULATE STRONG
> STEEL-LIKE MEASURES TO COPE WITH THIS NEW TYPE OF BOMB, IT
> WILL BE POSSIBLE TO KEEP THE DAMAGE AT A MINIMUM.
>
> WE MUST BE CAREFUL AT ALL TIMES SO THAT WE WILL NOT
> FALL VICTIM TO THE ENEMY'S MACHINATIONS.

With leaflets from the Marianas now falling over the home islands, Japanese authorities had no choice but to warn against enemy-

supplied news rather than against the Bomb. Although the device had generated horror only in the immediate environs of Hiroshima, censorship could not have kept it from the public for very long. And more bombs might fall.

Even in schools in the countryside—wherever people gathered—the news about Hiroshima spread rapidly. "From what I heard on the radio," Ichiro Hatano wrote in his diary, "I believed the raid to be a localized one." Yet his schoolmate Kinji had already declared that it was an "atom" bomb, an extraordinarily powerful weapon that would "kill every living thing" in its reach. "It must be a joke!" said Ichiro loyally, but Kinji "made a terrible face" and scoffed, "This is not the moment for joking. Three or four of these bombs and Japan might be completely destroyed."

Ichiro wondered how such weapons could be used if poison gas was banned by international agreements, and decided that Kinji was "too ready to believe what his teacher tells him." After all, Mr. Aoyama, the form master, was said to have "dangerous leftist ideas."

Still a survivor, unlike his assistant, Lieutenant Toshio Hashizume, whom he had left behind in Hiroshima, Captain Mitsuo Fuchida was in Yokosuka when the Navy decided to send its own investigative team to the blast site. Reports from Kure had quoted eyewitnesses as seeing a second device drop from a second B-29, possibly an unexploded bomb. If Fuchida's team could find it, the secret of the awesome explosive might be revealed. Fuchida rushed back alone, leaving the rest of his group to fly from the Atsugi air base by transport plane. He would meet them at General Hata's headquarters.

In charge of the nine engineering officers was Captain Yasukado Yasui, an expert on poison gas with little knowledge of radiation. With Fuchida, whom he had known since middle school days in Nara, they walked about the ruins, now stained with black rain or charred from fire and blast. The injured and dazed, a day later, still wandered, poking into the ashes for signs of identifiable dead. Along the rivers and canals, Fuchida saw bodies "piled six and seven feet high," corpses of those who had sought to relieve their burns or their thirst and found other relief instead.

Returning to Hata's underground shelter at dark, Fuchida heard again about the unexploded bomb. Reportedly it had come down by parachute. They would look for it the next day. But they were already convinced that the bomb that had gone off was atomic and that if they had possessed the weapon themselves, they would have dropped it on the United States: "That was war."

On the afternoon of the day after the Bomb, the War Cabinet met in Tokyo, with the War and Home Ministers offering reports on the devastation in Hiroshima. No one could be deluded about what had happened: President Truman's statement had been picked up in translation from Saipan and San Francisco radio. Copies were on the table. Stalling for time on behalf of the army, General Anami asked that they await the results of investigations then under way. The government radio announcement had minimized the danger. Togo rushed from the useless meeting to an audience, in the underground shelter of the Imperial Library, with the Emperor. "I said," Togo recalled, "that it was now all the more imperative that we end the war." The Bomb permitted them to "seize the opportunity."

Hirohito agreed, and "warned that we could no longer continue the struggle, now that a weapon of this devastating power was used against us." Recognizing the situation as desperate, the Emperor urged, "We should not let slip the opportunity by engaging in attempts to gain more favorable conditions." Bargaining for terms "had little prospect of success at this stage." All he wanted was "a prompt ending to hostilities," and he asked Togo to communicate his wishes to Premier Suzuki.

Going to the Premier would use traditional channels, but it was the Army that needed the Emperor's exhortation. Dutifully, Togo went to Suzuki, who asked that yet another cable be sent to Sato in Moscow. At 3:40 P.M. the Foreign Minister telegraphed a vague plea, picked up by "Magic":

> THE SITUATION IS BECOMING SO ACUTE THAT WE MUST HAVE
> A CLARIFICATION OF THE SOVIET ATTITUDE AS SOON AS POSSIBLE.
> PLEASE MAKE FURTHER EFFORTS TO OBTAIN A REPLY IMMEDIATELY.

At 7:50 P.M. Moscow time—it was ten minutes to midnight in Tokyo—Sato responded:

> AS SOON AS MOLOTOV RETURNED TO MOSCOW, I ARRANGED A
> MEETING. I ALSO ASKED LOZOVSKY TO HELP ARRANGE IT. . . .
> MOLOTOV NOTIFIED ME THAT HE WOULD SEE ME AT 1700 HOURS
> TOMORROW, THE EIGHTH.

All that Togo and Sato had done was to put off for another day any possibility of peace. By the time Sato would see Molotov, it would be the ninth in Tokyo.

Despite Togo's frantically misguided efforts, the military continued to gear up for the final phase of resistance. The key to the deployment of the new 43B *Okha* manned bomb was the turbojet *Kikka* aircraft, which was to undergo its first test flight that morning at the Kisarazu base in Chiba, across Tokyo Bay from Yokohama. At 10:20 forty American bombers roared in from Okinawa, raiding targets in the nearby Kanagawa area, and the air raid alert at Kisarazu was not lifted until well past noon. At 1:00 P.M. the *Kikka* was finally wheeled out of its underground shelter, given the go-ahead signal, and to the cheers of high-ranking officers lining the runway, took off and rose to about 1,500 feet, circled, and landed safely. Although it was in the air for a brief twelve minutes, the *Kikka* had worked. It was the first jet to fly in Japan.

The celebration was still going on at Kisarazu when a message was received from army headquarters that the bomb that had devastated Hiroshima the previous day had indeed been atomic. The *Kikka* and *Okha* now seemed useless. In any case, there were only 120 *Okhas* with pilots assigned to them, and the *Kikka* was not yet in production. The only practical move the army could make was to order radio jamming of the powerful transmitters beaming news of the atomic bomb from Saipan, Okinawa, and Manila. Returning to his base at Oita from Beppu, the big naval station at the southern end of the Inland Sea, Admiral Ugaki was given the text of Truman's announcement as picked up from San Francisco radio. "It is clear," he wrote, "that this was a uranium atom bomb, and it deserves to be regarded as a real wonder, making the outcome of the war more gloomy. We must think of some countermeasures against it immediately, and at the same time I wish we could create the same bomb." He knew the only countermeasure—surrender—but it was unpalatable.

It was 6:40 P.M. in Hiroshima when Toshiko Yokochi, with the help of a neighbor who had survived, loaded her husband, dead of burns, into a handcart and added to her burden the body of her daughter Chizuko. The Yutani Factory, where she had found Chizuko, still alive but disfigured, her clothing but for underpants burned away, had been a horror of bodies barely conscious or already dead. At one of many places in the smashed city where corpses were being burned, she left the bodies, returning later for the ashes. "The [remaining] children hardly said a word when, later that night, they helped me to pick up Chizuko's and their father's bones."

Shinoe Shoda, after searching for the remains of her child at an obliterated school, wrote a *tanka* about what she found:

> *Clustered with numerous small head bones*
> *Is a big bone, probably that of their teacher.*

In Manila, General Eichelberger talked with MacArthur at GHQ. MacArthur appeared convinced that Japan was on the verge of giving up because of the Bomb and that Russia's entry would make further resistance useless. He promised Eichelberger that he could take the Eighth Army into Japan for the surrender. Admiral Halsey was on the *Missouri*, off Japan, making a rendezvous with Admiral Rawlings and the British Pacific Fleet, when he learned of the results of the Hiroshima bomb. Orders from Nimitz remained unchanged. They were to continue carrier raids on the home islands. The day before, a carrier in the task force, the *Bonhomme Richard*, had sustained its first crew fatality aboard the ship, an index to how secure the fleet had become since the fading of the *kamikaze* raids off Okinawa. A seaman had been hit by friendly fire while planes practiced bombing and rocket attacks on a towed target. The ship's log for the seventh noted Halsey's orders for Task Forces 37 and 38 as well as the routine of the fleet. It ended with a rare personal note:

> Effected rendezvous with T.G. 30.8 and refueled. Various destroyers along for transfer of personnel stores and mail. Commenced run to launching point for strikes against Northern Honshu and Hokkaido. News of the "Atomic Bomb" dropped on Hiroshima received on board—the beginning of the end.

Also at sea was the *I-58*, which on surfacing picked up an American broadcast about the Bomb. Fluent in English, the diving officer, Lieutenant Nishimura, fully understood, and although listening to enemy radio was forbidden to all but senior officers he took Truman's statement to Commander Hashimoto. To admit what Nishimura had heard would damage the morale of the crew, and Hashimoto refused to let the lieutenant report what he had heard.

Survivors from the cruiser he had sunk were debarking in Guam, where they were taken to Base Hospital 18. Admiral Spruance went from bed to bed pinning Purple Heart medals on pajamas. The blackout on news about the *Indianapolis* continued. No one was to discuss why he had received his Purple Heart. Captain McVay expected to receive a court-martial summons with his medal, and it was no surprise to him to learn that an inquiry would begin on the ninth.

In the former Greater East Asia Co-Prosperity Sphere, the Japanese were preparing to grant independence to colonies from which they were attempting to withdraw. At noon the announcement was made establishing the Preparatory Committee for Independence in the East Indies, with committees in Java, the Celebes, Borneo, the Lesser Sundas, and Ambon. Formal independence was to come a month later, after which the new nation was to be recognized by Japan, then declare war on Britain, the Netherlands, and the United States. The scenario from Imperial General Headquarters in Tokyo included continued oversight after independence: "Japanese military personnel will control and guide the new State. . . . Important points relative to the government which affect the entire area will be referred to the supreme military commander. . . ." After the announcement of independence "an intense propaganda campaign of Thanks" was to be carried out.

The puppet government of Burma, in place since 1942, was still fleeing its Japanese masters. Every organized unit left on the Sittang was depleted. One 148-man-strong remnant staggered to the village of Dalazeik, on the Sittang, on the seventh. Down to four grenade launchers, they held off the British while making for the riverbank through the sodden, six-foot-high elephant grass. Soon the unit was down to 98, and had nothing but pistols, swords, and bayonets. By the time they reached the Sittang, several hundred yards across, they were down to 17. To the north, Colonel Hiroo Saitō's column, struggling toward Yele, was being picked off by guerrillas. His men were going crazy and he had the eerie sensation of watching himself go mad. Catching himself before he went too far, he rested for three hours in the branches of a tree. On the seventh, with about 350 men remaining, he reached the Sittang at Yele. The Japanese called the failed operation "Breakout."

Across Russia the news of the atomic bomb was stunning and impossible to conceal. *Pravda* and *Izvestiia* carried the official Tass bulletins summarizing Truman's statement and estimating the destruction. Readers were awed that the Bomb project had at its apex employed over 125,000 people—an index to American industrial power. Japan, it seemed clear, would be finished by the new weapon. And Russia, it seemed, would be diminished by the new factor in global politics.

At 4:30 P.M.—the morning after the Bomb in Washington—Stalin and Marshal Antonov signed an order committing the Red Army to war in Manchuria after midnight local time on August 9. The Far East General Army would have one more day to prepare.

Teaching the last of the term's lessons at the Polish agricultural college at Tarnobrzeg, Witold Sagajllo referred to the matter-energy relationship and observed that in theory a chain reaction that turned one into the other could create an atomic explosion of fantastic destructive power. Normally his students accepted what he said and merely wrote it down. This time they were full of questions, and he asked, "Why this sudden interest?"

"Sir," said a student, "yesterday, according to the BBC, the Americans dropped an atom bomb on Hiroshima."

He "froze." What was there politically safe to say? "Well," he struggled, "this is the end of an era and sooner or later it will be the end of civilization."

He went home and had a long talk with his wife, Irena. Poland under the Communists was dismal enough, but it could become an atomic battleground between East and West. They decided to leave the country. There was little time. Irena was pregnant. They would have to convert, secretly, almost everything they owned into dollars and buy a special pass, for use as a visa, to enter Czechoslovakia ostensibly in search of family members deported by the Germans. That itself would require an almost impossible fifty dollars. How to live afterward was not important.

Sagajllo's response to the Bomb was not unusual. Europeans caught between the two Great Powers recognized the Bomb in their future. In Lübeck, close to the new line between East and West, Arthur Dickens heard Germans say, "Thank God this came after we had been defeated and not before." His old housekeeper, a Latvian Catholic refugee who disliked the Russians almost as much as the Nazis and had her own racist views besides, told him, "Thank God the Yellow Race is finished and even the Russians cannot do much now, or they will get atom bombs dropped on them."

The German physicists lodged at Godmanchester spent the morning in avid reading of English newspaper reports about the Bomb. Otto Hahn wondered what percentage of the uranium in the bomb underwent fission. Heisenberg suggested "the whole lot," and improvised a short, confident lecture explaining why. (Actually only 2 percent underwent fission in the uranium bomb.)

Hahn was impressed by the amount of uranium he thought was needed for the test explosion and a bomb. Neither realized that the test was of a different kind of device, employing a laboratory-made element about which they knew almost nothing. Harteck guessed that another bomb would be ready "in a few months," and Weizsäcker exaggerated, "History will record that the Americans and the English made a bomb, and that at the same time the Germans, under the Hitler regime, produced a workable engine.* In other words, the peaceful development of the uranium engine was made in Germany under the Hitler regime, whereas the Americans and the English developed this ghastly weapon of war." The distortion of history pleased him, and Heisenberg later followed up the idea by telling Weizsäcker that had they, the Germans, dropped such a bomb they would have been executed as war criminals for having made "the most devilish thing imaginable."

Newspapers had speculated about how far the Germans may have proceeded on a nuclear bomb, and late in the evening the physicists decided to produce a statement they could sign that detailed the actual work on which they claimed to have been engaged. Wirtz reminded him that a patent for the production of an atomic bomb was taken out in 1941 on behalf of the Kaiser Wilhelm Institute for Physics, but it would not turn up in the statement drafted for the group by Heisenberg. A self-serving apologia, the Farm Hall statement was signed by all, although Bagge and Diebner objected to the special pleading and self-exoneration in the claims of being motivated only by moral scruples. In a letter to his son written the same day, Max von Laue, whose moral scruples were genuine, echoed the sentiments of the intended press release: "All of our uranium research was directed toward the achievement of a uranium machine

*German scientists had not yet produced a nuclear reactor, but were close.

as an energy source, first because no one believed in the possibility of a bomb in the foreseeable future, and second because fundamentally no one of us wanted to put such a weapon in Hitler's hands."

The Farm Hall manifesto was not published, but in later months and years Heisenberg and several of the others congratulated themselves in press interviews and articles that on principle they had never worked on a bomb. Few would demonstrate any moral anguish at having worked for the Hitler regime on other projects. And some, like Gerlach, had tried unsuccessfully to build a bomb. Their moral courage was safely and largely ex post facto.

Perhaps Sir James Chadwick, who gave up work at his own laboratory in Liverpool to oversee the British scientific team at Los Alamos, put the German response, which he knew nothing about, in the right perspective. "By God's mercy British and American science," he told the press, eager for every word on the project, "outpaced all German efforts. These were on a considerable scale but far behind. The possession of these powers by the Germans at any time might have altered the result of the war and profound anxiety was felt by those who were informed." And he underlined that anxiety by revealing that in the winter of 1942–1943 "most gallant attacks were made in Norway on two occasions by small parties of volunteers from the British Commandos and Norwegian forces at the very heavy loss of life, upon stores of what is called 'heavy water,' an element in one of the possible atomic bomb processes. The second of these attacks was completely successful."

The British embassy's report from Washington described the American reaction as "typical in the American nature. The lurid fantasies of the comic strips seemed suddenly to have come true." It deplored the questionable taste of the Washington Press Club's new Atomic Cocktail at sixty cents—"only one to a customer." The Bomb, the report predicted, would "do more than Pearl Harbor or the war to obliterate the last vestiges of the isolationist dream, and in this sense it is a new weapon in the hands of the internationalists. At the same time nationalists are insisting that if America can only keep the secret she will be powerfully placed to make other nations, not least the Soviet Union, behave."

The President could not have chosen a more auspicious day to return to an American harbor. Newspapers were full of stories about the

Bomb as an American (perhaps Anglo-American) achievement of un-precedented scope and the likelihood of a quick end to the war. Even the politically unfriendly New York *Herald-Tribune* was lavish in its praise. Truman's "flat statement" that the Bomb had an explosive force equal to all the bombs that could be carried in a fleet of two thousand B-29s was "more fateful for human history than the whole war it-self. . . . One forgets the effect on Japan or on the course of the war as one senses the foundations of one's own universe trembling a little."

That there was a sense of trembling as well as triumph emerged in page after page of stories about the Bomb. A sense of awe crept through the self-congratulation. There was extinction for everyone possible in its misuse.

The *Augusta* docked at Newport News at 4:54 P.M. with a flock of correspondents eager to file their stories. Truman's party boarded a special train for Washington. For security reasons, no advance advi-sory had been given out about where or when he would arrive, and some reporters expected him at Boston. But those who chanced Boston harbor found a story there anyway, as, with the Nazi swastika streaming out beneath the Stars and Stripes, two German destroyers manned by volunteer German crews with American officers steamed in. The Navy refused to say why they were there, but a spokesman "guessed" that "experimental" purposes were involved, probably by prearrangement at Potsdam with Britain and Russia.

By eleven, five members of Truman's cabinet had assembled to greet him at the White House, where, escorted by a fleet of Secret Ser-vice cars, he arrived alone at 11:07. The rest of the Potsdam group went separately from Union Station to their homes, and bed.

Truman invited the remainder, including three press secretaries, up to his study on the residence floor for a drink. Unable to resist the temptation once he saw his familiar piano, he sat down at it and played a few bars, then telephoned Mrs. Truman in Independence. Over drinks he filled in his guests on the conference. Most of all they wanted to know about Stalin. Whether or not one liked what Stalin said, Truman contended, he was a man of his word. "Stalin was one who if he said something one time would say the same thing next time."

They asked about the new British government, which Truman confessed had come as a surprise to him. He had formed little opin-ion of Attlee, he said, but Bevin reminded him of the cantankerous American mine workers leader, John L. Lewis—only that Bevin was more crude and uncouth. Stalin and Molotov might be rough men,

Truman said, but they knew the common courtesies. Bevin was lacking in all of them—"a boor."

At 11:45 a guest signaled that they all should leave and give the President some rest, and, still excited by events, Truman seemed genuinely disappointed. He lingered at the door with his press secretaries, speaking of troubles ahead. In Congress, he confessed, most of his troubles came from his friends. One knew what to expect from known enemies, and how to meet them. He started down the corridor to his bedroom. Charlie Ross, Matt Connelly, and Eben Ayers moved toward the stairs. Then, turning toward them again, Truman confided that he had been glad to leave Europe and never wanted to go back.

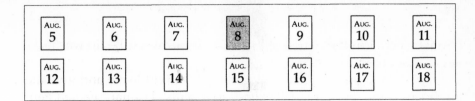

| Aug. 5 | Aug. 6 | Aug. 7 | Aug. 8 | Aug. 9 | Aug. 10 | Aug. 11 |
| Aug. 12 | Aug. 13 | Aug. 14 | Aug. 15 | Aug. 16 | Aug. 17 | Aug. 18 |

CHAPTER XXVII

# · AUGUST 8, 1945 ·

## *exchanging documents in Moscow*

At eight in the evening, Guam time—much earlier in Washington—the destroyers *Doyle* and *French* finally left the scene of the *Indianapolis* disaster. The last of the 316 survivors had been picked up five days earlier; the few identifiable bodies of the 880 missing had been located and recorded.

On Guam and Tinian, since the Japanese had not made the slightest move toward surrender since the Hiroshima catastrophe, bombers of the Twentieth Air Force prepared for further strikes. "Ultra" intercepts in Manila had picked up clear recognition of the enormity of the damage. A message to the Navy Minister from the Kure Naval Base, just far enough from Hiroshima to be spared, reported "the concussion was beyond imagination." Japanese signal intelligence had incorrectly identified Claude Eatherly's weather plane from its coded messages as from the 313th Bomber Wing on Tinian rather than the 509th, and had not yet realized that the parachuted package was not a bomb. Guessing that the chute retarded the atomic bomb's fall so that it would explode in the air to cause maximum blast damage, Imperial Headquarters ordered pilots to shoot down lone B-29s or at least to destroy any parachutes deployed.

Their own mission postponed for a day, Hays Gamble's 315th Wing convened a bull session on the possible next Bomb. "I believe," he wrote in his diary, "that if bomb is not used, war will be over by Dec. 21, '45 and if it is [used], by August 21, '45. A lot of boys believe it will be over by the end of this week."

Crews were less than eager to go up, assuming that the Japanese would put everything they had into preventing another atomic raid. The "big sweat" was the rescheduled daylight raid on Yawata, in which 245 B-29s took part. Opposition was aggressive. Thirty Zeros supplemented the heavy flak, although the bombers operated at 21,700 feet. From 20,700 feet other B-29s, again subjected to intense fire, bombed the Nakajima aircraft plant in Tokyo. Four planes and their crews were lost. Other damaged bombers limped to Okinawa. At the same time, ostensibly to confuse the enemy or inspire alarm, the 509th sent six B-29s to drop "pumpkin" bombs. One of the six had a more far-reaching mission. Chuck Sweeney had taken *The Great Artiste* out to sea to release a dummy bomb that duplicated "Fat Man" except for the plutonium core. All electrical and mechanical components worked as intended, which meant that the gadgetry on the actual bomb could be counted upon. When the plane returned to Tinian, Sweeney and his crew were told to prepare for delivery of the armed bomb the next morning. Bad weather was moving in and any delays might continue for five or more days after that.

Storms close to the home islands had already aborted most carrier attacks, but despite morning fog the Japanese were reconnoitering in unusual numbers, losing two planes to American air patrols circling the task forces. At 11:45 a fighter from the *Wasp* shot down another intruder.

From Okinawa a variety of aircraft struck targets on Kyushu, including the city of Usa, notorious in the late 1930s, when many Americans were boycotting Japanese products, for its deliberately obfuscating MADE IN USA labels. Other planes hit industrial targets in Osaka, one P-51 lost to ground fire. Later that day its pilot, Lieutenant Marcus McDilda, was interrogated at secret police headquarters in the city. He had been picked up from the water, brought to shore, and marched blindfolded through the streets while bystanders pummeled him. He was still bleeding as officers interrogated him.

They knew that his P-51 had come from Iwo Jima, and evasive answers drew further beatings.

Interrogators also raised the matter of the atomic bomb. After dark a general came in to conduct the questioning, drawing his sword to induce more informative answers. Although McDilda vowed he knew nothing, the general poked at the pilot's already swollen lip. Blood streamed down his chin onto his flying suit. "If you don't tell me about the bomb," the general warned before leaving the room, "I'll personally cut off your head!"

When underlings picked up the interrogation, McDilda determined to fabricate something to keep himself alive. He began talking in his nearly unintelligible Florida drawl about pluses and minuses and lead shields and how the "box" dropped from the bomber explodes and pushes back the atmosphere, knocking everything down beneath it with "a tremendous thunderclap."

The explosion atomized, he claimed, an area of six square miles. The box, he went on more confidently, was about thirty-six feet long and twenty-four feet wide—too big, the Japanese should have realized, to be true, as even a Superfortress could not have ferried an object of such size. It could not be dropped, he added, suggesting a technical flaw, at night or during a rainfall. McDilda knew only what he had heard on the radio, to which he had supplemented his fictional extrapolation. Since some of his "facts" tallied vaguely with what the interrogators also knew from American statements, they appeared satisfied. Yet they wanted to know more.

"Do you know the next target for the weapon?"

"I believe Kyoto and Tokyo," said McDilda, having thought about which cities would, if destroyed, agonize the Japanese most. "Tokyo is supposed to be bombed in the next few days."

One of the questioners exited hurriedly, very likely to telephone headquarters in Tokyo. That a telegraphed report of the entire interrogation was also sent from Osaka to Tokyo was known to Manila almost immediately. It had been picked up by "Ultra."

Into the smoldering environs of Hiroshima, which Captain Fuchida and Captain Yasui had overflown to search for the parachute and possible bomb, the pair set out once more, this time in a truck. Up a mountain road five miles north of the city they saw what appeared to be white silk billowing in the wind. Stopping, they climbed out and cautiously followed the parachute cords down to a metal cylinder three feet long and about a foot wide. It did not look like a bomb, but it resembled what observers had described. Tugging at a metal ring, they dislodged the contents—instruments connected by wires, including what appeared to be a thermometer and a radio transmitter. They had found Luis Alvarez's scientific package, which had measured and reported the performance of the Bomb. To Yasui, Fuchida explained the likely purpose of the contents, adding, "Whatever made us think we could beat America?"

Gingerly, they pushed the wires and instruments back into the cylinder, loaded it into the truck, and left the hills, from which they could still see the horror of Hiroshima.

The Army Second Bureau (Intelligence) investigation team, led by Lieutenant General Seizō Arisue, located three more calibration cylinders attached to parachutes. One was carrying, he reported, "a sort of barometer . . . fitted with an electric wave transmitter" to calculate and transmit "the changes in atmospheric pressure caused by the explosion." Writing his report at the Ujima Shipping Command, which was out of the blast zone, he added, inadvertently corroborating Lieutenant McDilda, "Rumor had it that the same kind of bomb will be dropped on Tokyo on August 12."

Professor Nishina had joined General Arisue on the eighth, first surveying Hiroshima from the air. "I decided at a glance," he wrote, "that nothing but an atomic bomb could have done such damage." Since he was working under Japanese Navy sponsorship on methods for uranium separation, he accepted American claims that uranium fission had been involved, but he wanted to prove it for himself and asked the crew that offered to drive him about the ruins in a truck, "Can you find a corpse without exterior injuries? I want to see it dissected post-mortem."

The body of a soldier was brought to the laboratory of the Daiwa Spinning Company, which had been outside the blast area. Nishina used a scalpel to expose the cadaver's entrails, and reached for the liver. "Do you see this inflammation?" he asked. "There's absolutely no doubt about it now. This is the atomic bomb."*

Fifteen years after Hiroshima, Edward Teller, labeled the father of the hydrogen bomb, suggested, "I can appreciate the reasons for the fateful decision to drop an atomic bomb without warning. The men who made the decision thought that a quick end to the war

---

*Nishina had constructed a cyclotron in his laboratory in Tokyo and was doing, by American standards, rudimentary studies of fission and radiation. They would be enough to cause his death in 1951 from liver cancer.

would save many lives, Japanese and American. But ... I am convinced that the tragic surprise bombing was not necessary. We could have exploded the bomb at a very high altitude over Tokyo in the evening. Triggered at a high altitude, the bomb would have created a sudden, frightening daylight over the city. But it would have killed no one." A dud under those conditions, he contended, would have done no strategic harm. A success high over Tokyo, "in full sight of Emperor Hirohito and his Cabinet, would have been just as terrifying as Hiroshima. And it would have frightened the right people." An ultimatum then, explaining the demonstration, Teller thought, might have brought a quick surrender. But that specific strategy, he admitted, had never been proposed, and recommendations for remote detonations had been rejected as unlikely to convince a culture in which suicide was glorious and surrender base. And even with the doomsday message of Hiroshima a reality to Hirohito's Cabinet, it again rejected capitulation.

In Tokyo, citing incontrovertible evidence, the Suzuki government filed a protest through the Swiss Minister against the United States for employing an inhumane weapon. Tokyo radio quoted a Japanese commentator as declaring that the methods Americans were now using in the war had "exceeded in horrible cruelty" the atrocities perpetrated by Genghis Khan.

On Tinian, bomb case F-31 was being metamorphosed into "Fat Man," with implosion sphere and boxed tail sprouting radar antennae. By ten in the evening it had been loaded in the forward bomb bay of *Bock's Car*, B-29 number 77, usually captained by Captain Frederick Bock but this time assigned to Major Charles W. Sweeney, who had piloted the observer plane over Hiroshima.

Most of the men involved in the mission assumed it would end the war, and the feeling across the Pacific seemed to be that Japan needed one more good push in the direction of peace. The feeling even reached into the distant Aleutians, where TF 92, comprising three cruisers and two destroyer divisions, had sortied from Massacre Bay, Attu (with Kiska one of the two islands in North American waters briefly occupied by the Japanese). It appeared to be a last chance to fire in anger against the enemy, and was labeled a shipping sweep of the Kuriles. On the eighth, TF 92 reported sinking a subchaser and three trawlers at what was then called Kurabu: "Return fire was heavy. Destroyer *McDermott* hit by machine gun fire." The Japanese were not giving up easily.

In the lower home islands, propagandists writing for newspapers and radio, however contradicted by their own carefully watered-down news reports, kept up a brave facade. The August 8 issue of *Asahi Shimbun*, one of the major Tokyo papers, featured an editorial, "Strength in the Citadel of the Spirit," in which it pointed out that regardless of the intensity of the bombing and the number of cities destroyed, "the foremost factor to decide the war is the will of the people to fight and how well they are united to fight. As human beings, we naturally were shocked by the rapid change in the war situation, but now we have to strengthen the citadel of the mind. The people in Tokyo can stand these difficulties better than the people in the provinces. The people in the country have had a sense of security so far, and now there is a lack of the will-power to resist, but the whole country has become the front. . . ." Japan, it warned, was at the crossroads of destiny.

How insecure country people actually were was obvious from a story censors let pass—that a man caught stealing vegetables from a field had been beaten so badly that he had died. Propagandists had passed it as an object lesson, but Hisoko Hatano wrote in her diary: "I can't simply blame him as a criminal. For it is impossible to find any food nowadays, even if you have plenty of money." Country people, she charged, could barter their rice and their vegetables for almost anything, and hold back food for exchange only "if they see the possibility of getting hold of fabrics or things which might be handy for their daughters' weddings." Others without "these treasures" had no choice "but to steal or die."

The censor had let slip a loaded word. "The man who died like that," Mrs. Hatano observed, "was an evacuee. The provincials always speak ill of evacuees; they never think . . . to what straits they have been reduced. We are evacuees too and I can easily see what must have happened. Probably the man did not steal for himself, but for his family; perhaps he had children and couldn't bear to see them without food." The monthly ration, she scorned, was only enough for ten meager days, "and even *that* is not rice, but half-rotten potatoes, peas and bran fit for fowls." Even cats, desperately, according to a *tanka* by Mokichi Saito, "try to eat pumpkin."

A single episode of August 8 encapsulates the aftermath in stricken Hiroshima. In the morning a neighbor had come to the outlying—and spared—house of Toshiko Yokochi to tell her that her son Shigemi was still alive but badly hurt and at the Oshiba Embankment. Pulling her handcart, Mrs. Yokochi hurried to the riverbank. Shigemi was indeed there with two of his schoolmates. They had been on a work detail, dismantling houses for firebreaks. While they were at morning roll call outside the Fukuya Department Store the Bomb had exploded. Instantly their clothes were burned from their backs. They beat out each other's flames with their hands and ran away from the fires toward Hiroshima Station, jumping into the river en route. When the tide went out they climbed to the embankment, where they had remained.

"I've brought the cart, so get on quickly," she said, and when he complained about how hot he was, she gave him her paper umbrella, which he clutched in his burned hands. Again and again he begged for water.

When they got as far as the bamboo wood at Gion, which was littered with charred bodies—people who had fled from the city only to die where they collapsed—she pulled the cart into the shade and asked Shigemi if he wanted a rice ball. He wanted only water. Some of the bodies still twitched with signs of life. A few croaked for water. "These groaning voices filled the whole wood and sounded like a dirge."

By early afternoon she had managed to pull Shigemi home, where he babbled of the fire—of watching, from the embankment, the city burn and people die. "People said," she remembered, "that powdered human bones were good for burns. So I got my husband's bones that we'd cremated the evening before and ground them up in an earthenware mortar. Then I put the powdered bone on Shigemi's burns. But it didn't work at all. My husband's bones had been [radiation] poisoned, so of course they wouldn't work. I realized that later. . . . All the same I was desperate to do anything. But it's a nightmare to think that . . . I ground up his father's bones, my husband's bones, in an earthenware mortar and put the powder on my boy's burns."

At no time as they trudged home, Mrs. Yokochi recalled, did her son inquire about his father or his elder sister, who were already dead. "He never asked about either of them. And I didn't say a word about them either." All he had worried about were the rules under which he had been conscripted for work. "We must tell the school that I am going back home. . . . We must tell the school. . . ."

With that on his lips he died at about four in the afternoon. Mrs. Yokochi and her remaining son, Hajime, set to work to build a coffin.

• • •

Day by day the news of the Bomb filtered down into the POW camps abroad. Bob Grafton of the British Sumatra Battalion was at a camp in the Thai paddy fields called Phra Putta Chai, near a temple with a pagoda and seated Buddhas, when he overheard the Japanese and Korean guards referring to a *"Takusan Bom Bom"* that had been dropped on Japan. Prisoners expected to be moved—where they didn't know. At the camp in Mukden, where survivors of the Philippines were gathered, Brigadier General W. E. Bougher noted in his diary for the eighth: " 'Rescript Day'—but no celebration. No flags up first time in 3½ years!" Something bad had happened when the monthly anniversary of Pearl Harbor was not marked. He gathered new hope.

News of the Bomb had even reached into the prison of Fresnes, where Pierre Laval, after a lengthy, politicized hearing, was awaiting his formal trial for treason. "I admit I am not surprised," he wrote in his diary. "I believed the Germans, who boasted so much about it, possessed such a device for use at the last moment. The weapon did exist, but in American hands. Will they be able to keep the secret for long?" He had once learned from Jean Bichelonne, a brilliant mineralogist and, before the surrender in 1940, deputy to the Minister of Armaments and later collaborationist Minister for Industrial Production in Laval's own vassal government, about the possibilities of using heavy water—deuterium oxide—to help make a uranium bomb. "This explains," Laval added, "his arrest by the Germans at the beginning of the Occupation." (He dated the occupation only from the German takeover of the Vichy puppet remnant.) Bichelonne, who might have known more than he was willing to share with the Nazis, then disappeared into Germany, where he died late in 1944 under mysterious circumstances following an apparently minor operation in an SS hospital in Berlin.

The Americans, Laval thought, might make political as well as military use of the weapon: "Japan would have no choice but to sue for peace and the realization of Stalin's dream might be delayed. In a few days we shall know the exact implications of this sensational discovery. . . ." Laval would never write about them. His diary ended a few lines later. The next day he was due to answer the charges brought against him.

The first Germans to be charged with war crimes were announced in London the same day, one of the outcomes of Potsdam. As befit the joint aspect of the tribunal to be set up in Nuremberg, the documents were signed in English, French, Russian, and, for the defendants, German. The first ten were Hermann Göring, Joachim von Ribbentrop, Franz von Papen, Alfred Rosenberg, General Wilhelm Keitel, Robert Ley, Julius Streicher, Arthur Seyss-Inquart, Karl Hermann, and General Alfred Jodl.* Learning that he was first on the list and that Dönitz had not yet been charged, Göring was delighted.

The German physicists at Godmanchester had not yet seen newspapers naming their compatriots. What interested them from press accounts was whether the Bomb scientists had "a running stabilized machine," as Bagge called it—a reactor—and what plutonium was. They also had no idea how such an efficient chain reaction had been achieved without heavy water. Heisenberg still professed to be baffled, especially about plutonium: "We could not see how we could do it because we did not have this element, and we saw no prospect of being able to obtain it. How they have obtained this element is still a mystery."

"Yes," said Wirtz, "but I believe that they have got it and I feel sure that the bomb is not big."

In London the news of the deployment of the Bomb had left Churchill even more disconsolate than he had been on the day the election results were posted. The biggest events of his life were occurring and he was removed from them. Dr. Moran called on him at Duncan Sandys's flat in Westminster Gardens. Sandys, an M.P., was his son-in-law, married to Diana Churchill. Moran found Churchill sitting on the edge of his bed, looking at the floor. He complained of waking at about four each morning and having to take a sleeping pill to keep "futile speculations" from his mind. His family wanted him to go away with his paints and brushes, perhaps to the Riviera. "If I'm ill," he suggested to Moran, "you could fly out." Churchill didn't care if he never saw England again.

"It's no use, Charles, pretending I'm not hard hit. I can't school myself to do nothing for the rest of my life. It would have been better to have been killed in an aeroplane, or to have died like Roosevelt. After I left Postdam," Churchill claimed, "Joe did what he liked.

*Ribbentrop had been Foreign Minister; Papen, once ambassador to Austria, had been instrumental in the *Anschluss;* Rosenberg, an anti-Semitic ideologue, had been chief civilian administrator of occupied Russian territory; Ley, head of the Labor Front, oversaw much of the use of slave labor; Streicher had been publisher of the organ of the SS and high priest of anti-Semitism; Hermann was the overseer of occupied Czechoslovakia.

I'd not have agreed and the Americans would have backed me."
(Neither part of his speculation was true, as he had agreed in principle to the new borders at Yalta.) "I get fits of depression. You know
how my days were filled: now it is all gone."

There was no question that Communism in some police state form or
other was the future for the liberated nations between newly swollen
Russia and truncated Germany. In the Sudeten lands of Czechoslovakia, ethnically German but transferred to the new nation at Versailles
in 1919 and recovered by the Nazis in 1938 at Munich, the new "People's Democracy" was still putting into internment camps those Germans not yet expelled. One was Maria Schubert, a Great War widow
of fifty-eight who had worked in a factory much of her life in a town
near the German border. "Never," her son contended, "did we have a
picture of Hitler in our home." Father Hermann Schubert, describing
the eviction of his mother, noted that all the belongings she could
take with her filled an old suitcase and a rucksack. And even from
that several pieces of clothing were stolen during her first night in
the camp.

On August 8 he bicycled to Hohenelbe to negotiate with the authorities for her release. A Czech woman at the camp office shouted
at him, "All Germans ought to be gassed! All Germans ought to be
murdered!" He managed ("through the help of someone I know") to
secure Frau Schubert's release to Trautenau, where he was still allowed to be pastor of his church. But he had to leave behind his aunt,
"aged 72 and completely blind." Dismissing his appeal, the medical
officer of the camp told him confidently, "As a Catholic priest you
will have very little work amongst us Czechs. Fundamentally the
Czech people do not believe in God."

The next day Father Schubert pushed his bicycle, with his
mother on it and her remaining possessions tied to it, the twenty-one
miles to Trautenau. Germans were not permitted to use the railway.
Three weeks later the three priests in his vicarage were arrested,
placed in a work camp at Ober Alstadt, and assigned to a factory for
the bleaching of yarn at Eipel, where Schubert remained until he was
expelled to Germany in February 1946.

Harry Truman was in his office early on Wednesday morning to prepare for a nine o'clock conference with aides and with the new Secretary of the Treasury, John Snyder. There was some talk of the atomic

bomb, and the President brought up Admiral Leahy's having said to the last that it would not go off. The Bomb was the subject of his morning appointment with Secretary Stimson, who wanted to discuss the likely surrender and occupation to follow, and the importance of Emperor Hirohito in accomplishing both objects. He knew, Stimson said, that the public had long considered Hirohito a war criminal of even a higher order than the Nazis to be brought to trial, yet he stressed "kindness" and "tact" in dealing with Japan. Trying the homely approach Truman himself often used, he cajoled, "When you punish your dog, you don't keep souring on him all day after the punishment is over." It was the "same way with Japan." After the war, Americans had to get along with the Japanese to rebuild that part of the world. Then he confided that he would soon be stepping down on the advice of his physicians. He was a month from his seventy-eighth birthday and had been in public service for most of the last forty years of his life. The next Secretary, he warned, would have the onerous job of downsizing the Army. It would not be much easier than making war.

In Moscow it was already five o'clock. Ambassador Sato had arrived at the Kremlin to see Foreign Commissar Molotov after waiting weeks for the appointment. The previous day Molotov had moved up the time from 8:00 P.M. to 5:00 P.M. Earlier on the eighth the Politburo had met urgently to instruct Gosplan, the State Planning Committee, to prepare a new Five-Year Plan for 1946–1950 that would emphasize "technological progress." Perhaps the earliest symbol of what that meant would be the Special Committee on the Atomic Bomb, set up secretly twelve days later under the chairmanship of NKVD boss Laventrii Beria. In statement after statement by Soviet bigwigs thereafter, including Molotov, "technological progress" seemed a barely disguised code for an accelerated atomic bomb project, for "monopoly capitalism"—which meant the West—remained the enemy. Given the opportunity it might even revive, as allies, Germany and Japan. As Molotov claimed years later, the atomic bombs dropped on Japan "were, of course, not against Japan, but against the Soviet Union. . . ."

As the Japanese ambassador was ushered into Molotov's study, he began congratulating him, in Russian, on his safe return from Potsdam, but Molotov interrupted, saying brusquely, "I have a communication to make in the name of the Soviet government." He asked

Sato to take a seat and began reading—in Russian—from a paper he had yet to let Sato see. "I had been prepared for the worst for some time past," the ambassador recalled, "so I did not lose my tranquility of mind. Since, however, our government had humbly solicited the good offices of the Soviet government in restoring peace, I thought it might not be altogether impossible for the Soviet Union to come forward and accept the noble role of mediator. Therefore I cannot deny that I was considerably shocked when I received the sudden notification. Feeling that what was to come had come at last, I maintained a calm attitude."

Molotov's paper was a declaration of war, based less upon the request Stalin had solicited from Truman—it was not sufficiently supplicatory—than upon the Potsdam ultimatum that the Soviets were not asked to sign:

> After the defeat and surrender of Hitlerite Germany, Japan remained the only great power which still held out for continuing the war.
>
> The demand of the three powers—the United States of America, Great Britain, and China—of July 26, 1945, concerning the unconditional surrender of the Japanese armed forces was refused by Japan. The proposal of the Japanese Government to the Soviet Union concerning mediation in the war in the Far East thereby loses all basis.
>
> Taking into consideration the refusal of Japan to surrender, the Allies approached the Soviet Government with a proposal to join the war against Japanese aggression and thereby shorten the length of the war, reduce the number of victims, and assist in the prompt reestablishment of general peace.
>
> Faithful to its obligations to its Allies, the Soviet Government accepted the proposal of the Allies and adheres to the statement of the Allied powers of July 26, 1945.
>
> The Soviet Government considers that its policy is the only means of hastening the coming peace, to deliver the people from further sacrifice and suffering, and enable the Japanese people to avoid those dangers and destructions which Germany suffered after its refusal to surrender unconditionally.
>
> In view of the foregoing, the Soviet Government declares

that as of tomorrow, that is, as of 9 August, the Soviet Union
will consider [that] it is in a state of war with Japan.

Sato scrutinized the statement and asked what was meant by the
words "to deliver the people from further sacrifice and suffering, and
enable the Japanese people to avoid those dangers and destructions
which Germany suffered. . . ." Molotov explained that the Soviet
government "wished to shorten the duration of the war and de-
crease sacrifices."

The Pacific war, now, Sato remarked ruefully, "would not be of
long duration."

In his car on the way back to the Japanese embassy, Sato observed to his secretary, "What had to come has come!" Molotov had
moved the meeting forward to present his war note before midnight
on the ninth in Manchuria, but before Sato could encode and rush the
news to Tokyo it was already morning in East Asia. The message was
relayed to the Emperor and the Prime Minister, who notified his
Supreme War Council. With Foreign Minister Togo, Suzuki hurried
to the palace, emerging to tell his private secretary that he was determined to end the war as quickly as possible. The Red Army had already gone into action, before dawn, against the remnant of the
Manchuria garrison, depleted to bolster the defenses in Kyushu.

In Moscow, after ushering Sato out into the bleak light of early
evening, Molotov telephoned the American and British ambassadors
with the news, explaining to Averell Harriman that while at one time
the Soviet government thought that it could not move before mid-
August it had now strictly lived up to its Yalta obligations. To the
British ambassador Molotov sounded almost regretful—an almost
unprecedented reaction from the cold Foreign Commissar—about his
treatment of Sato, who was "a kind-hearted man" with whom he had
always had good relations.

At 2:45 in Washington, press secretary Charlie Ross looked in on
waiting reporters at the White House. Announcing that the President
would have a brief statement to make at 3:00 P.M., he left no time for
newspapermen out on long lunches to return. In the oval office, Truman was sitting at his desk with Secretary Byrnes at his left. Admiral
Leahy entered and sat down at Truman's right, holding, like Byrnes, a
sheet of pink paper, which the reporters could see was headed in red
ink TOP SECRET. Rising, the President said, "I have only a simple announcement to make. I can't hold a regular press conference today, but

this announcement is so important I thought I would call you in. Russia has declared war on Japan. That is all." What Truman did not say may have been, in the long run, even more important. There was no word of gratification, no word of thanks, to Premier Stalin for his intervention to help end the war. As Truman now realized, it was ending—and soon. A B-29 had already been in the air for two hours en route to Japan. It carried a second and very likely decisive atomic bomb. Truman could not tell the reporters that the Russian declaration he had once looked forward to might now only complicate the peace.

There was a rush for the doors.

From the naval attaché in the Moscow embassy came a cable to the Chief of Naval Operations: "Red Navy . . . not alerted until late evening 8 August when huge liberty parties [in Japan were] recalled and wives [of] government officials started [to] evacuate." Although another cable read, "Senior Soviet convoy officer states each Russian vessel has sealed instructions to be opened in case of declaration of war against Japan . . .", it seemed likely that the decision to intervene had been made in a hurry.

From Khabarovsk in eastern Siberia the Russians lost no time in denouncing the evil machinations of the new enemy. A Soviet High Command radio station there charged violation of the Neutrality (Non-Aggression) Pact, recounted the aggressive behavior of Japan ("always . . . very wolf-like"), and indicted Japanese "right-wing Imperialists who are destroying the interests of the people." An American monitoring post picked up the broadcast and cabled the text to Washington.

Shortly there was another, and longer, cable in code to the White House from Harriman, in Moscow. "I saw Stalin and Molotov this evening," Harriman began. (He had arrived with Minister-Counselor George F. Kennan, his chief aide, fluent in Russian.) "Stalin said that his advance troops had already crossed the frontiers of Manchuria both from the west and the east not meeting heavy resistance on any front and had advanced 10 to 12 kilometers in some sections." Stalin described three main attacks from the west, one south, one east from Outer Mongolia, and another through the Gobi Desert toward southern Manchuria. From the Vladivostock area, which dipped southeast, cutting off Manchuria from the Sea of Japan, another thrust aimed at the key industrial city of Harbin, the heart of the puppet empire. The Russians had not yet attacked the long island of Sakhalin, just north of Hokkaido, but planned to do so.

In discussing the Japanese situation, Stalin—so Harriman continued—"said that he thought the Japanese were looking for a pretext to set up a government that would surrender and he thought that the atomic bomb might give this pretext." It was clear that the Bomb had precipitated Stalin's decision to rush into the war before that happened. "He showed great interest in the atomic bomb and said that it could mean the end of the war and aggression but that the secret would have to be well kept. He said that they had found in Berlin laboratories in which the Germans were working on the breaking of the atom but that he did not find that they had come to any results. Soviet scientists had also been working on the problem but had not been able to solve it."

Winging northwest in the forward bay of *Bock's Car* was the solution, a single bomb named "Fat Man" long before in a sardonic bow to Churchill. He was out of the war but his surrogate was carrying on for him.

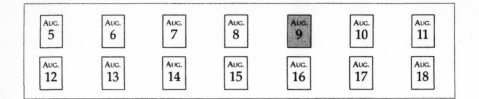

| Aug. 5 | Aug. 6 | Aug. 7 | Aug. 8 | Aug. 9 | Aug. 10 | Aug. 11 |
|---|---|---|---|---|---|---|
| Aug. 12 | Aug. 13 | Aug. 14 | Aug. 15 | Aug. 16 | Aug. 17 | Aug. 18 |

CHAPTER XXVIII

# · AUGUST 9, 1945 ·

## *Special Bombing Mission 16*

At 3:49 A.M. Tinian time the B-29 strike planes of Special Bombing Mission 16 began lifting off from North Field. Major Charles W. Sweeney had flown Number 89, *The Great Artiste*, on the Hiroshima run; his plane, second to take off, still fitted out to calibrate the atomic blast, had Captain Frederick Bock at the controls. Sweeney, in *Bock's Car*, was carrying "Fat Man," the plutonium bomb. Number 90, slightly late in departing, carried the cameras—but not the chief cameraman. Dr. Robert Serber, the 509th expert in high-speed photography, had turned up without his parachute and was ordered to get it. He returned to find his B-29 already in the air. General Farrell had to break radio silence to reach Major James I. Hopkins, Jr., and have the unhappy Serber furnish twenty minutes of instructions on operating his equipment.

Hopkins, the operations officer for the 509th, had cut and signed Order 39 that put him on the mission, which was beginning badly. Sergeant John Kuharek, the flight engineer for *Bock's Car*, had discovered before takeoff that an auxiliary transfer pump was defective. Of the plane's 7,250 gallons of fuel, 600 gallons in the reserve bomb bay tanks were inaccessible and represented a sharp cut in range—and, at eight pounds per gallon, more than two tons of useless weight. The alternative to going up with less fuel than was needed for the round-trip was to delay the mission until the typhoon moving up toward Iwo Jima toward Japan had dissipated. For Sweeney there was no alternative. Iwo and Okinawa were emergency landing sites en route home.

Although "Fat Man" was a message in itself, the instrument plane was carrying a special, personal, one. Taped to each of the three instrument cylinders to be dropped from *The Great Artiste* was a letter addressed to a Japanese nuclear physicist, Professor Ryukochi Sagane. Luis Alvarez, Philip Morrison, and Robert Serber remembered Sagane as a postdoctoral researcher at Berkeley in 1938. If anyone in Japan could explain the enormity of what would continue to happen to Japan if it did not surrender, they thought he could. They urged him to use his influence "as a reputable nuclear physicist" to explain the Bomb and the consequences of further resistance, as the "output" of American atomic bomb factories "will be exploded on your homeland" until the war ended. "We implore you to confirm these facts to your leaders and to do your utmost to stop the destruction and waste of life which can result in the total annihilation of your cities. . . . As scientists, we deplore the use to which a beautiful discovery has been put, but we can assure you that unless Japan surrenders at once, this rain of atomic bombs will increase many fold in fury."

An extra passenger in the instrument plane was William L. Laurence of *The New York Times,* in the interest of secrecy the only journalist permitted to cover the Manhattan Engineering District from beginning to deployment. It would be the most interesting ride he had taken since, at seventeen, a penniless Latvian Jew, he had been smuggled out of Czarist Russia in a barrel after the uprisings of 1905. Taking notes as his B-29 headed for the rendezvous point off Kyushu, he wrote, "Somewhere ahead of me lies Japan, the land of our enemy. In a few hours . . . one of its cities, making weapons of war for use against us, will be wiped off the map by the greatest weapon ever made by man. In a fraction of time immeasurable by any clock, a whirlwind from the skies will pulverize thousands of its buildings and tens of thousands of its inhabitants. Does one feel any pity or compassion for the poor devils about to die? Not when one thinks of Pearl Harbor and of the Death March on Bataan."

The primary target was Kokura, on the northern coast of Kyushu just east of Yawata. The aiming point would be its vast arsenal. The secondary target was Nagasaki, on the west coast of Kyushu, where four Mitsubishi plants dominated production. Niigata, the remaining city on the approved list, was excluded as too distant from the other two. This time the bomb could not be armed in the air as "Little Boy" had been. "Fat Man" was devised to be detonated by an implosion caused by the simultaneous explosion inward of sixty-three lens molds that surrounded the plutonium core. If anything could go wrong it would be an electrical malfunction—and there was one. In mid-flight Lieutenant Philip Barnes, overseer of the "black box" monitor of the bomb's circuitry, had to awaken Commander Frederick L. Ashworth, the mission weaponeer, when a red warning light began to flash. A mistake in the arming process had reversed two switches. After some frantic searching Barnes located the problem.

*Bock's Car* had been climbing toward its 31,000-foot rendezvous point over Yakujima, an island off the south coast of Kyushu, reaching it at nine minutes after nine, one minute ahead of schedule. Three minutes later it was joined by *The Great Artiste*. Its crew spotted the camera observation plane close to Yakujima, then lost visual contact. Hopkins, in the third plane, never saw the others, mistaking one of the smaller islands off Kyushu for Yakujima, but radio exchanges to reposition each other were forbidden. Using up precious fuel, Sweeney circled for forty-five minutes before wagging his wings to instruct Fred Bock to follow him. The weather planes that preceded them from Tinian at 2:30 A.M.—one was Number 82, the *Enola Gay*, now flown by George Marquardt—had reported clear skies, and *Bock's Car* turned toward northern Kyushu.

Over Kokura, the Twentieth Air Force paid the price for its earlier missions to pound Yawata. The wind had shifted slightly. Smoke still rising from the wreckage of Yawata, mixed with industrial haze, obscured the arsenal. The bombardier, Captain Kermit K. Beahan, could see a river running through the target area, and the streets of Kokura, but not his aiming point. The bomb bay doors opened, and as the steady humming signal indicating that the Bomb was ready for release warned the crew that fifty-two seconds remained before implosion, Sweeney called out, "No drop. Relax. We're going 'round again."

*Bock's Car* approached from another angle, but again the arsenal was obscured. Kuharek knew that there was no chance now of getting back to Tinian. There was barely enough fuel to make Iwo Jima. Still, Sweeney wanted one more bomb run. Electronics specialist Jake Beser, monitoring Japanese radio and radar signals, and the only crewman on both atomic strike planes, began to pick up indications that they were being intercepted—adjustments to AA direction and flak bursts—and he reported: "Zeros on the way up. About ten." Sweeney shook off the threat. Zeros could not reach his altitude.

A third try was visually no better. Consulting with Beahan and Ashworth, Sweeney decided to head southwest for Nagasaki, and not seeing Fred Bock's plane behind him, asked on his intercom, "Where's Bock?" But he had inadvertently pressed the wrong button and broken radio silence. Still circling the wrong island off Kyushu, Hopkins in the camera plane overheard and shouted, "Is that you, Chuck? Where the hell are you?"

Closing the open switch and hoping the Japanese had not picked him up, Sweeney offered no navigational clue to Hopkins, and flew on, wondering what to do if Nagasaki was also obscured. With no spare fuel, *Bock's Car* might have to ditch. His intention now was to make one run over the secondary target and drop the bomb— visually if possible, by radar at last resort. Ashworth was deputy to Deak Parsons and knew that no one in the chain of command would want the Bomb ditched in the sea with the plane, or wasted over open water. If they reached Iwo or Okinawa with it, they risked blowing up the island in a crash landing. Further, the entire military purpose in deploying the second bomb was to demonstrate American potential to obliterate Japan. Besides, carrying the five tons of bomb any longer might reduce their fuel below what was essential for an emergency landing. Fifty-five minutes circling back and forth over Kokura and two tons of unusable fuel had not been included in their contingency plans.

With the other alternatives seemingly worse than an instrument drop, Ashworth bit the bullet. "Drop it by radar if you can't do it visually," he told Beahan. "I'll take the responsibility."

As *Bock's Car* turned toward Nagasaki, clouds were closing in from the typhoon offshore to the south. Approaching the city, navigator James Van Pelt, Jr., realized that the orders requiring the bombardier to see an atomic target through the cross hairs were not going to apply. It would be Ashworth's drop. "I'll guarantee we come within a thousand feet of the target," Sweeney assured him, "and that's better than dropping it in the ocean."

Nagasaki had not been immune to bombs. Although on the restricted list, it had been hit three times during the summer by B-24s from Okinawa, the last time on August 1. An air raid warning had sounded earlier when a 509th weather plane was high overhead, but that threat had passed uneventfully. Inhabitants were back at their daily pursuits, which included weapons manufacturing at a reduced level because of shortages of materials. Among the morning activities was Mass in Our Lady of the Immaculate Conception, the largest Roman Catholic cathedral in the Far East, on a bluff overlooking the Urakami Valley. Nagasaki had long been the center of Catholicism in Japan. Americans and Europeans also knew the city as the setting for a beloved opera, Giacomo Puccini's *Madama Butterfly*, as Commodore Matthew Calbraith Perry had opened the port to the United States Navy in 1853, after which a succession of Lieutenant Pinkertons had witnessed the collisions of tradition and modernization in Japan.

At North Field on Tinian concern had deepened into alarm. It was approaching noon, Marianas time. *Bock's Car* was overdue. When a message arrived from Hopkins, piloting the wandering camera plane—"Has Number 77 aborted?"—Groves's deputy, General Farrell, was near panic.

"We could only pray," said Farrell when it was over, "that if it had aborted, it had dropped into the ocean rather than on Japan. We didn't feel our people were particularly welcome in Japan at that time."

At lunch, the shaken Farrell lost his. Returning to the North Field communications center, he sweated out the silence until he heard a radio operator say, "Stand by for a message from Number 77!"

At the moment of Hopkins's unfortunately phrased query, *Bock's Car* was approaching the rough X that Nagasaki formed, its upper arms populated valleys, its lower arms residential and industrial areas sloping down on either side to the harbor. The aiming point, to spread the blast across the least hilly land, was just above the Mitsubishi shipyards. Ground Zero was just below the crossing point of the diagonals, in the heart of the city toward the bay. At thirty seconds to release, Beahan thought he had found a hole in the 8/10 cloud layer and shouted, "I'll take it!" It was 11:58 A.M. in Tinian, an hour earlier in Nagasaki.

Sweeney banked sharply down from his 28,900-foot altitude and the bomb bay swung open for the fourth time. Sure he had the Mitsubishi Arms Manufacturing Plant, his secondary target, in his cross hairs, Beahan paused, then sang out the traditional "Bombs away!"—amending it immediately to "Bomb away!" "Fat Man"—a fat football in shape, with large, boxy fins at one end and a thousand pounds heavier than the Hiroshima bomb—fell from the plane at 12:01. Suddenly lightheaded, the B-29 jumped up as Sweeney put the plane into an immediate sharp, diving turn; behind him Bock executed a turn in reverse direction, dropping his instrument tubes with their chutes.

Radar proximity fuses did the rest, closing the final switches for the implosion of the radioactive material at 1,540 feet. The Bomb detonated just over the stadium in the Urakami Valley, three miles off target—but only a half mile northeast of the alternative aiming point, the sprawling arms complex. The dazzling blue-white flash caught the quarter million residents of Nagasaki by surprise. The upper valleys felt a crushing blast wave and searing heat. The Mitsubishi steel plant was smashed and the Mitsubishi-Urakami Torpedo Factory skeletonized. Just under a half mile to the northeast of the blast center the roof and masonry of the cathedral collapsed on the worshipers.

Only a mile from the epicenter, in the Mitsubishi Foundry for which Camp 14 furnished POW labor, Bernard O'Keefe of Warrnambool, a town south of Melbourne, looked up as a lone bomber flew past and saw a package float down by parachute. He had no idea that it was the instrument cylinder and that the flash and blast simultaneous with it were from a plane he hadn't seen. His top teeth went through his bottom lip but he managed to carry a fellow POW with an injured shoulder behind a huge boulder, and when they looked up again it seemed "like the end of the world was coming as the sun appeared to be falling towards the earth."

The terrible flash seemed to echo Shakespeare's Prospero:

> *I have bedimm'd*
> *The noontide sun, call'd forth the mutinous winds,*
> *And 'twixt the green sea and the azur'd vault*
> *Set roaring war.*

The boulder shielding Bernard O'Keefe enabled him to survive to eat horsemeat cooked with the heat of the bomb—his first meat in two years—and to live into 1977. Eight Dutch POWs and an Englishman died in the blast. Others, Jack Johnson, another Aussie, wrote, had "weeping flesh where the skin was blown from their bodies and hung about them like the skin of a potato that had been boiled in its jacket." Twenty-four Australians survived to cremate the eleven who did not on heaps of splintered wood from collapsed buildings.

Camp 2, in the dockyards, fared better, Bob Watkins recalling the heat and the noise "followed soon by a great rush of air" and dust that rose "knee high" after the shock of the concussion. The dockyards were spared but much of Nagasaki's industrial area was destroyed—and with it six hospitals, a prison, eighteen schools, and residential areas with about one hundred thousand people, of whom forty thousand died and sixty thousand were injured. Because of the contours of the land where tracks ran, no interruption in railway service occurred. The crew of an inbound train assisted in rescue work, and aid was quickly available from nearby cities. Of thirty-one thousand Second Army troops in the area, nearly seven thousand died in the blast; the others were put to work in relief efforts and removal of wreckage.

Head of the radiology department at the medical school of the University of Nagasaki, Dr. Takashi Nagai was swept into the air by the blast and buried under debris that had been his wing of the hospital. He crawled out, holding his forehead where, he could feel, an artery had been cut by a shard of glass. From outpatients to physicians, most people in the building who had survived found themselves nearly naked, scorched, and bleeding. "Covered with dirt and smoke," Nagai would write in *The Bells of Nagasaki*, "they were gray like phantoms, and it was difficult to believe that they were human. . . . Some, in whom a spark of life remained, extricated themselves from the vast and motionless heap of dead flesh and crawled up to me." Everyone appealed for some sort of help, yet whenever Nagai removed a hand from his injured head "the blood would spurt out like red ink from a water pistol. . . . But since it was a small artery, I thought my body would hold out for about three hours."

Professor Raisuke Shirabe of the medical school had come up from breakfast with other faculty members to note in his diary their talk of the "growing austerity" in Nagasaki that made their dining at the college easier to feed families at home. "My wife and I, only yesterday, had gone far out into the country to forage for food. . . . Even now, my face burns with shame at the memory of having to plead with farmers to sell us some food, which I, a university professor, then had to carry away on my back, like an ox." The morning air raid alarm had been lifted just in time for his nine o'clock class, after which he met with other senior professors to discuss how to indicate to enemy aircraft "that a hospital is on our campus." Beginning the next day, they decided, the roofs of all buildings would be painted with "a giant red cross." Back again in his office, he heard the drone of high-flying planes and rose to go to the shelter. "But I only got as far as the door before a pale light swept over me. I threw myself in the corner, closed my eyes and crouched in smallness as the building began to collapse around me." Everything around him fell down and it seemed to be twilight. The next thing he remembered was picking up the clock that had been on his desk. It had stopped at 11:02.

Most hospital buildings had collapsed into smoking rubble. Electricity was gone. There was no water. In Nagai's wing some nurses, doctors, students, and attendants were relatively uninjured, but a corner of the building was burning, the flames whipped by a hot wind. In the X-ray room a doctor and a nurse wound some gauze tightly about Nagai's forehead, but the hemorrhaging seeped through, dripping down his chin. A pair of clogs were found in the debris for him.

Twenty minutes had passed since the *pika*. He realized that someone had to organize those who were left and evacuate the area, carrying whatever was useful and salvageable, as well as those who might make it, up the hill behind the hospital to a safer location. He saw survivors of the blast and fire outside already moving in that direction. Two medical students and a technician looked back at the X-ray equipment. "The machines can wait," Nagai said. "Let's attend to the people."

What he saw of them horrified him:

Their clothes were torn and many of them were completely naked. From downtown they ran, climbing the mountain with tottering steps in an effort to escape the flames. Two children passed by dragging their father. A young woman ran clutching a headless child. An aged couple, hand in hand, slowly climbed the mountain. As she ran, a girl's clothes burst into flames and she fell writhing in a ball of fire. On top of a roof that was enveloped in flames, I saw a man dancing and singing wildly: he was out of his mind. Some people kept looking back, looking back as they ran; others did not even turn their heads.

The chief nurse ran to Nagai and handed him a sheet of paper. It was a leaflet headed "To the People of Japan"—one of thousands dropped by B-29s and now raised by the scalding winds. Glancing at it quickly, he shouted, "The atomic bomb!" Much of what he had already seen evidenced the effects of radioactivity but he had put it out of his mind. On the ground nearby lay a bamboo spear, left behind after an early morning drill of the "volunteer" *Kokumin Giyutai*. "I kicked it fiercely," he remembered, "and it made a dull, hollow sound. Grasping it in my hand, I raised it to the sky as tears rolled down my cheeks. The bamboo spear against the atomic bomb! What a tragic comedy this was! This was no longer a war."

As in Hiroshima, thousands of blackened and blistered remnants of the population were streaming out of the devastated sectors of the city, eastward over the hills into Nishiyama and south into the less damaged harbor areas. As in Hiroshima, many were not only burned and naked but had flaps of peeling and shredding skin hanging from their bodies. Some were hairless, even faceless. They moaned for water, or merely in pain. Radiation effect left them retching or running with diarrhea as they shuffled through debris-clogged, treeless streets. Rescue workers who rushed in by truck or by rail once Urakami Station was cleared sobbed as they collected corpses and piled them into mounds for cremation. There was no shortage of splintered wood to keep the pyres going.

As Mrs. Shoda had written three days earlier about Hiroshima,

*Gulping cupfuls of sake one after another,*
*A weeping man is burning bodies.*

They were reduced, Nagai realized, to "really primitive medicine." By the time they had dragged out what could be saved, and assembled people, it was two o'clock, almost two hours since the blast. The fires around them were stronger, now fed by a west wind.

Since the wind was blowing toward the university, the coal shed began to be in danger, and I decided that the patients must be taken to the field further up the hill. But what a task that proved to be! The path was narrow and blocked with the wreckage of houses, and we had to climb over bare rocks and stone fences carrying the patients one by one. I myself climbed up twice, each time taking a patient on my back. But when it came to a third, I knew that my strength had left me and I could not go on. My temple artery had not stopped bleeding and I had had to change the bandage three times. The chief nurse warned me that my face was ghastly pale and I realized that my pulse was very weak. . . .

A baby howled and howled. The mother, seriously wounded, lay unconscious. And beside her lay this baby, about two months old with a protruding navel, crying wildly. Since the fire was approaching rapidly, I felt that I must at least save the baby. So I took her in my arms and, climbing up the hill, laid her close to Nurse Hamazaki. Just at that moment Hamazaki uttered a deep groan and slumped over on her side. Sensing that her end had come, I took a scissors and cut a lock from the front of her hair and put it in my pocket.

As they moved patients and injured staff uphill at the back of the hospital, rain began to fall, "black rain the size of the tip of one's finger. When it splashed on something, it left a stain like that made by crude oil. . . . It seemed to come from the dark cloud above us." He sensed an "even more ghastly" phenomenon. "The oxygen in the air had been used up by the fire, and there was an extraordinary upsurge of carbon dioxide, so that it was difficult to breathe in this valley of flames. As we worked, we were panting like dogs."

From the slope they watched their documents, specimens, photographs, and equipment go up in flames, along with what proved to be only 8 percent of those who had been in the hospital—workers, students, and patients. From one of the wards a doctor had salvaged a large white sheet. Dabbing the blood that was still dripping from his own head and chin, Professor Nagai traced a huge circular Rising Sun and attached the sheet to a bamboo pole. "We lifted it up and watched it flutter loudly as the hot wind blew all around." As a student carried their improvised flag along the hill, now covered with black smoke from the city, the evacuees defiantly moved what was left of the medical school upwind from its ashes.

The energy released by plutonium implosion was almost identical to that of the earlier uranium bomb. Since the ridges and valleys reduced the shock wave and limited its range, no firestorm arose, as in Hiroshima, but there was fire enough through the narrow streets and tile-roofed wooden houses in the Urakami Valley, and a reprise of the deadly black, radioactive rain from the condensing, debris-laden mushroom cloud that quickly rose fifty thousand feet above Nagasaki. To one of the Allied prisoners in local camps, it was "a great columnar anvil."

Many of the POWs were survivors of Malaya, Java, and Sumatra—Dutch, British, and Anzac. The Americans were largely from the Philippines. Most who lived through the usual Japanese brutality, and were brutalized further by Korean guards, survived the Bomb—the blast, the fire, the spreading radiation—by being underground. They had been laboring in the mines that dotted the hills around Nagasaki. Once a crewman at Clark Field, Anton Bilek worked a coal shaft in Omura, across the bay, but had been hospitalized with beriberi. He had only known that American forces had neared the home islands because he had seen fighter planes. "They had to be within three hundred miles to send fighters." When the barracks shook, "We turned around and there's the big mushroom, way up in the air."

Only a mile and a half north of the fireball, Ensign Jolly of the Netherlands Navy saw the parachutes drop at almost the same time as the flash. Instinctively he dived under a table as the building collapsed, crushing POWs around him. Jack Madison, captured at Corregidor, was at a coal-washing pit only two miles from the fireball when *Bock's Car* passed overhead. The blast knocked him unconscious. Alf Carne—an Australian—worked a mine at Yoshikuma, side-by-side with Japanese men and women who toiled nearly naked a half mile below the surface. When above ground now he often saw his "own" planes, but on the morning of the ninth POWs noticed, across the bay, only a parachute, and then a second one. Another American said, "Some poor bastard has had it." Then "a tremendous flash lit the sky, and a great column of smoke went up. The explosion was several seconds after the flash, and shook us even where we were. The Nips went crazy and set about us with rifle butts and flats of bayonets as we cheered like mad. . . ." At Fukuoka Camp 24, well north of Nagasaki, Lieutenant Julien Goodman, once ward surgeon at the Fort McKinley hospital in Manila, was in a mine storeroom when he heard a roar resembling "a myriad of sixteen-inch naval batteries fired in unison." He fell to the floor, which shook, but except for the radio in Japanese headquarters, which chattered constantly, an ominous quiet followed. Prisoners sensed that something terrible had happened at Nagasaki, and soon the POW senior officer was informed that when the next shift emerged from the mine, no more would go down. The reason remained a mystery, but it was easy to relate the two events.

As the boiling mushroom cloud rose, Second Lieutenant Nobukazu Komatsu and two crew members were on patrol from Sasebo Naval Base toward Nagasaki to the south. Pilots had access to radios, and like others at Sasebo he had picked up President Truman's message about the Hiroshima bomb. They had all wondered what an atomic bomb really was, and Komatsu was eager to get "some first-hand information." At 11:05 the base radio had broadcast news of a "great bombing in Nagasaki City." He found his helmet and announced, "Follow me, those of you who want to," and went out to his floatplane. By 11:10 he was airborne. Nagasaki was forty miles distant.

The black pillar of smoke was already visible, still rising and expanding. At ten thousand feet he was well below its cap. As the cloud boiled, its colors changed, and Komatsu circled to get a better look, increasing the temperature inside his plane. Opening his cabin window, he poked out a gloved hand. The air felt like live steam and he drew in a blackened glove, but behind him Chief Petty Officer Umeda had inhaled the vapor and was instantly nauseous. The cabin window darkened with soot and Komatsu realized that he was flying through the widening column of cloud. The heat was intense, and the co-pilot, Lieutenant Tomimura, screamed. Suddenly they were blinded by sunlight. In eight minutes they had passed through an edge of the pillar.

Komatsu took the plane lower, and at a thousand feet he skirted Nagasaki. Black smoke rose as if from a crude oil fire. He splashed to a landing in the harbor, where the lack of damage surprised him, but up the Urakami Valley he saw what was obviously the area of the blast. Taking off his boots and carrying them, he got out in the shallow water with Tomimura, leaving the sick Umeda with the plane, and as they hurried uphill away from the waterfront they began to see the city in agony. The closer they came to the Urakami area the more the fleeing people became almost unidentifiable as humans, hopelessly burned, charred, speechless in silent screams. Bodies were sprawled everywhere. He had no water to offer, and most victims were beyond help.

The two pilots turned back, downhill, away from the fires. In shock at the horrors they had seen as they trudged upward, they had not noticed the imprint of the Bomb. Now they saw the railing of a vaporized bridge imprinted on the pavement, a diagonal stripe across a street that was once a telephone pole, the shadow of a man on the ground. Two hours after they had left their plane they found the harbor no longer empty. Bodies floated in it or were nearby on the wharves—victims seeking watery relief. They pushed corpses aside to make a path for takeoff, and flew north, shaken, to Sasebo. (They would pay a price for the venture into the cloud. Umeda died of leukemia in 1947, Tomimura in 1964; Komatsu would suffer from chronic anemia.)

At Isahaya, fifteen miles northeast of Nagasaki, just below Omura, Gunji Kitamura, chief of production at the aircraft factory, had heard the deep drumbeat of the blast, dropped a tool he had been holding, and rushed outside. With further rumbling came a strong wind, then quiet. He was about to return inside when he saw a huge column of smoke rising from the direction of Nagasaki, and moments later an office employee ran out to tell him that the air defense post at Shiroyama had reported a monster bomb dropped on the city—after which the message had broken off. When, at about one o'clock, two hours later, he received a message to come down to the research laboratory, Kitamura assumed that more news had arrived. He had been worried earlier when someone brought him a leaflet dropped on Nagasaki by a B-29 warning inhabitants to leave before further cities were destroyed like Hiroshima. Now, on a table in the lab, he saw a metal cylinder—or bomb—about five feet long and one and a half feet wide. It had been found, he was told, in a field near Uki. "They say it was dropped from a B-29 at about the same time as the other bomb, and that a parachute was attached to it."

There were, he could see, some small openings punched in the tube. Putting an ear against it, he could hear a steady ticking. It could be a bomb, he said. "I suggest that all leave and wait outside." Everyone in the room disappeared quickly, except for an assistant who offered loyally to stay.

At the back end of the cylinder, where there were stabilizing fins, Kitamura saw a screw cap. He tried it and it turned easily. Inside seemed to be dozens of tiny instruments. Taped to the cap was a white envelope. Despite his limited English he could make out what it said: "To Professor Sagane."

A lab technician knew of Ryukochi Sagane, who had taught him physics at Tokyo University. A half hour later they had translated the letter. Tears filled Kitamura's eyes. The message meant the end of the empire. It would take two weeks before Sagane could reach Isahaya and collect his mail.

As the towering mushroom cloud, now dark below but blood-red and white above, receded toward the northwest, radioman Abe Spitzer reported to Tinian that Nagasaki had been bombed visually with "effects about equal to Hiroshima." "Trouble in airplane," he added, required a stop en route back. "Fuel only to get to Okinawa." Ditching became a real possibility, but as they closed the 350 miles to Okinawa they saw no Dumbos or picket subs below. So much time had elapsed since *Bock's Car* had been expected on the route that rescue crews had assumed a safe passage home and left their posts. Closer to Yontan Field both Spitzer and Sweeney tried to contact Okinawa but raised no response. After nearly twelve hours in the air both Sweeney and his co-pilot, Captain Charles Albury, were exhausted. The B-29 was consuming three hundred gallons of aviation fuel per hour.

Estimating that they would reach empty fifty miles out, Sweeney reduced speed to conserve his supply and put the plane into a slight glide. When in sight of the Yontan tower, Spitzer sent increasingly frantic messages. He saw P-38s and B-25s take off and land undisturbed and realized that Sweeney would have to go directly in without circling. "Skipper," Kuharek reported on the intercom, "as of right now all the fuel gauges read empty. I don't know what we're flying on."

The right outboard engine quit, and Sweeney told Albury to increase power to the number three engine. "We've got to get this damn thing down before we spin in!" To Van Pelt and Lieutenant Fred Olivi, the spare co-pilot, Sweeney shouted to fire the red and green flares that were the identification colors for the day. Nothing changed on the runway after four flares had burst, and he yelled into his radio, "Give me the field! Mayday! Mayday!" With no reaction to his S.O.S. below and *Bock's Car* on a direct course to the airstrip, he tried again, "Mayday! Mayday! I want any goddam tower on Okinawa!" Then he called back to Van Pelt and Olivi, "Shoot every flare you've got!"

While Commander Ashworth, sitting on the floor just behind Sweeney, braced himself against a bulkhead, twenty flares went off around the plane, their colors signifying "heavy damage," "aircraft on fire," "dead and wounded on board," "aircraft out of fuel," and "prepare for crash landing." Even in the bright sunlight they were inescapable, and planes began peeling away from the runway. Sweeney could see fire trucks and ambulances moving in. At two thousand feet he nosed down more and warned Albury, "Tell the others to brace for a rough one." *Bock's Car* came in at 140 miles per hour, about 30 miles per hour too fast. The other outboard engine fluttered out and the plane veered sharply left, toward the line of parked B-24s. Sweeney reversed the props on the two inboard engines still running and hit his emergency brakes. Crewmen tumbled about but *Bock's Car* stayed upright and came to a full stop. Only ten feet of runway remained.

Later, Kuharek checked the remaining fuel. Of the usable 6,650 gallons with which they had taken off, 7 gallons were left.

A sergeant jumped from one of the crash wagons as the plane's door opened and poked his head in. "Where are the dead and wounded?" he inquired.

"Back there," said Sweeney. He was pointing toward Nagasaki.

While the crew arranged for refueling, *The Great Artiste* came in, having cautiously laid back to observe *Bock's Car*, which they knew had been in trouble and might ditch. "While we were refueling," Bill Laurence wrote, "we learned that Russia had this day entered the war against Japan."

For Sweeney the tension broke as he and Commander Ashworth paid a courtesy call on Lieutenant General Jimmy Doolittle, the new head of the Eighth Air Force. Doolittle's flight of B-25s from the *Hornet* for his epic raid on Tokyo five months after Pearl Harbor had foreshadowed the turn in the war. He asked for details, but all Sweeney could tell him was that smoke obscured the target after the blast.

"It's been a long time coming, Sweeney," Doolittle said. His own mission, about which synonyms for *daring* are inadequate, had been on April 18, 1942.

"Yes, sir. I hope it means the end."

Sweeney saluted and turned to leave. Doolittle called him back. "I can only tell you what they said to me. Well done!"

In Tokyo the chief of staff of the Air General Army telephoned the chief of staff of the newly formed 10th Air Division to notify him of the Nagasaki bomb, urging that the strongest possible efforts be made to continue the fight. Every enemy plane flying alone might be carrying another atomic bomb, and would have to be intercepted. Yet there was futility in his voice. The 10th Air Division, formed from four depleted air regiments, had only ninety-five fighters with the capability of reaching bomber altitude. Everything else that flew was capable only of *kamikaze* use when *Ketsu-Go* was activated against invasion.

In his fortieth month as a prisoner in Peking, a survivor of the Doolittle raid, dying of malnutrition and dysentery and covered with body boils, had become delirious. Possibly recognizing after Hiroshima that he might have to answer for his treatment of POWs, a Japanese medical officer gave Corporal Jacob DeShazer some unidentified injections to keep him alive. Awakening on August 9 in the Kiangwan Military Prison on the outskirts of Shanghai, he heard a voice inside him tell him to pray.

"What shall I pray about?" DeShazer wondered.

"Pray for peace and pray without ceasing," his voice answered—and he did, although until then he had rejected prayer as "useless." An all-powerful God "could stop the war at any time." At seven in the morning he began praying that "God would put a great desire in the hearts of the Japanese leaders for peace."

At two in the afternoon—it was one o'clock in Nagasaki—his voice, which he attributed now to the "Holy Spirit," advised him, "You don't need to pray anymore. The victory is won." He accepted the message as "quicker and better than the regular method of receiving world news" and determined to stay alive and "just wait and see what was to happen." Three other Doolittle flyers had cells and straw mats in the same prison—Lieutenants George Barr and Robert Hite, and Sergeant Chase Nielsen. Barr was near death. Three others who had flown from the *Hornet* were only ashes in urns stored in Shanghai. After a mock trial in September 1942, Lieutenants Dean Hallmark and William Farrow and Sergeant Harold Spatz had been sentenced to death and shot. The sentences of the four survivors in prison had been graciously reduced by the Emperor to life imprisonment.

Bock took off from Okinawa five minutes before Sweeney. They arrived in Tinian at 10:25 and 10:30 that night after a mission of twenty hours. The greeting party was thin—Colonel Tibbets and Admiral Purnell. No cameras. No medals. "Pretty rough, Chuck?" asked Tibbets.

"Pretty rough, Colonel."

•     •     •

About thirty minutes after the blast, Major Hopkins saw the mush-room cloud from his circles in the sky over an island that was not Yakujima. He closed in at a safe thirty-eight thousand feet, still twenty thousand feet below the top of the mushroom, and accom-plished what remained of his photographic mission. Following the others to Okinawa, he returned, still puzzled about what had hap-pened, to Tinian.

Navy search-and-rescue pickets had stopped looking for *Bock's Car* too early, but the Navy itself remained busy through the day, from the Panama Canal to the westernmost Pacific. "Olympic" was still on, but travel through the Canal in support of it was temporarily blocked by a circumstance feared through the war almost as much as attacks and sabotage. The troopship *General D. E. Hultman* had dam-aged a propeller and lost its steering. The vessel had to be towed to dry dock. It could have been worse.

On Guam, the Navy experienced a different kind of delay. With Rus-sia in the war, Vice Admiral Charles A. Lockwood, Jr., commanding the Pacific submarine fleet, could not be available to head the court of inquiry on the *Indianapolis* sinking. It had been scheduled to open on the ninth. A new date was scheduled—the thirteenth.

Between typhoons Admiral Halsey kept sending task forces to the home islands to bombard coastal industry. Far north of Tokyo was the Japan Iron Company's works at Kamaishi. It had been hit earlier, on July 15, the first major home installation attacked by naval gunfire. This time Rear Admiral John F. Shafroth returned with three battle-ships, four heavy cruisers, and ten destroyers to fire 2,186 more shells into the factories and docks, while a Royal Navy force of three cruis-ers and three destroyers commanded by Rear Admiral E. J. P. Brind added 733 more rounds.

Concentrating on airfields and shipping in overlooked harbors, another British force, headed by the carrier *Formidable*, explored Ona-gawa Wan, south of Kamaishi, and the 1841 Squadron went after five warships in the bay. Lieutenant Hampton Gray's section flew low over the water to evade shore batteries, but Gray's Corsair was rid-dled and caught fire. Keeping on course, he bombed and sank a de-stroyer before his plane hit the water. Gray, a Royal Canadian naval pilot, was awarded, posthumously, the only Victoria Cross received in the Pacific Fleet.

• • •

TF 38 was also ordered by Admiral Nimitz to disable a reported concentration of naval aircraft at Misawa, far to the north, east of Aomori, and a carrier force was detached for the mission. Pilots were briefed to root out camouflaged planes, and flew at treetop level to find them, claiming 251 destroyed and 141 damaged, one of the biggest hauls of the war. Most were carefully hoarded medium bombers for use as troop carriers in a suicide mission against B-29 bases in the Marianas. "Ultra" in Manila had found the mission out, one planned before "Fat Man" and "Little Boy" had been deployed. A major disaster was averted.

No *kamikazes* approached the carriers, but one went after a four-ship picket station standing by for ditched aircraft. Under fire from the four destroyers, a "Val" headed for the *Borie*'s stern and crashed near the bridge. Damage control needed two hectic hours, but the ship survived—although forty-eight crewmen did not.

No casualties were incurred when seamen from the destroyer *Cassin* boarded the *Kikku Maru* toward evening. Its destination had been Yokosuka. The *Cassin* had been destroyed in dry dock on the first day of the war. One of the memorable photos of the day showed it tangled with the *Downes*, with the battleship *Pennsylvania* hit by bombs behind it. Rebuilt from what remained, the *Cassin* was remembering Pearl Harbor.

Reporting some of the day's events in its log, the *Bonhomme Richard*, part of TF 38, closed its account with "The end approaches."

Hundreds of other aircraft were up during the day in addition to carrier planes and the B-29s of Special Bombing Mission 16. MacArthur's report that B-25s and P-38s supported ground forces in areas north of Baguio, southeast of Cervantes, and northwest of Infanta implicitly confessed how many places in the Philippines were still unpacified. Baguio had been the prewar summer capital. So many other B-24s, P-47s, and P-51s from Iwo and Okinawa were over southern Japan that if there had been any restriction on flights while the deployment of "Fat Man" was in progress, no one had paid any attention. Among them, also, was an eighty-six-plane raid on the Nippon Oil Refinery at Amagaski, near Osaka, which took off northward from Guam after *Bock's Car* had returned to Tinian. All but three found the target, which they reached through a tropical storm and failed to hit accurately. One of the three that aborted was Hays Gamble's B-29, which had mechanical problems soon after takeoff—

"so we turned around and dumped our bombs on Rota. . . ." A half hour out and halfway between Guam and Tinian, Rota was one of the many smaller islands in the Marianas that had been bypassed. One did not want to chance an emergency landing with a bellyful of bombs any more than with a single, imposing "Fat Man."

"Now this country is going to fight alone against the whole world," Admiral Ugaki deplored. "This is fate indeed! I won't grumble about anything at this moment. I only hope we do our best in the last battle so that we'll have nothing to regret even if destroyed." Russia's declaration of war had reflected in him the state of mind that also possessed Imperial General Headquarters in Tokyo and tied Premier Suzuki's hands.

On hearing the news, Suzuki telephoned the chairman of the Cabinet Planning Bureau, Sumihisa Ikeda, who had been in Manchuria in July. "Is the Kwantung Army capable of repulsing the Soviet Army?" Suzuki asked.

"The Kwantung Army is hopeless," said Ikeda.

"Is the Kwantung Army that weak?" sighed Suzuki. "Then the game is up."

The chief of the once-feared Kwantung Army in Manchuria was the thin, elderly Otozō Yamada. On the ninth the general had been scheduled to pay a courtesy call in the palace at Hsinking (Changchun), upon the puppet head of government in what the Japanese called Manchukuo, Henry P'u Yi. For four years, until 1912, when he was still only six, P'u Yi was, as Hsüän-t'ung, the last emperor of China, then a private citizen in Peking until co-opted in 1932 to be an august ventriloquist's dummy in a facade of a state.

Although Russian incursions had already begun on several fronts, a nervous Yamada offered P'u Yi an incoherent account of how the Kwantung Army was coping, and assured him of ultimate victory. Suddenly air raid warnings sounded and they rushed to the cellars, where they listened to bombs exploding. When the all-clear was heard and they emerged into daylight, the general found himself without further predictions. Half or more of his twenty-one divisions and eleven brigades were only on paper. During the summer he had been ordered to return one third of his ammunition stocks for defense of the homeland. The Russians had five times his artillery strength and twice the land-based aircraft. The Japanese Navy in the area had been reduced to nearly nothing, and had only 170 planes.

The Russians had a real fleet and 1,549 naval aircraft. The Japanese northern islands and Manchuria were helpless.

The Manchurian home army, supplementing the depleted regulars, was a ragtag of poorly trained men, including the husband of a kindergarten teacher, Yoshie Fukushima, called up the month before. They had a ten-month-old son and lived in a village near the Soviet border north of Vladivostock. She was feeding her dog when she heard *"Pa! Pa! Pa!"* and saw "silvery things falling." It was seven in the morning. She turned on her radio and heard that the Russians were coming. Villagers panicked. "Into the mountains!" shouted one. "Follow the rail lines!" urged another. There were no roads and she had never seen a map.

With others she followed the tracks they hoped led to Mukden. She had a rucksack and her son on her back. To evade the Russians they soon had to leave the railway and trudge into the hills, where they encountered some Japanese soldiers. One wore Red Cross insignia—a medic. By then her son had a high fever and labored breathing. She begged for help. "Measles," he said. "He probably won't make it, ma'am. It's better for you to reconcile yourself to that."

When he admitted that he had an ampule of German medicine intended for pneumonia, she pleaded for it. Although reluctant to waste even a child's-size dosage, he gave in to her tears. Masaaki got better. Conditions quickly got worse. She saw "heaps and heaps of bodies. . . . Japanese soldiers gave us women hand grenades and told how to place them against our own bodies." The Manchus, they explained, were just as vicious toward the Japanese as the Russians. "It would not be good for a Japanese woman to be raped." She threw her grenade away "somewhere in the mountains."

Somewhere in Manchuria Tomoichi Yamamoto wrote,

*Fearing Soviet troops closing in,*
*My wife holds our child tight,*
*Realizing that she cannot kill herself.*

Recognizing that the war with Russia was a reality, Togo politely brushed off a request from Ambassador Malik for a meeting. "I instructed my subordinates to tell him that I could not receive him on that day—which was taken up . . . with conferences of first importance—and that if his business was pressing he should see the Vice-Minister." Jacob Malik could pretend just as easily as Togo that the matter could wait. Each understood that Sato had, hours before, cabled urgently from Moscow, and each understood that the Manchurian frontier had been breached in half a dozen places. "The Ambassador replied, however, that the following day would do." Togo arranged a meeting for the tenth, Tokyo time, and he had been in no way dissembling when he spoke of conferences of the first importance, which had begun for him almost as soon as he had heard from Sato.

The American psychological warfare mill on Saipan did not wait for Malik's formal meeting, rushing out another leaflet to rain on Japan. Both as heading and as close it warned, "EVACUATE YOUR CITIES!" The text borrowed much from the earlier leaflet about the power of the Hiroshima bomb, and warned of employing the atomic weapon again if surrender were not immediate. A further result of Japanese rejection of Potsdam, it pointed out, was that the Soviet Union had declared war, and "all the powerful countries of the world are now at war against you." The final line before urging, again, all Japanese to flee their cities was the warning, "Act at once or we shall resolutely employ this bomb. . . ."

It was a day, in Tokyo, of almost nonstop conferences. The Lord Privy Seal, Marquis Kido, saw the Emperor on six occasions beginning at 9:55. His last meeting was at 11:25 P.M., nearly fourteen hours later. Even earlier, Togo had been at Premier Suzuki's house in Koishikawa, in north-central Tokyo, demanding a meeting of the Supreme War Council to discuss the previously unthinkable. Suzuki contacted the Chief Cabinet Secretary, Hisatsune Sakomizu, to handle arrangements, advising, "Let us, the present Cabinet, take the responsibility of seeing the country through the termination of the war." The circumstances suggested a complete failure of the sitting government, which would normally have resigned, but that would have delayed suing for peace. Six hundred miles to the south, *Bock's Car* was making landfall.

Togo went from Suzuki to Admiral Mitsumasa Yonai, the Navy Minister and an ally. Prince Takamatsu, a rear admiral and the Emperor's second brother, was with Yonai, and asked Togo what might be negotiated. Perhaps, said Togo, preservation of the national polity—the Throne. For the Emperor himself, Hiroshima had made the future of his Throne insignificant. What was crucial was preservation of the nation. In that interest he asked Kido to have the Premier do what Suzuki had already determined upon at Togo's insistence, and also to consult such senior statesmen of the *Jushin* who might help pressure the War Council to accept the idea of surrender.

At 10:30 A.M. the Council convened in the Imperial Palace. Togo opened the discussion by quoting the Emperor's words: "Continuation of the war has become impossible." The situation, Togo declared, was hopeless, and the Potsdam declaration had to be complied with, but for stipulations "absolutely essential for Japan." The Hiroshima bomb—and, now, the intervention of Russia—left no option but to end the war. Agreeing, Yonai, who had been Premier in 1940 but had been forced out when he opposed the alliance with Germany and Italy, quietly challenged the other military representatives: "We're not going to accomplish anything unless we speak out. Do we accept the enemy ultimatum unconditionally? Do we propose conditions? If so, we had better discuss them here and now."

All six quickly agreed that retaining the imperial house was "the indispensable condition of acceptance." Short of that they would fight to the bitter end. War Minister Anami and the two chiefs of staff laid down additional terms, described by Togo as "specifically, that occupation of Japan should if possible be avoided or, if inescapable, should be on a small scale and should not include such points as Tokyo; and that [our] disarmament should be carried out on our responsibility; and that war criminals should be dealt with by Japan."

Such conditions, Togo objected, would make peace impossible, and unless the military could offer some hope of victory should their terms be rejected, they were unrealistic. Gloomily, Anami confessed he had no such hopes, but felt that Japan was still capable of fighting on. Togo wanted specifics. Could they prevent the enemy from landing on the home islands? No, said General Umezu, but "we could inflict heavy losses on them."

Before the discussion could go further, news arrived of the atomic bombing of Nagasaki, but even that stunning development could not break the deadlock. Toyoda, the Navy chief of staff, expressed confidence that the United States could have little radioactive material left for more bombs. "All the radium-like elements in the world would not amount to much." Further, he doubted "whether the world would permit the United States to continue such an inhuman atrocity." (Rear Admiral Takijiro Onishi, who had initiated the *kamikazes*, was now Toyoda's vice chief, and may have influenced Toyoda's die-hard posture.) After more than two hours the six remained evenly split as they rose for lunch and to make way for a full Cabinet meeting at two-thirty at the Premier's official residence.

As the Council adjourned, the Emperor was meeting with Hiroshi Shimomura, Director of the Information Bureau, who had applied to the Imperial Household Ministry for an audience. He would not have applied on his own initiative. The suggestion may have emerged from one of Hirohito's increasingly frequent consultations with Marquis Kido—within those private meetings possibly from the Emperor himself. Shimomura's audience lasted two hours, after which he commented to his secretary, "It all went well. The Emperor has agreed to make a broadcast telling the nation whether we're to have peace or war."

Although once caught inadvertently by an open microphone, His Majesty, known for his shyness, had never before spoken to his people officially on radio. The idea seemed contrary to the carefully cultivated mystique of a demigod.

The Cabinet meeting that afternoon required a unanimous decision for action. Premier Suzuki hoped that the Russian intervention and the second atomic bombing might furnish the impetus, and he had the more articulate and energetic Togo open the meeting by reviewing the dire events in Manchuria and Nagasaki. Suzuki then asked for the opinions of the Navy Minister and the War Minister. Admiral Yonai sounded even more pessimistic than in the morning session. "We might win the first battle for Japan," he said, thinking of the first wave of invaders on the beaches of Kyushu, "but we won't win the second. The war is lost to us. Therefore we must forget about 'face'; we must surrender as quickly as we can, and we must consider at once how best to preserve our country."

General Anami took a more belligerent stance than he had earlier. "We cannot pretend," he began, "that victory is certain, but it is far too early to say the war is lost. That we will inflict severe losses on the enemy when he invades Japan is certain, and it is by no means impossible that we may be able to reverse the situation in our favor, pulling victory out of defeat. Furthermore, our Army will not submit to [forced] demobilization. Our men will not lay down their arms. And since they know they are not permitted to surrender, since they know that a fighting man who surrenders is liable to extremely heavy punishment [on his return home], there is really no alternative to us but to continue the war."

In turn, Suzuki called upon the Ministers of Agriculture, Commerce, Transportation, and Munitions, all of whom disagreed with Anami's hard line. The people of Japan, they contended, were on the verge of exhaustion and hunger, aggravated by the poorest rice crop since 1931. Air raids and coastal shelling had crippled transportation and industry. Japan, they concluded, did not have the means to continue the struggle.

"Yes! Yes!" Anami broke in. "Everyone understands the situation . . . but we must fight the war through to the end no matter how great the odds are against us!"

Supporting him, Genki Abe, the Home Minister, warned that if the Cabinet decided upon capitulation the country could be faced with massive civil disobedience. There would also be massive military disobedience. He recommended that they fight on.

After Togo again urged acceptance of Potsdam, Suzuki asked for other opinions, and two additional ministers supported surrender only if all Anami's conditions were met.

Following an hour's recess at five-thirty, they argued further until ten, still with no consensus. Admiral Yonai reminded the Cabinet that they could expect no better conditions if they went on with the war, but Anami stubbornly insisted that if they repelled, at least for a time, the invasion of the homeland, they might "find life out of death." Most agreed that Japan's "relative position"—they often resorted to euphemisms—would be "far worse" as time went on, but unanimity had clearly escaped Suzuki. Shortly after ten he called for an adjournment. The ministers bowed to each other and disappeared into the blacked-out and ruined streets.

Most of President Truman's broadcast to the nation on the evening of the ninth had been composed on the *Augusta*, but once back in Washington he had to revise it in the aftermath of Manchuria and Nagasaki. Going over issues with his press secretaries, Eben Ayers noted in his diary, Truman observed that August 15 had been the date set for "the entry of the Russians" but that after the Hiroshima bomb "Stalin hastened to get in before Japan could fold up." In his radio talk, without mentioning Yalta, and suggesting, rather, a decision at Potsdam, Truman declared that Russia, "before she had been informed of our new weapon, agreed to enter the war in the Pacific" and that he "gladly" welcomed the Soviets into the struggle. The half-truths were diplomatically necessary. As for Japan, he had said it all before: "We shall continue to use the Bomb until we completely destroy Japan's power to make war. Only a Japanese surrender will stop us."

That Truman was serious could be seen in the continuing intensity of operations. Another Bomb was scheduled to be ready by August 21, and further ones with increasing frequency after that. In Washington on the ninth, the "Logistic Plan for Land Based Forces—OLYMPIC" was under study by the Joint Chiefs of Staff Secretariat, along with plans for the invasion of northwest Kyushu "subsequent to the invasion of southern Kyushu." The United States meant business.

The events of the ninth came as the Empire of Japan was unraveling further. In a ceremony in Indochina, Southern Army General Headquarters, physically isolated from home, conceded independence to Indonesia. The army had withdrawn from Saigon to the hill station of Dalat, where, on the lawn of the resort's biggest hotel, under the shade of palm trees, the Indonesian delegation, led by Kusnasosro Sukarno, listened to a congratulatory speech from Field Marshal Terauchi. In Bangkok, Japanese unit commanders gathered to prepare to defend their forces against an expected Siamese insurrection. In Korea, colonial authorities began to approach influential locals about how to preserve order long enough to let Japanese occupation troops leave for home. Four high officials met with Song Chin-u at a Japanese house in Seoul to ask him to form an "administrative committee" to preserve the peace and prepare for Korean independence. Concerned that Allied forces and local Koreans might consider him a collaborator, he declined to cooperate.

In the home islands themselves, as the marathon meetings at the highest level were going on, and while Nagasaki was still reeling from the second Bomb, the civilian population was expecting a third, and hoping paradoxically that it would not happen—or that it would finally end the war. Rumor had it that the Americans had a huge signboard already painted and stored, because of its size, on "some battleship" off the coast. It allegedly read: "There was a city here called Tokyo." After Hiroshima, when Captain Fuchida heard of the bombing of Nagasaki, he requested permission to fly to Tokyo to urge peace on the Navy Ministry. He feared a bomb on Tokyo itself. That the Americans had only furnished an interval of three days between the two Bombs had not been enough time to negotiate, he said. It could happen again. To young Yukio Mishima, the Nagasaki Bomb was the final warning. Peace must come now. "It was our last chance.

People were saying that Tokyo would be next. Wearing white shirt and shorts, I walked about the streets. . . . People had reached the limits of desperation and were now going about their affairs with cheerful faces. . . . Everywhere there was an air of cheerful excitement. It was just as though one was continuing to blow up an already bulging balloon, wondering, 'Will it burst now? Will it burst now?' "

Inadvertently the hard-nosed Genki Abe, by raising fears of a recurrence on a larger scale of the insurrection of 1936, and the Emperor's desperate intervention, had suggested a solution that was already in the minds of both Togo and Suzuki. They lingered to talk privately. Earlier in the day, anticipating a deadlock, they had asked Chief Cabinet Secretary Sakomizu to persuade General Umezu and Admiral Toyoda to sign a petition enabling the Premier to call for a meeting of the Supreme War Council in the presence of the Emperor. Sakomizu's approach was that it would be convenient to have such a document ready in case of emergency. The two chiefs of staff had signed it without concern, for the government never brought any problem before the Throne until there was unanimous agreement to a solution. The Emperor's presence was a rubber stamp—but one that added dignity and authority to a decision already reached. Marquis Kido, however, in league with Togo and Suzuki, had met five times that day with Hirohito and kept him apprised of developments. The Emperor expected a late-night call from the Premier.

Suzuki and Togo were received by Hirohito as soon as they arrived at the palace. In the sweltering imperial study—it had been a hot and muggy day—Togo laid out the issues on which the government was deadlocked, and the warnings of military and civil disobedience. Hirohito was prepared to give his assent—and did—and Suzuki ordered a Council session to be convened immediately. A summons went out, and Suzuki and Togo went to wait in the palace bomb shelter, where they would convene. The Emperor called again for Marquis Kido before the conference was to begin. When Kido left the imperial presence once more he noted the time as 11:37 P.M. At ten minutes to midnight Hirohito, accompanied by an aide, entered the underground shelter. At forty-four, he had been Emperor of the allegedly 2,600-year dynasty for seventeen years. Like P'u Yi, he might be the last.

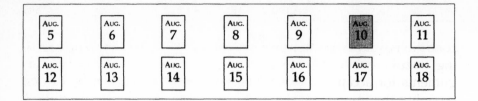

| AUG. 5 | AUG. 6 | AUG. 7 | AUG. 8 | AUG. 9 | AUG. 10 | AUG. 11 |
| AUG. 12 | AUG. 13 | AUG. 14 | AUG. 15 | AUG. 16 | AUG. 17 | AUG. 18 |

CHAPTER XXIX

## · AUGUST 10, 1945 ·

*". . . even if we have to chew grass and eat earth"*

At ten minutes to midnight, Emperor Hirohito and an aide entered the *Gobunko* underground shelter. The six members of the Supreme War Council, as well as Chief Cabinet Secretary Sakomizu and Privy Council President Hiranuma, were waiting, several with their own aides. Their formal morning attire or dress uniform for the imperial presence made the crowded, humid, windowless paneled vault oppressive. The men were dabbing at themselves with handkerchiefs when the Emperor entered. Rising slightly and bowing, they averted their eyes from the demigod figure who took the empty straight-backed chair at the head of two narrow, parallel, cloth-covered tables.

To a man they were exhausted after continuous meetings, and Premier Suzuki, weary as well from age, stood at the Emperor's left and asked Sakomizu to read aloud the Potsdam proclamation as a basis for discussion. No one took minutes. Each knew that the six voting members were divided evenly about the Potsdam ultimatum, while the Cabinet had split into those favoring acceptance if the imperial house were preserved, those insistent on Anami's additional conditions, and those somewhere between. For the Emperor's hearing, Suzuki reviewed the impasse, after which Togo repeated the arguments for acceptance without delay, but with the proviso about retaining the imperial system. "I agree with the Foreign Minister," said Admiral Yonai.

Protocol required recognizing the War Minister. Rising, General Anami declared his complete disagreement. One could not know the outcome of the battle for Japan, he insisted, until it was fought, and if it were not to be fought, the price should be the acceptance of his four conditions for national integrity. "If all the people go into the final battle resolved to display the utmost patriotism and fight to the last," he said, "I believe we can avoid this crisis." Then, turning to Premier Suzuki, he asked, "Suppose the enemy refuses to give you any assurance that the Imperial House will be preserved—will you go on fighting?"

"Yes," said the Premier—the meeting, after all, was in the presence of the Emperor, who looked on quietly—"we will continue the war."

Turning then to the Navy Minister, Anami asked the same question, and Admiral Yonai also agreed. Satisfied that no one would accept the Potsdam demands outright, the War Minister sat down.

Like Anami, said General Umezu, he would insist on all four conditions for national survival. Surrender would dishonor the war dead. Furthermore, he claimed, "Preparations for the decisive battle of the homeland are already completed, and we are confident of victory."

Protocol required recognizing next the hard-line navy chief, Admiral Toyoda, but Suzuki wanted to interrupt the ranks of the diehards, and he called on Kiichiro Hiranuma, President of the Privy Council, which had the constitutional role of ratification of treaties. Baron Hiranuma was meticulous about form. He asked about the likely war criminals, about what prolonged war with Russia might mean, about the chances of repelling an American invasion, about the possibility of civil disorder. He was convinced, he said finally, that all of Anami's points were worth negotiating. As for the national polity—that went without saying.

Given his opportunity, Admiral Toyoda backed Anami's hard-line position strongly and added that he could not guarantee that the navy would accept a surrender unless the disarming were accomplished by the Japanese themselves.

It was now past two o'clock on the tenth. The lines were drawn as before. Above the sweltering bomb shelter the war was going on unabated, and people waited to see whether Tokyo would be next after Hiroshima and Nagasaki. It was evident, Suzuki told the others, that no agreement could be reached. In view of the urgency of the situation there was only one recourse for the Council. Neither he, Togo, and Yonai; nor Anami, Umezu, and Toyoda had altered their positions in any way. Turning toward the quiet bespectacled man in the wing collar at the head of the table and bowing deeply, the Premier said, almost certainly to the shock of some in the stifling room, "It has already been nearly two and a half hours and we have yet to resolve our differences. Since the situation is so serious that it does not permit further delay, one wonders if we might not impose upon Your Majesty—however unprecedented it may be—to bring this meeting to a decision by expressing Your exalted views. Your Imperial Majesty's decision is requested as to which proposal should be adopted, the Foreign Minister's or the one with the four conditions."

Very likely primed by Marquis Kido, the Emperor had been awaiting his opportunity. Since no official transcript was made, only the recollections of participants about what in earlier days was called the Voice of the Crane—the pronouncement of an imperial command—can be pieced together. Hirohito was apparently harsh in his assessment of the military, possibly a strategy to embarrass the most hawkish into silence. "I have given serious thought to the situation prevailing at home and abroad," he began, "and have concluded that continuing the war can only mean destruction for the nation and a prolongation of bloodshed and cruelty in the world. Those who argue for continuing the war once assured me that our defenses and armaments would be ready in Kyushu by June. I realize now this cannot be fulfilled even by September. As for those who wish for one last battle here on our own soil, let me remind them of the disparity between their previous plans and what has taken place. Indeed, none of the military's plans seemed to be realized. Does anyone suppose we can win a war under the circumstances?"

The only way to relieve Japan "from the terrible distress with which it is burdened," he went on, was to end the war. He saw Japanese culture itself as in peril. He grieved for "the soldiers and sailors who have been killed or wounded in far-off battles, the families who have lost all their worldly goods, and often their lives as well, in the air raids at home. It goes without saying that it is unbearable for me to see the brave and loyal fighting men of Japan disarmed. It is equally unbearable that others who have rendered me devoted service should now be punished as instigators of war. Nevertheless, the time has come when we must bear the unbearable. It cannot be helped."

He understood, he said, referring to what had been in 1895 an embarrassment for Japan, how his grandfather, the Emperor Meiji, must have felt when France, Russia, and Germany in what Japanese histories called the "Triple Intervention" forced the return to China of the Liaotung Peninsula, an appendage to Manchuria. The Empire, Hirohito had no need to say further, would have to disgorge all its colonial gains.

"With tears in my eyes and for the sake of the country," the Emperor concluded, "I find myself agreeing with the Foreign Minister." He would go even farther, he added, knowing that Americans were calling for his prosecution as a war criminal. Neither concern about his person or the Imperial Household should stand in the way of peace.

Suzuki arose and bowed. "One is humbled," he said, "by such worthy sentiments. Surely in the light of them the decision of this body is clear."

Not waiting for what might come next, Hirohito walked from the room as the conferees bowed and their handkerchiefs reappeared. No one asked for, or wanted, a vote. Immediately, Suzuki ordered Sakomizu to convene a Cabinet meeting, however small the hours were—it was 2:20 A.M.—at the Premier's official residence. Another debate and ballot would be superfluous, but there had to be prepared a broadly based draft of a message offering surrender— with the unanimously accepted essential reservation retaining the imperial house. The "national polity" represented the continuation of Japanese tradition, and to preserve it they remained ready to commit national suicide.

With the Emperor out of sight, the respectful silence ended as they climbed wearily up the long flight of steps into the Tokyo night. Necessarily mute during the meeting, General Masao Yoshizumi, Umezu's deputy, rushed at the frail Suzuki and screamed, "Are you happy? Are you satisfied now?" General Anami stepped between them and wrapped his arms protectively around the Premier while others pulled Yoshizumi away.

Traditionally the Premier's offices, like those of major Cabinet members such as the Foreign Minister, were part of the official residence. It was there that officials with their chief secretaries argued until four in the morning over the language of the cable that was to go to ministers in two neutral countries—Switzerland and Sweden—

for transmission to the Allies. Most of the text was formal language responding to Potsdam affirmatively. The contentiousness occurred over how the preservation of the national polity was to be demanded as a condition for peace. As Togo's deputy, Toshikazu Kase, set down the text for the conferees, he felt doubts about Baron Hiranuma's phraseology, particularly the word *taiken*, which referred to powers inherent in the Throne, but he wrote (in Japanese) that his government was ready to accept Potsdam if its terms were understood as not including "any demand for modification of the prerogatives of His Majesty as a sovereign ruler." The understanding, it concluded, was crucial. And the envoys were assured in the cable that a translation of the text into English, which would be the official version, would be speedily forthcoming.

Sakomizu went to sleep in Suzuki's armchair. The others went home, Anami embarrassed and heartsick. The Emperor had made it clear that the army had been disgraced, and his die-hards would not take that easily. Yoshizumi's behavior had already made that predictable.

At 8:47 A.M. Tokyo time (according to "Magic") the Japanese text began clicking off in a deliberately low-security code from the Foreign Ministry Building to Bern and Stockholm. Unaware of the Japanese initiative, General Carl Spaatz, on Guam, cabled Hap Arnold's deputy, General Lauris Norstad, in Washington, to recommend dropping the next atomic bomb on Tokyo "for its psychological effect on government officials." Hurrying now to get their own message out, the very officials whom Spaatz had in mind cabled instructions that the Swedish mission was responsible for communication to Britain and Russia, the Swiss mission to the United States and China. If the message was picked up by American listening posts, so much the better. As Kase got on a tramcar to go home for a few hours' sleep the air raid sirens, quiet all night, began howling. But he had accomplished his last assignment for the beginning of the new day. To avoid publicity, as the Soviet Union was already unofficially but vigorously at war with Japan, he had arranged to have the postponed meeting of Togo and Malik take place in the little-used guest reception room of the House of Peers.

General Anami seemed able to work without sleep. He had to prepare the officer caste for the bad news before Dōmei released it for broadcast and before rumor worsened it. At the same time, Admiral

Toyoda ordered Naval General Staff officers "not to make any hasty move or take independent action." At nine-thirty that Friday morning all personnel in the War Ministry above the rank of major gathered at Anami's orders in the Ministry's underground bomb shelter. He explained his own position at the Imperial Conference and how the Emperor's own more pacific view had broken the deadlock. No one had talked openly about surrender and everyone had expected it, yet the bleak reality shocked the group into silence. The Emperor had hardly counted in all the years of wartime decisions, however much he was tacitly accepted as demigod. He had now overruled the most powerful entity in the Empire, the Army, and its commanders had accepted the decision. All of them faced dismal and possibly barren futures although the day before they had run Japan.

As Minister of War, Anami had to be obeyed; as subjects of the Emperor they were all theoretically loyal by oath. Anami understood that in many minds their loyalty was to the imperial design, not to a wayward decision by the transient object of their loyalty. "We have no alternative," he reminded them, "but to abide by the Emperor's decision. Whether we fight on or whether we surrender now depends on the enemy's reply to our note. No matter which we do, you must all remember that you are soldiers. You must obey orders. You must not deviate from strict military discipline. In the crisis that faces us, the uncontrolled actions of one man could bring about the ruin of the entire country."

"The War Minister," an officer challenged, rising at his place, "has told us to obey his orders whether we fight on or whether we surrender. Is the War Minister actually considering surrender?"

Anami slapped his swagger stick on the table with a loud crack. "Anyone who isn't willing to obey my orders," he warned, "will have to do so over my dead body."

Although Kase did the actual translation into English, Togo's catching some sleep after the surrender cable went out explains in part the gap in time between transmission of the Japanese text and the promised but delayed English equivalent that was to be the basis for negotiations. Officials in Tokyo waiting for some response from the enemy had no idea why none was forthcoming—one of the earliest of the confused signals from both sides. In mid-afternoon—still predawn in the United States, although the beginning of the workday in Europe—Togo, having collected his wits by three, held an audience at the Premier's official residence for the senior statesmen collectively referred to as the *Jushin*. Explaining the Supreme War Council and Cabinet negotiations that led up the Emperor's intervention, he was offering news that had yet to be publicly released. General Kuni-aki Koiso, "the Tiger of Korea," whom Suzuki had replaced as Premier and who had himself replaced Hideki Tojo as the war soured, asked strangely whether the Potsdam ultimatum was in conflict with Divine Will, as it laid down the necessity of disarmament. The divine national polity, he insisted, required a nation at arms to preserve it. Potsdam only proscribed militarism, Togo explained. Former premier Tojo opposed surrender under any conditions, but, he conceded, if it were the august wish of the sovereign, it could not be helped. Little enthusiasm for ending the war without honor emerged, but the Foreign Minister observed privately, "the government . . . had convened this meeting not to consult the *Jushin* as to what to do but to inform them of what had already been done. There was thus little need to heed their remarks."

At four he slipped away to meet Jacob Malik at the little-used House of Peers reception room, and at 4:10 the Russian ambassador was ushered in to deliver his overdue declaration of war. Togo knew well it was the purpose of the call Malik had wanted to make a day earlier, yet even at that it would have been many hours after hostilities had begun in Manchuria. As an ex post facto formality it would have been, even if presented twenty-four hours earlier, much on the order of Pearl Harbor, where a Japanese diplomatic paper had been delivered after the beginning of hostilities. Again the Foreign Minister—like Cordell Hull in Washington on December 7, 1941—had a copy of the ambassadorial statement in advance. The difference in 1945 was that the document in Malik's hand was a real declaration of war, not an intimation of war couched in an interruption of peace talks. Togo, who had been responsible for the statement delivered by Ambassadors Nomura and Kurusu as Japanese planes were bombing Pearl Harbor, expressed his regret at Russia's belligerency, which he had no idea had emerged from the secret Yalta protocol of February 11, 1945, rather than from Potsdam.

Later, Togo thought that the Russians had accelerated their declaration because of the Hiroshima bomb, "which suddenly brought the end of hostilities in sight." That the Red Army would move earlier than planned had been assumed in Washington after the Bomb had made Soviet intervention unnecessary and even awkward.

The encounter between Malik and Togo was one of the most

paradoxical in the annals of war, for on receiving the Russian declaration of war the Foreign Minister handed to Malik his surrender offer. It was not unconditional surrender on the basis of Potsdam, but nevertheless what had occurred was the exchange of diplomatic documents, one a declaration of war, the other a suit for peace. "He read me a statement concerning the Soviet Union's endorsement of the Potsdam Declaration, and the existence of a state of war with Japan," Togo wrote. He already knew the text. "I said in reply, 'It is very strange that the Soviet Union should declare the existence of a state of war without replying to our request for its good offices in restoring peace.'"

"Your Excellency is well aware of the position of the Japanese Royal Family," Togo went on, having had time to prepare for the encounter. "You know that the position of the Emperor in Japan is indivisible from the Japanese people. Our understanding [of Potsdam] on this point is absolute. Accordingly, I believe there will be no difficulty about the governments of the United Nations agreeing to this."

Although his own government's note on ending the war, Togo explained to Malik, was being sent via Sweden to utilize a mediator, "We desired him to [also] submit it to his government, if he had no objections.... The Ambassador said that he had no authority to receive our proposal, but that he would agree to send it on, on his own responsibility." In the confusion of cables that crossed each other, Minister Okamoto, in Stockholm, had waited impatiently for the promised English text of the note for transmission to the Soviet and British ambassadors, and finally delivered his own translation to Swedish Foreign Minister Östen Undén. Well aware of the Potsdam Declaration, Undén scanned Okamoto's translation and asked whether the statement about "maintaining the prerogatives of His Majesty as a sovereign ruler" meant that Japan insisted on "no changes in the State's governing system or no change in the position of His Imperial Majesty." At a loss for explanations from Tokyo, Okamoto said that he felt "the words included both interpretations." Undén politely expressed his feeling of "great honor" at receiving the request and offered to extend Sweden's "good offices at once."

Twenty-five minutes later the official English text arrived in Stockholm. The major difference was the "maintaining the prerogatives of His Majesty ..." had been Englished as "prejudiced the prerogatives ..." On such fine distinctions it was possible that the shooting would not stop. "Ultra" quickly had all three texts—the

Japanese one, the English translation, and the revised Japanese version to parallel the official surrender offer in English.

The English text Togo had cabled to his ministers in Bern and Stockholm was the "legal" one for purposes of negotiation: "We are handling the Japanese version as the translation and are correcting it [to conform to the English version]." An identical text was broadcast by Dōmei at 8:35 P.M. Tokyo time—7:35 A.M. in Washington. Even before "Ultra" had delivered the message to the President, Secretary Byrnes had received the text from Walter Stucki, Foreign Affairs chief for the Swiss government. Byrnes awakened Truman with the news, which suggested that the war was about over—but only if Unconditional Surrender was out.

The message clearly had come from the highest level, as it offered surrender "in obedience to the gracious command of His Majesty the Emperor" and specifically accepted the Potsdam terms with the single reservation of retaining not only the Emperor but his "prerogatives." In Japan that traditionally if not constitutionally encompassed everything. And the Japanese government wanted, "speedily forthcoming," the enemy's "explicit indication" that the sole, but possibly sweeping, condition was acceptable.

At seven in the morning, Washington time, Captain William Smedberg, who had been in the office of the Chief of Naval Operations at the time of Pearl Harbor, then commanded destroyers and cruisers in the Pacific, and was now back in Washington, telephoned Secretary Forrestal that he had "a very important message" and brought the "Magic" decrypts to Forrestal's house. At the same time copies were delivered to the President. Within two hours of White House receipt of the surrender proposal, Truman met with Leahy and the Secretaries of State, War, and Navy to frame a response. Ever the realist, Leahy urged in what Stimson called "a good plain horse-sense position" that the status of the Emperor was "a minor matter compared with delaying a victory in the war which was now in our hands." It did not mean, he explained in his memoirs, "that I favored the Emperor retaining all his prerogatives. I had no feelings about little Hirohito, but was convinced that it would be necessary to use him in effecting the surrender."

With his ear to the domestic situation—polls showed, still, that the public wanted Hirohito's head—Byrnes warned of press "crucifixion of the President." With the war won, concessions were unnecessary, he claimed, reminding the others that Roosevelt and Churchill had insisted since 1943 on unconditional surrender, and that Potsdam, with Britain and China as cosigners, had repeated the demand. "I don't see why we should retreat," he said. "That demand was presented to Japan before the Bomb and before the Soviet Union was a belligerent. If any conditions are to be accepted, I want the United States and not Japan to state the conditions."

Forrestal argued that retention of the Emperor would facilitate both the surrender and the occupation, creating a buffer between victors and possibly hostile defeated troops. He suggested some ambiguity—"an affirmative statement on our part in which we could see to it that the language of surrender accorded fully with our intent and view." Stimson went along with offering some assurances about the Emperor, observing, "We would have to continue the Emperor ourselves [anyway] under our command and supervision" in order to persuade "the many scattered armies of the Japanese" to lay down their arms, for the Emperor was "the only source of authority in Japan under the Japanese theory of the state."

Authorized to draft a reply, Byrnes hurried back to the State Department, where he enlisted the Department Counselor, Benjamin Cohen. He got all the tough assignments, and more advice than he wanted from the Pearl Harbor–era hands Joseph Grew, now the Undersecretary, and Eugene Dooman, who had been embassy counselor when he and Grew had served in Tokyo—as well as from Joseph Ballantine, who, as assistant to Cordell Hull, had ushered in ambassadors Kurusu and Nomura while the bombs neither envoy knew about were falling on Oahu. Byrnes had taken even a harder line about the Emperor than Truman, but had accepted Cohen's phraseology that acknowledged that the Emperor could remain while not guaranteeing what prerogatives he would keep.

In an hour the draft was on Truman's desk. He rushed copies to Leahy, Stimson, and Forrestal, and by noon Stimson had telephoned that he approved the language. The message was tough, but it recognized—and utilized—the Emperor, however much it fell short of Japanese hopes. As Truman noted in his diary about the Emperor, "We told 'em we'd tell 'em how to keep him, but we'd make the terms":

> From the moment of surrender, the authority of the Emperor and the Japanese Government to rule the state shall be subject to the Supreme Commander of the Allied

Powers who will take such steps as he deems proper to effectuate the surrender terms.

The Emperor will be required to authorize and ensure the signature by the Government of Japan and the Japanese Imperial General Headquarters of the surrender terms necessary to carry out the provisions of the Potsdam Declaration, and shall issue his command to all the Japanese military, naval and air authorities and to all the forces under their control wherever located to cease active operations and to surrender their arms, and to issue such other orders as the Supreme Commander may require to give effect to the surrender terms. . . .

Byrnes's final paragraphs were calculated to cause the most dismay to Japanese authorities, as they put the "national polity" at risk:

The ultimate form of government of Japan shall, in accordance with the Potsdam Declaration, be established by the freely expressed will of the Japanese people.

The armed forces of the Allied Powers will remain in Japan until the purposes set forth in the Potsdam Declaration are achieved.

When Stimson excused himself at ten o'clock for urgent War Department business there were excited crowds in the streets. Word of the Japanese surrender offer had leaked out—as the Japanese had hoped it would everywhere but in Japan.

Few in the West would worry that the conditions of surrender were humiliating—that was one of the purposes of surrender stipulations. But English novelist and poet Richard Aldington, of the "Imagist" generation of Ezra Pound and W. B. Yeats that earlier in the century had derived inspiration from Japanese culture, would write a friend later in the day that the Japanese would "have to give in" regardless of the shame. "I suppose you won't agree, but I feel the deepest sorrow for Japan and admiration for the heroism and devotion of the Japanese people. All they asked was to be left alone." Left alone, he failed to explain, to exploit East Asia in ways far more barbaric than what he characterized as "the howling pack of European nations" that had preceded Japan as colonizers. "They who had worked out so exquisite and beautiful a civilisation" now were being forced into "humiliating concessions" when all they had tried to do was "to revenge themselves" on the West. Aldington had made a career of contrariness, as had been clear in his cynical—and autobiographical—Great War novel, *Death of a Hero*. The war, and particularly the atomic bombs, kept him thinking, he claimed, of the *tanka**

> *Each time that an extra is circulated*
> *The widows of friends and foes*
> *Have increased in multitude.*

Although he would not concede it any more than would last-ditch holdouts in the Japanese military, peace on whatever terms would bring an end to the widowing.

Among those most anguished was Anami's brother-in-law, Lieutenant Colonel Masahiko Takeshita, who told him, "Since such a unique national polity as we enjoyed was beyond the understanding of foreign nations, there was little doubt that the occupation forces would eventually compel us to transform it as they wished. . . . It would be useless for the people to survive the war if the structure of the State itself was to be destroyed." While Potsdam guaranteed Japan a government of its own choice, militarists were not confident that the form that had perpetuated their role would survive a popular vote.

Civilians knew little yet about anything but their own plight. Under instructions from General Anami, Admiral Yonai, and Minister Togo, the director of the Information Bureau, Hiroshi Shimomura, drafted a bland statement for the afternoon radio news that changes to better meet the nation's serious challenges were being considered. More specifics would go into the evening broadcast—especially if there was an American response.

Another of Anami's listeners at the War Ministry Friday morning had been Lieutenant Colonel Masao Inaba of the Budget Branch, hardly a fighting unit, but Inaba possessed the fighting mood of what his former Axis ally would have called a *schreibitsch Offizier*—a desk officer. For the nation's honor, at least until the actual surrender, the army had to resist with increased ferocity. He tried the idea out on Anami, who saw no conflict in it with the imperial will, and then on the Vice Minis-

*Very likely Aldington's own.

ter and younger officers, including Colonel Okitsugu Arao of the Military Affairs Section (which included the Budget Branch).

When Shimomura reached his office with the Cabinet statement for the evening news, he discovered that Takeshita had delivered his special "Army" declaration under Anami's name. Shimomura telephoned the general and learned that Anami had seen some such text written by hothead patriots and was under pressure to release it. He had the impression that it did not violate the letter of the surrender text, however it violated its spirit. Shimomura read into Anami's response the feeling that the War Minister might be assassinated if it was not broadcast.

On the evening news at seven the Information Bureau arranged for the spurious Anami declaration to be read first, with the official Cabinet message as its antidote. Yet it would have been difficult for homeland listeners to detect in either text an admission that Japan had, that morning, sued for peace. The first statement began with the announcement of Russia's intervention. Whatever its excuses, the manifesto under the general's name explained, "her ambition to invade and seize Greater East Asia is very clear." The armed forces now had to "fight to the last" against enemies new and old. "What is there to say but that we will give our all. . . . We have but one choice. We must fight on until we win the sacred war to preserve our divine land. I firmly believe in fighting to the end, even if we have to chew grass and eat earth and sleep in the fields—for there is life in death. The hero [Masashige] Kusonoki pledged to live and die seven times in order to save Japan from disaster. We can do no less. . . ." (Kusonoki, a fourteenth-century samurai, had supported the Southern Court of the Emperor Godaigo against the dictatorial Northern Court shogunate, committing suicide in 1336 rather than face capture.) The radio audience, including townspeople and villagers listening at outdoor loudspeakers that had been a feature of life predating Pearl Harbor, would understand, as they would the references that followed to "the faith of Tokimune Hōjō that life springs from nonexistence, indestructibility from destruction." Hōjō, regent and military dictator under a weak emperor late in the thirteenth century, had fought off two Mongol invasions. The second, in 1281, had ended, according to tradition, when a *kamikaze*, or "divine wind," decimated the armada of Kublai Khan, leaving the survivors easy targets for the Japanese. One needed now, Anami's ghostwriter exhorted, the "spirit" of Kusonoki and the "faith" of Hōjō.

By comparison the Cabinet statement was bland. It acknowledged that the enemy was using a "new type" of bomb that was of
unparalleled barbarity and possibly preliminary to invasion. "Our
fighting forces," it went on unpersuasively, "will no doubt be able to
repulse the enemy's attack, but we must recognize that we are facing
a situation that is as bad as it can be. The government will do all it can
to defend the homeland and preserve the honor of the country, but it
expects that Japan's hundred million will also rise to the occasion,
overcoming whatever obstacles lie in the path of the preservation of
our national polity."

As preparation for a surrender announcement it may have been
intended to manipulate the people into a sense of relief—if, indeed,
the national polity had been rescued. But the announcement of the
conditional acceptance of Potsdam was made only in Morse code
broadcasts beamed away from Japan. The enemy capitals had not yet
released the news, and the Foreign Office wanted to force its release
without its own people knowing of it, to forestall the dropping of the
third atomic bomb on, it was feared, Tokyo. If the world knew that
Japan was suing for peace, Togo and Kase schemed, the potential
moral outrage at another atomic bombing could prevent it from happening. Further, public realization in the West that Japan wanted an
end to the war might put pressure on Allied governments to accept
the Japanese formula for surrender, backed up in the Ministry's release by a quotation from the post-Potsdam broadcast late in July by
Captain Zacharias.

In the War Ministry, where die-hards congratulated themselves
on their emotional broadcast, resentment boiled up at the Foreign
Ministry's evasion of army censorship. No one had worried about
Morse code transmissions. As Greater East Asia Minister—in effect,
wearing another hat as Colonial Minister—Togo also notified his representatives in Manchukuo, China, Indochina, Thailand, Burma, and
the segments of soon-to-be-independent Indonesia that because of
"various foreign and domestic circumstances" a surrender offer had
been made to the Allies.

With the Morse code message out, General MacArthur, implying that
he had something to do with it, sent his publicist, Brigadier General
LeGrande A. Diller—merely Major Diller in December 1941, when he
invented good news on MacArthur's behalf to feed journalists in
Manila—to inform the staff that Japan had accepted Potsdam. Yet

even Diller knew that an offer was not a surrender, and hundreds of sorties were flown by "MacArthur's men"—as, to the continuing indignation of the unidentified men and units, forces under his command were described.

Although Okinawa-based B-24s and B-25s, escorted by P-51s, attacked Kyushu and lower Honshu, and carrier-based fighters and dive-bombers from TF 38 hit airfields in northern Honshu, the major target of B-29s from the Marianas was Tokyo, which may have relieved Japanese concerns that the Twentieth Air Force was reserving the capital for the next atomic bomb. In his relatively posh POW building in Tokyo, Sergeant Frank Fujita listened to the B-29s as he lay doubled up with stomach cramps—from fear, he conceded, that even if the next big bomb didn't target Tokyo, prison guards, out of anger at what had happened to Hiroshima and Nagasaki, or despair over imminent defeat, would "eliminate us." He now kept a knife hidden in his bedding, intending to take some of his captors with him if it came to that.

For the Japanese there was no longer any question that the two "special bombs" had been atomic. On the tenth, two investigating teams gathered in a surviving Hiroshima arsenal to reach that joint conclusion, but they found little they could recommend for coping with future nuclear attacks. Charging the United States with immorality in deploying the weapon, they realized, was a useless tactic, and civilian grumbling at the hardships and the horrors was spreading into the military ranks. Still dumping corpses into crematory fires in Hiroshima on the tenth, soldiers in *Black Rain* sigh, "If only we'd not been born in this damn-fool country!" In the Mitsubishi aircraft factory in little-bombed Matsumoto, in central Honshu west of Tokyo, engineer Jiro Horikoshi noted in his diary: "The majority of the company's employees are now busily occupied with dispersal of their private belongings, and hiding factory machines and equipment. Their daily shop work has been forgotten. They seem to have accepted defeat as only a matter of time."

While with the Hiroshima investigating team, Captain Mitsuo Fuchida was telephoned by Rear Admiral Yokoi, an old friend and now chief of staff to Ugaki in Kyushu. "I favor surrendering to the United States," he suggested, "but not to the Soviet Union. I suggest we gather all our remaining air forces and send them against Vladivostock or wherever we can find enough Russians." The mission, he confessed, would be "without any hope of victory," but it would express "hatred and disgust at Russia's perfidy."

Fuchida liked the idea, and offered to try it on the Navy Ministry. Higher-ups, however, were no longer eager for *kamikaze* missions, and instead ordered him back to Tokyo. At Atsugi was Captain Yasuna Kozono, who had preceded Fuchida by a year at the naval academy at Eta Jima. Kozono was furious about the likelihood of national surrender, and assumed that Fuchida, whose influence exceeded his rank, had something to do with the Navy's acceptance of Potsdam. "In no case," Kozono insisted to Fuchida, "will I accept any order to lay down my arms. I will kill you if you agree to surrender, because two thousand *kamikaze* pilots are already dead from serving under your plan. How can you justify living with this knowledge?"

The question of loyalty to Emperor or loyalty to national honor would continue to tear at the officer corps, but Fuchida thought he had made up his mind. He had seen Hiroshima and he saw no reason for the nation to die from *genbaku sho*—atom bomb disease. "You may do as you like about this," said Fuchida, "but I shall also do as I please." He asked Kozono to take care of the plane, and went on to the Navy Ministry, where there would be little to do but wait.

American forces were not waiting. Pulled in opposite directions, planners were working on the logistics of surrender, ongoing offensive operations, and "Operation Olympic." On the tenth, the final replotting of beach assignments for landing in and around Kagoshima Bay was approved, ranging from 5,000 yards on Kyushu to as limited a diameter as 310 yards on smaller islands offshore in the Koshiki Retto. Advised of the possibility of peace, Admiral "Bull" Halsey growled, "Have we got enough fuel to turn around and hit the bastards once more before they quit?" But by evening the word was going out to minimize offensive activities until further notice, both to safeguard lives and to establish a climate to encourage surrender.

An outdoor screening of *Captain Eddie* on Okinawa had reached the sequence where Eddie Rickenbacker, home from the 1917–1918 war, was telling his bride that millions of doughboys now back from France were going fishing, when the film operator stopped the reel to announce, "Japan has asked for terms of surrender!" In the roaring and cheering that followed the rest of the movie was forgotten. Offshore on the *Montpelier*, Seaman Fahey noted, Captain William A. Gorry went on the intercom at 8:50 P.M., awakening some men on the next watch, to report the Japanese offer and its reservation about keeping the Emperor. "When the Captain finished speaking, everyone gave a big cheer. Some of the men were whistling and yelling. . . . Everyone went wild. Right after the men on Okinawa were informed of this news, we could hear guns firing; flares of all colors and star shells lit the sky. The searchlights were turning in all directions. . . . Some of the ships here fired their guns and others blew their foghorns. It was quite a celebration. This was the happiest day of our lives."

Whatever the war, premature peace celebrations were always the happiest, and the lower the rank the more spontaneous was the explosion of relief. On Guam, soldiers destined for "Olympic" shouted, "Let 'em keep the Emperor!" and celebrated through the night. Having missed the Yawata adventure because of crackups on the runways but then making up for it over Fukuyama on the night of the eighth, the 468th Bomb Group, on Tinian, had all day on the tenth to think about a strike on a well-defended industrial complex east of Nagoya. Briefing was at six and takeoff scheduled for three the next morning, but at eleven the news of the Japanese offer came through. "A fine film of perspiration began to appear," according to the Group's history. "At the very last minute, I mean the last minute, our mission was cancelled and everybody went back to the sack with a prayer on their lips." Few wanted a risky mission for the thrill of it. On Guam, Lieutenant Hays Gamble noted in his diary, the news reached the barracks area of the 315th at 10:30 "that the war was over. All hell broke loose and what a time—[the] place in a turmoil! Flares, guns, fires, yelling, etc. Bottles broken out and much gaiety all over the place. Can hardly believe it and seems too wonderful to be true. Hope there isn't a snag in it somewhere."

But there was. The United States could not respond to Japan until its allies had approved a response, and in Tokyo the silence seemed ominous in the wail of the air raid sirens. Truman's Cabinet had met at two—already early on the eleventh in Japan—and approved sending the Byrnes response, for concurrence, to London, Moscow, and Chungking, impressing each recipient of the importance of speed. Truman explained to the Cabinet the deliberate reference to a "Supreme Commander . . . to give effect to the surrender terms," rather than "Supreme Command," so that it would be explicitly clear, according to Forrestal, "that the United States would run this particular business and avoid a situation of composite responsibility such as has plagued us in Germany."

Truman expected, he told the Cabinet, that "we might not hear" from the Russians, and if so he intended to "act without them." Stimson predicted that the Russians would stall as an excuse "to push as far into Manchuria as possible," and Truman agreed that it was not in the American interest that the Red Army "push too far."

The British response was back by 9:48 P.M. Washington time. For Attlee and Bevin, Cadogan raised doubts about the requirement to have the Emperor personally sign the surrender. "The Emperor," the British cable suggested, "shall authorize and ensure the signature by the Government of Japan and the Japanese General Headquarters. . . ." Chiang Kaishek, on the other hand, cabled: "I especially concur in the condition to require the Emperor . . . to sign the surrender terms. . . ." Russia, from whom Truman did not hear until after midnight in Washington, in a cable from Molotov, was "skeptical" that Japan was really proposing unconditional surrender and intended to push on in Manchuria. "He gave me the definite impression," said Truman, "that he was quite willing to have the war continue." Ending a war, Japan was discovering painfully, was far more difficult than beginning it.

As Halsey and Spaatz had already made clear in the Pacific, whatever Washington wanted in the way of a slowdown that would promote the peace process, combat commanders could find reasons to flout it. Scores had to be paid, medals and promotions won, service rivalries served. But from the Pentagon, Admiral King dispatched a message apprising Admiral Nimitz of the Japanese offer. With deliberate irony it began, "This is a peace warning." (On November 27, 1941, General Marshall and Admiral Stark had warned overseas commands of Japanese intentions with cables beginning, "This dispatch is to be considered a war warning." But no one was paying attention then.) Supporting the Navy view, Stimson wanted Air Force commanders to "now cease sending our bombers over Japan," although Truman wanted the war kept up "at its present intensity" to maintain the pressure. A B-29 hiatus would be ordered, but no planes in the air were called back. More important from Stimson's standpoint, Truman declared a halt to the atomic bombing, conceding in the Cabinet (according to Secretary of Commerce Henry A. Wallace, Truman's predecessor as vice president) that "the thought of wiping out another

100,000 people was too horrible." He was thinking, he said, "of all those kids."

Few in the military or in the Manhattan District would have disagreed that the Bomb had added a new horror to war. Even fewer thought that the enemy would have denied itself an equivalent opportunity, or that the enemy had not perpetrated gross horrors of its own. While moral qualms had accompanied deployment of each atomic weapon, there would be more guilt about Nagasaki. Not only was the bombing a sequel, and to some unnecessary, but the radioactive components were different. "If anyone had tried to defend the first bomb, then I might have listened to him," says C. P. Snow's anguished nuclear physicist Walter Luke in *The New Men* (1954). "But if anyone dares to defend the second, then I'll see him in hell before I listen to a single word."

"The only point of dropping the second," agrees his agonized colleague, Martin Eliot, "must have been for purposes of comparison." Yet after Alamogordo another plutonium blast was not needed to furnish physicists with calculations. A second charge with even less basis further sickens Martin Eliot. "There was a good deal of discussion," he tells his brother Lewis, a Whitehall bureaucrat, "about how to drop it with maximum results. One ingenious idea was to start a really spectacularly pretty flare a few seconds before the bomb went off."

"Why?"

"To make sure that everyone in town was looking up."

"Why?"

"To make sure they were all blinded."

Such breast-beating allegations, in which fiction becomes inseparable from fact, would fuel the atomic debate for decades.

Although no new Bomb was ready on Tinian, General Groves had reported to Marshall that four days had been sliced off production time for the next "Fat Man" plutonium core and initiator. The components could be shipped out on August 12 or 13, with a Bomb "ready for delivery on the first suitable weather [date] after 17 or 18 August." Marshall told him to hold it.*

---

*A book by Frank Chinnock on the Nagasaki strike quotes weaponeer Deak Parsons as sending messages to Groves and Oppenheimer that on August 11 he would begin assembly of two additional "Fat Mans," completing one on August 12, which could be dropped the next day. On August 16 "F102 can be dropped"—a third plutonium bomb. But no deployable plutonium core was on Tinian.

As the United States began to gear down the war, the Russians were pushing quickly and easily into Manchuria. General Yamada returned to P'u Yi's palace to inform him that the army was withdrawing to positions in the south, both to avoid being trapped in a Red Army pincers movement and to form a defensive redoubt just above the Korean border. The capital would move to Tunghua, close to the Yalu River border with Korea. P'u Yi protested. His accumulation of property was too vast to be uprooted, and the Imperial Household was large. "If Your Majesty does not go," Lieutenant General Yasunori Yoshioka, ostensibly his military attaché, warned, "you will be the first one to be murdered by Soviet troops." P'u Yi began packing.

"We must take the mirror," he told an aide. Three sacred treasures were associated with the throne of China—a jewel, a sword, and the mirror, which was wrapped in yellow and white silk. Each required a ninety-degree bow from the reverent. Packed into a railway car with P'u Yi, they were never seen again.

The only impediments to the Russian advance were Japanese air attacks and the hordes of refugees. One of them, Yoshie Fukushima, had enough problems with a sick son at her breast, but as she walked along railway tracks that she hoped went south, she came upon an infant girl "in a good kimono, lying on a neatly arranged pile of her things. She even had a little shade to shield her from the sun. . . . Her parents must have . . . left her in the hope that someone else would take her." Carrying two infants was impossible. Although she felt "terrible remorse," she left the baby "near a Manchurian village where people would find her. When it comes to saving your own child, you become like that."

She caught frogs and snails and cooked them over a fire, and cooked leaves and grass, treasuring her hoard of dry matches. Luckily, she was offered a ride in a horse-drawn cart, literally a ride to survival.

In Hong Kong, a newspaper smuggled across the bay from Macau brought news of the atomic bombing of Hiroshima. When a Chinese employee of a Japanese firm reported the burning of documents, rumors spread that the Japanese were indeed defeated. In Stanley Internment Camp the rumors gained credibility when the Formosan guards became "friendly and excited." When orders came at 2:00 P.M. that men with "technical qualifications" were to assemble with their families in an hour, prepared to leave, rumors of every description flew. "I think we are being repatriated in exchange for Japanese technicians from Australia," one guessed. "My idea," said another gaunt internee, "is that the Japanese are evacuating Hong Kong and they are taking us out to run the city." Tom Spelbury, a pessimist, speculated, "They are taking us as a reprisal for something. We are to be hostages. They'll take us to Canton to get us out of the way as we know too much about the running of Hong Kong." There was pandemonium, with debts to be collected, farewells to be made.

In order to stay together, three couples married in the moments before leaving Stanley, and, counting family members, including a baby in a pram, 173 internees were packed onto a junk and towed across the harbor to a makeshift camp in Kowloon. Conditions were even worse than at Stanley, where one of the couples in prewedded bliss had made a love nest on a small landing in a stairwell. Told nothing, they waited—for something. For anything.

In Shanghai, word came of the Red Army attack far to the north when the Japanese began checking for Soviet passports. News of the atomic bombs spread, and on the tenth, Allied flags went up on some public buildings. Peace rumors flooded the Jewish ghetto; people danced in the streets. Russian, Chinese, and refugee inhabitants kissed each other in unheard-of solidarity—and pummeled passing Japanese. Yet the celebration was premature. The flags were hauled down by armed sentries, and some in the jubilant crowds were hauled away. Some rounded up were made to stand bareheaded in the broiling sun— until the *Jüdische Gemeinde* ("local authority") raised the matter with the Japanese commander, who validated the rumors by relenting. The shoe could be on the other foot in a matter of days.

In Hankow the Japanese-language *Continental News* headlined an article "ATOMIC BOMBING OF HIROSHIMA," and the local antiaircraft units began practicing firing at zero angle to defend cow pastures against tanks. From Yenan, the Communist Chinese army commander, Chu Teh, sent orders to forces in liberated areas beginning, prematurely, "Japan has announced her unconditional surrender." "Puppet" and Japanese troops were to be disarmed, and "All anti-Japanese forces in the Liberated Areas should resolutely wipe out all those enemy and armed puppet forces which refuse to surrender and hand over their arms." He also claimed "full authority . . . to take over and occupy any city, town, and communication line. . . ."

At a prison camp on Hainan, desperately ill B-25 pilot Eugene Harviell died. Japanese guards cremated the remains and buried his ashes, later retrieved and removed to the National War Memorial Cemetery of the Pacific on Oahu. But for POWs the sudden softening of the usual brutality seemed confirmation that the war was coming to an end—that they had to hang on just a little longer. In Thailand, Weary Dunlop noted in his diary that eight truckloads of Red Cross stores had arrived. They might have been held back for months or even years. Yet the improvement in conditions was not universal, even in the same occupied country. Four hundred POW officers in the Chon Buri camp were moved in the tropical rain by open cattle car to a camp at Hakhan Nayak, north of Bangkok, "in pitch blackness, the total illumination in the huge marshalling yards being provided by two small hurricane lamps and one candle without a candlestick." The new encampment consisted of roofed cattle cars, fifteen prisoners to a truck. The men hoped for a quick end to the war.

In what was still French Indochina, Ho Chi Minh, anticipating the Japanese surrender, convened sixty northern Viet Minh delegates to begin forming a National Liberation Committee of Vietnam. In the north, even in Hanoi, the Japanese had nearly disappeared. Ho called for general insurrection. The Japanese Southern Army headquarters in Indochina still existed in Saigon, where General Terauchi reigned, although his hot weather quarters was at the hill station of Dalat. *Reigned* was the operative word, as he was related to the imperial house and had been considered a favorite to succeed Tojo as Premier in July 1944 until Army stalwarts prevailed and pushed in General Koiso. Terauchi had suffered a cerebral hemorrhage on April 10, but his staff had kept his failing condition a secret from everyone but the Emperor, who sent him a telegram earlier in the month appealing, "Come back to Japan and report. Come to Tokyo on the understanding you will not be returning to a theater of war." Terauchi made plans to leave on the eighteenth, but on the tenth his headquarters picked up a broadcast that Japan had surrendered. It was yet another misunderstanding of the conditional offer to surrender, but it hastened the formal ceremony, held at Dalat, of independence for Sukarno's Indonesia. Although the move hastened the decolonialization of Southeast Asia, it did nothing to alleviate Terauchi's sense of entrapment. Could the Southern Army become an autonomous force, living off the land? He had at hand the benefit of captured and appropriated British, and even German, weapons.

In Burma the situation remained the worst for the Japanese—those that remained alive. Even east of the swollen Sittang the fields were strewn with the dead and dying. Despite British shelling, another three hundred crossed on the tenth, greeted, in yet another premature announcement, by airdrops of leaflets telling them that the Japanese had surrendered. Colonel Hiroo Saitō thought of the eight thousand men of the 55th Division he had left behind dead, futile sacrifices for Greater East Asia. Many had died on the march, as he recalled later, retaining the incredible discipline of politeness that left them whispering "Thank you for helping me" as they breathed their last. Whatever the truth of the surrender news, the Japanese goal was to find more tolerable terrain and regroup.

An Axis pact agreement in headier days under the code word *Lübeck* was that if one nation was defeated but the other continued fighting, the loser would turn over to the belligerent ally whatever war material was accessible. In East Asia that had meant port facilities that the Japanese had made available for German subs and blockade runners, and in May 1945 the subs themselves. While U-boats at sea had been ordered to radio their positions in the open and await surrender to Allied vessels, those in waters controlled by the Japanese came under the command of Admiral Paul Wenneker, German naval attaché in Tokyo, who called for recognition of "the decision *Lübeck.*" It meant, he conceded, "an uncertain fate" for German crews. Lieutenant Otto Giese, in Singapore harbor, had immediately thrown overboard the codebooks for the *U-181*, but orders were that it and the *U-862*, docked with it, were to be turned over to Japanese crews and the Germans were to submit to internment.

All U-boat and base personnel were transferred to a guarded camp in the Malayan village of Bata Pahat, just off the Strait of Malacca, where all the houses were built on stilts. Although the region was guerrilla-occupied and bandit-ridden, the Japanese were the enemy, and the Germans felt safe in their compound until they heard of the atomic bombs and the Russian intervention. When the initial Japanese surrender offer came on the tenth, Giese recalled, the jungle around them came to life. "Silent columns were marching. Now and then we could hear sticks breaking and branches brushing against unseen forces. We would often hear Chinese curse words." Japanese soldiers withdrew prudently to Johore, just north of the strait separating Malaya from Singapore, and their Malayan police took reprisals against suspicious-looking Chinese, which meant any Chinese. Giese's former sub commander, Captain Kurt Freiwald, the senior officer among the internees, received a feeler from the Chinese guerrillas asking what the Germans (who had small arms) would do if the guerrillas attempted to liquidate the police stations. Freiwald offered to remain neutral if the Germans were unharmed and their provisions left untouched. It was a new war.

In Lübeck itself, where thoughts of Japan did not exist, Arthur Dickens of the British military government was sent a demobilized young German officer described as "highly disgruntled and possibly dangerous." A Hitler Youth product, he seemed "innocent of any humane education." A Silesian as well, he complained about Potsdam, "I find it hardest of all to bear the thought of our lovely Silesia being handed over to the Poles." As for the Potsdam stipulation of "humane" expulsion of Germans from appropriated territories, it was, he said, mere hypocrisy—as it indeed was. Dickens reminded him that "the Germans had shown no compunction in staging brutal and unprovoked annexations and expulsions; they should not be the first to protest when the roles were reversed."

"Yes," he conceded, "acts of cruelty have been committed by both sides in the East."

Neither one had mentioned the most sadistic of Nazi acts, the mass murder of Europe's Jews, and until August 10, even the Supreme Commander in the West, Dwight Eisenhower, had taken the plight of surviving Jews less than seriously, attempting to circumvent the Secretary of War on the need for action. On August 3, Stimson had cabled Eisenhower to implement the report of Earl Harrison, Dean of the University of Pennsylvania Law School, who had found Jewish displaced persons still "living under guard behind barbed-wire fences, in camps ... built for slave laborers and Jews ... including some of the most notorious of the concentration camps, amidst crowded, frequently unsanitary and generally grim conditions. . . ." Stimson had added on his own, "I want to emphasize the importance we attach to this problem and request that everything possible be done to improve present situation."

Rabbi Stephen S. Wise of New York, possibly the most distinguished of the American rabbinate, had suggested that Eisenhower designate one of his own Jewish army chaplains as adviser on Jewish affairs, and the general had dismissed the idea only the day before. Now he reconsidered and intended to make the appointment, but, he cabled Stimson, his own staff had found Harrison's report "completely different" from their own observations. "I should call your attention to the fact," he lectured his boss, "that problems of this nature must not be over-simplified because each Jewish individual is presumably a national of some European country, and it is impossible to consider them all as stateless."

In harping on the technicality he knew he had begged the question; the very reconsideration had made that obvious. Finally, on August 22 he would issue a directive that Jews desiring to be repatriated to countries of which they were nationals would be returned, and that those who did not want to return or who were stateless would be cared for in new Jewish centers. "In establishing these special centers, particular attention will be paid to a high standard of accommodation."

Even Sir Alexander Cadogan, in London, was certain from the Japanese note on surrender that the war was over—that a compromise would be made to accommodate the imperial proviso. The Cabinet, meeting at 4:30, he noted, spent its time on "announcements [of peace], broadcasts, Parliament, public holiday, Day of Thanksgiving &c." The public was not waiting. As General Bernard Freyberg, VC, hero of two world wars, reported in his diary, "The streets of the West End were a snowstorm of torn up fragments of paper—a queer demonstration of joy." Driving from London to Chartwell for the weekend, Winston Churchill knew that victory had not yet arrived, but his secretary, Elizabeth Layton, saw with him that "it hung in the air, and the streets of London, as we left Westminster, were already filling with rejoicing people." As they approached Tower Bridge, Churchill told her sadly, "You know, not a single decision has been taken since we left office to have brought this about."

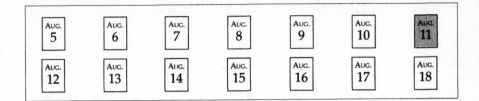

| Aug. 5 | Aug. 6 | Aug. 7 | Aug. 8 | Aug. 9 | Aug. 10 | **Aug. 11** |
| Aug. 12 | Aug. 13 | Aug. 14 | Aug. 15 | Aug. 16 | Aug. 17 | Aug. 18 |

## CHAPTER XXX

# · AUGUST 11, 1945 ·

*speaking with several voices*

Die-hards in Japan who had given no thought to how to end the war in the long-ago when they had begun it had no more idea how to conclude a losing war than they had a winning one, posturing with such exhortations as "Let us seek life in death itself!" As naval captain Masataka Chihaya would put it in a study of the war six months later, "They finally sent us an atomic bomb instead of a referee with a whistle, just to close the lid." The American decision not to ship a third atomic bomb to the Marianas and to hold back major bombing and shelling of the home islands was intended not to give Japan breathing room but negotiating space within an obviously divided leadership.

With the outcome no longer in doubt, telegrams sped from Washington on the eleventh cancelling $4 billion in military procurement orders (one third of that for ninety-five warships), holding munitions-laden freight trains, advising manufacturers to begin gearing up for civilian production. According to John W. Snyder, Director of the Office of War Mobilization and Reconversion, the bad news about imminent victory was that thirty days after "V-J Day" unemployment—including returning veterans—might reach 6 million. In Philadelphia the Cramp Shipyard began to lay off the first 2,875 of its 11,500 workers, offering those who volunteered to quit twenty hours' extra pay. At the Newport News Shipbuilding and Drydock Company the aircraft carrier *Iwo Jima*, looking like the rib cage of a whale, was abandoned.

Opinion polls in the country, reflecting nearly four years of war rather than the imminence of peace, still registered firmness on unseating and punishing Emperor Hirohito, an attitude that if hardened into policy would prolong the fighting. From the Marianas, the 40th Bomb Group report for the day noted that "civilian reaction . . . did not sit well and there was much gnashing of teeth and full bloom cursing on this expression of opinion. It was not appreciated. . . ." Orders from the White House in any case were to ground the B-29s pending a Japanese reply, and crews on Tinian, Guam, and Saipan unloaded bombs from planes being prepared for missions.

Although no heavy bombers went up, planes from Okinawa, Iwo Jima, and the Philippines flew 539 sorties, mostly strafing missions, less to keep the pressure on Tokyo than to keep Air Force pressure on a postwar Washington for separate status. Unwilling to halt the raids, the Air Force explained its activity as limited to "precision missions," yet fliers were less eager than their leadership. As Captain George Withee put it in a letter to his wife from Guam after the 331st Bomb Group's loudspeaker announced the Japanese peace offer, "I have prayed, I have honestly prayed, that this is the end of this ungodly slaughter. It is my opinion that Japan truly knows the meaning of war now . . . more than I hope we ever do know. I have never seen so much fire in all my life, and it must be much more impressive to one on the ground. . . . No artist could paint the horror—or the beauty—of such a spectacle."

Since an unacceptable Japanese offer would not end the war, each service chief took in his own fashion Truman's instructions to maintain some "intensity" while negotiations proceeded. Admiral Nimitz advised the Pacific Fleet: "The public announcement by the Japanese of counter proposals for the termination of the war must not be permitted to affect vigilance against Japanese attacks. Neither the Japanese nor Allied Forces have stopped fighting. Take precautions against treachery even if local or general surrender should be suddenly announced. Maintain all current reconnaissance and patrols.

Offensive action should be continued unless otherwise specifically directed." Little action would occur. As new storms were approaching from the south, the fleet took the opportunity to do widespread refueling. To the north, the six destroyers and two cruisers of Task Force 92, on an "anti-shipping scan" of the Kuriles, sank Japanese trawlers and shelled a seaplane base, drawing "ineffective" fire from coastal batteries. "We fired 500 rounds of 5-inch shells," Laird Shirk wrote from the *McGowan*, observing that unloading ordnance in that fashion was "a lot easier on the crew than having to hand carry it off the ship back in the States." They were still moving north, nosing into the Bering Sea and now picking up Russian radio.

Like Nimitz, General Marshall advised forces—and was advised himself—to be wary. In a memorandum on the eleventh, "Ultra Intelligence during and after Arrangements to Terminate the Japanese War," his G-2, Major General Clayton Bissell, warned that enemy orders for "general or isolated repudiation of the surrender" could escape detection. Terms should require that all Japanese military communications be sent in the clear, Bissell suggested, and in any case, decrypting had to continue round the clock:

> Cryptographic systems used for communication by the Japanese Foreign Office with its diplomatic officials in neutral countries . . . are being fully read with speed. If the Japanese are given no reason to suspect those systems are compromised . . . intelligence of importance may be obtained.

Bissell also thought that "substantial long-term benefits" accrued by continuing to listen in via "Magic." No beaten enemy could be fully trusted.

While the shooting war at least temporarily went into low gear along the Pacific rim, the Soviets were moving quickly to take over Manchuria. At 4:04 P.M. Tokyo time, still morning in Moscow, Hsinking radio was used by the Japanese to send a message that "Magic" picked up: "With this we are shutting down. Keep up the good fight!" The colonial adventure in Manchuria was itself shutting down. Yet "Magic" did not pick up Russian messages sent, in panic, in the clear, from motorized troops of the Trans-Baikal Army who had crossed into Manchuria from the west. After three days they had run out of fuel and had to shut down their own operation. The retreating Japanese heard it but could do nothing except recognize evidence that Stalin, after the wake-up call from Hiroshima, had rushed into the war before his stockpiles were in place. That had been evident in the north, also, where the Red Army had not prepared enough pontoon bridges to cross the Amur River. Manchuria was as vast as Alaska, and the Soviets had begun what was, but for Japanese weakness and Russian numbers, a rather plodding blitzkrieg.

Still, recognizing the inevitability of victory, the Soviets had responded to the draft American note on the peace feeler by suggesting the subordinating of Hirohito to a joint high command of an American and Russian general. Harriman told Molotov bluntly that the proposal was "unthinkable." After "heated discussion," with Molotov insisting that his proposal be forwarded, Harriman did so, warning him, he cabled Truman, that it would be "unacceptable" in Washington.

By the time Harriman had returned to his embassy, Molotov's interpreter and assistant, Pavlov, was on the telephone to explain the "misunderstanding." Stalin had agreed to withdraw the demand. The cynical attempt to co-rule occupied Japan on the basis of a two-days' war had been blocked. Used to being high-handed, the Russians understood, but in London the Foreign Office was piqued that the United States had accepted its amendment on the Emperor but not acknowledged it—as if cabling Whitehall a copy of the note to Japan revised by the British language was not an acknowledgment. The action, Pierson Dixon, Bevin's principal private secretary, complained in his diary, was characteristic of America's "healthy aggressive mood to take the lead and be the spokesman."

The Allied response was handed to Max Grassli, the Swiss Chargé d'Affaires in Washington, by Secretary Byrnes for transmittal to Tokyo. At the same time, 10:30 A.M., Truman held a press conference to announce that the relevant governments were consulting on the note, only to find that the State Department, without the President's advance knowledge, was releasing the text. Victory exuberance boiled up across the country in street crowds and ticker-tape flurries, and the White House had to warn that the Japanese had not yet accepted the terms. But there was little public concern, despite the opinion polls about hanging Hirohito, that the Government had wronged the war dead. Tense himself, Truman telephoned the American Minister in Bern, Leland Harrison, to ask for an immediate call when a Japanese reply came in. And General Arnold ordered mas-

sive airdrops of leaflets with the surrender texts in Japanese and English—a move that would put B-29s over the home islands again.
Radio messages were also beamed at Japan to increase the pressure
to accept the terms. And Truman had a message prepared for the Allied powers that he intended General MacArthur to be Supreme
Commander in Japan, and that MacArthur would be empowered to
instruct Mountbatten to accept surrenders in Southeast Asia, Chiang
in China, and the Soviet commander in the Far East to take the surrenders of forces facing him. No objections arrived.

Not waiting for discussions in Washington on the ramifications
of peacemaking, MacArthur told Weldon Rhoades to expect to fly to
Tokyo so that the general could "officially accept the surrender of
Emperor Hirohito." A planning committee headed by the State Department was quite willing to recommend MacArthur as sole American authorized to sign the surrender document—as splendid a
one-man show as he visualized. The Navy objected. Only the Navy
could realistically move in to accept an immediate surrender. Security matters were also raised, and the venue of a ship in Tokyo Bay
was broached. In any case, Hirohito would almost certainly absent
himself from any surrender ceremony.

Almost lost in the frenzy of winding down the war, the "Smyth
Report," *Atomic Energy for Military Purposes,* was released by the War
Department for publication in the Sunday papers the next day. *The
New York Times* would put the story on page 28.

State Department personnel had met into the night and almost
into breakfast on the eleventh on practical details of other surrenders.
Japanese troops still straddled thousands of miles of colonized and
captured territory. In Korea, for example, Byrnes wanted to accept a
surrender as far north as possible, to keep the Russians away from
Japan and to insure a noncommunized occupation. With the Red
Army storming across Manchuria, the Soviets would quickly pour
into the Korean peninsula. Two staff colonels from the War Department, one of them a future Secretary of State (Dean Rusk), proposed
the thirty-eighth parallel—which had come up earlier, in Potsdam—
on grounds that it took in the capital of the country, Seoul.

The Japanese, however, had not surrendered. On the morning of
the eleventh in Tokyo, newspapers appeared with the mixed signals
of the domestic radio broadcasts of the evening before. American radio and American leaflets would force the government to furnish
more details, but readers were being prepared by statements insist-

ing on the national polity and on preserving it to the death despite a situation that confessedly could not have been worse. Between the lines of the *Mainichi Shimbun* and the *Asahi Shimbun*, readers could sense surrender and its minimal conditions. The American response was not yet known in Tokyo on Saturday morning, thirteen hours later than Washington time, when Prince Takamatsu, Hirohito's naval officer brother, invited their army officer brother, Prince Mikasa, youngest of the family, and others of the imperial house below the Emperor himself, to a meeting to hear Foreign Minister Togo's assessment of the situation. Mikasa had already been visited by young officers who wanted to continue the war, and the prince had refused. Togo then went to confer with Marquis Kido, his conduit to the Emperor, as did Premier Suzuki and Information Director Shimomura. The Emperor himself received General Anami, addressing him with unusual familiarity as "Anami"—he had been military aide to Hirohito in the early 1930s—but reprimanding him for the fighting manifesto broadcast under his name. Under no circumstances, he assured Anami, would he accept a peace that failed to guarantee the national polity. Unable to admit that he had succumbed to pressure from junior ranks, Anami promised his personal loyalty and explained that the army, as a practical matter, would have to go on fighting until a legal end to the war existed.

The junior officers themselves were still plotting to derail the surrender. Meeting in a bomb shelter at the War Office on Ichigaya Hill, they took heart from the claims of Lieutenant Colonel Masahiko Takashita that he could persuade his brother-in-law—Anami. Using Anami as example, they would then win over Lieutenant General Takeshi Mori, commander of the Imperial Guards and protector of the Emperor's palace and person. If not, they would do away with him. Except for Colonel Okitsugu Arao, chief of the Military Affairs Section, whose loyalty to the coup was shaky, few of the plotters were known outside the ministry. Lieutenant Colonel Masao Inaba drafted Anami's speeches and press releases. Lieutenant Colonel Masataka Ida, Lieutenant Colonel Jiro Shiizaki, and Major Kenji Hatanaka were headquarters heroes. But the six had, already, their small victory to claim—the strident "Anami" appeal for *bushido* defiance, the first stage in rejecting the peace.

If the militarist system was to survive, they determined, the peace faction led by Suzuki, Togo, and Kido had to be disposed of, and the Emperor "protected" (code for "house arrest") from similar officials so that their version of the imperial polity could be continued in his name. National intransigence might then cow the enemy into accepting terms that would leave the sacred honor of the army and the nation unblemished. At worst, their honorable deaths— among many, they imagined—would cancel defeat by appeasing the souls of the battle dead.

The poorly ventilated and lighted bomb shelter below Ichigaya was heavy with cigarette smoke, emphasizing the conspiratorial atmosphere. They spoke excitedly of the brief time frame in which their coup had to succeed. The American response was due imminently. The government could not be permitted to receive and accept it. The key to everything was Anami. If he went along, they could win over Mori, and certainly Umezu. All they needed then would be General Shizuichi Tanaka, commander of the Eastern District Army that included Tokyo. Midnight on the thirteenth—half through the American twelfth—seemed the outside limit for gaining control.

Although only a major, Hatanaka was assigned the task of contacting Mori. If he proved impossible to persuade, they would have to subvert his subordinates. Anami would be left to his brother-in-law. This time they would not make the mistakes of 1936.

Officer plots and uprisings were not new to Japan. The bloodiest, known thereafter to Japanese as "two two-six," had taken place early on the morning of February 26, 1936. The Tokyo-based First Guards Division, which had seen no action since the war with Russia in 1904, had been ordered to Manchuria, a posting that hothead officers interpreted as a way to remove a politically militant force from Japan. A document titled *The Great Purpose*, written in large part by Captain Kiyosada Koda, claimed goals ranging from social justice to imperial expansion. Hardly moderate in aim, it declared that "the nation is destined to expand under Imperial Rule until it embraces all the world." But that manifest destiny could not happen under the "refractory men ... obstructing the true growth of the people." The country, it went on, was "on the verge of war with Russia, Britain and America, who wish to crush our ancestral lands." Patriots had to "rise and annihilate the unrighteous and disloyal creatures who surround the Imperial Throne."

Since coups require planning, and men talk, the hothead plot of 1936 was known for weeks before it happened, even at levels up into the Imperial Household and family, yet those who knew something, if not everything, felt safer going along with events. Insurgent officers recruited twelve hundred men from the division to occupy buildings and to form death squads. On the evening of the twenty-fifth, Ambassador Grew had invited a select group of Japanese officialdom, with wives, to dinner and a film. He had arranged to run a recent American musical, *Naughty Marietta*, with Jeanette MacDonald and Nelson Eddy.

In the early hours after midnight, as a light snow fell and the dinner guests were getting home to bed, the nine death squads fanned out. The first broke into the home of the War Minister, General Yoshiyuki Kawashima, and insisted on reading him their manifesto. To save his life he showed no indignation, but they put him under house arrest and screened his visitors.

The second squad, also encountering no resistance, took over the Metropolitan Police station opposite the Imperial Palace. The third broke into the home of the future premier, Baron Suzuki, who was then Grand Chamberlain to Hirohito, and had just returned from Grew's party. "You must have some reason for doing this. Tell me what it is," said the admiral, a veteran of 1904. But no one had a copy of *The Great Purpose,* and a sergeant shouted, "No time. We're going to shoot."

"Go ahead and shoot," said Suzuki. Three officers fired, and he crumpled with multiple wounds. *"Todome,"* said an officer to Suzuki's wife—"Coup de grace." He put a pistol to Suzuki's head, but she struggled with him, shouting, "Don't do it! I'll do it!" Unnerved, Captain Teruzo Ando ordered his men out. They knelt before Suzuki's body, then saluted the admiral, who appeared dead. "I'm particularly sorry about this," said Ando to Mrs. Suzuki, "but our views differ from His Excellency's, so it had to come to this." Yet Suzuki survived.

Four hundred men surrounded the official residence of Premier Keisuke Okada and killed four policemen at the gate. Still in his nightgown, Okada was hidden in a storeroom by a security guard and the Premier's brother-in-law, a retired colonel, Denzo Matsuo. Okada's private secretary and son-in-law, Hisatsune Sakomizu—Chief Cabinet Secretary in 1945—telephoned the already-occupied Metropolitan Police station for help. "The situation is out of control. What can we do?" was the answer. As Matsuo tried to escape—it was thought afterward that he was trying to substitute himself for the Premier—the rebel soldiers hesitated to shoot. "What's the matter?

You'll be fighting in Manchuria soon. Can't you kill a man or two?" demanded an officer.

As the soldiers fired, Matsuo shouted, "Long live the Emperor!" To make certain they had murdered the right man they compared the battered body to a framed photograph found in the bedroom. "Okada," they agreed. The actual Okada hid in a laundry closet until the body was removed for an official funeral; then, wearing a gauze surgical mask, as many Japanese still do in public to ward off winter colds, he joined the mourners at his own obsequies.

The fifth squad murdered Finance Minister Korekiyo Takahashi after shouting at him *"Tenchu!"*—"Punishment from heaven." "Idiot!" Takahashi shouted back as he went down. As the group left, the rebel officer in charge apologized to the hysterical household: "Excuse me for the annoyance I have caused." The sixth attacked Viscount Makato Saito—then Lord Privy Seal—in his bedroom, shooting him more than forty times. His wife had tried covering him with her body, but they forced her away by poking at her with their swords. When, bleeding, she refused to leave the body, they dispensed with cutting Saito's throat and gathered by the front gate to shout three *banzais* for the Emperor. The seventh gunned down and slit the throat of General Jotaro Watanabe, inspector general of military training. Another group occupied the *Asahi Shimbun* building, and a ninth squad sought out the former Privy Seal, Nobuaki Makino, burning down the hotel near Atami where he was on holiday, but failing to find him.

Emperor Hirohito remained unaware of the plot until he was awakened to reports of a litany of murders. As in 1945, he found the Cabinet and the military in disarray, with some of his leading advisers dead, disabled, or merely disloyal. Relieved that the rebellion seemed restricted to Tokyo, Hirohito ordered it put down, even if it meant that the loyal Navy had to fire on insurgent elements of the Army. Yet even palace checkpoints were manned by rebels. Not deemed important by the hotheads, Sakomizu managed to escape Okada's killers and get into the palace, arriving by taxi to inform Hirohito that the Premier was alive. But the remnants of the Cabinet and ostensibly loyal Army commanders could agree on no course of action except to announce the lie that Tokyo had been "placed under the jurisdiction of the First Division." When a statement was issued suggesting that the murders had official sanction, Hirohito raised his voice for the first time in his reign. "End this incident as quickly as possible!" he told the

War Minister, Kawashima, who had been cowed by the rebels. And the Emperor took charge (through Kawashima) in more than the meek way he would later do on August 10, 1945. An interim prime minister declared martial law and army commanders were ordered to disarm the mutineers "by force if necessary."

Reluctant to respond drastically, the Army hierarchy reported back through the Emperor's chief aide-de-camp, Shigeru Honjo—who was in fear of his and the Emperor's lives and had, besides, a son-in-law among the mutineers—that while the rebels could not be "entirely forgiven," the "spirit that moved them" was "the good of the nation." Rejecting the Army's view, Hirohito scoffed, "How can we not condemn even the spirit of those criminally brutal officers who killed my aged subjects who were my hands and feet?" Rising to real emotion, he characterized the conspiracy as "akin to gently strangling me with floss-silk."

The rebels, Honjo appealed, were "misguided," but he believed their actions were "the best way to serve the state." Yet as the Army dragged out its negotiations with the men whom the Emperor called rebels and the Army merely labeled "activists," Hirohito had had enough. At dawn on February 28, as the standoff was entering its third day, the Emperor issued an edict ordering rebels to "speedily withdraw" from places they had occupied and to return to their barracks. At 8:00 A.M. the next day the ultimatum ran out and tanks rolled through Tokyo. Planes dropped leaflets urging, "Return to your units. It is not yet too late. All who resist are rebels. We will shoot them. Your families weep to see you becoming traitors."

Pride kept officers from returning, but the others flooded back. Lower ranks filled the jails; officers who failed to commit suicide were arrested, tried, and, like Captain Koda, executed. Close to a nervous breakdown, Premier Okada was given a room in the palace but never functioned again as Premier. In May 1936 he was replaced by Koki Hirota, who proved too moderate for the army and lasted only until January 1937, worried throughout his brief ministry about another coup. August 1945 seemed now déjà vu: hothead plots, honor at stake, survivors of "two two-six" like Suzuki and Sakomizu in office, even airdropped leaflets. Hirohito's elusive "Voice of the Crane" had not been heard for nine years, but it had been heard before.

One of the new generation of plotters, Colonel Masataka Ida had used his desk job at Ichigaya to cut orders for an old friend, a secret police colonel, Makoto Tsukamoto, to be returned from *Kempeitai* duty in Formosa. Tsukamoto was shocked by the devastation in Tokyo when he arrived on August 6. By the time he saw Ida on the eleventh he was already aware of talk of a coup. "Suzuki is a Badoglio," Ida explained. Marshal Pietro Badoglio had double-crossed Benito Mussolini in 1943 and surrendered what he could of Italy to Eisenhower. Suzuki and other defeatists, said Ida, had "surrounded the Emperor and have talked him into surrendering. We intend to take him away from them. Will you join us?"

Tsukamoto was too much a *Kempeitai* hand not to exercise caution. He'd cooperate, he said, if the Army—not a faction here and there—was committed to fighting on and the Emperor was with them. He then reported to his superiors and was asked to observe developments at the War Ministry and to keep watch on Ida himself.

Had there been an index to senior die-hards, Admiral Ugaki would have been in it. That afternoon, with "a look of horror on his face," Ugaki noted in his diary, his chief intelligence officer brought him "the most hateful news," not transmitted from the Navy Ministry but plucked from San Francisco radio. The government had offered surrender "on condition that Emperor Hirohito be left as he was." The "clever fellows" who proposed that, Ugaki fumed, were "selfish weaklings." If the intention was to keep the nation from "the bitterness of war"—somehow Ugaki thought that hadn't happened— "the traditional Japanese spirit would be basically destroyed." With it, "the noble spirit of revenge" would be lost.

Even guerrilla warfare "under the Emperor" would be preferable, he wrote. It would force the enemy to "finally give up the war." He faced "a great problem" as a commander: "Though the Emperor's order must be followed, I can hardly stand to see us suspending attacks while still having ... fighting strength. I think many things remain to be done after consulting with those brave men willing to die."

The test flight of the *Kikka* jet plane took place at Kisarazu as scheduled on the eleventh. Taxiing down the runway, the pilot noticed a defect registering in the booster rocket but it was too late to decelerate. Overshooting the runway, the *Kikka* hit the edge of a ditch, snapping off its landing gear before it could be retracted. The plane crashed into the ocean, ending Japan's jet program. Also undergoing further tests, the Type 22 *Okha* was taken up by a *Ginga* mother plane, and at 2,400 feet the pilot turned on the rocket ignition. The manned bomb began shaking wildly and he shouted into his radio while pressing his emergency button, "Hold it! Don't drop the plane!" It was too late, and Ensign Kazutoshi Nagano died in the line of duty. The *Ginga* returned to Konoike and another detaching test was scheduled for August 15.

Some Japanese aircraft were reported to have achieved successes. A rumor reached Hiroshima, which needed all the optimism that wish-fulfillment fantasies could furnish, that Japan had, all along, possessed an atomic bomb, but, Dr. Hachiya was told, "had kept it a strict secret and had not used it because it was judged too horrible even to mention." According to the man from Fuchu—a nearby town—who had the story to tell and visited the bedridden Hachiya, "a special attack squad from the navy had now used the bomb on the mainland of America and . . ." His news had come from no less a source than General Headquarters. The blow had been dealt by a squadron of six-engined, trans-Pacific bombers, two of which failed to return. Those bombers were assumed to have dived right into their targets to make certain of success. If San Francisco, San Diego, and Los Angeles had been hit like Hiroshima, "what chaos there must be in those cities!"

The fantasy lifted the entire hospital ward. Patients joked; some even sang victory songs. Prayers were said for the dead heroes who had failed to return. "Everyone was now convinced that the tide of war had turned." But the uplifting report, for good reason, had not come to Admiral Ugaki's careworn intelligence officer.

Elsewhere the atomic bomb reports, although bad, were paradoxically good. To ward off another such attack, stories went, Japan was quitting the war. Ichiro Hatano, an evacuee from Tokyo, noted in his diary that his father had received a letter from a friend back home: "He advises us to return to the capital within two or three days and buy a house there. It seems that right now you can get hold of a house for next to nothing. But however low the price, we still haven't enough capital to buy a house. And even if we did, it would be razed tomorrow. That's quite obvious, so why does he give us such advice?"

The friend, however, held an important position in Tokyo, "and he doesn't say anything without having thought it over carefully. Father's deduction is that the war will soon be over." Obviously the family friend knew that no atomic bombs would now raze Tokyo, and that until that was publicly assured, property values would remain low. And that news, or some variant of it, had reached all the way to Frank Fujita's POW quarters in Tokyo, where his diary entry dated 11:30 A.M. that Saturday morning reported a rumor that Saipan radio had warned that "if Japan does not kick in by Monday midnight"—Monday would be the thirteenth—"Tokyo and its near vicinity would be destroyed by atomic bombs. A 72-hour armistice was declared last night. The Japanese have sent terms and are awaiting answers." News got around quickly enough, even if it was only partially accurate. After all, perception was reality of a sort as well. "If we are to be free, we will emerge emaciated, weary fragments of humanity into a strange world," Fujita speculated from memories of the "25th century" comic strip, into "the world of 'Buck Rogers.'"

But the atomic bombs, and imminent defeat, also meant scores to pay. In Fukuoka, one hundred miles north of what remained of Nagasaki, the army held B-29 crewmen who had chuted from crippled planes to the dubious safety of Japanese prison camps. On June 20, eight POWs had been executed. On the morning of the eleventh, a truck hauled eight more prisoners and twenty-four soldiers out of the camp to Aburayama, several miles to the south. The Americans were stripped to shorts or pants while the soldiers dug large holes in a field. First one prisoner was beheaded as he kneeled. By the fifth execution the tired headsman needed two strokes to do the job. The sixth flier, hands tied behind his back, was beaten by karate chops; then, as he slumped, his head was severed. The seventh was also beaten, then cut down bloodily through his shoulder and into his lungs as he pleaded, "Wait! Wait!" The last had endured the horror of seeing his seven companions hacked to death. Pushed into the center of the bloodcrazed soldiers, he was seated on the ground, hands tied behind him. An officer shot at him with a bow and arrow until one arrow hit above the left eye, and blood spurted. Then his head was chopped from his bleeding body and pushed into a hole in the ground.

From the distance of Sweden, remote from war zones in which he had served as a deputy to Field Marshal Hata, now in Hiroshima, Major General Makato Onodera—military attaché in Stockholm—told reporters besieging the legation for news that Japan and its adversaries "should now shake hands like after a tennis match." War, he said, was "a sporting affair mingled with heroism," although the atomic bomb, which he conceded had ended the war, was "no longer leaving room for chivalry." Soon, he predicted, Japanese and Americans would be competing on the golf links as good friends. "Anyone who is good at war is also good at peace."

Listening posts tuned in to Tokyo were learning that whatever form surrender took, headquarters considered the war over. Admiral Soemu Toyoda's daily order to fleet commanders was almost meaningless: "Further positive offensive operations against the United States, Great Britain, the Soviet Union and China will be suspended pending further orders." Although it appeared to validate the armistice rumors that Frank Fujita, a lowly POW, had heard, the Japanese were incapable now of offensive operations. Ugaki was outraged, but toward night learned, he wrote, that "there was some little doubt involved in . . . Imperial orders . . . which relieved me a great deal." The conspiracies to evade surrender were filtering down.

Reports of Japanese disintegration spread without the aid of radios and other sophisticated means. In Hong Kong a rations truck pulled into Shamshuipo Camp. Hidden in a crack in a hut floor was a scrap of paper—the informal communications system. A POW put it in his pocket. Quickly stories began circulating about an awesome new bomb that had devastated two Japanese cities. The news apparently also reached a POW camp in Celebes by a circuitous route. Two prisoners ordered the day before to repair bicycles at Japanese headquarters had gone off as usual on their detail to find instead of disabled bicycles a tray of hot coffee and local cakes. "The Nip," they reported back, sweetened their coffee and asked them to sit while he waited on them. Had he been sufficiently kind? If their situations should become reversed, he asked, would they remember that and treat him well? On Saturday all working parties were asked to clean up and then stop working. "I was bombarded with questions," said W. E. Johns. He knew nothing more than that "something was in the air." They were sure they knew what it was when they were told to return to camp "and take our rice with us." The Red Cross, from which they had never received a single parcel through the Japanese, was going to be permitted to visit. That seemed even more likely when they were ordered to don new white shirts and shorts.

The Japanese commandant mustered the prisoners that afternoon. Behind him were the senior Dutch, British, and American officers in the camp. They waited apprehensively as the senior Dutch officer climbed to the platform and began to speak. "We listened without comprehending, but as he spoke we began to sense his meaning, confirmed for us by Dutchmen in the ranks who muttered,

'The war is over. The war is over.' Then the English major, who had only recently joined us, told us tersely that there was a three-day armistice, that the war was not yet over, but that we would not go to work. We were to avoid any fuss or trouble; the guards were still in charge and would shoot if we did anything silly."

The war was not over; there was not even the three-day armistice the Japanese commandant had claimed. Yet the announcement from Tokyo of the "suspension" of offensive operations of which the military was incapable anyway was interpreted realistically everywhere it reached. The POWs looked at each other in silence. Most would now make it back. As soon as they were dismissed, "Pandemonium broke loose; tears, shouts, screams, kissing, and handshaking."

Elsewhere the trouble was just beginning. In China, claiming to be acting within the provisions of Potsdam, Mao's forces ordered Japanese troops to surrender to them, while Chiang claimed that the orders were "presumptuous and illegal," as he was the only authority delegated to receive surrenders. Many of the Nanking puppet government's troops, taking their equipment with them, would surrender to the Communists rather than risk the harsh treatment expected from the Nationalists. In Shanghai itself, Peggy Abkhazi wrote, "the bamboo wireless" was "up to standard" about the state of the war, but there, too, internment camps accepted Japanese anticipation of the end as the end itself. By evening, she wrote, the cry "The war is over! The war is over!" was being passed from hut to hut. "And then miraculously one heard the same cry echoing from the whole camp. And yet if you asked how they knew, or who had told them, nobody could say. They just heard someone calling the news, so they took up the cry. My first reaction: I don't believe it. And yet—it *could* be true."

Among signals from Tokyo was one from Shigenori Togo, wearing his other hat as Minister for Greater East Asia, advising envoys in the puppet governments that Japan would not object if local overtures "in concert with Japan" were made to the Allies. "Various foreign and domestic circumstances" had made the peace offer necessary. (The circumstances, a follow-up message explained, "of course include the problem of the atomic bomb.") However, Togo added, and "Magic" decrypted, he had not yet "received the agreement of the Army and Navy on this matter." The Foreign Minister was trying to pull the plug on incipient rebellion in the colonies.

As realism began to set in among those unlikely to find themselves in the war criminal dock, a long view began to take hold. The only way that Japan would revive from defeat and prosper, possibly even recover lost gains, would be in concert with the victors, especially the West, which had little chance itself to recover its former position in East Asia. A similar attitude had emerged from survivors of the German defeat. The director of British Naval Intelligence circulated, on August 11, the translation of the last directive to influential subordinates from Admiral Dönitz in his capacity as successor head of the German state. The fifteenth paragraph took a long view:

> Comrades, it must be clear to all of us that we are now fully in the enemy's hands. Our fate before us is dark. What they will do to us we do not know, but what we have to do we know very well. We have been set back a thousand years in our history. Land that was German for a thousand years has now fallen into Russian hands. Therefore the political line we must follow is very plain. It is clear that we have to go along with the western powers and work with them in the occupied territories in the west, for it is only through working with them that we can have hopes of later retrieving our land from the Russians.

Dönitz's next paragraph, following some national self-praise, could have been written three months later by a Japanese leader, substituting only the word *Japanese* for *German*:

> Our fight against the British and Americans can be viewed with pride and glory. We have nothing to be ashamed of. What the German armed forces and the German people accomplished and withstood during these six years has happened only once in world history. Such heroism has never before been displayed. There are no spots on our honour. It is therefore useless to set ourselves against our former enemies. What really matters is that they are here with us and you must treat them with civility and politeness. We must remain loyal to the terms of the unconditional surrender. . . . It is wrong for anyone to believe that he must continue the war wherever he can. . . .

While Russia was hardly eager to repatriate German—and, soon, Japanese—prisoners who would be kept for years doing slave labor and often dying, usually unacknowledged, in grim work sites in Siberia, the Soviet entrance into the war with Japan failed in any way to divert Stalin's attention from reclaiming alleged Russians from the West, even if the intention was to eliminate them on arrival or add them to the swelling Gulag population. A British Control Commission memorandum on August 11 emphasized that a displaced person's "personal wishes" had nothing to do with his future if Soviet citizenship was established. The return operation, the commission directive advised, was not working smoothly. The horror stories were many. At Kempten in Austria on August 11, British authorities announced that 410 persons found to be Soviet citizens, veterans of the German First Cossack Division and their families, would depart the next day. Half the internees slipped away during the night past a deliberately light security detail. In the morning, American troops called out names and no one came forward. Russians still huddled in their church resisted being pried out by hurling icons and anything else that was portable. Every person had to be dragged out by arms, legs, even hair. A survivor wrote, "People cut their throats and slashed their wrists, jumped out of upper story windows, and used any means they could think of to kill themselves to keep from falling into Soviet hands."

The commission paper on the problem saw no solution as long as the Yalta agreement remained "operative":

> Serious situations are arising over the forcible repatriation of DPs who have been established to be Soviet Citizens.
>
> DPs have threatened mass suicide and in certain cases have committed suicide. When they refuse to return they can only be put into transport for repatriation by physical force. British Officers are loath to order their men to carry out this unpleasant task and even if they issue the order there may be the possibility of their troops hesitating or refusing to comply with them.
>
> The British soldier will not bully civilians, especially children and old people, and even more so where the reason for doing so appears to him unjust and cruel.
>
> In one case the British Officer offered to withdraw his men so that the Russian L[iaison] O[fficer]s could force the

DPs into transport, but the Russians declared that it was the duty of the British Military Authorities to carry out this task.

As time goes on the above situation is bound to become aggravated, and if the existing regulations remain in force may well lead to mutinous conditions amongst the British troops concerned.

The practical solutions were to defy the agreement, which would exacerbate already worsening relations, render the problem moot by ridding the West of all allegedly Soviet prisoners and refugees, or permit the agreement to fall victim itself to relations inevitably worsened from other causes. For some American brass in Germany and Austria the latter alternative only recognized what had not yet been labeled a "Cold War." Generals of the Patton persuasion even saw a hot war ahead, and were already actively recruiting former Nazis into the rebuilding of civilian governments if they met Patton's sole test of anti-Communism. Claiming more expedient reasons, Patton explained to Eisenhower on August 11 that "a great many inexperienced or inefficient people" were running local governments as a result of the "so-called de-Nazification program." As the press already knew, to Eisenhower's embarrassment, Patton took pride in his reasoning. "It is no more possible for a man to be a civil servant in Germany and not have paid lip service to Naziism," he wrote to Eisenhower, "than it is possible for a man to be a postmaster in America and not have paid at least lip service to the Democratic Party, or the Republican Party when it is in power."

Eisenhower was anguished by the obstructiveness of an old friend and comrade-in-arms whom he knew he would have to dispense with if Naziism were to be extirpated in Germany. It was, Ike would explain to him, "a most delicate subject both here and at home."

At forty-five minutes after midnight in Tokyo—near the close of Eisenhower's workday in Frankfurt—the Foreign Office's radio listening station picked up, ahead of the official transmission from Washington via Bern, a broadcast response to its surrender offer based upon the State Department briefing. The United States was insisting that the authority of the Emperor to rule Japan was to be subject to the Supreme Commander of the Allied Powers—in effect, an American general. Would this mean another "two two-six"?

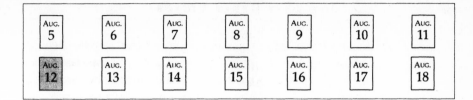

CHAPTER XXXI

# · AUGUST 12, 1945 ·

*". . . temporary disobedience of the Emperor"*

Although radio intercepts gave the Japanese Foreign Ministry the Four Power reply to its surrender proposal less than an hour into the morning of August 12, Tokyo time, official receipt of Byrnes's message came much later via Bern. In Stockholm, Minister Okamoto handed an identical copy to the Swedish Foreign Office. He cabled to Tokyo, "Since yesterday the BBC and other enemy broadcasts have stated that the United Nations accepted conditionally the Japanese proposal. It must be noted that they used the word 'accept.'" The machinery of peacemaking ground slowly through the international bureaucracies. The Swiss government had to send the official Allied response to functionaries in Karuizawa, the highland summer resort in central Honshu to which its legation had moved to escape the heat and the bombs.

Despite Okamoto's optimism, the service representatives on the Supreme War Council, except for the Navy Minister, Admiral Yonai, deplored the requirement that the Emperor authorize the surrender and submit to the authority of an occupation commander—and the earlier guarantee that the Japanese people would be free to decide their ultimate form of government—as infringements of the *Kokutai*, the national polity they had all sworn to uphold, even if that meant continuing the war. "I felt refreshed," Admiral Ugaki wrote, ". . . when a foreign broadcast reportedly said that the enemy refused our request [for peace] because they wouldn't recognize the continuation of the present position of Hirohito and his descendants."

The precise meaning of the Allied terms, and how their interpretation would sit with patriots, became the predawn problem of Togo's Vice Minister, Shunichi Matsumoto, and the Ministry's American specialist, Toshikazu Kase. At breakfast, "in low spirits," they met with Chief Cabinet Secretary Sakomizu, Matsumoto remembered, "believing that it was probably impossible for Japan to accept the terms outlined in this reply." That the Emperor would be "subject to" the Supreme Commander of the occupation forces eroded not only the constitutional basis of the state but the spiritual authority of the Throne. As for the "freely expressed will" clause, did "ultimate form of government" refer to the sacrosanct role of the Emperor or purely administrative matters? Much hung on the nuances of translation, as the wrong connotations could ignite the firebrands.

*Subject to* really meant "controlled by," but the Matsumoto group seized upon the less offensive "under the limitation of" as the safest alternative. Since the Emperor's will would be the people's will, the Foreign Office saw less danger in explaining that worrisome paragraph away. Rejection of the Byrnes-Cohen text loomed—as did an escalation of the war—if extremists could hang their own continuation in power on reverence for the ceremonial centrality of the Emperor.

Awakening Hirohito early, Marquis Kido, who had taken up residence within the palace grounds to reduce the chances of his own assassination by the ultras, brought the Emperor the Foreign Ministry interpretation, explaining that Togo had determined that the language met minimal needs on national polity. "No matter what happens to my safety," Hirohito insisted, "we must put an end to this war as speedily as possible."

Imperial General Headquarters had its own access to foreign broadcasts and its own interpretation of the Allied response. Armed forces' control of the Cabinet and direct access to the Throne would be lost on capitulation. The officer class, roughly equivalent to the *Jünker* military aristocracy of pre-1918 Prussia, preferred no surrender whatever, but if the facts required it, they insisted, at the least, upon firmer assurances that military honor would be preserved under disarmament and occupation, and that the imperial system remain. Die-hard delegations descended upon General Umezu and Admiral Toyoda to clamor for rejection even before Kido had met with the Emperor, and by 8:20 A.M.—still late at night on the eleventh in Washington—the two chiefs of staff were at the palace demanding access. Hirohito listened courteously, then played for time by claiming he had not yet received an official text to study.

Since neither service chief had requested Ministry permission to go to the palace, Admiral Yonai was outraged and General Anami merely unhappy. Anami knew that he could not have been asked, as he had not arrived at his office until ten, having gone first, accompanied by the legalistic Baron Hiranuma, to consult Premier Suzuki. Hiranuma brought the weight of his Privy Council position to bear on his argument that the American terms meant the end of 2,600 years of Imperial Japan. If the Emperor was indeed a demigod, how could his people be offered an opportunity to determine his status? How could he be "subject" to an Allied Supreme Commander? The Throne could not be subject to anyone. (In theory the Emperor was indeed supreme. In theory he even owned the country and its inhabitants. But it was not an authority he was expected to exercise.) For the same reasons, Hiranuma contended, the fifth paragraph of the American note, leaving the "ultimate" government of Japan to the "freely expressed will" of its people, was invalid. For Togo and Suzuki the facts had invalidated theory. Suzuki knew that the facts had also invalidated his broadcast promise to the people on the April day he had taken office: "Should I die, I hope that you will advance over my dead body to continue the fight against the enemy." Whether or not he would have to eat his own words, Suzuki revered the Throne and was struck by Hiranuma's argument.

Anami raised other questions that had dismayed his middle ranks, especially that of an orderly transition to peace that would protect the Army and its pride. "Provisions relating to troop disarmament and occupation zones," he insisted, "must be included in any agreement with the Allies." The general was restating the staff conviction that Japan's honor required self-disarmament and unobtrusive occupation away from large cities, especially Tokyo.

Suzuki promised that he would do nothing that would compromise the Throne, and the two power brokers left with confidence that they had halted the pacifist momentum.

Anami went on to call upon Prince Mikasa and ask that he intercede with his eldest brother, the Emperor. Mikasa was reputed to have radical, even Socialist, ideas about the welfare of the masses. He was the wrong member of the Imperial Household to whom to apply, but he was available. After listening politely, Mikasa exploded: "Since the Manchurian Incident, the Army has not acted once in accordance with the Imperial wish. It is most improper that you should still want to continue the war when things have come to this stage."

Abashed, the general drove back to his office with his aide, Major Saburō Hayashi, repeating the prince's words with which he had been scolded. It was his lot, he confided, for even his brother-in-law, insignificant as he was, had admonished Anami, in the hearing of other middle-level officers, to commit suicide with his own sword in repentance for surrender. Only a lieutenant colonel, Masahiko Takeshita was an outspoken insurrectionist and vital to the conspiracy because of the family connection that secured for him a certain immunity. "Takeshita said such cruel things to me," Anami told Hayashi. "Since I am nearly sixty years old, I don't think it would be difficult for me to die. Perhaps it would be difficult for a young man like you. . . ." His voice broke.

Takeshita's reasoning about imperial loyalty appealed to those who saw purity of motive in acting contrary to Hirohito's expressed wishes. In Baron Hiranuma's terms, *Kokutai* meant "to keep the Emperor's position unchanged." To Takeshita that could condone actions counter to the desire of a sovereign who betrayed the traditions of his Throne. As he reasoned with no little sophistry, "Although the result would be temporary disobedience of the present Emperor—a situation certainly to be avoided—to act in compliance with the wishes of his Imperial Ancestors would, in the final analysis, constitute a wiser and truer loyalty to the Throne." That militarists concealed their desire to retain political power behind reverence for a hereditary institution they deliberately kept weak and nominal remained unsaid.

At eleven, as Togo was being received by the Emperor and told to convey to Suzuki the imperial desire to accept the Allied terms, the coup cabal was gathering to confront Anami. Although Hirohito had no idea who the conspirators were, he understood from Kido and from the morning meeting with the uneasy service chiefs that something on the order of "two two-six" was brewing and had to be countered—or undermined. At about noon, the six key plotters crowded into Anami's office and exhorted him to join what they saw as a holy rebellion in the Emperor's interest. Anami's aide, Colonel Sato, warned, "Don't be so hasty about a coup!" and squabbling broke out as to which side was treasonous. "Come now," said Anami, rising, "military men must trust each other."

Another extraordinary Cabinet session was imminent, and the general had to excuse himself for it. "Takeshita," he said to his brother-in-law, "come to my home later. I will be happy to talk to you about it then." Although he should have ordered arrests, he only ordered the conspirators out.

At three the Cabinet convened at the Premier's residence. Suzuki began by reading a translation of the American note with the Foreign Ministry's gloss on the key words. The text, Suzuki hastened to point out, was unofficial, taken from the radio. The official note had not yet been delivered. Wrestling with the problem of surrender amid the intransigence of die-hards, Togo tried the traditional Japanese approach of indirection. The American response, he conceded, "could not be said to be entirely reassuring. This was not unforeseen; it is inevitable that under . . . occupation the sovereignty of the state will be limited to the extent requisite to implement the surrender terms." He saw no jeopardy to the national polity: "It was impossible to conceive that the overwhelmingly loyal majority of our people would not wish to preserve our traditional system." As for continuing the war, he saw that as "intolerable even if not impossible."

When Togo asked for opinions, Hiranuma and Anami weighed in with their familiar arguments. They recalled former Secretary of the Treasury Henry Morgenthau's recommendation to President Roosevelt to turn Germany into an agricultural economy, and he warned that surrender might reduce Japan to that state. America's history of rejection, even despisal, of monarchy, they contended, lay behind the promise of free choice of government for a future Japan, a covert threat to dispense with imperial tradition.

Rising in anger, Togo warned, "To add issues at this moment would make the Allies wonder at the integrity of the Japanese Government and at its sincerity in negotiating at all." He walked to the door, announcing before he slammed it behind him, "Acting like this is contrary to reason!"

From the adjoining room he telephoned his deputy, Shunichi Matsumoto, who urged Togo to return and adjourn the meeting before a vote could reject the peace. Barely in time, Togo reopened the door and heard Premier Suzuki, often swayed by the last, or loudest, voice he heard, confess that since the Allied note seemed not to guarantee imperial rule, as Baron Hiranuma had pointed out, perhaps Japan should insist upon further clarification—even guarantees. And as a military man he was also aware, he added, that "to be disarmed by the enemy would be unbearable for a soldier, and that under the circumstances there was no alternative to continuation of the war."

"Your words are worthy of careful consideration," Togo interrupted, "but at the same time, Japan should not continue the war irresponsibly without paying any attention to its outcome." He hardly needed to point to the Red Army overrunning Manchuria and nearing the borders of Korea, and the certain resumption of American bombing, including atomic bombing. "Unless there is some prospect for victory, Japan should negotiate for peace. I therefore propose that the meeting be adjourned and that the question be reopened after the official communication from the Allies has been received." The Cabinet rose with both sides angry and frustrated.

Remaining behind, Togo had it out with Suzuki, reminding him that his duty lay with the Emperor, who had firmly decided upon surrender as the only course possible to save what was left of Japan. Unless the Premier followed the Emperor on his own, Togo warned, he would ask Hirohito to command him to do so.

After consulting with aides at the Foreign Ministry, from which he arranged a meeting at the palace with Kido, Togo went on wearily to explain to the Marquis that imperial pressure had to be applied to Suzuki. Kido was already doing so. The Metropolitan Police were keeping watch on known conspirators and guarding strategic points in Tokyo, postings that were more show than reality because any military intervention would overwhelm them. At the same time, Matsumoto was taking a cue from the weekend of Pearl Harbor, when the Army had arranged with the Censorship Office that cables— except for those sent by the Japanese government itself—would be delayed in delivery five hours one day, ten hours the next. One cable then held back had been an eleventh-hour peace appeal from President Roosevelt to the Emperor. The day before the attack on Oahu (a Sunday in Tokyo) the lag had been ten hours.

Telephoning the Telegraph Section of the Foreign Ministry on yet another crucial Sunday, Matsumoto ordered the duty officer to date and delay any official communication that arrived during the remainder of the day and through the night as of Monday morning. It would give Togo and his allies time to update their strategy. As he and Togo realized, however, it also gave the conspirators equal time, although not equal information. Yet some information was intended for leakage. Cables from Bern and Stockholm, very likely encouraged somehow by Ministry people, came in hinting that positions in London, Moscow, Peking, Sydney, and elsewhere were hardening about surrender terms. Useless delays could lead to harsher demands.

Secretary Byrnes's official response, transmitted through Swiss intermediaries, arrived at 6:40 P.M. The duty officer receiving it dated it 7:40 A.M. on Monday morning—and filed it away.

At 9:30 P.M. Premier Suzuki was summoned to the palace by Marquis Kido. "If we do not accept the Allied position now," he explained, "we will be sacrificing hundreds of thousands of innocent people to the continued ravages of war.... Furthermore, it is His Majesty's wish...." Suzuki promised to stand by the Emperor.

Since a government that had to operate by consensus seemed to Toshikazu Kase almost hopeless in an emergency, on his own as Togo's deputy he had telephoned Mamoru Shigemetsu, once ambassador to London, and Prince Konoye, asking them to see him in Tokyo as soon as possible. Konoye was two hours away by train, and Shigemetsu—who knew the West well—was first to arrive, already late in the evening. Kase asked both to remain overnight, to see Marquis Kido in the morning, and to back him in pressing for acceptance of the Allied note. Also he asked them to visit and back up the unsteady Suzuki.

The quiet in the skies over Japan on the twelfth had been intended to create a climate for conciliation, but it was essentially a B-29 hiatus. For harried urban populations that was blessing enough, but neither side remained entirely quiet. Other American planes, closer to Japan, continued hitting what the Air Force called "targets of opportunity" on the home islands and as far north as Korea and as far south as Formosa. Active, too, were the Japanese, where commanders sensed last chances at strikes on an enemy temporarily in a state of diminished alertness. A plane from Kyushu managed to get close enough to Okinawa at twilight to send a torpedo into the somnolent *Pennsylvania*. At Pearl Harbor the battleship had been in dry dock, frustrating the torpedo planes, which could not launch a strike at it. The ship was left to the less effective dive-bombers. Soon repaired and at sea, the *Pennsylvania* had remained unscathed. Now, although only twenty died, the ship was without power. A thirty-foot gash at the fantail left its stern low in the water, and tugs in Buckner Bay worked at pumping out the hull and pushing the lifeless ship about.

Even a few *kaitens* were active off Okinawa, including those from the *I-58*, nemesis of the *Indianapolis*, but with no result other than the entry of the *kaitens* into their undersea nirvana. With the possibility looming that Japanese defenders would have to surrender themselves and their equipment, they were permitted chances formerly reserved for the final battle, and from Kagohara Air Base the last six Ki-43 Falcons took off to intercept carrier-based Grumman Hellcats. One was piloted by Ensign Ryuji Nagatsuka, once Western-minded with a love for French novels. Wrought up now to long only for a blazing *kamikaze* end, he headed for Kumagaya, the apparent enemy destination, and dived toward the small gray specks below—willing, even, to collide with an enemy fighter. From behind, machine gun fire from a second enemy squadron ricocheted off his fuselage. Then he was hit; his right arm hung limp and bleeding. With his left arm he grappled with the controls, pulling out of a spin in time to crash-land, wheels still up, in a paddyfield. The instinct to live had taken over. Unconscious, he was pulled from the wreckage and finished the war in a hospital bed.

Like twenty-seven other Japanese pilots that day, Nagatsuka had been denied an American target, but the others had managed to achieve death. Seldom in August had so many home islands planes been airborne, but others were never able to take off. American aircraft flying from TF 38 destroyed 254 planes on the ground and claimed many more damaged—equipment removed from wraps for *Ketsu.*

On Guam, the B-29 wings learned that if the Japanese failed to accept surrender terms the bombings would begin again, and Hays Gamble, keeping his misgivings to himself, jotted in his diary that Sunday, "Can't see why we should keep on fighting & dying just because of one man who is only a figurehead in his gov't anyway." A crewman on Tinian griped to a pilot, "Would you listen to those phonies back home? If they are so eager to carry on the war, why don't they come over and fly some missions to the Empire?"

Since "Olympic" might still have to take place—and ships at sea could not easily turn about when close to their destinations—thousands of troops reassigned in Italy and France poured off transports in the Philippines. As many had two years of service or more, and had accumulated discharge "points" that would give them priority over Pacific hands for rotation home, there was little cheering from troops already on Leyte and Luzon when the new arrivals marched down their gangplanks. MacArthur, however, was still claiming that his initial "Downfall" landing would have succeeded, using the past tense because he was convinced the Japanese would give up. He had been far less certain of the Kanto Plain offensive. "Coronet," he told Eichelberger, ". . . was the main blow and of necessity it had to be practically a frontal attack. You were to get it. The First Army movement in from the coast southeast of Tokyo was merely a token since the terrain did not permit a real blow from that area. The proposed attack north of [General Luther] Hodges' area was the one I had hoped to give to you because it would permit rapid movement, but we found the beaches would not permit a landing."

MacArthur remained certain, on the other hand, that "Olympic" would have gone well—far better than he had first predicted to Truman. "The main blow [from Tokyo Bay] would have been a deadly thing because the Japanese are fine in defending against what would have amounted to a frontal assault. Krueger's landing on Kyushu was a cinch and he would not have suffered over 15,000 casualties." Although neither MacArthur nor anyone else on the American side knew that Japanese intelligence had now broken enough of the army code to validate all of their assumptions about "Downfall," the boast would not be tested. To cheering troops in the streets of Manila on Sunday evening he said that he hoped, from the bottom of his heart, that the end was coming without an assault.

In Tokyo, the rumor grapevine reaching Frank Fujita's POW quarters was that "Ambassador Grew was in Okinawa and was conferring with a delegation of Japanese. The cessation of hostilities had been arranged and the only thing holding up the formal declaration of peace was the future position of the Emperor." Fujita had at least one fact right—the concern over the status of Hirohito. Newspapers had been given an ambiguous statement by the Board of Information suggesting that if the monarchial system was guaranteed, Japan was ready to lay down its arms. Newspapers had headlined Shimomura's statement, unidentified as a surrender offer, on the eleventh and again on the twelfth.

Whether or not that sticking point was resolved, Japanese war casualties continued to mount, especially in Hiroshima and Nagasaki, where burns and radiation sickness claimed more lives every day, and fires remained stoked to consume more corpses.

•     •     •

As the Japanese fell back everywhere in Asia—the Russians entered Korea on the twelfth—the Western allies were hurriedly organizing operations to rescue, guard, and care for their own behind the lines. All the information received from sympathizers, spies, and the rare escapees was that prisoners were deteriorating badly—less, now, through brutality than through exposure and starvation. On the night of the twelfth in Peking, a group of OSS volunteers had chuted onto a nearby field dressed in Japanese uniforms and entered the walled city, where they set up radio contact with their headquarters in Hsian, far to the southwest in safe territory. Their temporary base was the home of a commander of Chinese mercenaries working for the Japanese. He was ready, for money, to turn his coat. Besides, he knew his ostensible employers had lost the war. In the adjoining house were quartered some of the Japanese General Staff in northern China, but Major Jim Kellis was less interested in them than in what could be done quickly after they surrendered.

In Shanghai, internees were already behaving as if the war was over, breaking out hoarded tins of celebratory food. In the afternoon the barbed-wire grapevine reported that the Japanese commandant would be making a statement that evening, but when they gathered at F Block they found only their internee representative. "I am sorry," he apologized, "but I have no good news for you. The Japanese put forward proposals to the Allies, and it will take some days for them to be considered. Meanwhile, fighting is going on, and camp life will continue as usual." On the other side of the fence, villagers were setting off volleys of firecrackers, and the internees' own secret shortwave radio, hidden in a brick stove barely fifty yards from the commandant's bungalow, had picked up San Francisco and the report that peace hung on whether the Emperor would hang. There were always new local rumors that acted as antidotes to good news. That night one of the gloomiest was that the internees would be moved inland, to keep them as hostages, with only hand baggage to accompany them and a life of wretchedness to look forward to. Another rumor, which was no better, was that they would all be shot the moment the Allies landed.

In what was left of occupied Burma, the Japanese "ambassador" to the puppet state, U Nu remembered, remained "a perfect gentleman," unlike representatives of his army, and at Mudon, just south of Moulmein, he encouraged the erection of an "Independence Monument" to mark the completion of two years of Burmese satellite freedom under the Japanese. Independence under the Japanese was something of a fiction, but more to Burmese tastes than imperial British reality. Whatever time was left to the Greater East Asia Co-Prosperity Sphere, it had promoted nationalist beginnings in Southeast Asia that would not be undone.

The Burmese president, Ba Maw, had a residence nearby that the British had strafed and bombed for several days running. Hurrying to a shelter from Ba Maw's house, U Nu had to straddle barbed-wire fences that ripped his trousers. "For the past three months," U Nu mused, "there had been no attack on Dr. Ba Maw's house and it was very strange that they should attack it with machine-guns and bombs when the war was practically over. The whole house was damaged beyond repair. . . ." The British had recognized him in 1937 as prime minister of a Burma under colonial self-rule, not as *Adipati*—head of state—of a nation they recognized only as their colony.

China was a problem of priorities difficult to separate from Manchuria. The American theater commander, General Wedemeyer, cabled the Joint Chiefs of Staff that to keep strategic places away from Mao's Communists, Chinese and Manchurian seaports should be occupied by the U.S. Navy, which had more ships than it could possibly use in the region. Asia, he warned, was "an enormous pot, seething and boiling, the fumes of which may readily snuff out the advancements gained by Allied sacrifices the past several years. . . ." Both Nimitz and MacArthur would oppose the idea, and the decisions would have political consequences. The future of Korea, Manchuria, China, and Japan hung in part upon where the United States took calculated risks. Getting into someone else's civil war seemed, to Nimitz, absurd. The United States had to "avoid participation in fighting between the Chinese." MacArthur wanted nothing to get in the way of "the prompt occupation of Japan proper," although he recommended as an exception that two divisions of Marines be sent to Shanghai.

While Truman would suggest that both Dairen and Seoul be occupied, any territory in the Manchurian sector was already past redeeming. The Red Army was moving too fast and Mao's forces in northern China were assisting on the Soviet flank. For the Japanese in Manchuria, flight was replacing retreat. One group of 630 civilians from eight villages streamed out to avoid attacks not only by the Soviets but from angry Manchus and Koreans, hoping to reach Hsinganchen, sixteen miles to the south. The evacuees from Sakurada were all followers of the Lotus Sutra from the Jōsen Temple in Tokyo, and they chanted the *Nichiren* prayer as they left their village with the schoolmaster carrying the Sutra scroll in a portable tabernacle at the head of the column. Not trusting all their faith to the Sutra, they kept women and children in the center, while men carried Russo-Japanese rifles of 1904 vintage when they had them, barrel staves and knives when they did not. As they shuffled along, pelting rain turned the roadless plain into mud. Wind lashed them; children cried.

The question of who occupied what, and what nations would really be free, was central to the ongoing realignment of power. Nations that would have no border, or occupation border, with the West had little chance to develop other than as satellites of the East. The converse was not necessarily true because democratic societies usually permitted, even if they did less than encourage, the activity of political parties of every band in the spectrum, including Red. In a broadcast of August 12, Edward R. Murrow recognized that the Anglo-American withholding of atomic bomb secrets would affect the balance of power only briefly. "Other nations, by research and espionage, are likely to solve the problem before we have mastered the countermeasures." Writing from his internal exile at Kirchhorst, Ernst Jünger, like many others, was saying the same thing. The Bomb was more overwhelming than *"die Trompeten von Jericho,"* but the atomic monopoly would not last long.

The problem, said Murrow, who recognized a new and different kind of war emerging before the ongoing one had ended, required "a revolution in the relations between nations," but he saw no hope for that. What he found were problems that, despite the new international organization, would threaten to fragment nations. "When we entered Buchenwald," he said, "I discovered that the hatred of Czech for Czech, Pole for Pole, was much greater than their hatred for their German captors and butchers." The new division was "Communist versus non-Communist. For they believed, these miserable, emaciated Czechs and Poles, in different things. . . . Communism is an item for export. So is democracy. The two are bound to compete."

While in Moscow all was seemingly smiles and handshakes as Marshal Zhukov greeted General Eisenhower and praises rang out for American troops and arms, in Los Angeles, FBI director J. Edgar Hoover, at a fiftieth birthday banquet in his honor, prophesied nothing but gloom about American-Russian relations. The Socialist victory in Britain was only the beginning. The new enemy, even before the current one had acknowledged defeat, was Communism and "creeping socialism," the goals of "totalitarian liberals" who intended to dominate the private lives of free people. While 14,850 happy soldiers disembarked from the *Queen Elizabeth* in New York, Hoover called for American troops to remain in Europe. The bureaucrat who would intrude into more private lives of Americans than any other person in history brought his audience to their feet with the peroration, "You and I must not be marked as the generation who surrendered the heritage of America!"

In Washington, crowds gathered, and increased in numbers, all day along Pennsylvania Avenue opposite the White House and in Lafayette Park. It was Sunday, but they were not out on a weekend of sightseeing. They stood about talking or sat on the grass, hopefully waiting to celebrate news of a Japanese surrender. By early evening— darkness came late in mid-August—the White House staff began to feel claustrophobic. Little news was coming in, and as the crowds continued to grow, Truman's press secretaries and their secretaries, along with Judge Sam Rosenman, who had drafted speeches for FDR and was now assisting Truman, went out to a seafood restaurant along the Potomac. "As we were finishing," Eben Ayers noted in his diary, "there was the blaring of automobile horns, and waitresses told us the President had announced that Japan had surrendered. We knew this could not be true and I telephoned the White House."

In 1918 the "False Armistice"—an erroneous flash from France— had ignited celebrations across the nation four days before the actual Armistice on November 11. Now, in many places, it outdid the real thing. Ayers got the White House telephone operator, who knew nothing about it, but a helpful policeman in the lobby came to the telephone and told Ayers that an incorrect bulletin had been broadcast that Truman had made such an announcement. One of the secretaries, Terry Lorentz, had rushed back to the White House and telephoned the restaurant to report that a service operated by United Press, Washington City News, had carried a flash that the President had announced Japan's acceptance of the surrender note. It had been fed, somehow, onto its wires at 9:34 and two minutes later UP had quashed it with a curt "Editors. Hold up that flash." Hugh Baillie, the UP president, would offer a $5,000 reward for information on the tampering with United Press circuits, but found no culprit. In any case, it was too late to matter. The report had spread across the country to enliven a summer Sunday evening, sending happy throngs into the streets and triggering impromptu block parties in American cities where such blue-collar social occasions had become institutionalized by the war.

A working-class phenomenon in urban row house districts, the block party had begun to flourish when servicemen came home. A soldier returned from the war was greeted by hand-lettered banners of welcome, bare bulbs strung on wires across narrow streets, sawhorses at each end of the street to keep traffic out, and trestle tables or card tables set up with contributed food and drink. Often local establishments—bakeries, fruiteries, breweries—cooperated. A wired-up record player blared music. But the new "false armistice" also sent pleasure seekers into the major thoroughfares, the Times Squares, for more exuberant and uninhibited celebrations on the order of the V-E Day mob events in early May. In New Jersey, where the posh hotels along the Boardwalk at Atlantic City had long been wartime convalescent hospitals for servicemen, patients in pajamas leaned out of windows and poured the contents of torn pillows down on the boards and the beaches—the equivalent of a ticker-tape shower.

Across the country the din from industrial whistles, ships, trains, auto horns, and church bells swelled, and in Chinatowns in New York, Philadelphia, Los Angeles, and San Francisco fireworks flared. Honolulu went wild—for ten minutes. The correction to the first bulletin had arrived too soon. But in Ottawa the news had triggered a prerecorded victory message by Prime Minister Mackenzie King made only hours earlier, hailing peace and declaring the following Sunday as a day of national prayer and thanksgiving. Before the message had concluded on the CBC, liquor stores had been stormed in Halifax. In Australia, where it was Monday morning, wild rejoicing erupted in Melbourne and Sydney and Prime Minister Joseph Chifley declared national holidays for that day and Tuesday. Far to the west, in Perth, where the early morning rush hour had just begun— the city was closer to Singapore than to Sydney—Australians jitterbugged on the roofs of stalled automobiles.

At the White House, the staff remained until midnight, which was already midday on the thirteenth in Japan, with no further word from Tokyo. The celebrations across America wound down, and the revelers went home.

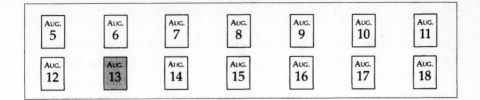

| Aug. 5 | Aug. 6 | Aug. 7 | Aug. 8 | Aug. 9 | Aug. 10 | Aug. 11 |
| Aug. 12 | Aug. 13 | Aug. 14 | Aug. 15 | Aug. 16 | Aug. 17 | Aug. 18 |

# CHAPTER XXXII

## · AUGUST 13, 1945 ·

*". . . a nation does not have the right to commit suicide"*

At Mokapu Head on Oahu, the tip of a peninsula east of Kaneohe where Japanese carrier planes had hit a Marine airbase on December 7, 1941, a shore battery was test-fired on August 13, 1945. It had been a fourteen-inch turret that salvage workers with cutting torches had removed from the sunken *Arizona* and reassembled with great effort and expense as a coastal artillery installation where none was needed. On the western side of the island another salvaged battery was still being installed, former turret IV. It would never be finished.

On Guam that morning, a secret court of inquiry chaired by Vice Admiral Charles A. Lockwood, Jr., as president, opened proceedings in the case of Captain Charles Butler McVay III and the loss of the *Indianapolis*. The prosecutor, Captain William Hilbert, had forty-three witnesses present, including McVay, but acknowledged that he was "starting the proceedings without having all the necessary data." It would quickly become clear that he was also starting with the aim of whitewashing the Navy of charges that it had failed to recognize that the cruiser was missing and overdue. Before survivors on Peleliu left aboard the hospital ship *Tranquility*, Commander George C. Attebury brought Lieutenant Wilbur C. Gwinn aboard, called the men from the *Indianapolis* to attention, and asked whether they would like to say hello to the pilot who had spotted them. Those crewmen who could walk rushed forward; those too weak to leave their bunks sobbed openly. It was almost more than the quiet Gwinn could take. Others being flown from Samar to Guam to be at the court of inquiry were invited to the transport's cockpit as the morning sun flooded the sea below. "For all we know," said the pilot, "there may be another group of survivors from another ship [below] waiting for rescue." The sailors could see nothing in the reflected glare, and understood.*

Elsewhere on Guam and other Marianas airstrips, bombs were again being hauled out to waiting B-29s. President Truman had told the chiefs of staff that in view of Japanese silence it would be necessary to reapply military pressure. Still, the day and its orders were a confusion of conflicting actions and signals. Vice Admiral Ben Moreell, the Navy's construction and logistics wizard, was ordered back to Washington from Kwajalein, as if he were no longer needed, and NCR order 1834 halted all shipments of torpedoes to the Pacific. Still, NCR 1680, with the same date, referred to the "undesirability of losing towing days in forward movement of [landing] craft on joint towing priority [for "Olympic"]. . . . In event war is prolonged it is recommended that all towing continue as presently scheduled." In particular it directed that floating dry docks and cranes, repair craft, and dredges continue on without letup. They might be needed for the occupation if not for the invasion.

While carrier planes continued to hit occupied atolls as close to the International Date Line as Wake, ships closer to Japan were warned that suicide craft might be out in large numbers if Japan rejected the peace note. The attack on the *Pennsylvania* was a foreshadowing of that, as was another *kamikaze* hit, on the service vessel *La Grange*, exploding in the radio room and penetrating

---

*On Guam, the Court of Inquiry on the *Indianapolis* completed its hearings on August 20, recommending Letters of Reprimand be issued to Captain McVay and to two officers on Leyte who failed to report that the cruiser was overdue. For wartime officers the slap on the wrist meant nothing. For a career man like McVay it was a disgrace—although he would make rear admiral before early retirement. Still disconsolate twenty-three years after, he shot himself.

three decks into the armory, demolishing the engine room and the piping and ventilating system. Then a second *kamikaze* struck the *La Grange* at foremast, starting new fires. By 5:00 P.M. all ships had been pulled out of Okinawa harbors for safety. Admiral John Mc-Cain was worried about enemy trickery. The plane that had hit the *Pennsylvania* had come in with its landing lights on, to confuse ships into assuming it was "friendly." Halsey ordered new strikes, as did LeMay and MacArthur, who sent 550 planes over Japan on the thirteenth.

The Japanese delay in responding created a new caution in MacArthur, who had envisioned an almost solo arrival in Tokyo as the new *shogun*. Since the Navy would be involved anyway—the White House had decided to have the formal surrender take place on Halsey's flagship, *Missouri*—MacArthur began contemplating a dramatic airborne beginning to the occupation culminating in his *deus ex machina* arrival on Japanese soil. As Eichelberger described the MacArthur scenario to his wife in the disparaging racist carica-turing that had caused the American military to underestimate the Japanese in 1941, "as soon as the bomb craters [on the airstrips] are filled, we will fly in." But first, "monkeys will come to Ma-nila where final peace terms will probably not be signed. . . ." Then he would "accompany a certain person on a boat" where "we would receive a number of goggle-eyed little bucktoothed birds and settle things."

Calling in Rhoades, MacArthur directed him to get Sutherland back from leave in the States. The general was no longer as important to his boss as he once had been, but running Japan was a tall order and Sutherland was an administrative hand. No one, however, could keep MacArthur from the imperial ways he had adopted long before he knew what his next role would be. The War Department team working on the surrender formalities had flown an Operations Division colonel to Manila to discuss a proposal with the general, and on the return of the colonel barely a week later he was asked about his "high-level con-versation." "Yes," he reported, "I had one high-level conversation with him. I walked into his headquarters and stepped into the elevator, and General MacArthur came along and stepped into the same elevator. He turned to me and said, 'You will take the next elevator, I presume.' That was my high-level conversation with General MacArthur." But he would be supreme in Tokyo nonetheless, and OPD was preparing a di-rective to him to be signed by the President in which "the authority of the Emperor and Japanese Government to rule the state will be subject to you. . . ." He would not need to adjust his style.*

The new openness of Japanese newspapers—encouraged, even ordered, by the Bureau of Information, which for years had been the major source of what the press printed—made it clear to the public that the sacred deaths of a hundred million, trumpeted as essential only a month earlier, had to give way to a new patriotic prudence. There was some value in continuing to live, after all. And even that modest aim had become admittedly difficult, Tokyo radio was now permitted to imply, as a Dr. Takemi announced, that used tea could now be eaten as a "foodstuff" in place of unobtainable vegetables. It was rich in vitamin C, and "as long as one takes tea, he can maintain sufficient nutrition." The advice revealed deep desperation. *Yomiuri Hochi* editorialized, "There is an ebb and flow in the tides of the affairs of every nation. Statesmen require the greatest courage when they think not of themselves but of the nation. Individuals must have the courage of self-immolation, but it may be said that a nation does not have the right to commit suicide." The editorial went on to recall the story of two nearly mythical states in China 2,500 years before. Yüeh, after suffering a humiliating defeat at the hands of rival Wu, lived in hardship and deprivation for twenty years and then recovered to win a great victory.

After the fevered propaganda of the nearer past, belief in the surrender leaflets fluttering down from the silvery B-29s was difficult except where the experience of the Bomb existed. Dōmei had even broadcast a report that its correspondent "who recently visited Hiroshima" discounted the atomic bomb's effects upon those housed in underground shelters—as if the Japanese could exist underground indefinitely while maintaining themselves as a nation. In the town of Okaya, in central Honshu, Ichiro Hatano determined not to believe the leaflets. "I was certainly tempted to take them seriously," he confessed in the diary he was keeping "to show Mother when times are more peaceful," but his new friends "convinced me they must be lies." Approvingly, he noted a column in the *Asahi* of Tokyo quoting a Swedish paper that had argued that the Americans should have

*When OPD paperwork for the signing was hand-carried by another Pentagon colonel to MacArthur, according to Dean Rusk, the liaison officer rushed from his plane to motor launch out to the *Missouri* "with the surrender documents in hand. One of MacArthur's staffers met him at the foot of the gangway, took the documents and said, 'General MacArthur says you will not be needed on board.' "

warned the people of Hiroshima and Nagasaki to leave their cities before dropping atomic bombs. Yet leaflets by the millions had been dropped to warn townspeople to flee B-29 raids, and almost no one had evacuated their cities until, like young Ichiro's family, they had been ordered to do so. In Tokyo, and even in Hiroshima, blocks of houses had been cordoned off by soldiers and knocked down to force departures to the country. Possessions had been left in the streets for outraged householders to carry with them, sell, or abandon. Only those forced to flee had left, as the authorities had not furnished them with an alternative home or the wherewithal to move.

In Hiroshima, burn patients were often treated with cucumber juice, a folk remedy of little value when the burns were massive and very likely fatal. A few casualties, like Dr. Michihiko Hachiya, were actually recovering. Hachiya felt well enough to borrow a bicycle to survey the damage. A week after the blast there were still blackened bodies in the ruins and gutted streetcars in the streets. He passed the Aioi Bridge, aiming point of the Bomb, "so buckled and sprung that its re-enforced concrete surface had been thrown into the water. . . ." On the east bank of the Ōta he gazed at what had been the Museum of Science and Industry, its bronze dome gone, its brick-and-stone walls crumbled, its interior gutted by fire. It seemed to him "the symbol and epitome of a destroyed city and its people."* He followed the streetcar line to the Prefectural Office to ask for more medical supplies for his hospital and was told, "Well, I've learned that no one will be able to live in Hiroshima for the next seventy-five years." Only after he left did Hachiya berate himself for failing to counter "an ugly rumor."

If the rumor was true, he wondered what to do with his staff and patients, then decided that the idea was "an enemy stratagem aimed to deprave a people already demoralized." There was hardly any need for additional demoralization, but the authorities were contributing to it in ways large and small. The same day, Shin Bok Su, a Korean housewife from one of many families brought to Japan as imported labor and required to take Japanese names (her own parents

*The skeletal ruins remain as a monument across the Ōta from the Peace Park. At the edge of the park is the Peace Memorial Museum, which recounts, in artifacts from the blast, what the aftermath of the Bomb was like. Not until 1994, forty-nine years later, was an annex built to place the event in the context of the war and fill in the historical amnesia that suggested that the bombing had victimized a somnolent, innocent Japan. The upper floors of the new museum, however, connected to the original building by a skywalk, politicize the bombing in their devotion to the postwar nuclear arms race with its deadly atmospheric testing of nuclear hardware.

had adopted *Shigemitsu* as surname), had received notification that she and her husband should come to the ruins of the school where their children had died, to retrieve the remains. "There we were given," she recalled, decades later, and still in Hiroshima, "two yellow envelopes. When we opened them, my husband said, 'These are from the backbones of adults.' Our kids were seven and four. So we released those bones into the river."

The recollection suggested the poignant *tanka* of Taira Yamazaki,

*Alas, my child has finally returned to me,*
*His remains only a few strands of black hair.*

Two weeks later Su's husband, who seemed only to have a scrape on his knee from the bombing, blackened and died from radiation sickness. She was living on a handout of one rice ball a day. A neighbor told her that the city authorities would give rehabilitation money to survivors of the bomb dead. Su filled out a form at the Prefectural Office. The clerk examined it and said, "You're a foreigner. We cannot give anything to Koreans." She asked him why. "My husband and two children died because we were Japanese. Who decided suddenly that we were aliens?"

"I don't know," he said. "The orders came from above."

In the Nagasaki area the day was cloudless and hot. Dr. Takashi Nagai, whose hospital had been destroyed and its surviving patients relocated to nearby villages, planned to visit those at Rokumai Ita, Toppomizu, Akamizu, and Odorise, the farthest only five miles away. By the time the medical team reached the first village, news of their visit had spread and the numbers to be seen burgeoned beyond expectations. In Rokumai Ita, his eyes filled with tears at the sight of a bowl of steaming rice offered by a grateful farmer. When they were about to leave Akamizu, having accomplished much of their work, they heard the sound of an airplane engine, presumably American. It was probably on a leaflet mission, but B-29s now terrified them. "No flash! Please, no flash!" Nagai prayed. The rumbling receded, but they marched cautiously and in single file, in the shadows of rocks where possible, so as not to be visible from the air. It was a curious group to make medical rounds, he thought:

Who would have guessed that we were a group of professors, associate professors, nurses, and students—

members of the medical faculty of a university? Our heads were wrapped in bandages, and some of those bandages were stained with new blood. Some among us were limping along on wounded legs. Some were wounded in the chest and could scarcely breathe. Others were deathly pale from radioactive injuries. Yet others had lost their glasses and were groping and stumbling on their way. Some were leaning on sticks; others were supporting themselves on the shoulder of a friend. . . . Some were wearing straw sandals; some wore wooden clogs; some were tripping along in ill-fitting rubber boots. Some wore bloodstained skirts; others had torn shirts or ragged trousers. There were headbands, handkerchiefs, steel helmets. And we all covered our shoulders with green leaves to serve as camouflage against enemy planes.

Although Togo had stalled another confrontation with the die-hards until morning, the continue-the-war faction had been active about Tokyo. As early as four in the morning, Anami had sent his aide, Colonel Hayashi, with a message to the Chief of Staff asking for support from Umezu for an appeal to Field Marshal Hata, in Hiroshima, to intercede with the Emperor. One of only two active field marshals in Japan—the other was Hajime Sugiyama of the Tokyo-based First Army—Hata had the stature to ask Hirohito to refuse the surrender terms. (The Emperor, Anami realized, had no faith in Sugiyama, who had made too many boastful forecasts about victories to come as the Army had withdrawn across the Pacific.) Umezu, who had been routed from bed, thought about the message, which Anami had not entrusted to paper, and said, "You must forgive me. I favor acceptance of the Potsdam Declaration."

Anami received Umezu's response with surprise, but by 7:10 A.M. he was at the palace and in Marquis Kido's office to press the suggestion that continued belligerence would force more acceptable conditions. Anami also needed, he thought, maneuvering room to pacify his reluctant headquarters officers. "No self-respecting nation," he opened, "could possibly accept the Allied terms."

Kido had heard all the arguments. "There is no way out," he said. "The Japanese have sued for peace. The Americans have given the terms. For Japan now to add conditions to conditions would result in certain rupture of negotiations and a renewed ferocity to the war. Look at it from the American position. What would they think the Japanese were plotting if, at this late stage, they put new rules into the game? If the Emperor changed his mind and rescinded the peace proposal, the Allies would consider him a fool or a lunatic." Kido and Anami had been aides in the palace at the same time, in the early 1930s. They understood each other and the constituencies each represented, and Kido knew he could not step back an inch from the Emperor's declared position.

"Pessimism," Anami argued, "never yields good results. We should make one last effort to achieve better terms."

"We must abide by the wishes of His Majesty," said Kido quietly. "We must accept the Allied reply in its present form."

"I understand your position very well," said Anami, rising to leave. "I knew you would say something like that. You don't know what it's like in the Ministry." And he went back to the fanatics to whom he felt hostage.

A morning meeting of the Supreme War Council offered Anami an opportunity to remain distant from the plotters, who still wanted his approval for their coup. An accomplished fact might make their ambitions moot. At nine, the six met once more in the air raid shelter below the Premier's residence. Formally they were still evenly divided, but Umezu had, if only privately, shifted. As Toshikazu Kase had learned, and had told Togo, the War Ministry ultras wanted to prevail upon the Emperor to proclaim a renewal of the war, and upon the War Minister to order resistance to the last man. Although the ultras knew that further fighting was suicidal, they looked to the judgment of Japan in history, and to their pride as soldiers. And they hoped that resistance at an intensity the Allies had not yet known might make the enemy reconsider its terms. With their chances to upset the momentum to surrender diminishing by the hour, peace resisters patrolled the corridors of the War Ministry, seeking converts and condoning whatever insubordination might be useful. A bomb causing little damage was thrown into the Foreign Minister's residence. Posters appeared in the streets with the declaration, "Down with Badoglio!" Other posters named Suzuki, Yonai, and Togo as abominable traitors to the national polity. And while the Cabinet was again sitting on the afternoon of the thirteenth a statement was delivered to all Tokyo newspapers purporting to be an announcement from GHQ that the Army had decided upon "an all-front and all-out war." Neither the War Minister nor the Chief of Staff had known of it.

"By a miracle," Kase wrote later, "we discovered this circular in time to prevent its publication."

At the morning meeting of the six, even after Toyoda and Umezu were called from it for an audience with the Emperor, no movement was perceptible. However, Hirohito was unusually direct for a sovereign whose traditional mode of communication was indirection. "A peace proposal is now being submitted to the Allies," he began. "What is your plan for air operations to be conducted while the negotiations are in progress?" Toyoda recalled letting Umezu speak for both of them. The armed forces, he explained, would "refrain" from aggressive action but would "return fire." The Emperor made it plain that he did not want military interference impeding progress toward peace, and returned them to the Council table before the usual deadlock and adjournment, this time at noon.

Although Hirohito feared the massive, possibly atomic, retaliation that might follow *kamikaze* air strikes or other die-hard gestures, Umezu, who may have feared assassination, cut no orders to comply with the Emperor's wishes until two days later. Exploiting the chaos, disaffected officers could flout orders anyway. For them the American atomic option had no reality, yet General Marshall's assistant, Lieutenant General John E. Hull, would call on Colonel L. E. Seeman of the Manhattan District that morning for an update on the Bomb production schedule "so we can determine how to use them." Marshall was considering whether to drop them all on further cities "as originally planned" or use them if necessary in direct support of "Olympic." Seven more bombs would be available by October 31, said Seeman, but they could endanger American troops. Marshall had in mind, said Hull, hitting troop concentrations and communication centers "a couple or three days" before the landings.

On Ichigaya Hill, the service ministers returned to their offices aware of confrontations to come and the need to make contingency plans to cope with mutinies. At the Navy Ministry, Admiral Yonai heard that complaints about his will to fight had been made by his chief of staff, Admiral Toyoda, and the Vice Chief, Rear Admiral Onishi. Loyally warning subordinates "not to resort to indiscreet actions" while he tried to moderate the surrender terms, Toyoda tried to have it both ways. At the War Ministry there was more talk of a coup, and Lieutenant General Masao Yoshizumi suggested to the Vice Minister, General Tadaichi Wakamatsu, that military police be permitted to round up suspected plotters and place them in preven-

tive detention. Wakamatsu tried the idea on Military Police headquarters, which refused on grounds that the very first arrest would
inflame the situation. Wakamatsu then called the commander of the
Imperial Guards Division, Lieutenant General Tadeshi Mori, who
was responsible for the palace, to warn him not to obey any troop
movement order unless he, Wakamatsu, issued it by telephone. All
written orders were to be considered suspect.

At the Ministry the die-hards finally had their moment to crowd
into Anami's offices and demand action. He had made sure, however, that he had some loyalists present. With hotheads, violence was
always a possibility. At first Anami listened but said nothing, leaving
it to Colonel Hiroo Sato, a section chief, to put them off with a skeptical, "With the situation as it is at present, I cannot agree to the imple-
mentation of your plan." Major Kenji Hatanaka screamed of treason
to the Army, and the general cautioned him quietly, as he had advised the ultras before, that they had to retain confidence in one another. As Anami rose to leave, hoping he had stalled rebellion a little
longer, one of the cabal assured him, "The officers in the Ministry of
War have determined to follow their Minister in whatever course he
takes. Please be assured of that." While it appeared to be a vow of
support, it left open their intent to change Anami's mind.

Absent from the Ministry was one of the most fanatical of the
die-hards, General Tojo's son-in-law. Major Hidemasa Koga, who
lived next door to the former Premier, had motorcycled home. Picking up his eleven-month-old son, he said to his wife, "I want to talk to
you alone." They walked down the stairs into the family air raid shelter. When he emerged to leave, his mother-in-law was watching. "I
came," said Koga to her questioning look, "to ask Makie if she had
my hair and nail clippings." Soldiers expecting to die left such physical tokens as legacies.

When the women told Tojo about the episode, he left immediately for Ichigaya, but General Anami was already at the Cabinet
meeting. Before it had opened, at four, the Foreign Minister had seen
Hirohito again and received encouragement for his stand, which by
seven had picked up a twelve-to-three majority, but not the required
unanimity. Home Minister Abe supported the War Minister, as did
Minister of Justice Hiromasa Matsuzaka, who insisted that following
popular will to choose a form of government was incompatible with
Japan's "unique national polity."

After the meeting, Anami stopped to ask Suzuki, "Will you give me just two more days before you go to the Emperor again?" The Premier knew that in two days a coup could alter every equation. "I'm sorry," he said. "Our opportunity is now—we must seize it at once."

After the general's departure a naval aide to the Premier who had overheard the exchange asked Suzuki, "Couldn't you possibly wait the two days?"

"Impossible," said the seventy-eight-year-old Premier, who had commanded a torpedo boat against the Russians in 1904. "If we don't act now, the Russians will penetrate not only Manchuria and Korea but northern Japan as well. If that happens, our country is finished. We must act now, while our chief adversary is still the United States."

"General Anami," the naval aide predicted, "will kill himself."

"Yes," Suzuki agreed; "that would be very regrettable."

Only suicide seemed likely to end the contradictions Anami faced in himself. By stalling the irreconcilables in the War Ministry he was fulfilling his vow to the Emperor; by loyalty to the Emperor he was forcing the Army into ignominious surrender. Anami might have resigned from the Cabinet to resolve his dilemma, but he also saw the survival of Japan as a higher interest than officer caste pride. Yet he could not say that to ultras, whose aspirations were beyond logic. Chief Cabinet Secretary Sakomizu had overheard Anami, in a telephone conversation with his headquarters during a break in the meeting, claiming that all he needed was the further patience of the ultras—"The Cabinet is beginning to agree with us." He knew it was untrue but he wanted time to run out on the hotheads.

Suzuki had already announced his intention to seek a decision—a reconsideration—from the Throne. Sakomizu had secured the signatures of the six for an Imperial Conference, but the chiefs of staff had signed at a price. Sakomizu had to promise that the petition would not be used without their further consent, and not before they could talk once more with Togo.

The Foreign Minister had returned to his own residence, where he had long planned a small dinner in honor of two retiring ambassadors for that evening. With the bombing in remission, it was a brief oasis of formality and calm in overheated Tokyo. Suddenly, as dinner proceeded, a messenger arrived with an urgent request from Umezu and Toyoda that Togo see them immediately. Parting from his guests at his own table, Togo pleaded the obvious urgency of the moment and offered to see the chiefs in Suzuki's conference room, where he was exasperated by yet another rehashing of the day's arguments.

Then Admiral Onishi burst in, announcing that he had come directly from having it out with Prince Takamatsu, to whom he had appealed as a fellow naval officer. Loyalty to the Navy now came second to the harried Takamatsu. Hirohito had quickly moved to control the royal princes, ordering them, despite their misgivings, to "unite solidly" behind his decision to surrender. Kido recalled the rancorous meeting as marked by "a very free and frank exchange of views"—the diplomatic euphemism for argument. After two hours the princes pledged their fealty. The family council was only one of many reasons why Kido called the thirteenth "the most trying day in our peace move."

Since the armed forces had lost the confidence of the Emperor, Admiral Onishi had told Takamatsu, whom he had confronted only after the palace council, "it is necessary to submit to the Emperor a plan to gain the victory, and to ask his reconsideration." The wild plan must have dumbfounded the prince, and as Onishi repeated it to Togo, Umezu, and Toyoda, they wondered about the admiral's sanity.

Japan would not be defeated, he explained, if the nation "resolutely risked the lives of twenty million Japanese as a Special Attack Corps." (Onishi took pride in his having invented the *kamikaze* concept.) Officially, until then, only 665 officers and 1,400 ranks had died in suicide attacks. Patriotism could do more. The service chiefs stared in disbelief. Turning then to Togo, Onishi demanded, "What is the Foreign Minister's opinion?"

"If only we had any real hope of victory," said Togo, "no one would for a moment think of accepting the Potsdam Declaration; but winning one battle will not win the war for us." Onishi was only rephrasing the unrealistic propaganda of months about "the Honourable Death of a Hundred Million." As the war wound down, legendary director Akiro Kurosawa, then a young filmmaker cranking out uplift for the military, thought it would happen. People "probably would have done what they were told, and died. And probably I would have done likewise. The Japanese see self-assertion as immoral and self-sacrifice as the sensible course to take in life. We were accustomed to this teaching and never thought to question it."

Returning to the Navy Ministry, Onishi looked in at the office of Captain Yoshio Kodama and told him, "We caused you people a lot of hardships over a long period of time, but it's already over. His Majesty the Emperor seems no longer to have any confidence in the Army and the Navy."

Leaving Suzuki's residence, Togo went to the Foreign Ministry to read the latest cables and transcripts of foreign broadcasts, "which bore in upon me the growing gravity of our peril. I pondered, in the car returning home, that even if we offered the sacrifice of twenty million Japanese lives, they would fall easy prey to machines and gunfire. . . . The soldiers' ignorance of the nature of modern warfare was beyond my understanding."

The deadlock in the military about how to lay down arms, if at all, was furnishing alluring opportunities for conspirators—or at least for their fantasies. One farfetched plot envisioned the kidnapping of a child of royal lineage who would then be brought up secretly as postoccupation successor to the discredited or dethroned Emperor. Navy Ministry funds were to be covertly used, and the scheme entrusted to Captain Minoru Genda, one of the planners of Pearl Harbor. Another navy plot had already enlisted the wavering interest of still another participant in the Pearl Harbor drama, Mitsuo Fuchida, and the die-hard Vice Minister, Onishi. The scenario included seizing the palace, the service ministries, the Metropolitan Police, and the government, but it was kept from army plotters, who were hatching a similar scheme. Day and night no longer had any meaning in the dim corridors of diminished military power that were the War and Navy ministries, and on his way to Onishi's office after nightfall Fuchida encountered his fellow officer Prince Takamatsu. The prince motioned him into an empty room and intimated that he knew everything. "I have just returned from the Palace," Takamatsu confided, "where I spoke with His Imperial Majesty personally. The Emperor most sincerely desires to surrender immediately and thus secure peace for the nation."

"All right," said Fuchida, deflated. "The coup d'état will be cancelled." He had been coaxed into it, and his role was over. But open knowledge of the Emperor's will, he urged the prince, had to be communicated to the officer corps, who would distrust surrender messages as having been coerced from the Throne. "May I request that all members of the royal family in the military service go to the various fronts as imperial messengers? They can perform a national service by convincing our military leaders that surrender is indeed His Imperial Majesty's sincere wish."

Without consulting Onishi, Fuchida, on leaving the prince, telephoned the air bases at Yokosuka and Atsugi, asking leaders there to call off their plans. At Atsugi, Captain Yasuna Kozono, commander of the 302nd Air Corps, refused to hear Fuchida out. In response,

Fuchida began drafting a manifesto, "We Believe This," in which in five pages he declared that the Navy had no reason to reproach itself and was fulfilling the command of the Emperor. The crucial leaflet, however, was American. Five and a half million copies of it were being dropped on Japanese cities; it contained the text of the Japanese surrender offer and the American reply. Domestic press and radio could no longer conceal the surrender plan or the precariousness of the Japanese situation. Rumors of both peace and coup abounded, one of the most curious recorded by Admiral Ugaki from Kyushu as he wrote up his diary at the end of the long day. "Nimitz at Guam," he claimed, "also called up Tokyo by the international call signal and said that, as it took time to communicate via Switzerland, communication should be made in plain English, and he also instructed what wave channel to use. What an insult!" In a reshuffle of commanders, Ugaki also learned that he was moving up to the new fleet headquarters at Otachi, to command the Thirty-fourth Air Fleet and Sixth Air Army—a consolidation made necessary because of depleted resources. He had gone to inspect his new facilities but could not move there. His replacement, Vice Admiral Jinichi Kusaka, had postponed the changeover. Ugaki telegraphed his ministry to suggest that he remain where he was. It was a better location from which to send *Tenzans* to strike ships at Okinawa. He felt sure that one had "rammed a carrier." Every plane that failed to return gave him hope that an enemy target had been hit.

While Togo was first hosting his dinner and then contending with the senior militarists, Anami was facing ten of his younger officers, who had descended on his official residence in Miyakezaka as the Minister returned from the Cabinet session. Major Hatanaka announced as spokesman that they could wait no longer: a coup would take place at ten the next morning, and they wanted Anami's approval. Further, he warned the Minister, the peace faction intended to assassinate him if he continued to oppose unconditional surrender. Realizing that the opposite was more likely to happen and that the threat came from the hotheads around him, Anami laughed and asked Colonel Okitsugu Arao, officially the group's leader, to outline what they had in mind. Knowing that Anami would never support a coup in effect against himself, Arao, chief of the Military Affairs Section of the ministry and senior in rank of the ten, explained in some discomfort what the insurrectionists had in mind. Surrender was to be delayed until the national polity was guaranteed. The pacifist influences around the Emperor—Kido, Suzuki, Togo, and Yonai, at the least—were to be removed from office and imprisoned. Martial law was to be proclaimed and the Imperial Palace isolated from treasonous influences. Backing for the coup was to be demanded from Anami, Umezu, Mori, and General Shizuichi Tanaka (Eastern District Army commander).

The plan, Anami ventured, was insufficiently detailed to have any chance of succeeding. He would not say whether he was in sympathy with it, but, playing for time, he asked Arao to return at midnight for further discussion and bade him good-night until then. "If you disapprove of the plan," Hayashi told Anami as Arao left, "it is necessary for you to say so definitely." Trying to string out the conspirators without committing himself to anything, Anami would say only, "Well, I'll have another talk with Arao." When Arao returned, alone, Anami confided that after much consideration of the proposals the officers had made, he saw no chance that a coup could succeed, but that he would have a more positive answer in the morning.

What he meant by "positive answer"—whether he meant "definitive" or "affirmative"—remained ambiguous. "I don't know," he confessed to Hayashi, "whether Arao will interpret my remark to mean that I am opposed to the coup."

In Manchuria, the forlorn followers of the Jōsen Temple reached Hsingan-chen at noon on the thirteenth, lit fires at the roadside, and tried to dry their sodden clothes and cook food. The Manchu villagers looked on and laughed. The Japanese presence was gone. The police station was empty. Even as they tried to reorganize their trek the refugees were attacked by Manchus until young Japanese with their few rifles drove the predators off. Abandoned to their fates, they discussed whether to go on, merely to escape the Russians, or commit suicide. Some opted for returning to Sakurada to die before their own temple. The new Manchuria for which they had left Japan had ceased to exist—if it ever had. Those from Hachijo village announced that it was hateful to throw life away. They would return. "As long as life goes on, we can do something which will serve our country in some way. We are sorry, but we will have to leave you." About twenty set off to the east. The others opted to return to the last settlement they had passed, but on arriving, they found it looted and burned. By then they were too tired to continue, and decided to go to sleep where they were and commit suicide the next morning.

P'u Yi had only slightly better luck. To avoid strafing from the air his imperial train bypassed Mukden, and at Meihokou the local commander came on board. The Japanese Army, he told P'u Yi, was winning, but the head of state saw enough frantic refugees begging vainly to board the train to understand the lie. On the thirteenth the train reached Talitzu, a mining town in the mountains. It seemed to be nowhere, but the train appeared not about to proceed farther.

In Yenan, speaking to Communist cadres, Mao Zedong boasted that the imminent defeat of Japan had been due to Russian intervention: "The decisive factor for Japan's surrender is the entry of the Soviet Union into the war. A million Red Army troops are entering China's northeast; their force is irresistible." Whether or not he was right about Russia, he could have boasted that his Communist forces had accomplished much more than Chiang's Kuomintang armies since the Manchurian invasion of 1931 to resist the Japanese. Chiang's governors and warlords were in constant communication— and cooperation—with the Japanese. Every Chinese general now coveted surrendered Japanese weapons, and the Japanese had little more than that with which to bargain for their safety. Yet Chiang blustered ineffectively, as if he could order Mao's army commander, Chu Teh, that he was "never again to take independent action" and was to "wait for further directions" from Chungking about taking over territory or accepting surrenders.

Everywhere in Southeast Asia the race was on to take power and territory before the Allies could have some role in the decision. In Hanoi and environs a National Liberation Committee of Vietnam was formed on the thirteenth to prevent the return of the French. "The defeat of the Japanese," the committee manifesto warned, "does not render us automatically free and independent.... Let us free ourselves by our own energies.... Onward under the flag of the Viet Minh." General Giap's troops moved into the city without opposition.

Theoretically the Japanese Southern Army under Field Marshal Terauchi was responsible for areas from the Indies north to China and west through Burma. Having left the heat and instability of Saigon, it had little effective control of anything but Moulmein in Burma, Bangkok, and Singapore. From the hill station of Dalat, Terauchi on the thirteenth called a conference of his staff. What was the Southern Army to do when—it seemed no longer *if*—Japan surrendered? It had been planned as a military empire responsible largely to itself, subsisting on local agriculture, defending itself with locally manufactured weapons, co-opting local troops and populations to do what natives in colonial regions always did. Some of his officers opted to continue that independence; others contended that if GHQ in Tokyo intended that Japan cease hostilities, the surrender included the Southern Army. "Study the question well, gentlemen," said Terauchi in the dry manner of a general in the army of British India, and left the officers to argue on their own. Summoning his chief of staff, Lieutenant General Takazō Numata, to his hotel room, Terauchi told him, "I'm not going back to Japan. Send a signal convoking a meeting of all [our] Area Army commanders-in-chief." The result would be his order: "The plans of the Southern Army have changed in no way whatever. Each Army under our command and jurisdiction, in no way confused and blinded by scheming propaganda, will establish a unified and firmly united military discipline, and will go ahead to strengthen its war preparations more and more."

The times had turned very sour for defeated commanders, as even the most elevated in rank at the end of the German war were learning. As delegates met in London to plan the first trial of war criminals, in Nuremberg on September 15, lumping together bureaucrats, industrialists, politicians, and generals—and wondering which side secretly held Martin Bormann—the star of the proceedings seemed certain to be the Nazi with the most elevated title. Hermann Göring had been named *Reichsmarschall* by Hitler. Now fifty pounds slimmer, he fit comfortably into a bucket seat on the C-47 that carried him from Luxembourg to Nuremberg. As the transport flew over the Rhine, which glistened in the morning sun, Göring, who chattered incessantly to his morose colleagues, looked out the window and quipped to his future companions in the dock, "Take your last look!"

Göring was still news elsewhere. From Florence came a dispatch that yet another hoard of art loot he had tried to spirit away had been found—works by Manet, Renoir, Cézanne, and other Impressionists. And in Amsterdam, art forger Han van Meegeren was busy proving that the old masters he had sold the *Reichsmarschall* were not by Vermeer but by van Meegeren. He offered to paint a Vermeer "before witnesses." Guarded by police and watched by critics, he began filling a large canvas with a scene of the young Jesus teaching in the Temple. It would not be finished until October, but it was already obvious that his ninth "Vermeer" was one of his best.

Yet he was neither charged nor set free. Was he guilty of forging a signature, or only of duping Göring? If the latter, it was the only patriotic act in his life.

In the United States, as Washington waited out a Japanese response, a very different work of art was unveiled—the first Ford civilian automobile since Pearl Harbor. A few sedans had been manufactured during the war, mostly for government use and deliberately drab in finish. But on August 13 the fifteen 1946 Fords completed that Monday rolled out of the factory at Edgewater, New Jersey. Resplendent in its chrome detail, the first gray, two-door vehicle had, for the cameras, onetime Captain Eddie Rickenbacker, an auto racer before he flew army planes in France in 1918, at the wheel and blond, leggy film star Carole Landis in the passenger seat.

The legal wartime speed limit, Rickenbacker warned, was still thirty-five miles an hour. And there was still a war on.

# CHAPTER XXXIII

# · AUGUST 14, 1945 ·

## *Rescript and Rebellion*

After three days of waiting for a response from Tokyo, Washington realized that the peace process inside Japan was in trouble. Informal listening stations in neutral embassies in Tokyo and military listening stations on Saipan and Okinawa and Guam intercepted disturbing signals of dissent in the Japanese Army and Navy. So did "Magic" in Manila. American ships and planes were readied to hammer again at Japan, even if most of the men assigned to the missions were unenthusiastic about putting their lives at risk. With Truman's assent, the generals and admirals had already cut new orders. Yet the air intrusion that had the most impact—leaflets—greeted the awakening, in his room at the palace, of Marquis Kido.

Early morning in Tokyo was evening on the thirteenth in Washington, where the President, exasperated by the silence from across the Pacific, would retire to bed early. Kido, awakened for what he expected would be a day of haggling and possibly insurrection, was silently handed a piece of paper by a court chamberlain. Addressed to "the Japanese people," it declared that B-29s were dropping leaflets rather than bombs "because the Japanese government has offered to surrender and every Japanese has a right to know the terms of the offer and the reply made to it. . . ." The leaflet reprinted the Foreign Ministry note of August 10 and the Byrnes reply.

Kido was horrified. The words from the sky intended to arouse an ill-informed Japanese public into pushing their government to act before the B-29s returned with bombs might instead stir the die-hards into rushing their coup. Since the official silence could not be strung out much longer, he asked to see the Emperor. If Hirohito himself called an Imperial Conference, the ultras might feel thwarted.

As Kido was beginning his day, Field Marshal Hata, having arrived at dawn from Hiroshima, was finishing an early breakfast with General Anami. Hata and Field Marshal Sugiyama, as well as Fleet Admiral Nagano, the three most senior officers in Japan, had been summoned by the Emperor in his strategy to demand loyalty to the Throne. Hata's headquarters was destroyed, as well as half of his troops in Hiroshima. The Bomb, he told Anami, was inhuman. The plight of the population was indescribably horrible. But although a Dōmei press release had only tried to minimize the effects, Hata claimed that the Bomb was defensible. As it exploded in the air (carried, he thought, by parachute), it was ineffective below ground. Deeply entrenched positions might survive and Japan could manage to withstand future blasts. "Be sure to mention this to the Emperor when you see him," Anami, grasping at straws, urged Hata. "Tell him the Bomb is not so deadly."

While Anami went on to Ichigaya Hill—high brass still had cars and fuel although the few buses and taxis in Tokyo sputtered on charcoal burners—Premier Suzuki arrived at the palace. Encountering Kido, who had finished his audience, Suzuki exchanged views on how to "command the termination of the war and [the] drafting of an Imperial Rescript," and went in to see the Emperor.

At the War Ministry, conspirators camped at Anami's office since seven o'clock were waiting for him. Disaffection seemed to be spreading. Decrypted in the United States as "Magic 1238," a message from General Okamura, commander of the army in China, was—to Anami—the strongest objection to surrender yet. "The limitation of our sovereignty to the home islands only," Okamura disparaged, "will take us back to when the race of Yamato was only thirty million. The existence of seventy million absolutely requires that we keep Formosa, Korea, and [south] Manchuria. . . . Such a disgrace as the surrender of several million troops without fighting is not paralleled in the world's military history and it is absolutely impossible to submit to the unconditional surrender of a million picked troops in perfectly healthy shape to the Chungking forces of defeated China."

The conspirators planned to begin their seizure of buildings and personnel at ten o'clock, and wanted the approval, if not the assistance, of key generals in the War Ministry and in Tokyo commands, but Anami would see only a single emissary, Colonel Arao. With Arao—who may have been playing a double role—Anami went to Umezu's office and sought his opinion. The Chief of Staff was unambiguous. A failed coup was useless, and whatever its merits, it would certainly fail. The group separated, Anami intending to return home to rest after nights of little sleep, but at 8:52 commands began going out for an Imperial Conference at 10:30 called by the Emperor himself. Suzuki and Kase had found no difficulty in persuading Hirohito to do what he had already determined to do—in Kido's words: "to command the government without further loss of time to go through the formalities of terminating the war."

By ten o'clock Hata, Sugiyama, and Nagano (naval chief of staff at the time of Pearl Harbor) were in audience with the Emperor to learn that the war would end at his insistence and that their support was expected. At ten, also, the ultras discovered that they were still being strung along by Anami. Rushing to catch him before he entered the palace grounds, they were too late.

Given the urgency of the occasion and the summer heat, Cabinet ministers had been instructed not to wear court dress. They came in a mix of uniforms and suits, but all respectfully wearing coats and ties. The parallel narrow tables in the clammy underground shelter below the library were covered with a cloth of gold brocade. At the Emperor's end was a straight-backed chair with arms, behind which was a six-panel gilded screen. At 10:30 the twenty-four Council and Cabinet officials and secretaries took seats, wiping their brows, and waited for Hirohito, who entered at 10:55 wearing a military uniform and white gloves. Suzuki opened the meeting by reviewing the impasse and called upon those in disagreement to offer rebuttal in the imperial presence.

Umezu began by describing the danger to the *Kokutai* that surrender under the Potsdam terms would bring. Toyoda worried that the people (and by implication, the military) "would not readily accept the wording of the [Byrnes] reply, which placed the Emperor in a position subordinate to that of the Supreme Commander of the occupation forces." Further, "Japan must not be occupied." It was a humiliation that "in practice" a defeated nation might have to accept, but not Japan. He wanted to hold out for more acceptable terms that would not "undermine the entire Japanese tradition." Anami spoke last, seconding the positions of both chiefs of staff.

Suzuki apologized for again asking the Emperor to advise a divided Cabinet. A number of versions of Hirohito's words survive, perhaps the most authoritative of them a composite prepared from memory by Minister of State Sakonji, Navy Minister Yonai, and Minister of Education Ōhta. As the Emperor spoke his eyes filled with tears, and as he went on, all of the twenty-four who heard him sobbed, recognizing, without the word *surrender* ever being spoken, what they were being commanded to do:

> If no one wishes to speak further, I wish to express my thoughts. I have listened carefully to the arguments of those who are not in agreement with me, but the opinions I have already expressed have not changed. Having carefully considered conditions in the world at large and conditions within our own country, I believe it would be unreasonable and fruitless to continue the war.
>
> There are all sorts of arguments concerning the question of national polity, but my interpretation of the purport of the [Byrnes] reply is that the other side is showing some good will. There is ground for some concern over the attitude of the other side, but I do not wish to be suspicious. The important question is the confidence and determination of the whole of my people, and that obliges me to believe that we must now consent to the proposal made to us.
>
> I can well understand the emotions of the officers and men of the armed services when they learn of such things as their being disarmed and of military occupation to insure the carrying out of the peace terms. Nevertheless, I am determined to save the lives of my people whatever may happen to me. If the war were to continue our country would be reduced to rubble, and I cannot bear to have my people suffer more anguish. I could not face the spirits of my ancestors. Although we naturally cannot place complete confidence in all

that the Allies might do, that concern is not to be compared with the inevitable destruction of Japan; if only some few seeds survive we will be able to see light in hopes of our country's resurrection.

In Toshikazu Kase's version the Emperor here warned that the nation faced "extermination" and that to rebuild they had to save something, "be it ever so little."

Hirohito went on as he had earlier about having to "tolerate the intolerable and suffer the insufferable" in the interest of national survival, and, he continued,

> I mourn for those who died on the battlefields and who died in doing their duty, and I mourn with those they left behind. I am anxious for those wounded in battle, for those [civilians] on whom fell the calamity of war, and also for those who lost their livelihood. . . . If there is anything I can do at this time I shall be glad to stand before the microphone. The people thus far have been allowed to know nothing, and I expect they will be greatly shocked when they hear of our decision. That will be especially the case with the officers and men of the armed services. I expect it will not be easy to calm them down, and I therefore ask that the Ministers of War and of the Navy will appreciate my feelings and will work together to the end that order is maintained. If necessary I would be ready personally to speak to them.
>
> As the issuance of an Imperial Rescript will probably be called for, I desire that the Government prepare a draft as soon as possible.
>
> My opinions are as I have stated them.

On past occasions when the Emperor had intervened in public affairs, he had done so guardedly, through palace functionaries like the Lord Privy Seal, or so ambiguously that others could interpret his wishes and issue the commands. As he left the room this time, to weeping as well as bowing, there was no ambiguity. The group recessed for an hour so that the Cabinet itself could reconvene at Suzuki's official residence for formal action. Conferees trudged through the underground corridor below the *Gobunko* and followed the stairs into the noon sunlight.

In the *Gobunko* itself, Hirohito met privately with Kido, who as a palace official had no role in the conference, and explained what had happened. The Council had gone as the Marquis expected, but he, too, could not hold back his tears.

Before the Cabinet meeting at one—midnight on the new day in Washington—most members gathered informally at lunch at the Premier's residence. The menu was stark fare symbolic of their straits— whale meat and black bread. Only Suzuki found he could eat it. Rising from the table, Anami went off separately with his adjutant, pulling him aside to suggest, "Hayashi! You've heard the rumor that the enemy has a huge landing force near Tokyo Bay. I want to hit that hard while we're still talking peace—then maybe we'll get the kind of peace terms we want." (With almost the same vindictiveness in mind—but intended as a public relations gambit for the Air Force— Spaatz and LeMay were gearing up eight hundred B-29s in the Marianas and Okinawa for a huge assault on the home islands.)

"But the Emperor has already given us his decision," said Hayashi in surprise. "Anyway, we don't know definitely where the landing forces are now—it's only a rumor that they're near Tokyo." In fact, there were no troops at sea, but the War Ministry had been fearing both phases of "Downfall" for weeks, and only hours seemed left to assuage military pride.

Anami shook his head sadly. There was his brother-in-law hanging about in a corner, waiting to plead the ultra cause once more, and no gesture seemed possible to placate the die-hards. With the coup still in limbo, Takeshita wanted Anami to "mobilize troops for the purpose of maintaining security." The suggestion was transparent: "Furthermore, there is a lot you could do at the Cabinet meeting. You have power; you could use it. As you know, the Chief of Staff has changed his mind. Why don't you?"

Umezu had not joined the die-hards, but had sought safety in ambiguity. Speaking only for himself, Anami reminded Takeshita that the decision had been the Emperor's. "As a Japanese soldier, I must obey my Emperor." But there was another alternative, Takeshita suggested. Anami could resign, bringing down the Cabinet before it could ratify the surrender. The war would go on until a new War Minister could be seated. Since the Army had its veto over the choice, it could avoid surrender by deferring a new government. "Admiral Onishi," Takeshita confided, "told an officers' meeting that even if the Emperor decided to end the war, he himself, at the risk of being branded a traitor, would advocate continuing the war for the sake of a higher justice."

Outspokenly insubordinate, Onishi had told Rear Admiral Sadatoshi Tomioka of the Naval General Staff, "Even the Emperor sometimes makes foolish mistakes," and to Captain Kazuo Yatsugi he announced, "It was not I who lost the war, but the Emperor."

Onishi's intemperate talk failed to move Anami. "The war will end even if I resign," he told his brother-in-law. "That is definite. And if I resign, I would not see the Emperor again." Takeshita understood the rejection and the hint of *bushido* code.

A quick appearance at the War Ministry seemed essential, and before the Cabinet reassembled, Anami and Hayashi went off to Ichigaya Hill. The die-hards were still milling about, and the general called them in to review what the Emperor had said. "With tears in his eyes, he asked me to persevere, however difficult the duty," Anami explained, as if Hirohito had pleaded with him personally. "I can no longer oppose my view to the Emperor's decision." When the muttering about mutiny continued, he affirmed, "The Emperor has spoken his decision, and we have no choice whatever but to obey it. Anyone who disagrees will have to do so over my dead body." Anami rebuckled the ceremonial sword that he had leaned against a wall.

To manipulate the mood for insurrection, ultras had to spread the bad news quickly, even before the Imperial Rescript formalized surrender. Acceptance of defeat, unit commanders knew, would be difficult after years of the opposite kind of indoctrination. (Earlier in the war the forces of the West were only "armed robbers in the Asian garden" and "even weaker than the Chinese army," while their military equipment, from tanks to aircraft, was "a collection of rattling relics.") At the Oppama air base, officers were summoned at three to hear their commandant, in a faltering voice, warn of what was to come, perhaps before the day ended. Listening with the others was Lieutenant Saburo Sakai, who claimed sixty-four aircraft kills, including the B-17 captained by Colin Kelly over the Philippines on December 10, 1941. Head injuries, including the loss of an eye, now restricted him to pilot training. "What I am about to tell you," he recalled the commandant as saying, "is of the utmost importance, and must be regarded as absolutely top secret, and I rely upon your integrity as officers of the Imperial Navy to keep this information strictly to yourselves."

He stared at them vacantly, supporting himself against his desk.

"Japan has decided to accept the enemy's terms. We will abide by the Potsdam Declaration. The surrender orders may be announced at any moment. I want all officers to cooperate with me to the fullest. Order must be maintained at this base. There may be hotheads who will refuse to accept the decision to surrender. We cannot afford to have our men violate whatever conditions our country accepts. Remember—and never forget it—that His Majesty's orders come before anything else."

The men stood dazed and unbelieving. "Some of the officers were crying," Sakai recalled, "others cursing." For comfort he went out to lean weakly against his Zero. But Japan was only *about* to surrender. The B-29s might be over once more. A friend, Ensign Jiro Kawachi, reading Sakai's mind, came over and suggested, "We just can't quit like this. We have to draw blood once more." For weeks they had been forbidden opposition, to preserve planes and fuel for the last battle. Kawachi was not preaching insurrection—but what he was suggesting was at least insubordination. In case the Superforts crossed Tokyo Bay after dark, they had the ground crew move their planes out to the runway.

In Suzuki's underground shelter, Hiroshi Shimomura, director of the Information Bureau, was holding a pre-Cabinet background briefing for the Tokyo press. When peace came, however humiliating, the Japanese people had to know that the Emperor himself had decreed it. Like everyone else, Shimomura could not restrain his tears. None of the news was for release yet, but the journalists asked questions more freely than any could remember doing before, and would talk freely afterward.

Since the Premier's deafness prevented him from handling subtleties of language, he had his son Hajime at his side when the Cabinet convened. The agenda was the draft of a surrender note. That they had to rely upon the Emperor to force them into uneasy consensus had embarrassed Suzuki. "It was an affront to the Throne," he told the nineteen Cabinet officers and aides at the round table. "It happened only because we didn't try hard enough." As a beginning, then, they passed a resolution, unanimously, begging the Emperor's pardon. Then came the agonizing work of approving language for the Imperial Rescript ending the war, and a communication to the Swiss authorities for transmittal to Washington.

At the same time as the Cabinet convened, three directors of the Japan Broadcasting Corporation—NHK—were meeting at the Information Bureau at Hiroshi Shimomura's request. Since he was at Suzuki's residence himself, an aide met Hachiro Ohashi, Kenjiro Yabe, and Daitaro Arakawa to inform them that a rescript declaring the surrender would be forthcoming within hours and that the Emperor himself would read the rescript on NHK. A collective gasp arose from the broadcast officials. It seemed close to sacrilege to have the Emperor go before a microphone, yet no other gesture would convey to the people the alteration in their lives. The Cabinet, Shimomura's deputy went on, was even then considering whether the broadcast should be live or from a recording. "Meanwhile, will you make all preparations for either eventuality?"

NHK chairman Ohashi accepted the charge, and as they left, Yabe—the Domestic Bureau chief—recalled to the others the horror of the December 2, 1928, incident only a month after Hirohito's enthronement when, at the Yoyogi Parade Grounds in Kyoto, words of the Emperor's address to the Army were picked up on the radio through an acoustical quirk. It seemed an act of blasphemy and was a dark moment for NHK. Since then the voice of the Emperor had never been heard by his people. Now the responsibility would fall upon Arakawa, director of the Technical Bureau, to carry off the awesome assignment.

Chief Cabinet Secretary Sakomizu's surrender draft was the basis of discussion at the Premier's conference. Anami objected to having the Emperor say, "The war situation grows more unfavorable to us every day." He wanted language more palatable to the Army, and proposed, "The war situation has not turned in our favor"—as if defeat had been an act of fate rather than arms. Admiral Yonai opposed the dishonesty but thought better of it and withdrew his objection. The words would be changed again in later editing. Anami also insisted upon the phrase, opening one paragraph, "Having been able to safeguard and maintain the structure of the Imperial State . . ." It almost made surrender sound like a sort of victory, and peace as accomplished with honor.

The Foreign Ministry had the task of preparing the actual surrender notes, which accepted Potsdam but hopefully attempted to limit the "points in Japanese territory" to be occupied to a "minimum number" not to include Tokyo, to request advising the Japanese authorities in advance of entry of troops or ships "so that arrangements can be made for reception," and to have disarming of troops take place "under the command of His Majesty the Emperor," with a "rea-sonable time" permitted for orders to reach "remote places."

The rescript itself was prepared in two copies, brushed onto heavy paper. After one was reviewed by the Cabinet, which had re-mained in session, it was brought by Marquis Kido to the Emperor. On reading it, Hirohito asked for five changes, each duly approved, but rather than prepare fresh copies, each containing more than eight hundred characters, the two copyists, frantically trying to meet the Foreign Ministry's deadline of six o'clock, pasted blank bits of paper over the sections to be altered, then, when the paste dried, brushed in new characters. One change turned Anami's line about the "war situ-ation" to "the war situation has developed not necessarily to Japan's advantage"—still a large understatement. Then an omission was dis-covered in one copy. The final participial phrase had been omitted from the sentence

> Moreover, the enemy has begun to employ a new and most cruel bomb, the power of which to do damage is indeed in-calculable, taking the toll of many innocent lives.

Across the world at Godmanchester in Huntingdonshire, Wer-ner Heisenberg, having read all the newspaper accounts he could find at Farm Hall, was giving a lecture to his colleagues on how he thought the Hiroshima bomb had been made. He had figured a lot of it out. "Obviously," he explained, "they put the [uranium] sphere to-gether from two hemispheres."

"Hemispheres are difficult to put together," said Horst Korsching.

"A possible construction," said Heisenberg, "would be to have the hemisphere . . . able to move in a gun-barrel, to be fired in this gun against the other hemisphere." Oppenheimer had expected "a brilliant luminescence," and achieved it. "The first thing one will see," Heisenberg explained to the Farm Hall physicists, "will be a glowing ball of about 20 meters diameter, glowing white because of the absorbed X-rays. This radiation sends out further radiation and so the affair gradually spreads out."

Carl von Weizsäcker interrupted to theorize about the "pressure wave," and Heisenberg went on, "At the beginning the affair has wonderfully spherical symmetry, and then gradually convection phenomena enter to complicate it."

•      •      •

Where the phenomena had actually occurred, it was now closer to eight in the evening than six, and there seemed no way to get the documents completed in time for the war to end earlier than the next day. Reports were already in that American bombers were again over Japan, this time with explosives rather than leaflets. The abashed copyist was instructed, against all precedent, to insert the missing words in tiny characters between the lines. When the sheets were brought to Premier Suzuki before they went to Hirohito for signature (and broadcast), the Premier was seen to grimace at the patched and pasted document. It was less than artistic, but would have to do. At eight-thirty the Emperor signed "Hirohito" at the bottom of each rescript, and the imperial seal was affixed. Next to the seal the document was dated "The Fourteenth Day of the Eighth Month of the Twentieth Year of Showa"—the name which Hirohito had chosen for his reign at his enthronement. *Showa* meant "Enlightened Peace."

After Suzuki bowed out of the imperial presence, Kido asked for a word with him. Had the Premier any further intimations of a rising? Kido had heard through Prince Konoye of disaffection in the Imperial Guards Division. Suzuki refused to believe that loyalty would not prevail, especially with General Mori in charge. "The Imperial Guards," assured the Premier, "are the last people in the world I would worry about."

Through the Guards' officers, however—especially Major Hidemasa Koga and Major Sadakichi Ishihara, who had been brought into the conspiracy—the coup leaders had learned that the Emperor would be recording a surrender broadcast. Once it was aired, a mutiny would very likely fall apart. Major Hatanaka and Lieutenant Colonel Shiizaki realized that they needed to prevent its broadcast. Even more, they needed the cooperation of General Mori. The palace was under his protection.

In a corner of the nearly dark pressroom at the Premier's official residence, Toshio Shibata of the *Asahi Shimbun* sat waiting for things to happen. He had been to Shimomura's afternoon briefing and, moving about Tokyo since, he had heard that the Imperial Rescript would be promulgated that night, which was still day in the United States; that a huge occupying force was lying off Japan, ready to take over the home islands in the morning and subject the women of Japan to methodical rape; and that the Emperor would be immediately exiled to Okinawa or an even more remote place. NHK radio was piped into the pressroom, and the nine o'clock news began with the usual reports from Army and Navy sources, few of them believable. Then came a bland voice announcing that an important broadcast would be made at noon the following day. Following it came the customary martial music. Shibata realized that at noon on the fifteenth the war would be over. Few others listening had any idea what to expect, which gave Hatanaka and his plotters some room to maneuver.

With the long meeting on the rescript ended, Anami had been driven through blacked-out Tokyo back to the War Ministry, which he found largely deserted. There were no sentries at the front gate. It was clear that the scare about an American landing had spread; few troops intended to be in the way. Although he knew that the rescript ending the war would be in the next day's newspapers as well as on radio in the very Voice of the Crane, Anami sat down at his desk and drafted a message to all units in his and Umezu's names:

> . . . The Emperor has made his decision. The Army expects you to obey that decision and make no unauthorized moves that would put to shame the glorious traditions of the Imperial Army. . . . You must behave in such a way that you need never fear the judgment of posterity, and it is expected that your conduct will enhance the honor and the glory of the Imperial Japanese Forces in the eyes of the entire world. . . .
>
> The Minister of War and the Chief of Staff dispatch this order with grief in their hearts, and they expect you to appreciate the emotions of the Emperor when he himself broadcasts the Imperial Rescript terminating the war at twelve noon tomorrow.

From the Navy Ministry, Chief of Staff Toyoda had already issued the blunt order, "Further offensive operations against the United States, Great Britain, the USSR and China will be suspended pending further orders." Now the Minister, Yonai, followed up Toyoda's message with the explanation that the end to hostilities was the Emperor's command. "His, and only his, decision" was that "for the Empire's future, the only thing to do was to accept the Potsdam Declaration on condition that the structure of the nation be left intact."

At Ichigaya, Anami also wrote out a letter of resignation to take with him to the resumption of the marathon Cabinet meeting. Once the surrender had become effective, Baron Suzuki would ask the entire Cabinet to resign. As Anami prepared to leave, the tall figure of his aide, Colonel Arao, appeared in the doorway. "Arao, I don't want our young officers to do anything foolish and heroic," Anami said. "The country needs them. I want them to go on living. No *seppuku*, eh? You can help."

Arao asked what he could do. "Talk to them; tell them what I said. Help them join the police force . . ." He trailed off. Army-trained men would need work, and the occupation would need men to maintain order—and become the nucleus of the next Japanese army. As Anami continued, Arao realized that the War Minister was talking in the past tense. On the way out, Anami picked up a box of cigars from his desk and, before he wrapped it in a sheet of newspaper, took out two. "I'd like you to have these, Arao," he said. "I'll be seeing you." They disappeared separately into the night.

At the Premier's residence the rescript lay on the conference table awaiting the signatures of the Cabinet. A new inkstone and brush lay beside the sheets. Until ministers returned to sign, the Foreign Ministry could not send either its note to Bern and Stockholm formalizing the end or a follow-up message on the modalities of surrender. At 9:30 Anami was one of the first to return. At the Foreign Ministry, Vice Minister Matsumoto had his draft to the four warring powers ready:

> With reference to the Japanese Government's note of August 10 regarding their acceptance of the provisions of the Potsdam Declaration and the reply of the Governments of the United States, Great Britain, the Soviet Union, and China sent by American Secretary of State Byrnes under the date of August 11, the Japanese Government have the honor to communicate to the Governments of the four powers as follows:
> 1. His Majesty the Emperor has issued an Imperial Rescript regarding Japan's acceptance of the provisions of the Potsdam Declaration.
> 2. His Majesty the Emperor is prepared to authorize and ensure the signature by his government and the Imperial General Headquarters of the necessary terms for carrying out the provisions of the Potsdam Declaration. His Majesty is also prepared to issue his commands to all the military, naval, and air authorities of Japan and all the forces

under their control wherever located to cease active operations, to surrender arms and to issue such other orders as
may be required by the Supreme Commander of the Allied
Forces for the execution of the above-mentioned terms.

Each action depended upon an immediately preceding action,
but as far as the ultras were concerned, no command was valid if
they could convince key people that the Emperor had been coerced
into acting against the interest of the sacred national polity. Only a
few hours remained before even that strategy became moot. To iso-
late the palace, Major Hatanaka and Lieutenant Colonel Shiizaki
went out into the night to locate Colonel Toyojirō Haga, commander
of the Second Regiment of the Imperial Guards. The Emperor, they
urged Haga, had to be protected from the "traitors" who had persuaded him to act against Japan's interests. If the army rose against
the dishonorable minority, the Japanese would either overwhelm the
enemy or die gloriously in the effort.

When Haga remained unconvinced, the two plotters volunteered their big secret—the generals were for it, from the Minister of
War down to the Colonel's own division commander. Haga found it
odd that he had to find out about the turn in events in such a conspiratorial fashion, but seemed ready to join the coup. Yet Hatanaka and
Shiizaki realized that to make good on their impulsive invention,
they still had to convince General Mori, from whom Haga took his
orders. They left to arrange that.

By then Information Bureau chief Shimomura had left for the
palace to oversee the imperial recording. Officials were exhausted
from the heat and the tension and the endless day, but for Shimomura it had hardly begun. And he and his secretary, Nobumasa
Kawamoto, had the additional problem of deciding what to wear in
the imperial presence. They chose *kokuminfuku*, the austerity national
male work uniform, a khaki shirt and trousers with puttees wrapped
around the calves, and an army cap without insignia. Shimomura
pinned on his civilian decorations, and the two went off in a sputter-
ing police car to the palace. While they moved slowly through the
darkness the Director's secretary took comfort in the annual August
meteor shower dotting the Tokyo sky. Soon only such reassuring natural phenomena would be crossing the skies.

As the Emperor left his temporary apartments in the *Gobunko* for
the Imperial Household Ministry, where, in the *Goseimu* Room, he

was to record his broadcast, an air raid warning sounded. Although he preferred to chance the palace grounds anyway, Chamberlain Sukemasa Irie urged him into the bomb shelter beneath the *Gobunko*. They waited while American planes were spreading across the Japanese skies from south to north. It was already eleven, and at the Premier's residence the straggling in of signatories to the rescript was still going on. Transportation Minister Naoto Kobiyama would be the last to brush in his name, making the agreement to surrender official. As Ministers were rising to leave, Anami walked over to Togo, bowed, and thanked him for the language in which the note on the modalities of surrender was couched. Concessions that Anami had insisted upon and that would have delayed ending the war had been requested, from self-disarmament to limitations on occupation. Togo was willing to ask for honorable remedies but not to demand them. "I owe an apology," Anami continued, "for some of the things I may have said in the heat of argument." Togo returned a fifteen-degree bow.

White-gloved and dressed again complete to sword, Anami looked into Suzuki's private office next to the conference room, the newspaper-wrapped box of cigars in hand. Again he offered apologies for strong words, and Suzuki, twenty-one years older, put his hand on the stocky Anami's shoulder in fatherly fashion and explained that he understood that only patriotism had motivated the Minister's stubbornness. "Set your mind at rest. The Emperor is safe."

After some words of agreement that Japan would recover and prosper, Anami handed Suzuki the package. "They're cigars from the southern front, and since I don't smoke, I think the Premier should make use of them." He saluted, turned, and left without a further word.

Chief Cabinet Secretary Sakomizu saw Anami off and then returned to Suzuki's desk. He had something to say but Suzuki got the words out first: "I think the War Minister came to say goodbye."

Bright lights were unusual in frugal wartime Japan, but in the curtained room where Hirohito was to read his rescript, garish extra illumination had been arranged to prevent his faltering on any of the words. Although the air raid alert was still in force, a telephoned report was that B-29s were ranging north of Tokyo, bombing Kumagaya. Moving within the palace grounds was deemed safe, and functionaries bowed deeply as he entered. The Emperor positioned himself at a microphone in the center of the *Goseimu*, asking, "How loudly should I speak?"

Shimomura suggested that ordinary tones would be best, and Hirohito began:

TO OUR GOOD AND LOYAL SUBJECTS:

After pondering deeply the general trends of the world and the actual conditions obtaining in Our Empire today, We have decided to effect a settlement of the present situation by resorting to an extraordinary measure.

We have ordered our Government to communicate to the Governments of the United States, Great Britain, China and the Soviet Union that Our Empire accepts the provisions of their Joint Declaration.

To strive for the common prosperity and happiness of all nations as well as the security and well-being of Our subjects is the solemn obligation which has been handed down by Our Imperial Ancestors and which lies close to Our heart.

Indeed, We declared war on America and Britain out of Our sincere desire to ensure Japan's self-preservation and the stabilization of East Asia, it being far from Our thought either to infringe upon the sovereignty of other nations or to embark upon territorial aggrandizement.

But now the war has lasted for nearly four years. Despite the best that has been done by everyone—the gallant fighting of the military and naval forces, the diligence and assiduity of Our servants of the State, and the devoted service of Our one hundred million people—the war situation has developed not necessarily to Japan's advantage, while the general trends of the world have all turned against her interest.

Moreover, the enemy has begun to employ a new and most cruel bomb, the power of which to do damage is indeed incalculable, taking the toll of many innocent lives. Should We continue to fight, not only would it result in an ultimate collapse and obliteration of the Japanese nation, but also it would lead to the total extinction of human civilization.

Such being the case, how are We to save the millions of Our subjects, or to atone Ourselves before the hallowed spirits of Our Imperial Ancestors? This is the reason why We have ordered the acceptance of the provisions of the Joint Declaration of the Powers.

We cannot but express the deepest sense of regret to Our Allied nations of East Asia, who have consistently cooperated with the Empire towards the emancipation of East Asia.

The thought of those officers and men as well as others who have fallen in the fields of battle, those who died at their posts of duty, or those who met with untimely death and all their bereaved families, pains Our heart night and day.

The welfare of the wounded and the war-sufferers, and of those who have lost their homes and livelihood, are the objects of Our profound solicitude.

The hardships and sufferings to which Our nation is to be subjected hereafter will be certainly great. We are keenly aware of the inmost feelings of all of you, Our subjects. However, it is according to the dictates of time and fate that We have resolved to pave the way for a grand peace for all the generations to come by enduring the unendurable and suffering what is insufferable.

Having been able to safeguard and maintain the structure of the Imperial State, We are always with you, Our good and loyal subjects, relying upon your sincerity and integrity.

Beware most strictly of any outbursts of emotion which may engender needless complications, or any fraternal contention and strife which may create confusion, lead you astray and cause you to lose the confidence of the world.

Let the entire nation continue as one family from generation to generation, ever firm in its faith in the imperishability of its sacred land, and mindful of its heavy burden of responsibility and of the long road before it.

Unite your total strength, to be devoted to construction for the future. Cultivate the ways of rectitude, foster nobility of spirit, and work with resolution—so that you may enhance the innate glory of the Imperial State and keep pace with the progress of the world.

"Was it all right?" he asked.

The NHK engineer confessed that a few words "were not entirely clear," and Hirohito offered to make another attempt—that his voice may have been pitched too low. The second time he was more tense, and his voice too high. He even missed a word. But hearing the humiliating concession twice was quite enough for the others, many of whom were in tears at the end. "I am quite willing to make a third," the Emperor volunteered.

Shimomura intervened. In the imperial presence it was bad manners to discuss the qualities of each recording. It would be too great an ordeal for the Emperor to record the rescript a third time, Shimomura said. One or the other would do. Everyone bowed deeply as Hirohito left for the *Gobunko*—and sleep. It was already past midnight on the fifteenth, nearly noon on the fourteenth in Washington, where Truman and Byrnes still awaited some word. Nearly a hundred hours had passed since their own message had been sent to Japan.

At 11:48 P.M.—only 10:48 A.M. Eastern War Time—the Foreign Ministry began sending a series of long coded messages to Bern, then to Stockholm.

As one date melted into another in Tokyo, Hatanaka, Shiizaki, and their fellow die-hard Masatake Ida pondered how to turn General Mori to their side. Without control of the palace there could be no coup. "We may have to kill," said Hatanaka, frustrated by the failure of persuasion. "We'll kill if there's no other way to give the country what it needs. I think you had better make up your mind to that. Isn't Japan worth a death or two?"

Without access to vehicles, the three, pedaling worn bicycles, went off in the darkness to confront Mori. Before long one of Lieutenant Colonel Ida's tires flattened, delaying the insurrection further.

In the Household Ministry, NHK technicians had checked the recordings and chosen the first as the superior disk. After some discussions about how and where to store both sets until playback, Motohike Kakei of the Ministry asked two chamberlains to put them in a secure place. They concealed both in cotton uniform bags in a safe belonging to the Empress's retinue.

At the official residence of the War Minister in Miyakezaka, near the palace, General Anami was drinking sake to prepare himself for *seppuku*. His brother-in-law, sitting with him through the night, had opted out of the coup and was waiting out the hours until Anami had achieved the tranquility created by the warmed rice wine and his desire not to live out the night. He showed Takeshita a poem:

> *After tasting the profound benevolence*
> *of the Emperor,*
> *I have no words to speak.*

Another sheet of heavy paper had three additional lines:

> For my supreme crime,
> I beg forgiveness
> through the Act of Death.

Anami had dated both "The night of August 14th, 1945." He had technically overstayed his time, he admitted, but "the broadcast of the Emperor's recording will be made at noon tomorrow—I could not bear to hear it."

It was about four when Takeshita was called out to an anteroom to see Captain Uehara. He claimed that the coup was succeeding. "Did General Mori agree?" Takeshita asked.

"Actually no," said Uehara, growing excited in a way that frightened Takeshita. "He didn't. That's why Major Hatanaka had to kill him. . . . Everything is going beautifully!"

Uehara wanted to know whether there was any news of Anami, to whom Takeshita had been sent hours earlier to convert to the coup. "Not yet," he said. He knew that the insurrection had no chance now, and felt some guilt about its imminent failure. But he had promised to stay with Anami in case he needed a coup de grace.

Because secrecy seemed vital to conspirators, none of the attempts at insurrection under way in the Tokyo area were coordinated with each other, yet rumors of mutiny were so pervasive that the NHK technicians had not ventured to carry the rescript recordings back through the dark Tokyo streets to their studios. One of the plots was that of Mitsuo Fuchida's hothead friend at the Atsugi naval air base. Captain Yasuna Kozono commanded the 302nd Air Corps, whose officers he summoned to proclaim his refusal to call the war over: "Surrender is not only against our traditions; it is against our law. Japan *cannot* surrender! Are you with me?" There were shouts of *"Banzai!"*—but from the noncom pilots and crews rather than the officers. Still, the new *Raiden* fighter flew from Atsugi, and Kozono intended to take over the base and oppose the occupiers.

Knowing nothing of what was going on at Atsugi, nearby was Yokohama Guards captain Takeo Sasaki, who thought he controlled a battalion and intended to follow the formula of "two two-six" and murder the Premier. But he had no willing officers, and grimly set out to find some men.

The Hatanaka plot was the most serious of the conspiracies. Yet his support was eroding. A key to his mutiny was Anami's brother-in-law, but Takeshita had been unable to enlist Anami, and with the rescript recorded and the surrender approved by the Cabinet, prospects seemed bleak. "Isn't it better," Takeshita had pleaded even before leaving for the War Minister's residence, "to take the point of view that everything has ended? We've failed to win over the four most important officers in the Army—"

Hatanaka had dismissed the impasse with a fanatic's confidence. His most solid ally, Lieutenant Colonel Ida, was on his way to win over Mori even if it took force. No one in the officer corps in Tokyo seemed to be sleeping that night, and Ida and his companion, Lieutenant Colonel Shiizaki, found the general in his tiny, sweltering Imperial Guards office. After fifteen minutes of futile talk—Mori would not disobey an imperial command—the interview seemed over, but they had not counted upon Hatanaka, who turned up late, and with a new disciple, Air Corps Academy captain Shigetaro Uehara. Sweaty and disheveled after a hectic ride to Guards' headquarters, they brusquely dismissed Ida and Shiizaki to have it out with Mori themselves. Predictably, again he said *no*. Hatanaka drew a pistol, and Mori's earlier visitor, still at his side in the office, raised an arm in defense. Lieutenant Colonel Michinori Shiraishi, the general's brother-in-law and a survivor of Hiroshima, had evaded the Bomb, but Uehara swung at him with a sword as Hatanaka shot Mori dead. Crazed by the blood spurting from the decapitated Shiraishi, Uehara plunged his dripping blade into the prone body of Mori.

Snapping eerily to attention, the murderers saluted the butchered corpses, put away their weapons, and seized gory advantage of their opportunity. They had come with a document for Mori to sign, prepared by Major Koga and Major Ishihara, "Imperial Guards Division Strategic Order No. 584." Dated two o'clock, it called for the Guards to occupy the palace and the NHK building, and for the severing of communication between the palace and the outside. Hatanaka rifled the dead man's desk for his seal, then affixed it to copies of the forged order. Couriers were instructed to deliver them to appropriate commanders for action. Then Hatanaka and Shiizaki, who a few minutes before had been pedaling dilapidated bicycles, drove off in Mori's staff car flying the colors of the First Imperial Guards. Their destination was Colonel Haga's regimental headquarters. Reluctant earlier, Haga could not help now believing that he had legitimate instructions to quarantine the palace.

Koga's next objective was General Tanaka's Eastern District Army, charged with the defense of Tokyo. Telephoning hysterically that Mori's Guards had risen against the surrender and wanted the Eastern Army to join, he aroused the suspicions of the duty officer, Lieutenant Colonel Hiroshi Fuha, who alerted the unsleeping General Tanaka, then conferring with his chief of staff, Major General Tatsuhiko Takashima. Tanaka assumed a drunk, and put no credence in the call. They knew Mori.

Tanaka had just returned to his own office when Ida and Mori's aide, Colonel Kazuo Mizutani, was at the door with the news of Mori's murder. Hysterical, Mizutani collapsed. Ida struggled shakenly to justify the killing as a positive act. If the Eastern Army acted with the Guards, he explained, the imperial system would be preserved. They had only until noon. Ida no longer believed in the coup himself, but was trapped in his own rhetoric.

Stalling him, Takashima explained that he could do nothing without the approval of General Tanaka. If Ida would wait . . .

By two, the Imperial Guards had already been acting on their faked orders. The palace police were being disarmed, the telephone lines cut, the grounds surrounded, and persons trying to enter or leave arrested. In one small Guards hut NHK personnel found themselves cooped up with Shimomura and his secretary. No news was emerging from the palace, but even under blackout conditions—the raid alert was still on—the city's newspapers were preparing morning editions. They had the news of the rescript, which could not be printed before noon, but they could publish the announcement of the Emperor's forthcoming speech and other guarded bulletins that implied the war was over. But they also had Hatanaka's proclamation, prominently displaying Mori's seal, that the Army had rejected the traitorous government that had persuaded the Emperor to terminate the war. The *Asahi* was cautiously preparing two front pages, one to discard when confirmation of either version of reality came.

Tanaka wanted to go directly to the palace and find out what was happening, but Takashima reminded him of the fate of Mori. It was already clear that Hatanaka had control of the Guards. The hothead major was after the recording, and was sending soldiers hunting through the palace for it. He and Koga personally questioned the NHK prisoners, but the radio personnel knew little more than that the recording had not left the labyrinthine buildings of the Imperial Household Ministry. The Household Minister himself was hidden in an underground room, and soon Kido would be concealed by chamberlains.

Puzzled by his release by unsympathetic Eastern Army commanders, who expected that he would report to other mutineers that the game was up, Ida was in the palace grounds before four o'clock. "There isn't a chance," he warned Hatanaka. "The Eastern Army is absolutely opposed to us. If you occupy the Palace any longer, you'll find yourself fighting a battle against the entire Eastern Army." Hatanaka laughed. He had the palace, he said, and he had hostages. But the Eastern Army was preparing orders under Tanaka's signature to go to every Guards unit messengers could reach:

1. The Commander of the First Imperial Guards Division has been killed by insubordinate officers.
2. The First Imperial Guards Division will until further orders be under the direct command of the Commander of the Eastern District Army.
3. The First Imperial Guards Division orders issued as of today's date are false. They are herewith cancelled.
4. All troops surrounding the Imperial Palace are ordered to disperse.

In the Household Ministry, frustrated by the inaccessibility of the recording, Guards soldiers were making a shambles of each tiny, look-alike room. In still another reverse, the once-credulous Colonel Haga of Mori's Second Infantry Regiment was having doubts. Hatanaka had told him that the War Minister was on his way to the palace to ask the Emperor to reverse his decision. That had been three hours earlier. Anami had not come. The sky was beginning to lighten. Hatanaka offered to "telephone" Anami to find out whether he had left, but Koga sensed that Haga could no longer be fooled by patent falsities. "General Mori is dead," he confessed. "The Colonel must take command of the Guards Division."

"How did he die?" Haga asked. No answer came. When he found out, Koga realized, it would be all over.

In Yokohama, none of Captain Sasaki's four company commanders was willing to disobey orders and journey into Tokyo to assassinate Japanese elder statesmen. Furiously, Sasaki went off into the night to find hotheads on his own. By four he had dragooned thirty soldiers, five students, and two boys from the Youth Corps, all headed on National Highway 2 in a car and a truck toward Tokyo. They had pistols, swords, and two light machine guns, and intended to assassinate Premier Suzuki. They raked the front of the house with machine gun fire while the inhabitants fled out the back. Then Sasaki poured some heavy oil on the carpet in the front corridor, which first failed to light and then flamed up. A frightened guard at the gate whispered that Suzuki was really at his private residence, to which the self-styled *kamikazes* rushed while a telephone call alerting Suzuki got him out the back door to his car in the alleyway. The car failed to start—possibly because of the inferior gasoline then available—and policemen had to push it until the engine turned over. Sasaki arrived and burned the house down. Then he had to decide on another victim, and at a few minutes before seven fired the house of Baron Hiranuma. "He would like to deliver our sacred country into the hands of the enemy!" Sasaki shouted. Only the garage survived, but Hiranuma was safely in the country. Then the frustrated saviors of their country turned back toward Yokohama.

At 4:30, as Sasaki's heroes were beginning their work, guards at the residence of Marquis Kido in Akasaka were attacked by seven men from a radical element of the *Kempeitai*. A guard was wounded but they were driven off. Kido was in the palace, hiding from still another group of self-anointed patriots.

The next coup visitor to Anami—it was now close to five—was Lieutenant Colonel Ida, who seemed to be everywhere in central Tokyo in his beflagged and appropriated staff car. A noncom on guard outside the official residence stopped him. No one could go in, he confided, because the War Minister was preparing to kill himself. Takeshita, however, had heard the car idling loudly in the street and came out to explain why Anami would be unavailable for the coup. Since Ida could see the general through the window, deep in a corridor, naked from the waist up and kneeling on mats for the ritual act, Takeshita, his sobriety sapped by sake, led the visitor in for a farewell, and Anami, knowing nothing of the palace takeover or Mori's murder, asked cheerfully what Ida thought of *seppuku*.

"I think it is a glorious thing to do," said Ida. Then he added, choking on his tears, "I'll follow you."

The idea angered Anami, who saw no need for Ida's suicide. Ida, however, did, his ardor for insurrection having already died. "You must do your best to help rebuild Japan," Anami urged, and asked Takeshita to pour all three more sake.

"If you drink too much," Takeshita appealed to Anami, "your hand might slip, you might not succeed in killing yourself." Anami told him not to worry. And when Ida left, the Minister asked for his uniform and decorations, which he pinned to it and folded before him, and a photograph of his second son, Koreakira, who had died at twenty-one during the China Incident. It would be after six, kneeling alone, before he plunged in the knife. When Takeshita felt it safe to return he found Anami bleeding and unconscious but still kneeling. He took the dagger that lay at Anami's side and thrust it into his brother-in-law's neck. The body fell. Takeshita had made his contribution to the war.*

At Studio 2 in the Japan Broadcasting Corporation building, just before five, Morio Tateno was sorting papers for the hourly news. NHK was on the air around the clock. At nearly the same time in the early morning hours 1,346 days earlier, he had broadcast to a jubilant nation the first reports from Pearl Harbor. Looking up from his papers he saw, waving a pistol, a wild-eyed officer with a major's insignia, followed by a second lieutenant and two soldiers. Kenji Hatanaka was about to take over the five o'clock news. With the defection of Colonel Haga's troops and the likely arrival of General Tanaka's other battalions at first light, Hatanaka knew he would lose the palace, but an appeal to the Army and the people by radio might stir national resistance to surrender.

Tateno refused, even at gunpoint, to turn his microphone over to Hatanaka. The air raid warning was still in effect, he explained; they could not broadcast at all without a go-ahead from Eastern Army headquarters. In another part of the studio Hatanaka saw someone sit down at a mike, possibly the actual broadcaster. Moving over to intimidate Tateno's associate, he was interrupted by a telephone call. Someone at NHK had informed General Tanaka's offices, and now a staff officer at Eastern Army wanted to speak to Hatanaka. As the radio personnel listened, Hatanaka opened with a harangue that the surrender be cancelled and the war continue; after he heard the Eastern Army's responses he began reducing his demands to five minutes of radio time.

Apparently that irreducible minimum was also refused, for

*A contradictory story is that Tanaka sent a surgeon to put the unconscious Anami out with an injection.

Hatanaka sighed, "Very well, it can't be helped." Putting down the receiver and swaying with fatigue, he turned to the other soldiers and added, "We've done everything we could. Let's go!" While he had been arguing his case, NHK technicians had disconnected the building from the transmission tower, and Hatanaka must have learned that the manifesto to the nation he had demanded would go nowhere.

While everything was going wrong for Hatanaka at NHK, General Tanaka arrived with an overwhelming force at Guards Division headquarters to demand personally that the false "Order No. 584" be rescinded. There Major Ishihara, ostensibly Mori's deputy, was placed under arrest. In the already hot morning sun, Tanaka's troops swarmed about the palace entrances, and from the Inui Gate the general himself telephoned Haga to meet him forthwith. The *Gobunko*, in which the Emperor was still asleep, had been barred and shuttered by chamberlains, who knew nothing yet of the coup's reverses. But with the hour approaching seven, it seemed time to approach the imperial bedchamber and warn the Emperor and Empress Nagako about what was happening.

"Is it a coup d'état then?" asked Hirohito. "What actually has happened?"

Chamberlain Yasuhide Toda explained what he knew about a Guards uprising and the failed search for the recording. "I will go outside myself," said the Emperor. "Gather the men together in the garden, and I will speak to them. I will explain my decision to the Imperial Guards." He also called for various aides, and the chamberlains did not know how to explain that key officials were being held prisoner—as all of them in fact might be.

At the Inui Gate, Tanaka effectively took over the Guards Division and, as he hurried toward the *Gobunko* to inform the Emperor that all was, again, well, there occurred a scene that could have happened only in Japan. As Tanaka approached, a chamberlain, Yasuya Mitsui, came running awkwardly in kimono and clogs, and shook with anxiety as he answered the general's questions about Hirohito's whereabouts. "Why do you keep trembling?" Tanaka asked. "The revolt's over—you have nothing to worry about." And in the custom of first meetings he handed his card to Mitsui, who examined the name, drew a long breath, and extricated one of his own cards, offering it to Tanaka. They exchanged bows.

It was 7:00 P.M. on the fourteenth in Washington.

• • •

Anticipating the outcome of the anguished Cabinet session that was more a pronouncement of last rites than an exercise in polemics, the Dōmei News Agency had issued a bulletin at 2:49 P.M. Tokyo time, beamed outward only: IT IS LEARNED THAT AN IMPERIAL MESSAGE AC-CEPTING THE POTSDAM PROCLAMATION IS FORTHCOMING SOON. It caused waves of cheering in the Marianas when the flash had broken into an Armed Forces Radio Network broadcast, but it was not offered to Japanese home audiences and was followed by no confirmation, leading high brass to regard it as a ruse to head off further bombing. In Washington, where the fourteenth had barely entered the calendar, nothing but waiting remained. Orders had long been in place to bomb the hell out of the Japanese until the promised surrender happened.

General Arnold wanted a thousand planes over Japan on the fourteenth, and although official accounts vary, the action was heavy. Daylight strikes involved 449 B-29s, with all radiomen briefed to listen for the message "Break Utah Utah Utah Break," which meant that the war had ended and all planes were to return to base. The air-sea rescue stations on the "Empire" route consisted of fourteen submarines and five surface ships, twenty-one Dumbos, and nine Superdumbos—search-and-rescue B-29s. One Dumbo (according to NCR 2522) was lost in Tokyo Bay with all hands, two P-38s, one P-47, and two B-25s, all from the seven hundred additional sorties made from Okinawa. Navy planes from Eniwetok hit targets on Ponape in the Carolines and carrier planes roamed the home islands.

The B-29s firebombing Kumagaya had taken off at 6:07 P.M. on Tuesday—the first Superfort mission of Jimmy Doolittle's Eighth Air Force, transplanted (with new aircraft) from the ETO to Okinawa for "Olympic." Even after their briefing, correspondent Homer Bigart wrote, crews hoped they would not have to go up. "No one wants to die in the closing moments of a war."

The 314th Bomb Wing chaplain led the men in prayer, after which the group commander, Colonel Carl R. Storrie of Denton, Texas, exhorted, "This is the last mission. Make it the best we ever ran. We've got 'em on the one-yard line. Let's push the ball over." Switching metaphors, he went on, "This should be the final knockout blow of the war. . . ."

The plane in which Bigart rode was *City of Saco*, after the hometown in Maine of its bombardier. A few minutes before the briefing, crewmen had heard reports of Japan's acceptance of the peace terms, but the "Utah" code had not confirmed it. "Look at the sweat pour off me," said one pilot, Major William Marchesi of Brooklyn. "I've never sweated out a mission like this one." Still, everyone expected to jettison bombs and turn around. "Boy, we're going to kill a lot of fish today," said Karl L. Braley, the sergeant from Saco.

The *Saco,* piloted by Lieutenant Theodore Lamb of Queens, was hardly in the air when its radio picked up San Francisco, already— perhaps prematurely—celebrating. "I hope all you boys out there are as happy as we are this moment," the announcer bubbled. "People are yelling and screaming, and [harbor] whistles are blowing."

"Yeah," said a crewman. "They're screaming and we're flying." 'Frisco, a sailor's mecca, would have a boisterous three-day blowout.

"We caught every news broadcast," Bigart wrote, "listening to hours of intolerable rot in the hope that the announcer would break in with the news that would send us home." None came, nor did any come to the other eighty-one Superforts on the way to firebomb Isesaki, just to the north of Kumagawa. Crews saw feeble AA-fire and groping searchlights, but no enemy aircraft. There were no bombs left for the fish.

En route from Okinawa, Eighth Air Force planes came within ten miles of Tokyo, delaying the Emperor's recording of his rescript, and Saburo Sakai claimed in his memoirs that from the Oppama air base he had gone up in his Zero after the Americans, led into the air, because of his own poor night vision, by Jiro Kawachi. Still, he and Kawachi claimed a final kill, a B-29 forced to ditch off Ō Shima, east of Tokyo Bay. His account is dramatic, but it was dark, and he had only one eye. Yet it was true that the Japanese had not ceased fighting. In Buckner Bay, Okinawa, a cargo ship was hit by the last successful *Baka* bomb. The war wasn't over yet. Not nearly, as Admirals McCain and Halsey at 4:11 A.M. Japan time ordered new carrier strikes. Two hours later, Halsey received an order from Nimitz suspending further operations. At 6:35 McCain recalled his second strike, already in the air, and ordered all bombs jettisoned over the open sea. The first strike was already over Tokorozawa Airfield—six Hellcats from the *Yorktown.* Air Group 302 at Atsugi had no reason to hoard their best aircraft further in underground hangars. Four *Raidens* and eight Zeros went up after the Americans, shooting down four F6Fs. Americans claimed nine of the enemy in a wild encounter as meaningful as Andrew Jackson's Battle of New Orleans in 1815— fought, although he didn't know it, *after* the peace treaty had been signed across the Atlantic in Ghent.

The fliers who had gone up from Oppama with Sakai returned to the wrath of the commandant. "I suppose I can't blame you," he said, "but we can't have any repetition of what occurred tonight. From this moment on, all planes are grounded." And he told them of "wild riots" at Atsugi, where Captain Kozono had stirred up pilots, if not their senior officers. "Men who could not accept the idea of a surrender . . . tried to get their planes into the air. They lost their heads and defied the officers, swearing that they would fight until their last breath. Reinforcements were moved in. . . ."

For the second time American troops were being told to cease offensive operations but, as in Nimitz's orders, to "continue searches and patrols" and to "maintain defensive and internal security measures at the highest level and beware of treachery." No one knew whether, as at Atsugi, there would be organized attempts to keep fighting, or whether there would be further *kamikaze* actions. The Japanese had secreted a lot of hardware for *Ketsu*. All of it would be dangerous until placed under control.

To the west of the home islands the fighting went on as the outgunned Japanese frantically defended themselves against the Red Army, which showed no intentions of stopping the war until Soviet gains were ensured. The Russians were also demonstrating little desire to coordinate actions with the United States, however much in Moscow they had toasted Eisenhower and Allied friendship. The Pacific Fleet, for example, reported to Washington on the fourteenth, nearly a week into Soviet intervention, "We still have no Russian-U.S. recognition signals." Now that it was almost too late to matter, B-29s were permitted to ferry equipment to Khabarovsk, just above the northeast edge of Manchuria, to set up a weather station run by the Russians as they had insisted upon at Potsdam.

On the afternoon of the fourteenth, General Otozō Yamada, commander of the quasi-autonomous Kwantung Army, learned by radio that an announcement from Tokyo at noon the next day would very likely end the war. He had returned to the nearly abandoned capital, Hsinking, from which he ordered troops to fall back to defend the border with Korea. Even that border was already porous, as the Russians had made amphibious landings below it the previous day, and armored columns had already virtually cut off Yamada's Fourth Army in the north. The Russians were taking vast numbers of prisoners, many of them unable to retreat because refugees clogged every road and pass, many maddened by hunger, fright, and sleeplessness.

The Lotus Sutra followers, returned to Halahei on the thirteenth bedraggled and weary, found their settlement already looted by bandits. Some buildings were afire. After struggling to a nearby hamlet to sleep, they gathered the next morning before their own ravaged temple for mass suicide. They had washed their clothes in order to arrive in the beyond in suitable condition, and as they intoned prayers in which the many repetitions were to put them in a properly hypnotic state for collective death, a young man posted as sentry on the hillside came running to report that close by, near Hsingan, the Japanese and Russians were battling each other.

The news broke the spell. Some hope might be left. To set out again they had to reassemble, and as leaders went to find everyone, they discovered suicides accomplished or in progress under individual roofs, and the intoning of the monotonous *Daimoku* preparatory to death. One aged man emerged and asked to be left alone. "We've had enough walking backwards and forwards across Manchuria. Why should we die in the middle of some barren desert? If we are going to die, it may as well be in the house we have known. Please leave without us!"

Fleeing settlers trudged in increasing panic as hunger and heat maddened them. The elderly and ill were abandoned; children died. The pathetic remnants comforted themselves as they struggled on from day into darkness in endless recitations of the *Daimoku*.

The insanity that overtook desperate refugees and equally desperate troops in the shimmering heat of Manchuria as they tried to evade the legendary barbarian invaders was evoked nearly a decade later in Kobo Abe's surreal story, "Record of a Transformation." The narrator, a Japanese soldier abandoned on the fourteenth because he is dying of cholera, is shot by an officer retreating with others in a truck. All are desperate men, all going mad, all destined to die. They have killed the cholera sufferers so the unit will survive. "Our mission," declares a crazed colonel, "is to cross into the mountains, hole up, and fight to the last. Ten thousand soldiers hand-picked from every unit will rendezvous there. Even if the homeland falls, we are to go on fighting: the Empire is always with us, wherever our feet tread the earth!"

The dead all walk together, observing the madness of the retreat. There are more and more of them, including a Japanese general who, pushing aside the waves of tall, dry grasses, sees a child nearby whose body he inhabits in order to steal a new life. But the child, too, is dying of cholera. And the stolen Empire is dying, little more, now, than a wraith. Like the general.

With the only factor slowing down the Soviet overrunning of Manchuria its vastness, the outcome was never in doubt. Four massive field armies were spreading across former Manchukuo. The Red Army was also in Korea, and had begun moving into southern Sakhalin, threatening the home island of Hokkaido, just to the south. To try to save the occupation army in Korea from massacre, the Japanese approached Un-hyong Yo to ask him to form a Korean peacekeeping administration. Their wooing of Chin-u Song had, earlier, failed. As the night of the fourteenth faded into the fifteenth, Yo met with Ruysaku Endō, the Secretary for Political Affairs under the Governor-General. Like so many others marooned in the Empire, Endō was desperate. "Japan is now defeated," he confessed. "It will be announced today or tomorrow. At this time we must keep the peace. From now on, the preservation of our lives depends on this."

   Yo placed conditions on his acceptance. All political prisoners had to be released immediately. Food for the population had to be guaranteed for the next three months. No interference was to be made with independence movements or parties, or with the training of students, workers, and farmers. The Japanese feared the demonstrativeness of Korean students, who seemed always in eruption or about to erupt, and hoped that Yo could rein them in. But the Russians, Endō predicted, would shortly occupy all of Korea, and he saw a "somewhat radical" and anti-Western facade for the caretaker government as its most prudent strategy. Washington had similar concerns, but no way yet to get near Korea.

In occupied China the soldiers of the puppet Chinese Army began melting away for their own safety, but the Japanese had nowhere to go. From Nanking, General Okamura fired off a new protest to the War Ministry at 8:25 P.M. that was full of poetic hyperbole about Japan's fighting possibilities. The people had already been "transformed into a bullet of flame . . . advancing along the road which leads to the destruction of an arrogant enemy." The Army in the empire had "a strength of seven million men," all of them confident that they would "find life in the midst of death"—a cliché of the ultras.

The empire was still "shining in all its glory," which made it "humiliating" and "absolutely impossible" for the China Expeditionary Force to submit to the Potsdam terms. "At this fateful moment of our Empire's history," he appealed, "our innermost thoughts must reach out to the Emperor to be heard, and we offer our respectful prayer that he will proclaim an Imperial Rescript to prosecute the war to a final conclusion."

By the time the telegram reached Umezu's office at midnight the rescript had not only been approved and signed but recorded for broadcast. By then, even Okamura's own headquarters city was slipping away from him. Clandestine listeners to Allied radio broadcasts were many, and word-of-mouth rapid. Eager to seize control before Mao's forces did, Chiang's agents were spreading reports of imminent surrender, and a large banner had already appeared outside the Central Chupei Bank: LONG LIVE GENERALISSIMO CHIANG KAISHEK! Supporters of the puppet regime were defecting to Chungking; self-styled claimants to Chiang's favor were already openly exacting contributions from Nanking banks that would never reach the Chinese government.

The same day, a Sino-Soviet Treaty of Friendship and Alliance was signed across the world in Moscow. For concessions in Manchuria, especially the inclusion of Dairen in the Soviet military zone in exchange for a promise not to exert military authority there during peacetime, Stalin agreed to recognize the Chungking government in an ambiguous way as the legitimate authority in China. T. V. Soong, who negotiated the agreement, justified it to the skeptical Averell Harriman as in the end "a matter of faith." For Russia it was a paper transaction to validate agreements made at Yalta and Potsdam.

Briefings had begun in mid-afternoon for the air raids that few crews in the Marianas wanted. Missions that had been cancelled on Friday, Saturday, and Sunday as Washington waited were rescheduled, including a raid on the Hikari Arsenal, southeast of Kure. The 793rd Bomb Squadron history recalled, "It was a hard thing to send crews out thinking that peace would come momentarily.... Some wanted to wait and not endanger another life; others wanted to drop a few more persuaders, while others said we shouldn't even let the bastards surrender. Our planes took off."

In Hiroshima, Dr. Michihiko Hachiya could hear "the noisy clamor of planes" from his hospital in the Hakushima district. Ambulatory patients rushed to shelter. It was "a helpless feeling," he noted, to be able to do nothing for the bedridden, but the planes over Kure stayed south of Hiroshima Bay and they listened with fear, but safely, to the distant sounds of bombs and answering fire. How awkward it was, he observed, to worry about death when one's life "has once before been miraculously spared." A visitor from the Prefectural Office told him that "an important radio broadcast had been announced for tomorrow. Everyone was urged to listen, so we could guess that an announcement of tremendous importance was in the offing."

Each bomber wing aloft expected a radio code message to abort the mission. The 331st stopped listening for a recall signal once past Iwo Jima. The 315th, on the same mission, to the Nippon Oil Company refinery at Tsuchizaki, far north on Honshu, was on the runway on Guam when a jeep drove up and an officer signaled to cut engines. "Admiral Nimitz," he called out, "says the war is over." Minutes later another jeep arrived and the driver yelled, "Get going! [General] LeMay hasn't received word that the war is over!"

The mission of the 315th would be the longest combat flight of the war, 3,470 miles from Guam and return. Sitting in the lead plane with the Wing Commander, Brigadier General Frank Armstrong, Major Bill Leasure was gunning the engines of the *Fluffy Fuz III* when radioed orders again put the takeoff on hold. The war might be over. They idled on the airstrip until 4:47 and then took off—143 aircraft from several wings, with a thousand tons of 100-pound and 250-pound bombs, a curious load that caused flight histories thereafter to add a correction that very likely the bombs were 1,000-pounders and a zero had been omitted. Yet the mission was as peculiar as its bomb loads: 100-pounders that had to be loaded into the bays by hand. Was the Air Force trying to get rid of surplus ordnance? The crews didn't know, but they did know that each Superfort would use up 6,785 gallons of aviation fuel in the process.

Delayed in takeoff because of "word that Japan had sent acceptance note to Swiss," Hays Gamble's plane was not airborne from Guam until 5:15: "Expected at any moment to be called back and . . . was on continual watch on radio."

Eight hours into the seventeen-hour flight the *Fluffy Fuz* radio picked up the news that Washington had announced that the war was over, but received no "Utah" signal. "Did you hear anything?" Armstrong asked.

"Hell, I didn't hear anything," said Leasure. And the flight con-

tinued to the target, in a traffic jam of B-29s that left pilots looking
into the exhaust stacks of the preceding plane's engines—hazardous
running lights often only fifty feet above or below. Colonel Boyd
Hubbard, Jr., ordered his own planes to turn on their landing lights
to keep them from running into each other—perhaps the only combat
mission flown with landing lights. But combat was a misnomer. No
one was firing at them.

At "Bombs Away!" from eleven thousand feet each pilot pulled
up, climbing another thousand feet, though not high enough to
evade the hot cloud of smoke and debris that the first payloads had
created. Gamble took his B-29 to fifteen thousand feet to avoid "severe thermal currents" after going through "cinders and burning em-
bers" over the "seething mass of flames." The mission had been
effective—if its job had been to empty warehouses on Guam of small
bombs. As for the refinery, which Japan needed in the transition to
peace, production had been down to 4 percent of capacity before the
strike. It was now down to zero.

As the planes turned back toward Guam, crews spotted a late-
comer. Captain Don Trask's aptly named *The Uninvited*, forty-three
minutes late because of a malfunction, roared by, following the fire
and smoke to Tsuchizaki. At 3:39 A.M. on the fifteenth, Tokyo time,
Trask dropped the last bombs of the war on Japan. "Sort of evens up
score for Pearl Harbor," Gamble noted in his diary.

In the southern remnants of the empire—Java, Malaya, and Thailand—POWs learned of imminent surrender from clandestine radios
and comments by Japanese and Korean guards. In Thailand, prisoners
could see villagers on the other side of the wire raise fingers with the
"V" sign, and Weary Dunlop jotted in his diary, "Hope is rising in my
head, but who knows to the last minute what will be decided in
Japan?" He quietly contacted his "100 emergency men" to plan protection for POWs and essential stores: "We are working on the basis of
doing our best to enforce discipline upon the camp at a time when
exuberance, or failure to maintain coordination and order, could be
fatal." In every camp senior officers were working on similar contingencies. The captors could become vindictive and violent, courteous
and turncoat—or merely melt away and leave debilitated prisoners to
the mercy of local bandits, rebels, and others with their own agendas.

Allied concern over the thousands of prisoners still at the sadistic mercies of the Japanese in Southeast Asia had resulted in the for-

mation of intelligence teams to be airdropped into Malaya, Thailand, and the Dutch Indies for contact with the captors immediately upon surrender. The missions were hazardous, but Mountbatten's staff left no doubts about the urgency to reach the debilitated and dying Australians, New Zealanders, British, and Dutch in dozens of camps as distant as Sumatra and Java. One group dropped early in August was led by an Afrikaner major, Gideon Jacobs of the Royal Marines, with two Australian radiomen, a Dutch sergeant, Albert Plesman, and a Chinese-speaking native of Java known only as Tjoeng. In north-central Sumatra, near Medan, they waited for the evening when, tuned to Radio India, they heard of the atomic bombs and the surrender of Japan. The next morning, according to plan, they were to raft down the river until they came to civilization, then try to reach Japanese headquarters in Medan and assess the condition of prisoners and prison camps in Sumatra. There were eighty thousand undefeated enemy troops on the 1,100-mile-long island flanking Malaya and Singapore; all over the Indies in dozens if not hundreds of POW camps, more than a hundred thousand prisoners, male and female, had moldered in stark confinement since early in 1942. In one of the most fertile agricultural areas in the world they were—given the notorious Japanese abuse of captives—undoubtedly starving.

On the evening of the fourteenth in Moulmein, Ba Maw called the ministers of the puppet Burmese government to his house and read to them a letter from the Japanese ambassador—a title that in the Greater East Asia Co-Prosperity Sphere suggested less than the ambassador's proconsular role. Suddenly the *Adipati* was on the verge of becoming a real head of state. The letter reported the atomic bombs, the Russian intervention, and the intention of Japan to surrender. His news, the ambassador advised, had to be kept confidential until the troops were informed. U Nu thought sadly of the thirty resistance leaders whom the Japanese had executed only ten days earlier—and then of his wife, who had been too jumpy to be able to eat or sleep since the air attack by the British on Ba Maw's house. He rushed to his house and whispered to her, "Ma Mya Yi, the Japanese have surrendered. The war is over." He explained that she was to tell no one. "She was thrilled with delight. But it was not because the war was over; it was because this was the first time I had ever told her a political secret."

In Washington the morning of the fourteenth had begun with reports to Truman that the Japanese reply was "in the mill"—on the way. "When I saw the President at midday on Tuesday morning," Sir Michael Wright, Head of Chancery at the British embassy, reported to London, "he was a very worried man, pinned down in his office at the White House by a mob of news-hungry journalists parked on a twenty-four-hour vigil in the anteroom. He had just received a report that the messages intercepted from Japan did not contain the expected reply, and he sorrowfully remarked that another atomic bomb now seemed the only way to hasten the end."

Given the chaos and delays in Tokyo it took until mid-afternoon Washington time before the actual message for which Truman had been waiting was received in Bern. Minister Kase had to decipher it and take it to the Swiss authorities, who then had to call in the American Minister, Leland Harrison, to receive it. Secretary Byrnes could not wait, and kept Harrison's office on the telephone. At 4:05 Byrnes learned that the surrender text was in transit, and he telephoned Bevin in London and ambassadors Harriman and Hurley in Moscow and Chungking to arrange simultaneous announcements at 7:00 P.M. Washington time. It was just past midnight in Moscow. Eisenhower had been visiting as the guest of Marshal Zhukov, and at a glittering formal dinner two evenings before, Stalin had asked "Ike" what he would like as a remembrance of Russia. Eisenhower thought a diplomatic moment and suggested a portrait of Stalin. The Generalissimo would not forget it. Now, on Eisenhower's last night in Moscow, Ambassador Harriman, his host at a farewell reception, was called away to the telephone. When he returned it was with the dramatic news that the Japanese had surrendered.

Outside the White House, reporters and onlookers eager to glimpse a moment of history gathered waiting, crowds growing larger as the afternoon waned. Finally, at 6:10 Max Grassli formally delivered the Swiss note that—but for stopping the actual shooting— concluded the war. An Imperial Rescript had been issued, and the Emperor was "prepared to authorize and ensure the signature by his Government and the Imperial General Headquarters of the necessary terms for carrying out the provisions of the Potsdam declaration."

It was, Byrnes remembered in his memoirs, "the longest wait I have ever experienced." The end might have come sooner but the messenger rushing the text from the RCA offices on Connecticut Avenue to the Swiss Legation, sixteen-year-old Thomas Jones, had been stopped by Washington police for making a U-turn.

Calls were put through to the service chiefs to come to the White

House for the announcement, and Admiral King set aside a message from Nimitz about holding fire. He called instead for his flag secretary, Neil Dietrich. "Sit down, Neil," he said, invoking a first name, which he seldom did. "I have to go to the White House soon. The President is going to announce the Japanese surrender. . . . Well, it's all over. I wonder what I'm going to do tomorrow."

"If you think you had problems during the war," said Dietrich, "it's nothing compared to the problems you're going to have trying to hold everything together now that the war is over."

Among the people called to the White House was Cordell Hull, who had been Secretary of State on December 7, 1941, and had received the Japanese envoys as the bombs were falling on Pearl Harbor. Elderly and ailing, Hull was slow in getting to 1600 Pennsylvania Avenue, impeded, too, by the crush of cars and people clogging the streets behind ineffective police barriers near Lafayette Square. At seven o'clock, as Truman stood behind his desk to make the announcement, with Bess nearby and members of the Cabinet and the JCS behind him and journalists jammed everywhere, Hull had not yet arrived, but the President had to go on. Klieg lights for the newsreel cameras brightened. Truman, in double-breasted blue suit and striped tie, read from a prepared statement that closed with the text of the Japanese note:

> I have received this afternoon a message from the Japanese Government. . . . I deem this a full acceptance of the Potsdam Declaration which specifies the unconditional surrender of Japan. In the reply there is no qualification. . . . The proclamation of V-J Day must wait upon the formal signing of the surrender terms by Japan.

As reporters rushed for the door, cameramen came forward and Truman made room for Cordell Hull—for a picture with Leahy, Byrnes, and the President. Hull had been there at the beginning, and now the end.

With Bess, Truman went out to the fountain on the north lawn and, to cheers of the swelling crowd, made a Churchillian "V" gesture. Then he went in again to telephone Grandview, Missouri. Martha Ellen Truman, his mother, had to be among the first to know. "Yes, I'm all right," she said. She knew all about it. "I've been listening to the radio."

"That was Harry," she told a houseguest. "Harry's a wonderful man. . . . I knew he'd call. . . ."

By then White House personnel were setting up loudspeakers on the lawn so that the President could be heard over the din of auto horns and the surging crowds who had begun chanting "We want Truman! We want Truman!" Streetcars and automobiles unable to move became perches for more people, some, conspicuously in their white garb, sailors. His call to his mother over, Truman went to the microphone on the White House portico and told the crowd, "This is a great day, the day we've been waiting for. This is the day we've been looking for since December 7, 1941. This is the day for free governments in the world. This is the day that fascism and police government ceases in the world." He knew better, especially after Potsdam, but this was a moment for idealism and hope. "We will need the help of all you," he concluded. "And I know we will get it." Another reach, he knew, for idealism and hope. Truman was a constant reader of history, and, besides, an adult and returning veteran in 1919 when Americans had begun an earlier retreat from world responsibilities.

Moving closer to the high iron fence that kept the throng from the White House lawn, Truman waved and drew more shouts of approval, then went inside to an evening of work.

In London, Prime Minister Attlee broadcast at midnight. "Here at home," he said, "you have earned a short rest from the unceasing exertions which you all have borne without flinching or complaint for so many years." And he ushered in two official days of holiday as ships in the Thames began to hoot and country bonfires, long prepared, began to blaze. Pubs, already closed, remained dark.

In Moscow, Stalin's announcement came in early morning darkness, and celebrations were muted even the next day. The Russians had no intention, yet, to call a cease-fire in their war. The Red Army still had territory to seize. But in Paris, where the ETO edition of *Stars and Stripes* was printed, the army staff prepared an extra headlined in "Second Coming" type, **PEACE**. It would be distributed free.

In the United States, despite the impromptu jubilation the previous Sunday evening, people were eager to celebrate the real thing— "You hugged and kissed total strangers," a straitlaced family man put it—but some of the enthusiasm may have been artifice. The much-photographed conga line of servicemen and civilians in Lafayette Park, published in newspapers the next day, seemed similar to what a later generation would have called a "photo opportunity" encouraged by cameramen.

The announcement that the next two days would be considered national holidays did nothing to disguise the foreboding that for many there would be more holidays as layoffs from war work began. There would even be delayed bad news, beginning the same day with the Navy's announcement that the *Indianapolis* had been sunk, late in the previous month, with "every man aboard" lost. All 1,196 had been "lost"—by the Navy. The erroneous report failed to note the survivors.

In the Hudson and East rivers flanking Manhattan, tugs and ships let loose with whistles and horns, and the cacophony spread through New York and across the nation. New York's noise was the loudest only because among American cities it was the largest. Wealthy recluse Arthur Inman wrote in his diary from a tall apartment building that the cheering in the United States was out of proportion. "No more Americans were killed ... than were killed on either side in the Civil War. It was more an outpouring of men, money, production, energy, natural resources than it was a concentrated business of getting killed." He resented the length more than the magnitude of the celebration, as it had begun early enough not to have continued into his sleeping hours. "People yelled. Automobile horns blew. Toy horns screeched. Firecrackers popped. Planes zoomed. Fire engines screamed. Kids in the alleys upset garbage cans and broke bottles. And always automobile horns blew frantically. It was very hot and very humid. Four o'clock found me wide awake."

In Philadelphia, a sixteen-year-old who had managed to push through the crowds the previous Sunday only to see the flickering bulbs on the *Evening Bulletin*'s newsboard flash a disclaimer to JAPAN ACCEPTS SURRENDER TERMS OF ALLIES, rushed up Broad Street again with his friends. The City Hall area was again packed with happy people. The white hats of sailors from the Navy Yard were everywhere. The men of the fleet seemed unable to keep their caps or to fend off the hordes of embraceable—or at least willing—females of every age and shape.

The teenagers waded in, mostly unsuccessfully. "Get lost, kid!" said a painted lady reaching past him for a sailor. "This ain't no kid's war!"

The streets were impassable for trolleys. Stanley Weintraub walked home to wait for the next war.

•   •   •

Three time zones away, an Okinawa casualty who had been left for dead, but then retrieved and put back together on Saipan, was asleep in the Balboa Park naval hospital in San Diego when church bells ringing across the city awakened him, even though among his more minor injuries were two ruptured eardrums. A nurse in starched white came running, and William Manchester asked what was happening. "The war's over! The Japs have surrendered," she explained.

"Thank you," he said.

In Los Alamos, only two time zones from Washington, bells clanged, sirens whined, and the ubiquitous automobile horns blared—possibly among them one in Klaus Fuchs's old Buick—and George Kistiakowsky set off a pile of leftover explosives near the Alamogordo blast site. But where the two bombs designed at Los Alamos had broken the militarist spell and forced the imperial hand, morning had come and the unspecified broadcast to which the nation was directed to listen was only a few hours away. The long day through which Truman had waited in Washington had been an agonizing night in Tokyo, and the agony was not yet over.

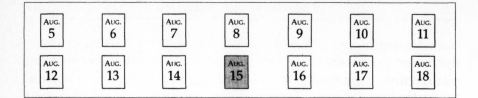

## CHAPTER XXXIV

# · AUGUST 15,1945 ·

### *The Voice of the Crane*

At 7:21 A.M., thirty-nine minutes before President Truman's announcement from the White House, where it was still Tuesday evening, Morio Tateno went on the air from NHK, which had resumed broadcasting, with a special announcement. "His Imperial Majesty the Emperor," Tateno read, "has issued a Rescript. It will be broadcast at noon today. Let us all respectfully listen to the voice of the Emperor. Let us all listen to the voice of the Emperor at noon today."

Since electric power barely existed in most of Japan he added, "Power will be specially transmitted to those districts where it is not usually available during daylight hours. Receivers should be prepared and ready at all railroad stations, postal departments, and offices both government and private." And, twice more, he repeated the time, which had already appeared in some morning newspapers. Despite hints of surrender from government sources for nearly a week, many expected the rescript to be an exhortation to fight to the death.

Press releases prepared while Major Hatanaka held the Imperial Palace hostage had not identified the august speaker. In the confusion, Hatanaka and Shiizaki had disappeared. Still without sleep, they were producing a protest pamphlet that implied a continuing insurrection. Expecting to resist arrest, each looked forward eagerly to martyrdom. Received in audience by the Emperor at 8:10, Grand Chamberlain Hisanori Fujita found him wan and exhausted as if he had gone without sleep, still confused by what had happened during the night. "Why couldn't they"—the ultras—"understand what was in my mind?" he asked. Fujita could not tell him that "they" did. But the important fact was that the Emperor's recordings had survived, and NHK was prepared to broadcast the Emperor's voice. One record was stamped "ORIGINAL" and the other "COPY." Each had been brought separately to the NHK studios.* NHK's domestic power, reduced on August 1 to ten kilowatts, was increased to sixty—still feeble for reaching throughout the home islands.

At Premier Suzuki's official residence, its entrance burned but the rest habitable, Suzuki's son and secretary, Hajime, prepared a draft of a resignation letter to be submitted after the broadcast. One more formality remained—the Privy Council's rubber-stamping of the rescript. At 11:20, in the underground conference room of the *Gobunko*, used for the last time in war, the Emperor sat impassively as Baron Hiranuma read the Imperial Message recognizing that the Council should have considered the question of accepting the Allied terms before the enemy powers had been notified, but "pressed for time," the government had accepted the presence of the Council president as the equivalent. Holding the message, rolled up like a scroll, high above his head, Hiranuma made a deep bow to the Emperor. The other Councillors rose and bowed, accepting the extralegal procedure; then they sat waiting for the broadcast to begin. Chamberlain Yoshihiro Tokugawa had brought in an old RCA portable radio and checked its reception. In a special chair in an anteroom the Emperor would listen to his own voice.

With pride in his own role in concealing the recording from the ultras, Tokugawa would brush a verse,

> *While frantically trying to abort the rebellion,*
> *I greeted the dawn with the naval attaché.*

As the Privy Council gathered, Major Hidemasa Koga slipped into the headquarters of the Guards Division, where General Mori's

---

*The call letters of the Tokyo station were JOAK.

body now lay in state. In his own Guards uniform, Koga had no difficulty mingling with other mourners. Insurrection had turned sour.
By supporting it he had contributed to the murder of his commanding officer, whom he had admired. Koga knelt at the open wooden
coffin, pointed a pistol at his chest, and joined Mori in death.

Left as harmless fanatics to be dealt with later, Hatanaka, riding a
motorcycle, and Shiizaki, astride a horse, were seen in the hour before
the broadcast handing leaflets to the faithful gathering before the
palace. They proclaimed their intention to protect the Emperor and the
sacred *Kokutai,* and "pray[ed] that the Japanese people and the members of the Armed Forces will appreciate the significance of our actions
and join with us to fight for the preservation of our country and the
elimination of the traitors around the Emperor, thus confounding the
schemes of the enemy." No one seemed to want the leaflets, and they
had to press them on people wary of being seen with them.

They reached the swath of green in front of the palace, between
the Double Bridge Gate and the Sakashita Gate, just before noon. The
sun was high and hot. There, employing the pistol with which he had
murdered Mori, Major Hatanaka put a bullet into his own forehead.
Lieutenant Colonel Shiizaki followed by plunging a sword into his
abdomen, then allegedly giving himself his own coup de grace with a
bullet to the head.

At noon, traffic halted all over Japan. Awaiting the Emperor,
people gathered about radios, public and private. In Morio Kita's *The
House of Nire,* Tetsukichi Nire rinses his mouth, washes his hands,
and changes into traditional *haori* and *hakama.* Admonished to do the
same, Ryuku responds, "I don't have a single kimono left." As others
in the novel, returning from the fields, bustle with excitement, Jiemon
tells her children morosely, "I guess it'll be the one-hundred-million
sacrifice at last."

"When we hear His Majesty's voice," Iku acknowledges, "then
I'm sure we'll all be ready to die at any time."

In Miyagi prefecture, north of Sendai, where Naokata Sasaki's sixth
grade class from the Asakusa district of Tokyo had been evacuated,
students were awakened as usual for 6:00 A.M. calisthenics. Summer
or winter, girls and boys alike stripped to the waist and shouted
rhythmically in time to the exercises: "Annihilate America and England! One-two-three-four! Annihilate America and England! One-
two-three-four!" Then they tended their mountainside pumpkin

patch before returning to listen to the Emperor. But the sacred words were lost in static and even the teachers could not understand the message. The next morning the exercise chant was no different.

Where the broadcast came through, many knelt before their radios until NHK announcer Nobutaka Wada followed the noonday tone with "His Imperial Majesty has graciously agreed to broadcast to us. Let us listen with reverence. All listeners will please rise." While "Kimigayo," the national anthem, played, able-bodied citizens across the home islands stood at attention, awaiting the Emperor's "To my good and loyal subjects. . . ."

Shigeo Hatanaka—no kin to the maniacal major—was not permitted to listen to a radio. Arrested by the Special Higher Police—the *Kempeitai*'s "thought police"—in January 1944, he had been languishing in prison for violating the Peace Preservation Law as editor of *Chuo Koron*, the house magazine of the publishers of that name. He had printed articles, it was charged, opposing the emperor system and supporting Communism. Under torture he had confessed to whatever fictions had been composed for him, although *Chuo Koron* had published its share of required propaganda, including political caricatures as biased as their equivalents in the Western press. A guard had confided to him a few days earlier, "I don't like it. I don't like it. I can't stand it! Unconditional surrender?" Hatanaka was prepared when on the afternoon of the fifteenth a janitor told him, "Japan's like this!"—and he held up both hands to symbolize surrender. Suddenly Hatanaka's rations increased and he was permitted a bath with other convicts, including Karoku Hosokawa, a journalist arrested under the same statute in September 1942. They were afraid to say to each other "Japan has lost." But both knew.

The imperial voice was high and difficult to follow over the buzz and crackle of static, especially in areas remote from Tokyo. Even the strengthened signal was too weak to carry clearly. Evacuated to a highland village, Tennessee-born Gwen Terasaki, whose husband, Hidenari, had been press secretary at the embassy in Washington when the war began, understood without making out the words. The Terasakis had known it was all but over when the contents of the American leaflets about the Bomb were passed by word of mouth after the leaflets were dutifully turned over to the police. "Japan is beaten already," Terasaki told his wife. "Russia has only come in for the kill: the Four Horsemen will ride across the night." Now "Terry" sobbed, "It is over; no more bloodshed at last, at last. My poor country!"

Evacuated to a farm, Yoko Matsuoka, who had spent seven years at school in Ohio and Pennsylvania while her father was a journalist on assignment in the United States and was now married to a newsman for Dōmei, listened in tears. Although her father had spoken happily of breaking "the yoke of white imperialism," she had realized from the first day that her country had embarked upon a war it could not win. Feeling no humiliation, she blamed emotional letdown after years of tension and privation: "I just stood there, as if all my bones had become disjointed." A neighboring farmer broke the silence. "Would it be unpatriotic," he asked, "if we continue fighting against the will of the *Tenno*?" The idea dismayed her.

Ryosaku Sato, a housewife, listened with a group that "sank into silence and didn't say a word" after the *Tenno* finished. She felt "dazed, exasperated, resentful, relieved, anxious for the future"—probably the sequence of feeling of most Japanese civilians. At one end of the spectrum were emotional holdouts whose responses ranged from "Japan cannot be defeated!" or "It's a filthy lie!" to "I'll kill my wife and children, then commit suicide!" Some authority figures shifted blame, as did a schoolmaster who chastised his class after the broadcast: "It's your fault. Did you work as hard as you could for the nation? Didn't you forget it was a war ordered by the Emperor?" At the other extreme were the hopeful, who saw "shining promise for the future," or the patriotically patient, who saw victory as only postponed: "Endure this and let's bide our time for the sake of the Empire."

Young people accepted the surrender more easily. Ichiro Hatano, yet another evacuee, wrote in his diary, "It was the Emperor's decision; his wisdom is great! Once again I marvel at his power, and his kindness toward his people." Yet Hatano was at once exhilarated and despondent: "There is a rumor that, since Japan has lost, all the young men will be drafted into agriculture and the girls will be sold to the enemy as prostitutes." He was bewildered about how much truth there could be in such fears, but the reality was that his family could return to their suburb west of Tokyo: "The war has ended before we all are dead and we are going back to the house at Suwa." For Yukio Mishima, who was older, "It meant that fearful days were beginning," that "whether I would or no, and despite everything that had deceived me into believing such a day would never come to pass, the very next day I must begin life as an ordinary

member of society." Determining his own future was the most frightening prospect of all, more disconcerting than death.*

For eleven-year-old Wakana Wada in Numazu, an industrial city
west of Tokyo but quiet since a fire raid on July 16, the neighbors
flocking into her family's unscathed house made the already
crowded living spaces more stifling. But the Wadas had a radio. They
also had relatives from burned-out homes camping with them, one
family to a room. Of the few who could understand the Emperor's
high-pitched voice, one was her father, who "wiped away tears with
his fist and groaned loudly." But he had wept for the nation, not for
his son Minoru, a *kaiten*, who no one yet knew had died in a harbor
accident at Hikari on July 25. A telegram arrived a month later announcing his "public death." The family assumed suicide in the aftermath of defeat, but their lamentation would end with the truth and
turn into mere misery.

In Hiroshima, a city of lamentation, Dr. Michihiko Hachiya concluded that the broadcast would announce "an enemy invasion on
our shores . . . [and] order us to fight to the bitter end." He wondered
about the best escape route into the hills although he knew that fleeing would be futile. The local communications bureau had set up a
radio in a large room, already crowded when Hachiya arrived. Over
the hum and crackle he caught an indistinct voice and a phrase that
sounded like "bear the unbearable." The official standing closest to
the radio switched it off at the close and announced for those who
understood few of the words, "The broadcast was in the Emperor's
voice, and he has just said that we've lost the war. Until further notice
I want you to go about your duties."

The recommendation stunned Hachiya almost as much as his realization that the Emperor himself had read the proclamation of surrender. "My psychic apparatus stopped working, and my tear glands
stopped, too." For a while the throng lingered in silence; then people
melted away. He returned to the hospital and resumed his patient
status by retreating to bed, but uneasy there, he got up to make

*Fourteen years later, in *The Temple of the Golden Pavilion*, Mishima would create the tale of a young
acolyte of a Buddhist temple in Kyoto, a national treasure since the fourteenth century, who de-
stroys the *Kinkaku-ji* by fire because he is so obsessed by its beauty. By no coincidence, the act of ar-
son by which Mizoguchi severs his dependence upon the object that has him in thrall occurs on the
last night of the war. (The incident upon which the novel was based actually happened in 1950.) Between the lines, the golden temple may be Mishima's symbol for the *Kokutai*, beautiful in concept although holding the people in emotional bondage, and now sacrificed to a new if not better Japan.

rounds, largely to calm the new fears. "The Emperor has so ordered," he kept repeating. Then Hachiya slipped outside, sat on a ventilator shaft, and gazed over the ruins.

Less resigned to Hirohito's unwillingness to intervene until catastrophe had come, Tatsuichiro Akizaki composed a bitter *tanka*,

> *While I read the Emperor's rescript that came too late,*
> *Atomic bomb victims writhe on the scorched ground.*

Dr. Takashi Nagai, in Nagasaki, rejected the news of surrender with "It's a lie!" A deliveryman unloading supplies at the university hospital confirmed the imperial order. "Some people said it was the voice of His Majesty himself. But the military people kept driving about the city in trucks, shouting that the noon broadcast was a trick of the enemy and we shouldn't believe it. They said we would fight to the end—even on our own soil. Several people who said the war was over were beaten up by the young men standing nearby."

That night Nagai dreamed of defending himself with a bamboo spear against a ticking atomic bomb. The spear would not penetrate the bomb, and it bent—and he seized spear after spear, each of which bent and broke as he made desperate thrusts. "My breathing becomes painful; sweat breaks out all over my body. The bomb will certainly explode. I'm trembling with fear. The rumbling sound has begun. Now the awful flash of light! The rays are striking my face." Nagai screamed, and his chief nurse appeared. "You have a fever," she said, placing her hand on his forehead and wiping the perspiration away.

Later, novelist Kensaburo Ōe would combine images of the broadcast and the Bomb into a surreal end-of-war story, "The Day He Himself Shall Wipe My Tears Away" (1972). On August 15, 1945, he is a ten-year-old on remote Shikoku, where his sake-sodden father and his followers listen to the rescript, read by a divine voice turned human, on a radio "capable of producing a noise no bigger than the whining of a mosquito." Enough of a voice "work[s] its way through the static" to leave them shaken by the humiliation of defeat, and the elder Ōe leads his son and a band of army deserters out of the valley in a vain attempt to reverse the surrender.

The quixotic incident is transmuted into ironic magical realism as, on their march from the mountain village, they sing in German the refrain of a Bach cantata they had learned from a record the night before. His father, until then uncommunicative with the boy, explains that *"da wischt mir die Tranen mein Heiland selbst ab. . . . Komm, O Tod, du Schlafes Bruder"* ("then the Savior himself wipes my tears away. . . . Come, O Death, you Brother of Sleep") means that the Emperor himself in his demigod state will wipe away their tears "with his own hand."

The men are aspiring *kamikazes*, ready to bomb the Imperial Palace if they can to save the Emperor, and in Ōe's paradoxically exalted prose, his father is shot down, and the living god who is His Majesty consecrates the death and the insurrection in a mystical transfiguration that outdoes the possibilities of mere plutonium. "A gold chrysanthemum flower 675,000 miles square, surrounded by, yes, a purple aurora, high enough in the sky to cover entirely the islands of Japan" rises like a mushroom cloud from the explosion, "even managing to increase the glittering radiance of the sun in the blue, midsummer sky. . . ."

Later, the boy's mother explains the absurdity of the affair and one is unsure whether the father is dead, in jail, or in a less romantic state, and instead of a divine emperor wiping away the narrator's tears, it is his mother's "scratchy thumbs that expertly wipe away the tears in the corners of his closed eyes." The mythical descent of the god, by radio, into mortal guise, and the *Götterdämmerung* of the Bomb, are reduced to very human disappointment.

While the Japanese had no atomic bomb, they did have stores of poison gas, and it was at a gas installation in Chiba that Yoshimi Nakajima was lined up to hear the rescript read. "I fainted. A couple of people carried me off. It made me really sad. We worked to win without rest." Across Tokyo Bay at Combined Fleet Headquarters, Admiral Jisaburo Ozawa called in his senior officers, one of whom was Mitsuo Fuchida. "We fought the war," Ozawa said, "according to the will of the Emperor. I have killed, and been injured, following the Imperial policy. Now I will accept surrender in the same spirit of loyalty. We must carry out the surrender in good faith and to the letter. We must withhold nothing—not one sword, not one gun. . . ."

It was very different nearby at Atsugi, where Captain Kozono's patriotic hysteria was heightened by sake and then by a feverish recurrence of malaria. Surrender, Kozono shouted, was "not the will of the Emperor!"—and he ordered planes up to litter the Kanto area with tens of thousands of leaflets urging a general uprising and "thorough resistance" to America. A message from Admiral Yonai at the Navy Ministry led to a wild reply from Kozono breaking off relations with the defeatist Ministry. From a sickbed he declared Atsugi's independent war against alleged "Red demons." Claiming to represent the Emperor, he sent hothead pilots to other bases with bundles of leaflets exhorting: "Stand against the surrender! Continue the fight!" A few units seemed willing, including Army squadrons at Sayama and Kodama, in central Honshu.

At the naval air station at Hiro, near Kure, the reaction paralleled the one at Atsugi. Corporal Kuwahara, now a *kamikaze* pilot without a mission, stood with officers and men "as mute as stones." Through the static they picked out enough to realize that they were being commanded to surrender. "I looked at the stricken faces, watched the expressions alter. Suddenly a cry went up. . . ." Purpose for living had vanished. "Are we women?" one cried. "Let us strike this very moment—before it is too late! We are expendable!"

Men sprang toward their planes and would have taken off to nowhere had the commander not intervened, but once he left and men returned to barracks, at least two pilots slipped out, took off, and determinedly crashed their planes. A wave of suicides followed, some by placing pistols in mouths and squeezing the triggers. Other pilots cut their throats or, more traditionally, their bellies. A few hanged themselves. Several took off with leaflets exhorting: "Continue the war! Don't surrender!" Some leaflets fell on Hiroshima, twenty-five miles to the north.

Admiral Matome Ugaki could make out little of the broadcast— "but I could guess most of it," he wrote in the last entry in his diary. ". . . I've never been so ashamed of myself. Alas!" He had been awake all night awaiting the inevitable, and talked openly of suicide. Ordering five "Judy" bombers readied, he had his chief of staff write out an order: "The Oita Unit of the 701st Flying Corps will attack enemy warships in Okinawa with five carrier dive-bombers. I shall lead the attack myself." Ugaki signed it, drank a farewell cup of sake with his staff, and added a last line to his diary—that it "must never be placed in enemy hands."

Ugaki had his badge of rank cut from his uniform before he climbed aboard. "Although our commander is going to launch a special attack by himself," Lieutenant Tatsuo Nakatsuru shouted above the roaring of the motors, "we can't stand by and see only five planes dispatched. My unit is going to accompany him with full strength!"

To ensure that for each man it was a voluntary decision, Ugaki asked to see hands raised, and when all twenty-two crewmen complied, he thanked them. With the volunteers the five two-man *Suesei* bombers became eleven, their warming engines whipping the dry summer grass. Boarding Nakatsuru's plane, Ugaki asked Warrant Officer Endo for his seat. Refusing to leave, Endo squeezed down between the admiral's legs. As they taxied down the strip, Ugaki waved his most precious possession, a dagger that had belonged to Admiral Yamamoto. By five the entire unit was airborne, but three planes soon returned with mechanical problems. The last heard from the remaining eight was Ugaki's message at 7:24 P.M.: "We have succeeded in making a surprise attack." Yet none reached Okinawa or crashed into anything but the sea.

Among the papers Ugaki left was a last note,

*Having a dream,*
*I will go up into the sky.*

Admiral Onishi's legacy was 5,350 *kamikaze* planes still ready for use, along with 12,000 other aircraft of all types for general purpose— or suicide—defense. An obsolete fighter or slow trainer was as good as any other plane as an instant *kamikaze*. Fuel for all of them for *Ketsu-Go* was stored underground all over Japan. The capability remained to inflict grievous casualties, although not nearly enough to win an invasion battle, let alone the war.

In the Imperial Palace plaza, near the bypassed bodies of Major Hatanaka and Lieutenant Colonel Shiizaki, weeping citizens were still prostrate in grief, foreheads to the ground. Their numbers had multiplied following the reading of the rescript. Sculptor-poet Kōtarō Takamura, living obscurely in Hanamaki, far to the north of Tokyo, since his studio had been incinerated by the fire raids,

*. . . heard that broadcast.*
*Sitting upright, I was trembling.*
*Japan was stripped bare,*
*the people's heart fell, down to the bottom.*

On radio, Dōmei explained that the desolate crowds at the Double Bridge outside the palace were bowed in "shame" that their wartime efforts were "not enough." And Dōmei went on, "How shall the hundred million people, filled with trepidation, reply to the Emperor? His Majesty's subjects are moved to tears by His Majesty's boundless and infinite solicitude." The language still evoked the demigod, but as Takamura was writing in his "End of the War," the burden of that belief had been lifted, although not yet recognizably so, by the broadcast, as

> . . . the Emperor stepped forward
> and explained that he was not a living god.

General Eichelberger, who had been listening from Manila, wryly observed, "The Emperor's statement to his people sounds like he's just a good-hearted fellow who had been trying to bring peace to the world." And, in fact, nothing in the rescript had mentioned surrender.

While Ugaki had radioed a farewell message from his *Suesei* that ended loyally with "Long live the Emperor!" the events had overwhelmed his Navy Ministry colleague in Tokyo, Takijiro Onishi. The Emperor had betrayed him, and unlike the people prostrate at the double-arched *Niju-Bashi*, Onishi could weep only for the *kamikazes* he had sent up to die for a failed ideal. He brushed a farewell message "to the spirits of the departed special-attack pilots," who had offered their lives "in the firm belief that we would win the final victory." Since their sacrifice had come to nothing, he closed, "I apologize to your spirits and to your bereaved families with my own death." That night he slit his abdomen in the manner of General Anami.

Although the American press had speculated that Premier Suzuki might atone for the surrender with his life, he had been chosen for the thankless post to do exactly what he had accomplished. He offered his resignation to Hirohito effective on a replacement likely to be acceptable to the occupiers. Tokyo radio quoted him as saying that the war was "lost by the enemy's use of the new-type bomb," but he knew better. The Bomb had created the conditions to end a war already well lost at the time he had taken office, but it had also been a useful excuse to help accept surrender, much like the *Dolchstoss*—"stab in the back"—fantasy in 1918 supported the claim that Imperial Germany had lost because the home front had failed the Kaiser's forces. "With an uncheckable flow of tears," he declared, "we face the situation. The defense of the national polity is our duty now. . . ."

That afternoon, after conferring with Baron Hiranuma of the Privy Council, Marquis Kido recommended that Prince Higashikuni become Premier. Hirohito's uncle (by marriage to Toshiko, Emperor Meiji's youngest daughter), he was the first member of the royal family to head a Cabinet in the sixty-year history of the institution, and the appointment demonstrated to the people that the imperial system still functioned. Further, the War Ministry trusted him. He had the reputation of being a militarist and a nationalist, yet, as royalty, might seem safe to the victors. Two days later he would formally succeed Suzuki, who was relieved to step down.

Although Tokyo avoided using *surrender* at home, it had no choice in dealing with military units and satellite governments. "Magic 1238" picked up instructions to handle imperial portraits carefully, to protect the lives of Japanese residents abroad, to maintain essential jobs and services such as clinics and utilities, to refrain from destroying industrial machinery that had civilian uses—and to destroy codes and cryptographic equipment. Commander Hashimoto, aboard the *I-58*, received a more laconic message: "Do not attack enemy except in self-defense." He called his officers to the bridge to tell them, but warned them not to inform the crew.

Where the Japanese installation was only a POW camp with nothing to surrender but prisoners, the hints of peace brought greater brutality or improved conditions that occurred without announcement. Laboring near Lake Biwa, Robert Haney was surprised when at eleven in the morning all prisoners were told to drop their shovels and return to camp. "The Japanese never leave a tool uncleaned, so this is really an occasion to think about. We were told to rest until 2 P.M., and at noon all the sentries but two left the camp. Some said it was for a lecture (hand opening and closing in front of the mouth); others said it was for a radio broadcast (hand cupped over the ear)." Haney knew that the work hiatus had enabled guards to hear the Emperor's surrender speech. No one told POWs that the war was over. At 3:30 they were back cleaning their tools. Only the next day, when guards left the compound and prisoners seemed to be on their own, did they realize what had happened.

At Private Jack Brady's camp at Sendai, where prisoners had been working at a steel mill, all were lined up to hear what they were told was the Emperor talking on the radio, and "some of the guys," he recalled, "picked up something about *senso*—the war—and *owari*, the end. . . . The next thing we noticed was that all the guards had gone." At Corporal Kenneth Day's camp at Toyama, prisoners had to peek out from behind a horizontal board fence to watch guards gathered around a small radio. The voice was too scratchy to make out, but "All at once the Japanese took their hats off. We could guess what that must mean. . . . They listened carefully for a few minutes, then put their hats on and went back to work. . . . They came and got us." In Nagasaki, where Corporal Harry Douthitt and his buddies knew from the reaction of Japanese soldiers that something significant had happened, a teenaged guard released the Marines from their stockade, asking as he did that they be sure to tell the Americans when they came that he had been good to them. "Some bullshit!" Douthitt exploded—but the guard failed to understand, going on to explain that it had all come about because of "one little bitty bomb." No, the POWs said, it must have been lots of bombs, but the guard insisted, "No, one little bitty bomb." Nearby at Omuta, a POW chaplain was able to borrow Captain Thomas Hewlett's Bible to lead a memorial service for their dead, the first permitted. It convinced Hewlett that the war was over. Chaplain Carel Hamel read the 90th Psalm, which included the lines,

> For all our days are passed away in thy wrath:
> we spend our years as a tale that is told.

Tom Cartwright of *The Lonesome Lady* was still isolated at a camp near Yokohama, unaware that his buddies in Hiroshima were all dead. Over the loudspeaker system, previously used only for commands, music played that seemed funereal, and he worried that the palace had been bombed and the Emperor killed. Yet he could see everyone standing in "stony silence" as they listened to a faint voice that followed the music. A somber mood prevailed; then the formerly authoritarian guards came in with some dried fish to supplement his daily rice ball, and greeted him in English: "Are you well?" "How are your parents?" "Are they old?" "We will take you to a better place and then see that you are reunited with your parents." He could scarcely believe what all the signs surely meant.

At Sergeant Frank Fujita's urban prison in Tokyo a Major Hifumi simply assembled the prisoners and told them that the war was over "for the time being." Fujita knew it was really over when Hifumi dismissed his staff and they turned to the POWs and bowed.

In one of the camps servicing the copper mines on Hokkaido,

medic James J. O'Keefe—captured in the Philippines—was told by a Japanese lieutenant, "You're our enemy, and I don't like you and never will." But he explained that the war was over and he would try to get the prisoners better food. A prisoner even longer, since the seizure of Wake Island, Sergeant Walter Bowsher was in another copper mine camp, where four other Wake survivors had escaped a few days before, two of them recaptured the day of the Emperor's announcement. The rescript saved their lives. The Japanese called off the night shift for the mines and declared a four-day holiday. From camp to camp the public admission of defeat occurred over several days, and a relaxation in discipline usually followed as commandants and underlings realized that war criminal charges could arise. At Tangsan, in Korea, the authorities released a Red Cross package to each man, and in Mukden the next day, six OSS parachutists, the first of many such teams deployed, flew in from China to effect the release of prisoners. Greeted by a Japanese MP detachment, the OSS men were blindfolded, threatened, and handled roughly until confirmation of the surrender came. After the commandant cabled Tokyo for instructions, he began transferring administration of the camp to the POWs.

Another commandant, turning over his camp at Omachi, in central Honshu, to the senior prisoner, was told by Captain Jerome McDavitt, "Captain Omura, the first thing I want for you to do is remove all the Japanese and Koreans who have been supervising my men and forcing them to work. I want them taken some place where they cannot ever be seen again by my men. Second, I want you, Captain Omura, to start bringing food into this camp, the kind and quality that I designate, including fresh meat, even if it's on a rope. . . . Next, I want you to report to me for further instructions every morning at eight o'clock until we leave this camp."

"Is that all?" said Omura in all seriousness. Then he bowed, unbuckled his sword, and handed it to McDavitt by the handle. "No, Captain Omura," said McDavitt. "I know what that sword means to you and your family, and I hereby give you another direct order. Take that sword home with you and don't ever give it to any American."

Omura withdrew the sword with tears in his eyes. It may have been the first formal surrender attempted in Japan.

The War Ministry was busy around the clock sending orders to cease hostilities and to destroy all "confidential documents." At POW camps that meant the evidences of harsh treatment and executions. From the Philippines, Okinawa, and the Marianas, American over-flights of camps began with dropped instructions—one came tied to a wrench—to paint "POW" on roofs. The note attached, like many, asked that if the group needed medicines to paint a "1" on the roof; food, a "2"; and clothes, a "3." Most roofs quickly displayed all three.

The prisoners now, all but in fact, were the Japanese troops trapped everywhere. Some, holdouts hiding in Okinawa, saw flares lofted like fireworks from shore and from ship, yellow and red and green, and hoped that the long-awaited *kamikazes* had come. Flouting orders, a few pilots bent upon suicide did take to the air, but the rate of hits was zero. Eight left the Kisarazu base in Chiba before the Emperor's broadcast and were shot down by Task Group 38.1. A *Judy* and a *Kate* diving at H.M.S. *Indefatigable* splashed down short of the ship at 11:35. At noon, Admiral Halsey raised his flag on the *Missouri* and ordered the whistle blown a full minute. Other ships followed, raising a victory cacophony repeated across the Pacific just as American celebrations the night before—which was in real time the same moment—were reaching a peak. Still, sufficient danger remained for Nimitz to radio the fleet that Japan had been warned that "approaches to ships" of any kind would be treated as hostile action.

MacArthur had already issued similar warnings as he opened communications with Tokyo. And right through to his final communiqués his cult of personality continued. On the fifteenth the *Free Philippines Daily* (distributed by his headquarters), under the bold headline JAPAN ACCEPTS, printed a story, "MacArthur's Airmen Blast 41,000 Tons of Shipping." A later extra the same day trumpeted, "IT'S OVER!" in red, the words on two separate lines divided by a black headline, MACARTHUR NAMED OCCUPATION CHIEF. The surrender news was brought to notorious Billibid Prison in Manila, where the Japanese had routinely tortured prisoners and where the former occupiers were now held. Many remained disbelieving.

Even more disbelieving were Japanese troops still fighting on Luzon who had heard neither MacArthur's announcement months earlier that the Philippines had been retaken nor the Emperor's instructions to stand down. At 10:00 A.M. Manila time, an hour earlier than Tokyo, the command post of Company A, 128th Infantry Regiment, was attacked and an American killed. A few hours later another unit in the hills of northern Luzon was assaulted. "Yeah, the war's over," said a frustrated GI. "It's all over this goddam hill."

Ready to move on the occupation, MacArthur's office radioed a first message in the clear to Japan in his name as Supreme Commander. He directed that a radio station be designated to handle communications at a specified frequency and in English text. And he gave the frequency for sending messages.

A second message in the clear ordered "the immediate cessation of hostilities" and directed "the Japanese Imperial Government to send . . . a Competent Representative empowered to receive . . . certain requirements for carrying into effect the terms of surrender." The emissary would have to come with "a document authenticated by the Emperor of Japan empowering him. . . ." Ranking officers of the Japanese army, navy, and air forces, MacArthur stipulated, were to accompany the imperial representative. In elaborate detail, the message set out time and procedure for the envoys to fly south to Ie Shima in an unarmed plane painted white with green crosses. From there they would be flown to Manila in an American plane. "In communications regarding this flight," the instructions concluded, "the code designation 'Bataan' will be employed." The directive was vintage MacArthur.

Two of the Supreme Commander's visitors on the fifteenth were colonels, Willard W. Wilson, commander of the 331st Bomb Group, and Albert T. Wilson, Jr., LeMay's communications officer. After flying a B-29 in from Guam they were cooling their heels in MacArthur's office, although authorized to see him by General George Kenney, the command's air chief. Their father, the senior Albert T. Wilson, had been a prisoner of the Japanese in Mukden almost since the fall of Bataan. MacArthur had known him since they served together in the Philippines in 1911. With a Russian-speaking lieutenant colonel, Roland K. Barnick, they wanted permission to fly to Manchuria to extricate their father. "Thus began a daily routine," Willard Wilson remembered in 1987. "We would go to MacArthur's headquarters and sit in the outside office and wait several hours, knowing that he was in. . . . His senior aide would inform the general that we were out there and why we were there, but he was always too busy to see us. . . . All we needed was about two minutes of his time." Eventually, without MacArthur's authorization, they loaded up with Red Cross supplies at Clark Field and flew off to China.

Although MacArthur was indeed busy with plans for the formal surrender and occupation, one operation rendered moot by events was formally disposed of by radiogram CCS 381/JIS 158/4/M from the Joint Logistics Plans Committee in Washington with the subject heading "Cancellation of Directive." The invasion of Kyushu was off.

In Manila, on the same date, Major General S. J. Chamberlin, Assistant Chief of Staff to the absent Richard Sutherland, issued to senior officers authorized top-secret clearance the staff study for "Coronet," for which "Y-Day" was to have been March 1, 1946. The thirty-one legal-size pages were being furnished in their "present incomplete form," Chamberlin explained, "as a matter of interest only and for completion of files of all concerned." Some of the troops scheduled for the invasion of Honshu would be going anyway—for the occupation.

In Hong Kong, where internee emotions had risen and fallen for days, a Japanese Lutheran minister, Kiyoshi Watanabe, revealed what the commandant at Stanley Camp was not yet ready to confess—that the war was ending. Finally, with the rescript public, block monitors were permitted to announce: "Ladies and Gentlemen, the war is over." At noon—an hour later than Tokyo time—the Japanese handed control of the camp to the Swiss consulate. Union Jacks, Peggy Abkhazi remembered, "blossomed suddenly from the most surprising places, including the top of the water tower." And as POWs were returning from an afternoon work detail to the wooden barracks of Shamshuipo Camp, a group of Portuguese women, safely neutral through the war, slyly raised their voices as if in conversation with each other, announcing, in English, "It's all over."

Yau Tam Shang learned of the end in the crowded Sai Kung Market and happily informed passengers on the harbor ferry. Deceived often by rumors, no one aboard believed him, but on arriving home he instructed his aged mother not to cook any more detested sweet potatoes. They could start on their rice reserve. Tai Ngau ("Big Cow") Wu, who on the first day of the war had bought all the rice he could get and advised his family, "The thieves are bound to lose sooner or later," returned from work with the happy news: "I've heard that the Japanese devils are going to surrender!" A friend who had secretly listened to the radio had told him, but did not know when it would actually happen.

"Big Cow," said a neighbor from the next flat, "at noon I saw that the flags of the Japanese devil's institutions and warships have been lowered. This should be paid attention to!" Those who had seen soldiers complete to swords and boots kneeling in front of the Gloucester Building at Des Voeux Road Central as they awaited the imperial broadcast understood, but the news was not offered in Chinese until six, followed by a warning that residents were not to be disorderly. Behind the walls of Stanley Camp its inmates, attired in "carefully hoarded respectable clothes" (according to Peggy Abkhazi's diary), held a thanksgiving service and sang the Allied national anthems, including "the old Imperial Russian one, but probably nobody knows the Internationale, which I suppose would be the correct one for the Soviet Union." Then, on the roof of E block, they danced under a moonlit night to old records on a windup phonograph, not having to be in billets at 8:30 ever again.

After dark the cautious Hong Kong Chinese celebrated behind closed doors. Food and beverage shops had long been emptied, and unobtainable alcoholic drinks materialized in bars on the island and in Kowloon. Even the firecracker sellers sold out their stocks, although not an explosion was heard. Everyone was waiting for the Japanese police to leave.

In Shanghai the narrow ghetto lanes exploded with dancing and shouting. In the suburban internee camp of Lunghua, where Jim Ballard had matured since 1941 into a street-smart fifteen, he laughed at the thought that the creaky voice of the Emperor would make any Japanese surrender, but he had also seen, a week earlier, from the scorched grass at the center of an abandoned football stadium, an eerie blink in the morning sky that might have been the distant flash of the Nagasaki bomb. When American reconnaissance planes cruised only a few hundred feet above Lunghua and the antiaircraft guns remained silent, he discovered that the guards had disappeared with the war.

At Gene Lawlis's POW camp at Sanya, on Hainan, when the guard opened cell doors and beckoned prisoners to follow, they guessed the worst and assumed they were going to be shot. Like Lawlis, many were barely ambulatory. Instead, they found themselves at a hospital with "immaculate private rooms" and hot meals. Baths and clean kimonos followed, and also Dr. Miyao, the head surgeon, who asked whether there was anything they wanted. "Please bring me lots of writing paper and a pencil or two," said Lawlis, who proceeded to put down on thin sheets of rice paper all he had been carefully remembering. He hardly needed to be told—as he was— that the war was over. Miyao explained that the end had come when the United States had dropped "automatic" bombs on Japanese cities. "Later it seemed strange to me that he omitted the great loss of Japanese life in those cities; instead, he was awed, as the guards were, by the bombs themselves—by the fact of their destructive power, and how that power had changed, overnight, the whole nature of war. He explained that the Emperor had ordered all Japanese forces to lay down their arms and that American forces would be arriving soon to take us home."

Fourteen miles from the mainland, and the largest Chinese island after Taiwan, to the north, Hainan had been occupied only since 1939. Above the home islands, the clawlike southern half of forbidding Sakhalin, a Czarist prison island until 1904, was in the process of reoccupation, the Russians having crossed the frontier at the same time as they had invaded Manchuria. In Manchuria itself, the Japanese ambassador, stranded at Talitzu with the terrified Emperor P'u Yi, broke the news to him of the surrender rescript. "The American Government," he lied, "has given guarantees for the safety and position of Your Majesty." Both plunged to their knees to thank heaven for protecting the Japanese Imperial Crown, which indeed was true, and the ambassador told P'u Yi and his brother P'u Jie, at thirty-eight a year younger and heir to the tottering Manchu throne, that they would be evacuated to Japan. The promise was empty. The Russians were closing in, and the Americans had no compensatory presence in Manchuria.

Dramatizing the dilemma of the Kwantung army in the colony the Japanese had reinvented as a state, Toyoko Yamasaki's realistic novel *The Barren Zone* (1976) finds Japanese officers unable to reconcile the command for unconditional surrender with the order, only six days earlier, to "crush the Soviets." Although their situation seems hopeless, one young officer asks, "How do we know that the Allied Powers will honor any pledge following a surrender that's unconditional?" Openly belligerent, another, representing the generation of the 1930s, argues, "Whether we win or lose the battle is of little consequence. Our duty is to fight to the last man. If Japan survives, the memory of our annihilation will be an inspiration to our people as they rebuild the country."

Breaking his silence, General Yamada in the novel asks his planner, Colonel Iki, what had undermined the position of Imperial General Headquarters to fight the final, decisive, battle on Japanese soil. Iki rises to describe the plans to defend southern Kyushu and the Kanto plain around Tokyo. "But," he adds, "the realities are different." And he goes on to describe how bombings have destroyed productive capacity and exhausted fuel reserves: "The only alternative left was for each man and each tank to fight an individual suicidal battle. . . . His Majesty said that he did not wish to see his people subjected to more misery, and he rejected the Army's request for a decisive last stand on the home islands."

First there is silence, then protests about abandoning the people of Manchukuo "to a fate no one dares to guess. You're telling us to submit to the shame of being taken captive!" Mutiny hangs in the air.

"Settle down!" shouts Chief of Staff Yuzaburo Hata. How can one preserve the nation, he challenges, by flouting the Emperor's "sacred wish"? "If you insist on continuing this war, do so. But strike off my head first. Then do what you wish."

Agreeing to surrender, Yamada says quietly, "Anyone who disobeys the Emperor becomes an outlaw or a guerrilla. . . . Whether in victory or defeat, we have one duty only—to obey the imperial wish." He orders sake and cups brought to the table for the ritual of parting, and they drink in silence. Then he commands Iki to fly to Tokyo to report that the Kwantung Army has accepted the cease-fire. But Iki finds an excuse to stay. Like many of the others, he feels guilty about surviving a lost war. Those in the novel who become Russian prisoners will later regret the missed opportunity for death.

The Southern Army, with units stretching from Rabaul to Burma, offered verbal resistance only a little longer, claiming that no explicit orders had followed the rescript, but hours later officers and men were commanded to "observe strict discipline and obey orders to the last, thus proving to the world their fidelity to the Emperor." Later orders would speak of "united obedience to the Emperor," a clear validation of the decision to retain Hirohito in the interests of orderly surrender.

In Rabaul itself, just north of New Guinea, more than a hundred thousand troops had been cut off for more than a year. Lieutenant General Isamu Tanida had received his last promotion, an empty honor, by radio. The closest strong radio signal was Sydney, but at eight-thirty on the morning of the fifteenth a communications officer handed him a slip of paper: "San Francisco broadcast: Japan Surrenders to Us—Truman." At noon his radio specialists picked up the Emperor's broadcast, and the area commander, General Kin Imamura, called in senior officers to warn that order had to be maintained and that with so many ships sunk it might take as long as four years to get all troops home. It would take only until December 1946.

There were far fewer of them than the conquerors of 1942. New Guinea and New Britain were a ghastly green grave for hundreds of thousands dead of exposure, starvation, and disease, some eaten (usually flesh from the thigh) by survivors who later went mad, some shot for desertion on returning from hopeless deserts of coral. A Japanese saying was "Burma is hell; from New Guinea no one returns alive." Tamotsu Ogawa saw two flags go up from the enemy camp in the distance—a Union Jack and the Rising Sun, and he heard cries of *"Banzai! Banzai!"* After some silence, enemy planes dropped leaflets proclaiming "Peace has come to the Orient." He was the only one of 261 in his company to survive. They had shipped out to Rabaul on New Year's Day 1943.

In Southeast Asia improvised flags went up over prisoner of war camps where emaciated POWs seized control of what remained of their destinies, and few Japanese officers had any chance of escaping back to an occupied homeland that would be safer than a vindictive former colony. The night before the Emperor's proclamation, Colonel Masanobu Tsuji, who had been instrumental in the quick seizure of Malaya in December 1941, was in Bangkok trying to figure out how, short of suicide, to evade surrender. The actual commander in Thailand, Ambassador Yamamoto, was more interested in relinquishing Japanese arms to the Thais, and securing Thai protection for himself, before the British arrived. The next morning—it was two hours earlier than in Tokyo—Tsuji stood with the rest of the headquarters staff to hear the high, halting voice of the Emperor; then he disappeared, with the help of friendly Thai politicians, in the guise of a Buddhist devotee. When a staff officer of the Thirty-third Army in North Burma, according to Allied charges, Tsuji had a captured American flier executed and had taken part in a cannibal feast in which the dead man's corpse had been consumed. Now Tsuji claimed he would go underground to await "the reconstruction of Japan," but he had other reasons to vanish.

At a camp in Bandung, in the Dutch Indies, Yoshikichi Kasayama, a Korean POW guard who had adopted a Japanese name, was surprised when his prisoners knew, from clandestine radios, about the surrender before he did and demanded food at the expense of the staff. "We had to salute them now, because they'd won," he recalled. "We had to do it." When he went to Japan for the first time, it was to Sugamo Prison as a war criminal. One POW group went "house hunting" for better quarters and took over, to Japanese protests, one of their hospitals, with real beds and mattresses and pillows. Weak and emaciated as they were, they chanced telling the "Nips" to go to hell and saw them give way. The Sixteenth Army commander on Java, General Nagano, could not make out the actual words of the imperial voice as it disintegrated into the buzz of atmospherics, but he and his staff choked back sobs of grief and understood that the rising and dying broadcast sounds meant surrender. Conceding independence to Sukarno's nationalists seemed now a mixed blessing to some Indonesian revolutionaries, who looked on it as tarnished recognition. Rather than be seen as Japanese puppets, they preferred the appearance of seizing power, and planned riots to begin in Djakarta at midnight.

In Indochina, Field Marshal Terauchi listened to the Emperor in the hill station radio room of Dōmei Tsushin, which pulled in the best shortwave signals locally. He closed his eyes and let the tears fall. His aides worried about suicide, and concealed all likely instruments from Terauchi, but he had no intention of doing anything other than to return to Saigon and fulfill "the Imperial will." In what was left of Japanese Burma, Lieutenant General Shōzō Sakurai arrived at the headquarters of the 53rd Division at Shanywa, in the panhandle, where soldiers had rigged up a wooden archway painted with SAKU KANGEI—"Welcome 28th Army." There wasn't much left of the army, but he accepted a telegram of congratulations from Terauchi and put it in his pocket. A few hours later he heard of the surrender. The costly breakout from the jungle had come to nothing.

For the British forces, orders from the absent Mountbatten's headquarters were to "suspend offensive operations forthwith insofar as is consistent with safety. . . . You will accept all surrenders. . . ." It would be a week before there were any to take.

At a vast staging area near Marseilles, Maxine Andrews of the famous singing sisters recalled, "Our last show was packed with eight thousand GIs, and it was the unhappiest audience you ever saw.

These guys knew they were being shipped out to another long, bloody, and hard war, the one in the Pacific with Japan. Some of them hadn't been home in four years. We were just trying to put them into good spirits." Patty Andrews was doing a skit with Arthur Treacher when a soldier motioned Maxine offstage and told her that he had a message for Patty to read onstage. "I'm not kidding," he insisted. "It's from the C.O."

When she protested that it could not be done in the middle of the show, he said, "You're going to get me into trouble." With a whisper she slipped the paper to Patty, who turned to the audience with the remark, "Look, there's a big joke going on up here. I have a note *supposedly* from the C.O." And without examining it first she read the announcement of the end of the war. When not a sound came from the audience, she looked at the note again, then said, "No, fellas—this *is* from the C.O. This is an announcement that"— and she raised her voice—"*the war with Japan is over.* You don't have to go to the Pacific."

She began to cry, as did Maxine and LaVerne, and still there was no reaction from the troops. "This is the end! This is the end!" Patty said once more—and the area erupted in yells, screams—and clamor to see the rest of the show. It was the Andrews Sisters' last show of the war, and an appropriate one, as they had also done the first—in Cincinnati on December 7, 1941. That Sunday Maxine had walked out to the street to see how the box office was doing, and found neither crowds nor queues. Puzzled, she returned backstage to find stagehands sitting around a radio and talking about Pearl Harbor. "Where *is* Pearl Harbor?" she asked. Nearly four years later her geographical education had improved—on the job.

At the replacement depots sprawled around Marseilles, combat units shorn of veterans who had logged the most overseas time "were stretched for miles," Rifleman John B. Savard, who had been wounded in Normandy and frostbitten in the Bulge, remembered, "and most still had their personal weapons as they were headed for the invasion of Japan." But French extras headlined, "LE JAPON ACCEPTE DE CAPITULER," and Savard wrote home, "Sometimes I think the GI is crazy. Everyone that had a gun was shooting as fast as he could. They say there were 40 men wounded. I sure hope the war *is* over, as I wouldn't like to go through that again."

In front of the Hebbel Theater on Stresemannstrasse in Berlin, cars carrying leading figures from the occupying forces disgorged ticketholders for the best seats. The theater was opening with a new production of *The Three Penny Opera*: "The Beggar's Opera," Ruth Andreas-Friedrich wrote, "what coincidental symbolism." The lines themselves, she added, had resonance in rubble-strewn Germany:

> "You masters who tell us to lead an honest life, to avoid crime and sins," we hear them sing.
> I feel choked with emotion. It was the song of our illegal days. Providing solace and comfort during many desperate hours.
> "... First give us something to eat, then talk: that's how it begins."
> A storm of applause breaks out. ...

While most Germans struggled to escape the incubus of Nazism, its transplantation across the Atlantic into Argentina was going well. In Mar del Plata the *U-977* docked and surrendered a hundred days after V-E Day, the second sub announced to have reached Argentina, where, reputedly, Nazi bigwigs, many of them war criminals, had begun to go underground. In Buenos Aires itself, so-called Nationalists intervened in victory celebrations with brass knuckles, clubs, and revolvers. Two celebrants were killed and sixty-three injured before heavy rains blanketed the city. Then the violence erupted anew. Uniformed soldiers with civilian supporters of Colonel Juan Domingo Perón—the vice president, aspiring, as Hitler did, to move up—besieged the building housing the liberal newspaper *Critica* and tried to set it afire. Repeatedly crowds cheered Perón, Hitler, and Mussolini and blamed Communists for whatever internal troubles they sought to have Perón alleviate. "Down with Democracy!" they chanted, along with "Long Live Germany!" and "Death to the Jews!" Growing more vicious, the mob shouted "Long live Perón!" and assaulted onlookers who failed to remove their hats. Two died and thirty more were wounded as police prudently looked the other way. Perónists had little interest in the surrender of Japan, but upstaging the celebration offered an opportunity to rescue some of the discredited past for the future.

In London, Prime Minister Attlee's private secretary, John Colville, picked the surrender news off the Downing Street ticker tape and brought the strip into the Cabinet Room, where Attlee was closeted with Lord Louis Mountbatten, "who was professing Labour sympathies." The admiral was lobbying for a postwar role before returning to preside over the formal East Asia capitulations. (In Ceylon, his headquarters was getting along very well without him.) His chiefs of staff met to deal with surrenders and reoccupations and ordered Vice Admiral Sir Cecil Harcourt to proceed with elements of the British Pacific Fleet to Hong Kong. "I must say," Admiral Sir Andrew Cunningham, the naval chief, recalled, "that the Americans by no means approved of our action in this matter." All three of the despised colonial powers in Southeast Asia—the British, Dutch, and French—were in haste to retrieve possessions before local claims intervened.

Outside Westminster Gardens, the block of flats where Winston Churchill was living, celebrants gathered to cheer him, and when he ventured out to Whitehall, the exuberant crowds loyally gave him larger ovations than Clement Attlee. From General Marshall in Washington came a message to Churchill. "With the termination of hostilities," Marshall cabled, "my thoughts turn to you and the long hard pull up the heights to the final triumph of your labor."

In Washington, priorities shifted to conversion to peace, emphasized by the sign that Byron Price, director of the Office of Censorship, posted on his door: OUT OF BUSINESS. Harold Ickes, Petroleum Administrator as well as Secretary of the Interior, announced the end of gasoline and fuel oil rationing. Military requirements, despite the huge transfers of forces home and the needs of two occupations half a world apart, had dropped instantly by 565 million gallons per month. Chester Bowles, Price Administrator and rationing czar for nearly everything else, announced the beginning of the end of rationing of canned fruit and vegetables, clothing and shoes. American submission to wartime controls had been reluctant and grudging, and his job had been thankless. The Selective Service director, Lewis Hershey, directed a slowdown in conscription, which would continue for occupation needs, and in California the local office that had sent violinist Yehudi Menuhin his draft notice issued a cancellation order.

Harry Truman's lot was more complicated. In his first peacetime glitch he had to reexplain an executive order prepared in the Department of Labor that authorized for millions time-and-a-half pay for the two-day holiday he had announced the evening before. Neither August 15 nor the next day, the White House noted with some pain, was V-J Day, which would come when the formal surrender was signed by Japan under MacArthur's auspices, perhaps two or three weeks away. But the White House and the military departments could release diversionary news long withheld, both good and bad. The Navy began revealing, one at a time, a litany of embarrassments accumulated since Pearl Harbor—the loss of the *Houston* off Java with nearly all hands in 1942, the collision of the new battleships *Washington* and *Indiana* off Kwajalein in 1944, the torpedoing of the *Pennsylvania* by a lone Japanese plane off Okinawa as recently as the last days of the war, and the hits on the destroyer *Aaron Ward* off Okinawa in May by six *kamikazes*, five of which exploded. There would be even more. The Navy had already confessed to the *Indianapolis* sinking. Also, the first disclosure was made via military authorities in Seattle of the Japanese balloon offensive, with the deaths at Lakeview, Oregon, and the one hitherto concealed enemy triumph of the paper balloons. One had hit and severed a power line from the Bonneville Dam to the atomic bomb plant at Hanford, Washington, temporarily halting production.

Exhausted from the strain of his job, Secretary of War Stimson, now ready to quit, had left for his mountain retreat, St. Hubert's, in the Adirondacks, where John McCloy, his Acting Secretary, visited and shared "long and painful thoughts about the atomic triumph." Was it practical, they asked each other (as Stimson recalled), "to hope that the 'atomic secret'—so fragile and short-lived—could be used to win concessions from the Russian leaders as to their cherished, if frightful, police state?" A month later he conceded in a memo to Truman that the Bomb could not be "a direct lever to produce ... change." Stalin, it had been clear at Potsdam, had already had his suspicions of the West raised by the ease with which Allied armies overran Germany while the Red Army had to contest every inch. The West seemed recognized by the Germans, in the Soviet view, as a future ally against Communism—something Dönitz had predicted in his last message as Hitler's successor. And it was already clear to Stimson and McCloy that beneath the surface camaraderie of Potsdam what would soon be called a Cold War was being waged by Stalinists against the West, even exploiting the buffer satellites Stalin now controlled in eastern Europe. The Bomb had little to do with it: the Soviets were not talking to the West about their own atomic projects, and had hardly expected openness from the Capitalist adversary.

As for Moscow itself, the 2:00 A.M. announcement had worked to

Stalin's advantage. He was not ready to halt Soviet penetration of Manchuria, Korea, and Sakhalin. Public celebration would be as muted as the omnipresent police could inhibit it. *Izvestia*, the party paper, declared that the Soviet Union, "which carried the main burden of the war against the most dangerous aggressor—Hitlerite Germany—has made a great investment in the destruction of imperialistic Japan." *Pravda* declared that the situation of Japan "became hopeless" once the Russians entered the war. Neither newspaper mentioned the American air-and-sea war of attrition against Japan, nor the two atomic bombs. Further evidence that the wartime collaboration was perceived by Russia in terms of rivalry came when the Mexican ambassador in Washington proposed, as senior member of the diplomatic corps, to lead heads of other missions now allied within the United Nations to the White House to express congratulations to the President. The Russian chargé d'affaires demanded to know what the ambassador proposed to say, and when he discovered no explicit mention of the Soviet Union's contribution to victory over Japan, refused to pay his respects.

American celebrations went into a second night, even in tiny (population: twelve) Japan, Missouri, a hilltop village that had ignored, since Pearl Harbor, entreaties to change its name. "PEACE: IT'S WONDERFUL!" Movietone News screened nationwide. While some revelry got out of hand across the country, resulting in a few deaths and thousands of minor injuries, the only city where jubilation reached criminally wholesale dimensions was San Francisco. An area of naval installations, it became a riotous carnival of drunken sailors and crazed civilians. Women were thrown to the streets and publicly raped to public cheers. Liquor stores were looted bare and shop windows smashed. Outnumbered policemen stood aside. Thousands were injured. At least twelve people died. Describing the carnage to publisher James Laughlin, Kenneth Rexroth used his poet's license to make light of it. Contrasting the outburst to November 1918, Rexroth faulted August 1945 for lack of "creative expression." Armistice Day had included "dancing and singing and all sorts of spontaneous group expression in the streets" and, he claimed, a "class conscious" response. "This time everybody just milled around, drunk. The first night was uproarious, but well tempered; the third, which I didn't see, was apparently a bastard. Most of the windows on Market St. broken, hundreds of naked girls. (The emergency wards ran a douche service all night for the rapes. Honest.) It took 2,000 city regular and special bulls, 3,000 SPs and MPs to keep them from tearing the city to bits. . . ."

Pearl Harbor, where the Pacific war had begun, was relatively sedate, yet by evening the scene over the harbor evoked déjà vu. Colored flares from dozens of ships in the harbor lit the sky much in the manner of December 7, 1941. But when it was over, all the ships were still afloat—but for the sunken hulks of the *Utah* and the *Arizona,* each still poking a rusting remnant out of the water.

On Guam, captured on the first day of fighting, a B-29 of the Twentieth Air Force had replacement lettering painted on its nose, a poster for the new peacetime:

TOKYO TOURS

FREE          FREE          FREE

SEE THE EMPEROR'S PALACE

FUJIYAMA

RIDE THE [EMPEROR'S] WHITE HORSE

NO ACK-ACK

NO KAMIKAZE[S]

16 HOURS ROUND TRIP

# CHAPTER XXXV

## · SURRENDERS ·

On the morning of August 16, General MacArthur's publicist, Le-Grande Diller, issued communiqué 1227, declaring the end of the fighting. It would take more than that to convince holdout Japanese, who in some sectors doubted even the authentic if unimpressive voice of the Son of Heaven. The Southern Army issued orders, pending confirmation from Tokyo, to "all units in the East Indies to maintain a strict lookout and precautions, and if the enemy makes a visit, they are to make every effort to annihilate him." From the signal traffic picked up, Allied forces worried that the Japanese might try to hold strategic positions around Singapore with troops withdrawn from outlying areas. As the initial responses in the chaos of defeat seemed much like procrastination, evasion, impenitence, and outright defiance, a Washington witticism was, "Do you think Japan's surrender will shorten the war?"

Washington—at least its Democratic Party wing—had been questioning MacArthur's appointment since Truman had first announced it. Texas senator Tom Connally worried that "Dugout Doug" would use his visible new post to run for President in 1948 as a Republican, while Secretary Ickes warned that MacArthur was too dangerous a man to be Supreme Commander and "would take every advantage of his dramatic situation to get himself spread all over the papers." The Japanese shogunate would also obscure the fiasco of his Philippines record, Ickes contended. "MacArthur would probably be a candidate anyway," said Truman. He did not tell Ickes that he had his own candidate in mind to run against MacArthur in 1948—Dwight D. Eisenhower.

Despite the lingering bitterness about the sneak attack on Pearl Harbor and nearly four years of orchestrated hatred of the enemy, on the first postwar morning Admiral Nimitz issued an order to all Navy forces in the Pacific that would set a standard for what would be a benign occupation:

WITH THE TERMINATION OF HOSTILITIES AGAINST JAPAN IT IS IN-CUMBENT ON ALL OFFICERS TO CONDUCT THEMSELVES WITH DIG-NITY AND DECORUM IN THEIR TREATMENT OF THE JAPANESE AND [IN] THEIR PUBLIC UTTERANCES IN CONNECTION WITH THE JAPA-NESE. THE JAPANESE ARE STILL THE SAME NATION WHICH INITI-ATED THE WAR BY A TREACHEROUS ATTACK ON THE PACIFIC FLEET AND WHICH HAS SUBJECTED OUR BROTHERS IN ARMS WHO BECAME PRISONERS TO TORTURE STARVATION AND MURDER. HOWEVER THE USE OF INSULTING EPITHETS IN CONNECTION WITH THE JAPANESE AS A RACE OR AS INDIVIDUALS DOES NOT NOW BECOME THE OFFI-CERS OF THE UNITED STATES NAVY. OFFICERS OF THE PACIFIC FLEET WILL TAKE STEPS TO REQUIRE OF ALL PERSONNEL UNDER THEIR COMMAND A HIGH STANDARD OF CONDUCT IN THIS MATTER. NEI-THER FAMILIARITY AND OPEN FORGIVENESS NOR ABUSE AND VITU-PERATION SHOULD BE PERMITTED.

Although MacArthur's instructions to the Japanese were to send a surrender delegation to Manila on the seventeenth, the formation of the Higashikuni government only took place that day, and even then Air Force hotheads threatened to shoot down any surrender mission. No responsible Japanese officials, civilian or military, wanted to serve on the delegation. Worries were real about being attacked en route or assassinated by ultras upon return. The government radioed its objections to the demeaning "Bataan" code and suggested the letters "JNP." MacArthur rejected the alternative.

By the nineteenth, Premier Higashikuni had assembled the required sixteen men. General Umezu had ordered his deputy chief of the general staff, Lieutenant General Torashiro Kawabe, to head the group, which took off secretly from the Kazarazu air base in the early Sunday morning darkness for Ie Shima. The two Mitsubishi "Betty" bombers were painted white with green crosses, as ordered. To evade rebel air patrols the planes flew out to sea before turning south while a white-painted "Betty" decoy flew toward Kyushu radioing messages that suggested it was carrying the emissaries. Near Ie Shima the two authentic planes were challenged by American interceptors and duly signaled "Bataan." The leader of the American squadron flashed back, "We are Bataan's watchdog. Follow us"—and escorted the planes to the island off Okinawa where a C-54 was waiting to fly the delegation to Manila, 750 miles to the south. It was late afternoon before they touched down.

The American command had little idea of the difficulties the Japanese military had in bringing about an orderly surrender. Japanese histories had stressed that in 2,600 years, however many of them were mythical, the empire had never lost a war or given up its arms. Paragraph 8 of the Army Field Code, which in its entirety never used the word *surrender*, ordered, "Never be taken alive; never accept the humiliation of becoming a prisoner of war." On the nineteenth and for several days thereafter, Special Attack Corps planes of the Imperial Navy were still dropping leaflets urging, "Don't surrender. Don't believe the Imperial Rescript. That is a false document." In Tokyo, posters and handbills surfaced wherever crowds gathered, not disclaiming the rescript as false but alleging that traitorous statesmen had misguided the Emperor into acting against Japan's interest. Weary of privation, the civilian population was grateful for peace and grateful to the Emperor. On the day the delegation left for Manila, blackouts ended and censorship of the mails was lifted. Air raid sirens were dismantled. Perhaps there would even be more food.

The services saw only humiliation, and military professionals saw proud careers curtailed. The contagion of suicide spread. On the morning of the sixteenth Admiral Onishi's body was cremated, his spirit joining the *kamikazes* he had sent off. Marshal Sugiyama, the former chief of staff, shot himself in his office, and on hearing the news his wife donned a ceremonial white kimono and disemboweled herself with a short sword. On August 24 General Tanaka made amends for failing to protect the Imperial Palace from rebels by killing himself. Officers down to lieutenant and ensign would take pride in such gestures, and some would follow, but former Premier Tojo, his hand trembling as he aimed at his head, failed to succumb instantly. Rushed to a hospital, he was saved for a war crimes trial—and a death sentence.

At the Yokosuka naval base, where midget sub crews were based for suicide defense, some loaded their submarines to resist the occupation armada, but loyalists prevailed in time. At the Kure naval base ultra officers led by Lieutenant Akira Kikuchi urged that all subs go to sea rather than surrender. He managed to get crews for six small coastal submarines to set out against the Third Fleet, only to come upon Commander Hashimoto of the *I-58* entering Kure harbor. Kikuchi tried to persuade Hashimoto to join them, but the nemesis of the *Indianapolis* refused. As he continued on toward Kure he saw the small subs turning about. They had recognized futility.

At Atsugi, where Captain Ozono had been trying to persuade naval fliers to go out en masse to throw themselves against the Third Fleet, Prince Takamatsu arrived to rouse respect for the Throne. Loyalists punched holes in gasoline tanks and removed propellers from aircraft, making them unflyable to hotheads as well as unusable to the occupiers. Removal of propellers would become widespread, and hardly a plane in Japan carried one two weeks later.

Resentment over surrender seemed strongest among naval airmen, who proved the most suicidal. No publicity was given their deaths, which were recorded as training accidents. At Admiral Ugaki's former command, Vice Admiral Kusaka finally appeared to take over, and found Oita seething with mutiny. There had already been crashes into the sea on the eighteenth when Kusaka convened a meeting of officers. The speeches preceding his own were bitter, and officers shouted, "Continue the war! The decisive battle should be on Japanese soil!" Seizing his turn while he could, Kusaka confided, whether in all honesty or not, "As your commander-in-chief, I came to Kyushu with the firm intention of dying with all of you. However, whether we fight or not is absolutely subject to the Imperial mandate. If the Emperor says stop fighting, I must do my utmost to bring the war to an end. I hope you will understand and cooperate. At the same time, I know some of you feel differently. But I will have my own way as long as I live. If you disagree with that, kill me before you take any action! I'm ready. Do it immediately!" He sat down, closed his eyes, crossed his arms, and waited.

Most officers filed quietly out of the room. One squadron leader approached Kusaka and saluted. Hearing him, Kusaka opened his eyes and said, "Whatever happens, do not act blindly or in haste. Be as patient as you can. Hard times are waiting for all of us, but everything is up to you young people. Do your best!"

By August 22 the men were being disbanded. Officers were allocated 3,000 yen, petty officers 2,880 yen. All planes but "Bettys" (to take the men back to the airfield closest to their homes) had their propellers removed.

Also on the morning of the eighteenth, the day when the sense of resignation cut deep, *kamikaze* pilot Yasuo Kuwahara heard his commander at the Hiro air base order the removal of propellers from planes, and only the arms and ammunition needed by guards retained. His face was weary as he told them, "You are all aware now that we have received orders to refrain from further aggression. Regardless of our own personal feelings, there will be no more fighting. Japan has lost the war. The time has come for us to consider the future—to face reality. Our Emperor has spoken." He wept, and his men wept. The days that followed, Kuwahara—a corporal—recalled, were the strangest in his abbreviated military life. Although men in the ranks had long piloted aircraft, the social barriers between officers and men had remained rigid. In their last days as a unit these barriers disappeared: "Officers who had dealt unjustly with their men fled by night. . . . Others were killed trying to escape." Men deserted before being officially disbanded—to vanish into civilian status in case the Americans might be vindictive toward *kamikazes*. Records and documents were destroyed to prevent identification by the enemy. It was only ten years after his discharge order appeared on the bulletin board at Hiro that Kuwahara learned that among the documents destroyed was one that would have put him in the air on August 8. "I was to have been part of a final desperation attack, involving thousands of men and planes—all that was left. The great bomb that had destroyed so many of my countrymen [at Hiroshima] had saved me."

Truman's orders to MacArthur about supervising the occupation of Japan left him in charge at a dimension of authority the general relished while the Russians fumed. The Soviet representative in Manila, Lieutenant General Kuzma Nikolaevich Derevyanko, a chunky man with huge shoulderboards and a ceremonial dagger, brought Stalin's Potsdam-like plan to MacArthur despite the signals from Washington that there would be only one supreme commander for Japan, and no dismemberment of the home islands into zones. Awarded all of Sakhalin and the Kuriles at Yalta, largely a return to the Czarist borders of 1904, Russia additionally proposed an occupation zone for itself of all of Hokkaido and northern Honshu as far south as the thirty-eighth parallel at Niigata. The rest of Japan, Derevyanko offered, would be American. "Why are you wasting your time with these ridiculous demands?" MacArthur replied. "I am the Supreme Commander here." He threatened to send the astonished Derevyanko back to Moscow if he took his observer status any more seriously than that. When he reported his rebuff, there was no response from Stalin. But the Generalissimo cabled Truman on August 22, about being denied even Hokkaido, "I have to say to you that I and my colleagues did not expect such an answer from you." (Yet no provision for a Soviet zone in Japan was made at Yalta or at Potsdam.)

Soviet duplicity had already gone well beyond Stalin's demand for a role in Hokkaido. Before either Potsdam or the Bomb, the Politburo, on June 26–27, had discussed occupying at least northern Hokkaido. Zhukov opposed it as militarily unwise, while Molotov warned at violating the Yalta accords, as they could then be violated by the West. Still, Stalin supported the invasion and operational plans were prepared. On August 19, despite Truman's rejection of Stalin's occupation proposal, Marshal Vassilevsky ordered his First East Asian Army, about to move into southern Sakhalin, to push across the Soya Strait into Hokkaido. As late as August 21 the invasion was scheduled for August 23, but the day before the Army was to jump off, Stalin communicated sudden misgivings. Admiral Nimitz's armadas controlled Japanese home waters. Any Soviet intrusion risked an armed incident with vast potential for trouble. "To avoid the creation of conflicts and misunderstanding," General S. P. Ivanov, chief of staff of the Red Army in Asia, ordered, almost certainly on orders from Moscow, "it is categorically forbidden to send any ships or planes at all in the direction of Hokkaido." Stalin settled for what he had been conceded at Yalta.

Perhaps as a diversion, he claimed to be more exercised about an American request, to secure the safety of an air route over the North Pacific to Japan, for an air base in the Kuriles. "Demands of such a nature are usually laid before a conquered state," Stalin carped. The Cold War had long existed in parallel with the official one against the Axis in which Russia and the United States were allies, and Derevyanko was not recalled. He would take his ceremonial authority with him to Tokyo, where MacArthur from time to time would write notes to the general appreciative of his empty advisory role.

A reading of diplomatic intercepts suggested that the resourceful Japanese expected to rise again as an Asian power. The noble task in East Asia by the "Divine Land" was only interrupted, and could be revived, Minister Okamoto suggested from Stockholm, by exploiting the inevitable rift between Russia and the Anglo-Americans. Further, he thought, America could be isolated morally and diplomatically "by skillfully emphasizing the extreme inhumanity of the Bomb."

Tokyo had already reported its difficulty in arranging a surrender in Manchuria as the Russians had ignored all efforts at a cease-fire. Even the Americans seemed unable to wait for mutual arrangements to be made, the Japanese firing back in self-defense as troops landed on Chishima (Jino-Shima), an islet just west of the Ashiya airbase off Kyushu. Still the Imperial representatives came with a document signed by Hirohito and validated with the seal of the empire "at Our Palace in Tokyo this eighteenth day of the eighth month of the twentieth year of Showa. . . ." As befit his own imperial style, MacArthur conducted the negotiations indirectly through lower-ranking officers.

The initial greeting of the Japanese at Nichols Field was that of dozens of correspondents' cameras—like machine guns, Katsuo Okazaki of the Foreign Office thought. Despite the presence of Americans in the convoy of cars that brought the Japanese into Manila, some Filipinos threw stones; others shouted curses. Yamashita's troops had torched the city when they abandoned it in February. The entire occupation had been a searing memory. That Americans would not forget the brutality visited upon the defenders of Bataan and Corregidor was obvious when General Kawabe offered his hand to Colonel Sidney Mashbir, the chief staff interpreter, whom he had known in Japan in the 1930s. Mashbir instinctively reached out his own, then thought better of it and jerked his thumb toward the waiting cars. This set the tone for the negotiations, run in the second-floor conference room of the repaired Manila City Hall.

The house put at the disposal of the delegation also fixed the tone. LeGrande Diller issued a release describing the "small house on Dewey [now Roxas] Boulevard," adding, "The harbor, with its great fleet of ships, can be seen from the front windows . . . and from the upstairs windows one can see the acres of desolation that was once a fine residential section of Manila."

In charge, to the relief of Eichelberger and Kenney, was the returned Richard Sutherland. In the chief of staff's absence, MacArthur, who would not meet the Japanese, had put his operations officer, Major

General Stephen J. Chamberlin, in charge of the surrender plans, with the haughty intelligence chief, Charles Willoughby, to assist. Neither Eichelberger nor Kenney would accept Chamberlin's authority, and Sutherland, unchastened by the slap on the wrist that had sent him Stateside, restored order within the staff. The rivalries for publicity and preeminence were open. Chamberlin told Eichelberger that Kenney would try "to steal the show by landing early," and MacArthur himself wanted to make sure that Nimitz didn't precede him into Honshu.

Still feeling his oats as the Japanese, in inappropriate woolen uniforms for the sweltering Manila heat, filed into the battered City Hall at nine in the evening, Willoughby ordered them to remove their ceremonial swords. Then Sutherland, with studied contempt in his voice, read to the perspiring and exhausted delegates what their duties were to be when they returned to the home islands, and, unnecessarily, read MacArthur's first general order, which they already had received: the Russians were to take the surrenders in Sakhalin, the Kuriles, Manchuria, and northern Korea; Chiang's armies in China, Formosa, and Indochina (the latter to be a sore point with both the French and the Vietnamese); and the British and Americans in other areas. The Japanese listened in silence until Sutherland announced that American forces would begin landing at Atsugi on August 23, only four days away. "The Japanese side would sincerely advise you not to land so quickly," Kawabe broke in. "You should know that we are still having trouble at home with some of the *kamikaze* units. At least ten days are needed to prepare. They delayed our trip, in fact."

Insisting on his tough line, Sutherland agreed only to a delay until August 26, and planned to have MacArthur receive the formal surrender on August 28. Fortunately for both sides, a typhoon would move across the home islands, disrupting communications and halting American aircraft and shipping. The target dates would be moved back again.

Even more upsetting to the delegation was the opening of the proposed surrender document, which began (in Japanese), "I, Hirohito, Emperor of Japan. . . ." The Emperor always referred to himself in official documents (as he did in the rescript) with the royal "We." Kawabe could hardly return to Tokyo with that insult in hand, yet the American brass was unmoved. A petty insult followed and was almost as galling. The delegation was given a directive spelling out occupation privileges for officers—three maids for each general, for example, down to one for every lieutenant. When no arguments overrode the implied arrogance, Kawabe impulsively slammed his hand down on the table.

Finally, to prepare for the first landings, the American side wanted detailed data on mine fields, coast artillery, and *kaiten* and *kamikaze* bases. The Japanese had come prepared to cooperate, hoping for an occupation that would not be vindictive. Kawabe's aides supplied information, even minutiae, into the early hours of the twentieth, telephoning Tokyo when necessary. At 4:00 A.M. the meeting adjourned and the delegation returned to the house on Dewey Boulevard for four hours of sleep.

Before their second session at the City Hall, the sixteen emissaries were awakened to an un-Japanese breakfast of bacon and eggs, but matters improved after that. Nothing further was heard about the allocation of maids, which had disappeared overnight from the documents they were to take home. Also, Sidney Mashbir had managed to get the imperial pronouns put right. A revised document was handed to Kawabe with apologies on behalf of General Willoughby. Policy from Washington, which had been spelled out before the B-29 raids began, and was meant to safeguard the Imperial Palace, cautioned, "The Emperor of Japan is not at present a liability and may later become an asset." The strategy had proved itself, and when Colonel Mashbir later explained the changes in text to MacArthur he said, "Mashbir, you handled that exactly right. I have no desire whatever to debase him in the eyes of his own people."

With the Japanese pleased with the modifications, the brief morning session ended in an atmosphere of goodwill, and at 1:00 P.M. a C-54 took off in the rain for the four-hour flight to Ie Shima. But from there only eight could leave for Japan. One of the "Bettys" developed mechanical trouble, and its party had to remain overnight. The other, too, turned out to be in trouble—it developed a fuel leak as it neared Japan. Kawabe asked the Foreign Office delegate, "Okazaki, are you still a good swimmer?" (He had competed for Japan in the 1924 Olympics in Paris.) Okazaki reached for the surrender documents and—in case—tucked them inside his shirt.

As a lower Honshu beach materialized in the moonlight, the pilot came in low and hit the water just short of the shoreline. The plane bounced into knee-deep water and the passengers lifted the canopy and climbed out—all but Okazaki, who had hit his head as the plane crash-landed. Stunned and bleeding, he was pulled from the wreckage, the surrender papers with him.

Two fishermen found the group wandering on the beach, and police sent a truck to fetch them. In Tokyo, Premier Higashikuni had no idea what had happened to the plane, which had vanished in the night. It had evaded the rebels en route to Ie Shima, but had ultras managed nevertheless to forestall the surrender? Finally a police report arrived after the dazed passengers and crew had been taken to an air base to recover. At dawn a plane that still functioned took them north to Tokyo, where Kawabe, embraced gratefully by Higashikuni, delivered the documents and learned that military discord had diminished, but was not yet over.

Peace brought little relief to Hiroshima and Nagasaki. The uninjured as well as the burned and maimed survived in terror that the legacy of the *pika* was in them, and that their internal organs could be decaying even as they lived. Every day more inhabitants festered, blackened, and died, and families already decimated lost further members to the busy crematoria. In Hiroshima, Dr. Michihiko Hachiya felt well enough to conduct autopsies in which his curiosity about the causes of death overpowered his sorrow. Mosquitoes, flies, and fleas often clustered in the summer heat about a body not yet a corpse, and on August 24, sleepless because of the close night and the mosquitoes, he thought, he had a "frightful" dream—not about the Bomb but about the 1923 Kanto earthquake—yet the transference is obvious. "Around me," so he wrote in his diary, "were decomposing bodies heaped in piles, all of whom were looking right at me. I saw an eye sitting on the palm of a girl's hand. Suddenly it turned and leaped into the sky and then came flying back towards me, so that, looking up, I could see a great bare eyeball, bigger than life, hovering over my head, staring point blank at me. I was powerless to move." He awakened "short of breath and with my heart pounding."

While the Tokyo government worked out occupation matters with Manila it also bombarded MacArthur with appeals about Soviet behavior in Manchuria, northern China, and northern Korea. "Disarmed Japanese forces and civilians," message 27 on August 23 explained, "are being made victims of illegitimate firing, looting, acts of violence, rape and other outrages, rendering it almost impossible to maintain law and order.... Although we are making sincere efforts to carry out your requirements faithfully, it is requested to permit our forces to retain the necessary arms in these localities until Japanese residents have been removed to places of safety." Message

34, the next day, reported continuing Russian attacks, even by sub-marine, on civilian coastal shipping in Hokkaido waters, from shellings to torpedoings. On August 22 a Japanese ship repatriating civilians from Sakhalin went down with 1,700 aboard. In China itself hostilities were still continuing where orders had not yet reached dis-tant or isolated units. Further, neither Mao's nor Chiang's troops had stopped shooting, as each side attempted to extend its effective bor-ders. In Burma and Borneo and the Pacific islands the Japanese had not been able to communicate with Southern Army forces by radio, and now depended upon Allied airdrops. Lieutenant General S. G. Savige of the 2nd Australian Corps ordered leaflets dropped as far off as Bougainville; the leaflets were headed, in Japanese, "The War Is Ended," ordering Japanese troops to "remain in your present posi-tions and to cease all hostile actions." Recommendations to surrender parties were that they "will advance under a white flag and will be accompanied by NOT more than one (1) other personnel." On Luzon the Japanese still holed up in the northern highlands were left notes by local Filipinos whose livestock was being raided for food: "The war ended on August 15. Come down from the mountains!" A year later B-17s were still dropping copies of the surrender order signed by General Yamashita to remnants of the Fourteenth Area Army.

At the POW camp for senior officers near Mukden, a plane sent by General Wedemeyer parachuted six men, including a Nisei corporal who spoke Japanese, and reported what K. M. Hoeffel, a naval offi-cer, heard described as an "armistice." Conditions improved, but the camp remained under Japanese control until August 19, the day be-fore the Russians came. For the captors there was no opportunity to flee, and on the evening of August 20, Hoeffel wrote, the Russians "staged a remarkable ceremony . . . for our benefit. They marched the 12 Japanese officers and 50 men out in front of us, disarmed the men, turning their rifles over to American soldiers. The Jap officers were allowed to retain their sabres however; but all of the Japs were de-clared our prisoners." The officers were confined and the guards be-gan doing fatigue duty. Writing to his friend Aubrey Fitch, now an admiral, Hoeffel described the camp population as "20 U.S. Generals, 60 or so British Generals and Brigadiers, 10 Dutch Generals. Also 120 American Colonels, 40 British Colonels and 50 Dutch Colonels. Other than listed above we have 12 Navy officers and warrant officers and 106 men. Also total of 5 Marine officers and 87 men."

Where the Japanese could manage it, their covering up of evidence of war crimes went on simultaneously with ostensible cooperation. While working on returning POWs to Allied control, the Prisoner of War Bureau sent a message to camp commandants: "Personnel who mistreated prisoners of war and internees or who are held in extremely bad sentiment by them are permitted to take care of it by immediately transferring or by fleeing without a trace. Moreover, documents which would be unfavorable for us in the hands of the enemy are to be treated in the same way as secret documents and destroyed. . . ." In a few cases, open solicitousness, from bowing to bringing food and medicines, went to the extreme of the commandant at the Hakodate POW Camp 2, who posted a notice nine days after the Emperor's rescript—the first the prisoners heard of the apparent surrender—that closed,

> As the war came to an end, so let it be with Enmity. If any of you happens to hold a grudge against any particular man of the staff or sentries, let us shake hands and forget the dark hours for the sake of peace and love.
> Lastly, the commandant, with good grace, has prepared to drink a toast to your health and happiness. Are you all going to accept this invitation? Yes? Very well.
> > Congratulations to each of you.
> > Lieutenant Jiro Tendo

Few starved and brutalized prisoners accepted such invitations, but many, while awaiting retrieval, struck out on their own to see what was on the other side of the barbed wire. In Hokkaido, a lieutenant traded a GI raincoat for a kimono from a woman who had been hanging out washing. Seven officers found themselves guests at the private club of a Hokkaido mining company where there had never been a food shortage. Near Kyoto a group of Marine POWs commandeered a police car and visited the posh Miyako Hotel, untouched by bombing like the city itself.

With over two hundred thousand prisoners of war to retrieve, Allied commanders faced huge logistical problems. After finding them they had to feed and clothe them and get them into medical shape for movement out of their camps. Many were near death from malnutrition and exposure, only walking skeletons—when they could walk. A parachuted medical team found Lieutenant General Jonathan Wainwright, who had surrendered Corregidor on May 6,

1942, at a camp in Hsian, in Manchuria. Lieutenant Colonel James Devereux, who had led the defense of Wake Island until December 23, 1941, was found in a camp near Peking. On August 19, ten days after Sergeant DeShazer of the Doolittle raiders had experienced his vision of victory, a prison officer opened the cell doors of the surviving four fliers and said, simply, "The war is over. You can go home now." They were presented the clothes in which they were captured in April 1942, offered haircuts and shaves, and taken to a Shanghai hotel. Captain George Barr was too ill to be moved farther.

Two weeks later, several Japanese slipped into an undertaker's storage area in Shanghai looking for the ashes of Dean Hallmark, William Farrow, and Harold Spatz, who had been executed, and directed that the names on the urns be changed to "J. Smith," "H. E. Gande," and "E. L. Brister." American investigators would later find the original records.

At the Thai camp of Nakon Paton, where the Japanese had been gathering British officers from smaller camps, guards disappeared, and an American paratrooper floated down to tell the POWs that the war was over and he would radio their position. The next day a plane dropped food supplies. As the men waited for transportation to Bangkok they rummaged through the camp and discovered Japanese orders that would have moved them from Nakon Paton to be machine-gunned on August 26.

The Siamese surrenders released thousands of prisoners held since early 1942. At Weary Dunlop's camp the Japanese commandant spoke on August 16, through an interpreter, of an armistice rather than a surrender, and continued, "All fronts are at peace and we have received instructions that we are to cease to regard you as POWs. We cease to guard you. The maintenance of discipline is your own responsibility. Your repatriation will be soon. I advise you to keep your health, and to cultivate the papaya trees." The Japanese had done little to encourage prisoner health. Forty percent of the malnourished POWs had died. Dr. Dunlop looked at the "gaunt, rapt, and mostly tear-stained faces" around him and wrote in his diary later in the day, "This has been a war against monstrous things, but one for which we all share responsibility because of the selfish preoccupations which allowed matters to reach such hideous proportions." Now that "this long dark night of captivity" was ending, he realized, "there will be strenuous and exciting days working to get the last of these maimed and damaged men on their way home. I have resolved to make their care and welfare a life-long mission." And he did—until 1993.

At the Nahon Nayak camp for officers, Colonel Philip Toosey needed two parades for his hundreds of POWs. At each he warned against "indiscriminately going out of camp to get food for yourselves or getting mixed up with women, because the last thing I want is to get a lot of you full of venereal disease before we go home." Given the poor shape of the men, he expected low sexual desire, but he radioed Delhi for an airdrop that would include "10,000 French letters." The "girl wireless operator in the Royal Air Force," he recalled ... "must have been astonished at our virility after so many years in captivity." After the surrender the men were ferried, twenty to a Dakota (C-47), to Rangoon. (Verifying, at the least, a positive state of mind, one Aussie POW claimed that the newly lettered sign on a hut roof, PW CAMP 21, 608 MEN, was placed so that supply planes would know "how many blondes to drop.")

The Twentieth Air Force began airdrops to previously unknown camps once lists and locations were furnished by the Japanese. Food—most of it in cans—came with warnings about overindulgence. Vitamins came with instructions on usage. Clothing was often wildly wrong—long winter underwear for semitropical Fukuoka went unappreciated, although the parachutes and the fifty-five-gallon drums often proved useful themselves. Between August 27 and September 20, 1,066 POW missions were flown, of which only 900 were considered effective. Poor weather and poor aiming took a toll, but 4,470 tons of supplies reached an estimated 63,500 prisoners in 154 camps. Eight aircraft and seventy-seven crew were lost. Some parachuted loads injured overly eager prisoners, a drum in Korea breaking the legs of Captain Oliver Orson. One B-29 from the 73rd Wing attempting to supply a camp in Korea was attacked by Soviet fighters and damaged so badly that it had to crash-land. The Russians called it a "mistake" (yet the Japanese had no such aircraft).

Although the airlift was desperately needed, at the same time piles of Red Cross food parcels suddenly materialized after being denied to prisoners for years. At Toosey's camp the commandant tried to persuade him to backdate receipts for them, but he refused. At the same time, in POW camps all over Southeast Asia, the Japanese hastily distributed tens of thousands of withheld letters from loved ones. Much of the mail had been stored in the very stockades in which the recipients were imprisoned, kept from them in senseless cruelty since 1942.

POW evacuations were to begin only after the formal surrender, but political and logistical circumstances speeded up some operations. MacArthur was ordered to have the haggard Wainwright, who was too weak to walk without a cane, on the *Missouri* with him at the formal surrender, as well as General Arthur Percival, who had suffered the ignominy of surrendering Singapore. It would take until the third week of September, five weeks after the shooting had stopped, to reclaim all of the twelve thousand surviving American POWs from camps in Manchuria, Korea, Formosa, and Japan. Ten thousand were beyond return. Curiously, no women prisoners (all nurses) had died, although their average weight loss was 30 percent.

Among the prisoners gathered for convenience on Omari, a small dredged island in Tokyo Bay, was B-24 pilot Tom Cartwright, who had survived Hiroshima by being removed for questioning. Some, like the Australians, had been there a long time, working as dockhands. Others, like future Medal of Honor recipient Gregory ("Pappy") Boyington, who had flown with the "Flying Tigers" in China and then as a Marine over Bougainville, were newcomers, as was Frank Fujita, moved from Tokyo. Work parties had ceased by the twenty-third and the Americans were largely on their own. Summoned to the "Head Shed," once occupied by the Japanese commandant, "Foo" expected the usual beating. "Come in, Sergeant," said Major Boyington, holding out his hand for a shake. "I'm Pappy. Are you the half-Japanese sergeant that was captured with that bunch of Texans down in Java?"

"Yes, sir," said Fujita.

Boyington wanted to know if the other side had been rough on him for being part Japanese, and Fujita conceded it. "By damn I'm glad to meet you!" said the ace who had twenty-six enemy planes to his credit. "Always stand tall and don't ever be ashamed of your heritage."

During the night of August 27 all Japanese personnel vanished from the island—just in time for American planes to begin dropping supplies. The first was a gull-winged carrier plane. Passing low over their heads, the pilot opened his canopy and tossed out a half-empty cigarette pack with a note attached: "Hang on! It won't be long now!" Soon B-29s were parachuting supplies, the first a food package in two welded-together fifty-five-gallon drums that broke apart on hitting the ground, everyone running for cover as the cans flew. Another drop hit a building, and POWs rushed to letter on a barracks roof, "DROP OUTSIDE. THANK YOU." (Supplying a compound near Sendai,

B-29 crewman Joe Keenan discovered that the prisoners had spelled out "PW" in white stones—across the river from camp.)

The supplies for Omari included toothbrushes, soap, razors, and rations from soup and chocolate to coffee. "The mood was ecstatic—in fact a bit wild," Cartwright remembered. "Boyington, a rather compulsive fellow, overdosed on caffeine . . . and several of us took turns sitting up and talking with him the night through. Some of the old-hand Aussies swam ashore with cigarettes, soap and candy wrapped in condoms. They reported great success in bartering their supplies to friendly women."

The next day the Navy was in Tokyo Bay and a flotilla of landing craft led by Commander Harold Stassen "landed among a jubilant group of POWs who cooperatively rushed on board and were spirited away to various U.S. Navy ships." Unable to wait for them, "Foo" Fujita began swimming, but made only about forty yards. "I began taking on water and started to sink," he recalled. ". . . I was expecting the boat's propellers to chop me to bits." He regretted his stupidity in ending his life "just at the moment of liberation." In his panic he surfaced in time for two large hands to pull him to safety.

Surrenders across the expanse of Asia and the Pacific that the Japanese still clung to would take months rather than weeks. Some came easily. A few days after the Imperial Rescript, his leaflet war over, Lieutenant Paul Boller, on Guam, was recruited to interpret for the surrender of about three thousand Japanese on Rota, forty miles to the north. In full dress uniform, the commander on Rota, a Major Imagawa, faced Marine Lieutenant Colonel Kenneth King and turned over his sword. Boller asked such questions as "Have you attempted to bring in all stragglers?" and King seemed pleased. "Tell him, Boller," King added amiably, "that they are now on good behavior."

Boller could not think of a Japanese military equivalent and framed something literal that offended Major Imagawa. "Look," the major said, "we've done everything your commanding officer instructed us to do. . . . Why, why, after all of this, do you make such an insulting remark to us?"

The ceremony in the broiling sun had taken two hours, and Boller was at a loss for an answer. "It's very simple," he said. "I'm only a *chūi*"—a junior lieutenant. "My CO is a Marine colonel. He ordered me to say that to you." Imagawa laughed, and his staff joined in. The surrender had become easier to take.

Large island groups and smaller bits of coral contained isolated forces. Some had little food or drinkable water, and improvised intention-to-surrender symbols that could be seen out at sea or from the air. Someone on Mili Atoll, in the Marshalls, painted a large white cross on the lone runway, and on August 23 Captain H. B. Grow in the destroyer escort *Levy* was ordered over to reoccupy it and save 2,395 ragged Japanese soldiers, sailors, and construction workers from starvation. On the twenty-ninth Major General H. H. Johnson took some troops from Morotai to accept the surrender of 41,700 troops and civilians in the Halmahera group, east of Celebes. Two days later 2,500 emaciated troops trapped on Marcus Island surrendered to Rear Admiral F. E. M. Whiting of the destroyer *Bagley*.

Two surrender ceremonies followed in the South Pacific. The first was held on board the H.M.S. *Glory*, an aircraft carrier, in Rabaul Roads on September 6, with the Australians in charge. "The Japanese," Air Commodore Sir Geoffrey N. Roberts remembered—he represented New Zealand—"were brought out on a small pinnace from Rabaul . . . and were lined up on the aft aircraft lift facing the stern. . . . They thought for a moment they were going to be marched over the stern into the sea. An about turn order fixed that, but they suffered the indignity of having to march up the entire length of the flight deck heavily lined with sailors to the surrender table in the bow." Roberts was also at the surrender for the Bougainville area on September 8, under a large tent erected in a jungle clearing. The Australians also took the surrenders of 2,500 long-isolated Japanese on phosphate-rich Nauru and on Ocean Island, 2,300 miles northeast of Sydney, signed aboard the H.M.A.S. *Diamentina* on September 13, after which survivors furnished harrowing accounts of atrocities, starvation, and cannibalism during the occupation.

One of the more contested surrenders occurred in Hong Kong. The British, French, and Dutch had expected to return to their former colonies on much the same terms that had existed before losing them to the Japanese, and when Generalissimo Chiang notified London that he expected to take the surrender in Hong Kong, the Foreign Office warned on August 18, "Hong Kong is a part of the British Empire and we intend to occupy it just as any other part." Hong Kong remained in the control of the Japanese police until August 30, when Rear Admiral Harcourt arrived with a British fleet, but the formal instrument of surrender was only signed at Government House on September 16. As would be Chiang's pattern, he was even late in sending troops to the mainland portion of Hong Kong colony, Kowloon. They arrived the day after Harcourt. Not wanting to send unsafe troops to accept surrenders, Chiang had ordered Chinese forces far to the south to take over territories that required moving long distances, and the delays offered Mao's Communists opportunities.

The first of the occupation forces on Japanese soil was a pilot from the carrier *Yorktown* who landed at Atsugi while laborers were still filling in bomb craters on gravel runways. At his orders on the twenty-seventh, the ground crews painted a sign, WELCOME TO THE U.S. ARMY FROM THIRD FLEET. His prank completed, he flew back to the *Yorktown*, certain he would raise the ire of the paratroops due the next day.

In preparation for the occupation, ships of Halsey's Third Fleet, including transports with the Fleet Landing Force, had been anchoring in Sagami Wan. Separated from Tokyo Bay by the peninsula on which was the Yokosuka naval base, it offered a view of Mount Fuji, its peak now nearly clear of snow. Sagami Wan seemed less threatening as a cover than a conspicuous presence within sight of Tokyo. While battleships remained in the outer bay as fire support if needed, the carriers roamed outside for wider surveillance and minesweepers began clearing the entrance to Tokyo Bay, using charts supplied during a rendezvous with Navy Ministry officials ferried out on the destroyer *Hatzuzakura* to the battleship *Missouri*.

As the destroyer *Waldron* approached Sagami Wan, its decks crowded with war correspondents covering the history to be made, the ship's alarm sounded General Quarters. Captain Peckham's voice came over the loudspeakers with the traditional exhortation that all hands would do their duty. The sneaky Nips had one unaccounted sub and the *Waldron* had made sonar contact with it. There was a rush to "Sad Sam" Alexander at the sonar shack. "I told the Captain," he explained, "that the target was making twenty knots at a hundred feet, and no Jap sub can make ten knots submerged. He just does not trust me."

Depth charges set shallow exploded and shook the destroyer, which was beginning a turning maneuver. Those looking down, Lieutenant Richard Bullis recalled, spotted "blood and the huge hulk of a whale with its eyes hanging loose from their huge sockets." It was the closest to battle action off Japan the press would experience.

Sagami Wan was already congested. The Fleet Flagship Group gathering for the surrender ceremonies was also arriving. At dawn on the twenty-eighth, as ships began moving into Tokyo Bay, an air um-

brella of land-based and carrier fighters escorted the first C-47s from
Okinawa into Atsugi. The Japanese were as surprised as the Americans. The flight had been due at nine but the first transport touched
down at 8:28. Circling before landing for a look at Tokyo, twenty-
seven miles northeast, or to make certain that it was safe to come in,
the contingent must have been amazed to see hundreds of planes
stripped of their propellers on both sides of the field. The Manila
agreement had called for weaponry including aircraft to be held for
destruction by occupation forces. Then, as the C-47 came to a halt,
and Colonel Charles Tench and his men emerged, dozens of shouting
soldiers came running toward them. Worried, Tench drew his
sidearm. But what they were shouting was that the C-47 had landed
at the wrong end of the runway.

At the other end, the Japanese had laid out a welcoming buffet,
including turtle soup and assorted sandwiches that seemed to them
appropriately American, but when the Atsugi commander offered
Tench an orangeade, he cautiously declined it. After the Japanese
raised their glasses and drank, Tench understood, and accepted a
drink. Then he radioed, "No hostile action encountered," and the
hovering transports landed 30 officers and 120 men, with their jeeps
and signal equipment.

Sampling the fare at the buffet, Colonel John R. Lackey, Jr., pilot
of Tench's C-47, pronounced the soup "damned good." The Japanese
apparently had not run out of Tokyo Bay turtles.

Atsugi's pool of battered trucks were lined up for further incoming
troops, and by the end of the day 4,200 men and 123 aircraft carrying
fuel and maintenance equipment had landed. What awed the coopera-
tive Japanese crews assisting the Americans were the navy fighters that,
even as they landed and taxied, folded their wings "like cicadas."

On the twenty-ninth, as reinforcements arrived and fanned out
toward Yokohama, Admiral Nimitz arrived by air to join his flagship,
South Dakota, and the prisoner of war rescues from Tokyo Bay camps
began. On the thirtieth, Admiral Badger landed his Marines and
sailor force at Yokosuka.

From the New Jersey, Admiral Halsey ordered officers ashore to
secure houses of prostitution for the fleet. Once ashore they had little
difficulty instructing the Japanese to maintain the same services that
had existed in the past, now for a new clientele. "We established," an
officer recalled, "one house for flag officers, several houses for senior
officers, and special houses for junior officers and enlisted men. This

operation did get off the ground, and was in operation for about a week after the fleet arrived—until MacArthur found out about it. . . ."

MacArthur arrived at Atsugi in the first of a stream of C-54s, having been awakened from a nap in time to view the serene beauty of Fujiyama. Two steps down from the open door of the plane he paused dramatically for the corps of press photographers. Eichelberger greeted him at the bottom with a salute and a handshake. "Well, Bob," said the Supreme Commander, "it's been a long road from Melbourne to Tokyo, but as they say in the movies, this is the payoff."

Symbolic of the condition in which Japan came out of the war was the fleet of vehicles MacArthur had stipulated be provided for his entourage for the journey to the Yokohama customs house and nearby hotel that were to serve as temporary headquarters. None of the automobiles was in good shape, and most were charcoal-retrofitted, including an ancient red fire engine. The Supreme Commander—with Eichelberger—was offered an old American Lincoln, which, like the other cars, broke down en route. It was, "Miss Em" was told, "a dusty ride of about an hour and a half," and Yokohama was "to a large extent burned down."

It had already become clear that the August 31 date for the surrender ceremony was overly optimistic, perhaps chosen by MacArthur for its symbolism. The fighting had begun with the German invasion of Poland on September 1, 1939. A signing on the last day of August would close the world war neatly at the six-year mark. However, all the parties to the signing could not arrive in time, nor could the formalities be planned with all the dignity and coordinated display of military power MacArthur envisioned. Besides, MacArthur wanted to gain control of the shores of Tokyo Bay, except for Tokyo itself, by the time of the ceremony. As journalist Theodore White, who flew in from China to cover the event, put it, "This was to be no cloistered surrender, as had been the surrender of the Germans at Reims three months earlier. MacArthur wanted everyone there, and the world to watch."

On Sunday morning September 2, still early evening on September 1 in Washington, the veranda deck to starboard on the *Missouri*, in Tokyo Bay, was prepared for the signing of the surrender documents. Massed in the vicinity were 257 other vessels, mostly American, but some representing other nations that had fought Japan. Guests to the ceremony began arriving by destroyer and launch at seven. Admiral Nimitz came aboard at 8:05 but MacArthur did not come up the gangway until 8:43. Three minutes later the Japanese delegation mounted the starboard gangway, led, with painful difficulty, by the morning-coated Foreign Minister, Mamoru Shigemitsu. A survivor, years before, of an assassin's bomb, he limped on a badly fitting artificial leg and required a cane. Following him was General Yoshijiro Umezu, still chief of staff, with headquarters gold braid cord over one shoulder. Nine representatives were all that Japan was allowed, three each from the Foreign Office, the Army, and the Navy. With Shigemitsu was Toshikazu Kase, who had been in his ministry at the beginning. "We waited a few minutes," he recalled, "standing in the public gaze like penitent schoolboys awaiting the dreaded schoolmaster." As bombers had warmed up on the decks of Japanese carriers off Pearl Harbor, Kase had stood at Foreign Minister Togo's side while Ambassador Grew tried to deliver a twelfth-hour peace appeal from President Roosevelt to Emperor Hirohito. Now Kase was present at the end.

A mess table covered with a green felt cloth held the documents to be signed, so the Japanese credentials read, on behalf of "Hirohito, by the Grace of Heaven, Emperor of Japan, seated on the Throne occupied by the same Dynasty changeless through ages eternal...." The formal instrument as drafted in Washington and amended in Manila committed Japan literally to "unconditional surrender," commanded all civil and military officials to obey and enforce Allied orders, and directed them "to remain at their posts and to continue to perform noncombatant duties unless specifically relieved...."

As the proceedings opened at 9:08 A.M., 450 aircraft from TF 38 roared overhead. Flanking MacArthur at his microphone, flown from prison camps in Manchuria, were Generals Wainwright and Percival, gaunt in their fresh uniforms. "We are gathered here," MacArthur began, "to conclude a solemn agreement whereby Peace may be restored." He asked for a disavowal of "distrust, malice, or hatred," and said he hoped "that both victors and vanquished ... [would] rise to that higher dignity which alone befits the sacred purposes we are about to serve."

The Japanese signatories walked forward and bent over the documents, looking for their places. Seated because of his infirmities, Shigemitsu slowly removed his silk top hat and yellow gloves and placed them on the table. As he fumbled, MacArthur snapped to Sutherland, "Show him where to sign!" As Umezu finished signing and straightened up, the sun broke through the gray overcast. After MacArthur signed for the Allied Powers, their representatives followed to sign, but confusion arose after the United States, China, Britain, the U.S.S.R. (in the person of the stolid Derevyanko),* and Australia had inscribed both sets of papers. Possibly dazzled by sunlight, the Canadian delegate signed on the line for France. Shrugging helplessly at being put out of place, the French representative signed on the Netherlands line, forcing the New Zealand delegate, who then lost his space to the Dutch, to sign an empty space.

Observing the disorder, General Sutherland walked over and drew arrows on each copy to restore identities. (The instrument would win no prizes for neatness, but the Imperial Rescript that had begun the peace process had itself been corrected and patched.)

MacArthur announced in a ringing voice that seemed to require no microphone, "These proceedings are closed," and then added quietly to Halsey, "Bill, where the hell are those airplanes?" As if stage-managed—and it was—400 B-29s and 1,500 carrier aircraft swept over from the north and thundered toward the mists overhanging Fujiyama. The United States had been at war for 1,365 days.

September 2 would not enter, any more than May 8 or August 15, into the great calendar of American (or international) holidays. World War II would have too many endings—and different beginnings, as well—for the participants. For the United States, laws that applied for the "duration" of the war could not be erased by decree, and some, like the draft, or the winding down of war agencies, required acts of Congress to change them. Carefully sidestepping the legal mine field, Harry Truman announced from a White House microphone, "As President . . . I proclaim Sunday, September 2, 1945, to be V-J Day—the day of formal surrender by Japan. It is not yet the day for formal proclamation of the end of the war or of the cessation of hostilities." But it was, Truman declared, the "day of retribution" for the "day of infamy."

In most war zones the surrenders awaited the signing on the *Missouri*. The Russians refused to stop shooting in Manchuria and Korea

*Secretary of State Byrnes, in *Speaking Frankly*, recalled being shown in Moscow in December 1945 a documentary about the Japanese war. The Red Army was pictured crossing the frontier and being greeted tumultuously by the people of Manchuria. The signing of the surrender document was filmed as largely an affair between Japanese and Soviet representatives that had taken place on "a battleship" not identified as American. "The scene might very well impress many Russians as the ending, on a battleship, of a private war between Russia and Japan."

until September 1, intending to seize what they could on the technicality that no peace yet existed. Yoshie Fukushima, who had been fleeing since the Soviets attacked, held her son and jumped from a moving train at Harbin. "He was all I could hold." In her clothes she had pinned a tiny Buddhist sutra. "The whole area was in total confusion. Japanese beggars, Manchurians, and boastful Russians [were] now settling in to run it, all mixed up together." In 1955 she received a letter from a former POW recently returned from a Soviet prison camp "four hundred miles from Moscow." Her husband, Masaichi, he wrote, had died there on May 18, 1946. The Russians claimed to have killed 83,737 Japanese soldiers but would never confess to the widespread atrocities committed against civilians and refugees. Of the 594,000 prisoners taken, many would be worked to death as Russian slave labor well into the 1950s and even beyond. Heavy industry equipment was stripped and taken across the border into Siberia. The Kwantung Army's war matériel revitalized the burgeoning armies of Mao Zedong. And in a speech at the Kremlin, Stalin declared, "For forty years we, the men of the older generation, have waited for this day. And now this day has come." The shame of 1904 was expunged.

Peace came only briefly to the rest of China. After the surrender some of the great cities belonged to no one. In Shanghai, Japanese police vainly tried to keep order as the soldiers withdrew. Everyone looted. In Shanghai luxury goods unobtainable for years suddenly turned up on the black markets—whiskey, silks, refrigerators, cameras, typewriters, tobacco. Chinese warlords and gangsters had never been out of business, but free enterprise was never freer.

Jewish refugees from Russia now had their turn to worry, although "White" Russians had been anti-Communist and many had lived in the East since the 1917 revolution. To the Japanese, looking for revenge against the Soviet stab in the back, differentiation between one Russian and another was seldom observed, but the Japanese had little opportunity to search the Shanghai ghetto, and remained in nominal control only until August 22, when the ghetto-pass system collapsed. On August 30 Americans began arriving in strange vehicles they called "jeeps," and brought with them Manuel Siegel, the onetime Joint Distribution Committee representative who had negotiated American-Jewish aid to the refugees until thrown into an internment camp. The Stars and Stripes were hoisted in a school compound and refugees sang "God Bless America" and took to the streets, dancing—even with the impassive Chinese.

Near Nanking, American parachutists landed on August 17 to check on the Wse-hsien internment camp but were then confined to the camp. The Japanese claimed "the dangerous state of affairs in the surrounding area." And there *was* chaos as the Communist Eighth Route Army was eager to move in. Negotiations with the puppet Nanking Army took place, under American auspices but involving Chiang's remote government, on August 21. Four days later Nanking itself was visited by a Chungking delegation, but only on September 6 did General Ho Ying-chin enter the city, covered by a squadron of fighter planes. On the ninth, in the name of Chiang, he accepted the formal surrender of all Japanese armies in China (but not Manchuria), Formosa (which again became Taiwan), and Indochina north of the sixteenth parallel. More than two million men were actually involved, and it took round-trips running into June 1946 to repatriate all of them in eighty-five American LSTs, one Liberty ship, and various captured Japanese vessels.

Although the ceremony was colorful, held at the Central Military Academy in Whampoa in the presence of senior Allied officials, Mao's forces stayed away and in violation of the Potsdam accords took their own regional surrenders and their own booty. Chu Teh, the Communist army chief, had already announced his own interpretation of Potsdam—"All anti-Japanese armed forces in the Liberated Areas should resolutely wipe out all those enemy and armed puppet forces which refuse to surrender and hand over their arms." He also claimed "full authority . . . to take over and occupy any city, town or communication line . . . to maintain order and to appoint commissioners to take charge of all administrative matters there." Most of the pacified Nanking troops—nearly one hundred thousand—went over to the Communists with their weapons.

Chu claimed that his troops did most of the fighting, while Chiang's American-supplied Army stayed largely in place as Chungking let the Americans fight their war. For Chiang the real conflict was the post-Japanese civil war for control of China. Bolstered by fresh troops and vast caches of enemy arms, much of them turned over by the Russians, Mao fielded a formidable and motivated force. General Wedemeyer appealed to Washington to fly Kuomintang troops into the big coastal cities before the Communists secured them, but Chiang had his own ideas about which forces were most trustworthy for the assignment and had units airlifted from Burma and Indochina, or sent by sea, creating delays that Chu exploited. In Tientsin, in northern

China, the American consul reported to Washington in October 1945 that Marines depended upon former puppet troops and the Japanese to keep order, and Kwantung Army officers who had escaped the Russians turned up as advisers to Chiang's units. Deals were made with Japanese commanders that their troops would not be disarmed if they fought the Communists, and as late as April 1946 a Japanese general in full imperial uniform would inspect Chinese troops who not only cheered him with "Long Live the Republic of China!" but followed their salute with "Long Live the Empire of Japan!" In 1947, eighteen months after General Okamura had formally surrendered his troops in Nanking, Japanese soldiers commanded by their own officers—but all now in Chinese uniforms—were still fighting for Chiang in what had become a very hot civil war that Chiang was nevertheless losing.

Although the British retaking of Hong Kong was slow to come, on August 16, when the commandant of Shamshuipo Camp on Kowloon ordered the usual roll call of prisoners, Lieutenant Simon White stepped forward and told him that with Japan's surrender such controls were over. The commandant claimed to know nothing of it, and White showed him the front page of the *Hong Kong News*. After that the POWs began taking over, and demanded food. When a delivery arrived with toilet paper but no food, the prisoners armed themselves with iron bedposts and took the truck to the once-posh Peninsula Hotel, emptying the kitchens. By the eighteenth the guards had disappeared and a victory parade was held, marked by the singing of "God Save the King." Despite the presence of Japanese police, a Union Jack was hoisted to the Peak to symbolize British administration, and the next day Colonel White and the interned Colonial Secretary for Hong Kong, Franklin Gimson, tried to send a radio message to the Colonial Office in London through the International Red Cross, but the Japanese had sabotaged the radio equipment. Moving freely now, the British sent another former prisoner, Arthur May, across the bay to Macau to use Portuguese facilities, and learned of the impending arrival of Rear Admiral Harcourt with a fleet.

During the fortnight in limbo, gaunt and poorly clad British civil servants took over while armed Japanese kept order, dress swords clanging. On the thirtieth, minesweepers leading the way, the British fleet entered Victoria Harbor and Harcourt went out to visit Stanley Camp, where his skipper of the H.M.S. *Maidstone* gave a short speech reviewing the last years of the war. To one half-starved lady, Captain Shadwell "was so lovely and cheerful, plump and priceless."

The Chinese population was far less orderly and out for retribution, throwing Japanese passengers off ferries and buses and looting warehouses and stores. The chaos ended when two thousand British marines arrived on September 10 on the overworked *Empress of Australia*. Two days later the first lot of new bank notes printed in London arrived, and all remaining British internees (most left on the eleventh for Liverpool on the ship that had brought in the marines) received a credit of two hundred Hong Kong dollars. The British empire was back. On the sixteenth came the formal surrender at Government House, but not until the third week in November were all the Japanese troops still on duty in the New Territories relieved, disarmed, and repatriated.

Attempting to fend off rival interests in Korea, on August 24 the Shigemitsu government formally relinquished claims to sovereignty over Korea but left disposition to a future peace conference. On August 29 it authorized Japanese forces in Korea to minesweep Inchon harbor in advance of American landings intended to occupy nearby Seoul, and the Americans established a line of communication through a Japanese editor on the *Seoul Press*, Miyanaga Akiyoshi. On September 3, Lieutenant General John Hodge of the 24th Army Corps, with no briefing about Korea nor a Korean-speaking staff, arrived with a landing force, preceded by transport planes headed for Kimpo Airfield, near Seoul. Of the eighteen aircraft, only three did not turn back after encountering bad weather. It might have been better had the three turned back also, as one ferried the military government officer, Brigadier General Charles Harris, whose ideas about Korea began with retaining the Japanese system of administration and instructing the Japanese police to keep order until the Koreans could be trained. Hodge arrived on the seventh and his twenty-five-vessel flotilla disembarked troops the next day. To maintain order the Japanese forbade any but essential personnel to be on the streets of Inchon when the Americans landed, but Koreans crowded in anyway, and Japanese police fired to disperse what was becoming a mob. People were killed and wounded, and the Koreans used the funerals as occasions for anti-Japanese demonstrations that became, also, anti-American when the Army defended the Japanese as having acted legally.

Although the occupation (to the thirty-eighth parallel) was off to a bad start, the American political adviser made the situation worse. Merrell Benninghoff had been on the staff of the Tokyo embassy on December 7, 1941, and had proved an excellent improviser. On his own authority now, he blamed the "misbehaving" American press and Korean radicals for the bad relations. MacArthur replaced him on October 10 with William R. Langdon, but it was too late. Langdon explained that in "excluding popular leftwingers from Military Government, it is quite probable that at the beginning we may have picked out a disproportionate number of rich and conservative persons. But how were we to know who was who among this unfamiliar people? For practical purposes we had to hire persons who spoke English, and it so happened that these persons and their moneyed friends came largely from moneyed classes because English had been a luxury among Koreans." Not so the Soviets, who had trained cadres of Koreans in Moscow for their share of the occupation. Out of sight and out of mind, Korea had been ignored by American planners and as late as October 17, Hodge was confiding, "Japanese are still needed here, that is an undeniable fact." The bitterness among Koreans that Americans were prepared to act indefinitely through the hated Japanese was never overcome, and the hostility of Korean radicals only pushed the United States closer to Korean conservatives. Ignorance and incompetence set the stage for the Korean War of 1950–1953 between the efficiently Sovietized north and the unpopular government to the south, which appeared easy to overthrow and which the Americans had to return to save, if only because of the threat the Red alternative posed to Japan. The United States had gone to Korea only to disarm the Japanese, but could never get out.

The American strategy to have Chiang accept the surrenders in the northern half of Indochina was intended to outmaneuver the French while strengthening Chiang's hand against the Communists. Roosevelt had advised then-Secretary of State Cordell Hull in December 1943 that Indochina under the French thumb was worse off than it had been in precolonial days: "France has milked it dry for one hundred years. The people of Indo-China are entitled to something better than that." He wanted a United Nations trusteeship until the country was ready to be on its own, but both the French and the forces of Ho and Giap had other ideas, and the United States would eventually be caught, catastrophically, in the middle. In Hanoi on August 20, the viceroy of the puppet emperor, Bao Dai, surrendered to the Viet

Minh, and five days later Bao Dai abdicated. A delegation of Viet
Minh moved quickly south through Hue and central Annam toward
Saigon, where, from the governor's palace, Hoang Quoc Viet, its
leader, telegraphed Ho in Hanoi: "IN 21 PROVINCES I HAVE CROSSED
POWER IS IN OUR HANDS EVERYTHING HAS GONE SMOOTHLY. . . ." But
Mountbatten was authorized at Potsdam to take over the south of the
country, and his headquarters had no way of coping with the vast
additional responsibilities—all of the Dutch Indies and almost all
of Southeast Asia below the Chinese border except for what had
been assigned above the sixteenth parallel, even less realistically, to
Chiang. The SEAC also had well over a hundred thousand prisoners
and internees to extricate and support.

At a meeting in Rangoon with the chief of staff to Marshal Terauchi
on August 27, Mountbatten arranged for token Allied forces to enter
Siam and Indochina, and on the day after the surrender in Tokyo Bay
an advance party of his 7th Indian Division flew into Bangkok to prepare to move troops onward into Saigon. A brigade began flying in
on the thirteenth, with instructions to secure military control for
French administrators. The British agreed on little with the French,
but the two countries thought in parallel about recovering lost
colonies. The arrangement did not sit well with the Americans, nor
was it acceptable to the Viet Minh, who agreed with the United States
on little else, but General Sir Douglas Gracey in effect did de Gaulle's
business in Indochina.

   Flying in from Paris, General Jacques Leclerc stopped in Kandy
and persuaded Mountbatten to assist the French in pacifying the
southern half of the colony. The civil war that would last until the
Americans left in 1974 was on. There were murders, even massacres,
on both sides while armed Japanese troops stood aside. On September 26, the first American of what would be a long list over four
decades in Indochina was killed—OSS colonel Peter Dewey. Realizing when his jeep was attacked in Saigon that he had been mistaken
for a Frenchman, he cried out, "*Je suis Américain!*" The Vietnamese
even carted away his body.

Conditions were no better above the sixteenth parallel. To support
Chiang, General Wedemeyer blocked Jean Sainteny from leaving
Kunming for Hanoi, enabling Ho Chi Minh to arrive a day ahead of
Sainteny, on August 21. By the twenty-ninth, Ho had announced a

"nationalist"—rather than Communist—government with himself as president, addressing the people as "My children," which, from a colonial ruler, would have been an outrageous but expected condescension. His wispy beard blowing in the hot wind, he would appear to enthusiastic crowds to blame the French rather than the Japanese for the wartime hunger and the postwar chaos. The Japanese troops seemed hardly to exist. In mid-September, when their surrender was taken by Chiang's Chinese, who looted like Russians, the Greater East Asia Co-Prosperity Sphere seemed to many like the good old days. The Chinese did not begin withdrawing until March 1946—and then to Leclerc's French.

In Malaya a different breed of Chinese was operating. Long at odds, the Chinese and Malays who shared the land for centuries had different ideas about the Japanese, who knew their game was up and awaited the end. A Chinese guerrilla insurgency with Communist backing had long been under way, while the Malays had accepted the Japanese as another change of masters. With the Japanese losing control, Malays, who had been employed as the colonial police, began rounding up Chinese and murdering them, then dumping the bodies in the fast-moving rivers, which took the evidence out to sea. From their internment camp the German seamen of the *U-181* watched and listened, hoping to be extricated before the violence reached them. Toward the end of August the Japanese informed them that they would be taken to Singapore so that all Axis forces could be surrendered there. At a meeting of the German officers the feeling was to remain and protect themselves, and the Chinese irregulars offered to cooperate, as they had no use for the British either, but the Japanese had their way. The Germans were piled into trucks on top of the cargo.

At night, Lieutenant Otto Giese recalled, the jittery Japanese "fired wildly into the jungle with their rifles and machine guns," wounding some of their own men as the trucks, in the darkness, drove around sharp bends. Reaching Singapore over the Johore causeway, they saw "many flags in the streets, the Union Jack, the Stars and Stripes, the Soviet banner, and the Chungking flag, a very strange sight. Suddenly the world had become international again." In Singapore business as usual prevailed. Commander Wolfgang Ehrhardt had sold the opium and other valuable commodities his U-boat had been hauling to Germany and that had been removed to the Empire Dock to Chinese and Malay go-betweens for a price in gold bars. The gold was retrieved and a secret account opened for the men of the *U-181*, giving them "a sort of clandestine war pay and enabling them to buy provisions and clothing up to the very day we shipped to England." Captain Kurt Freiwald, the senior internee officer for all the Germans, signed for the account, which stipulated that the residue would be turned over to the next legal German government. Giese kept a copy inside the aluminum paper from a cigarette pack, folded into a tube of toothpaste, where it remained until 1948.

On September 4 the Germans watched from the beaches as the first British warships appeared off Singapore. Giese recognized the heavy cruiser *Sussex*. Up the peninsula to the north, British forces landed at Port Swettenham on September 9, and on the twelfth the formal surrender of Malaya was signed by nine ranking Japanese representatives of their forces and Mountbatten. The Germans wandered freely, Indian troops unaware that the smartly attired naval officers were the former enemy. "Suddenly the streets were jammed with cars again, cars that had been scarce for so many years." His "provisions corporal," Friedemann, told him about how clever the Chinese had been during the occupation: "They took their vehicles apart when the Japanese conquered Singapore and distributed the parts among their kinfolk, waiting for this moment to resurrect them."

The Germans were discovered on September 7 and Ehrhardt was escorted to the city jail as a possible war criminal. On October 17 they were marched twenty-two miles across the island to Changi Prison, on the eastern edge, the 260 seamen and officers of former U-boats and surface raiders singing enthusiastically "Lili Marlene" and other German songs despite the oppressive heat, to demonstrate the spirit missing from the disarmed Japanese. Crowds gathered. The Gurkha guards, who could not keep up to the quick German pace, were relieved by Indian troops. The afternoon sun became merciless but pride would not permit the seamen to slow down. Some fainted and collapsed, to be picked up by trucks. Before Changi loomed, their voices had cracked, and they marched on in silence on blistered feet, sweat dripping down into their shoes. Not until they boarded the busy, dilapidated *Empress of Australia* on June 26, 1946, did they venture again beyond the walls of Changi. Passing through Suez they saw deeply tanned POWs, former soldiers in the Afrika Korps, toiling along the banks. Shouting down, they threw cigarette packs. When Rommel's veterans heard that their compatriots had come from Singapore they were surprised that there had been Germans fighting so far east.

In Bangkok, Field Marshal Pibul, the strongman who had cooperated with the December 1941 velvet occupation, had long been in touch with Mountbatten. Thailand had survived by regularly playing both sides. The British landed at Don Muang Airfield with an advance force of 1,250 on September 3, and two days later Lady Mountbatten herself flew in to see to the welfare of prisoners who had survived the building of the Siam-Burma railway. POWs, who had been reduced to foraging in Japanese feces for the occasional undigested black bean, were shocked and delighted to see her, but Edwina Mountbatten was a free and unpredictable spirit. One of the first British officers into the upjungle areas was Major Andrew Gilchrist, who had been military attaché in the embassy at Bangkok when the war began, and who would become Deputy Political Adviser to the British commander in Siam, General Geoffrey Evans. When, before the formal surrender, he found the Japanese commander, Lieutenant General Minoru Hamada, who was ultimately responsible for some of the most criminal brutalities inflicted upon POWs on the part of a nation that considered a surrendered soldier a worthless thing, he asked how Hamada was going to handle his situation. Through an interpreter the general answered, "The Japanese esteem the carp. When this fish is placed on the chopping block, ready to be cooked, it does not jump and bounce; it stays still and submits to its fate quietly." In November, Gilchrist asked about him, and was told that Hamada had sent Evans a poem,

> The evening breeze moves the clouds to the horizon,
> But the flowers in the garden are fading.

It had arrived after Hamada had committed *seppuku*. "Not easy to understand, those Japs, are they?" wondered Evans.

In the sprawling Dutch Indies, the Sukarno declaration of independence for Indonesia on August 16 had been rushed by the Imperial Rescript the day before. Not until September 8 did a small advance party of eight officers from Mountbatten's forces parachute into Java to assess the situation. The Dutch were waiting in Brisbane to reassume colonial administration. To them, Sukarno was a corrupt Quisling who had sold out his people, to whom the Dutch had brought modernity and were grooming for a sort of partnership with the Netherlands. When a Dutch civil affairs team on board the H.M.S. *Cumberland* attempted to land, the infant republic forbade it. The Allies could land forces to disarm the Japanese and remove POWs, but no political interference would be tolerated. The standoff left the Japanese in a quandary. They had been appreciated for throwing the Dutch out, but now the Indonesians wanted the Japanese out too, yet prevented their surrendering to the Allies. On October 1 the Indonesians attacked Japanese garrisons in central Java, shouting the familiar independence cry, *"Merdeka!"*—"Freedom!" Most surrenders were made to the Indonesians, who secured further weaponry, while the outraged Dutch complained that according to the Tokyo Bay capitulation agreement the Japanese had to surrender to the Allies. By October the Indonesians were in full warfare with the Dutch, with the British military caught in the middle. It took a month for the Dutch to recapture the big Javanese city of Surabaja, but it was an empty and temporary triumph. Mountbatten's own British-Indian divisions employed in Java were decimated with Japanese weapons and a British brigadier was killed. In November 1949 the Dutch, after embarrassingly costly "police actions," relinquished their colonial dream and recognized Indonesian sovereignty. The war foreshadowed Vietnam.

The British dilemma in Burma mirrored Dutch frustrations in the Indies. The Burmese had taken no part in the negotiations leading up to surrender, nor had they—but for hill country Karen guerrillas—fought the Japanese, who had given them a government of their own. Japanese-style independence was at least independence. After the Japanese were shipped home the British had a new war with the Burmese, leading to recognition of their independence on January 4, 1948. The pro-British Karens felt betrayed. They wanted their own state, yet were left as a colony of lower Burma. Terror and violence became a long-term legacy of an unstable Burma, unhappier as a nation than it had been as a ward of the empire.

While India gained no taste of self-rule under the Co-Prosperity Sphere, it did gain an army. The Indian communities in Southeast Asia, plus the Indian army prisoners of war acquired in Malaya, Burma, and Singapore, became fertile soil for cultivating an Indian National Army. Out of sixty-five thousand Indian POWs in Malaya and Singapore, twenty-five thousand were recruited into an *Azad Hind Fauj* by Mohan Singh, who was too effective for the Japanese. When he began to suspect Japanese aims for India as another Manchukuo, he was jailed.

A new leader was available. Subhas Chandra Bose had slipped out of India in early 1941 to attempt to recruit Desert Army prisoners from North Africa into an Indian army for Hitler, but the *Führer* was not interested in India, which in dividing the future world with Japan he had rejected. Bose went back to Asia via the still-neutral Soviet Union, reconstituted Singh's army, and employed it in Burma until he had to flee in May 1945 to Siam, where he broadcast propaganda to India. Going south to Singapore, he solicited help from Marshal Terauchi to try to get to Manchuria, where he hoped quixotically to continue the struggle to free India through Siberia. Taking off from Formosa to fly north, his overloaded plane crashed, and Bose died in a hospital a few days after the rescript broadcast in August.

The surviving leaders, prisoners of war twice, much like the Vlasov Army in Germany, were put on trial for treason by the British in Delhi. The Indian National Congress raised money for the defense, and one of its star attorneys, who had not practiced law for thirty years, was Jawaharlal Nehru. Demonstrations all over India supported the defendants, and the British backed down, finding them guilty but suspending their sentences of forced exile for life. Supporting the INA leaders required some political agility. They had advocated violence in a nonviolent culture. They had allied themselves with a fascist power. They had violated their military oaths. But the verdict and the hostility raised were further nails in the coffin of colonialism, and an India divided into Moslem and Hindu nations was given its independence in 1947, the transition overseen in his new political role by Governor General Mountbatten. In effect, the Japanese had indirectly liberated much of Asia.

Forcible repatriation of the Vlasov Army and related prisoners exacerbated Western relations with the Soviets well after the Japanese surrender. The last group doomed to return to Russia was shipped from Fort Dix, New Jersey, to Germany on August 31, the date apparently intended to ensure Russian participation in the Tokyo Bay ceremonies. In Italy, Field Marshal Alexander was increasingly appalled by the tragedies of the transfers, and early in September he sent a message to the War Office describing how the Soviet mission required "use of force including handcuffs and travel under escort in locked box-cars. . . . We believe that the handing over of these individuals would almost certainly involve their death." He foresaw "many more such cases" and implied that he wanted the practice stopped.

In Russia the operation officially did not exist. Newspapers filled their columns instead with praise for the Red Army's "dealing the death blow to Japanese imperialism." On his way by rail from Moscow to Warsaw on a Red Cross mission, Russell Johnston watched, going in the opposite direction, "a line of boxcars loaded with Red Army soldiers, who lean from the open doors. . . . The tops of the boxcars are piled high with used bicycles, odd pieces of furniture, and hundreds of baby carriages." Victorious troops traveled in boxcars, too—with their loot.

Life remained miserable for the defeated, innocent and guilty alike. Writing for the London *News Chronicle* from Berlin, Norman Clark reported seeing, late in August, the Danzig train come in at the Stettiner Station crowded with tearful women and famished children who had been forced by young Poles looting the train to give up any possessions of value they still had. As he watched, the Poles were waiting for the next train out to repeat the process. In Lindenau, in Polonized Upper Silesia, Germans were still being forcibly expelled. "Quite early in the morning of August 24," Josef Buhl, the local photographer, reported, "the village had been surrounded by militia, making flight impossible. The old basket-maker Scheurel was shot when he attempted to flee, and bled to death. Wagner, whose wife was already dead, hanged himself in desperation. . . . We had to pack the most necessary things together in haste and get out of the house, for drunken militia had already arrived to drive us out with truncheons." Russian soldiers pulled aside those they wanted to do alleged threshing work, chiefly young girls. One by one the others were searched, first their baggage, then their bodies. "Nothing escaped these bloodhounds. From me they took all I had, tobacco and pipe, mirror and comb, and of course my money. I came out again stripped and looked for my rucksack which I saw lying empty on the ground: the rucksack had also been thoroughly searched. Next to it lay half a loaf and my carving knife. The rest of the contents were gone. Blanket, working trousers, stockings, soap and towel, everything was gone."

Instead of being permitted to continue, the miserable procession was herded to Lärchenain, now Ciescowic, where they were shut up, men separated from women and children, in an old castle without food for three days. They were left unguarded, to encourage escape. They had nowhere to go but westward.

Life was incomparably worse for many German prisoners of war. Even in the West conditions remained squalid for those still unreleased. At a Belgian camp 9,700 SS prisoners were incarcerated where 40,000 political prisoners of the Nazis had been housed, a former brick factory still piled high with the shoes of earlier victims. Few had bunks; officers had narrow duckboards. Food and sanitary conditions were bad. Learning that a relative of his had died in Belsen, a guard reached for his Sten gun and promptly shot seven Germans. The Dutch were equally embittered but could do less about it, distracted by events in the Indies as the war wound down. And they would not forget Japan any more than Germany. (In 1971, when Emperor Hirohito made what was billed as a "redemption tour" of Western Europe, objects were thrown at his car, and in Amsterdam he was greeted by crowds carrying placards reading, "Where is my father? Give me back my father!" He asked his Grand Chamberlain to advise Japanese newsmen not to report it.)

In Lübeck, Arthur Dickens wondered on September 2 whether "the thousands of authenticated cases of cruelty by Germans in war and occupation" suggested that "when the Nazis called for *Brutalität*, there must have existed an all-too-common answering chord in the national character." Yet the experience of war and its aftermath was evidence enough that the capacity for cruelty, lust, and greed overwhelmed flags and faiths and frontiers. Just before the Allied Control Council met for its first session on August 30, its first object the elimination of all traces of Nazi rule from Germany, Ruth Andreas-Friedrich wrote in her diary about the dilemma of German women raped in the last weeks of war, and since, who now bore the results. Article 218 of the Nazi criminal code forbade aborting a fetus. Even if extenuating circumstances were proved, mandatory sentences of six months were required. Public health officials met at the Charité hospital to discuss the problem, one of them explaining afterward that the law could not be repealed "without legislative power." But he added, "Its enforcement will cease temporarily."

In Paris, Cyrus Sulzberger, war correspondent for *The New York Times*, met for tea with fat, amiable Gertrude Stein and her companion, "cozy, hideous Alice Toklas." Gertrude Stein bubbled, "I am completely drowned in the American army and I eat, think and sleep

GI." But she worried about their lack of "any active interest in things." They had no political or spiritual interests and seemed ready to return to isolation. "I was on a plane with some soldiers. I asked them if they had any Bibles with them. One soldier said, 'Why do we need Bibles? If you have a good ground crew your plane stays up.' They knew all the percentages of error."

A few days later, on August 28, Sulzberger met with the British ambassador, Churchill's friend Alfred Duff Cooper, who worried more about England than about France, which had "a great gift for recovering from wars." France had lost many wars before and had always revived quickly, he noted. "If Great Britain had been overrun, I doubt if we could ever have recovered." Yet Churchill, the man who had overseen Britain's recovery in 1940 after the fall of France, was, on the day the war ended in Tokyo Bay, out of a job and out of Britain, leaving that morning in Field Marshal Alexander's Dakota for Italy, where he would be Alexander's guest in a villa on the edge of Lake Como. He was thinking now of using his daily minutes to write his war memoirs. "People say my speeches after Dunkirk were the thing," he told Charles Moran on the plane. "That was a part, not the chief part. They forget I made all the main military decisions."

From Met Lab in Chicago, Leo Szilard used the end of the war and wartime constraints as his reason for appealing to the President through his secretary, Matthew J. Connelly, for permission to make public the petition to Truman from atomic scientists on the morality of dropping the Bomb on civilian populations. His petition was forwarded—very likely Truman never knew of it—to the Corps of Engineers, under which the Manhattan Engineering District ostensibly operated, and he was told that the contract of employment he had signed forbade it. Stories about the Bomb abounded in the press, but none disclosed what Szilard and Franck had wanted released. The August 20 issue of *Life* magazine was full of articles on the making of the atomic bomb and illustrated with photographs of scientists involved in nuclear research over the years, including Otto Hahn, who was shown a copy at Farm Hall. Weizsäcker pored over the pictures and remarked, "Of course they are mostly Germans."

From Los Alamos, J. Robert Oppenheimer wrote to the Secretary of War about the Interim Committee Scientific Panel's concerns about atomic energy and future wars. "We have been unable to devise or propose effective military countermeasures for atomic weapons," he conceded. Further, "We are not only unable to outline a program that would assure to this nation for the next decades hegemony in the field of atomic weapons; we are equally unable to insure that such hegemony, if achieved, could protect us from the most terrible destruction."

Not all the delayed surrenders occurred on isolated coral atolls. Excluding the hermit Japanese who survived for years in remote places, Rip van Winkles of reefs and rain forests, the very last holdouts were the ultimate Nazis—the SS. The myth of an Alpine redoubt where German die-hards would disappear only to fight on had been widespread in 1945, but searches turned up only deserters in hiding and soldiers who had shed uniforms to evade POW stockades. Just before Christmas 1945 a report to American G2 in Austria claimed that SS troops were wintering near Hitler's mountain aerie of Berchtesgaden. The 9th Reconnaissance Troop of the 9th Infantry Division in Bavaria was issued snow gear and sent to flush them out.

Although nothing was found, follow-up tips in February alleged that SS forces had slipped westward to the Reit im Winkl area, and Lieutenant Edward W. Samuell, Jr., was ordered with his infantry unit to Tutzing, on the Starnberger See below Munich. The local population disclaimed any knowledge of soldiers in the area, and GIs of the 9th saw no traces of recent habitation. Then French occupation troops in the Tyrol reported SS sightings to the south along the Austrian-German frontier.

With reports continuing early in April that fixed the alleged SS activity as south of the Tegernsee, near the frontier at the Achenpass, a joint French-U.S. operation was mounted on April 10 with a French liaison officer, Captain La Roux, joining the 9th for it. They were to search and occupy a snowy ridge on the common border between the American zone of Germany and the French zone of Austria. The 9th Reconnaissance Troop was to move south toward the ridge while the French climbed north. A second French force was to attack westward down the ridge line. Samuell's unwritten instructions were to let any prisoners be taken by the French and to let them claim credit for the operation if anything came of it.

The Americans deployed from Tutzing toward Wildbad Kreuth, and for three days, according to the official operations report, "Sent patrols out into the surrounding mountains both during [the] day and at night, set up road blocks, checked all civilians for proper identification and raided suspected houses. Some evidence of former enemy equipment was found—bayonets, ammunition (small arm), one radio, Nazi flags, steel helmets, etc." But, the report added, "no SS or former SS troops were captured. Constant liaison with the French was maintained. . . . Mutual help, smooth and reciprocal cooperation and relations were had at all times during this operation."

The laconic report implied something more. The American patrols, according to Samuell, deliberately made "considerable noise," to drive whatever there was of the enemy toward the French. "The SS apparently observed our attack and pulled off the ridge southward. They walked directly into the hands of the French. . . . I had taken no prisoners and no SS were inside the American zone of Germany."

Late that night Samuell met the French lieutenant colonel in charge of the other and larger side of the operation. "He was elated over its success. At the time he was interrogating 22 SS people but gave me no hint of the size of the units he captured. I did not ask. His people had gotten involved in a fire fight with the SS but took no casualties." And so, in early April 1946, eleven months after the surrender at Reims, the last German surrender, never reported in the press, concluded World War II.

The second world war in its century had lasted, counting only until the formal surrender in Tokyo Bay, six years and two days, and had produced as many new crises as it had settled. Even after the last instrument of surrender was signed the war continued, and a "Cold War" of unforeseen consequences arose between the victors. Collapsing colonialisms were already spawning new imperialisms and colliding nationalisms. Decaying economies, expanding economies, and economies imploding from their inner contradictions would determine whether the world could recover from its propensity for wars as solutions to problems—or as diversions from them. New technologies born from war—atomic energy, electronics, computers, chemistry, medicine, engineering, agriculture, aviation, and rocketry—would become enormous stimuli, for better and for worse.

No formal peace conference, or comprehensive treaty, on the order of Vienna or Versailles, emerged when the shooting stopped. There was nothing to ratify but a recognition of discord. Still, the majestic *Missouri* in Tokyo Bay on September 2, 1945, remains an ironic image of the end. The final month of the war had made such formidable floating worlds as the battleship obsolete. World War II may even have made world wars obsolete.

# · Sources ·

Full references are furnished only with the first citation. After that citations are shortened and a cross-reference is supplied to the notes for the chapter where the first citation occurs. References are in order of appearance of data in the text. Names are generally family name last; however, exceptions appear in the cases of Chinese and Southeast Asian names otherwise unrecognizable.

## PROLOGUE

The history of the balloon bomb offensive, with charts of recorded impacts and discoveries of debris, is in Robert C. Mikesh, *Japan's World War II Balloon Bomb Attacks on North America* (Washington, D.C., 1973). An oral history account of making the devices is that of Tetsuno Tanaka, then a Kokura schoolgirl, in Haruko Taya Cook and Theodore F. Cook, eds., *Japan at War* (New York, 1992). The search for what German scientists knew about an atomic bomb is described by a participant, Samuel Goudsmit, in *Alsos* (Annapolis, 1947); Tom Bower in *The Paperclip Conspiracy* (Boston, 1987); and Sir Charles Frank in *Operation Epsilon: The Farm Hall Transcripts* (Berkeley, Calif., 1993).

Future "Flashman" novelist George MacDonald Fraser's memoir of Burma in 1945 is *Quartered Safe Out Here* (London, 1992). Quotations are with his permission.

British embassy reports to the Foreign Office, written largely by Isaiah Berlin, are in H. G. Nicholas, ed., *Washington Despatches* (Chicago, 1981). Bill Dunn's war correspondent memoir is *Pacific Microphone* (College Station, Tex., 1988).

Admiral Zacharias's papers are in the Hoover Institution Library, Stanford. His 1945 broadcasts were published in the national press and further described in his *Secret Missions* (New York, 1946).

## I. THE ROAD TO POTSDAM

The "88" for "Heil Hitler" was observed by Douglas Botting in *From the Ruins of the Third Reich* (New York, 1985). Allied signs declaring, "Here ends the civilized world . . ." are described by Sabine Richel in *What Did You Do in the War, Daddy?* (New York, 1989). Graffiti ironically thanking Hitler in Third Reich formula are noted in *Ruins* and in an oral history by Libussa Fritz-Krockow, *Hour of the Women* (New York, 1991), transcribed by Christian von Krockow and translated by Krishna Winston. Heinrich Böll's *The Silent Angel* was published in 1992 in Cologne. The translation of *Der Engel schweig* by Breon Mitchell, used here, was published in New York in 1994.

The definitive biography of Vidkun Quisling is Oddvar K. Hoidal, *Quisling: A Study in Treason* (Oslo, 1989). Hitler's admiring comment to Belgian fascist Leon Degrelle is quoted in AP reports of his death, April 1, 1994. The situation in Denmark at the surrender is described in chapter 22 of a privately printed memoir by Robert Strauss and in letters from RS to SW. William Colt MacDonald's *Cartridge Carnival* was published by Doubleday in New York in 1945 in a trade edition; it went immediately, as servicemen were avid for Westerns, into an Armed Forces Edition. Eisenhower mentions reading the novel while surrender parleying went on in a letter to Mamie, May 6, 1945. The confusion over the surrender is described in the chapter "Bungling V-E Day," in Nigel Hamilton, *Monty: Final Years of the Field-Marshal, 1944–1976* (New York, 1987). Jimmy Carter at Annapolis, presumably a memory offered to his biographer, is in James Wooten, *Dasher: The Roots and Rising of Jimmy Carter* (New York, 1978).

Aleksandr Solzhenitsyn's prison memories are quoted from his published writings by Michael Scammell in *Solzhenitsyn: A Biography* (New York, 1984). The surrender of the *U-234* is described in delayed press accounts and in Edwin P. Hoyt, *U-Boats* (New York, 1987). Churchill's exchanges with his Foreign Office are quoted in Martin Gilbert, *Winston S. Churchill, VIII: "Never Despair," 1945–1965* (Boston, 1988). Norman Turgel's arrest of Manstein is described in Gena and Norman Turgel, with Veronica Groocock, *I Light a Candle* (London, 1987). Kesselring describes his arrest in *Memoirs of Field-Marshal Kesselring* (Novato, Calif., 1988). Albert Speer describes the other Nazis at Mondorf in *Inside the Third Reich*, translated by Richard and Clara Winston (New York, 1970). Dönitz's unrepentant orders for surrender are quoted in Peter Padfield, *Dönitz: The Last Führer* (New York, 1984). Von Krosigk's broadcast was reported in *The Times* of London. *Leutnant* Boettger and Private Leverkus (and, later in the chapter, Konrad Adenauer) are quoted in Edward N. Peterson, *The Many Faces of Defeat* (New York, 1990), an excellent source for 1945 German testimony.

Michael Dembo described the Linz incident in a letter to SW. Offers of guns to kill Germans are common in 1945 testimony by DPs. (An equivalent from a released American prisoner is that of turret gunner Darr Coates, May 5, 1945, from Stalag 17B in Brannau, Austria, in the Hoover Library.) Dozens if not hundreds of books exist on the DP experience; the most useful for this book was Mark Wyman, *DP: Europe's Displaced Persons, 1945–1951* (Philadelphia, 1989). Other studies utilized were Robert H. Abzug, *Inside the Vicious Heart: Americans and the Liberation* (New York, 1985); and Jon Bridgman, *The End of the Holocaust: The Liberation of the Camps* (Portland, Oreg., 1990).

My major sources for the Vlasov Army, used throughout unless otherwise cited, were Jürgen Thorwald, *The Illusion: Soviet Soldiers in Hitler's Armies*, translated by Richard and Clara Winston (New York, 1977); and Frederick Anderson's *The Vlassov Movement*, a typescript in the Hoover Institution Library. The Yugoslav attempts at encroachment upon Austria and Italy are also covered in Mather, and I have further utilized David W. Ellwood, *Italy 1943–1945* (New York, 1985); Milovan Djilas, *Wartime* (New York, 1977); and Harold Macmillan, *The Blast of War: 1939–1945* (London, 1967).

James Krüss's 1965 memoir of his march home from the war is *Coming Home from the War: An Idyll*, translated by Edelgard von Heydekampf Bruehl (New York, 1977). The most graphic of many personal accounts of rape by Russian troops are those of Libussa Fritz-Krockow (above) and Lalli Horstmann, quoted by Ruth Andreas-Friedrich in her diary, *Battleground Berlin* (New York, 1990). W. L. White reports the Berliner congratulations on not being in the Soviet zone in *Report on the Germans* (New York, 1947). Lord Strang, in *Home and Abroad* (London, 1956), recollecting his tenure as Permanent Undersecretary for Foreign Affairs, describes the "smiling countryside"—as opposed to devastation in the large cities—in much of the British zone in the summer of 1945. Anne Morrow Lindbergh, in *A Gift for Life* (New York, 1992), quotes her husband in his journals as "preachily" castigating isolated American military atrocities, observing that at the same time he could not bring himself to recant "his admiration of the Nazis." The visiting congressman was F. Edward Hebert of Louisiana, who published in paperback pamphlet form (at thirty-five cents) his European diary as *I Went * I Saw * I Heard* (Washington, D.C., 1945).

Herschel Liebowitz (then a Pfc.) was interviewed by SW, as was Ed Buss (then a major). Judge Roy Wilkinson (then a major on Eisenhower's legal staff) was interviewed by SW on American soldiers and the capital crime problem. Heinz Kosok, then a boy in northern Germany, was interviewed by SW on the dangers of unexploded ammunition as toys. His unpublished memoir also deals with growing up in immediate postwar Germany. A similar account, with a Berlin venue, is a brief oral history by Leo Welt in *Voices from the Third Reich*, edited by Johannes Steinhoff, Peter Pechel, and Dennis Showalter (Washington, D.C., 1989). The protective angle iron on jeep bumpers in the summer of 1945, familiar to GIs in the ETO, is described in Joseph E. Persico, *Nuremberg: Infamy on Trial* (New York, 1994).

The mock circular quoted on eligibility for release is in the Austin E. Fife collection in the Hoover Institution Library. Accounts of Kissinger as occupation mayor are in Marvin Kalb and Bernard Kalb, *Kissinger* (New York, 1974); and Walter Isaacson, *Kissinger* (New York, 1992).

Kay Summersby Morgan is quoted from her posthumously published *Past Forgetting: My Love Affair with Dwight D. Eisenhower* (New York, 1976). Representative Hebert is quoted from his pamphlet. Libussa von Oldershausen is referred to under a different surname in chapter I. *The Papers of Dwight David Eisenhower: Occupation,*

*1945: VI* (Baltimore, 1970), edited by Alfred D. Chandler, Jr., Louis Galambos, and others, will be the source for Eisenhower correspondence of this period, including his chastisement of Patton. Additional background for the workings of the occupation can be found in *The Papers of General Lucius D. Clay: Germany 1945–1949*, I, edited by Jean Edward Smith (Bloomington, Ind., 1974).

For Leslie Groves and James Bryant Conant, see chapters III and IV. The competition to spirit away Nazi scientists is discussed in *The Paperclip Conspiracy* (see notes to Prologue). The role of Klaus Fuchs and his cohorts is dealt with in H. Montgomery Hyde, *The Atom Bomb Spies* (New York, 1980). Churchill's election campaigning is detailed in Gilbert, VIII, and in Robert Rhodes James, *Anthony Eden* (London, 1986).

## II. Summer Grasses

The epigraph verse by Bashō has been translated many times and in many ways, but always with the same point being made. The present text is my own adaptation.

The long weeks in Japan in which leaders tried to reach a consensus about fighting, or ending, the war are dealt with from the Japanese perspective best in the Pacific War Research Society's *Japan's Longest Day*, edited by Kazutoshi Hando (Tokyo, 1968); and the same group's *The Day Man Lost* (Tokyo, 1967), both of which were able to secure testimony from surviving participants twenty years after. They are relied upon throughout except where testimony is contradicted by known facts. An excellent source by a participant is Toshikazu Kase's *Journey to the Missouri* (New Haven, Conn., 1950). "Magic" intercepts (National Archives) also expose Japan's diplomatic dialogue.

Wesley F. Craven and James L. Cate, in *The Army Air Forces in World War II*, vol. 7 (Chicago, 1958), often useful for statistics, note the value of Iwo Jima as a safe haven for B-29s. Susumu Ushioda's recollections of the summer fire raids is in a letter to SW. Shiji Nire appears in the autobiographical family chronicle novel *The House of Nire* by Morio Kita, translated by Dennis Keene (Tokyo, 1984 and 1985). The wry Japanese joke about Mount Fuji and the war situation is from Saburo Ienaga's *The Pacific War: World War II and the Japanese, 1931–1945* (New York, 1978). Juro Kara is quoted in Ian Buruma's *The Wages of Guilt: Memories of War in Germany and Japan* (New York, 1994). Yukio Mishima's early memoir is *Confessions of a Mask*, translated by M. Weatherby (New York, 1960). Hiromi Tanaka's recollection is in a letter to SW.

Mitsuru Yoshida, a junior radar officer on the *Yamato* and one of its few survivors, wrote its story as *Senkan Yamato no saigo* (The End of the Battleship *Yamato*). It was translated by Richard Minear as *Requiem for Battleship Yamato* (Seattle, 1985). The most graphically detailed account of the Okinawa invasion is George Feifer's *Tennozan* (New York, 1992), supplemented here by reports to the Chief of Naval Operations (Admiral King) in the National Archives.

Cabinet meetings on ending the Japanese war are minuted in copies in the National Archives, which also have the "Olympic" and "Coronet" planning documents overseen by Sutherland and MacArthur. The final meeting is crucial to postwar arguments about use of the Bomb, as the casualty projections by someone as cautious (and anti-Bomb) as Admiral Leahy forecast very stark figures based upon the Okinawa experience—and on the home islands themselves the resistance would not have been less. Leahy estimated 268,465 dead and wounded for the first phase of

"Olympic." The OSS geographer was E. Willard Miller, who confided the quarter-million casualty estimate to SW in November 1994. Stewart Udall, in *The Myths of August* (New York, 1994), basing his argument on historical revisionists, talks of "the shifting numbers that Truman and others used to justify the atomic bombings" and is skeptical of Truman's "quarter of a million" estimate in later years, calling it "popular myth" in the making. The figures were the crusty Admiral Leahy's. The planners who projected lesser figures were promoting the invasion; Leahy was not. The greatest invasion in history would not have had modest losses. Truman's meeting with senators prior to Potsdam is described in his diaries.

## III. JULY 15, 1945

Truman's own record of Potsdam appears in his *Memoirs* (I, 1955); diaries (*Off the Record,* edited by Robert Ferrell); letters to his wife, daughter, and sister; and memoranda in the official State Department compilation on Potsdam (see chapter V). The family letters are in *Letters Home by Harry Truman,* edited by Monte M. Poen (New York, 1984). They are usefully padded by some nonfamily letters, as those to Assistant Press Secretary Eben Ayers. See also David McCullough, *Truman* (New York, 1992).

"Magic" intercepts and JCS documents are in the National Archives. Some JCS memoranda and minutes are in the Potsdam volume, a few of these deliberately incomplete. The memoirs of Secretary of State James Byrnes, *Speaking Frankly* (New York, 1947); his assistant and interpreter, Charles Bohlen, *Witness to History* (New York, 1973); and Admiral William D. Leahy, *I Was There* (New York, 1950), flesh out the Potsdam record. Forrestal's comments are from his highly selective published diaries. Weldon Rhoades's diaries are in the Hoover Institution Library. The report from the Japanese consul-general in Harbin is a "Magic" intercept. Navy reports to Washington are in the National Archives. The Pentagon's order for Purple Heart medals in anticipation of the invasion of Japan was reported on "The MacNeil-Lehrer Newshour" during its telecast of November 23, 1994.

That "Rosie the Riveter" and "Remember Pearl Harbor!" fail to suggest the considerable foot-dragging in the war effort in the United States can be confirmed by the daily press (see almost any issue of *The New York Times* or *Washington Post* between 1941 and 1945) and the *Congressional Record.* John Morton Blum's *V Was for Victory: Politics and American Culture in World War II* (New York, 1976); and William L. O'Neill's *Democracy at War: America's Fight at Home and Abroad in World War II* (New York, 1993), persuasively detail the politics, the prejudice, the bickering, the disorganization, the "group selfishness" (O'Neill), the compromises, the inefficiency, the dawdling, and the callousness that were at odds with the public posture of commitment and idealism. As Blum puts it, "At work at home or at arms abroad, Americans wanted it that way."

The identity of the evicted owners of the house in Babelsberg occupied by Truman is reported in McCullough. German refugee testimonies are in Peterson (see notes to chapter I) and in Arthur Dickens, *Lübeck Diary* (London, 1947). James J. Fahey's *Montpelier* diary is *Pacific War Diary 1942–1945* (New York, 1963). Sergeant Fujita's account is *Foo: A Japanese-American Prisoner of the Rising Sun. The Secret Prison Diary of Frank "Foo" Fujita,* with notes by Stanley L. Faulk (Denton, Tex., 1993).

The primary works that focus entirely upon the Trinity experimental blast at

Alamogordo are Lansing Lamont's *Day of Trinity* (New York, 1965) and Ferenc Morton Szasz's *The Day the Sun Rose Twice: The Story of the Trinity Site Nuclear Explosion* (Albuquerque, N.M., 1984). Other works utilized here that deal crucially with Trinity are William L. Laurence's *Dawn Over Zero* (New York, 1946); *The New World, 1939–1946,* by Richard G. Hewlett and Oscar E. Anderson (University Park, Pa., 1962); and General Leslie Groves's own memoir, utilized more fully in later chapters (see chapter VII). The most informative and detailed book on a much written-about subject is Richard Rhodes, *The Making of the Atomic Bomb* (New York, 1986). It also covers both uses of the Bomb in war.

Hays Gamble's diaries and papers, still in his personal collection, offer striking insights into the lives and thoughts of B-29 pilots in the Marianas. I have made use of his papers throughout the narrative.

## IV. JULY 16, 1945

Balloon bomb data is from Mikesh (see Prologue). Eugene Dooman's manuscript memoirs about his years with Joseph Grew are at the Hoover Library. Dooman's additional papers are also in the Hoover Library. Douglas Fairbanks, Jr., writes of his role in preparing the Potsdam ultimatum in *A Hell of a War* (New York, 1993).

Allen Dulles's messages to the State Department are in the National Archives. General Montgomery's letter to the War Office is in *Monty.* Dr. Moran's diary is published as *Churchill: Taken from the Diaries of Lord Moran* (Boston, 1966). Sir Alexander Cadogan's diary is *The Cadogan Diaries,* edited by David Dilks (London, 1971). Ronald McKie's memoir is *Echoes from Forgotten Wars* (Sydney, 1980). The *Lübeck Anzeiger* is quoted from Dickens's *Lübeck Diary* (see chapter III).

Some Trinity sources were cited in chapter III. Additionally, Fermi's paper-strip experiment is recalled by Joseph O. Hirschfelder in "Scientific-Technological Miracle at Los Alamos," in L. Badash, J. O. Hirschfelder, and H. P. Broida, eds., *Reminiscences of Los Alamos 1943–1945* (Boston, 1980). James Conant's recollection of Fermi's "black-humored" bet is in James G. Hershberg, *James B. Conant: Harvard to Hiroshima and the Making of the Nuclear Age* (New York, 1993). Richard P. Feynman's account of his watching the blast too eagerly is in his *"Surely You're Joking, Mr. Feynman!"* as told to Ralph Leighton (New York, 1985). Edward Teller's role is self-explained in his *Legacy of Hiroshima,* written with Allen Brown (New York, 1962).

The *Tachibana Maru* episode is detailed in radiograms intercepted by "Magic" and Navy reports to Washington, both in the National Archives. The Chinese mess is described in messages to the Chinese Combat Command Headquarters in the R. D. Weigle Papers in the Hoover Library, which also describe Wedemeyer's posh C-47.

## V. JULY 17, 1945

Potsdam minutes, diplomatic papers, memoranda, and other relevant documents utilized here through August 2 (chapter XXI) are in the State Department volumes *Foreign Relations of the United States. Diplomatic papers. The Conference of Berlin (The Potsdam Conference), 1945,* 2 vols. (Washington, D.C., 1960).

Laird Shirk's destroyer *McGowan* diary was made available to me by his son, Vaughan Shirk. Ernest Heppner wrote about the Shanghai ghetto in *Shanghai Refuge* (Lincoln, Neb., 1993). Foreign Minister Togo's memoir is *The Cause of Japan* (New York, 1956). Diplomatic intercepts are in the National Archives. The funeral of Field Marshal von Busch is described from Lieutenant Colonel Grondona's testimony, in *Thresholds of Peace: Four Hundred Thousand German Prisoners and the People of Britain, 1944–1948*, by Matthew Barry Sullivan (London, 1979).

Anthony Eden's diary extracts are from Robert Rhodes James's biography (see chapter II). Some details of Truman at Potsdam, from interviews with underlings, are from McCullough (see chapter III).

Dorothy Strachey Bussy's letter to André Gide is from Richard Tedeschi, ed., *Selected Letters of André Gide and Dorothy Bussy* (Oxford, 1983).

## VI. JULY 18, 1945

General Robert Eichelberger's comments were made in letters to his wife, published as *Dear Miss Em*, edited by Jay Luvaas (Westport, Conn., 1972). Ryuji Nagatsuka writes of his unexpected survival in *I Was a Kamikaze*, translated by Nina Rootes (New York, 1956). Captain Chihaya's report is in "An Intimate Look at the Japanese Navy," in the misnamed *The Pearl Harbor Papers*, edited by Donald M. Goldstein and Katherine V. Dillon (New York, 1993). The book covers 1941–1945. For Eisenhower's letters and papers, see chapter II. Colonel Leavel's letter of July 18 is in the Hoover Library. For Truman, see chapter II. The Potsdam conference documents are supplemented here by McCullough and the Stimson, Moran, and Cadogan diaries (see chapter X for Stimson, chapter IV for the last two). De Gaulle's remark to Nixon is quoted by William Safire, Nixon's speechwriter, in *The New York Times*, April 25, 1994. Dooman's comments are from his papers in the Hoover Library and his memoir. Bohlen is quoted from his memoir (see chapter III). German scientists as taped are quoted from the Farm Hall transcripts in *Operation Epsilon* (see Prologue), Ruth Andreas-Friedrich from her diary.

## VII. JULY 19, 1945

Admiral Ugaki's diaries, translated by Masataka Chihaya and edited by Donald M. Goldstein and Katherine V. Dillon, are *Fading Victory: The Diary of Admiral Matome Ugaki, 1941–1945* (Pittsburgh, 1991). Yoshio Kodama's boast is quoted in his *I Was Defeated* (Tokyo, 1959), translated by Taro Fukuda. Kodama was head of his navy's *Kodama Kikan* in Shanghai and served a term in Sugamo Prison as a suspected war criminal, where he wrote his memoirs in 1947.

Leo Szilard's petitions and letters to higher authority, and the responses received, are in *Leo Szilard: His Version of the Facts* (Cambridge, Mass., 1978). General Groves's memoir, which quotes many documents usefully, is *Now It Can Be Told: The Story of the Manhattan Project* (New York, 1962). Arthur Compton's is *Atomic Quest: A Personal Narrative* (New York, 1956), which deals in part with his bureaucratic war with Szilard. Göring and his jailers are quoted in David Irving, *Göring* (New York, 1989). The life of

Han van Meegeren is in John Godley's *Master Art Forger* (New York, 1951). German war prisoner accounts are from Peterson and W. L. White. German expellee accounts from first-person testimonies are recorded in full in the compendious and invaluable multivolume *Documents on the Expulsion of the Germans from East-Central Europe,* edited by Theodor Scheider, translated by G. H. de Sausmarez and associates, published by the Federal Ministry for Expellees, Refugees and War Victims (Bonn, 1960). Although the project had an obvious Cold War bias, the cumulative effect of the oral histories is compelling. Extracts appear throughout this book. Rosemarie Hebek Steinfeld is quoted from letters to SW. Germans quoted on *Fragenbogen* are from Dickens's *Lübeck Diary* (see chapter III). *Fragenbogen* themselves are in the Hoover Library. Occupation news here and elsewhere is from the U.S.-published (from Frankfurt) English-language *News of Germany.* Spiriting of Nazi scientists out of Germany is detailed in *Paperclip Conspiracy* (see Prologue). The Fort Dix incident is in Nicholas Bethell, *The Last Secret* (New York, 1974). The "Magic" intercept from the German diplomat dated May 5, 1945, was released only on August 10, 1993, in a batch of previously withheld intercepts, and published in *The New York Times* on August 11, 1993.

The "Italian solution" on war criminal punishment is quoted in Buruma, *Wages of Guilt* (see chapter II).

The historian of codebreaking is Ronald Lewin, in *The Other Ultra* (London, 1982): "The historian has to shed hindsight and consider what the situation looked like *at the time*. . . ."


## VIII. JULY 20, 1945

Balloon bomb impacts are charted in Mikesh. The Oregon logger was quoted in press accounts. Ugaki's comments are from his diary. Sato's exchanges with Togo are "Magic" intercepts. "Hypothetical Defense of Kyushu," as CINCPAC-CINCPOA Bulletin 158-45, is in the National Archives, as is the July 20 report to Marshall. Lieutenant Hakata's tracking of Twentieth Air Force groups and planes carrying orange bombs is described in *The Day Man Lost* (see chapter II).

The log of the *Shangri-La* was made available to me by Mrs. A. O. Rule, widow of its commander in 1945. The Southeast Asia situation is described in Louis Allen's *The End of the War in Asia* (London, 1976); Terence O'Brien's *The Moonlight War* (London, 1987); and Hiroshi Abe's "Building the Burma-Siam Railroad," an oral history in *Japan at War* (see Prologue).

The "day of Witzleben and Stauffenberg" remark is by Ruth Andreas-Friedrich. Omar Bradley's memoir is *A Soldier's Story* (New York, 1951). The USMG questionnaire is in the Hoover Library. Potsdam minutes and conversations through to August 2, unless otherwise cited, are from the State Department's Berlin conference volumes.


## IX. JULY 21, 1945

The Zacharias broadcast-to-Japan saga is fleshed out beyond his own memoir in Maria Wilhelm's *The Man Who Watched the Rising Sun* (New York, 1967). Zacharias references through August 4 are from this volume and from the *Washington Post*. Japan's efforts to develop an atomic bomb are recounted in Robert K. Wilcox's *Japan's Secret War* (New York, 1985). Ernst Jünger's *Tagebücher* (Stuttgart, 1982) includes a volume on his wartime years.

William Manchester's *American Caesar* (Boston, 1978) notes MacArthur's inconsistency on employing the Soviets against Japan, and his later lying about it. Supplementing the Potsdam State Department documents regarding discussions on Russian involvement against Japan is a War Department typed transcript made at the time, "The Entry of the Soviet Union into the War against Japan: Military Plans, 1941–1945," an extensively detailed briefing book. It includes the text of MacArthur's telegram to Marshall urging a Russian attack against Japan "launched from Siberia" in advance of "Olympic"—a strategy MacArthur later denied he promoted. It appears on page 80 of the document in the National Archives.

George Taylor and Ralph Bard are quoted in Udall (see chapter II). *The Myths of August* (1994). Bard's memo is in the Harrison-Bundy files, Office of the Chief of Army Engineers, folder 77.

Charles Bohlen's *Witness to History 1929–1969* (New York, 1973) observes Potsdam from the vantage of his being Truman's Russian interpreter. Andrei Gromyko's *Memoirs*, translated by Harold Shukman (New York, 1989), are the closest counterpart, as the envoy to Washington knew English but had higher status than the nominal interpreter, Pavlov. The Emilio Collado story about Truman appears in McCullough (see chapter III). The carping about taking productive areas from Germany is in George Kennan's *Memoirs 1925–1950*, called there "pernicious" although the West had no control over the territories and little leverage to challenge the Soviet fait accompli.

## X. JULY 22, 1945

Stimson's diaries and recollections are in *On Active Service in Peace and War*, edited by McGeorge Bundy (New York, 1947). Curtis Cate is co-author of the Craven and Cate Air Force history (see chapter II). Air Force commander Henry H. Arnold's memoir is *Global Mission* (New York, 1949).

The "piece of paper" was first reproduced in Hewlett and Anderson and is reproduced as an illustration in this book. A copy is in the National Archives; another is in the Hoover Library.

Dooman's account of the MacLeish broadcast is in Dooman's oral history at Columbia University. Zacharias's role is detailed in his own memoir and in Wilhelm (see chapter IX). Aircraft engineer Jiro Horikoshi's memoir is *Zero!* (New York, 1956), with added chapters by Masatake Okumiya, all written with Martin Caidin. Hugh V. Clarke recalled the misdropped aerial mine in *Last Stop Nagasaki!* (Sydney, 1984).

Hedi Smuk Fried's *Fragments of a Life: The Road to Auschwitz* (Bath, n.d.) was translated from the Swedish by Michael Meyer. C. L. Sulzberger's interview with Vladimir Macek is extracted from his diaries in his *A Long Row of Candles: Memoirs and Diaries 1934–1954* (New York, 1969).

## XI. JULY 23, 1945

"Olympic" messages are in the "Olympic" and COMINCH files in the National Archives. David Kaufman, who worked in a Tel Aviv shipyard in 1945, told SW about the all-wood minesweepers. Martin Berkowitz wrote to SW about training for "Olympic." The report of the 73rd Bomb Wing flak officer is in the National Archives, dated July 23. General John B. Montgomery's explanation for bombing civilian targets near industrial areas is in an interview filmed for the Twentieth Air Force, later transferred to television cassette (Hays Gamble papers).

The dropping of a pumpkin on Kobe is from *The Day Man Lost* (see chapter II). The oil liquefaction plant bombings are described in Hays Gamble's diaries and papers. The shift in the decision making from *whether* to drop the Bomb to *how* is discussed by Len Giovannitti and Fred Freed in *The Decision to Drop the Bomb* (New York, 1965), where it is considered more a Cold War matter than an end-the-war strategy. Groves's "little boy on a toboggan" line applied to Truman is quoted by Rhodes (see chapter III) but must be seen in the light of the general's emphasizing his own importance, not untypical in his case. The letter requested from Groves by Spaatz the day before on dropping the Bomb was discussed with Handy (for Marshall) on the twenty-third but was dated July 25.

Göring's prison situation is described by Irving. Field Marshal Alan Brooke's presence at Potsdam is described in Arthur Bryant's *Triumph in the West* (New York, 1959), based upon Brooke's diaries.

## XII. JULY 24, 1945

Rescue techniques in the Pacific in the summer of 1945 were described by Bill Leonard in a letter to SW. Biographies of Japanese naval pilots here and elsewhere are from Ikuhiko Hata and Yasuho Izawa, *Japanese Naval Aces and Fighter Units in World War II*, translated by Don Cyril Gorham (Annapolis, 1989, based upon the 1975 Japanese edition). Ugaki is quoted from his diary. The "volunteer fighting corps" is described, and pictured, in the "Spears and Awls" chapter of Thomas Havens's *Valley of Darkness: The Japanese People and World War II* (New York, 1968). Toki Tanaka's oral history is in *Japan at War* (see Prologue). Isoko Hatano's diary is in Ichiro and Isoko Hatani, *Mother and Son* (Cambridge, Mass., 1962); Shuhei Hayama and Yukiko Kasai are quoted in Havens, who also quotes the drillmaster on the need for pine stumps. Colonel Cunningham's warning about Japanese civilian volunteers is from the R. D. Weigle papers at the Hoover Library. The report of Japanese killed and captured on already-occupied Pacific islands is in Navy reports to COMINCH in the National Archives.

Potsdam is largely from the conference proceedings. Gromyko's remarks are from his memoirs (see chapter IX). The revelations about Chelyabinsk-40 were in *The European* in August 1993. Stalin's order to have Russian scientists hurry up with atomic research is from Zhukov's memoirs, quoted by McCullough (see chapter III). Truman, Bohlen, Churchill, Cadogan, Byrnes, and others all told of the bomb revelation to Stalin from their varying perspectives. What Truman said, how Stalin responded, and what others saw, is discussed by David Holloway in *Stalin and the Bomb* (New Haven, Conn., 1994). He quotes Pavlov from V. G. Trukhanovskii, *Angliiskoe iadernoe oruzhie* (Moscow, 1985). No one suggests that Truman told Stalin that the new weapon would be used against Japan, but Truman claimed that Stalin wished him success with it. Holloway also writes, "There is some evidence that Soviet intelligence learned of the test within a day or two of its taking place," citing I. N. Golovin in an interview with Oleg Moroz, "Nikogda me dolzhno byt' primeneno!" in *Literaturnaia Gazeta*, July 25, 1984. Yet the behavior of Soviet leaders lends no credence to that. They did know that the Alamogordo test was imminent, but Fuchs would not be able to deliver his report about it to Gold until September 19, describing in it his sense of awe.

Cairncross's role as spy is described by KGB desk officer Yuri Modin in his *My Five Cambridge Friends* (New York, 1995), trans. by Anthony Roberts.

The deliberate Japanese blindness to Russian orders home for all diplomatic dependents in Japan is noted in *The Day Man Lost* (see chapter II).

## XIII. JULY 25, 1945

The requests to Marshall and Nimitz for surrender scenarios, and their responses, are in the "Olympic" materials in the National Archives. An early postwar look at the invasion and surrender options from the Navy-Marine perspective is K. Jack Bauer and Alan C. Coox, "Olympic/Ketsu Go," in *Marine Corps Gazette*, August 1965. The Japanese meager diet is described in *The Day Man Lost*. Maps and specifications for "Olympic," as updated several times in 1945 with various annexes, are dated, finally, June 23, 1945, as "Brief of Olympic," National Archives. It is this version that Truman and his advisers debated before Potsdam. The annexes include engineering and intelligence studies, plans for communications, military government, meteorology of the area, and a terrain study with refraction diagrams for beaches outlined in red. The beach maps were further updated in August.

In *First Rough Draft: A Journalist's Journal of Our Times* (New York, 1973), Chalmers M. Roberts recalled his Strategic Bombing Survey team's examination of how "Olympic" might have fared on the beaches at Miyazaki. Despite his observations to the contrary, the Strategic Bombing Survey, for which Roberts worked, would conclude, based upon the testimony of "surviving Japanese leaders" at the end of the war, "that certainly prior to 31st December 1945, and in all probability prior to 1st November 1945"—that is, before "Olympic"—"Japan would have surrendered, even if the atomic bomb had not been dropped, even if Russia had not entered the war, and even if no invasion had been planned or contemplated." That the Strategic Bombing Survey accepted the self-serving contentions of Japanese wartime leaders was naive in the extreme. The military hierarchy had been adamant about continuing the war, and made every effort to do so until the post-Nagasaki intervention of the Emperor. Persuasion of Survey brass that the Bombs were unnecessary seems to have been intended to plant nuclear guilt to obfuscate Japanese war guilt. In the *International Herald Tribune*, Paris, August 26, 1994, Roberts, in "The Revisionists Err: The Bomb Was to Save Lives," updates his findings but gets the projected date of X-Day for "Olympic" wrong. It is incontrovertible from evidence of Japanese intentions known to the United States in August 1945 that only powerless diplomats wanted a surrender. The military hierarchy wanted to fight on in *kamikaze* fashion on

Japanese soil, just as Hitler insisted upon fighting to the end on German soil in the spring of 1945 although Nazi leadership knew the war had long been lost.

Eisenhower's letter to Corporal Jarvis is in the Eisenhower occupation papers. Hays Gamble's description of the buildup in the Marianas is from an interview with SW. Supply officer Philip Habermann's perspective from the Philippines, based upon the experience of Samar, comes from letters to SW and Habermann's personal papers. John Dudley's reminiscence of his assigned role in "Olympic" is from *Los Alamos Chronicle, 1943–1983* (Fortieth Anniversary Special Issue, "Los Alamos: The Lab, the Town, the People"). Eichelberger's comes from his letters to his wife.

The order for Pacific shipping to have Japanese harbor anchorage charts is NCR 7764, 250431, July 25, 1945, National Archives. Wakana Wada's oral history is from *Japan at War* (see Prologue). Descriptions of B-29 raids as unreported in communiqués are from Hays Gamble's Twentieth Air Force papers, which include "Anthologies," a privately printed (September 1977) series of Twentieth Air Force reminiscences and extracts from letters.

Nakon Paton POW Camp in Thailand is described from *The War Diaries of Weary Dunlop: Java and the Burma-Thailand Railway 1942–1945* (London, 1989).

The Lozovsky-Sato nonnegotiations were overheard by "Magic." Potsdam dialogue is from the proceedings. Lindbergh was reported in the national press. The long-running negotiations over war crimes trials are seen in greatest detail in Telford Taylor, *The Anatomy of the Nuremberg Trials: A Personal Memoir* (New York, 1992).

## XIV. July 26, 1945

Francis Birch's comment about "screwing the nozzle" on the Bomb was quoted in a letter from Barbara Birch, his widow, to SW.

Churchill's awakening premonition of his election defeat appears in the closing pages of his *The Second World War*, vol. 6 (Boston, 1953). The last stages of the voyage of the *Indianapolis* are described in Samuel Eliot Morison's *Victory in the Pacific 1945* (Boston, 1960), used here and elsewhere for naval details; and especially—for first-person accounts—Richard F. Newcomb's *Abandon Ship! Death of the U.S.S. Indianapolis* (New York, 1958); Thomas Helm's *Ordeal by Sea: The Tragedy of the U.S.S. Indianapolis* (New York, 1963); and Dan Kurzman's *Fatal Voyage: The Sinking of the U.S.S. Indianapolis* (New York, 1990). The 40th Bomb Group's experiences are drawn from papers in the collection of the 40th Bomb Group Associates in the Hoover Library. U Nu is quoted from his memoir. John Luff wrote about captivity in Hong Kong in *The Hidden Years* (Hong Kong, 1967).

Extracts from Raemer Schreiber's diary are from a letter to SW from Schreiber. The effect of the exposure of plutonium to seawater (". . . it forms a heavy insoluble material") is described by Rear Admiral Edward Sheafer, Jr., Director of Naval Intelligence, in a letter to *The New York Times*, June 17, 1993.

Churchill's mournful day as the understanding of electoral loss became apparent is from the Gilbert biography (see chapter I); Churchill's *The Second World War*; Colville's diary; *The Diary of Evelyn Waugh*, edited by Michael Davie (Boston, 1977); Mary Churchill Soames's memoir; Anthony Eden's diary (see chapter V); and the Moran and Cadogan diaries (see chapter IV for both).

Heisenberg and his associates are quoted from the Farm Hall transcripts in *Operation Epsilon* (see Prologue). General Freyberg's analysis of the election is from Paul Freyberg, *General Bernard Freyberg, V.C.* (London, 1991), from a private letter. Dialogue from the Potsdam meetings not in the published Department of State volume, particularly the exchanges between General Marshall and General Antonov on Russian entrance in the war with Japan, are from a postwar Department of Defense transcript in the National Archives.

## XV. JULY 27, 1945

The leaflet war is described from the preparation side by Paul Boller, Jr., then a lieutenant on Guam, in *Memoirs of an Obscure Professor* (Fort Worth, Tex., 1992), and in letters to SW. One of his leaflets is reproduced as an illustration in this volume. A different warning leaflet is on display in Los Alamos. The dilemmas of the War Cabinet in Tokyo are described in the Pacific War Research Society's two volumes (see chapter II), in the memoirs of Togo and Kase, and in Kido's diaries. The PWRS also described the partial evacuation of Hiroshima and Katsuyama's radio monitoring. For the Navy/Marine side of "Olympic," see Bauer and Coox (chapter XIII). Syngman Rhee's exchanges with Nimitz are in the COMINCH papers in the National Archives, as are the Sato-Lozovsky "Magic" intercepts with Togo.

John Luff's account of Stanley Camp is *The Hidden Years* (see chapter XIV). George MacDonald Fraser's Burmese dialogue is from his memoir (see chapter I). Churchill's day is based upon the same sources cited in chapter XIV. The Bonhoeffer memorial service is described in Eberhard Bethge, *Dietrich Bonhoeffer*, translated by Eric Mosbacher (London, 1970). Ben Helfgott's experience is in Anton Gill's memorable oral history, *The Journey Back from Hell: Conversations with Concentration Camp Survivors* (New York, 1988). The cargo of half-dead children arriving in Berlin is in Amity Schlaes, *Germany: The Empire Within* (New York, 1990). Solzhenitsyn's prison memories are quoted in Scammell (see chapter I).

For Schreiber's diaries, see chapter XIV. McCloy's reminiscence is in Udall (see chapter II).

## XVI. JULY 28, 1945

The Rairich rescue mission is described by Morison and others. Tom Cartwright wrote to SW and included a typescript memoir utilized here and continuing. The Burmese war is adapted from Louis Allen (see chapter VIII), who writes about the "comfort girls"—a dirty secret to which the Japanese government would not admit complicity until the early 1990s. "Operation Dagwood" is named in a memo from the Undersecretary of the Navy (the Secretary was away) to the 12th Naval District, NCR 8587/272132, National Archives. The *Laggin' Dragon* story is from *Dawn Over Zero* (see chapter III). Maxwell Taylor's account of his meeting with Marshall is in his *Swords and Plowshares* (New York, 1972). German civilian problems in dealing with the American occupation bureaucracy are evidenced in the "U.S. Occupation/Bavaria" file in the Hoover Library. Bevin's smug remark that dealing with

Stalin and Truman was little different from labor negotiations "about unloading a ship" is quoted from John Saville, *The Politics of Continuity: British Foreign Policy and the Labour Government, 1945–46* (London, 1993).

## XVII. JULY 29, 1945

Navy "Blue" summaries are in the National Archives and often contain revealing data left out of communiqués. Most accounts claim that Spaatz did not deliver MacArthur's copy of the A-Bomb directive until the fifth but he was ordered to deliver it personally and flew to Manila soon after his arrival in Guam.

*Indianapolis*, Tokyo, Marianas, and Potsdam data are from sources cited earlier. Forrestal's quotes from Bevin are in the Forrestal diaries. Data from Pauley and other subordinate officials at Potsdam are in the "Supplementary Papers" to the Potsdam proceedings. Accounts of German refugees expelled from Siberia, Prussia, and eastern Europe are from Peterson and Scheider. Ursula von Kardorff's account is from her *Diary of a Nightmare: Berlin 1942–1945* (New York, 1966). The Empire State Building telescope entrepreneur is quoted from *The New York Times*.

## XVIII. JULY 30, 1945

Navy activities are from "Blue" summaries, National Archives. What Manila—and therefore MacArthur—knew is from Edward J. Drea, *MacArthur's Ultra: Codebreaking and the War Against Japan, 1942–1945* (Lawrence, Kans., 1992). "Pastel Two"—the disinformation plan to shield "Olympic"—is in the National Archives. The Palestine problem is delineated in the Potsdam supplementary papers, Forrestal's diaries, and in the international press. The directive from the Occupation's Civil Affairs Division, "Denazification and Demilitarization of German Street Names and Memorials," is in the "Germany/Office of Military Government" file in the Hoover Library.

William Deakin's letter to Churchill is quoted by Gilbert. Dylan Thomas's letter to Oscar Williams is in Paul Ferris, ed., *Dylan Thomas: The Collected Letters* (New York, 1985).

## XIX. JULY 31, 1945

The buildup of supplies and equipment for "Olympic," awesome in scale, is described by Charles Hosler and Philip Habermann in letters to SW, and in Hays Gamble's diary. For their postwar dumping into the sea, see Daniel J. Lenihan, "Pacific Requiem," in *Natural History*, August 1994, which describes thousands of "seemingly sound vehicles" still arrayed across lagoon bottoms "like Matchbox toys in a bathtub." The pumpkin missions are listed in Rhodes. Fleet operations, unless otherwise identified, are from "Blue" summaries and from Morison. Edwin Reischauer is quoted from his *My Life Between Japan and America* (New York, 1986). Momo Iida's story is from Tessa Suzuki-Morris's *Shōwa, an Inside History of Hirohito's Japan* (New York, 1985). Witold Sagajllo is quoted from *Man in the Middle: A Story of the Polish Resistance 1940–45* (New

York, 1985). Luba Zindel's story is in Abzug's *Inside the Vicious Heart* (see chapter I). Earl Harrison is quoted from Wyman's *DP*. Oral histories of the German expellees from Czechoslovakia are in volume 4 of Scheider (see chapter VII). Lola Potok's experience is recaptured in John Sack's striking *An Eye for an Eye* (New York, 1993). Churchill's farewell exchanges with George VI are in Gilbert.

## XX. AUGUST 1, 1945

The dialogue of B-29 pilots is from Wilbur Morrison's *Hellbirds* (New York, 1979). Frank Fujita's diary is *Foo*. The rumors leading to life raft improvisation in Hiroshima are described in *The Day Man Lost* (see chapter II). Richard Downie described the first big raid on Nagasaki in *Last Stop Nagasaki!* (see chapter X). The tests on new Japanese plane prototypes are described in Hata and Izawa, *Japanese Naval Aces and Fighting Units*. Masuo Kato writes about travel in raid-prone Japan in *The Lost War: A Japanese Reporter's Inside Story* (New York, 1946). Yasuo Kuwahara's memoir is *Kamikaze* (New York, 1957). Claire Chennault's final exploits in China are recounted in Joseph W. Alsop's *"I've Seen the Best of It"* (New York, 1992), written with Adam Platt.

General W. E. Brougher's POW diary is *South to Bataan, North to Mukden* (Athens, Ga., 1977).

Robert Boothby's return to Parliament is described in Robert Rhodes James, *Robert Boothby: A Portrait of Churchill's Ally* (New York, 1991).

German POW skepticism in Australia about the films taken inside Belsen are from Barbara Winter, *Stalag Australia* (Sydney, 1986).

## XXI. AUGUST 2, 1945

Japanese experimental plane results are in Izawa and Hata, *Thunder Gods* (New York, 1989), and Yasuo Kuwahara's *Kamikaze*. The Navy Munitions Assignment Board's assignment of PT boats to Russia is its directive 706-718 in Navy Department file MAC (N) 284/TAL/258 in the National Archives. Truman on board the *Augusta* en route home is described from the Truman sources noted earlier with the addition of Merriman Smith's *Thank You, Mr. President: A White House Notebook* (New York, 1946). German expellee testimony and the Czechoslovak expulsion order text are from Scheider.

The "Ultra" intercept from Manchuria is from the August 2 summary in the National Archives. The "Magic" intercept of Togo-Sato communications is also in the Archives.

## XXII. AUGUST 3, 1945

Japanese film watchers in the Marianas, and pilferage of food, were both related to SW in an interview with Hays Gamble. Eugene Lawlis's experiences as a POW on Hainan were described to SW in letters from Lawlis and from his unpublished typescript memoir. Jean Sainteny writes of his Indochinese experiences in *Ho Chi Minh and His Vietnam,* translated by Herma Briffault (Chicago, 1970). A vast scholarly and first-person literature exists on Vietnam prior to broad American involvement there. Commander Weddell's hospital report on John Kennedy is quoted by Nigel Hamilton in his *JFK: Reckless Youth* (New York, 1993). Solzhenitsyn is quoted from his *Gulag Archipelago,* in Scammell (see chapter I).

## XXIII. AUGUST 4, 1945

The identification of "floating dead" and landing of *Indianapolis* survivors is NCR 6194 in the National Archives. As late as 1950 the Navy was collecting data on the survivors, the dead, and the belated rescue efforts (Archives). The *Juneau* catastrophe is described scathingly by Dan Kurzman in *Left to Die: The Tragedy of the U.S.S. Juneau* (New York, 1994). Tibbets describes his own role with the *Enola Gay* in his *The Tibbets Story* (New York, 1978); the best third-person account is that of Richard Rhodes (see chapter III). Decrypts of Japanese communications are in the National Archives.

The air raid *tanka* by Iwane Kawanami is from Takeo Nakao's *The Japanese Mind: Wartime Japanese Feelings as Expressed in Tanka Poems* (Tokyo, 1992). Other civilian-composed *tankas,* unless cited from other sources, are from this volume. The English adaptations are SW's own, based upon Nakao.

Intelligence summaries in the Archives include intercepts on the *Sea Truk* leading to its seizure. Corporal Kuwahara is quoted from *Kamikaze* (see chapter XX). Burma details are from Louis Allen's *Burma: The Longest War* (London, 1984).

The late Robert Sherrod wrote to SW about the leakage of atomic bomb information to *Time.*

## XXIV. AUGUST 5, 1945

The rare sinking of a factory is reported in Hays Gamble's diary and papers, in particular the 315th's report on its mission 8. Professor Mimura's lecture is described in *The Day Man Lost* (see chapter II). Fuchida's autobiography is *God's Samurai,* edited by Prange, Goldstein, and Dillon (McLean, Va., 1990). The raid on Saga is described in the 40th Bomb Group's papers (Hoover Library). The loading of the Bomb and the takeoff are described in many more sources, each adding a bit or contradicting a bit. My narrative is largely a composite of LeMay, Tibbets, Laurence, Rhodes, and Hewlett/Anderson.

Kuwahara's account of going to Hiroshima early on the morning of the Bomb is from *Kamikaze.*

## XXV. AUGUST 6, 1945

Okumiya's recollections of fielding news on the Bomb are a separate chapter (28), "The Atomic Bombings: Personal Observations of Masatake Okumiya," in Jiro Horikoshi's *Zero!* (see chapter X). Satoshi Nakamura is described from *The Day Man*

*Lost.* Tosh Kano's memoir and a typescript translation are in the Imperial War Museum, London. Hiroko Nakamoto's memoir, as told to Mildred Mastin Pace, is *My Japan 1930–1951* (New York, 1970). Corporal Kuwahara's memoir is *Kamikaze.* Yōko Ōta's experiences are described by her in *Hiroshima: Three Witnesses,* edited and translated by Richard H. Minear (Princeton, N.J., 1990). Shinobu Hazume's account is one of nineteen in *Widows of Hiroshima,* edited by Mikio Kanda and translated by Taeko Midorikawa (New York, 1989). Dr. Hachiya's memoir, perhaps the most memorable account outside of fictionalized versions, is Michihiko Hachiya, *Hiroshima Diary: The Journal of a Japanese Physician August 6–September 30, 1945,* edited and translated by Warner Wells (Chapel Hill, N.C., 1955). Hidenari Terasaki's pages of notes of conversations with the Emperor were rediscovered after his death by his half-American daughter, Mariko Terasaki Miller, and published many years later in the Japanese monthly *Bengei Shunju* (November 16, 1990). Takaaki Aikawa's memoir is *Unwilling Patriot* (Tokyo, 1960). Momo Iida and Mutsuo Saitō are quoted in *Shōwa* (see chapter XIX). Constantine Petrovsky's memoir is in the Oral History Archives, Republic of Singapore. Gregory Boyington's account is in his *Baa Baa Black Sheep* (New York, 1958). Tom Lamb's recollections are from a letter to SW. Laurens van der Post wrote of his POW experience in *The Night of the New Moon* (London, 1970). Theodore White and Sam Hynes wrote about the Bomb in their war memoirs, as did Sy Kahn in his *Between Tedium and Terror* (New York, 1993).

"Nine-Section" in Burma is quoted from Fraser. The Flossenburg recollection is from Reichel, *What Did You Do in the War, Daddy?* (see chapter I) and Kenneth Rexroth, in Lee Bartlett, ed., *Kenneth Rexroth and James Laughlin: Selected Letters* (New York, 1991). Albert Einstein's Yiddish groan is quoted from Michael White and John Gribbin, *Einstein: A Life in Science* (New York, 1993). Rosemarie Hebek Steinfeld is quoted from a letter to SW.

Albert Speer recalled Nazi interests in an atomic bomb in his *Inside the Third Reich* (see chapter I); the Farm Hall intercepts are from *Operation Epsilon* [edited by Sir Charles Frank] (Berkeley, Calif., 1993).

## XXVI. AUGUST 7, 1945

The atomic bomb leaflet is in the Larson file at the Hoover Library. Churchill's confidence to Lord Camrose is in Gilbert. Karl Compton was quoted by Weldon Rhoades (Hoover). Stalin's exhortation to his atomic scientists is from David Holloway, *Stalin and the Bomb,* quoting A. Lavret'yeva in *"Stroiteli novogo mira," V mire knig* 9 (1970)— "Builders of the New World," in *In the World of Books,* vol. 9.

Soviet knowledge of atomic bomb theories and processes was largely due to Klaus Fuchs, imported as part of the British scientific team, but it appears impossible that some of the scientific/technological talk generated by Szilard's petition and by official surveys of possible options for bomb usage did not leak out. There were too many knowledgeable people in the loop. A dismissal of overt espionage by respected physicists in the Manhattan District is in Richard Rhodes's persuasive "Atomic Spies, or Atomic Lies?" in *The New York Times,* May 3, 1994. Conant's description of the atomic blast, and his abortive request to the Harvard Librarian, are in Hershberg, *James B. Conant* (see chapter IV).

Nishina and Tamura are quoted from *The Day Man Lost* (see chapter II). Hachiya is quoted from *Hiroshima Diary* (see chapter XXV). The Japanese broadcast about the atomic attack was intercepted and transcribed by an Office of War Information monitoring station. Hatano is quoted from the diary *Mother and Son* (see chapter XII). Fuchida's account is from his *God's Samurai* (see chapter XXIV), Togo's from his *The Cause of Japan* (see chapter V). The *Kikka* test flight is described in *Thunder Gods* (see chapter XXI).

Politics in Indonesia is from Louis Allen's *The End of the War in Asia* (see chapter VIII), Burma from his *Burma: The Longest War* (see chapter XXIII). Sagajllo is quoted from his *Man in the Middle* (see chapter XIX). Truman's return is largely from Eben Ayers's diary.

## XXVII. AUGUST 8, 1945

Marcus McDilda's ordeal is described from William Craig, *The Fall of Japan* (New York, 1967). Fuchida is quoted from *God's Samurai*. Nishina's visit to Hiroshima is from *The Day Man Lost*. Edward Teller is quoted from *The Legacy of Hiroshima* (see chapter IV). Navy activity is from "Blue" summaries in the National Archives. The Hatano family is quoted from *Mother and Son*. Mrs. Yokochi's ordeal is from *Widows of Hiroshima*, edited by Mikio Kanda, translated by Takeo Midorokawa (New York, 1989). Grafton is quoted from *The Sumatra Battalion* (see chapter XXXV) and Brougher from *South to Bataan* (see chapter XX). Laval is quoted from *The Diary of Pierre Laval* (New York, 1948). Data on Jean Bichelonne is from Bertrand Goldschmidt, *Atomic Rivals* (New Brunswick, N.J., 1993) and a letter from Jean-Claude Amalric to SW.

The Sudeten German plight is described in oral histories in Scheider (see chapter VII). Sato's encounter with Molotov was described in a message to Togo intercepted by "Magic." Molotov's claim that the A-Bombs against Japan were actually intended to intimidate Russia appears in *Sto sorok besed s Molotovym: iz dnevnika F. Chueva* (Moscow, 1991), as quoted in Holloway's *Stalin and the Bomb* (see chapter XII). Eben Ayers described Truman's press conference. The cable from Moscow to the CNO is in the National Archives. Harriman's reports are in W. Averell Harriman and Elie Abel, *Special Envoy to Churchill and Stalin, 1941–1946* (New York, 1975).

## XXVIII. AUGUST 9, 1945

The basic books utilized on the Nagasaki raid, apart from documents and individual accounts, are Joseph Laurence Marx, *Nagasaki: The Necessary Bomb?* (New York, 1961); Frank W. Chinnock, *Nagasaki: The Forgotten Bomb* (New York, 1969); Takashi Nagai, *The Bells of Nagasaki*, translated by William Johnston (Tokyo and New York, 1984; first published in Japanese in 1948); and Richard Rhodes, *The Making of the Atomic Bomb*, and W. L. Laurence, *Dawn Over Zero* (see chapter III for both). *Japan's Longest Day* (see chapter II) also has much on Nagasaki, and Masanobu Ibuse's documentary novel *Black Rain* (Tokyo and Palo Alto, 1969) is a vital source. Aussie POWs Bernard O'Keefe and Bob Watkins are quoted in *Last Stop Nagasaki!* (see chapter X). The instructions to the 10th Air Division are reported in *Homeland Air Defense Opera-*

*tions Record,* prepared by Headquarters, USAFFE and Eighth U.S. Army (1952) from Japanese war records.

The vision of Sergeant DeShazer is described in Carroll V. Glines, *Doolittle's Tokyo Raiders* (New York, 1964). Anton Bilek's POW memory is an oral history account in Studs Terkel's *The Good War* (New York, 1984). The atomic scientists' letter to Professor Sagane is printed in full in Marx's *Nagasaki.*

The war at sea off Japan is described in Clark G. Reynolds, *The Fast Carriers* (New York, 1968); the account of Royal Navy pilot Hampton Gray is in Wilbur H. Morrison, *Above and Beyond* (New York, 1983). The boarding of the *Kikku Maru* by the *Cassin* is NCR 0701; the loss of steering of the *Hultman* in the Panama Canal is NCR 8628 in the CNO files in the National Archives.

The Manchurian situation is in Louis Allen, *The End of the War in Asia* (see chapter VIII); however, the story of Yoshie Fukushima is an oral history account in *Japan at War* (see Prologue). Malik's attempt to meet with Togo is retold in Togo's *The Cause of Japan* (see chapter V). The "Evacuate Your Cities" leaflet is in both the Hoover Library and the National Archives. The rounds of high-level meetings in Tokyo are detailed in *Japan's Longest Day.*

The plans for a northern Kyushu follow-up landing to "Olympic"—if necessary—are in the National Archives. Fuchida's movements are detailed in *God's Samurai* (see chapter XXIV). Yukio Mishima's memory of the day is in *Confessions of a Mask* (see chapter II).

## XXIX. AUGUST 10, 1945

The Tokyo high-level meetings, now nearly around the clock, are best described in *Japan's Longest Day* (see chapter II), which is paralleled in many places by Craig's *Fall of Japan* (see chapter XXVII). Additional details are in Kase's *Journey to the Missouri* (see chapter II) and Togo's *The Cause of Japan* (see chapter V). Kase utilizes his own memories as well as Marquis Kido's diaries. At least as important a source as these are the "Magic" diplomatic extracts and summaries, SRS 1756, 11 August 1945, not declassified from top secret until 1993. The three variant texts of the surrender offer from Japan are set off in parallel columns in SRS 1756, National Archives.

Washington's reaction comes from the Stimson, Forrestal, Truman, and Ayers diaries, as well as from Byrnes's memoir. Richard Aldington's *tanka* on the situation is from Norman Gates, ed., *Richard Aldington: A Life in Letters* (University Park, Pa., 1992). LeGrande Diller's handout for MacArthur is in the Rhoades papers, Hoover Library. The "Olympic" beach replottings are in the National Archives, reproduced as an illustration to this book.

Manchurian developments are from sources noted in chapter XXVIII. Hong Kong matters are taken from *The Hidden Years* (see chapter XIV), Korea from *The Origins of the Korean War* (see chapter XXXV), Shanghai from *Shanghai Refuge* (see chapter V), Indochina from Allen, and Malaya from Otto Giese, with James Wise, *Bridge Watch: Memoirs of a World War Two U-Boat Officer* (Annapolis, Md., 1994).

Eisenhower's attempts to circumvent Stimson on Jewish DP affairs are seen in the Eisenhower occupation papers (see chapter II). Freyberg is quoted from his diaries, as is Cadogan (see chapter IV); Churchill and Miss Layton are from Gilbert (see chapter I).

## XXX. August 11, 1945

Captain Chihaya is quoted from his *An Intimate Look at the Japanese Navy*, published in translation (by himself) in *The Pearl Harbor Papers*, edited by Goldstein and Dillon (see chapter VI). Captain Withee's letter to his wife is in the Hoover Library, as is the 40th Bomb Group report. Clayton Bissell's memo to Marshall is in Ronald Lewin, *The American Magic* (New York, 1982). Other references to "Magic" intercepts are in the National Archives. The Rhoades diary is in the Hoover Library. For Japanese internal negotiations, see sources noted in chapter XXIX. The 1936 Tokyo mutiny is described in Edward Behr, *Hirohito* (New York, 1989). The new flight of the *Kikka* is in *Thunder Gods* (see chapter XXI). Hachiya's account is in *Hiroshima Diary* (see chapter XXV). Onodera's interview in Sweden is from a press account.

Hong Kong developments are from *The Hidden Years*. Togo's message is a "Magic" intercept in the National Archives. The Hsinking radio intercept is SRS-1757 in the Archives. Russian military preparations and movements in Manchuria in 1945, including the fuel shortages brought on by hasty intervention, are detailed in *Japanese Special Studies on Manchuria XIII: Study of Strategical and Tactical Peculiarities of Far Eastern Russia and Soviet Far East Forces*, prepared by the Military History Section, Headquarters, Army Forces Far East (Department of the Army, 1955).

Dönitz's farewell message as *Führer* is from Padfield, *Dönitz: The Last Führer* (see chapter I). The "Cossack" plight is from Mark R. Elliott, *Pawns of Yalta: Soviet Refugees and America's Role in Their Reparations* (Urbana, Ill., 1982). The Patton-Eisenhower exchange is from the Eisenhower occupation papers.

## XXXI. August 12, 1945

A basic source for this chapter and the following two is the once top-secret SRH-090, "Japan's Surrender Manoeuvers," a State Department compilation dated August 29, 1945, of U.S. exchanges and Japanese "Magic" intercepts, National Archives. Supplementing it are *Longest Day*, Kase (see chapter for both), and Togo (see chapter V).

The attack on the *Pennsylvania*, temporarily kept from the press, is NCR 3075, National Archives. Nagatsuka's memoir is *I Was a Kamikaze* (see chapter VI). MacArthur's glib dismissal of "Downfall" casualties appears in Eichelberger's letters to "Miss Em." "Goodbye to All That" was a Murrow CBS broadcast on August 12, 1945, quoted in Ann M. Sperber's *Murrow, His Life and Times* (New York, 1986). Ernst Jünger's are from his *Tagebücher* (see chapter IX). J. Edgar Hoover's speech was covered by the national press. Other sources can be inferred from the text; many are press dispatches, as with Hugh Baillie's offer of a reward to find the false peace culprit, and reports on premature celebrations.

## XXXII. August 13, 1945

The salvage of the *Arizona* turrets is described in Michael Slackman's *Target: Pearl Harbor* (Honolulu, Hawaii, 1990). Damage by *kamikazes* to the *La Grange* is reported in NCR 6211, National Archives. The number of *kamikaze* aircraft the Japanese had in readiness (or stockpiled) differs from source to source depending upon whether the planes of both armed services are counted—and when the tallies were made. Accounts agree, however, that upward of ten thousand existed, with fuel for them. *The Sacred Warriors* estimates 12,725 in mid-August, with new construction still at over a thousand a month in underground plants. There were more planes than trained pilots.

The order to return Sutherland is in Rhoades (Hoover Library) and in Paul P. Rogers, *The Bitter Years: MacArthur and Sutherland* (New York, 1991). Dean Rusk's unflattering description of MacArthur's behavior to ranking subordinates is in his *As I Saw It* (New York, 1990).

Ichiro Hatano's diary comment is from *Mother and Son* (see chapter XII). Dr. Hachiya is the physician of *Hiroshima Diary* (see chapter XXV). Shin Bok Su's oral history is in *Japan at War* (see Prologue). Dr. Nagai is the physician of *The Bells of Nagasaki* (see chapter XXVIII). Fuchida's movements are from *God's Samurai* (see chapter XXIV). Manchurian and Chinese developments are from Allen, *The End of the War in Asia* (see chapter VIII). Göring's last flight is described by Irving; Van Meegeren's painting exploit is from Godley, *Master Art Forger* (see chapter VII for both).

The planned further use of still-unproduced nuclear bombs is described in Marc Gallichio, "After Nagasaki, General Marshall's Plan for Tactical Nuclear Weapons in Japan," *Prologue* 23 (Winter 1991), as quoted by John Ray Skates in *The Invasion of Japan* (Columbia, S.C., 1994). Skates's elegant study of "Olympic" and "Coronet," which appeared when *The Last Great Victory* was in press, is recommended to readers seeking further specifics from archive material.

# XXXIII. AUGUST 14, 1945

One version of the Emperor's address to the Cabinet is in Kase; another is in *Japan's Longest Day* (see chapter II for both). A third is a composite of texts reconstructed by Sakonji, Yonai, and Ohta; this one is in the Dooman papers at the Hoover Library. The lines about the West as relics and robbers are from a soldiers' manual prepared in 1941 by Masanobu Tsuji; it is quoted at greater length in Weintraub, *Long Day's Journey into War*. Saburo Sakai is quoted from his memoir, *Samurai*.

Heisenberg is quoted from the Farm Hall papers in *Operation Epsilon* (see Prologue).

Japanese intrigue and deliberations are described from sources largely listed in chapter XXIX; other sources will be clear from the text. Homer Bigart wrote his story for the New York *Herald-Tribune*. Other Air Force sources are 40th Bomb Group papers (Hoover Library) for the "Break Utah . . ." code; Hays Gamble's diary and papers; Major General Haywood Hansell's *Strategic Air War Against Japan* (Washington, D.C., 1986); Robert F. Griffin's "Last Mission" report in the 331st Bomb Group's publication; the 315th Bomb Group's *Anthologies*; Wilbur H. Morrison's *Hellbirds*; and interviews with Hays Gamble and Bill Leasure, pilot of the *Fluffy Fuz*.

Naval sources are NCR reports in the National Archives; Morison's *Victory in the Pacific* (see chapter XIV); Thomas B. Buell's biography of Admiral King, *Master of Sea Power* (New York, 1980); the log of the *Bonhomme Richard*; and Edwin Hoyt's *Closing the Circle* (New York, 1982).

Manchurian events are from "Magic" intercepts (Archives), and Allen's *End of the War in Asia* (see chapter VII); Kobo Abe's "Record of a Transformation" (1954) is from his *Beyond the Curve* (New York, 1991), translated by J. W. Carpenter; and Toyoko Yamasaki's *The Barren Zone*, translated by James T. Araki (Honolulu, Hawaii, 1985; original publication 1976). General Okamura's protests from China to Tokyo are "Magic" intercepts in the Archives. The Southeast Asia POW situation is represented by Weary Dunlop's diary and G. F. Jacob's *Prelude to the Monsoon: Assignment in Sumatra* (Philadelphia, 1982). U Nu's day in Burma from his memoirs.

American celebrations are taken from William Manchester's *Goodbye, Darkness* (New York, 1980); *The Diaries of Arthur Inman*, edited by Daniel Aaron (Cambridge, Mass., 1985); *Day of Trinity* (for Kistiakowsky); press accounts; Ayers; McCullough (see chapter III for *Trinity* and McCullough); and SW's memories in his "A Kid's War," *Contemporary Autobiography Series*, 20, ed. Joyce Nakamura (Detroit, 1994).

# XXXIV. AUGUST 15, 1945

Shigeo Hatanaka, Naokaka Sasaki, Wakana Wada, and Ryosaku Sato are quoted from *Japan at War* (see Prologue). Gwen Terasaki is quoted from her *Bridge to the Sun* (Chapel Hill, N.C., [1957]), Yoko Matsuoka from her *Daughter of the Pacific* (New York, [1952]). Kōtarō Nakamura's verse is from *Chieko and other Poems*, translated by Hiroaki Sato (Honolulu, Hawaii, 1980). Kenzaburo Ōe's "Tears" is translated by John Nathan in *Teach Us to Outgrow Our Madness* (New York, 1977). An interesting comparison of Ōe's story with the postwar German *The Tin Drum*, by Günter Grass, is Reiko Tachibana Nemoto's "A Study of Convergence," in *Contemporary Literature* 34 (1993).

Pilots Nakajima, Kuwahara, Fuchida, and Ogaki were all referred to earlier; Onishi's end, and statistics about his aircraft stockpile, are in "The Kamikaze Attack Corps," by Rikihei Inoguchi and Tadashi Nakajima, a chapter in David C. Evans, ed. and trans., *The Japanese Navy in World War II in the Words of Former Japanese Naval Officers* (Annapolis, Md., 1969; revised 1986).

James O'Keefe was quoted in "Kindness, Brutality in Japan," in *Altoona Mirror*, September 20, 1992; Harry Douthitt in a letter to SW; Thomas Hewlett, Kenneth Day, Jerome McDavitt, and Jack Brady in Donald Knox, ed., *Death March* (New York, 1981). Willard Wilson's reminiscence about MacArthur is from the 315th Bomb Wing's *Anthologies*, September 1987. Various presurrender directives are in JLPC, JSC, and NCR files in the National Archives.

Hong Kong happenings are from the Oral History Project, Centre for East Asian Studies, Chinese University of Hong Kong, as translated by Kay Li. (For earlier references to Big Cow Wu, see Weintraub, *Long Day's Journey into War*.) Also see Jean Gittin's *Stanley [Camp]: Behind Barbed Wire* (Hong Kong, 1982); G. A. Leiper's *A Yen for My Thoughts* (Hong Kong, 1982); and Alan Birch and Martin Cole's *Captive Years: The Occupation of Hong Kong, 1941–1945* (Hong Kong, 1982). J. G. Ballard's Shanghai account is from his *The Kindness of Women* (New York, 1991); he also appears earlier in *Long Day's Journey into War*. Gene Lawlis's typescript memoir is from SW's files, courtesy Eugene Lawlis.

Yoshikichi Kasayama's oral history is in *Japan at War*, as is that of Tamotsu

Ogawa. Maxine Andrews's last wartime gig is described by her in *Over Here, Over There* (New York, 1993). John Savard wrote to SW. Kenneth Rexroth's letter is Bartlett (see chapter XXV). The B-29 lettering was in an account, with photo, in *The New York Times*.

## XXXV. SURRENDERS

Nimitz's order on relations with the Japanese is in CNO files, National Archives. The Japanese flight to Manila, and negotiations with MacArthur's staff, are documented in *Japan's Longest Day*; Clayton James's *Years of MacArthur*, II (Boston, 1975); William Manchester's *American Caesar* (see chapter IX); Weldon E. Rhoades's papers at the Hoover Library and his *Flying MacArthur to Victory* (College Station, Tex., 1987); Paul P. Rogers's *The Bitter Years* (see chapter XXXII); and intelligence summaries in the National Archives.

Demobilization of Japanese airmen is described in Kuwahara, Fuchida, Nagatsuka, and Izawa/Hata (see chapter XXI). The removal of propellers and other key running parts of aircraft is best described, with many illustrations, in Robert Mikesh, *Broken Wings of the Samurai: The Destruction of the Japanese Air Force* (Annapolis, Md., 1993). Diplomatic intercepts then being read in Washington and Manila (the Japanese continued using wartime codes) are in the National Archives. The "Magic" diplomatic summary dated August 21, 1945 (SRS 1766), in the National Archives deals with intercepts on Japanese handling of POWs and on the problems of various surrenders, especially in China. British, and especially Dutch, chilliness toward Hirohito in 1971 over memories of Japanese treatment of POWs is described in Toshio Iritani, *Group Psychology of the Japanese in Wartime* (London, 1991). It is notable that as late as May 1994 the Japanese Justice Minister was forced by international outrage to resign after downplaying wartime atrocities. In August 1994 Japanese Prime Minister Tomiichi Murayama declared that his government was "considering seriously" how best to express its "apology and remorse on the issue of comfort women," another group atrocity. Estimates then were that 200,000 women had been forced into sex slavery for the military.

Minister Okamoto's suggestion from Stockholm that the Japanese attempt to deflect criticism of its own guilt by isolating the United States "morally" on the "Extreme inhumanity of the Bomb" is a "Magic" intercept in the National Archives. (Okamoto had not been listened to in war but apparently was successful here.)

Soviet plans for Hokkaido and General Ivanov's order cancelling them are in Dimitri Volkogonov, *Triumf i tragediia*, II (2nd ed., Moscow, 1990), quoted in Holloway.

K. M. Hoeffel's POW letter from Mukden is in the Aubrey Fitch papers, Hoover Library. The Doolittle raiders' story is from Glines (see chapter XXVIII). Accounts of the Omari POW camp are from Fujita, Cartwright, and Boyington. That the Japanese had planned to kill their remaining POWs in Malaya and Siam is claimed by A. A. Apthorp, *The British Sumatra Battalion* (Lewes, Sussex, 1988) and Peter N. Davies, *The Man Behind the Bridge: Colonel Toosey and the River Kwai* (London, 1991), which also quotes Toosey's radioed request to India for condoms. Kate Caffrey's *Out in the Midday Sun* (London, 1973), reports the facetious requisition for blondes. Toosey's refusal to sign back-date receipts for Red Cross parcels is in Rohan D. Rivett, *Behind Bamboo* (Sydney and London, 1946).

The report of the confinement of American chutists because of the alleged "dangerous" situation in the Nanking area is in SRS 1768, National Archives. SRS 1769 reports on the likely collisions between Chungking and Yenan forces. The complicated history of the use by both sides of Japanese soldiers in China is in a Donald G. Gillin letter to SW as well as in Gillin's *The Japanese in China, 1945–1949*. Theodore H. White reported on the temporary vacuum of government in major Chinese cities in *Life*, September 24, 1945.

The Mili, Marcus, and Morotai surrenders are described in bulletins to the CNO in the National Archives. Sir Geoffrey N. Roberts wrote to SW with documents and photos. The Nauru and Ocean Island surrender instruments were documented in the catalog of their sale at Sothebys in 1992.

The end of Hong Kong occupation and the surrender of the colony are described in far greater detail than possible here in Birch (see chapter XXXIV), Gittins (see chapter XXXIV), and G. B. Endacott's *Hong Kong Eclipse*, as well as in "*Sai Kung 1940–1950*," the Oral History Project at the Chinese University of Hong Kong.

The *Waldron*'s encounter with Japan is described in the privately printed *History of the United States Ship Waldron: Destroyer 699*, by Richard Bullis and Jack Melnick (1991), a copy of which is in the Hoover Library in the Bullis file. The Japanese Bureau of Military Affairs order to "render non-operational" all suicide craft is an intercept in Far East Summary 536, National Archives. Colonel Tench's encounter with enemy hospitality is described in Mikesh's *Broken Wings* (see above). The abortive effort to establish sanctioned whorehouses for the U.S. Fleet is described in the Bullis papers.

The surrender ceremonies were covered in great detail in the press. Kase's personal memories are from his *Journey to the Missouri*.

For surrenders throughout Southeast Asia the most comprehensive account is in Louis Allen (see chapter VII). Yoshie Fukushima's oral history is in *Japan at War*. For Korea, see also Bruce Cumings, *The Origins of the Korean War: Liberation and the Emergence of Separate Regimes, 1945–1947* (Princeton, 1981). For Singapore, see Otto Giese's *Bridge Watch* (see chapter XXIX). General Minoru Hamada's poem—and the description of his end—are from Allen. That Chandra Bose's name has become celebrated by streets across India is reported by Peter Ward Fay in *The Forgotten Army: India's Armed Struggle for Independence 1942–1945* (Ann Arbor, Mich., 1993).

Josef Buhl's expellee account is from Scheider (see chapter VII). Weizsäcker's comment is from *Operation Epsilon* (see Prologue). Cy Sulzberger's diary entry on Gertrude Stein in Paris is in *A Long Row of Candles* (see chapter X). Oppenheimer's report to Stimson is in Alice Kimball Smith and Charles Weiner, eds., *Robert Oppenheimer: Letters and Recollections* (Cambridge, Mass., 1980). Szilard's campaign, including his letter to Matthew Connelly, is documented in *Szilard: His Version* (see chapter VII). Churchill's departure for Italy, and General Marshall's cable to him before departure, are in Gilbert (see chapter I).

For the last German surrender, I am indebted to letters from Lawrence Rhatican and Edward W. Samuell, Jr., and to Maria Hanna of the Suitland Reference Branch of the National Archives, who turned up the April 1946 operations report of the 9th Cavalry Reconnaissance Troop, 9th Infantry Division.

# · ACKNOWLEDGMENTS ·

I am indebted to the people and institutions identified below for their memories, their good offices, and their access to materials relevant to my research. Interviews, oral history materials, letters, and documents used significantly are cited in the source notes or in picture credits.

Lucy Addington; Harold M. Agnew; Jean-Claude Amalric; Martin Berkowitz; Paul F. Boller, Jr.; Edward Buss; Thomas Cartwright; Harry P. Clark; Fred Crawford, Michael M. Dembo; Robert C. Doyle; the Reverend Roberts E. Ehrgott; Robert S. Elegant; George MacDonald Fraser; Hays Gamble; Norman T. Gates; Donald G. Gillin; David Gordon; Elwira Grossman; Philip Habermann; George H. Heacox; Frank Q. Helms; Charles L. Hosler; Jürgen Kamm; David Kaufman; Heinz Kosok; James Krüss; Tom Lamb; Eugene Lawlis; Bill Leasure; William Leonard; Laurent LeSage; Kay Li; Herschel Liebowitz; Charles W. Mann, Jr.; Junko Matoba; Marianne Mauner; Jean Nakhnikian; Reiko Nemoto; Ruth Nuzum; Richard B. Posey; Shirley Rader; Norman Ramsey; Colonel Richard S. Rauschkolb; Susan Reighard; Lawrence Rhatican; John Rich, Jr.; Sir Geoffrey Roberts; Edmund B. Roney; Mrs. A. O.

Rule; Colonel (Ret.); Edward W. Samuell; John Savard; Raemer Schreiber; Ernst Schurer; Harold Segal; the late Robert K. Sherrod; Laird Shirk; Vaughan Shirk; Brigadier General (Ret.) E. H. Simmons; Richard J. Sommers; Rosemarie Hebek Steinfeld; Gerhard Strasser; Robert K. Strauss; Catherine Styles-McLeod; Truman M. Talley; Hiromi Tanaka; John Taylor; Gilbert Thompson; Susumu Ushioda; Bud Voorhes; Mary Alison Kennedy Weintraub; David Weintraub; Rodelle Weintraub; Mark Bennett Weintraub; Roy Wilkinson; Meriel Wilmot-Wright; Richard Winslow.

Air Force Historical Center, Maxwell Air Force Base, Alabama Army Historical Center, Washington, D.C.; Atomic Bomb Memorial Museum, Hiroshima; Australian War Memorial, Canberra; British Library, London; Hong Kong University Library, Hong Kong; Hoover Institution Library, Stanford, California; Imperial War Museum, London; International House Library, Tokyo; Marine Corps Historical Center, Washington, D.C.; National Archives, Washington, D.C.; National Aeronautics and Space Museum, Washington, D.C.; Naval Institute, Washington, D.C.; Oral History Archives, Singapore; Pattee Library, the Pennsylvania State University; U.S. Army Military Institute, Carlisle, Pennsylvania.

# . INDEX .

*Texas,* 326

Thälmann, Ernst, 39

Thoma, Wilhelm Ritter von, 104

Thomas, Dylan, 324–25

Thompson, Cmdr. C. R. ("Tommy"), 80

Tibbets, Col. Paul W., Jr., 75, 176, 329, 372, 386, 397–98, 414–24, 435, 493

Tiernan, The Rev. Curtis, 175

Tito, Josip Broz, 27–28, 122–23, 132, 184, 318

Toda, Yasuhide, 603

Togo, Shigenori, 41, 52–53, 63–67, 93, 97–98, 131, 143–44, 162, 232–33, 266–68, 239–90, 299, 320–21, 380–81, 400, 454–55, 498–501, 505–12, 517, 534, 543, 548–53, 568–75, 572–73, 666

Toguchi, Jiro, 163

Tojo, Gen. Hideki, 163, 266, 570, 648–49

Toklas, Alice, 680

Tokugawa, Yoshihiro, 619

Tokyo Rose (Iva Toguri), 373

Tomimura, Lt., 489–90

Tomioka, Rear Adm. Sadatoshi, 585

*Tone,* 203

Toosey, Col. Philip, 659

*Top Secret,* 415

Toshiko, Princess, 629

Toyoda, Adm. Soemu, 499–500, 503, 505–06, 542, 549, 569, 581–82, 590

*Tranquility,* 562

Trask, Capt. Don, 611

Treacher, Arthur, 640

Troger, Michael, 292

Trukhanovskii, V. G., 694

Truman, Bess, 108, 122, 133, 361, 461, 614

Truman, Harry, 4, 16, 39–41, 50, 54–58, 61–63, 66–69, 78–83, 99–103, 105–09, 114–23, 135, 150–57, 167–76, 180–84, 194–200, 207–18, 222, 233–242, 247, 251, 254, 259–60, 267, 275–76, 291–94, 299–303, 318, 322, 332–35, 358–63, 374–76, 391–92, 404, 420–22, 426, 460–62, 472–76, 501–02, 513, 521, 530, 532–33, 557, 559, 562, 596, 612–18, 638, 642–43, 646, 650–51, 667, 681

Truman, Sgt. Harry, 116

Truman, Margaret, 61, 291, 299

Truman, Martha Ellen, 116, 171, 318, 614–15

Truman, Vivian, 116

Tsuchiya, Eiichi, 285

Tsuji, Masanobu, 638

Tsukamoto, Col. Makoto, 539

*Tube Alloys,* 194

Turgel, Gena, 22

Turgel, Sgt. Norman, 22

Turnage, Maj. Gen. Allen, 163

Turner, Mark, 152

Turner, Adm. Richmond Kelly, 227

Twible, Ens. Harlan, 308, 370

Twining, Lt. Gen. Nathan, 371

*U–181,* 526, 674–75

*U–862,* 526

*U–977,* 641

Udall, Stewart, 688

Uehara, Flt. Lt., 112

Uehara, Capt. Shigetaro, 597

Ugaki, Adm. Matome, 126–28, 143, 145, 179, 203, 230, 269, 281, 351–52, 373, 386–87, 408, 455, 496, 518, 539, 548, 574, 626–28

Ulbricht, Walther, 39–40

Umeda, Chief Petty Officer, 489–90

Umezu, Gen. Yoshijiro, 162, 499, 503, 506, 535, 549, 567–69, 575, 581, 584, 609, 647, 666

· A NOTE ON THE TYPE ·

The typeface used in this book is a version of Palatino, originally designed in 1950 by Hermann Zapf (b. 1918), one of the
most prolific contemporary type designers, who has also created Melior and Optima. Palatino was first used to set the in-
troduction of a book of Zapf's hand lettering, in an edition of
eighty copies on Japan paper handbound by his wife, Gudrun
von Hesse—also a type designer of note; the book sold out
quickly and Zapf's name was made. (Remarkably, the lettering had actually been done when the self-taught calligrapher
was only twenty-one.) Intended mainly for "display" (title
pages, headings), Palatino owes its appearance both to calligraphy and the requirements of the cheap German paper at the
time—perhaps why it is also one of the best-looking fonts on
low-end computer printers. It was soon used to set text, however, causing Zapf to redraw its more elaborate letters.